PAUL SAMUELSON ON THE HISTORY OF ECONOMIC ANALYSIS

Selected Essays

As one of the most famous economists of the twentieth century, Paul Anthony Samuelson revolutionized many branches of economic theory. As a diligent student of his predecessors, he reconstructed their economic analyses in the mathematical idiom he pioneered. Out of Samuelson's more than eighty articles, essays, and memoirs, the editors of this collection have selected seventeen. Twelve are mathematical reconstructions of some of the most famous work in the history of economic thought: work by David Hume, Francois Quesnay, Adam Smith, Karl Marx, and others. One is a methodological essay defending the Whig history that Samuelson was sometimes accused of promulgating; two deal with the achievements of Joseph Schumpeter and Denis Robertson; and two review theoretical developments of his own time: Keynesian economics and monopolistic competition. The collection provides readers with a sense of the depth and breadth of Samuelson's contributions to the study of the history of economics.

Steven G. Medema is Distinguished Professor of Economics at the University of Colorado Denver. His articles have appeared in journals including the *Journal of the History of Economic Thought*, *History of Political Economy*, the *Journal of Economic Perspectives*, and *Economica*. His latest book, *The Hesitant Hand: Taming Self-Interest in the History of Economic Ideas* (2009), was awarded the 2010 ESHET Book Prize. Dr. Medema served as president of the History of Economics Society for 2009–2010 term.

Anthony M. C. Waterman is a Fellow of St. John's College, Winnipeg, and Professor Emeritus of Economics in the University of Manitoba. He is the author of nine previous books, including *Revolution, Economics and Religion* (Cambridge University Press), for which he was awarded the Forkosch Prize for Intellectual History in 1992, and *Political Economy and Christian Theology since the Enlightenment*. He was elected Distinguished Fellow of the History of Economics Society in 2007 and Honorary Member of the European Society for the History of Economic Thought in 2014.

HISTORICAL PERSPECTIVES ON MODERN ECONOMICS

General Editor

Craufurd D. Goodwin, *Duke University*

This series contains original works that challenge and enlighten historians of economics. For the profession as a whole, it promotes better understanding of the origin and content of modern economics

Other books in the series:

Floris Heukelom, *Behavioral Economics* (2014)

Roger E. Backhouse, Mauro Boianovsky, *Transforming Modern Macroeconomics* (2013)

Susan Howson, *Lionel Robbins* (2012)

Robert Van Horn, Philip Mirowski, Thomas A. Stapleford *(eds.) Building Chicago Economics* (2012)

Arie Arnon, *Monetary Theory and Policy from Hume and Smith to Wicksell* (2011)

Malcolm Rutherford, *The Institutionalist Movement in American Economics, 1918–1947: Science and Social Control* (2011)

Samuel Hollander, *The Economics of Karl Marx* (2008)

Donald Moggridge, *Harry Johnson: A Life in Economics* (2008)

Filippo Cesarano, *Monetary Theory and Bretton Woods: The Construction of an International Monetary Order* (2006)

Timothy Davis, *Ricardo's Macroeconomics: Money, Trade Cycles, and Growth* (2005)

Jerry Evensky, *Adam Smith's Moral Philosophy: A Historical and Contemporary Perspective on Markets, Law, Ethics, and Culture* (2005)

Harro Maas, *William Stanley Jevons and the Making of Modern Economics* (2005)

David Laidler, *Fabricating the Keynesian Revolution: Studies of the Inter-War Literature on Money, the Cycle, and Unemployment* (1999)

Esther-Mirjam Sent, *The Evolving Rationality of Rational Expectations: An Assessment of Thomas Sargent's Achievements* (1998)

Heath Pearson, *Origins of Law and Economics: The Economists' New Science of Law, 1830–1930* (1997)

Odd Langholm, *The Legacy of Scholasticism in Economic Thought: Antecedents of Choice and Power* (1998)

Yuichi Shionoya, *Schumpeter and the Idea of Social Science* (1997)

J. Daniel Hammond, *Theory and Measurement: Causality Issues in Milton Friedman's Monetary Economics* (1996)

William J. Barber, *Designs within Disorder: Franklin D. Roosevelt, the Economists, and the Shaping of American Economic Policy, 1933–1945* (1996)

Juan Gabriel Valdes, *Pinochet's Economists: The Chicago School of Economics in Chile* (1995)

Philip Mirowski *(ed.)*, *Natural Images in Economic Thought: "Markets Read in Tooth and Claw"* (1994)

Malcolm Rutherford, *Institutions in Economics: The Old and the New Institutionalism* (1994)

Karen I. Vaughn, *Austrian Economics in America: The Migration of a Tradition* (1994)

Lars Jonung *(ed.)*, *The Stockholm School of Economics Revisited* (1991)

E. Roy Weintraub, *Stabilizing Dynamics: Constructing Economic Knowledge* (1991)

M. June Flanders, *International Monetary Economics, 1870–1960: Between the Classical and the New Classical* (1990)

Philip Mirowski, *More Heat Than Light: Economics as Social Physics, Physics as Nature's Economics* (1990)

Mary S. Morgan, *The History of Econometric Ideas* (1990)

Gerald M. Koot, *English Historical Economics, 1870–1926: The Rise of Economic History and Mercantilism* (1988)

Kim Kyun, *Equilibrium Business Cycle Theory in Historical Perspective* (1988)

William J. Barber, *From New Era to New Deal: Herbert Hoover, the Economists, and American Economic Policy, 1921–1933* (1985)

Takashi Negishi, *Economic Theories in a Non-Walrasian Tradition* (1985)

Paul Samuelson on the History of Economic Analysis

Selected Essays

Edited by

STEVEN G. MEDEMA
University of Colorado Denver

ANTHONY M. C. WATERMAN
University of Manitoba, Winnipeg

CAMBRIDGE
UNIVERSITY PRESS

32 Avenue of the Americas, New York NY 10013-2473, USA

Cambridge University Press is part of the University of Cambridge.

It furthers the University's mission by disseminating knowledge in the pursuit of
education, learning and research at the highest international levels of excellence.

www.cambridge.org
Information on this title: www.cambridge.org/9781107029934

© Cambridge University Press 2015

First published 2015

A catalogue record for this publication is available from the British Library

Library of Congress Cataloguing in Publication data
Samuelson, Paul A. (Paul Anthony), 1915–2009.
[Essays. Selections]
Paul Samuelson on the history of economic analysis : selected essays / Steven G. Medema,
Anthony M. C. Waterman.
pages   cm
Includes bibliographical references and index.
ISBN 978-1-107-02993-4 (alk. paper : hbk)
1. Economics – History.   2. Mathematical economics – History.   I. Medema, Steven G.
II. Waterman, Anthony Michael C.   III. Title.
HB75.S2924   2015
330.09–dc23
2014035049

ISBN 978-1-107-02993-4 Hardback

Contents

Acknowledgments   *page* ix

    Introduction   1

I. Historiography   23
    "Out of the Closet: A Program for the Whig History of Economic
    Science." *History of Economics Society Bulletin* 9 No. 1 (1987):
    51–60.   25

II. Before Adam Smith   37
    "A Corrected Version of Hume's Equilibrating Mechanisms for
    International Trade." In John S. Chipman and Charles
    P. Kindleburger, eds., *Flexible Exchange Rates and the Balance
    of Payments: Essays in Memory of Egon Sohmen*. Amsterdam:
    North-Holland, 1980, pp. 141–158.   39
    "Quesnay's 'Tableau Economique' as a Theorist would Formulate
    it Today." In Ian Bradley and Michael Howard, eds., *Classical
    and Marxian Political Economy: Essays in Honor of Ronald
    L. Meek*. New York: St. Martin's Press, 1982, pp. 45–78.   59

III. Wealth of Nations and the "Canonical Classical Model"   87
    "The Canonical Classical Model of Political Economy." *Journal
    of Economic Literature* 16 (December 1978): 1415–1434.   89
    "A Modern Theorist's Vindication of Adam Smith." *American
    Economic Review* 67 (February 1977): 42–49.   117

IV. David Ricardo   131
    "A Modern Treatment of the Ricardian Economy: I. The Pricing
    of Goods and of Labor and Land Services." *Quarterly Journal
    of Economics* 73 (February 1959): 1–35.   133

"A Modern Treatment of the Ricardian Economy: II. Capital
and Interest Aspects of the Pricing Process." *Quarterly
Journal of Economics* 73 (May 1959): 217–231.   168

"Mathematical Vindication of Ricardo on Machinery." *Journal
of Political Economy* 96 (April 1988): 274–282.   183

V.   Johann Heinrich von Thünen   193

"Thünen at Two Hundred." *Journal of Economic Literature* 21
(December 1983): 1468–1488.   195

VI.   Karl Marx   227

"Wages and Interest: A Modern Dissection of Marxian
Economic Models." *American Economic Review* 47
(December 1957): 884–912.   229

"Marx as Mathematical Economist: Steady-State and Exponential
Growth Equilibrium." In George Horwich and Paul
A. Samuelson, eds., *Trade, Stability and Macroeconomics: Essays
in Honor of Lloyd A. Metzler*. New York: Academic Press, 1974,
pp. 269–307.   260

VII.   Post-"Classical" Political Economy   303

"What Classical and Neoclassical Monetary Theory Really Was."
Canadian Journal of Economics 1 (February 1968): 1–15.   305

"A Modern Post-Mortem on Böhm's Capital Theory: Its Vital
Normative Flaw Shared by Pre-Sraffian Mainstream Capital
Theory." *Journal of the History of Economic Thought* 23
(September 2001): 301–317.   324

VIII.   Retrospectives on Early Modern Economists   345

"Schumpeter as an Economic Theorist." In Helmut Frisch, ed.,
Schumpeterian Economics. London: Praeger, 1982, pp. 1–27.   347

"D. H. Robertson (1890–1963)." 77 (November 1963): 517–536.   375

IX.   Revolutions in Twentieth-Century Economics   395

"Lord Keynes and the General Theory." *Econometrica* 14 (July
1946): 187–200.   397

"The Monopolistic Competition Revolution." In R. E. Kuenne,
ed., *Monopolistic Competition Theory: Studies in Impact.
Essays in Honor of Edward H. Chamberlin*. New York: John
Wiley, 1967, pp. 105–138.   412

Samuelson's Publications in the History of Economic Thought   447

Index   457

ACKNOWLEDGMENTS

We are grateful to the following organizations, publishers, and copyright holders for granting us permission to reprint the articles included in this collection.

The History of Economics Society: "Out of the Closet: A Program for the Whig History of Economic Science." *History of Economics Society Bulletin* 9 No. 1 (1987): 51-60; and "A Modern Post-Mortem on Böhm's Capital Theory: Its Vital Normative Flaw Shared by Pre-Sraffian Mainstream Capital Theory." *Journal of the History of Economic Thought* 23 (September 2001): 301-317.

American Economic Association: "The Canonical Classical Model of Political Economy." *Journal of Economic Literature* 16 (December 1978): 1415-1434; "A Modern Theorist's Vindication of Adam Smith." *American Economic Review* 67 (February 1977): 42-49; "Thünen at Two Hundred." *Journal of Economic Literature* 21 (December 1983): 1468-1488; and "Wages and Interest: A Modern Dissection of Marxian Economic Models." *American Economic Review* 47 (December 1957): 884-912.

Elsevier: "A Corrected Version of Hume's Equilibrating Mechanism for International Trade." In John S. Chipman and Charles P. Kindleburger, eds., *Flexible Exchange Rates and the Balance of Payments: Essays in Memory of Egon Sohmen*. Amsterdam: North-Holland, 1980, pp. 141-158; and "Marx as Mathematical Economist: Steady-State and Exponential Growth Equilibrium." In George Horwich and Paul A. Samuelson, eds., *Trade, Stability and Macroeconomics: Essays in Honor of Lloyd A. Metzler*. New York: Academic Press, 1974, pp. 269-307.

The Econometric Society: "Lord Keynes and the General Theory." *Econometrica* 14 (July 1946): 187-200.

Oxford University Press: "A Modern Treatment of the Ricardian Economy: The Pricing of Goods and of Labor and Land Services."

Quarterly Journal of Economics 73 (February 1959): 1–35; "A Modern Treatment of the Ricardian Economy: Capital and Interest Aspects of the Pricing Problem." *Quarterly Journal of Economics* 73 (May 1959): 217–231; and "D. H. Robertson (1890–1963)." *Quarterly Journal of Economics* 77 (November 1963): 517–536.

The University of Chicago Press: "Mathematical Vindication of Ricardo on Machinery." *Journal of Political Economy* 96 (April 1988): 274–282.

John Wiley and Sons, Ltd.: "What Classical and Neoclassical Monetary Theory Really Was." *Canadian Journal of Economics* 1 (February 1968): 1–15; and "The Monopolistic Competition Revolution." In R. E. Kuenne, ed., *Monopolistic Competition Theory: Studies in Impact. Essays in Honor of Edward H. Chamberlin.* New York: John Wiley, 1967, pp. 105–138.

The estate of Paul A. Samuelson: "Quesnay's 'Tableau Economique' as a Theorist Would Formulate It Today." In Ian Bradley and Michael Howard, eds., *Classical and Marxian Political Economy: Essays in Honor of Ronald L. Meek.* New York: St. Martin's Press, 1982, pp. 45–78. "Schumpeter as Economic Theorist." In Helmut Frisch, ed., *Schumpeterian Economics.* London: Praeger, 1982, pp. 1–27.

A special word of thanks goes to the permissions managers who worked so efficiently with us to navigate the permissions process.

We would like to thank Scott Parris, Karen Maloney, Adam Levine, Kristin Purdy, and Kate Gavino of Cambridge University Press for shepherding this volume through the publication process. Scott Parris is due a special debt of gratitude for his support and encouragement of this project from its inception. Craufurd Goodwin, the editor of the "Historical Perspectives on Modern Economics" series in which this volume appears, was a tremendous source of both encouragement and constructive criticism as we assembled this volume and prepared the Introduction. Roger Backhouse and the two anonymous referees employed by the Press provided invaluable feedback along the way and, along with Craufurd Goodwin, led us to modify our conceptualization of this project in a way that has allowed us to produce a stronger end product.

Finally, there is no one who has mastered the details of Paul Samuelson's published oeuvre like Janice Murray, his longtime assistant. Janice was a valuable source of information for us as we prepared this volume, and her cheerful interest in helping us in whatever way possible made our work just that much easier.

Steven G. Medema
Anthony M. C. Waterman

Introduction

Steven G. Medema and Anthony M. C. Waterman

The editors of this volume approached Paul Samuelson during the last year of his life with the suggestion that we might celebrate his unique and influential contribution to the history of economic thought by collecting his many papers in this field and publishing a selection. It seemed to us that the title of the series for which we proposed our book, "Historical Perspectives on Modern Economics," almost exactly described his heuristic intentions in at least the most formal and best-known of his historical studies.[1] We assured him that the project would not go ahead without his approval. To our delight, Samuelson warmly encouraged our initiative, offered his advice, began to comment on our selection, and interested himself in the thorny question of permissions. But his health began to deteriorate soon after his last communication with us (4 August 2009), and he was unable to write again before his death on 13 December 2009.

Samuelson's reputation as one of the greatest economists of the twentieth century rests on his classic *Foundations of Economic Analysis* (1947), his pioneering work with Robert Dorfman and Robert Solow (1958) on linear programming as a tool of economic analysis, and on hundreds of articles in almost every branch of economic theory, many of which are regarded as seminal. Why then did he bother with the history of economic thought? How did it relate to the rest of his intellectual enterprise? How did he go about doing the history of economic thought? What did he tell us about what he was doing? What did others think of his historiographic method? And what of permanent value can we identify in his historical writing? We

---

[1] Some would undoubtedly argue that Samuelson's research in this vein was more of a "modern perspective on historical economics." Our position is that this volume shows that the reality is much more complex than that.

Introduction

address these questions in what follows, and we conclude with an explanation of what we have selected and why.

1. The Historian

Paul Samuelson once referred, self-disparagingly, to "the 5 per cent of my published papers that deal with the history of economic science" (**54**, 3).[2] But D.P. O'Brien (2007, 336) regards this as a "significant underestimate." Nearly 140 articles, essays, or memoirs listed at the end of this volume, appearing over a period of forty-four years from 1946 to 2009 and comprising perhaps 20 percent of his scholarly publications, are clearly identifiable as studies of the history of economic thought. Many full-time specialists in this subdiscipline have achieved far less. We have selected seventeen of what we believe to be the most important of Samuelson's contributions to history of economic thought for inclusion in this volume.

Samuelson's earliest journal articles in history of economic thought were published in the 1950s. But *Foundations* (1947), based on his doctoral dissertation, refers to nearly forty of his more famous forerunners over the previous two centuries, ranging from Barone, Bastiat, Bentham, Böhm-Bawerk, and Bortkiewicz to Adam Smith, Thünen, Veblen, Viner, Walras, Wicksell, and Allyn Young, and including such relatively unexpected authors as Engels, Paley, and Sidgwick.[3] It is characteristic that he should have chosen to illustrate a purely mathematical conception, that of "one-sided stability-instability," with Malthus's population theory (1947, 296–299), so formulating a Malthusian production function, the germ of his famous "Canonical Classical Model" (**29**). Among major figures, only Marx is ignored in *Foundations*, for which Samuelson amply made up in later years.

Even in the 1940s, such attention to his predecessors by the author of a work of pure theory was unusual. When Samuelson began his graduate studies in the 1930s, "history of thought was a dying industry" (**48**, 51).

But it was still a presence in the required curriculum to be reckoned with. Jacob Viner was cracking the whip at the University of Chicago. Edwin Seligmann[sic] at Columbia and Jacob Hollander at Johns Hopkins occupied their professorial chairs. (ibid.)

---

[2] Unless otherwise noted, all references are to the numbered list of Samuelson's publications in the history of economics, which appears at the end of this volume.
[3] O'Brien (2007) provides an excellent discussion of the use of the history of economics in Samuelson's *Foundations*.

O'Brien (2007, 339) believes that "the importance of the influence of Jacob Viner on Samuelson's intellectual development cannot be overrated." Moreover, at Harvard in the 1930s, graduate students facing general oral exams were often expected to elucidate developments in analysis made by important figures back to Adam Smith and even before (**48**, 51). And at many other universities around the world, possibly because of "the decadence of literary economics from 1919 to 1930" (ibid.), the study of theory was intertwined with that of the great theorists to a far greater extent than is now the case. Thus the sixteen-year-old Paul Samuelson was "born again"

at 8:00 a.m., January 2, 1932, when I first walked into the University of Chicago lecture hall. That day's lecture was on Malthus's theory that human populations would reproduce like rabbits until their density per acre of land reduced their wage to a bare subsistence level where an increased death rate came to equal the birth rate. So easy was it to understand all this simple differential equation stuff that I suspected (wrongly) that I was missing out on some mysterious complexity. (Samuelson 2003, 1)

To this "accidental, blind chance" did Samuelson attribute his decision to study economics.

Samuelson himself believed that the science of economics "burst to life" shortly after this date in the eruption of four revolutions: "the *monopolistic competition* revolution, the *Keynesian macro* revolution, the *mathematicization* revolution, and the *econometric inference* revolution" (**48**, 52). The attention of the best economists therefore became focused on the exciting present. The study of past doctrinal controversy was left to those whom Donald Winch (1996, 421) later referred to as "incompetent or retired" practitioners. How then to explain that fascination with economic analysis of the past, and commitment to its elucidation, that Samuelson evinced to the end of his life?

As he was mastering the existing corpus of economic theory during the 1930s, he came to understand that "some unity of method and logic" underlay most of his researches. Two hypotheses – maximization by rational individuals and stability of market equilibrium (Samuelson 1947, 5) – were sufficient to unify "much of current *and historical* economic theory" (**64**, 1377; emphasis added). The analytical framework of *Foundations* thus had the effect of foreshortening the temporal distance between Samuelson's "heroes in economics" – Walras, Cournot, Edgeworth, Pareto, Fisher and Wicksell – and his fellow "working economists" such as J.R. Hicks and Ragnar Frisch (**64**, 1381). Perhaps for this reason, Samuelson sometimes wrote as though all the neoclassical masters were in fact contemporaries with whom he was engaged in dialogue. As for earlier generations from David Hume and Adam Smith to

J.S. Mill and Karl Marx, he habitually maintained that "within every classical economist there is to be discerned a modern economist trying to be born" (e.g., **29**, 1415). His discussions of Heinrich von Thünen (**43**, **47**, **75**) recognize "a prophet way ahead of his own times" who "anticipated the kind of mathematics later employed" by Jevons, Walras, Edgeworth, and Pareto (**75**, 1).

Samuelson's understanding of the conceptually unitary foundations of economic analysis, and his confidence in the power of mathematics to lay bare those foundations, allowed him to analyze a wide range of seemingly disparate problems with a common technical apparatus, and thus to think of himself as "the last generalist in economics" (e.g., Samuelson 1985, 52). His 1979 essay on "Land and the Rate of Interest" (**45**) is typical. In applying Modigliani and Ando's (1963) life-cycle model to appraise an off-the-cuff insight of Keynes (1936, 242), it invokes (and formalizes) Turgot's (1766) analysis and alludes to Henry George, Frank Ramsay, Böhm-Bawerk, Wicksell, Fisher, and Cannan. One of his last papers, "Where Ricardo and Mill Rebut and Confirm Arguments of Mainstream Economists Supporting Globalization" (**73**), affords striking testimony to Samuelson's perception of the essential contemporaneity of all good economics. His penchant for hyphenating chronologically distant authors, as in "Minkowski-Ricardo-Leontief-Metzler matrices" (**8**, 1) or "Smith-Allyn Young-Ohlin-Krugman trade paradigms" (**73**, 143), though sometimes half-humorous, was always a true index of his unique vision.

Lastly, and closely related to his view of the conceptual unity of economic analysis, Samuelson's long-standing devotion to history of economic thought may have been in part simply a consequence of his insatiable appetite for hard work, a characteristic noted by O'Brien (2007, 336–338). For seventy years he produced scholarly articles at an average rate of nearly one a month, not to mention several books and hundreds of popular pieces in newspapers and magazines. When he was awarded the Nobel Prize in 1970, he remarked that "it was nice to be recognized for hard work." At the Nobel banquet Samuelson listed five necessary conditions for academic success in his discipline: the fourth condition, "an important one from a scholarly point of view," was that "you must read the works of the great masters."[4] Few other economists have "read the works of the great masters" from Adam Smith to Kenneth Arrow with the diligence and penetration of Paul Samuelson. Fewer still have written of this literature so widely, or with such insight into its analytical core.

---

[4] http://nobelprize.org/nobel_prizes/economics/laureates/1970/samuelson-speech.html.

2. Historiography

Nevertheless, Samuelson occupies a controversial place among historians of economics. Because of his vision of the conceptual unity of all economic analysis, his historiographic method when reaching deep into the past was to formalize the analysis of his predecessors (and he saw them as such) using modern mathematical tools and theoretical constructs. Contextual elements such as historical background, influences, and ideology – important to most other historians – were ruthlessly ignored. When we move closer to the present, however, and witness Samuelson analyzing the work of contemporaries and near-contemporaries through what he describes as a historical lens,[5] we see a different approach, one that brings in the role of personalities, contexts, and scholarly communities in the creation of path-breaking ideas – that is, invoking elements of history that, as we shall see in this volume, he tended to dismiss in certain of his commentaries on writing the history of the economics of the distant past.

Samuelson sometimes identified his work as "Whig history," albeit with qualifications. Others have described it, privately, as an illustration of its worst excesses. This strikes us as excessively harsh. Samuelson himself hoped that "When meeting St Peter my worst crime will be the espousal of a Whig-History approach to the history of science" (**54**, 3). To understand Samuelson's contributions to the history of economics, and to apprehend their nature and import, we must appreciate the perspective that motivated his work – though, as we shall see later, that perspective does not wholly account for the historiographical importance of those contributions.

The starting point is Samuelson's orthodox view of economics as a *science*, and thus of the history of economics as the *history of science*. But his conception of history of science was very different from the contemporary approach that focuses on the production of scientific knowledge and its background conditions, sometimes to the exclusion of scientific knowledge itself. Samuelson labeled that approach, rather unkindly, as "antiquarian." His own view was roughly 180 degrees opposed:

When I read a Smith or a Keynes, it is the system that they are formulating that first interests me – the system discernible there and not primarily *their* understanding or misunderstanding of it. . . . The historian of science is interested primarily in the history of various scientific models and understanding. (**54**, 7)

---

[5] Many of these essays appear in his *Collected Scientific Papers* under headings such as "Essays in the History of Economics."

Samuelson found "antiquarian" approaches to the subject problematic. "History as it happened," he wrote, "is neither attainable in principle nor, where the history of a *cumulative* science is concerned, is it a desirable end" (**54**, 5). Sometimes he associated the antiquarian approach with "gossip" (e.g., **8**, 2). Elsewhere, however, he took a more charitable view: "I applaud those who study history of scholars – their writings, ideologies, influence, and changing reputations." But his own special interest was "in the history of economic theories, models, paradigms, measurements, hypotheses, etc." (**55**, 149), which is "in many ways ... easier to write precisely because it need not involve the determination of social influencings" (**8**, 5).

But how can one claim to be faithful to the ideas of the past when merely translating them into modern mathematics, without attending to what may be crucial contextual elements? Mark Blaug (1990, 32) has charged Samuelson with passing off "rational reconstructions" as "historical reconstructions," against which Samuelson often defended himself. He was well aware that we cannot know with certainty what an author was thinking when he formulated an idea. However, he observed that writers of the past often "imperfectly understood their own theories" (**48**, 56), not least because of limitations of the literary form in specifying relations and implications. As he wrote to Patinkin in 1990, "I agree that we humans are often imperfect logical machines – particularly in the early stages of discovery and exploration" (**55**, 150). But for Samuelson this simply required care to avoid overreaching in one's analysis, not evading the analysis of what might be implicit, conceivably even present, in a past author's mind:

Truly, I would not want to write, "If A implies B and Cohen asserts that A obtains, then he asserts (and understands) that B does obtain." ... But also, in pursuing my study of the history of (A,B, logical relationships, empirical relevances), I'd reproach myself for failing to recognize when the A's do imply the B's.[6] (**55**, 150)

This may not yield true history, but it gives us "the best-case understanding" of that model (**54**, 8).[7] One can then investigate consistency and logical correctness in the model, and how it relates to other ideas past and present.

---

[6] Patinkin, for his part, responds that he does not quarrel with Samuelson's demonstration that ideas are implicit in the work of particular scholars; his quarrel goes to "the cerebral distance between the implicit and the explicit, the width of the synaptic gap between the two" (**55**, 152–153).

[7] Samuelson goes on to advocate that the historian of science "should also work out [the author's] worst-case understandings" (**54**, 8).

Samuelson seemed to recognize that there is a fine line between exploring the ideas of the past and abusing them, and was highly critical of "attempts to read into" the ideas of the past "formalisms that are *not* there" (**67**, 333; see also **54**, 10; **48**, 56). His own goal was to determine by rigorous probing what *could have been* there. Of course, such probing can expose problematic elements in past ideas; and though he considered it "idle to castigate 18th-century writers for not being 20th-century virtuosi," Samuelson also considered it "mandatory to point out their errors in describing their own systems and scenarios." This is particularly important given that "top modern commentators (Schumpeter, Sraffa, Stigler, Blaug, S. Hollander, Kaldor, Wicksell, . . .) sometimes share their errors of omission and commission" (**67**, 333). If we are "standing on the shoulders of giants," we must be sure that the giant's skeletal structure is not deformed. The work of Ricardo and the treatment and use of it by Marx and by subsequent commentators is a case in point for Samuelson.

While there can be no doubt that Samuelson's approach to analyzing the economics of the eighteenth and nineteenth centuries has a certain Whiggish character, his is not a classic form of Whig history. Traditional formulation of the concept, owing to Herbert Butterfield (1931), paints the present as "the latest and best and *final* thing" (**54**, 6). Samuelson did not reject the Whig label – and at times even gloried in it – but he saw himself as putting forward a different and better version of Whig history: "That part of the past which is relevant to the present – that is, relevant to one *or more* of today's competing paradigms – is to be an object of special historical interest." He further suggested that instead of labeling this "Whig history," we might better speak of "history that is given special importance and attention because of its relevance to the present" and that "A good, if ugly, title might be 'Presentistic history'" (**54**, 6).

Although cognizant of the idiosyncratic nature of his approach, Samuelson was evangelistic about it, arguing in his 1987 keynote address to the History of Economics Society that the adoption of his method by other historians of economics offered a possibility of rescuing the field from the professional wilderness.[8] In doing so, Samuelson located the study of the history of economics, and the audience for such studies, in the economics profession rather than among historians. In effect, the market tests the interest and sensibilities of *economists* rather than historians, and with significant import. For Samuelson considered science, including economics,

---

[8]   A contrasting view is found in Schabas (1992). See also the responses to Schabas's argument in the same volume.

as progressive, and saw a characteristic difference between science and the humanities in explaining the fact that the ideas of period A are eventually replaced by those of period B:

A later [scientific] paradigm is likely to be a better paradigm and be more lasting. Einstein's 1915 system does not so much reject Newton's 1558 [sic] system as give it a *dominating* generalization. In the creative arts, Shakespeare is not better than Homer because he comes later. To think that economics is merely like poetry is both to downgrade it as a serious attempt to be a science and is to grossly misdescribe economics. (**54**, 6)

This has implications for the professional acceptance of work done by historians of economics, since "working scientists have some contempt for those historians and philosophers of science who regard efforts in the past that failed as being on par with those that succeeded, success being measurable by latest-day scientific juries who want to utilize hindsight and ex post knowledge" (**54**, 52–53).

Samuelson came to see that his approach has not served to raise the profile of the history of economic science in the larger economics profession:

When Samuelson (**48**) proclaimed a manifesto for Whig history of economic science, the argument was made that old-fashioned antiquarians had lost their market and maybe something different would sell better. Kurdas reminds me that empirical experience showed that the market for history of economics remains small despite the shift toward using present-day tools in that area. (**54**, 12; see Kurdas 1988)

Yet he remained unrepentant, and was happy to abandon the market test and instead make the case for his approach on its intellectual merits: that "economics is in some degree a cumulative science," and that "If the study of the past is worth doing, it is worth doing as well as we can." (**54**, 12) And that, for Samuelson, meant forsaking antiquarian approaches in favor of what he considered to be a more scientific approach to history.

But as we move closer to the present, a rather different Samuelson emerges – one that further belies his self-proclaimed Whiggishness and which relies increasingly on historical elements that he labeled antiquarianism and gossip when referring to the more distant past. Though the image of Samuelson as a historian of economics has been formed almost exclusively through his work on figures of the eighteenth and nineteenth centuries, he wrote an amazing amount on the history of twentieth-century economics. Here, the subjects were his contemporaries and near-contemporaries, and his analyses ranged from close-in-time retrospectives on individuals and ideas to the development of particular "schools" of economic analysis, and he did so for outlets ranging from scholarly journals to *festschriften* to funeral orations.

Samuelson's output on this front, too, is staggering: more than eighty articles spanning a period of roughly fifty years.[9] The topics covered a range from early assessments of the monopolistic competition and Keynesian revolutions to reflections on fellow Nobel Laureates, teachers, and colleagues. The perspective evinced throughout these works is historical – not judging by the standards of the present, but focusing on the place of ideas at their inception and their relationship to those of the past – attempting to bring out the role of personalities, perspectives, relationships, and contexts in the generation of ideas and in the development of economists and communities of economists.

The obvious question that this raises is how one reconciles this work with Samuelson's own comments to the effect that concern with such matters amounts to little more than antiquarianism and gossip. One possible answer is that he did not see himself doing "history" when he penned such works. But that claim is refuted by multiple elements of the record, including the fact that he or his editors (but presumably with his approval) specifically classified these essays as in the "history of economics" in his *Collected Scientific Papers* and the publication of many of these works in the same outlets as his more mathematically oriented articles. It is difficult to imagine that Samuelson would be so inconsistent as to offer prestigious academic journals and *festschriften* puff pieces in certain situations and serious scholarly work in others. A more reasonable conjecture, we believe, is that Samuelson's attitude toward contextual elements and the like was very different when he was considering the work of contemporaries and near-contemporaries than it was when he was working with the ideas of the distant past. When it comes to the history of twentieth-century economics, Samuelson was writing as a participant-observer, an observer, or as one who was at least in some way (e.g., as a student) connected to nearly all of his subjects. In this respect Samuelson's work as an author resembled that of Winston Churchill in the latter's history of *The Second World War* (1948–1953). The historical "facts" that he laid out, then, were the facts as he knew them, and in many cases had observed them; the impressions formed by professional and nonprofessional interactions at the office, at professional conferences, or based on things said to him by individuals on

---

[9] There are, in addition, roughly three-dozen speeches and items written for the popular press on these topics.

whom he felt he could rely. It may be that Samuelson believed that he was on much firmer ground in talking about the role of contextual elements in the genesis of modern economic ideas and was unwilling to make such leaps when it came to discussing the ideas of earlier centuries and with generations of scholars with whom he had no first- or even second-hand acquaintance.

Of course, this is only a conjecture, one that may be refuted, validated, or supplemented by the work of others who attempt to assess Samuelson's contributions to the history of economics in the coming decades. But whatever the explanation, the fact remains that these essays on modern economists and modern economics are far more than puff pieces written by a long-retired professor celebrating the great advances of economics during his salad days. They are both historical analyses in and of themselves and the source of a treasure trove of data for other historians of modern economics. They also reveal that there is far more to Samuelson as a historian of economics than the translation of the ideas of the past into modern mathematics. To get the proper scope of the man, both as economist and as historian of economics, requires coming to grips with the totality of this work. This introductory essay and the articles reprinted in the present collection represent only a partial view, one limited by multiple factors, including the highly selective nature of this volume and the fact that only time will allow us to digest the magnitude and import of Samuelson's contributions.

3. Mathematics and the History of Economic Analysis

For intellectual historians who attempt to get inside the minds of our predecessors in order to understand what they were trying to do in their day, "Whig History" is a term of abuse. Spinoza's dictum, *Non ridere, non lugere, nequedetestari; sedintelligere* (Not to laugh, not to lament, not to deprecate, but to understand), is their motto (Cassirer 1951, x). Context is all-important. It is therefore regrettable that Samuelson's provocative flaunting of his red rag should have induced a violent allergic reaction in many other historians of economic thought, blinding them to the important fact that Samuelson's method – whatever he himself may have said or thought about it – though certainly not able to produce genuine *history*, is a valid and often valuable *tool* of intellectual history. For it is undoubtedly the case that one of the reasons, perhaps the chief reason, why we are interested in Adam Smith and other "economic" thinkers of the last three centuries is that we can recognize what we now call the "economic analysis" that affords provisional coherence to their arguments and prescriptions.

When Smith tells us, for example, that "the demand for men, like that for any other commodity, necessarily regulates the production of men," and that "the demand for those who live by wages ... cannot increase but in proportion to the increase in the funds which are destined for the payment of wages" (*WN* I.viii.40), he is writing – and appears to be thinking – like a twenty-first-century economist. He has formulated a pair of related *theorems* that we can understand and criticize both on theoretical and empirical grounds; and thus in a sense we can still engage in conversation with him. Whatever else he was doing (which, of course, in the case of Smith, is quite a lot), he and his successors, both in the English School and on the Continent, constructed their "economic analysis" on a logical foundation composed of theorems and their elements: quasi-axiomatic assumptions about human behavior and the state of the world, and putatively causal relations among a few magnitudes abstracted from the welter of our experience for scrutiny and investigation.

Therefore, if we want to be good intellectual historians and get inside the thought-world of our subjects, and if our subjects happen to have written importantly about what we now call "political economy" or "economics," we have no option but to master their "economic analysis." Having done so we can begin to understand what our subjects were talking about: why Malthus and Ricardo disagreed about many things (and why they agreed about so many others); what Marx learned from Ricardo, and why both were confused about value theory; and why Jevons thought that "that able but wrong-headed man, David Ricardo, shunted the car of economic science on a wrong line." The so-called history of economic analysis in this narrow, focused sense is a drastic abstraction from what actually happened, and therefore is not true history. But it is an indispensable tool for the genuine intellectual history of "economic thought."

The formal study of economic analysis is inescapably mathematical and so, therefore, is the history of economic analysis. An early example is William Whewell's (1831) "Mathematical Exposition of Some of the Leading Doctrines in Mr. Ricardo's 'Principles of Political Economy and Taxation'," soon followed by J.E. Tozer's (1838) mathematical paper on the analyses of Barton, Sismondi, McCulloch, and Ricardo. The celebrated *Studies in the Theory of International Trade* (1937) by Samuelson's mentor, Jacob Viner, was largely literary, as befits a work of intellectual history. But mathematics was used when purely analytical content had to be elucidated. More recently there have been influential mathematical studies of the history of economic analysis by K. May (1949–1950), G. Stigler (1952), P. Sraffa (1960), L.L. Pasinetti (1960), L. Johansen (1967), W. Eltis (1975), and many more since. Even Samuel Hollander, the last great exponent of literary history of economic analysis, has been obliged to employ mathematics in some of his work (e.g., Hollander 2008, 114–129). Whig history may or may not be in the eye of the beholder, but it would be difficult to sustain the claim that each of these authors was "guilty" of it, and it is likely that none of them would admit to having committed it.

It would appear from this that there is no connection in general between mathematical history of economic analysis and "Whig History." Neither is necessary or sufficient for the other. Samuelson's historiographic method does not entail, nor is it entailed by, his claim to be doing "Whig History." The latter may have motivated the former in his case – but it need not have done so. And even if it did, the unintended consequence has been a brilliant illumination of the analytical structure of the work of many of the greatest economic thinkers of the past. Other historical methods may offer us alternative – and some would say better – ways of understanding the ideas of the past. But there is a purpose to be served by these modernist renderings, as Samuelson pointed out on several occasions when defending his approach against the critics, and the limiting nature of the notion of "Samuelson as a Whig historian" does a disservice to the assessment of his work and his legacy.

However, the illumination afforded by mathematical methods, though powerful, is not unproblematic. The same text can be made to yield very different results. Eltis (1984) and Costabile and Rowthorn (1985) used Keynesian categories to determine the "optimum propensity to save" at which Malthus believed a "general glut" could be avoided. But Negishi (1993) used a Neumann-type growth model to represent Malthus not so much as "an underconsumptionist as a supply-sider." Samuelson's (**12**) account of Marx's "transformation problem" is in conflict with that of Morishima (1973, chap 4). Do seeming anomalies of this type (and there are many) call into question the value of mathematical methods in history of economic analysis?

In the history of economic analysis, a mathematical model is an observational instrument, allowing us to see things invisible to the naked eye. But as with all observational instruments, what we can see depends both on the instrument and on how we use it. For example, even with the same microscope, the same sample of tissue looks very different under varying degrees of magnification. A slightly different metaphor supplied by Samuelson himself (**1** and **2**), "a modern *dissection* of Marxian models" (our italics), may be helpful.

When a zoological specimen is dissected in the laboratory, the biologist cuts away all that obscures the particular tissue to be studied. The knowledge so obtained is genuine but partial. To understand the organism as a whole, he must supplement his (anatomical) knowledge of the pulmonary system, say, with his fellow investigators' knowledge of viscera, glands, muscles, and so forth. And "complete" anatomical knowledge so obtained must be supplemented by general systemic (physiological) knowledge obtained by other methods.

Likewise, the economist who employs the scalpel of mathematical modeling to "dissect" out some particular line of argument in *Wealth of Nations* or *Capital* obtains genuine but partial knowledge. Now because analysts may and often do dissect out different tissues from the same dead rat, it is obvious that mathematical exegeses of the same text may differ. Thus Pasinetti (1960) attends to diminishing returns and rent in Ricardo's *Principles*, whereas Sraffa (1960) ignores these and attends to labor inputs and relative values. Such differences are only *apparent* when the diverse results could in principle be harmonized in a more general model that has correctly captured, and exhibited the relations among, all elements of the text that have been so far "dissected." But they are *real* when this is not possible because the incompatibility of various mathematical exegeses arises from inconsistency or incoherence in the original text or from the fact that the original author's formulation is such that mathematical tools do not generate a faithful rendering. And from the standpoint of intellectual history, this too is knowledge. (See Waterman 2003, on which the foregoing argument is based.)

4. History as Polemic

Although economics deals with much that lies at the center of political controversy, it is orthodox to suppose that economists apply their analyses without regard to their ideological commitments. In this respect, economists sometimes contrast themselves complacently with other social scientists – for whom the tail of ideology often seems to wag the analytical dog.

Paul Samuelson both deeply approved of and was strongly committed to this view of economic science. Yet his writing sometimes suggests doubt. For example, "It was the tragedy of my teachers' generation that, as they grew older, economics grew more liberal, and even radical. It has been the comedy of my era that, as we grew older, our profession has become more conservative" (**51**, 108). But how can *economics* possibly be "liberal" or "conservative"? We must assume that this was a slip: for "economics" and "our profession" we should read "economists" and "the members of our profession."

Now if economics be truly scientific, then at any one time all economists ought to be equally "conservative" or "liberal" because all have the same access to the latest and best economic theory, and relevant facts about the real world, with which to *rationalize* their normative preferences (Schumpeter 1954, 35–36). Yet this is manifestly not the case, as Samuelson, who never made any secret of his own "liberal" political sentiments, was well aware:

[A]round 1970 when I accepted a lecture engagement at the Western Economic Association, I never encountered so unanimous a gang of free marketeers. It was a pleasure to see those fellows losing their chips at the rigged gaming tables. (51, 108)

Writing in 1983, he reported:

For a decade now mainstream economics has been moving a bit rightward. But I have not been tempted to chase it. ... I have a dream of a humane economy that is at the same time efficient and respecting of personal (if not business) freedoms. (Samuelson 1983, 6–7)

The movement in "mainstream economics" that Samuelson was least tempted to chase was the "new classical school that believes in full employment and neutral money even in the short run of a few years. Like herpes, this condition caught us unawares" (57, 109).

It follows from the orthodox view that ideological differences among economists must be a consequence *either* of the fact that some are imperfectly acquainted with the best current theory, *or* because there is disagreement about the relevant facts, *or* both. Samuelson was never oblivious of the latter, and his objections to Chicago School macroeconomics were based on the obvious dissonance between its predictions and what often seems to happen in the real world. But he did very little empirical work, and his strongest interest always lay in theory. The element of ideological polemic in his historical writing, therefore, consists chiefly of demonstrating the theoretical inadequacy of all attempts to show that an "alternative" economics might better serve the political needs of left-wing causes than "mainstream" economics. His two principal targets were Marx and Sraffa. But Dobb, Meek, and Morishima, as also Stigler, Hollander, and Blaug – all of whom, in various ways, Samuelson believed, failed or refused to see the vacuity of much of the Ricardo/Marx analyses – also drew his fire (62, 192).

Indeed, Samuelson was more inclined to absolve his distant predecessors of their sins. As he noted in a 1998 retrospective on his work, "The real objects of Samuelson's more heated criticisms were his own time's contemporaneous historians of economic thought, rather than ancient heroic scholars" (**67**, 333).

In view of the bitter attack mounted against him and his economics by "radical" political economists after 1969, one might have conjectured that Samuelson's sustained critique of Marxian economics was the injured response of a man who had prided himself as a progressive and whose famous textbook was reviled as subversive in 1948, but who was now suddenly become "the personification of all that was bad about the running jackals of capitalism" (**63**, 159). But his response was temperate, and he saw the New Left as "the continuation of an important strand in the development of economics" (Samuelson 1971, i). Moreover, he had begun his studies of Marx "around 1955" (**62**, 190), twenty-two years before the unwelcome appearance of *Anti-Samuelson* (Linder 1977), perhaps stimulated by Joan Robinson's brief *Essay on Marxian Economics* (1942) which he admired and often cited.

No fewer than sixteen out of Samuelson's seventy-nine papers on pre-1930s history of economic thought – 20 percent of the whole – concern Marx (**1**, **2**, **11**, **12**, **13**, **19**, **20**, **21**, **22**, **23**, **24**, **25**, **41**, **42**, **57**, **62**), three of which are replies. Indeed, one could argue that Samuelson was a greater Marx scholar than many a professed Marxian. But at the end of his life their author thought this had been too much: "thirteen articles on Marx is ridiculous. He was a terrible economist and a poor prophet" (P.A.S. to A.M.C.W. 7 July 2009). Nevertheless, one of the most elaborate of these essays expounds and pays generous tribute to Marx's analyses of simple and extended reproduction in volume II of *Capital*: "Marx's advance on Quesnay's *Tableau* should win him a place inside the Pantheon" (**19**, 270). However, although this achievement gets occasional mention in several of the other papers, their general thrust is strongly critical. "The labor theory of value has much mischief to answer for," he says, "particularly for how it has served to obscure analysis and understanding of inequality" (**57**, 159). Marx's "1867 novelties concerning rates of surplus value and exploitation represented a sterile detour that renders zero or negative insight into the laws of motion of real-life capitalism and into the forces that create inequality of wealth and income" (**54**, 5). Bortkiewicz's "transformation" of Marxian values to competitive prices is "logically of the form: 'Anything' equals 'anything else' multiplied by 'anything/anything else'" (**12**, 423). A socialist planner maximizing steady-state consumption must eschew Marxian "values" and use "bourgeois prices" (Von Weizsäcker and Samuelson 1971, 1192). And in his foreword to the Japanese edition of *Collected Scientific Papers* he declared that, "No real light of understanding has *ever* come from the Marxian novelties of analysis" (1982, 874). Aside from his one genuine contribution, Marx as an economist was, in Samuelson's view, but a "minor post-Ricardian" (**1**, 911).

Samuelson was more than willing to attribute some of the blame for Marx's analytical failures to Ricardo, whom he considered "the most over-rated of economists" (**8**, 9). Samuelson was unimpressed by "the backward and forward groupings of a scholar who from his 1814 entrance into micro-economics until his 1823 death makes almost no progress in solving his self-created ambiguities and problematics" (**48**, 53). Like Marx, Ricardo was an "autodidact," but Marx at least had the excuse of having been "cut off in his lifetime from proper criticism and stimulus" (**1**, 911), quite unlike Ricardo, who blandly ignored the cogent criticisms of his friend Malthus and others. Ricardo did get some things gloriously right, notably the theory of comparative advantage and his highly controversial conclusion that a viable invention can reduce wages and national income. But his confusion about value theory muddied the analytical waters for decades. "How," Samuelson asks, "could Ricardo and the classicals have missed understanding how the complication of land is as logically damaging to the LTV [labor theory of value] as the complication of time and interest is?" (**66**, 35) Moreover, where there are many goods, "there are no 'natural' prices definable independently of how consumers choose to spend their incomes" (**70**, 13332). Yet "A deep student of Ricardo will gain insight into the simple truth *that David did not operationally pursue a model in which the labour theory of value obtained,* even though his twentieth century editor chose not to stress this substantive fact" (**48**, 55; emphasis added).

Ricardo's twentieth-century editor was Piero Sraffa, praised by Samuelson both for his exemplary Ricardo scholarship and for his famous 1960 mono-graph – but not for the elucidation of Ricardo's analysis in his "Introduction," which has been extolled by some for its "reconstruction of Ricardo's surplus theory" and for "the analytical role of the labor theory of value," thereby underwriting Marx's critique of capitalism (Eatwell 1984). Samuelson was dissatisfied with Sraffa's unwillingness to admit either the uselessness of "surplus theory" or the impossibility of any labor theory of value outside Smith's "early and rude state of society," and was tempted to attribute this to ideological bias: "A deep student of Piero Sraffa will not find it irrelevant information that he was more prone ideologically to Karl Marx than to Ludwig von Mises" (**48**, 55). Consequently Samuelson "perceived the need to audit objectively the claims for David Ricardo generated and augmented by" Sraffa; and "by comparison to dispel the Schumpeterian and other disparaging of Smith" (**67**, 329). To "the fascinating question whether classical political economy does, or can be made to, offer an *'alternative paradigm'* to modern mainstream economics" (**29**, 1415), Samuelson's answers were "no" and "no."

5. Samuelson's Contributions to the History of Economic Thought

The list of Samuelson's publications in the history of economic thought, presented at the end of this volume, includes 139 papers, only a small number of which could be included here. While we have argued earlier in this introductory essay that there is much more to Samuelson as a historian of economics than mathematical reconstruction, the contents of the present volume emphasize this aspect of the Samuelson corpus, for two reasons. First, the majority of Samuelson's substantive pieces on the history of economics are of the mathematical reconstruction variety, and the uniqueness of his approach on this front and the numerous contributions in this vein demand significant attention. Second, the largest share of his historical writings on modern economics appear in volumes 6 and 7 of Samuelson's *Collected Scientific Papers*, lately published by the MIT Press. Our publisher's request that we avoid significant overlap with these volumes has implications for the amount of this work that can be included in the present volume, as well as for which of the pieces analyzing eighteenth- and nineteenth-century economics were selected for inclusion.

It has been our goal to assemble a collection that provides a representative sample of Samuelson's published writings in the history of economics – no easy task for a subject whose works range from David Hume (1711–1776) to economists of the late twentieth century, and whose audiences for these writings ranged from academic economists generally to international trade theorists to historians of economics to the lay public.

We begin with one of Samuelson's several essays on historiography, both to illustrate his own perspective on his manner of working and to give the reader a sense for Samuelson's larger views on writing the history of economics. From there we move to two essays on pre-Smithian economics, the first dealing with Hume's trade theory (**31**) and the second with Quesnay's *Tableau* (**44**), the latter being the subject of several essays by Samuelson over the years.

Samuelson's case for Adam Smith as the leading figure in the pantheon of great economic minds ranges across a vast array of essays, two of which are included here. The first, on what Samuelson labeled "the canonical classical model" (**29**), is perhaps the most famous of all of Samuelson's works on the history of economics, while the second presents a bicentennial vindication of Adam Smith's triumphs in *The Wealth of Nations* (**28**) from the perspective of modern economics.

Though Samuelson thought both Ricardo and Marx overrated by their contemporaries and by many of his own, he nonetheless devoted a significant share of his historical work to each of these great thinkers. The three articles on Ricardo included in this volume (**3, 4, 49**) convey to the reader an excellent sense of what Samuelson saw as the strengths and weaknesses of Ricardo's corpus, while the essays on Marx (**1, 19**) are illustrative of those aspects of Marx's analysis that were a continual source of intrigue (both positive and negative) for Samuelson.

One rationale for Samuelson's greater or lesser interest in particular figures of the past lies in the resonance of their work with modern economics and/or the amenability of that work to analysis using modern mathematical techniques. We see this in his fascination with Quesnay, noted earlier in this Introduction, and also in his soft spot for Johann Heinrich von Thünen, whose legacy Samuelson perhaps has done more to preserve than has any other historian of economics. His high regard for Thünen's work is reflected in his essay, "Thünen at Two-Hundred" (**43**), included here.

One of Samuelson's favorite themes from the marginal revolution period is the theory of capital, perhaps because this is a subject that has perplexed so many leading minds across the centuries and lends itself to a wide range of mathematical formulations. Böhm-Bawerk, long a character of great interest to Samuelson, became the subject of a significant amount of published work in the later years of Samuelson's life, and we have included one of those essays (**72**) here. We have also chosen to include his article on classical and neoclassical monetary theory for its perspective on Samuelson's own views about the relationship between these two epochs in economic thinking and the insights into this that can be provided by formal analysis. Though there is a great deal of editorial challenge in determining which among Samuelson's many writings in the aforementioned areas to include in a volume such as this, one confronts a rather different problem when we arrive at the modern age. Here, the diffuse nature of the subjects treated by Samuelson requires some type of organizational principle, or principles. In the end, we determined that it would be useful to include two essays of a biographical nature and two essays on important "revolutions" in economics through which Samuelson lived. In the case of biography, we have selected one of Samuelson's essays on his teacher, Joseph Schumpeter, and another on D.H. Robertson. Articles on the Keynesian and monopolistic competition revolutions close the volume, the former because of Samuelson's prominent role in bringing Keynesian analysis into the scholarly and textbook arenas, and the latter because it gives the reader Samuelson's perspective on a revolution in which he did not play a major role but which he observed first-hand and which involved so many figures with whom he had professional relationships. The inclusion of these four papers, so sensitive to context as they are, reveals a Samuelson who cannot be neatly classified as a "Whig Historian," whether by his or any other definition, and enroll him among those from whom he pretended to distance himself: "those who study history of scholars – their writings, ideologies, influence, and changing reputations."

We did not arrive at this particular subset of seventeen papers without the assistance of others, including the late Paul Samuelson himself. We are grateful for the comments and suggestions provided by two anonymous readers selected by the Press, by Craufurd Goodwin, the General Editor of the "Historical Perspectives on Modern Economics" series, and by Scott Parris, our editor at the Press. Each forced us to think long and hard about the scope of this volume and the articles to be included in it, and the end product is all the better for their efforts.

This volume does not, and does not pretend to, present all that there is to Paul Samuelson as a historian of economics. A full understanding of Samuelson as a historian, like that of Samuelson as an economist *qua* economist, will have to wait many years and no doubt will be the product of the efforts of many scholars, with the analysis of Samuelson's work in the history of economics being set against and interpreted in light of his larger contributions, the contents of his personal papers (which now reside in the Economists Papers Project at Duke University), conversations with his contemporaries, and so on. It is our hope, however, that the present volume will be, for some, a stimulus to such work and for others will provide a collection of interesting and important contributions to the history of economics. The lengthy bibliography included at the end of this volume will give the reader a sense of the totality of Samuelson's contributions and, we hope, provide a map for many hours of enjoyable and stimulating further reading.

REFERENCES

Blaug, M. 1990, "On the Historiography of Economics," *Journal of the History of Economic Thought*, 12, 1, 27–37.
—1996, *Economic Theory in Retrospect*, 5th ed. Cambridge: Cambridge University Press.
Butterfield, H. 1931, *The Whig Interpretation of History*. London: G. Bell & Sons.

Cassirer, Ernst. 1951, *The Philosophy of the Enlightenment*. Princeton NJ: Princeton University Press.

Churchill, Winston S. 1948–1953, *The Second World War*, 6 vols. Boston: Houghton Mifflin.

Costabile, L. and B. Rowthorn. 1985, "Maltus's Theory of Wages and Growth," *Economic Journal* 95, 378, 418–437.

Dorfman, R. 1986, "Comment: P. A. Samuelson, 'Thünen at Two Hundred'," *Journal of Economic Literature* 24, 4, 1773–1776.

Dorfman, R., P. Samuelson, and R. Solow. 1958, *Linear Programming and Economic Analysis*. New York: McGraw-Hill.

Eltis, Walter. 1975, "Adam Smith's Theory of Economic Growth," in A. S. Skinner and T. Wilson (eds.), *Essays on Adam Smith*. Oxford: Clarendon Press.

—1984, *The Classical Theory of Economic Growth*. London: Macmillan.

Hollander, S. 1987, *Classical Economics*. Oxford: Basil Blackwell.

—2008, *The Economics of Karl Marx: Analysis and Applications*. Cambridge: Cambridge University Press.

Johansen, L. 1967, "A Classical Model of Economic Growth," in C. H. Feinstein (ed.), *Socialism, Capitalism, and Economic Growth*. Cambridge: Cambridge University Press.

Keynes, J. M. 1936, *The General Theory of Employment, Interest and Money*. London: Macmillan.

Kurdas, C. 1988, "The 'Whig Historian' on Adam Smith: Paul Samuelson's Canonical Classical Model," *History of Economics Society Bulletin* 10, 13–24.

Linder, M. 1977, *The Anti-Samuelson*, 2 vols. New York: Urizen Books.

Modigliani, F. and A. Ando. 1963, "The 'Life-Cycle' Hypothesis of Saving: Aggregate Implications and Tests," *American Economic Review* 53, 55–84.

Morishima, M. 1973, *Marx's Economics: A Dual Theory of Value and Growth*. Cambridge: Cambridge University Press.

Negishi, T. 1989, *History of Economic Theory*. Amsterdam: Elsevier Science Publishers.

—1993, "A Smithian-Growth Model and Malthus's Optimum Propensity to Save," *European Journal of the History of Economic Thought* 1, 1, 115–127.

O'Brien, D. P. 2007, "Samuelson: The Theorist as Historian of Economic Thought," chap. 12 in *History of Economic Thought as an Intellectual Discipline*. Cheltenham: Edward Elgar Publishing.

Pasinetti, L. L. 1960, "A Mathematical Formulation of the Ricardian System," *Review of Economic Studies* 27, 2, 78–98.

Robinson, J. 1942, *An Essay on Marxian Economics*. London: Macmillan.

Samuelson, P. A. 1947, *Foundations of Economic Analysis*. Cambridge, MA: Harvard University Press.

—1966–1986, *The Collected Scientific Papers of Paul A. Samuelson* (abbreviated *CSP*), 5 vols., Joseph E. Stiglitz, Robert C. Merton, Hiroake Nagatani, and Kate Crowley (eds.). Cambridge, MA: The MIT Press.

—1971, "Foreword," in A. Lindbeck, *The Political Economy of the New Left–An Outsider's View*. New York: Harper & Row.

—1982, "Forewords to the Japanese Edition of *The Collected Scientific Papers of Paul A. Samuelson*, vols. 1, 2, 4, 5, 6, 8, 9, M. Shinohara and R. Sato (eds.).

Tokyo: KeisoShobo. Reprinted in 1986, *The Collected Scientific Papers of Paul Samuelson*, vol. 5, 858–875. Cambridge, MA: MIT Press.

—1983, "My Life Philosophy," *The American Economist* 27, 2, 5–12.

—1995, "Economics in My Time," in W. Breit and R. W. Spencer (eds.), *Lives of the Laureates: Thirteen Nobel Economists*. Cambridge: MIT Press.

—2003, "How I became an Economist," Nobelprize.org. Accessed 9 June 2010, http://nobelprize.org/nobel prizes/economics/laureates/1970/samuelson-article2.html

—2009, Letter to A.M.C. Waterman, 7 July.

Schabas, M. 1992, "Breaking Away: History of Economics as History of Science," *History of Political Economy* 24, 1, 187–203.

Schumpeter, P. A. 1954, *History of Economic Analysis*. New York: Oxford University Press.

Smith, A. 1976 [1776], *An Inquiry into the Nature and Causes of the Wealth of Nations*. Oxford: Oxford University Press.

Sraffa, P. 1960, *Production of Commodities by Means of Commodities*, Cambridge: Cambridge University Press.

Stigler, G. J. 1952, "The Ricardian Theory of Value and Distribution," *Journal of Political Economy* 60, 3, 187–207.

Tozer, J. E. 1838, *Mathematical Investigation of the Effect of Machinery on the Wealth of a Community in Which It Is Employed and on the Fund for the Payment of Wages*. Transactions of the Cambridge Philosophical Society, vol. VI, part III, 507–522.

Turgot, A. R. J. 1963 [1776], *Reflections on the Formation and the Distribution of Riches*. New York: A.M. Kelley.

Viner, J. 1937, *Studies in the Theory of International Trade*. New York: Harper and Brothers.

Von Weizsäcker, C. C. and P. A. Samuelson. 1971, "A New Labor Theory of Value for Rational Planning Through Use of the Bourgeois Profit Rate," *Proceedings of the National Academy of Sciences* 68, 6, 1192–1194.

Waterman, A. M. C. 2003, "Mathematical Modeling as an Exegetical Tool: Rational Reconstruction," chap 33 in *Blackwell Companion to the History of Economic Thought*, W. J. Samuels, J. E. Biddle, and J. B. Davis (eds.). Oxford: Blackwell.

Whewell W. 1831, *Mathematical Exposition of Some of the Leading Doctrines in Mr. Ricardo's Principles of Political Economy and Taxation*, Transactions of the Cambridge Philosophical Society, vol. IV, part I, 155–198.

Winch, D. N. 1996, *Riches and Poverty: An Intellectual History of Political Economy in Britain, 1750–1834*. Cambridge: Cambridge University Press.

PART I

HISTORIOGRAPHY

Out of the Closet: A Program for the Whig History of Economic Science

A spectre haunts the history of economic thought. Someone is walking over our grave and we shudder involuntarily.

Like the press covering Mark Twain, do I exaggerate the death of our specialty? Yes I do. Our presence here belies the literal truth of any such pronouncement. But I exaggerate in a good cause and I repeat only what we all are complaining about in the privacies of our own boudoirs. And undoubtedly at those final family reunions of the dinosaurs, keynote speakers protested too much when claiming vaingloriously, "We're as good as we ever were." Better to run scared, I say, than to wind down with a whimper.

When I began graduate study a million years ago, history of thought was a dying industry. But it was still a presence in the required curriculum to be reckoned with. Jacob Viner was cracking the whip at the University of Chicago. Edwin Seligmann at Columbia and Jacob Hollander at Johns Hopkins occupied their professorial chairs. Edwin Cannan, though emeritus in London, carried into retirement his scorpion's bite.

The cash value of a subject in the curriculum is the ice it cuts in the examination ordeal. The general oral exams at Harvard in the 1930s were a game of Russian roulette: if you drew the lottery ticket of Leontief or Schumpeter in economic theory, you had better know how Frisch was able to measure cardinal utility and what adjusted demand concavity did to size of total output of a discriminating monopolist. [Aside: there's history of analysis for you.] If you drew Ed Chamberlin, there was of course only one subject you had to know. But if you drew Arthur Eli Monroe – or, just before my time, Frank Taussig or C.J. Bullock – your theory exam might well never get up to the time of Adam Smith.

Keynote Address at History of Economics Society Boston Meeting, June 20, 1987. I owe thanks for partial support to my Gordon Y Billard postdoctoral fellowship at the MIT Sloan School of Management and, for editorial aids, to Aase Huggins and Ruth Pelizzon.

It was even worse in the 1920 s: Douglass V. Brown told me that Bullock asked him: "What economic texts would you assign in Fifth Century B.C. Athens? In Fourth Century? In Third Century?" I only repeat the story as it was told to me.

All this was more than the traffic would subsequently bear. The decadence of literary economics from 1910 to 1930 perhaps explains the atavistic survival of *Dogmengeschichte* until so late a date. When physics is in a vibrant state of progress, a Fermi is contemptuous of any preoccupation with history of the subject. Thus, after he wrote up his Columbia lectures on thermodynamics for publication, he assigned a junior assistant the chore of filling in a few references. In the time you wasted pondering over the paradoxes and foundations of the second law of thermodynamics, Fermi felt you might be discovering a new elementary particle or be theorizing concerning a neutrino that keeps total energy conserved.

I wish I could assert that the present disdain for history of economics was occasioned by on-going Kuhnian breakthroughs in current economic science. Alas, as attendance at National Bureau seminars will reveal, ours is not an age of heady accomplishments and new exciting syntheses. But that does not blunt the following point.

Shortly after 1930 economics burst out into new life. At least four revolutions erupted: the *monopolistic competition* revolution, the *Keynesian macro* revolution, the *mathematicization* revolution, and the *econometric inference* revolution. Graduate students need at least 4 hours a night of sleep: that is a universal constant. So something had to give in the economics curriculum. What gave, and gave out, was history of thought – followed quickly by attrition of foreign language requirements and of minima for economic history.

As they say in the *Vogue* cigarette ads, "We've come a long way, Baby." Here's how far. A Scandinavian scholar has been spending a sojourn at Harvard. Undeterred by the leagues separating Littauer Center from the MIT Sloan Building, he has been auditing a macro course by one of my colleagues. "I did not expect that there would be copious assignments in Wicksell, Cassel, and Marshall," he confided to me. "But imagine my surprise that there were no items on the reading list earlier than 1985!" I answered him that, although the goatskins were brand new, some of the wine contained therein would have been recognizable to Harrod and Hicks and maybe to Ricardo as well.

So much for diagnosis of our subject's lack of Darwinian fitness in the struggle for existence.

I turn to prescribing what we might do about it.

PRESCRIPTION

I begin with the dogma that The Customer is always right. I take a leaf from the book of one of my contemporaries who, after being told by the Ford Foundation that it did not give grants for the kind of research he had proposed in his application, asked by return mail: "What *are* you giving grants for?"

I propose that history of economics more purposefully reorient itself toward studying the past from the standpoint of the present state of economic science. To use a pejorative word unpejoratively, I am suggesting Whig Economic History of Economic Analysis.[1]

The history of humane letters involves only history. Sam Johnson's mistakes may be more interesting than his correct observations. To the antiquarian, antiquarianism is all there is to the history of the humanities.

The history of scientific thought is a two-fold matter. We are interested in Newton's alchemy and biblical prophecy because we are interested in Newton the man and scientist. At the same time his stepbrother's theology is likely to elicit a yawn from even the most besotted antiquarian. How Newton discerned that a homogeneous sphere of non-zero radius attracts as if all its mass were at its center point, that is part of the history of cumulative science. Say that this attitude involves an element of Whig history if you will, but remember that working scientists have some contempt for those historians and philosophers of science who regard efforts in the past that failed as being on a par with those that succeeded, success being measurable by latest-day scientific juries who want to utilize hindsight and ex post knowledge. [Because Thomas Babington Macaulay judged the past completely in terms of how it led toward, or resisted movement to, the present of his own day the name Whig History was coined.]

Economics is in between belles-lettres and cold science. To illustrate the approach I am recommending, let us take a fresh look at Piero Sraffa's magnificent edition of David Ricardo's works, Sraffa [1951].

Serious economists below the age of 60 will judge Sraffa's edition of Ricardo both for its antiquarian and its scientific interests and insights. How then will they judge it?

From an antiquarian view the work is a jewel of perfection. Reviewers' enthusiasm has been unbounded. By luck and Sraffa's energetic skills,

---

[1] The following several paragraphs are paraphrased closely from my article *Sraffian Economics*, prepared for the *New Palgrave*.

virtually every scrap written by David Ricardo has been made available to the interested reader. This is a boon to scholars who lack the slightest interest in the history of thought for its own sake: Baconian scientific observation of Ricardo's economics has now been made possible by Sraffa's labors.

Editorial emendations have also been done in the new edition with skill and brevity. You might almost say that the editor has for the most part stayed chastely out of the act, letting David and his friends speak their pieces without an accompaniment of Greek Chorus expressions of approval or disapproval.

From the scientific viewpoint, and now a minority viewpoint is being expressed here, there is something anticlimactic about the great Sraffa edition of Ricardo. It is not just that we see, as if imprisoned in amber, the backward and forward gropings of a scholar who from his 1814 entrance into microeconomics until his 1823 death makes almost no progress in resolving his self-created ambiguities and problematics. Somehow one had hoped that the whole picture would be a prettier scientific picture, so that the editor's Herculean framings would be for a more worthwhile object.

There is, however, no point in lamenting that Ricardo was only what he was. It is the "road not taken" by the editor that occasions a twinge of regret. From the scientists, rather than the antiquarians' viewpoint, we appreciate from an editor and commentator what Jacob Viner gave economists in his magnificent 1937 *Studies in the Theory of International Trade* and what Eli Hackscher supplied in his *Mercantilism*. It is what Clifford Truesdell's lengthy introductions to the collected works of Euler provide, and what Abraham Pais succeeds in bringing off in his 1984 survey of the scientific physics of Albert Eienstein. Admittedly, old Edwin Cannan carried to excess his patronizing reviews of past economic giants, not only faulting them for their sins in failing to believe what Cannan believed in 1928 but also managing to convict them of the crime of not being so smart as himself. Surely, there is a golden mean somewhere between Cannan's dominating the act and Sraffa's avoiding getting into it?

Fortunately, in the Introduction to Ricardo's *Principles*, Piero Sraffa does seem to let himself go a little bit. Thus, it is conjectured that Ricardo may have, in a lost 1814 manuscript or letter or conversation, worked out a model in which the profit rate is determined within agriculture, as a ratio of so to speak corn to corn; and, Sraffa seems to all but say, in such a model distribution theory is successfully emancipated from value theory. Unlike Viner and Cannan, who can be very hard indeed on the guinea pigs they are judging, one reads Sraffa in the Introduction as being quite indulgent of

Ricardo. When he quotes Ricardo as purporting to get rid of the complication of rent by concentrating on the external margin, Sraffa never seems tempted to add that this is a *non sequitur*. When Ricardo tries to over-differentiate his product from Smith's, Sraffa never writes: "Of course, when Smith made the emergence of positive interest cause a divergence of price from labor contents, he was doing what Ricardo often admits must be done – namely formulating a two-factor rather than a one-factor model of pricing."

Let me now depart from my quoted text to relate an antiquarian's story. In 1982 I received an emergency call from the leading Italian newspaper, telling me that Piero Sraffa was dying and asking if I could hurry, hurry, hurry and write an obituary for him. Admiring him professionally and personally, I hurried, hurried, hurried: but Sraffa did not die. They saved the obituary, though. And when Piero died in 1983, the obituary appeared.

Two features in it are perhaps worthy of comment. Sraffa's exact relationship with the Left was always a matter of some ambiguity if not mystery. Of course he was a friend of Gramsci, who provided Gramsci in Mussolini's jail books and other helps. As his friend Ludwig Wittgenstein has said, "On that of which we cannot speak, we must perforce be silent." So I merely retold the old Kalecki story, in which Kalecki sought to meet "an English gentleman." "But," he related, "in the whole of the British Isles I could find only two English gentlemen. One turned out to be a communist and the other an Italian." Kalecki was understood to mean Maurice Dobb, who made no bones about his active participation in the British Communist Party; and to mean Piero Sraffa, who was the gentlest person that ever *graced* a Senior Common Room–and I choose my verb advisedly. So, allusively, I wrote: "Perhaps Kalecki met more than one communist."

When I came to write on Sraffa for the *New Palgrave*, my first draft merely said that his relationship to the Left was problematic. The Editors reproached me sternly, informing me that there was no mystery about the matter and that Sraffa "was a member of the C.P." So I decided to omit this antiquarianism and stick to Sraffa's square non-negative matrixes.

That is not quite the end of the story. Very recently in the *Proceedings of the British Academy*, there appeared a nice obituary on Piero by Nicholas Kaldor, his Cambridge colleague and old friend. This posthumous piece may be the last article Nicky every wrote. Now, as they say in court, I connect up. Kaldor states categorically that Sraffa was never a member of the Party. So, once again I stood corrected. But I did write to my Palgrave editor, voicing a mild complaint in this matter and in the matter of the 1959 *Introduction* to Ricardo's *Principles* that I shall presently discuss. This careful scholar apologized handsomely, reporting that his sources now admitted to some confusion.

The second point in my obituary concerned the authorship of the crucial *Introduction* to the Royal Economic Society's edition of the *Principles*. Once leafing through the new *Cambridge Journal of Economics*, I chanced upon a brief autobiography of Maurice Dobb, written Henry-Adams-like as if in the third person. I almost swallowed my gum when I encountered the sentence in which the modest Dobb took some pride in having written this *Introduction*, the flagship editorial piece of the whole magnificent *Works and Correspondence of David Ricardo*. Knowing Dobb to be a person of great integrity and modesty, I was literally dumbfounded.

And in a curious way I was relieved. For, as my quoted words revealed, I had been disappointed in Sraffa's *Introduction* as both thin and uncritical. I could have hoped for more from this giant historian of economics in the present Age, whereas Dobb was a mere mortal like the rest of us.

After my Sraffa obituary mentioned Dobb's authorship, Dobb's biographer at Trinity complained to Frank Hahn that Samuelson was traducing the good names of Dobb and Sraffa. The crime I committed was that of translating at literal face value Dobb's written sentence. Everyone knew that Dobb had aided in the editorial process, as indicated by the designation of "Piero Sraffa with the assistance of Maurice Dobb" on the title page of the *Works*. So again I stood corrected, even though no malice need be read into my American literalism.

Here are some asides concerning relevant Cambridge gossip. Richard Kahn had told me in 1948 that Sraffa was still blocked over Volume I's *Introduction*. Years earlier it had been found that, provided his secretary sat in the room with him, Sraffa could make some progress on the write-up job. But she, poor thing, began to go beyond the bloom of youth and when finally she had to leave to carry forward her own life plans, progress ground to a halt – until it was discovered that, so long as Maurice Dobb sat in the room, discernible motion could resume. Of course Dobb aided also in the arduous tasks of editing, and it was reasonable to infer that some of the editorial glosses came from his quill.

There matters stood until the recent appearance of Kaldor's eulogy of Sraffa. Kaldor seems to say plainly that Dobb and not Sraffa did write the *Introduction*. So apparently my corrections need to be uncorrected. The moral of the story for future researchers into Ricardo and into his collected works is to realize how severe Sraffa's writer's block had become and how uncertain must be attributions to drafters. Fortunately the ambiguities are primarily of antiquarian interest only, since we are entitled to believe that

Sraffa read any and all of Dobb's drafts and would have made explicit objection to any clauses with which he could not possibly agree.[2]

Notice that in this speech advocating Whig history, your humble Cretan servant – Cretan not spelled with an "i", please – I have allocated much

[2] The reader can study the documentation on the Dobb-Sraffa collaboration.

A. Dobb's autobiography, which I now realize was a posthumous publication, is entitled "Random Biographical Notes," *Cambridge Journal of Economics* 2 (1978), 115–120. On p. 119 appears the sentence: "At the same time [1948] he [Dobbs, I] started collaborating with P. Sraffa in completing the editing of the 10-volume edition of the *Works and Correspondence* of David Ricardo and in writing several editorial Notes and Introductions (including the Introduction to Vol. I).

B. From Kaldor's posthumous obituary commentary, "Piero Sraffa: 1898–1983" in *Proceedings of the British Academy*, 1986, 615–640–which includes a good picture of the elderly Sraffa, the whole of footnote 1, p. 631, is worth quoting: "Sraffa's extreme inhibitions against speaking or *writing* for publication (to which reference has already been made) provided another serious obstacle to the early completion of the work, since Sraffa could never bring himself to put pen to paper for writing a 'final' text of Introduction, even when the ideas which he wished to express in it were clearly worked out in his mind. The obstacle was overcome by calling in the assistance of M. H. Dobb, whose qualities were complementary to those of Sraffa; he was not a deep original thinker but had considerable powers of exposition with a clear and fluent style. Hence, as Sraffa explains in the General Preface, I. x, the actual writing of the Introductions to vols. I, II, V and VI, was due to Dobb-though the ideas were Sraffa's (this is particularly important in connection with the Introduction to vol. I, which gives a wholly new interpretation of Ricardo's theory of value").

C. The words cited by Kaldor concerning Sraffa's acknowledgement to Dobb on p. x of the *General Preface* to *The Works and Correspondence of David Ricardo, Volume I* (Cambridge, Cambridge University Press, 1951) seem to be
    "In 1948 Mr. Maurice Dobb came in to assist with the editorial work, in particular being associated in the writing of the Introductions to vols. I, II, V and VI."

Now, what to think in 1987?

a) Once my original reading of Dobb was challenged, I deemed it reasonable to infer that Dobb meant only to claim he had been "collaborating with P. Sraffa ... in writing ... (.. the Introduction to Vol. I)."

b) Although Kaldor's words are unequivocal ... "the actual writing of the Introductions to vols. I, II, V and VI was due to Dobb..", one must wonder whether he had literal warrant for saying this other than his words, "Hence, as Sraffa explains in the General Perface, Ix.."

c) For, when we read that cited Preface of Sraffa's, we find no more said than that ".. Dobb came to assist with the editorial work.." being associated in the writing of the Introductions to vols. I, II, V and VI."

In sum, it is still an open question whether Dobb did literally draft the Volume I Introduction or rather assist in its composition. Richard Kahn, Austin Robinson, or some other Cambridge friends of Sraffa and Dobb are needed to help us settle this antiquarian issue.

time to antiquarian gossip. Am I inconsistent? Very well, I plead guilty to
that. But I do claim minor extenuating circumstances. A deep student of
Piero Sraffa will not find it irrelevant information that he was more prone
ideologically to Karl Marx than to Ludwig von Mises. And a deep student
of Ricardo will gain insight into the simple truth that David did *not*
operationally pursue a model in which the labour theory of value obtained,
even though his twentieth century editor chose not to stress this substantive fact.

BRIEF SUBMITTED FOR THE COURT

If this session is not to be a monologue, my remaining time is infinitesimal.
So let me conclude with examples of what I consider to be Whig history of
economic science.

1. Schumpeter's great posthumous *History* is an evident leading example.
   It is even greater than its reputation but, alas, it is a sadly unfinished
   work. God permitted Moses to come near to the Promised Land but
   refused him final entrance.
2. Go to any economics library, as I have done at MIT and Harvard, and
   you will find the pages are dirtier in Mark Blaug's *Economic Theory in
   Retrospect* than in the well known texts of Gide and Rist, Alexander
   Gray, Eric Roll, or even Blaug's own *Ricardian Economics*. I could rest
   my case after these exhibitions of revealed preference by our hoped-for
   clients.
3. That I do practise what I preach, putting my pen where my mouth is, is
   shown by the following of my writings submitted in evidence to this
   court of opinion.

a) *Thünen at 200.* Here as midwife I draw from this genius's writings the
   complete model that is there. A rose by any name would smell as
   sweet. My use of modern notations and methods requires no apology
   since, on my oath, I did not put the baby there nor forge any of its
   parts. (I recognize the perils of reading into an older author what is
   only in your own mind and I would submit as an instance Milton
   Friedman's purported demonstration that Alfred Marshall intended
   his demand curve to be a Slutsky-compensated one. His evidence does
   not wash with Robert Bishop nor with me.)
b) The 1978 *Canonical Classical Model.* In one diagram there is captured what is held in common by Ricardo, J. S. Mill, Malthus,
   Marx and Smith. The fact that contemporaries quarrel must be

understood against the background of an age in which writers imperfectly understood their own theories. One consequence of the end-of-century Cliowhiggism approach has been the significant bull market in the stock of Adam Smith at the expense of the paper of David Ricardo.

c) *Quesnay's "Tableau Economique" as a Theorist Would Formulate It Today*, [1982]. Unlike the above two items, which were widely read and favorably received, this item was buried in a *Festschrift*, the posthumous one for Ronald Meek. And no one of its two-dozen readers has evinced approval. Yet I am unrepentant. The *Tableau* was a comic case of puffery and mystification but it did foreshadow general equilibrium: Quesnay did stimulate Marx, Schumpeter, Leontief, and indirectly Sraffa; and, in our times, Malanos, Almarin Phillips, Maital, Barna, Harry Johnson, Eltis, and Meek have related it to the input/output models of Leontief and to the Keynes-Metzler-Goodwin-Chipman multiplier models.

Nonetheless, it was still necessary in 1982 to develop two crucial points: the fatal inadequacies of Quesnay's dynamic *zig-zags*; and the asymmetric role of fixed-supply of land in the Physiocratic *Weltanschauung*, which underlay the notion of the "sterility" of manufacturing and justified land as the sole source of *produit net*, and which became lost in the modern generalizations of the analysis.

d) *Ricardo on machinery, 1987*. As well as providing examples of what I deem to be good Whig history of science, I should specify examples that are primarily of antiquarian interest only. Near the end of this life Ricardo added to his third edition of the *Principles* the notorious Chapter 31 on machinery. It scandalized his own followers and was hailed by the advocates of socialism as a damning concession concerning the demerits of capitalism – namely admission that invention of machinery could reduce the demand for labor, and in decimating the population could reduce in the long run *Ricardo's* defined *net national product*. The modern jury has ruled thumbs down on Ricardo's analysis of the matter: Wicksell's indictment of Ricardo's logic has been joined in by Kaldor, George Stigler, and almost all of the modern pack.

I must strongly dissent and have long used this issue as a *Rorschach* blot to test the minds of modern analysts. How people react to the smudge is more important than the blot itself. In two unpublished papers I have argued the details. Although I have rarely over the years been able to score Ricardo's logic high, in this case he is essentially

right and right for the right reasons. That means his critics are plain
wrong.

This is why, in summing up, I had to say that the machinery
chapter is the best chapter in Ricardo's *Principles*. It addresses a
problem important in economic theory, and it gets the analysis
right. To calibrate me, let me depose that the worst chapter in
Ricardo's book is his first chapter, the one on value and in which he
parades the criticisms of Smith's *Wealth of Nations* that motivated
him as a mere broker to become an author of microeconomics.
Literary economics at its worst and most boring: that is my report
card on Ricardo's first-chapter effort. Attempts by moderns, such as
Sraffa with his defined *standard commodity*, to provide justification
for Ricardo's labour theory of value – once you understand them–are
quite uninteresting. As the physicist Pauli once said of a new theory:
"It isn't even wrong." Over certain intervals of the interest rate, there
are definable market baskets of goods in terms of which the wage rate
paid post factum drops linearly with the interest rate. That is a
standard theorem for Perron-Frobenius matrixes. But from this fact
no modern Ricardian can get around the failures of the labour theory
of value: changes in consumers' demands must still generally alter
wage/profit shares, even when the profit rate does not change
(as Ricardo at times knew); changes in profit rates do (generally)
alter relative prices; and so it goes.

The conductor Leopold Stokowski once said, "I have talked a long time
about my own work. So in all fairness I should now ask you to talk about
me." Having provided examples from my own writings of the Whig history
of science that can thrive in the ahistoric times to come, let me conclude
with one of the most famous and most successful jewels in the crown of
Whig history of science.

I refer to von Bortkiewicz's 1907 resolution of what Marx called the
"transformation problem." Not only the critics of Marx, but also his
followers (such as Sweezy, Winternitz, Dobb, Meek, . . .) have followed
Bortkiewcz's lead. However, because the muse of history has a sense of
humor, it took a child to identify what clothes the Emperor wore – a child
who pointed out in 1971 that Bortkiewicz "transforms" to bourgeois
"prices" from 1867 "(marked-up) values" by erasing the latter's equations
and filling in the blanks by the former's. As Hans Christian Andersen
failed to relate about the fable, of course no one believed what the child
was saying!

FINALE

This concluding example illustrates that we Whig historians will never run out of work. In the course of discussing the works of past scientists, we are producing works that will be grist for the mills of those who will *follow* us–I mean who will come after us, after us with scalpels and hemp.

You in the audience can now proceed to make this a self-justifying prophecy.

REFERENCES

Blaug, M. *Economic Theory in Retrospect*, (London: Cambridge University Press, 1962, 1968, 1978).

Samuelson, P. A. "Quesnay's Tableau Economique' as a Theorist would Formulate it Today," in *Classical and Marxian Political Economy: Essays in Honor of Ronald L. Meek*. Ian Bradley and Michael Howard (eds.). New York: St. Martin's Press, 1982, 45–78; also published in *Collected Scientific Papers of Paul A. Samuelson*, chapter 343, Vol. V, (ed.) Kate Crowley, (Cambridge: MIT Press, 1986).

—"The Canonical Classical Model of Political Economy," *Journal of Economic Literature* vol. 16, Dec. 1978, 1415–1434; also published in *Collected Scientific Papers of Paul A. Samuelson*, chapter 340, Vol. V, (ed.) Kate Crowley, (Cambridge: MIT Press, 1986).

—"Thünen at Two Hundred," *Journal of Economic Literature*, Vol. 21, Dec. 1983, 1468–1488; also published in *Collected Scientific Papers of Paul A. Samuelson*, chapter 339, Vol. V, (ed.) Kate Crowley, (Cambridge: MIT Press, 1986).

—"Mathematical Vindication of Ricardo on Machinery," submitted for publication to *Journal of Political Economy*, 1987.

—"Ricardo Was Right," submitted for publication to *Scandinavian Journal of Economics*, 1987.

Schumpeter, J. *History of Economic Analysis*, Oxford University Press, 1954.

Sraffa, P. (Ed.) with the collaboration of M.H. Dobb, *The Works and Correspondence of David Ricardo*, Vol. I, *On The Principles of Political Economy and Taxation*, Published for The Royal Economic Society. Cambridge University Press. 1951.

PART II

BEFORE ADAM SMITH

A Corrected Version of Hume's Equilibrating Mechanisms for International Trade[*]

1. Introduction

David Hume put to rest in 1752 the fear that free international trade will drain a nation of its money. His doctrine of how an outflow of specie is self-correcting and eventually equilibrating still prevails in our textbooks and treatises after more than two centuries and is still appealed to in our definitive policy debates.

But, actually, Hume's account is both wrong and incomplete. If incompleteness were its only fault, that would be a forgivable blemish in an early masterpiece. Hume's classical followers – Ricardo and Mill, if not Adam Smith – could have been expected to fill in the gaps in Hume's brief exposition. But they did not. Nor did such modern giants as Haberler or Viner do so, though both these authors show clearly that they perceived a need to modify Hume's own syllogisms. And Ohlin, who deserves credit for emphasizing that transfer payments from one country to another will shift demand schedules in both places, did not rectify the classical mechanism that he hoped to supplement with his own innovations.

Never underestimate the blinding power of a beautiful mistake. Hume's inadequate analysis, both because of its brilliant simplicity and its obvious nearness to a correct truth, so satisfied the economists who followed him that they felt no need to provide correct alternative explanations. When Jacob Frenkel and Harry Johnson tried to puff up the case for something they called "the monetary approach to the balance of payments," they cited David Hume as one of its many precursors. But a line-by-line reading of Hume's essay "Of the Balance of Trade" will

[*] I owe thanks to the National Science Foundation for financial aid, and to Aase Huggins for editorial assistance.

demonstrate that – however close Gervaise, Longfield, Mill, Cairnes, and some other writers had come to the direct effects of money supply on demand-at-unchanged-prices in their momentary *deviations* from mainstream foreign-trade theory – David Hume's treatment of specie flows managed to miss completely that key element.[1]

Once we are alerted to Hume's sins of commission and omission, it is an easy exercise to assign to a modern analyst. Provide a correct version of what Hume sought: a self-equilibrating model of the balance of payments that recognizes the unity of price for competitive goods freely transportable in international trade.

This exercise I propose to provide here – with impressionistic brevity.

2. What Hume said

Here are quotations, selective but complete so far as logic is concerned.

... there still prevails ... in nations ... a strong jealousy with regard to the balance of trade, and a fear that all their gold and silver may be leaving them. This seems to me, almost in every case, a groundless apprehension; ...

Suppose four-fifths of all the money in Great Britain to be annihilated in one night ... Must not the price of all labour and commodities sink in proportion, and everything be sold as cheap [as in earlier days when *M* was one-fifth]? ... What nation could then dispute with us in any foreign market, or pretend to navigate or to sell manufactures at the same price, which to us would afford sufficient profit? In how little time, therefore, must this bring back the money which we had lost, and raise us to the level of all the neighbouring nations? Where, after we have arrived, we immediately lose the advantage of the cheapness of labour and commodities; and the farther flowing in of money is stopped by our fullness and repletion. [When *M* rises, the opposite happens.]

... Now, it is evident, that the same causes, which would correct these exorbitant inequalities, ... must preserve money nearly proportionable to the art and industry of each nation. All water, wherever it communicates, remains always at a level ...

[Similarly, Hume asserts,] it is impossible to heap up money, more than any fluid, beyond its proper level ...

How is the balance kept [internally] in the provinces of every kingdom among themselves, but by the force of this principle, which makes it impossible for money

---

[1]   See G. Haberler (1936), J. Viner (1937), B. Ohlin (1933); also J. Frenkel and H. G. Johnson (1974). The latter do give a quotation from another Hume essay, "Of the Jealousy of Trade," but the words cited there do not deal with the essential element of the *money stock's* direct effect on ceteris paribus demand, as stressed for example in Prais (1961), J. J. Polak (1957) or R. Dornbusch (1973).

to lose its level, and either to rise or sink beyond the proportion of labour and commodities which are in each province?[2]

Now to put Hume in crudest equation form. Let P stand for gold price(s) at home, P^* for price(s) abroad; M^* stands for their (gold) money supply, M for our gold supply; Q and Q^* for the total outputs at home and abroad. Finally, ignoring capital movements, let B be the (algebraic) gold value of our balance of trade – the surplus of our exports over our imports if positive, our deficit if negative.

Crudely put, here is a version of Hume's paradigm:

$$B = f[P/P^*], \quad \frac{df[\ ]}{d(P/P^*)} < 0; \qquad (1)$$

$$P = kM = (\gamma/Q)M, \ P^* = k^*M^* = (\gamma/Q^*)M^*; \qquad (2)$$

$$\frac{dM}{dt} = -\frac{dM^*}{dt} = B = f[P/P^*]; \qquad (3)$$

$$M + M^* = \mu, \text{the world supply of specie.} \qquad (4)$$

---

[2] These quotations are from Hume's 1752 essay "Of the Balance of Trade," and are taken from E. Rotwein, ed., *David Hume: Writings on Economics* (London: Nelson, 1955), pp. 61–65. Hume's essay that follows, "Of the Jealousy of Trade," has no words on the equilibrating macroeconomic mechanism, but does make the nice point that diversity among nations will assure that our nation has [what we would call] comparative advantage in some goods. Hume's April, 1749 correspondence with Montesquieu, Rotwein (1955, pp. 188–189), covers no new ground; his exchange of 1750 with Oswald (Rotwein, 1955, pp. 190–199), needlessly denies Oswald's valid point that our P's never rise as much as M alone does, precisely because we are an open trading economy.

Hume (Rotwein, 1955, p. 64, n.1), also has an acute footnote recognizing the equilibrating effect for a deficit country of the depreciation of its exchange rate down to the export *gold point* set by cost of "carriage and insurance" of the specie used as money. He also recognizes that transport costs make possible limited deviations between a good's competitive prices in two places a distance apart. Hume's words show he would understand there being a different water level at the two ends of the Panama Canal; since they are so far apart, the slight friction associated with distance accumulates to a sizable deviation in their equilibrium levels. My exposition will first assume zero transport costs for gold M and for *all* goods. Then I introduce nontraded goods, or goods that trade only when their transport costs are matched by their spatial price differentials. Finally, I briefly treat the case of inconvertible moneys – paper acceptable only at home, or M stuffs so nontransportable as never to enter into international exchange.

Equation (2) states the Quantity Theory of Prices in crudest one-nation form. Equation (3) is the definitional form of the balance of payments or trade when specie is alone used to settle deficits: you lose M^* to us, $-dM^*/dt = B$, when we enjoy a trade surplus of B.

Equation (1) states what Hume regarded as obvious without worrying his head about inelasticities of net demand that violate so-called Marshall–Lerner conditions. As will be seen, this first relation is vitiated by the fact that the same good must have the same price everywhere in a competitive world without transport costs.[3]

Let's give David Hume rope. For fixed total world gold, there is a unique equilibrium distribution of (M, M^*) implied by his system (1)–(4). Although Hume does not explicitly specify that trade balances when prices are equal, $P/P^* = 1$, suppose I do adjoin that relationship:

$$B = 0 = f[1], \quad P/P^* = 1. \tag{1'}$$

Then in longest-term equilibrium

$$M(t) \to \frac{Q}{Q + Q^*}\mu, \quad M^*(t) \to \frac{Q^*}{Q + Q^*}\mu,$$

$$B(t) \to 0, \quad P(t)/P^*(t) \to 1. \tag{5}$$

Proof. W. Substituting the Quantity Theory relations of (2) into (3) and writing $M^*(t)$ as $\mu - M(t)$, (3) becomes the self-correcting differential equation:

$$\frac{dM}{dt} = f\left[\frac{MQ^*}{(\mu - M)Q}\right]. \tag{6}$$

From any initial condition different from $M(\infty) = Q(Q + Q^*)^{-1}\mu$,

$$M(t) \to M(\infty).$$

Indeed, *penultimately*, $M(t) - M(\infty)$ decays away to zero exponentially at the same rate that $B(t)$ or any of the other deviations from equilibrium $[M^*(t) - M^*(\infty), P(t) - P(\infty), P^*(t) - P^*(\infty)]$ decay away to zero.

---

[3]   It won't help to interpret P and P^* as vectors of prices:

$$P = (p_1, \ldots, p_n); P^* = (p_1^*, \ldots p_n^*).$$

Then

$$B = f(P_1, \ldots, P_n; P_1^*, \ldots, P_n^*).$$

Were Hume to claim that raising *all* P_j^* fivefold while holding *all* P_j constant would raise B, we'd still have to ask how *any* P_j^* could stay above its respective P_j under free trade.

This ultimate speed of adjusting depends of course on how rapidly each change in P/P^* corrects B – the quantitative strength of what some call the Marshall–Lerner criterion – and on how near to the same size are the two countries and are their equilibrium shares of world money supply.[4]

3. Where Davie nodded

As Schumpeter used to put it, we can applaud Hume's performance in specifying a self-correcting mechanism that impressed people for two hundred years. But 1980 is not 1752. And neither was 1900. Hume's model is defective.

To see why, recall a stupid point that is attributed to J. L. Laughlin, bowdlerizing editor of J. S. Mill and first chairman of the Chicago economics department. Laughlin objected, saying in effect:

In these modern times of cable and quick transport, the specie-flow corrective mechanisms no longer work. Prices of the same goods are virtually *instantaneously* equilibrated. So it's quite impossible for Great Britain's prices to go down by Hume's postulated four-fifths to thereby restore Britain's dearth of M.

We speak of Laughlin's Fallacy. Orthodox writers, such as Haberler and Viner, refute Laughlin with words like the following:

Professor [J.] L. Laughlin has objected that between modern markets which are connected by railroads, telegraph, telephone, etc., price differentials cannot exist long enough to produce sufficiently large movements of goods. This criticism of the classical doctrine can be disposed of by pointing out that modern means of communication equalise prices by inducing transactions between the cheap and dear market; far from being an objection, this statement calls attention to circumstances which make for a rapid functioning of the mechanism. (Haberler, 1936, p. 29)

When, therefore, critics of the classical theory [like Laughlin, 1903] have taken it to task on the ground that it explained the adjustment of international balances by the influence on the course of trade of divergent market prices in different markets of identical [freely] transportable commodities, ... they have misinterpreted the classical doctrine.

... It is relative changes in *supply* prices of identical commodities as between different potential sources of supply, and, above all, relative changes in the actual sales prices of *different* commodities which, through their influence on the direction

---

[4] $M(t) - M(\infty)$ grows penultimately like ae^{-bt}, where

$$b = f'[1][(1/M_\infty) + (1/M_\infty^*)].$$

Note: If $B = 0$ at $f(\pi) = 0$, where $\pi = P_\infty/P_\infty^*$ is not unity, and if in (2) the countries' velocities of circulation are not the same so that on the right y must be replaced by y^*, then the formulas in (5) will require obvious modifications. Hume would not be surprised once we called his attention to these possible complications.

and extent of trade, exercise a significant role in the mechanism of adjustment of international balances. (Viner, 1937, pp. 316–318)

Haberler and Viner are right to attack Laughlin, but that does not mean Laughlin's critique of the Hume mechanism of the last section misses *its* mark. If $P(t)$ and $P^*(t)$ must be identical, then Equations (1)–(4) are indeed falsified. In effect, Haberler and Viner are agreeing with my present contention that the Hume reasoning is fundamentally defective.

Curiously, as the reader thumbs through the Haberler and Viner texts, she does not find a simple and correct replacement for the defective Hume exposition. To get that alternative, you must infer from between the lines how such a complete account would go. Arnold Collery (1974) has persuaded me that there remains a gap in Viner's exposition. To fill it, you would have to go to the advanced treatise by Viner's student, Jacob Mosak (1944). And even there you will not find the dynamic non-neutral-money adjustments that Frenkel and Johnson (1976) now emphasize shrilly.

Moreover, the Laughlin fallacy still lives, propagating with the vigor of a weed. It could as well be called the Laffer fallacy, or the Wall Street Journal fallacy.

Worse than that. Turn to the advanced modern rebuttals of what is essentially the Laughlin fallacy. You will be a lucky reader if you do not find yourself fobbed off with both or one of the following sophisticated fallacies:

Non-traded goods fallacy. It is by differential movements of 2 countries' nontraded goods' price levels, relative to their necessarily equal price levels of freely traded goods, that we save the faulty Hume mechanism and prove the stability and self-correction of the international trade mechanism. This is alleged to be especially applicable to small, open economies.

Terms-of-trade fallacy. It is not the lowering of price(s) in the deficit country relative to the respective prices in the surplus country of the identical tradeable good(s) that restores equilibrium. What accomplishes the essential equilibrium is the lowering of the price(s) and price level of the deficit country's export goods, relative to the price(s) and price level of the surplus country's export goods – at least this effects the equilibration if the Marshall–Lerner criterion is not perverse.

Neither of these rebuttals is correct logically or applicable in certain important empirical cases. Instead, I shall show:

1. Even with no changes in any relative or absolute prices – here or abroad, between tradeable and nontradeable goods, between export and import goods – a properly reformulated Hume model can be shown to be self-correcting and stable. This can be independent of the Marshall–Lerner criterion, whose importance has to do with microeconomic not macroeconomic stability.

2. If there are zero nontradeable goods, if transport costs and trade impediments are made to shrink to zero, the efficacy and speed of the monetary adjustment is preserved and not emasculated, and indeed may even be *accelerated.*

My words will shock some sophisticated readers. But that is only confirmatory to my charge that the fallacious Hume account has been so seductively plausible as to have eclipsed serious correct analysis. It is a scandal that, as late as 1937, Joan Robinson (1937, pp. 183–209) had to demonstrate that the terms of trade may go either way when a country depreciates its currency and thereby successfully restores micro-equilibrium of the Bickerdike (1920) model. And I do not know where, prior to the exposition of Dornbusch, Fischer, and Samuelson (1977, p. 836) there appeared explicitly in print a demonstration where gold flows *heal themselves faster when zero money is spent on nontradeable goods* than when much is spent on nontradeable items.

A digression. I fault Hume only on his fundamentals. I view as but a venial sin Hume's vagueness concerning his analogy between the equilibrium levels of M and M^* and the common level of water in communicating lakes or vessels. Ignoring friction, I can assert that water in two tubes settles at *identical heights.* That is different from saying, "A rope hanging in its equilibrium shape of a catenary has its parts at *different* heights." What is common in these last cases is the physicist's perception that a self-regulating physical process is involved in each case (and, as it happens, both cases can be subsumed under the principle that the statical equilibrium configuration is that which yields *minimum center of gravity* of the system subject to its constraints).

When I made $y = y^*$ in (2), I made the most favorable case for Hume, and for the notion he shared with such earlier writers as Malynes, Locke, Gervaise, and Cantillon – that M and M^* become respectively proportional to the economic sizes (populations, outputs) of the respective countries. Hume himself realized that a country could change its habits concerning the use of *paper* money and thereby alter y relative to y^* and thus affect ultimate M/M^* and make gold M/Q and gold M^*/Q^* be at different heights.

Gold's finding its proper geographical distribution by analogy with the way water finds its own level is merely a persuasive metaphor. If Hume had bothered to think the matter through, he'd have recognized that the analogy would have fit better if he likened the common price of wheat in two places to the common level of water in two places – a P rather than a Q or M analogy.

No later writers have been harmed by Hume's level-of-water analogy.

4. What Hume omitted

Along with the above-described errors of commission note an interesting Humean error of omission.

Hume fails to allow a drop in M to have direct contracting effects on our home country's spending. For him, it is only the changes in home prices relative to those abroad that brings about the healing increase in exports and the reduction in the imports of the deficit nation.

We could modify (1) in the manner of Prais (1961) and Dornbusch (1973) to make Hume more like what Frenkel and Johnson would like for him to have been. Now

$$B = f[P/P^*, M - M(\infty), M^* - M^*(\infty)], \qquad (1'')$$

$$\frac{\partial B}{\partial (P/P^*)} < 0, \quad \frac{\partial B}{\partial [M - M(\infty)]} < 0, \quad \frac{\partial B}{\partial [M^* - M^*(\infty)]} > 0.$$

Now, even if P/P^* were somehow frozen at unity and (2) somehow relaxed in the short run, $(1'')$ and (3) would constitute a stable, self-correcting mechanism that could work without regard to the Marshall–Lerner condition's determination of a perverse positive value for $\partial B/\partial (P/P^*)$. We could now write

$$dM/dt = f[1, M - M(\infty), -M + M(\infty)],$$

$$0 = f[1, 0, 0],$$

$$M(t) \rightarrow \frac{Q}{Q + Q^*}\mu,$$

$$M(t) - M(\infty) \simeq e^{-bt}, \text{ etc.} \qquad (6')$$

However, rather than patch up the faulty Hume model, the time has come to sketch a correct model.

5. Equilibration sans price changes

Begin with the challenge of tradeable goods only. With zero tariffs and transport costs, the upper and lower "gold points" are only an infinitesimal distance apart and exchange rates can't deviate from their parities. The same holds for all goods: wheat, cloth, cars, ... Their competitive prices must always be exactly the same as a result of quick arbitrage alone:

$$P_j = P_j^*, \ (j = 1, 2, ..., J). \tag{7}$$

Only factor inputs are immobile between nations. The gold wage rates need not be equal: $W \gtrless W^*$.

To sidestep the special problems involved in "capital" and time-phasing, if there be a second factor of production, let it be "land." The gold rents of immobile land need not be equal: $R \lessgtr R^*$.

Suppose we began in a Ricardian world of constant labor costs. If they were *uniformly* the same in both places, with no comparative advantages being involved, wage rates would be equalized and no profitable trade would occur.

There still would operate a self-correcting specie-flow mechanism. Here is how Hume should have formulated it.

Suppose we begin with twice our quota of world gold. Our initial excess of $M(0)$ will cause us in good Quantity Theory fashion to spend on consumption more than our incomes earned on production – as we try to work our excess money holdings towards their desired level. Abroad, their initial deficiency of $M^*(0)$ causes an opposite deficiency of consumption over output as they try to replenish their M^* balances over time. Short-run equilibrium involves an initial trade deficit, $B(0) < 0$ financed by an outflow of gold from us: $dM/dt = B(0) < 0$. So our $M(t) - M(\infty)$ is being corrected, and their deficiency $M^*(\infty) - M^*(t)$ is being corrected. The $-dM/dt$ hemorrhage ceases only when $[M(t), M^*(t)] \to [M(\infty), M^*(\infty)]$, their long-run normal values. If, as in the present case, the micro-model calls for no changes at all in relative (or even absolute) prices, that does not invalidate the self-correcting specie-flow mechanism.

The above would still hold in a world where, instead of all labor productivities being uniformly the same in all places, labor productivities were twice as great here as abroad so that our money and real wage rates were twice theirs. It would also be true in the more realistic case where we had comparative advantage in some goods and they in others. But now we must examine different cases.

(i) Suppose we *both* produce one of the goods, before the $[M(0), M^*(0)]$ initial disturbance, during the transition, and in the final permanent equilibrium. Then, even if we spend our increment of $M(0)$ differently from how they cut down on their spending, no price or wage changes will ever take place. But still the specie-flow correction works exactly as above.

(ii) Alternatively, suppose we produce goods $(1, 2, \ldots, r)$ and they produce goods $(r+1, \ldots, j)$. If the switch of $M(0)$ to us, and of $M^*(0)$ away from them, results in our incremental spending going toward the same goods they now cut their spending on – a not implausible Ohlin case in a world of zero transport cost and nonlocalization of demand! – no absolute or relative price changes will be induced. So, again, the specie-flow mechanism does the whole job by itself.

(iii) It could be that our incremental spending goes more toward the goods in which they have a comparative advantage, and their cut in spending is more on our goods than theirs. If so, the initial $[M(0), M^*(0)]$ switch will have turned the terms of trade in their favor: initially, they'll have higher W^*/W than before. This may force us to produce some good $r + 1$ or $r + k$, that previously they produced. So our products' prices will start a bit lower relative to their products' prices. $(P_1/P_j = P_1^*/P_j^*$ falls, but never does any P_J/P_J^* fall below unity!) This could add a bit to our initial trade deficit if the Marshall–Lerner conditions are "normal." So more specie will flow out initially. But still the self-correction sketched here will apply – even though money is not "neutral" in the transition phase, and *crude* purchasing-power-parity is violated since our weighted price level drops relative to theirs while exchange-rate parity never changes. Ultimately, gold gets relocated and the terms-of-trade revert to their long-run equilibrium level.

(iv) Finally, it could be that all the initial spending increments go more toward our goods $(1, 2, \ldots)$ than toward theirs. Then, W/W^* will be initially raised. Possibly we no longer produce good r previously produced. Our terms of trade have improved: $P_1/P_J = P_1^*/P_J^*$ rises by the gain in W/W^*. Under normal Marshall–Lerner conditions this subtracts from the size of our initial deficit. We have less initial rate of specie outflow and the transition to new equilibrium takes a bit longer. But the specie-flow mechanism is self-correcting.

Do all these reassuring results in the Ricardian world still hold in a neoclassical Ohlin-Haberler world of labor-cum-land? They do.

If labor/land endowments are close enough together and production-function knowledge the same in all regions, factor prices will be equalized. And through an initial $M(0)/\mu$ perturbation and subsequent correction, they will stay equalized. If our new spending generated by $M(t) - M(\infty)$ excess is directed toward the same goods their $M^*(\infty) - M^*(t)$ deficiency is withdrawn from, all absolute prices of goods and factors will be unaffected by the specie-flow corrections.

$$\frac{dM}{dt} \text{ has the opposite sign to } M(t) - M(\infty);$$

$$M(t) \rightarrow M(\infty) \text{ from any initial } M(0). \tag{8}$$

If technologies differ geographically, the same applies without necessary factor-price equalization.

If tastes are not the same at the margin in the different regions, then our $M(0)$ excess and its induced excess of consumption over income may alter the relative prices of the goods we export on balance relative to those we import. So the relative income share earned by the factor we are most abundantly endowed with may initially be perturbed and only gradually be restored to long-run equilibrium levels. Under normal Marshall–Lerner conditions,[5] there may be a slightly larger or smaller initial specie outflow, and a somewhat faster or slower period of adjustment of the self-correcting specie flow.

Warning: My corrected Hume model validates long-run purchasing-power-parity only in applications where the sole disturbance is in (M, M^*) stocks. In the short run, changes in these stocks need not be "neutral." Although P_j/P_j^* never deviates from unity set by zero transport costs and assumed gold-standard constancy of exchange rate, $P_{\text{export}}/P_{\text{import}}$ may change in either direction in the short run and so may any $P_i/P_j = P_i^*/P_j^*$ or W/W^* or Rent/Rent*. Furthermore, if the initial shock comes from something other than an $M/(M + M^*)$ perturbation, all bets are off concerning how some weighted $\sum P_j a_j$ behaves relative to some weighted $\sum P_j^* a_j^*$. With Cassel's bad example before them, why should zealots for the "monetary approach to the balance of payments" put his dunce's cap on their own heads?

6. Impediments to trade

Now I can dispose of the case on nontradeable goods, those with such heavy transport costs as to make them never exported or imported. More generally, with every good having some positive cost of transportation, it

---

[5] Dornbusch and Mussa (1975) have specified an optimal control model in which constancy of the consumption velocity of money is rationally derived. Even if we relax its strong assumptions, so long as an (algebraic) excessive M holding generates an excess of consumption spending over income, equilibrium will be stable.

becomes an *endogenous* problem to deduce which will be traded and which will not be.

As Ricardo knew, one important reason why gold is used as money domestically and internationally is the fact that its transport costs are unimportant in comparison with those of most goods. I begin by assuming gold has virtually zero transport costs; the gold points virtually coincide, and exchange rate parities never deviate from par.

Now prices of the same goods can deviate from unity within the interval set by transport costs per unit:

$$-t_i^* \leq p_i - p_i^* \leq t_i, \quad (i = 1, \dots, J) \tag{9}$$

where t_i is the (gold) cost of moving a unit of good i from there to here, and t_i^* is the cost of moving it from here to there. These transport costs need not be equal; they need not be constants, but it will suffice here to treat them as given positive constants. (For gold, they are provisionally taken to be zero.)

In long-run equilibrium, those goods with very high t_i or t_i^*, relative to their disparities in comparative advantage and domestic costs of production, will be produced and consumed within the same country. They won't be traded before or after a transitional disturbance. Any good that we do export, say good 1, will be at its "export point" where (9) becomes

$$p_1^* - p_1 = t_1^*.$$

Any good we do import, say good J, obeys (9) in the form of

$$P_J - P_J^* = t_j.$$

Some goods will have such disparities in geographical costs that they will continue to be traded in the same direction throughout the initial perturbation of $M(0)$ and the ensuing transition back to equilibrium. Some goods may cease to be traded and become nontradeable. Some that were nontradeable may now be forced into trade. And some goods may change the direction in which they are traded. All this comes about *endogenously* from the postulated disturbance and induced adjustment.

Even if we could assume that ultimate tastes are the same here and abroad and between rich and poor anywhere (so-called "uniform homothetic demand"), we must now expect transport costs to localize demand. An excess of $M(0)$ here in the California-gold discovery region must raise prices here more than abroad in Yorkshire. The price ratios for permanently nontradeable items, say P_k/P_k^*, are perturbed upward and only gradually recede to their normal long-run level. Now we Californians import goods we previously produced for ourselves as nontradeables: eggs are imported at dollars per egg, ice from abroad can be sold here. Hume and even Laughlin can agree than an index of less tradeable goods, $\sum P_k \alpha_k / \sum P_k^* \alpha_k$, will be bid up initially.

At the same time, easily tradeable goods keep their P_i/P_i^* near unity. So an index of them, relative to nontradeables, also rises: $\sum P_i a_i / \sum P_k a_k$ is perturbed upward and only gradually falls toward normalcy. We shift resources toward nontradeables, away from export goods. We substitute imports for home-produced goods where we can, running a trade deficit. But, to the degree that there are nontradeables whose prices can be bid up here, some of our excess consuming is offset by rises in our incomes and our trade deficit with abroad is thereby lessened.

Nontradeable goods, far from making the equilibration mechanism work, will if anything be presumed *to slow down* the correct version of the Hume specie-flow self-correction process (but not to the point of negating it).

Purchasing-power-parity will ultimately be restored if only an $M/(M^* + M)$ disturbance is involved and if that disturbance impinges on a system with but one micro equilibrium: this means that even an index number of nontradeables will return to its same level relative to an identically weighted index number abroad; this says no more than that, in a neutral-money world system, *every* price anywhere ends up in an exact proportion to world gold supply $\mu = M + M^*$!

During the transition, purchasing-power-parity must be false in the only form of it that experts consider to be useful. I.e., under a gold standard, index numbers of all prices inclusive of nontradeables, if compared geographically with *identical* (!) weights, show that the deficit country has an exchange rate higher than its calculated p-p-p rate. For a speculator to gamble that this will force the deficit country off the gold standard is just like betting that Saudi Arabia's prosperity will force *it* into a depreciation. (In real life, I find p-p-p valuable only if I don't apply it mechanically, but always try to allow for "substantive" changes in the *real* equilibrium relations.)

All this can be formalized. Thus, Dornbusch, Fischer and Samuelson (1977) showed that when we put into the differential equation for $M(t)$ a parameter depending on the percentage importance of nontradeable goods – call it δ – then the greater their importance the *slower* the process of self-correction. I.e.

$$-\frac{dM(t)}{M(t)dt} \to \text{constant that } \textit{diminishes with } \delta. \qquad (10)$$

In summary, the conventional defenses of Hume against himself and against the Laughlin fallacy are ill thought out, and are often 180° off in their references to the role of nontradeables in the adjustment mechanism.[6]

7. Gold's transport costs

My analysis can end with a paradox! Suppose gold's transport costs are appreciable. An example would be a model in which it costs s percent of gold's value to ship it from one country to the other. If all other goods moved freely, arbitrage would impose only the following limits on the gold prices of a good here and abroad:

---

[6] Here is a mathematical example. Each good gets one-third of anyone's total expenditure. Consumption expenditure (in gold/period) is proportional to the respective holdings of our gold or your gold, M or M^*, with a velocity of $\frac{1}{3}$/period. It costs $(\frac{1}{2}, 1, 2)$ units of L here to produce 1 of (food, housing, clothing). It costs $(2, 1, \frac{1}{2})$ units of your L^* to produce those respective goods. Both labor supplies are equal, $L = L^*$.

With zero transportation costs, $M(\infty) = M^*(\infty) = \frac{1}{2}\mu$. $W(\infty) = W^*(\infty)$. $(P_1, P_2, P_3) = (P_1^*, P_2^*, P_3^*) = (\frac{1}{2}W, 1W = 1W^*, \frac{1}{2}W^*)$. Two-thirds of our L produces food, one-third produces housing. Two-thirds of your L^* produces clothing, one-third produces housing. We export half our food production, import half your clothing production, are self-sufficient in housing.

Now let our gold M double and your gold M^* not change. Eventually, we'll each end with half the 50%-larger world μ supply. Hume errs if he makes our P's initially double and your P^*'s stay the same. Actually, *all* world prices now go up by the 50% rise in μ. So do *both* wage rates. But now our total consumption, $\Sigma_1^3 P_j C_j$, rises by more than the 50% rise in the nominal value of our total production, $\Sigma_1^2 P_j Q_j = WL$; our consumption doubles in nominal terms, or by 50% in real terms. Thus, we run a trade deficit. Your nominal incomes rise by 50%, your nominal consumption stays the same as before and your real consumptions each fall by 50%. Now you export half your housing production to us and half of the clothing you had previously been producing for yourself; also, you import only half the food you used to. So your surplus (or half your earlier income) matches our deficit (of half our earlier income): gold flows from us to you.

As we lose gold and fall below holding 2/3 of world μ, all these discrepancies are reduced but still exist qualitatively: so gold continues to be drained, but at a lower rate. The gold drain ends when our M has fallen to our long-run half of expanded world μ. Then the self-correcting mechanism turns itself off.

How will making housing a nontradeable alter the story? We begin as before. But now W is initially bid up by more than W^* is. Now we expand our imports and, diverting L from food production to housing production, expand our housing consumption and reduce our exports to you. Our improved initial terms of trade, $P_{\text{food}}/P_{\text{clothing}} = P_{\text{food}}^*/P_{\text{clothing}}^*$, have contributed to our deficit as we lose export sales and expand clothing costs. But even if the Marshall–Lerner condition only barely held, the excess of our consumption over our production would produce the gold drain that eventually rights itself. On a reduced-from basis we deduce

$$dM/dt = f[M/\mu]; 0 = f[\bar{x}], f'[\,] < 0; M(t)/\mu \to \bar{x}.$$

See my brief mathematical appendix for a proof that handles the continuum Ricardian case.

$$(1 - s) \leq P_i/P_i^* \leq (1 - s)^{-1}. \tag{11}$$

The exchange rate between an ounce of gold here and an ounce of gold there, expressed as the price in ounces here of 1 ounce delivered there, can be called e: its reciprocal is e^*. Then

$$(1 - s) \leq e \leq (1 - s)^{-1}, \quad (1 - s) \leq e^* \leq (1 - s)^{-1}. \tag{12}$$

A sophisticated reader can test her understanding of the correct Hume analysis by proving that *the world allocation of μ between M and M^* is rendered somewhat indeterminate in the long run by the cost of transporting gold.* And so is the long-run equilibrium deviation of e from unity. Viner (1937, p. 379) realized that there is no need for the gold-standard exchange rate to find its equilibrium at *par* (the geometric mean of the two gold points, where $e = 1 = e^*$), rather than at a random determinate point between the gold points. But I have seen no notice taken anywhere hitherto that $M/(M + M^*)$ is *indeterminate* in long-run equilibrium within a percentage interval determined by the discrepancy between $1 - s$ and one.

Thus, begin with countries the same size, with identical money velocities with each having exactly half the world money supply, $M = M^* = \frac{1}{2}\mu$. And let the past equilibrium be at $e = 1 = e^*$.

Now I wave my wand and transfer a bit of M^* to M. I shall now demonstrate that the correct Hume mechanism does *not* restore the old equilibrium. Instead, to within the limits of the gold points, every P_i and W is bid up in a balanced proportion relative to every P_i^* and W^*, which are bid down in balance. By how much will each P_i exceed each P_i^* initially and forevermore? By the postulated small percentage deviation between $M(0)$ and $M^*(0)$, which measures the permanent rise in e.

Note: This divergence must not exceed the permissible limits set by (8).

$$1 < e(0) = P_i(0)/P_i^*(0) < (1 - s)^{-1}, \quad e(0) = e(\infty). \tag{13}$$

Ever after all variables remain at their perturbed values dictated by p-p-p applied to the small percentage changes in the money supply. By how far from $\frac{1}{2}\mu$ can $M(\infty)$ persist in being? I calculate the limits to be

$$(1 - s)\frac{1}{2 - s}\mu \leq M(\infty) \leq \frac{1}{2 - s}\mu. \tag{14}$$

For $s = .01$, this gives the narrow interval around $\frac{1}{2}$ of

$$\frac{.99}{1.99}\mu = .495\mu \leqslant M(\infty) \leqslant .5028\mu = \frac{1}{1.99}\mu. \tag{15}$$

Note: Replace $(2 - s)^{-1}$ by $Q(Q + Q^* - sQ)^{-1}$ for the general case.[7]

Under inconvertible paper M and M^*, it is as if $s \rightarrow 1$ and then either country is free *permanently* to swell or shrink its money supply as it wishes relative to the other country's given supply.

I leave to the reader the task of working out how transport costs in a good and in gold interact to widen the limits within which the gold prices P_i and P_i^* may deviate; and how a cheaply transportable third good might narrow down the interval set by arbitrage.

8. Summary

David Hume correctly glimpsed how free trade might involve a self-correcting gold-flow mechanism. But he made the mistake of supposing that the Quantity Theory of Money linked every price in a region to the money in that region alone. This overlooked the forces that keep the competitive prices of the same transportable good virtually the same in all regions. Mesmerized by Hume's elegance, subsequent economists failed to recast Hume's analysis in the correct form that makes it immune to criticism. Instead they left the corrected version implicit, and often provided faulty rebuttals to Hume's critics, rebuttals that gratuitously pretended to locate the equilibrating mechanism in differential movements between a country's nontradeable and tradeable goods or in differential term-of-trade movements between a country's export and import goods.

Such rebuttals fail to notice that (i) the *absence* of nontradeable goods can actually speed up the rate at which an excess of money supply corrects itself;

---

[7] The above macroeconomic indeterminacy is not to be confused with multiplicity of *micro* equilibrium. It obtains even when the real equilibrium of price ratios and physical quantities is unique. There is a second, less interesting macro indeterminacy when the long-run equilibrium involves *autarky* with all goods except gold having finite transport costs. Thus, suppose positive σ is the minimum of s_i in $1 - s_i \leqslant P_i/P_i^* \leqslant (1 - s_i)^{-1}$ and gold's s is zero. Then $[\mu - M(\infty)]/M(\infty)$ can vary over an interval that shrinks to zero as $\sigma \rightarrow 0$. If the long-run equilibrium involves some trade, even ever so little, this second kind of macro indeterminacy disappears.

Why is gold different from other goods? Because it has a low transport cost s? In part that does help to make gold serve as a good money stuff. But also in my model and Hume's gold is the only good *not* wanted for its own sake but only for its convenience in making transaction purchases. If gold has dental, industrial, and jewelry utilities, the Quantity Theory story needs qualifying in its homogeneity.

and (ii), even in the absence of any terms-of-trade shifts (or indeed of *any* price changes at all), a gold drain will shut itself off when people run out of the excess money supply that is causing them as a nation to consume more than they produce.

My present analysis is too brief to do justice to the problem. I have been able to analyze only one kind of adjustment to disequilibrium – namely, the adjustment to an initial perturbed stock of money in one or more countries (as, e.g., when the conquistadors splashed Spaniards with new ownership of gold). One defect in early writers is their failure to understand and spell out just which exogenous change they are purporting to analyze. My readers are warned that the present exposition has not gone into the transfer problem, a shift in tastes toward the goods of one of the regions, a specified technical change, a reduction in supply of an important good like oil, and so forth.[8] These need their own analysis in the Hume model and I warn against overpreoccupation with a purely monetary approach to current international problems.

Mathematical appendix

Here is a corrected version for the Hume model in the manageable case of a continuum of goods. I utilize the notations of Dornbusch, Fischer, and Samuelson (1977), setting $e = 1 = e^*$.

Our long-run equilibrium conditions will be shown to impose 6 independent relations on the 6 long-run unknowns: $[\bar{z}_\infty, W_\infty, W_\infty^*, M_\infty, M_\infty^*, \dot{M}_\infty]$. These relations depend on the known value of the constants $(\gamma = V, \gamma^* = V^*, 1 - k, \mu = \bar{G}, L, L^*)$, which refer to velocities, share in total expenditure of nontradeable goods, world gold supply, and regional labor supplies. Our Ricardian labor costs for tradeable goods indexed by $z, 0 \leq z \leq 1$, are at home and abroad respectively given by $a(z)$ and $a^*(z)$, with $A(z) = a^*(z)/a(z)$ a monotone-decreasing function. Tastes are Mill–Cobb–Douglas, with the fraction of expenditure going for tradeable goods produced at home, those with z such that $0 \leq z < \tilde{z} < 1$, being given by the monotone-increasing function

$$\vartheta[\tilde{z}] = \int_0^{\tilde{z}} b(z)dz, \; b(z) > 0,$$
$$\vartheta[1] = k. \tag{A1}$$

---

[8]   I have covered some of the ground in Samuelson (1971a, 1971b); see also Dornbusch, Fischer, and Samuelson (1977).

The fraction of expenditure going for tradeables produced abroad is then $k - \vartheta[\tilde{z}]$, with k going for tradeables: $\vartheta[\tilde{z}] + (k - \vartheta[\tilde{z}]) + (1 - k) = 1$.

Our six relations are

$$WL + W^*L^* = VM + V^*M^* \tag{A2}$$

$$WL = \vartheta[\tilde{z}](VM + V^*M^*) + (1 - k)VM \tag{A3}$$

$$W/W^* = A(\tilde{z}) \tag{A4}$$

$$M/M^* = \mu \text{ or } \bar{G} \tag{A5}$$

$$dM/dt \equiv \dot{M} = WL - VM \tag{A6}$$

$$0 = \dot{M} \tag{A7}$$

Given the monotone nature of the $A(\tilde{z})$ and $\vartheta[\tilde{z}]$ functions, these 6 relations have unique roots for our respective 6 unknowns: $[\tilde{z}_\infty, W_\infty, W^*_\infty, M_\infty, M^*_\infty, \dot{M}_\infty = 0]$.

Actually,

$$\begin{aligned} M_\infty &= m_\infty \mu, M^*_\infty = (1 - m_\infty)\mu \\ W_\infty &= m_\infty \mu / L, W^*_\infty = (1 - m_\infty)\mu \end{aligned} \tag{A8}$$

where $(m_\infty, \tilde{z})$ are unique *real* roots of the following 2 long-run real relations deducible from (A2)–(A7):

$$(L/L^*)A(\tilde{z}) = \frac{\theta[\tilde{z}] + (1 - k)m_\infty V}{k - \vartheta[\tilde{z}] + (1 - k)(1 - m_\infty)V^*}; \tag{A9a}$$

$$m_\infty = A(\tilde{z}) \frac{L}{A(\tilde{z})L + L^*} V^{-1}. \tag{A9b}$$

Also, note that from relations (A2)–(A5), we can eliminate the 4 variables $(\tilde{z}, W, W^*, M^*)$, expressing them all in terms of M. Substituting the results into (A6) gives us the reduced-form relation

$$\dot{M} = \mu f[M/\mu], f[m_\infty] = 0 > f'[m_\infty]. \tag{A6'}$$

So (A2)–(A7) is equivalent to (A6')–(A7) as far as long-run M_∞ is concerned.

To determine our 5 short-run unknowns, $[\tilde{z}(t), W(t), W^*(t), M^*(t), M(t)]$ in terms of each given $M(t)$, we suspend (A7)'s requirement of long-run trade balance sans specie flow. The remaining 5 independent relations suffice to give our differential equation(s) of self-correction. Again, as far as $M(t)$ alone is concerned, we can use (A6')'s reduced-form relation

$$\dot{M} = \mu f[M/\mu],\qquad\qquad\text{(A6')}$$

and derive

$$\lim_{t\to\infty}[\dot{M}(t), M(t)] = [0, m_\infty\,\mu],\qquad\qquad\text{(A10)}$$

$$\lim_{t\to\infty}\frac{M(t) - m_\infty\mu}{\exp(-f'[m_\infty]t)} = \text{constant.}\qquad\qquad\text{(A11)}$$

Dornbusch, Fischer, and Samuelson (1977) have already given the above relations for $V = V^*$, it being understood that the 1977 Equation (16) refers to the limiting approximation of (A11). When there are no nontradeables, $k = 1$, $\tilde{z}(t)$ never departs from $\tilde{z}_\infty$ and $\dot{M}(t)/[M(t) - M(\infty)]$ is strictly constant. The greater the weight of the nontradeables the *slower* will be the correction of any $M(0) - M(\infty)$ discrepancy, as the 1977 Equation (16) suggested and as can be worked out by evaluating $f'[m_\infty]$ as a function of k when V and V^* take on *any* values.

Non-Ricardian cases, such as those of Heckscher–Ohlin or Jones (1971) and Samuelson (1971), create no new problems for the corrected Humean formulation.

REFERENCES

Bickerdike, C. F., 1920, "The Instability of Foreign Exchange," *Economic Journal* 30, March, 118–122.

Collery, Arnold, 1974, "Relative Prices in Monetary and 'Classical' Theories of Adjustment of the Balance of Payments," Privately circulated.

Dornbusch, Rudiger, 1973, "Devaluation, Money and Nontraded Goods," *American Economic Review* 63, December, 871–880.

Dornbusch, Rudiger, Fischer, Stanley, and Samuelson, Paul A., 1977, "Comparative Advantage, Trade, and Payments in a Ricardian Model with a Continuum of Goods," *American Economic Review* 67, December, 823–839.

Dornbusch, Rudiger, and Mussa, Michael, 1975, "Consumption, Real Balances and the Hoarding Function," *International Economic Review* 16, June, 415–421.

Frenkel, Jacob A., and Johnson, Harry G., 1976, "The Monetary Approach to the Balance of Payments: Essential Concepts and Historical Origins." In Jacob A. Frenkel and Harry G. Johnson, eds., *The Monetary Approach to the Balance of Payments* (London: George Allen & Unwin Ltd.), pp. 21–45.

Haberler, Gotifried, 1936, *The Theory of International Trade* (London: Wm. Hodge & Co.).

Hume, David, 1752, "Of the Balance of Trade," in *Political Discourses*, T. H. Green and T. H. Grose, eds., 1875 of Hume's, *Essays, Moral, Political, and Literary*, Part II (London). See Rotwein (1955) for source of Hume quotations used here.

Jones, Ronald W., 1971, "A Three-Factor Model in Theory, Trade and History," In Jagdish Bhagwati et al., eds., *Trade, Balance of Payments and Growth: Papers in International Economics in Honor of Charles P. Kindleberger* (Amsterdam: North-Holland Publishing Co.), pp. 3–21.

Laughlin, J. L., 1903, *The Principles of Money* (New York).

Mosak, Jacob L., 1944, *General Equilibrium Theory in International Trade*, Cowles Commission Monograph No. 7 (Bloomington, Ind.: Principia Press).

Ohlin, Bertil, 1933, *The Theory of Interregional and International Trade* (Cambridge, MA.: Harvard University Press).

Polak, Jacques J., 1957, "Monetary Analysis of Income Formation and Payments Problems." In *The Monetary Approach to the Balance of Payments* (Washington, DC: International Monetary Fund, 1977), pp. 15–64.

Prais, Sigmund J., 1961, "Some Mathematical Notes on the Quantity Theory of Money in an Open Economy." In *The Monetary Approach to the Balance of Payments* (Washington, D.C.: International Monetary Fund, 1977), pp. 147–161.

Robinson, Joan, 1937, *Essays in the Theory of Employment* (New York: The Macmillan Company), pp. 183–209.

Rotwein, Eugene, ed., 1955, *David Hume: Writings on Economics* (Edinburgh: Thomes Nelson & Sons Ltd.). Hume's essay, "Of the Balance of Trade," appears on pages 60–75.

Samuelson, Paul A., 1971a, "An Exact Hume-Ricardo-Marshall Model of International Trade," *Journal of International Economics* 1, February, 1–18. Reproduced in *Collected Scientific Papers of Paul A. Samuelson* (Cambridge, MA: MIT Press, 1972), Vol. III, Ch. 162.

Samuelson, Paul A., 1971b, "On the Trail of Conventional Beliefs about the Transfer Problem." In Jagdish Bhagwati et al., eds., *Trade, Balance of Payments and Growth: Papers in International Economics in Honor of Charles P. Kindleberger* (Amsterdam: North-Holland Publishing Co.). Reproduced in *Collected Scientific Papers of Paul A. Samuelson* (Cambridge, MA: MIT Press, 1972), Vol. III, Ch. 163.

Samuelson, Paul A., 1971, "Ohlin Was Right," *Swedish Journal of Economics* 73, 365–384. Reproduced in *Collected Scientific Papers of Paul A. Samuelson* (Cambridge, MA: MIT Press, 1977), Vol. IV, Ch. 254.

Viner, Jacob, 1937, *Studies in the Theory of International Trade* (New York: Harper & Brothers Publishers).

Quesnay's 'Tableau Economique' as a Theorist would Formulate it Today[1]

1 Introduction

Schumpeter used to shock his Harvard classes by declaring that of the four greatest economists three were French.

In view of Schumpeter's boundless admiration for the Newtonian general equilibrium of Walras, and his delight in the elegance of Cournot's partial-equilibrium analysis, two-thirds of his contention we could understand. But to admit François Quesnay into the Pantheon – presumably because his *Tableau Economique* was a precursor of general equilibrium and of Schumpeter's own beloved *circular flow* – that seemed a bit much.

The *Tableau* begain in comedy. Mirabeau (1760), who is known not to have understood it, is quoted maliciously by Adam Smith for his extravagant puffery:

There has been since the world began, three great inventions ... The first is the invention of writing ... The second is the invention of money ... The third is the Oeconomical Table ... the great discovery of our age.

Fire, the wheel and the invention of brandy must apparently come further down the list.

Overvaluation invites short selling. Contemporaries of the Physiocrats, such as Linguet, cast scorn upon the *Tableau* as the mystic mumbo-jumbo of a mad sect, dismissing it as charlatanical nonsense. Alexander Gray's (1931) useful compact history refers to the *Tableau* as 'an embarrassing footnote' in the history of economics. Gide and Rist (1926) consider the degree of enthusiasm expressed by Mirabeau and other idolisers as 'almost

---

[1] The author owes thanks to the American National Science Foundation for financial aid, and to Kate Crowley and Aase Huggins for editorial assistance.

incredible'. Schumpeter, when he came to write down his magisterial
History of Economic Analysis (1954), treats Quesnay as a bit of a bore and
a crank: there Schumpeter writes with patronising coolness about the
Tableau.

It was Karl Marx who resurrected the *Tableau Economique*, devoting a
whole chapter in his *Theories of Surplus Value* to the *Tableau* and writing:
'Never before had thinking in political economy reached such heights of
genius.' Marx's own analytical work on models of *steady reproduction*, and
of *expanded* (exponential) *reproduction*, seems to have been stimulated by
his puzzling over Quesnay's arithmetic. To be able to say this heaps much
praise on the Physiocrats since, I would argue, Marx's own finest *analytical*
work came in this area of circular interdependence.

My old teacher Wassily Leontief (1941) had Quesnay very much in mind
when he referred to his own endeavour to construct a statistical '*Tableau
Economique* of the United States'. It is thus not surprising that members of
Leontief's workshop – the late George Malanos (1946), Almarin Phillips
(1955), Shlomo Maital (1972), and others – should have offered interpretations of the *Tableau* in terms of modern Leontief–Sraffa input–output
systems. (Dialectically, Harry Johnson (1974) reacted against such a *technological* interpretation, preferring a Keynesian *multiplier–expenditure*
interpretation to an input–output one.) Tibor Barna (1975) gives a version
of the *Tableau* in modern guise, disaggregating the sectoral flows and
providing an expanded matrix of transactions.

W. A. Eltis (1975, p. 168), who has analysed the various tableaux against
the background of all the writings of Quesnay and Mirabeau, states:

Almost all the problems (assertions that have no clear logical basis . . . apparent gaps
in the arguments, inconsistencies, and puzzling calculations . . .) are solved, however, and the inconsistencies removed when Quesnay's published works are read as
a whole.

Eltis is one of the few modern authors bold enough to tackle Quesnay's zig-
zags or diminishing geometric progressions.

Although I recognise the role obscurity can play in commanding respect
and evoking attention to a scientific work, my own bent is against mystification and abracadabra. Hume and Cantillon, Quesnay's predecessors, and
Turgot, Quesnay's successor, are more to my personal taste than Mirabeau
and Quesnay. But in recalling the praises and abuses the *Tableau* has
evoked, I shall give Ronald Meek (1962, pp. 259–60) the last word:

The *Tableau* is far from being the ideal and airy thing which it is sometimes made
out to be: on the contrary, it is one of the most striking examples in the whole history

of economic thought of the achievement of a harmonious unity between abstract theory and concrete investigation.

2 Present Purpose

I shall not add one more explication of the many versions of the *Tableau* and its appended materials. Instead, my intent here is to try to put the fundamental Physiocratic insights into modern goatskins.

How would a student of Robert Solow or Piero Sraffa, starting from scratch, draw up a table that illuminates the envisaged equilibrium? My interest is theoretical and methodological. The point is not to capture the quantitative and sociological features of the *ancien regime*, and it is not to illuminate Quesnay's own modes of thought and exposition. Although my debts to Phillips (1955), and particularly to Maital (1972), will be obvious, the programme set out here hitherto seems never to have been carried through to completion.

Two features are central to Quesnay:

(1) Land enjoys a special asymmetric position in the Physiocratic system, and our model must reflect that.

(2) By the same token, if labour's 'sterility' is to stand in stark contrast to land's, logic requires us to push to the limit the Classical hypothesis that an unlimited supply of labour can be endogenously created at a specifiable subsistence wage (which could involve only agricultural food – 'corn' – but which could also involve manufactures).

When I first began to lecture on *Dogmengeschichte* several decades ago, I hoped to be able to understand Quesnay's zig-zag notions. It would be nice in this modern formulation to be able to clear up definitively these mysterious geometric progressions; for, I am sure, it is these puzzling patterns of spending flows that captivated the *Tableau's* admirers and critics. Alas, even the recent explorations of Izumi Hishiyama (1960) and Eltis (1975) do not satisfy my analytical conscience. So the best I can do is to use the complete model introduced here to indicate why Quesnay's zig-zags never did fulfil a useful purpose in the analysis of his own system and the crystallisation of his own insights.

3 Assumptions

Assume two industries or departments: *agriculture*, which produces food and raw materials; *manufacturing*, which produces clothing, shelter, other finished goods, and (in later elaborated versions of the model) various capital goods.

(1) Farm products – (Ricardian) 'corn' for short – are produced by the given supply of (scarce) land and by labour. (Later, you can allow for durable capital goods' inputs, for seed and other raw materials produced in agriculture.)

Quesnay deals with three classes of people: landowners or *proprietors* (possibly including the Crown and the clergy); the *productive class* of 'farmers' and farm labourers; and *artisans*, the 'sterile' class of people who labour on manufactures (and which includes what we would call 'bourgeois' employers of their own and other people's labour).

As Barna observes, one can easily disaggregate or consolidate the particular classifications of Quesnay. In a first pass at the subject, I find it useful to divide factors of production into fixed *land* (used exclusively, or primarily, in agriculture) owned by landowners or proprietors, and into *labour*, whether employed in manufacturing (as artisans) or in agriculture (as farmers or hired workers). Prior to complicating the model by explicitly introducing time-phasing and pure interest into it, the difference between a rural farmer and a rural labourer is only one of degree of skill and status. Like the Physiocrats, I envisage one farmer as a congealed unit of more than one unskilled labourer; so long as the gear ratio in this equivalence is not allowed to be an endogenous economic variable, we can avail ourselves of the simplification used later by Marx and speak simply of so many units of socially necessary ('least-common-denominator') labour without regard to the break-down by industry and occupation.

(2) Manufactures are produced by labour (with land of negligible use in the simplest model) and by raw materials produced on the farm. For simplicity, I begin with the assumption of *fixed proportions* among labour, co-operating raw materials, and output of manufactures.

A caveat is in order concerning the preliminary neglect of time-phasing. For land to be truly the only ultimate source of net product, à *la* Quesnay and Henry George, we are best advised to contemplate a model that is essentially *timeless*. (Or, if the steady states do involve synchronised time leads and lags, either these intervals are so short that the interest component of total costs and incomes is negligible; or else the rate of interest and profit – these are the same thing in the absence of uncertainty and market imperfections – have been established at so low a rate per period as to be effectively ignorable. In any case, as Barna observes, the *Tableau Economique* must be supplemented by a separate statement on capital account, since its own explicit current flows do not register the needed capital information.)

I do justice to the Physiocrats' vision that land's return is the only *produit net*, the only true surplus by virtue of the fact that its supply is given by nature without a needed cost. By contrast, labour's productivity merely repays labour's needed cost of subsistence; and raw materials' contribution to competitive revenue merely repays its competitive purchase price (which is, in turn, the sum of the land inputs in it and the subsistence cost of the labour needed for it as inputs). To do full justice to this essentially correct Physiocratic vision, I best sacrifice Quesnay's own ambiguous terminologies: the contribution of farm *labourers* is just as 'sterile' as the contribution of manufacturing *labourers*; the former are not 'the productive class' in the true sense of the word 'productive' – for the reason that it is the land they work with *that is alone productive* in producing the Physiocrats' *produit net*. Personally, like Adam Smith, I would avoid the adjective 'sterile' and merely insist that those costs that are paid to labour merely recoup in long-run equilibrium the subsistence cost whereby labour is maintained. Later, when one admits that manufactures also require some land, one realises that it is not the industry that is 'sterile' in the sense of lacking *net* product but rather only the labour and raw materials used there and anywhere which are 'sterile'. In departing from Quesnay's precise categories and terminologies, I actually better bring out his essential vision.

My technological stage directions will be complete after I have given the quantitative *technical coefficients* of labour and raw materials in manufacturing, and have given for agriculture what we would today call the 'production function' relating corn output to the land supply and the varying quantities of farm labour. But before doing this, I need to specify the composition and scale of the *subsistence real wage*. And I need to specify, as Quesnay's models do, how landowners spend their *produit net* or land rents on the consumption of farm products or of manufactures.

Quesnay's zig-zags must have seemed simpler to him if he always assumed 50–50 allocation of spendings. So I partially indulge that penchant and assume that landlords spend half their rents on manufactures and half on farm products.

But, with a bow towards greater realism, I postulate that the subsistence wage consists only of agricultural products (of 'corn'). It is immaterial how high or low I assume the subsistence wage to be, provided only that the quality of the land and the laws of technology enable a finite population of landless labour to be supported by the given land under a regime of competition for their services.

Quesnay and earlier writers definitely glimpsed at least vaguely the notion of what would today be called a 'production function'. They realised that under better technology France would be able to enjoy a higher level of total land rent while still paying the same competitive subsistence wage. Since mine is to be a modern treatment, I go beyond their vague perceptions and assume in Ricardo's fashion that the greater the rural labour supply employed, the lower must be its corn wage and the higher must be the total of landowners' *produit net*. The equilibrium that we will observe in the *Tableau Economique* for this society will involve a quantity of agricultural labour that is endogenously determinate. Here are the modern equations:

$$\text{Agriculture } Q = F(\text{land}, \text{farm labour}) = F(T, L_F) \atop = Tf(L_F/T), f'(\ ) > 0 > f''(\ ) \tag{1.1}$$

For fixed land (or lands), we can set T equal to unity and ignore it in all our equations.

West (1815), Malthus (1798), Ricardo (1817), and J. B. Clark (1899) realised that under a regime of competition by landowners for labourers, there would be a determinate level of farm L_F^* that would just earn the stipulated corn wage, $\bar{w}$. This L_F^* is the root of the equation (that the neoclassicals would call marginal productivity):

$$f'(L_F^*) = \bar{w} \tag{1.2}$$

Rent (in corn) can then be computed as the residual:

$$R^* = f(L_F^*) - \bar{w}L_F^* \tag{1.3}$$

To keep the arithmetic simple, I will let rent be half of total farm product, the rest being farm workers' wages.

Half of this rent goes for corn consumption. The other half goes to buy manufacturing product, the only source of demand for such product. Under competition these manufactures sell only at their cost of production – the sum of the subsistence corn needed to feed the manufacturing artisans and the corn raw material needed for production of manufactures. Thus the residual rent, left over after farm labour gets its subsistence and the only *produit net* in the system, is divided three ways: into landowners' own corn consumption, into the corn needed for *manufacturing* labour's subsistence, and into the corn needed by industry as raw materials. (What the ratio of these last two components is depends upon the technology in manufactures: to keep the arithmetic simple, I pick one-to-one as that ratio in my examples.)

4 Bird's-eye view

The stage has now been completely set. The play must now go on for ever more according to its coded laws of motion:

(1) Landowners buy from agricultural and manufacturing producers, paying from their stream of competitive money rents and receiving in return the physical goods that constitute their standard of life.

(2) The farm sector, besides selling to landowners, sells its product to labourers who need subsistence – i.e. they sell both to farm labour and to manufacturing labour. The farm sector also sells its product as raw materials for industry.

(3) Out of the total revenues it receives, the farm sector pays competitive rents for the land it needs. It also pays out wages to farm labour, paying the competitive wage that the existing supply of such labour can command (at auction, so to speak).

(4) The size of the farm population supplied is determined in final equilibrium at that level which will fetch the needed subsistence wage. (Were L_F too large, the corn wage would sink below the subsistence $\bar{w}$ and the population would decline; were L_F below L_F^*, the corn wage would exceed $\bar{w}$, thereby evoking a growing supply of farm labour. QED.)

(5) The sole receipts of the industrial sector, under my first simplifying assumptions, come from consumption purchases by landowners spending their rent incomes. In the competitive equilibrium these receipts are just enough to offset the subsistence wages that are forced by competition out of the industrial employers (who may be self-employed) plus the cost of the raw materials that have to be bought from the farm sector. There are no land factors in the industrial sector that can earn a *produit net*; the labour and raw-material inputs merely recover their costs of production and reproduction.

A picture or numerical table to sum this all up might well have pedagogical convenience. But it is an illusion to think that such a picture or *gestalt* provides a magic engine of analysis for the discovery of new truth and the marshalling of rigorous proof. Consider, for example, a typical problem propounded by Quesnay: What if landowners alter their 50–50 spending of rents, and increase the fraction spent on manufacturing products? A one-point-in-time *tableau*, geared to the previous spending proportions, cannot answer the question of what the new equilibrium will be. Barna (1975, p. 493) cogently criticises Quesnay's procedures:

Quesnay, as usual, begins the computation with the landlords spending their income. At the end of the first round landlords find that they did not collect in rent as much as they had originally spent, and hence the second round starts with a smaller outlay. There is thus a cumulative decline in the 'base' of the *Tableau* and everybody will be worse off then before.

This conclusion clearly does not follow from the *Tableau's* assumptions. Within the framework of a static Leontief model, a shift in demand from agricultural produce to manufactures should bring about a reduction in agricultural activity and an increase in manufacturing. There will be a redistribution of incomes away from landlords. But there is no reason why total national income should change.

In the rockbottom Physiocratic model adumbrated here, the effect of the specified change in tastes is clear. And its correct description seems not to have been achieved by Quesnay and Mirabeau or, according to my best recollection, by any of the commentators on them. Here is that correct description:

A shift in landowners' tastes towards manufacturers must lead to a new long-run equilibrium with *increased* labour population, all of which goes into manufacturing. Total rent (*produit net*) is *just as before* (whether measured in terms of corn or in terms of manufactures)! What Ricardo calls 'gross revenue' – which, in the Kuznets manner, adds the total of wages to the total of Ricardian 'net revenue' (equals rent or *produit net* in this interestless world) – will be *higher* in the new equilibrium, precisely as Ricardo came to argue in the notorious chapter on machinery that he added to his third edition. (See p. 393 in the 1951 Sraffa edition of Ricardo's *Principles*.)

Barna's point is well taken that you could never conclude all this from the *Tableau Economique* itself. You would have to go to the table's underlying logic to arrive at this result.[2]

---

[2]   In Barna's short run, when the total of farm and manufacturing labour has not yet grown, some L_F will shift to manufacturing. Corn rent will fall. The real wage will rise, both in terms of manufactures and subsistence corn, but more in terms of the latter. Kuznets's national income (Ricardo's gross revenue) will necessarily *rise* reckoned in corn and fall reckoned in manufactures. The terms of trade will temporarily shift against agriculture. All this, however, was not worked out in its entirety until the time of Stolper and Samuelson (1940). What needs mentioning in connection with the short-run case is that *it* does *not* constitute a Leontief–Sraffa one-primary-factor model. With homogeneous land and labour *both* primary factors, Leontief's assumption of fixity of production coefficients would lead to indeterminacies of equilibrium; under the Ricardian assumption of *land–labour substitution*, as in equation (1.1) above, the classical model apes neoclassical properties.

Quesnay's arithmetic never seems to have led him to the *fundamental theorem of Physiocracy*: that is, no change in tastes can alter the total of long-run *produit net* in a homogeneous-land model where *all other* output and inputs are producible at constant returns out of themselves.

5 At last A Table

Three sectors are in our model: agricultural production, manufacturing production, and the production of labour (out of subsistence wages). Table 1.1, with three columns, shows the costs of these respective industries broken down by the inputs those costs are spent on. Each input appears in its respective row – including the input of land (which is not itself producible in the system and so appears as a row appended *outside* the 3 × 3 input–output elements of the system). Finally, I append a final column to show how landowners spend their incomes.

I end up with a familiar *open-end* Leontief *tableau*, consisting of 3 × 3 internal elements plus appended exogenous row and column for Physiocrats' land and landowners. The *tableau* is expressed in money terms: dollars, livres, pounds, corn-*numéraire* units, etc. It can also be given a physical-units interpretation.[3]

Table 1.1. *Tableau Economique*

Output	Purchasing sector			Landowners	Totals
	Agriculture	Manufacturing	Labour		
Agriculture (product)	0	25	*125*	**50**	200
Manufacturing (product)	0	0	0	**50**	50
Labour (supply)	*100*	*25*	0	0	*125*
Land	**100**	0	0	0	**100** }
Value totals	200	50	*125*	100	(475)

---

[3] The base of 100 for land rent is arbitrary: we can define our units of homogeneous land so that there are initially 100 of them. Then, if their number should double or halve, the equilibrium level of *all* other *extensive* variables will double or halve, while all *intensive* price and quantity ratios will be invariants. We can select as our physical units of agricultural product exactly what half a land unit produces (when it has the matching labour to work with). For our units of labour, we define as one labour unit the amount needed (along with land) to produce two units of corn. In terms of these units the subsistence wage is one corn per period. It follows that the price of corn in *numéraire* units of land rent will be exactly one. Similarly, we are free to select as our physical unit for manufactures the amount of it that requires as raw materials exactly one-half of our farm-product units. Then our example's technology tells us that $P_M/P_F \equiv 1 \equiv P_M/$rent rate.

Adopting the above conventional definitional units, every item in the table becomes a physical magnitude as well as a dollar or livre magnitude. Thus, in column 1, 100 units of land along with 100 workers produce 200 of corn; in column 2, 50 of manufactures is produced by 25 workers and 25 units of farm-product raw materials. The rows can still be added to get totals of physical items. Interpreted as a *physical tableau*, the table's columns cannot be added since cheese-plus-chalk or corn-plus-manufactures-plus-labour-plus-land makes no sense.

The bold-face numerals denote *produit net* items, the only true surplus in the Physiocratic system and attributable to land alone, with its *zero cost* and *positive productivity*. *Produit net* (or Ricardian '*net* revenue') is **100**, and reckonable in two equivalent ways: as a flow of rent *income* (or cost), it is the **100** in the first column and land row (carried over in the totals column on the right as the last row's item); as a flow of (final) product, it is shown as **50** and **50** in the landowners' column of consumption expenditure.

To get modern national income of *225 à la* Kuznets (or Ricardo's '*gross* revenue'), we must add wage incomes to rent income. I have italicised these wage value-added items: in the third row for labour, note the wage items *100* and *25*, and their sum on the far right. As a matching Kuznets flow of (non-intermediate) product, we must add to landowners' consumptions of corn and manufactures the corn that goes for workers' subsistence. This is shown in the first agricultural row in labour's third column – by the italicised numeral there, *125*. (This last of course appears as a repetition in column 3's bottom total, where *125* is seen.) To relate modern national income to the smaller Physiocrats' *produit net*, I have introduced brackets to enclose the two magnitudes.

Finally, as is well known to users of input–output tables, the grossness of our data depends upon the arbitrary fineness of our disaggregation. The over-all total of 475, shown at lower right in the circle as a grand total of the whole table, has no intrinsic significance: it involves not only the double counting of the agricultural output that is used as raw-material input for industry; but, more singularly in modern eyes, it includes labour power as a produced item in the system; and, of course, it includes both landowners' earnings *and* their equivalent spendings, a palpable case of double-counting.

To help relate my presentation to that of Quesnay, Meek, Phillips, and Maital, I consolidate my 4 × 4 (open-end) table into the more conventional 3 × 3 (*open*-end!) format. Now labour will no longer be given its own row and column. Instead, I now put the farm labour back in the 'productive' sector of agriculture, treating the subsistence wage that workers receive there as 'corn raw-material input necessary to produce corn output'. Likewise the manufacturing labour and their corn wages are treated merely as the costs of the sterile classes ('artisans'), who produce manufactures out of an equivalent market value of farm product as input – out of actual raw farm materials themselves used in manufactures *plus* the subsistence corn in the artisans' stomachs while they produce manufactures.

Arithmetically, this consolidation involves eliminating column 3 and row 3 but adding row 3's items into the respective first-row items. This gives

Table 1.2. *Tableau Economique*

Sectoral outputs	Agriculture (productive classes)	Manufacturing (sterile artisans)	Landowners	Totals
Agriculture	100	50	**50**	200
Manufacturing	0	0	**50**	50
Land	**100**	0	0	**100**
Value totals	200	50	**100**	⃝350

Table 1.2, a formal variant of Table 1.1. The *produit net* items are again put in bold face, both on the side of income earned and the side of equivalent flow of final product (net, after allowances to keep labour alive and recouping their human reproduction costs). Table 1.2 does not conveniently tabulate Kuznets's national income of 225, since intermediate product of corn used to produce manufactures is mixed up with the requisite numbers.

Both my tables side with Maital against Phillips on the issue of whether Quesnay's *Tableau Economique* is best rendered by a *closed*-end Leontief table or by an *open*-end one. In Phillips's closed-end case, land and landowners are treated symmetrically with any other input or class. To make wine you really do need grapes; but it is stretching convention to say that to produce proprietors you need so many luxuries of this kind and so many of that. It is better to open end the array, pulling land out as a *primary* input and pulling landowners' final consumptions out as items dictated by exogenous tastes.

The Physiocratic asymmetry of land comes of course from their theory of reality. The table is made to reflect it, and it would not be useful to say that the *Tableau Economique* somehow 'proves' the correctness of this insight. Nor would it be useful to blame it for failing to provide such 'proof'.

I shall leave to the interested reader the task of making a pretty picture of my table, with pedagogically useful arrows indicative of spending channels. Perhaps there is a best, canonical pattern that such a diagram should take, but I do not dare to pronounce on the matter.

* * *

There remain two quite different tasks. There is the task of discussing zig-zags, the geometric progressions somehow supposed to be indicative of 'dynamic' spending processes. And also there is the task of facing up to time-phasing and to some of the durable capital-goods processes that Quesnay had explicitly in mind. (This will involve not only Quesnay's 'depreciation of capital' but also Turgot's true interest rate.) On both these issues I shall be very brief.

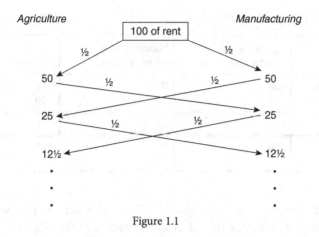

Figure 1.1

6 The Chimera of zig-zags

So far there has been no need to even mention the mysterious zig-zags of the Quesnay literature. A typical one, I suppose, is very roughly of the form shown in Figure 1.1. Or, since my model has neither workers spending their subsistence wages on manufactures nor corn producers needing manufactures as raw material or durable capital, after the second round no new flows come to the sterile sector of manufacturing. So the slightly less transparent pattern shown in Figure 1.2 might perhaps be the indicated zig-zag.

In the preceding paragraph I have used the tentative words 'I suppose' and 'might perhaps' because no definite prescriptions are possible until one has already settled what the intrinsic logic of the zig-zag is – which is the objective of the immediate investigation and ought not to be presumed settled in advance.

First, let me dispose of an empty point. Formally, unity can be written as

$$1 = \frac{1}{2} + \frac{1}{4} + \frac{1}{8} + \dots + \left(\frac{1}{2}\right)^n + \dots$$

And, for any positive x, we can write the convergent series

$$1 + x = 1 + [x/(1+x)] + [x/(1+x)]^2 + \dots$$

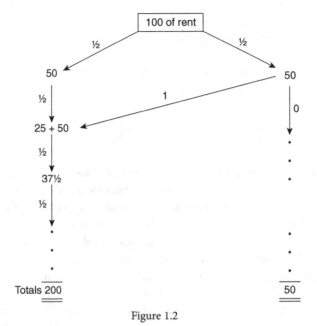

Figure 1.2

But *cui bono?* In the first flush of the Keynesian dawn many of us could write one-plus-one only as $1/(1 - \frac{1}{2})$. At least we then had the excuse that the Kahn–Keynes–Metzler dynamic multiplier could usefully take the difference-equation form:[4]

---

[4] If $y(t)$ is a column vector of n elements, B a vector of constants, 1 is replaced by the n-by-n identity matrix I, and $\frac{1}{2}$ is replaced by $a = [a_{ij}]$, a matrix of positive elements with column sums positive proper fractions, then expression (1.4) generalises to the 'matrix geometric progression'

$$y(t+1) = ay(t) + B$$
$$y(t) \quad = [I - a]^{-1}B + y(0)a^t$$
$$y(t) \quad = [I - a]^{-1}B + [y(0) - (I - a)^{-1}B]a^t \tag{1.4a}$$
$$\lim_{t \to \infty} y(t) = [I - a]^{-1}B = [I + a + a^2 + \dots]B > 0$$

The respective elements in a^t or $a^t B$ do not themselves decay in simple geometric progressions (being the *sum* of exponentials), but for a a *primitive* matrix such elements *asymptotically* decay at a common exponential rate. However, as seen in my text, the matrix generalisation cannot vindicate the Johnson spending-chain interpretation but if anything its reverse in time.

$$y(t + 1) = \frac{1}{2}y(t) + b$$

$$y(t) = \frac{1}{1 - \frac{1}{2}} + [y(0) - 2]\left(\frac{1}{2}\right)^t \tag{1.4}$$

$$\lim_{t \to \infty} y(t) = 2b = \left[1 + \frac{1}{2} + \left(\frac{1}{2}\right)^2 + \ldots\right]b$$

No doubt Harry Johnson (1974) had something like this in mind when he hankered for a multiplier – expenditure interpretation of the Quesnay zig-zag *Tableau* in preference to a technical input – output approach of the Phillips (1955) type. But I am not aware that Johnson ever made good his claim that the Quesnay zig-zag could usefully model *the* actual dynamic steps forward either (i) when the system is in its postulated steady state, or (ii) when it is dynamically being perturbed from an old steady state to a new one.

The essence of circular flow – the essence of what Schumpeter admired in Quesnay – is the repetition *without leakage* of the equilibrium. From this viewpoint we do not want to break 100 down into dwindling fractions, but instead want it and all the other elements to *repeat* in conserved magnitude:

$$100 = \ldots = R(t - 1) = R(t) = R(t + 1) = \ldots \tag{1.5}$$

No doubt the keen reader will cogently reply to my argument of the previous paragraph:

True, equilibrium involves stationariness. But every student of J. M. Keynes (1936) and Fritz Machlup (1939) knows that a plateau can be made up of the convergent sum of (an infinity of) overlapping elements – just as a stationary population can be the sum of all the age classes, with each cohort of new births forming a dwindling sequence as each passing year adds a year of age.

This logic is impeccable. But it leaves moot whether there is a *useful* dynamic paradigm that moves forward in time according to the Keynesian manner and which is in some measure illuminated by Quesnay's traditional zig-zags.

My own desultory researches make me agnostic. Code the elements in Table 1.2 as follows:

$$\begin{bmatrix} 100 & 50 & 50 \\ 0 & 0 & 50 \\ 100 & 0 & 0 \end{bmatrix} = \begin{bmatrix} z_1 & z_2 & z_3 \\ & & z_4 \\ z_5 & & \end{bmatrix} \tag{1.6}$$

My stage directions, and Quesnay's when he accepts my assumptions about tastes and technology, lead to the homogeneous difference equations:

$$z_3(t+1) = \frac{1}{2}z_5(t) = z_4(t+1)$$

$$z_1(t-1) = \frac{1}{2}[z_1(t) + z_2(t) + z_3(t)] = z_5(t-1) \tag{1.7}$$

$$z_2(t-1) = z_4(t)$$

These are incapable of being put in 'causal form' either forward or backward in time. Thus, for arbitrary $[z_j(0)]$ it is not the case that a unique sequence is generated for $[z_j(+|t|)]$ or for $[z_j(-|t|)]$. However, for $[z_j(0)]$ proportional to Table 1.2's equilibrium values, that same set of values gives a solution that satisfies the equations forever more. This suggests that Quesnay's attempted use of the tableau was flawed at the core: once he altered his parameters and ruptured the old equilibrium, its initial conditions could not begin a path to the new equilibrium. What he inferred to be a property of the real world was only a property of his misconceived programme – something his readers might have come to realise.

Is it quite hopeless, then, to seek some kind of geometric progression that correctly relates to our equilibrium system? Not quite. There is the teleological backward-in-time process known in the input–output literature as a Cornfield–Leontief (matrix) multiplier (and which is not to be confused with the dual pricing multiplier of Gaitskell–Dosso).[5]

Here is how to describe the process. Begin with 100 units of landowner expenditure that generates 50 each of the two sectors' consumptions. To produce these at initial $t = 0$, we needed to produce at $t = -1$ the raw materials and worker fodder called for by the paradigm's technology of input–output coefficients. But to produce these inputs at $t = -1$, we needed *their* inputs to be produced at $t = -2$. These in turn needed their inputs to be produced three periods back.

We are in an infinite regress, going not forward into the far future, but hypothetically backward to the beginning of time. Although the span of time is infinite, the series is a dwindling one with a convergent sum. It is actually the matrix power series of note 4 (see p. 71).

It would be somewhat farfetched to claim that Quesnay's zig-zags were a vague anticipation of the planner's teleological matrix multiplier. There is, however, one instance of the matrix multiplier in which its elements are *exactly* in geometric progression from the very beginning (and not just

[5] See Dorfman, Samuelson and Solow (1958) for details.

asymptotically *à la* note 4). Consider a two-sector example in which land and raw materials produce those sectoral outputs without explicit mention of labour. Let half of the cost of manufactures be agricultural raw materials and half of corn's cost be manufacturing raw materials, the other half being land rent in each sector. This singular case involves neither sector requiring its own self as input.

Figure 1.3 shows the Cornfield–Leontief teleology in quasi zig-zag form. This is not much of a harvest for several decades of mulling over Quesnay's zig-zags, you will agree. But it is the best I can do, and that best does not seem good enough.[6] It seems gratuitous to read this interpretation into Quesnay himself.

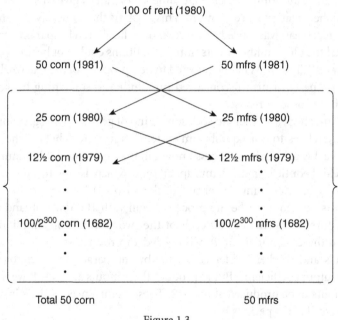

Figure 1.3

[6] For steady-state purposes, there is no harm in netting out each sector's *own* raw-material requirements. But when the pre-1980 pattern is a genuine planner's programme, phased in real time, technology usually will not allow us to have an $[a_{ij}]$ matrix with zeros in the diagonal. And then the matrix series of note 4, $B + aB + a^2B \ldots$ will *not* be the simple geometric progressions of Hishiyama (1960) and Eltis (1975), except penultimately.

   Remark: the 1980 and earlier *land* inputs needed to produce the 1980 consumptions are not shown in my zig-zag table. The reader may use the blank middle column to write in the requisite entries 25 (1980), $12\frac{1}{2}$ (1979), ... The sum there will be 50 of land units, representing the *direct* land requirements of the (50 corn and 50 mfrs); the missing 50 of land units is the *indirect* land embodied in the outer columns' totals.

7 Capital goods

Quesnay was one of the first Classical economists to concentrate on 'advances' – as when the farmer begins with a barn and with seed, and a worker is provided with the subsistence he needs to last out the growing season. Turgot, not quite a Physiocrat but at heart a 'fellow traveller', gave what Böhm-Bawerk called the first scientific theory of the interest rate: if land with a permanent annual *produit net* sells for a finite price, as in the medieval 'twenty years' purchase', then that interest rate calculated as annual-yield-to-principal sets the level that capitalists must competitively earn on their outlays for wages, for raw materials, and for barns or durable tools.

Neither Quesnay nor the *Tableau Economique* adequately handles the fundamentals of the profit rate and the time-phasing problem. That would be too much to ask of the eighteenth century. What I shall do is provide the simplest *Tableau* that consistently recognises interest.

My model preserves the subsistence-wage theory. It sticks to the stationary state. Just as rent income is spent half-and-half on agriculture and manufactures, so will be the profit-interest income of capitalists. Indeed, we could for the present purpose alternatively lump together *proprietors* and *rentiers* into the *capitalists*.

Since it already had the circulating-capital item of raw materials needed for manufacturing and had subsistence workers who were 'advanced' their subsistence pay, my previous model can be made to serve the present purpose – once we alter its 'timeless' properties and time phase it so that all outputs come one period *after* the application of all inputs. For brevity, I stick with the earlier model and forbear to introduce durable-capital items.

Where shall I get a determinate positive rate of profit from? Turgot's vision of the process is good enough for us, and recently in the Abba Lerner *festschrift*, Samuelson (1979) sketched a Turgot–Modigliani life-cycle model of interest. Here is its thumbnail outline.

At a zero interest rate, land would be of infinite value. Capitalists looking forward to a finite life (for themselves and the next few generations they care about) would overspend their incomes. So equilibrium can take place only at some positive rate of interest. If that rate per period, call it r, is too high, the capitalised value of land will be less than people need for their old-age livelihoods, and would-be savers will bid up assets' values until *the interest rate is at that equilibrium level where generation after generation there will be zero net saving.* So r^* will be the determinate long-run rate of interest.[7]

---

[7] Admittedly, r^* will be determined *simultaneously* along with the other equilibrium values (L_F^*, L_M^*, P_M^*/P_F^*, ...). For brevity I shall take r^* as already given: at 50 per cent, $r^* = 0.5$, in Table 1.3's dramatic example (p. 77). I mention, but ignore, the possibility of multiple equilibria.

At a positive profit rate the same land cannot support so many workers if their competitive wage rate is to equal the needed subsistence level in corn. So L_F^* will be lower than in the zero-r* case. That means that landowners' corn rent, R*, payable at the end of the harvest, will be lower than before. The determinate levels for these will be given as $(L_F^*, \ R^*)$ roots of

$$\bar{w} = f'(L_F^*)/(1 + r^*) \tag{1.8}$$

$$R^* = f(L_F^*) - \bar{w}f'(L_F^*) \tag{1.9}$$

$$\text{Agricultural profit}^* = \bar{w}L_F^*r^* \tag{1.10}$$

The rentier group of capitalists, who advance farm workers their wages, are seen to earn the profit rate on these advances (just as the landowners' rent earns them the same percentage on the capitalised value of their acres).

Now that the population working the land has been lowered by the presence of interest, it takes relatively more land to produce each unit of corn. This tends to raise the price of corn relative to the rent per acre, an effect that is reinforced by the profit mark-up on the wage component of corn's cost. The price of manufactures includes *two* profit mark-ups in my model's technology: the one mark-up already in the price of the corn raw material, and the profit mark-up on the wage and raw-material components of manufactures' cost.

* * *

To dramatise the effect upon the *tableau* of profit, I shall assume a 50 per cent interest rate. The task of writing down a new *Tableau Economique* consistent with the technology and tastes of our previous zero-profit *Tableau Economique* provides a testing for a modern theorist. So it is no wonder that the eighteenth-century writers fall short of accomplishing this goal.

Table 1.3 bases itself on a quasi-realistic agricultural production function in expression (1.1) above (p. 64). Raising r* from zero to 50 per cent per period reduces total population by more than half – from 125 to 60; lowers land rent by 20 per cent, from 100 of corn to 80; raises P_M/P_F from 1 to 1.5. With landowners and rentiers each spending half their incomes on farm goods and manufactures, the composition of the new *tableau* becomes determinate and takes the magnitudes shown in Table 1.3.[8]

With positive profit, my open-end *tableau* enlarges from a 4 × 4 to a 5 × 5 array: a new (fourth) row has been added for the profit component of sectors'

---

[8] See the mathematical appendix (pp. 83–4) for precise equilibrium conditions behind Tables 1.3 and 1.4.

Table 1.3. *Tableau Economique (cum profit)*[a]

Purchases by → Sales of ↓	Agriculture	Manufacturing	Labour	Capitalists	Landowners	Totals
Agriculture	0	20	60	20	40	40
Manufacturing	0	0	0	20	40	60
Labour	40	20	0	0	0	60
Profit (or interest)	20	20	0	0	0	40
Land rent	80	0	0	0	0	80
Totals	140	60	60	40	80	⃝380

$r^* = 0.5$.

[a] All these values are in terms of corn as *numéraire*. If desired in manufactures as *numéraire*, multiply every item by two-thirds. Values in monetary units (dollars, livres, ...) depend upon monetary assumptions – such as the money supply and its transactions velocity.

costs; and a new (fourth) column has been added for capitalists' consumption expenditure of their profit on agricultural and manufacturing products.

The brackets show modern national income, equal in corn *numéraire* units to 180. Land's share of the reduced total product has dropped from one-half to four-ninths, now that profit usurps a share; Labour's share has dropped from one-half to three-ninths. The real value of land's rent has dropped by one-fifth in terms of corn, and by even more in terms of manufactures. Each worker gets the same subsistence wage in corn as before, but now the real wage in terms of manufactures is down by one-third.

To pierce the veil of market values, Table 1.4 presents the exact physical magnitudes underlying Table 1.3.

8 Clouding up *produit net*

Once Turgot and Quesnay admit profit into their system, there arises some embarrassment in treating land rent as the sole component of *produit net*. Or, to sidestep circularity in the defining of *produit net*, I can put it this way:

(1) Manufacturing revenues no longer *merely* cover the 'cost elements' in manufactures. Subsistence fodder to reproduce workers seems to be a more legitimate 'cost' than capitalists' interest and profit is.[9]

[9] See Samuelson (1959a, 1959b) for the Physiocratic version of Ricardo, a version I have essentially plagiarised for Table 1.3. In that version the supply price needed to keep saving neither negative nor positive was the Pickwickian 'cost of reproduction of capital' and all market value was expressible in terms of 'embodied-dated-land-content-marked-up-by-that-profit-rate'.

Table 1.4. *Tableau's physical magnitudes*[a]

Sectors	Agriculture	Manufacturing	Labour	Capitalists' consumption	Landowners' consumption	Totals
Agriculture	0	20 corn	60 corn	20 corn	40 corn	140 corn
Manufacturing[b]	0	0	0	13 mfrs	26 mfrs	40 mfrs
Labour	40 labourers	20 labourers	0	0	0	60 labourers
Land		1 land unit (of 100 acres)	1 land unit (of 100 acres)			1 land unit

[a] The sole capital in this model is 80 of corn, 20 advanced as raw materials for manufacturing and 60 advanced as subsistence wages.
[b] Second-row items are those of Table 1.3 multiplied by two-thirds.

Unless one elevates 'waiting and abstinence' to the level of genuine real costs, they could seem to involve elements of 'surplus' or even of 'exploitation'. Land rent is indeed a surplus, but with the saving grace that the land is at least 'productive' whatever be the demerits of the land's owners.

(2) There are models in which interest can be given a semblance of true productivity but my Table 1.3's example differs from Table 1.1's not a bit in technology. Involving less of population and of farm raw material needed for manufactures, Table 1.3 possesses even less of useful capital goods than Table 1.2 did. So one can understand why Marx would not have been tempted to regard its profits as either legitimate costs or as the return to a 'productive' input.[10]

Twentieth-century theorists try harder than eighteenth-century theorists did to keep normative attitudes from contaminating correct analysis of positivistic fact. So it is as well if the honorific category of *produit net* begins to get complicated in realistic models.

9 Conclusion

Embarrassing or not, the *Tableau Economique* has been an interesting footnote in the history of economic thought. Dr. Quesnay was not a young man when he first fabricated it. After studying Quesnay's many jousts with the problems it raises, one is not surprised to learn that Madame Pompadour's physician believed he had matched his contribution to economics by his contribution to mathematics in the form of a successful squaring of the circle.

Where early pioneers are concerned, posterity must be grateful for what they accomplished and must not scold over mere imperfections.

MATHEMATICAL APPENDIX

1. Here is how the *Tableau Economique* of my Tables 1.1 and 1.2 are rigorously determined when $r^* = 0$. The steady-state production functions for the agriculture and manufacturing sectors are given by

---

[10] Quesnay used the term 'interest' to name what we call 'capital depreciation'. Suppose we stay with $r^* = 0$ and postulate *exponential* depreciation, with d_{ij} being the fraction of each intermediate input that is used up in any single period's use. Then we can still accomplish what Karl Marx struggled over and doubted could be done: we can express final goods' values in terms of the sum of the values added by land rent and profit or interest on capital items. See the mathematical appendix for some of the details.

$$Q_1 = F[T, L_1]$$
$$= f(L_1) \text{ if } T = 1, f'() > 0 > f''() \tag{A.1}$$

$$Q_2 = \text{Min}[Q_{12}/a_{12}, L_2/a_{L2}]$$
$$= \text{Min}\left[Q_{12}/\tfrac{1}{2}, L_2/\tfrac{1}{2}\right] \text{in my example} \tag{A.2}$$

The corn subsistence wage of $\bar{w}$, which can be unity by proper choice of corn and labour units, determines L_1^* by

$$f'(L_1^*) = \bar{w}$$
$$= f'(100) = 1 \text{ in my example} \tag{A.3}$$

Corn output and corn rent are given by

$$Q_1^* = f_1(L_1^*)$$
$$= f_1(100) = 200 \text{ in my example} \tag{A.4}$$

$$R^* = Q_1^* - \bar{w}L_1^*$$
$$= 200 - 1(100) = \frac{1}{2}Q_1^* = 100 \text{ in my example} \tag{A.5}$$

In the equilibrium of (A.1) every competitive farm firm has production coefficients given by

$$\begin{bmatrix} a_{L1}^* \\ a_{T1}^* \end{bmatrix} = \begin{bmatrix} L_1^*/Q_1^* \\ T/Q_1^* \end{bmatrix} = \begin{bmatrix} L_1^*/f_1(Q_1^*) \\ 1/f_1(Q_1^*) \end{bmatrix}$$
$$= \begin{bmatrix} 1/2 \\ 1/200 \end{bmatrix} \text{ in my example} \tag{A.6}$$

The following prices can be set at unity by virtue of my choice of units and coefficients $[P_1^*, P_2^*, W^*, W/P_1 = \bar{w}]$. With $T = 1$ earning 100 units of rent, the rate per unit is 100:

$$P_1^* = W^* a_{L1}^* + (\text{rent rate})a_{T1}^*$$
$$= 1\left(\frac{1}{2}\right) + 100(1/200) = 1 \text{ in my example} \tag{A.7}$$

$$P_2^* = W^* a_{L2} + P_1^* a_{12}$$
$$= 1\left(\frac{1}{2}\right) + 1\left(\frac{1}{2}\right) = 1 \text{ in my example} \tag{A.8}$$

Since $R^* = 100$ and I have made Quesnay's assumption that half of the income is spent on agriculture and on manufacturing:

$$P_1 C_1^* = R^* = P_2 C_2^* \tag{A.9}$$

$$C_1^* = 1(50) = \frac{1}{2}(100) = 50 = C_2^* \text{ in my example} \tag{A.10}$$

$$\begin{aligned} L_2^* &= a_{L2} Q_2^* = a_{L2}(C_2^* + 0) \\ &= \frac{1}{2}(100) = 50 \text{ in my example} \end{aligned} \tag{A.11}$$

Total corn must equal subsistence for all $(L_1^* + L_2^*)$ workers plus raw materials for manufacturing plus landowners' corn consumption:

$$\begin{aligned} Q_1^* &= \bar{w}(L_1 + L_2) + Q_{12} + C_1 \\ &= 1(150) + 25 + 50 = 225 \text{ in my example} \end{aligned} \tag{A.12}$$

Also

$$\begin{aligned} Q_2^* &= C_2^* + (Q_{21}^* + Q_{22}^*) \\ &= C_2^* + 0 = 50 \text{ in my example} \end{aligned} \tag{A.13}$$

This completes my Table 1.1 as:

$P_1^* Q_{11}^*$	$P_1^* Q_{12}^*$	$P_1 \bar{w}(L_1^* + L_2^*)$	$P_1^* C_1^*$	$P_1^* C_1^*$
$P_2^* Q_{21}^*$	$P_2^* Q_{22}^*$	0	$P_2^* C_2^*$	$P_2^* Q_{22}^*$
$W^* L_1^*$	$W^* L_2^*$	0	0	$W(L_1^* + L_2^*)$
R^*	0	0	0	R^*
Σ	Σ	Σ	Σ	$\Sigma\Sigma$

which is equal to

0	25	125	50	200
0	0	0	50	50
100	25	0	0	125
100	0	0	0	100
200	50	125	100	(375)

2. An equivalent treatment of the subsistence wage requirements involves eliminating the row and column for labour. Instead, add the subsistence

corn requirements of industries to the first row's a_{1j}^* coefficients. These now become $a_{1j}^* + \bar{w}a_{Lj}$. My Table 1.2 is then given by:

$P_1^* Q_{11}^* + P_1^* \bar{w} L_1$	$P_1^* Q_{12}^* + P_1^* \bar{w} L_2^*$	$P_1^* C_1^*$	$P_1^* Q_1^*$
$P_2^* Q_{21}^* + 0$	$P_2^* Q_{22}^* + 0$	$P_2^* C_2^*$	$P_2^* Q_2^*$
R^*	0	0	R^*
Σ	Σ	Σ	$\Sigma\Sigma$

which is equal to

100	50	50	200
0	0	50	50
100	0	0	100
200	50	100	(350)

3. There is no reason why, in models more general than my version of Quesnay, land might not be required in more than the first sector. Then $(a_{Tj}) = (a_{T1}, a_{T2}, \ldots)$ might have a_{T2} and other a_{Tj} non-zero.

Also, there is no reason why subsistence should be solely in corn. Instead, the ration needed per worker for subsistence could be the column vector $[m_i]$, with

$$\begin{bmatrix} m_1 \\ m_2 \end{bmatrix} = \begin{bmatrix} \bar{w} \\ 0 \end{bmatrix} \text{ in my example} \tag{A.14}$$

But in general m_2, and m_j other than m_1, could *also* be positive.

It would still be true, in the case of $r^* = 0$, that *produit net* equals land rent. Our equilibrium would be given by

$$1 = \sum_1^n (P_j/W) m_j \tag{A.15}$$

If land is a homogeneous scalar – or even if it were a vector of different-quality lands but with each quality of land having the *same* relative efficiency in every use (as when grade B has half grade A's effectiveness in every sector)[11] – the relation (A.15) together with the minimum-cost conditions

---

[11] If, however, T is a vector of heterogeneous lands $(T_1, T_2, \ldots)$ that do not enter into *all* production functions in the same linear aggregate, $\alpha_1 T_{1j} + \alpha_2 T_{2j} + \ldots$, then a change in

would determine real wage rates, real rent rates, relative prices, and L_j^*/Q_j^* ratios that are independent of the pattern of landlord tastes for consumption. And the real *produit net* would be a total independent of such tastes. See Samuelson (1977b, equations 25) for an 'Adam Smith' model of this type.

4. Recognising time-phasing, the production functions for the two sectors become

$$Q_1(t+1) = F_1[T(t), L_1(t)]$$
$$= f_1[L_1(t)] \text{ for } T(t) \equiv 1 \tag{A.16}$$

$$f_1'[\ ] > 0 > f_1''[\ ]$$
$$Q_2(t+1) = \text{Min}[L_2(t)/a_{L2}], Q_{12}(t)/a_{12} \tag{A.17}$$

$$[L_2(t), Q_{12}(t)] = [a_{L2}, a_{12}]Q_2(t+1) \tag{A.17'}$$

$Q_{12}(t)$ is the corn raw material used up in producing manufactures.

Writing $[c_j(t), C_j(t)]$ for consumptions of good j by capitalists and landowners respectively, total outputs are allocated according to

$$Q_2(t) = c_2(t) + C_2(t) + 0 \tag{A.18}$$

$$Q_1(t) = c_1(t) + C_1(t) + \bar{w}[L_1(t) + L_2(t)] + Q_{12}(t) \tag{A.19}$$

In the steady state

$$[Q_j(t), Q_{ij}, c_j(t), C_j(t), L_j(t)] \equiv [Q_j, Q_{ij}, c_i, C_j, L_j] \tag{A.20}$$

$$W/P_1 = \bar{w} = f_1'(L_1)/(1+r^*)$$
$$= f_1'(40)/(1+0.5) = 1 \text{ in Table 1.3} \tag{A.21}$$

$$Q_1 = f_1(L_1)$$
$$= f_1(40) = 140 \text{ in Table 1.3} \tag{A.22}$$

$$R = Q_1 - L_1 f_1'(L_1)$$
$$= 140 - (40)(1.5) = 80 \text{ in Table 1.3} \tag{A.23}$$

landowners' tastes might well affect $(P_j/P_1)^*$ and (L_j^*/Q_j^*) ratios. Also, real *produit net*, reckoned as $\sum_k(R_kT_k/P_j)$, will then generally be altered by changes in tastes.

$$P_2 = (Wa_{L2} + P_1 a_{12})(1 + r^*)$$
$$= P_1(\bar{w}a_{L2} + a_{12})(1 + r^*)$$
$$= P_1\left(\frac{1}{2} + \frac{1}{2}\right)(1 + 0.5) = P_1(1.5) \text{ in Table 1.3} \qquad (A.24)$$

$$c_1 + C_1 = \frac{1}{2}[\text{Total profit} + \text{Rent}]$$
$$= \frac{1}{2}[r^*(L_1 + L_2) + r^*Q_{12} + R] \qquad (A.25)$$

$$c_2 + C_2 = (P_2/P_1)^{-1}[r^*(L_1 + L_2) + r^*Q_{12} + R] \qquad (A.26)$$

$$L_2 = a_{12}Q_2 = \frac{1}{2}(c_2 + C_2) = Q_{12} \qquad (A.27)$$

Solving (A.25) – (A.27) simultaneously determines for Table 1.3

$$[L_2^*, Q_2^*, Q_{12}^*, c_1^*, C_1^*, c_2^*, C_2^*] = \left[20, \ 40, \ 20, \ 20, \ 40, \ \frac{2}{3}20, \frac{2}{3}40\right]$$

5. Quesnay's durable capital goods can be handled expeditiously if any such good is assumed to depreciate exponentially. Thus, replace the Q_{ij} symbol in (A.17) appropriate for the case where the input is all used up in one use by K_{ij}, with $d_{ij}K_{ij}$ being used up in one-period's use. For $d_{ij} = 1$, we have our previous case.

Now, in (A.19), replace the symbol $Q_{ij}(t)$ by $[K_{ij}(t) - K_{ij}(t-1)] + d_{ij}K_{ij}(t-1)$. This takes account of the fact that net investment equals gross investment minus depreciation. Then (A.24) becomes

$$P_2/P_1 = \bar{w}a_{L2}(1 + r^*) + a_{12}(d_{12} + r^*) \qquad (A.28)$$

Generally, if we are given for all input–output coefficients the depreciation fractions $[d_{ij}]$, what Leontief and Sraffa write for circulating-capital systems as

$$[I - a_{ij}(1 + r^*)]^{-1} \qquad (A.29)$$

we now merely write as

$$[I - a_{ij}(d_{ij} + r^*)]^{-1} \qquad (A.30)$$

My text skips such inessential complications.

REFERENCES

Barna, T. (1975) 'Quesnay's "Tableau" in Modern Guise', *Economic Journal*, vol. 85, pp. 485–96.

Clark, J. B. (1899) *The Distribution of Wealth: A Theory of Wages, Interest and Profits* (New York, Macmillan).

Dorfman, R., Samuelson, P. A. and Solow, R. (1958) *Linear Programming and Economic Analysis* (New York, McGraw-Hill).

Eltis, W. A. (1975) 'Francois Quesnay: a reinterpretation I: the Tableau Economique', *Oxford Economic Papers*, vol. 27, pp. 167–200.

Gide, C. and Rist, C. (1926) *A History of Economic Doctrines*, 2nd English edn (Paris, Société anonyme du Recueil Sirey).

Gray, A. (1931) *The Development of Economic Doctrine* (London, Longman, Green).

Hishiyama, I. (1960) 'The Tableau économique of Quesnay: Its analysis, reconstruction and application', *Kyoto University Economic Review*, vol. 30, no. 1, pp. 1–46.

Johnson, H. (1974) 'Some reflections on Quesnay's *Tableau Econmique*', (in Spanish), *Economie*, vol. 2, pp. 76–85; also in French, *Revue d'Economic Politique*, vol. 2, 1975, pp. 397–407.

Keynes, J. M. (1936) *The General Theory of Employment, Interest and Money* (London, Macmillan).

Kuczynski, M. and Meek, R. L. (1972) *Quesnay's Tableau Economique* (London, Macmillan).

Leontief, W. (1941) *The Structure of the American Economy, 1919–39* (New York, Oxford University Press).

Machlup, F. (1939) 'Period analysis and multiplier theory', *Quarterly Journal of Economics*, vol. 54, pp. 1–27.

Maital, S. (1972) 'The Tableau Economique as a Leontief model', *Quarterly Journal of Economics*, vol. 84, pp. 504–7.

Malanos, G. J. (1946) 'The evolution of the General Theory', Ph.D. thesis, Harvard University.

Malthus, T. R. (1798) *An Essay on the Principle of Population* (First Essay on Population) (London, J. Johnson).

Meek, R. L. (1962) 'Problems of the 'Tableau Economique', in *The Economics of Physiocracy* (London, Allen & Unwin).

Mirabeau, Marquis De (1756–60) *L'ami des hommes (Friend of Mankind)*, (Avignon). (Reprinted by Scientia, Verlag Aalen, 1970.)

Phillips, A. (1955) 'The Tableau Economique as a simple Leontief model', *Quarterly Journal of Economics*, vol. 69, pp. 137–44.

Quesnay, F. (1758) *Tableau Oeconomique* (so-called 'first edition' as reproduced and translated in appendix A of Kuczynski and Meek, 1972).

Ricardo, D. (1817) *On the Principles of Political Economy and Taxation* (London, J. Murray).

Samuelson, P. A. (1959a) 'A modern treatment of the Ricardian economy: I. the pricing of goods and of labor and land services', *Quarterly Journal of Economics*, vol. 73, pp. 1–35. Reprinted in *The Collected Scientific Papers of Paul A. Samuelson*, vol. 1, ch. 31, ed. J. E. Stiglitz (Cambridge, Mass., MIT Press, 1966).

Samuelson, P. A. (1959b) 'A modern treatment of the Ricardian economy: II. capital and interest aspects of the pricing process', *Quarterly Journal of Economics*, vol. 73, pp. 217–31. Reprinted in *Collected Scientific Papers of Paul A. Samuelson*, vol. 1, ch. 32.

Samuelson, P. A. (1977a) 'Correcting the Ricardo error spotted in Harry Johnson's maiden paper', *Quarterly Journal of Economics*, vol. 91, pp. 519–30.

Samuelson, P. A. (1977b) 'A modern theorist's vindication of Adam Smith', *American Economic Review*, vol. 67, pp. 42–9.

Samuelson, P. A. (1979) 'Land and the rate of interest', in *Theory for Economic Efficiency: Essays in Honor of Abba P. Lerner*, ed. H. I. Greenfield (Cambridge, Mass., MIT Press).

Schumpeter, J. A. (1954) *History of Economic Analysis* (Oxford University Press).

Sraffa, P. (1951) *The Works and Correspondence of David Ricardo*, vol. 1 (Cambridge, University Press) Editor's Introduction, pp. xiii–lxii.

Stolper, W. F., and Samuelson, P. A. (1940) 'Protection and real wages', *Review of Economic Studies*, vol. 9, pp. 58–73. Reprinted in *The Collected Scientific Papers of Paul A. Samuelson*, vol. 2, ch. 66, ed. J. E. Stiglitz (Cambridge, Mass., MIT Press, 1966).

Turgot, A. R. J. (1769) *Reflections on the Formation and the Distribution of Riches* (New York, A. M. Kelley, 1963).

West, Sir E. (1815) *Essay on the Application of Capital to Land* (Baltimore, Johns Hopkins Press, 1903).

PART III

WEALTH OF NATIONS AND THE "CANONICAL CLASSICAL MODEL"

The Canonical Classical Model of Political Economy

1. Adam Smith, David Ricardo, Thomas Robert Malthus, and John Stuart Mill shared in common essentially one dynamic model of equilibrium, growth, and distribution. When the limitation of land and natural resources is added to the model of Karl Marx, he also ends up with this same canonical classical model.

In its present version the model is stripped down to its minimal essentials. For brevity I employ modern mathematical tools, but only to characterize in modern terms the relations that were actually common to all these writers.

The reader should of course be warned that any simple codification of the classical economists' discursive writings must be an oversimplification: in some of their passages they qualify what they have written elsewhere; in some they provide negations and contradictions. Not a few of the stereotypes about the classical writers are, to paraphrase Voltaire, myths agreed-upon by later commentators – distortions that both improve and libel the originals. The relevant object of study for a modern scholar is the corpus of original texts and the commentaries on them, the latter not being genuinely of less interest than the former once we have succeeded in telling them apart.

To the fascinating question of whether classical political economy does, or can be made to, offer an *"alternative paradigm"* – in the sense of Thomas Kuhn [11, 1962] – to modern mainstream economics, the present investigation provides an instructive answer. So to speak, within every classical economist there is to be discerned a modern economist trying to be born. A Ricardo or Mill did not so much replace supply and demand by quite different mechanisms but rather sought to be able to say something significant and limiting about their properties, quite in the same way that we moderns endeavor to do. I describe and analyze here the basic classical model in its essential form.

2. Real output is divided interchangeably between *consumption* and *capital formation* (on a net or gross saving-investment basis). Ignoring details concerning the input-intensity differences between goods of different industries (much as can be done in a modern one-sector one-capital-good model), the classicists in effect assume that output is produced by a production function involving land input and a *dose* of labor-*cum*-capital input. Competition among (1) landowners, (2) entrepreneurs who hire labor and needed raw materials to work with hired land, and (3) owners of labor and capital goods out to make the most favorable terms for themselves – all this leads to a determinate breakdown of competitive earnings and cost between (a) land rent and (b) the *combined return to the composite dose of labor-capital*. The breakdown of the combined return to the dose between its two components would be indeterminate as far as the demand side of the problem is concerned (at least this would be so if we stick literally to the fixed-proportions assumption usually alleged to be adhered to by the classical writers). The needed conditions come from the supply side.

3. The classical long-run theory postulates that the workers' wage rate is ultimately determined by (α) the real *subsistence* level needed to ensure reproduction and maintenance of the working population. Just as the classicists had a long-run horizontal supply curve for the subsistence wage, so they had a long-run horizontal supply curve for capital at (β) the *minimum-effective rate of accumulation*, that profit rate just low enough and just high enough to cause capital to be *maintained* with zero net algebraic saving. The long-run equilibrium number of total doses, with the implied long-run plateau of population and of capital stock, is just big enough so that the law of diminishing returns brings down the combined return of the dose to the *sum* of the needed wage-subsistence and needed minimum-profit rates. When accumulation has gone that far and population has grown in balanced proper degree, then in the absence of further technical change total land rent is *maximal*. Equilibrium prevails forever. (Mill went on to emphasize that technological innovation, continued in the long-run steady state, would imply *rising output forever*; we can show on Mill's behalf that, if the technical change is *land-augmenting* at a steady exponential rate, then labor and capital will grow forever at the same balanced exponential rate, just enough to match the growth of land measured in "efficiency units" and with the long-run wage rate and profit rate each just high enough above their respective bare minima to elicit the implied growth rates of the factors.)

4. The long-run equilibrium is stable in the sense that the system, if disturbed from it, will spontaneously return toward it. To grasp the short-run transient development of the system, suppose labor and capital goods

begin in the balanced proportions needed for the technological dose, but with each at a level short of the long-run equilibrium level. Land rent then will begin below its long-run equilibrium; by the same token, the aggregate return to the composite dose will begin in excess of the long-run subsistence levels. The short-run breakdown of the dose's aggregate return among capital and labor will be determined by competitive auctioneering at that fractional breakdown just *needed to keep the two components of the dose growing at the same balanced rate* (which will be a uniquely determinate growth rate).

Thus, if population adjusts so rapidly to any surplus of real wage above subsistence that we can practically assume the truth of (what can be termed) Ricardo's "short-circuited" approximation, then the transient wage rate will be insignificantly different from the long-run subsistence level. The rate of profit is then determinate as a *residual* in the short run. And being thus determined *above* the long-run minimal profit rate, the system's saving propensities will determine the rate at which capital accumulates and population grows apace. Asymptotically, the growth of doses of capital as applied to a limited supply of land leads down the trail of diminishing returns to the rendezvous of long-run equilibrium.

Suppose we go beyond the short-circuited version and recognize that just as it takes an increment of profit rate to elicit positive saving and growth of capital, so too there must be an increment of real wage rate over the subsistence level to elicit the needed transient growth in population. Still, we shall find that there is a determinate short-term breakdown between the components of the dose's aggregate return that will be just enough to keep both labor and capital growing in the needed fixed-proportions way. The only difference in this more realistic scenario is what Smith envisioned so much more clearly than Ricardo – namely, that the real wage is higher in the transient state of progressive growth. Only in the final equilibrium when growth ceases is society in Smith's *dull* state of minimal real wages. Ricardo's predecessor and successor, Smith and Mill, are both more realistic than is Ricardo himself on wages adjustments. (By contrast, Ricardo is more realistic in 1817 [21] than Smith in 1776 [29] when it comes to recognizing that continuing new inventions will greatly delay the fall of the profit rate to its minimum and perhaps continue to do so permanently.)

Even Mill is not realistic enough in his modelling of innovation and the lagging supply of population in advanced economies. What observers like Kuznets have observed this past century is that the growth of technology has been enough *to keep the real wage growing at something like an exponential rate*, with the growth in population and saving not being fast enough to wipe out the rising trend in real wages. By contrast, the rate of profit has mean-dered more or less trendlessly depending on the qualitative structure of technical change, much as if population growth were more a bottleneck than were saving. It is curious that the Marxian variant of classicism, with its soft-pedalling of the limitations of land and natural resources, ought logi-cally to have led to an even more optimistic scenario for the laws of motion of capitalistic profits than the Ricardo-Smith version.

LONG-RUN EQUILIBRIUM DIAGRAMMED

5. *Figure 1* shows the canonical classical equilibrium in the long run or steady state. The DD' relation, which looks like a modern demand relation, gives the competitive return to the composite dose of capital-*cum*-labor: the greater the number of doses competing for the same fixed supply of various qualities of land, the higher will be bid up land rents and the lower will be the dose price available to be divided between labor's wage rate and capital's profit-or-interest rate.

The DD' relation looks like a Clarkian neoclassical marginal-product curve for the variable composite doses applied to fixed land(s). But we shall be more in tune with the classicists' own mode of thinking if we delay giving DD' that admissible interpretation.[1] Perusal of the accompanying footnote shows

---

[1]   The numerical tables in the last part of Chapter II on rent of Ricardo [21, 1817] leave sketchy his notion that "successive portions of capital [doses 1, 2, 3, and 4] yielded 100, 90, 80, 70 [with total rent therefore being $(100-70) + (90-70) + (80-70) + 0 = 60$ and the total return to the 4 units of doses being $\{(100 + 90 + 80 + 70) - 60\}/4 = 280/4 = 70$]." It is clear that Ricardo believed that extra available doses would both work with lands of lower quality not previously worth cultivating and work old lands more intensively, thus altering both the *extensive* and *intensive* margins of cultivation.

Until the last half century, no one seems to have worked out rigorously the processes going on implicitly in the background, although Mountifort Longfield [12, 1834] came close to doing so as far as "reduced-form" descriptions are concerned. We shall outdo the classicists and underplay neoclassical versions of marginalism by first utilizing the follow-ing model, which is analyzed in Samuelson [24, 1959; 28, 1977].

(a) A strip of land declines continuously "eastward" in "fertility." (b) Every grade of land is cultivated by composite doses of exactly the same internal *relative* labor-capital pro-portions. (c) Fixed proportions of dose to land prevail at each grade's longitude, with (d) return of product per doses applied declining continuously as we move eastward. Then, when total available doses are few, all land to the east is not worth cultivating; as doses increase in availability, they all are applied ever further eastward (with no change in density of doses on prime westward land, but of course with increased *differential* rent earned on those prime acres). For each total of doses available, there is an external frontier of zero-rent land: the height of DD' at any given V is the *average product* (not the yet-to-be invented "marginal product") of output per unit of V, namely Q/V there. Footnote 7 below will show when DD' also can be interpreted as a true marginal product of the variable composite dose, V.

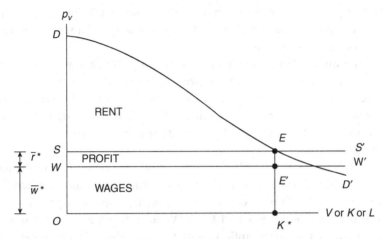

Figure 1. Long-run equilibrium is at E, where the DD' curve of return to the doses of V, made up of balanced proportions of L and K applied to a fixed profile of lands, just intersects the SS' supply curve that measures the wage subsistence and the minimum profit rate needed for steady reproduction of labor and capital. The equilibrium long-run wage rate is $\bar{w}^*$ and the long-run profit rate is $\bar{r}^*$, both exogenous parameters. Distribution of total product, OK^*ED, is between the residual rent triangle SED and the dose's rectangle OK^*ES. The breakdown between wages and profit is given by the rectangle's breakdown into $OKE^{*'}W$ and $WE'ES$. (Possibly $\bar{r}^*$ could be zero. DD' can be given the ultra-classical interpretation as the *average product* of the dose on the *external margin* of a continuum of lands of different grades; but, also, it could be the dose's common *marginal product* at the varying *intensive* margins of all lands used.)

how we might also interpret DD' as the curve of *average product of the varied dose* out at the moving external frontier of zero-rent grade of land.

6. The supply of labor is given by the horizontal line WW', representing the subsistence cost of reproduction of labor in steady-state numbers. Followers of Smith, Ricardo, and Mill were prepared to recognize non-physiological components in the subsistence level of wages required by workers before their patterns of marriage, procreation, migration, and labor-force participation were just adequate to keep total labor employed constant. Marx shifted the determinants of WW' away from Malthus's emphasis on biological elements of marriage, procreation, and mortality toward his own emphasis on the reserve army of the unemployed, labor-saving inventions, and in-migration to the industrial regions from the over-populated rural areas.

So long as we choose conventional units for labor, capital goods (or "leets"), and composite doses that agree in numerical magnitude, the height of WW' represents the *real wage rate* per unit of labor, $\bar{w}^*$, that must prevail when labor power's cost of reproduction is just achieved and its long-run total is in stationary equilibrium.

7. Superimposed on WW', to achieve the long-run supply response SS' for the composite dose, is the long-run profit per unit of capital goods needed if the profit rate per annum is to be at the effective rate of accumulation, $\bar{r}^*$, just enough to choke off further net saving but not so low as to cause dissaving and eating up of the previously existing stock of capital goods.

8. The distance WS, or $E'E$, represents both the rental rate of capital goods *and* the ("own") profit rate per unit time (such as .10 when 10 percent is the rate of profit to be earned on assets) when our numeraire for output is capital-goods per unit time. When differences in factor intensities between the consumption- and the capital-goods industries are ignorable, as in *Figure* 1, there is no difference between using consumption goods or capital goods as numeraire provided both kinds of goods are actually being produced – as will be the case for any stationary or growing system.

This long-run profit rate might, in some theories, be zero (after, of course, all allowances for depreciation and replacement of principal have separately been allowed for; after any needed actuarial premia for probable accidents and losses had been properly allowed for; and after any wages of managing capital assets had been provided for). If $\bar{r}^*$ is zero, SS' would coincide with WW' and E with the intersection of DD' and WW': the vertical distance between them measures the long-run *perpetual net rental* (if any) to be earned by owners of maintained capital-goods (leets) in the steady state when they are just motivated to cease net saving or dissaving.

9. The *residual of land rent* is measured on the diagram by the curvilinear triangle SED. It is what is left of total product, OK^*ED, after the composite doses are paid their needed long-run aggregate of OK^*ES. Whereas J. B. Clark and such neo-classicals as Philip H. Wicksteed, Knut Wicksell, Léon Walras, and Paul Douglas would split up the non-rent aggregate between labor and capital by a marginal product calculation in which variability of the labor-to-leets components is brought to the optimal degree of substitution, the present classical paradigm denies such smooth substitutability *within* the composite dose and at best tolerates it between land and the composite of the fixed components dose.

From the horizontal long-run supply curves of the components, WW' and SS', and from them alone comes the classical system's determinate *long-run* distribution theory of the non-land factor shares.[2]

10. As noted in the Physiocratic version of the classical system of Samuelson [23, 1959], under long-run equilibrium all goods can be decomposed into their (marked-up) socially-necessary *land* contents: a shift in tastes and final demand from one good to another, toward more cloth and less corn, would have no effect on long-run prices. But such a shift toward less–land-intensive and more–labor-intensive goods would lower rent's share in ultimate national income; it would also raise the plateaux of population and of capital in any model where they combine in doses of the same proportions in all industries (an implausible special case). The point is obvious that any classicist who thinks he can separate "value" from "distribution" commits a logical blunder. He also blunders if he thinks that he can "get rid of land and rent as a complication for pricing" by concentrating on the external margin of no-rent land: where that external margin falls is an *endogenous* variable that shifts with tastes and demand changes so as to vitiate a hoped-for labor theory of value or a wage-*cum*-profit-rate theory of value.

11. For given technological knowledge, there is defined a unique steady-state ("factor-price") frontier relating (α) the *profit or interest rate* to (β) the *real wage rate* (expressed in terms of market basket of subsistence goods or in terms of any specified good) and (γ) the *rate of land rent* earnable by a composite unit of *all* grades of land weighted by their actual importance in the system. With the profit rate and the real wage given at their long-run supply levels, the rent rate is maximal at the long-run rendezvous of the system. (For fixed profit rate, the trade-off between real wage and rent rates can be shown to be convex, no matter how many the sectors or capital goods.)

Any reader uninterested in the rigorous analysis of this classical model may skip the next section's mathematical exposition and concentrate on the subsequent section's graphical analysis of classical growth and development.

---

[2] If $V = \text{Min}[L, K]$ were replaced by a neoclassical-first-degree-homogeneous smooth function, $v[L, K]$ with well-defined partial derivative, $\partial v[L, K]/\partial L$, the same $\bar{w}^*$ and $\bar{r}^*$ levels would prevail in the long run: but now the 2-dimensional *Figure* 1 would be inadequate to depict the determination of the resulting L^* and K^* levels: marginal productivity conditions, involving DD' and $\partial v[L, K]/\partial L$ would be the necessary and sufficient conditions to determine the extra unknowns of the rephrased problem, as in §19 below.

MATHEMATICAL VERSION OF THE CANONICAL SYSTEM

12. To define the system's behavior both in long-run equilibrium and also in transient movements toward equilibrium, here are the equations implied by this version of the classical system.

Real output, Q, is divided into real consumption, C, and net capital formation, dK/dt. It is produced at time t out of land and a composite dose of labor and capital goods ("leets"), $V_t = \text{Min}[L_t, K_t]$, where the units in the dose and in L_t and K_t are related so that one dose involves one unit of labor and one unit of capital goods. With land (possibly of various grades) fixed, we can omit the symbol for it (T, standing for a scalar, a vector, or even possibly a function of a parameter denoting a continuum of grades) in the economy's production function.

The basic production function becomes

$$Q = 1(C) + 1(dK/dt) = f(V). \tag{1}$$

$$V = \text{Min}[L, K], \tag{2}$$

where $f(V)$ is a *concave* function with $f'(V) \geq 0, f''(V) \leq 0$. [Warning: only the expositional need to compress the model into a single sector and the desire to exaggerate the differences between classical and neoclassical writers can justify so simple and strong an axiom of fixed proportions. When we relax this by quoting passages in classical writings, we need to augment the system with extra equations that help determine the extra unknowns.]

Total land rent, R, is given residually by

$$R = f(V) - Vf'(V). \tag{3}$$

The non-rent real return to the total dose, p_V, expressed in output units as numeraire, is equal to the sum of the wage component and the profit component: it is given by

$$f'(V) = p_V = 1w + 1r, \tag{4}$$

where w is the real wage in output units, r is both the own rate of interest and the real rental rate of capital goods expressed in output units (*i.e.*, interchangeably in capital-good or consumption units), $f'(V)$ is the increment in product resulting from an extra dose of V, applied to fixed land(s); its reciprocal is the competitive marginal cost of output in terms of extra needed V requirements.[3]

13. As *Figure* 1's WW' and SS' horizontal lines indicated, w and r have to be at the well-defined $\bar{w}^*$ and $\bar{r}^*$ levels in long-run equilibrium. Thus, *Figure* 1's E is defined by the long-run equilibrium equations:

$$f'(V^*) = \bar{w}^* + \bar{r}^* = p_V \qquad (4^*)$$

$$R^* = f(V^*) - V^* f'(V^*) \qquad (3^*)$$

$$L^* = K^* = V^* \qquad (2^*)$$

$$Q^* = C^* + 0 = f(V^*). \qquad (1^*)$$

Any increase in the subsistence wage, $\bar{w}^*$, or in $\bar{r}^*$, must lower V^*, R^*, K^*, and L^*, Q^*, and C^*. The absolute shares $(\bar{r}^* K^*, \bar{w}^* L^*)$ can move in either direction relative to R^* : if $\bar{r}^*/\bar{w}^*$ rises, the profit/wage share rises, but how a change in $\bar{w}^* + \bar{r}^*$ affects the $(\bar{w}^* + \bar{r}^*)V^*/R^*$ ratio must depend on how changes in V affect the elasticity of the $f(V)$ curve (more precisely, on what we today call the elasticity of substitution of the $f(V)$ production function).

For all their talk about the importance of the problem of distribution between land rent, labor wages, and profits, the classicists succeeded in saying little definite (and correct!) on levels of and changes in relative factor shares.

14. The dynamic laws of growth of population, $(dL/dt)/L$, and of the accumulating stock of capital, $(dK/dt)/K$, must be specified for the canonical model. When the real wage rate, w, is above the subsistence real wage rate, $\bar{w}^*$, the population grows – and grows at a greater rate the greater is the excess in wage rates:

---

[3] As will be seen later, when one of the L or K inputs exceeds its needed proportions – *i.e.*, when $L/K > 1$ or $K/L > 1$ – the price of the redundant input in (4) is zero, corresponding to a free good. So (4) must be augmented under ruthless perfect competition by

$$w = 0, \; L > K \qquad (4a)$$

$$r = 0, \; K > L \qquad (4b)$$

$$w + r = f'(\text{Min}[L, K]), \; L \gtrless K. \qquad (4c)$$

$$\varepsilon(dL/dt)/L = \lambda[w - \bar{w}^*];$$
$$\lambda[0] = 0, \ \lambda'[\ ] > 0.$$

(5)

Here ε is a non-negative parameter determining the slowness of the growth response of labor supply to surpluses over subsistence wages: if $\varepsilon = 0$, the adjustment is instantaneous of short-run w^* to long-run $\bar{w}^*$ level of subsistence as L grows at whatever pace is needed to achieve $\bar{w}^*$; this is what I call the Ricardian "short-circuited" version of dynamics. If ε is a large positive parameter, evidently the more realistic case historically, the population grows only slowly during a high-wage era. By definition, in the long run, $(dL/dt)/L = 0$ when $w = \bar{w}^*$.

15. For Smith, Ricardo, and Mill, saving and investing never fail to be equated at full-employment conditions; only Malthus expressed doubts, envisaging in 1820 [15] the possibility of oversaving and violation of what we know loosely as "Say's Law". The rate of saving-investment is positive when r exceeds $\bar{r}^*$, the effective rate at which net accumulation ceases. Crudely, we write:

$$(dL/dt)/K = \sigma[r - \bar{r}^*];$$
$$\sigma[0] = 0, \sigma'[\ ] > 0,$$

(6)

where $\sigma[r - \bar{r}^*]/r$ is the fraction that saving will bear to total profit incomes.

16. Our dynamic canonical classical system is almost complete.[4] If it *always* started with initial L_0/K_0 in the balanced configuration of unity and remained always in a balanced configuration, it would in fact generate determinate motions of all our variables: $L(t)$, $K(t)$, $V(t)$, $w(t)$, $r(t)$, $p_V(t)$, $C(t)$, $Q(t)$.

One such complete version is the "short-circuited" case already referred to. In it, we make the unrealistic polar Ricardian assumption that population adjusts virtually instantly, so that w falls or rises immediately to the $\bar{w}^*$ subsistence wage rate. Now (5) is replaced by:

$$w = \bar{w}^*, L(t) \equiv K(t) \equiv V(t)$$

(5')

Our new system [(1)–(4), (5'), (6)] can now be reduced to

---

[4]   With the (4a) and (4b) relations of footnote 3, the dynamic system would be complete (as will be discussed later in footnote 6).

$$(dK/dt)/K = \sigma[f'(K) - \bar{w}^* - \bar{r}^*],$$
$$K(t_0) = K_0 \tag{7.1}$$

$$Q = f(K) \tag{7.2}$$

$$C = f(K) - dK/dt \tag{7.3}$$

$$L = V = K \tag{7.4}$$

$$w = \bar{w}^* \tag{7.5}$$

$$R = f(K) - Kf'(K). \tag{7.6}$$

The equilibrium at the K^* root of $f'(K) = \bar{w}^* + \bar{r}^*$ is globally stable: for any initial positive K_0,

$$\lim_{t \to \infty}[K(t), L(t), r(t), R(t), \ldots]$$
$$= [K^*, L^*, \bar{r}^*, R^*, \ldots], \tag{7.7}$$

where the starred long-run equilibria are precisely those of $(1^*)-(4^*)$. The global stability follows from the fact that $\sigma[x]$ always has the sign of x and $-dK/dt$ therefore always the sign of $K - K^*$.

17. Not even Ricardo adhered to the short-circuited version in which the population is instantly variable so that the wage rate could be regarded as adjusting to the long-run $\bar{w}^*$ rate instantaneously. Ricardo realized that labor as well as capital would have to share in the transient surplus of the dose's return: how much of the maximum "wage fund" that could go to wages rather than to profits was never worked out in proper supply-and-demand detail by the classical writers but was left implicit by Ricardo and his contemporaries. Our supply relations (5) and (6) explicitly bridge the logical gap. (See *Figures* 3(a) and 3(b) for the diagrammatic details.) The full classical system of (1)–(6), if started out with initially balanced (K_0, L_0) sufficiently near to (K^*, L^*), will forever after grow with K/L in the needed balance and with neither factor redundantly free. Subject to such balanced conditions, the canonical system of (1)–(6) can be reduced to the determinate dynamical system:

$$(dK/dt)/K = \sigma[f'(K) - w - \bar{r}^*],$$
$$K_0 = L_0 = V_0 \tag{8.1}$$

$$(dK/dt)/K = (dL/dt)/L$$
$$= \sigma[f'(K) - w - \bar{r}^*] \qquad (8.2)$$
$$= \varepsilon^{-1}\lambda[w - \bar{w}^*].$$

Between (8.1) and (8.2) we can eliminate w as an unknown, solving for it uniquely in terms of K:

$$w = \omega(K; \varepsilon)$$
$$\partial w(K; \varepsilon)/\partial K < 0, \qquad (8.2')$$
$$w(K^*; \varepsilon) \equiv \bar{w}^*.$$

The less is ε, the faster w approaches final equilibrium, the sign of $\partial \omega/\partial \varepsilon$ being that of $-(K - K^*)$.

Our determinate system becomes:

$$(dK/dt)/K$$
$$= \sigma[f'(K) - \omega(K; \varepsilon) - \bar{r}^*]$$
$$0 \equiv \sigma[f'(K^*) - \omega(K^*; \varepsilon) - \bar{r}^*] \qquad (9.1)$$
$$\lim_{t \to \infty} K(t) = K^*$$

for all K_0 near enough to K^* for (8.2) to have the solution of (8.2'). The smaller is ε, the closer the solution of the full-fledged canonical system (1)–(6) to the short-circuited version.

18. There remains only the task of showing that the canonical system is determinate and globally stable from any *initial conditions* of positive K and L, balanced or unbalanced.[5]

Suppose we start the system off with excess supply of one of the factors – say with more of capital goods (leets) than can be manned by labor. With $K_0 > L_0$, the short-term rentals of redundant capital goods would fall to zero under ruthless competition. At a current profit rate of zero (really negative if we recognized depreciation), there would be no profit income to save, and presumably there would be every incentive for all holders of capital assets to want to dissave at as rapid a rate as possible. Meantime

---

[5] Strictly speaking, if initial L_0 is astronomically large, starvation and insurrection might kill off the system in one fell swoop. To do justice to this realism, we would have to make $\lambda[w - \bar{w}^*]$ minus infinity at $w = 0$ and perhaps make $f(V)$ turn down for overly large V. Along with the classical writers, I forbear from modelling scenarios of *extinction* from over-population. Darwin would no doubt deem this a fault.

labor's wage is getting all of the gross return to the composite dose, and population growth will be rapid. Therefore, very quickly, K/L will diminish toward balanced proportions without redundancy – the case already analyzed in (8) or (9).

Similarly, if we begin with redundant L/K, labor will be a free good with a zero competitive price or wage. Under laissez faire, people will die like flies; even if poor-law relief slows down the process of genocide, after an interval L/K will have dropped to balanced proportions suitable for the earlier analysis. (If one more realistically replaces perfectly fixed proportions by some variability of techniques, the r/w factor-price ratio will not gyrate so violently to zero or infinity and the more neoclassical model of §19 will better approximate reality.)

In every case, ours is a deterministic system for $(L, K, dL/dt, dK/dt)$ and the other variables.[6]

DIGRESSION ON NEOCLASSICAL ELABORATION OF THE CLASSICAL MODEL

19. Ricardo and Marx were not so naive observers as to believe literally in fixed proportions between capital goods and labor. Their knowledgeable commentaries on current events presuppose recognition that, at certain price and profit rates, substitutions will be made that would not be competitively viable at other price and profit rates. So it is a caricature to insist on fixed-proportion doses, $V = \text{Min}[L, K]$.

On the other hand it would be ahistorical to read into the classicists a full-fledged post-Clarkian model of neoclassical type. Nonetheless, if we wish to flesh out the torsos of their logically incomplete models, we must supply the equations missing for their additional unknowns. And, once we commit ourselves to (α) free-entry and widely-shared knowledge, (β) constant-returns-to-scale technology, and (γ) smooth variability of the (L_t, K_t) components of the V_t dose, ruthless competition will enforce the neoclassical marginal productivity relations in the canonical model whether or not the

---

[6] The dynamic system is most generally defined by

$$dL/dt = \varepsilon^{-1}\lambda[g_1(L, K) - \bar{w}^*]$$
$$dK/dt = \sigma[g_2(L, K) - \bar{r}^*]$$
$$g_1(L, K) + g_2(L, K) = f'(\text{Min}[L, K]), K \gtreqless L$$
$$g_1(L, K) \equiv 0, L > K; g_2(L, K) \equiv 0, K > L.$$

For any initial (L_0, K_0), this system will approach §13's (L^*, K^*) asymptotically.

classicist is yet aware of those relations and is able to apprehend them. (Before Isaac N.'s birth, apples and the moon fell toward the earth in accordance with inverse-square-of-distance gravitational laws!)

To evaluate the question of how different the classical paradigm was from today's mainstream economics, it is worth sketching briefly the consequences of replacing $f(\text{Min}[L, K])$ by smooth constant-returns-to-scale technology. To relate the discussion more easily to classical "wage-fund" notions, I work with discrete-time variables, $K_{t+1} - K_t$ instead of dK/dt, and so forth. Writing $(T_1, T_2, \ldots) = \text{T}$ for prescribed amounts of different grades of land, we have:

$$Q_{t+1} = C_{t+1} + K_{t+1} - K_t$$
$$= F(L_t, K_t; T_1, T_2, \ldots), \qquad (10.1)$$

where $F()$ is a first-degree-homogeneous, concave function.[7] For this section, F's partial derivatives are assumed to be well-defined everywhere, in contrast to $\text{Min}[L_t, K_t]$'s assumed non-substitutability. The present section does not rule out that $F()$ might have the separability property of $F(v[L, K]; T_1, T_2, \ldots) \equiv f(v[L, K])$, where $v[L, K]$ is now a smoothly

---

[7]   As Ricardo and J. H. von Thünen understood, larger totals of L and K involve more intense cultivation of previously cultivated grades of good land – say of T_1, at the same time that T_2 newly comes into cultivation. In the background, the function $F()$ has been defined implicitly *as if* by a maximization process. Thus

$$F(L, K; T_1, T_2, \ldots) = \underset{L_i, K}{\text{Max}}\{F_1(L_1, K_1, T_1) + F_2(L_2, K_2, T_2) + \ldots\}$$

subject to

$$L_1 + L_2 + \ldots = L,$$
$$K_1 + K_2 + \ldots = K.$$

If $F_i()$ are concave in (L_i, K_i) and $\partial F_i()/\partial L_i$ and $\partial F_i()/\partial K_i$ are well-defined, or if, for the composite dose $V_i = \text{Min}[L_i, K_i]$, $\partial F_i(V_i, T_i)/\partial V_i$ is well-defined for $F_i()$ concave in V_i, then for all lands actually in use, there will be common marginal productivities of the transferable factors, equal as the case may be to $\partial F(L, K; T_1, T_2, \ldots)/\partial L$ or $\partial F(L, K; T_1, T_2, \ldots)/\partial K$ or to $\partial F(V; T_1, T_2, \ldots)/\partial V$. Therefore, in *Figure* 1 and later figures, the DD' curve of $f'(V)$ represents not merely the *average* product at the *external margin* of continuous-grade lands (as in my footnote 1's' ultra-classical interpretation); DD' alternatively represents the true *marginal* product (at the *internal* margin on every land used of whatever grade) of the variable dose there applied. Note that residual rent, $R = F(V; T_1, T_2, \ldots) - V\partial F(V; T_1, T_2, \ldots)/\partial V$, can *also* be given the post-classical interpretation as being a *marginal-product imputation to lands*: it is logically $R = [T_1\partial F(V; T_1, T_2, \ldots)/\partial T_1] + [T_2\partial F(V; T_1, T_2, \ldots)/\partial T_2] + \ldots$ when $F(V; T_1, T_2, \ldots)$ is smooth and obeys constant-returns-to-scale – whether or not Adam Smith had ever known anything of the work of his contemporary, Leonhard Euler!

substitutable first-degree-homogeneous and concave function. In this last case, $\partial F/\partial L$ and $\partial F/\partial K$ would be equivalent to $f'(v[L, K])\partial v[L, K]/\partial L$ and $f'(v[L, K])\partial v[L, K]/\partial K$, with $wL + rK = f'(v[L, K])V$ still.

We complete our system with the relations:

$$r_t = \partial F(L_t, K_t, T_1, \dots)/\partial K_t \tag{10.2}$$

$$w_t = \frac{\partial F(L_t, K_t, T_t \dots)/\partial K_t}{1 + r_t} \tag{10.3}$$

$$R_{t+1} = F(L_t, K_t, T_1, \dots) - r_t K_t - w_t L_t(1 + r_t). \tag{10.4}$$

Note that the workers who are paid *at the beginning* of the period receive only their *discounted* marginal productivity. Note that the total of profit includes (α) interest on wages advanced to the workers (in consumable output) plus (β) the interest earned on the capital-goods used in production K_t. Land gets as residual rent under competitive bidding that part of end-of-period product not preempted by competitive bidding for laborers and capital goods; if rent is payable in advance, competitive arbitrage will ensure that it too will be discounted by the $1/(1 + r_t)$ factor.

Long-run equilibrium comes when all dated variables are starred constants determined by (10.1)–(10.4), when (10.2)–(10.4) have had inserted inside them $\bar{w}^*$ and $\bar{r}^*$ exactly as in §13.

To generate the dynamic growth path of the classical system, we complete it by the supply conditions of saving and of population growth:

$$\frac{K_{t+1} - K_t}{K_t} = \sigma[r_t - \bar{r}^*], \ \sigma[0] = 0 < \sigma'[\ ] \tag{10.5}$$

$$\frac{L_{t+1} - L_t}{L_t} = \lambda[w_t - \bar{w}^*], \ \lambda[0] = 0 < \lambda'[\ ] \tag{10.6}$$

$$\lim_{t \to \infty} [L_t, K_t, r_t, w_t, \dots] = [L^*, K^*, \bar{r}^*, \bar{w}^*, \dots]. \tag{10.7}$$

The stability property of (10.7) holds under wide conditions.[8]

---

[8] For $\sigma'[\ ]$ and $\lambda'[\ ]$ sufficiently small, the difference equations of the above neoclassical model will be at least locally stable. For any number of factors, $(T, L, K, \dots) = (x_0, x_1, x_2, \dots)$, the following version will be stable:

$$(dx_i/dt)/x_i = s_i[p_i - \bar{p}_i^*],$$

$$(i = 1, \dots, n)$$

It would not be hard to include in (10.5) explicit handling of the wage-fund component in the total asset base upon which capitalists earn profits. For that matter, the capitalized value of land could, in the fashion of A. R. J. Turgot [34, 1770] and Franco Modigliani [18, 1966], be included in the asset base of life-cycle saving. But to handle these items and the public debt rigorously would be to mete out more than justice to the classical writers.

Actually, the classical economists did less than justice to their own model. To suppose that the real wage of any period must merely be the ratio of however many workers present themselves for jobs, divided into that part of

---

$$p_i = \partial F(1, x_1, \ldots, x_n)/\partial x_i = \partial f(x_1, \ldots, x_n)/\partial x_i$$

$$s_i[0] = 0 \le z s_i[z] x_i, \ x_i > 0$$

$$F(x_0, x_1, \ldots, x_n) = x_0 f(x_1/x_0, \ldots, x_n/x_0)$$

$f(x_1, \ldots, x_n)$ a strictly-concave function

We may set $x_0 = 1$; and denote by $(x_1^*, \ldots, x_n^*)$ the unique roots of

$$\bar{p}_i^* = \partial f(x_1, \ldots, x_n)/\partial x_i$$

$$(i = 1, \ldots, n).$$

Then, for all positive (x_i^0),

$$\lim_{t \to \infty} x_i(t) = x_i^*, \ (i = 1, \ldots, n).$$

To prove this theorem on global stability, consider the following maximization process of *total rent*,

$$R(x_1, \ldots, x_n) = F(\bar{x}_0, x_1, \ldots, x_n) - \sum_1^n \bar{p}_j^* x_j$$

$$\dot{R} = \sum_1^n [F_j(\bar{x}_0, x_1, \ldots, x_n) - \bar{p}_j^*] \dot{x}_i = \sum_1^n [F_j(\ ) - \bar{p}_j^*] x_j$$

$$s_j[F_j(\ ) - \bar{p}_j^*] > 0 \text{ when } x_j \not\equiv x_j^*$$

$$\therefore \lim_{t \to \infty} R(t) = \text{Max } R \equiv R^*$$

$$\lim_{t \to \infty} x_j(t) = x_j^*, \ (j = 1, \ldots, n).$$

Note that $\dot{R} = dR/dt$, etc., and that the sign-preserving property of $z_j s_j[z_i] x_j$ has been exploited in the above proof of global stability. I owe thanks to Hiroaki Nagatani of the MIT graduate school for suggesting that $d\{R^* - R(t)\}/dt$ be used as a Lyapunov function for this stability proof. When dx_i/dt is replaced in this footnote's first equation by $x_i(t+1) - x_i(t)$, it can be shown that the resulting difference equations will assuredly be locally stable provided all $s_i'[0]$ are small enough positive numbers.

C_t which capitalists have decided not to consume but instead have dedicated to the wage fund is not so much a falsehood as a triviality. There could be a period so short in which that version of the wage fund might even be formally correct. (But even this is dubious: the potatoes coming into Manchester need not go by that night into some worker's belly; they might be stored for another day or be destined for the stomach of one of Jane Austen's genteel rentiers.) For a more sympathetic appraisal of wage-fund, see George Stigler [32, 1976].

In the long-run steady state, the fraction of C^* that is adapted to wage-earner's consumption will have been *endogenously* determined. In the transient growth phase of the classical system where each month or year is not very different from its predecessor or successor, the competitive system will anticipate and forestall unpleasant surprises: so the "wage fund" will have been adapted to the viable real wage and total of employed population rather than itself constituting a *deus ex machina* to predetermine wages. John Stuart Mill had reason to dither when various of his wage-fund expositions came under attack – which is not to disagree with the attack in Frank W. Taussing [33, 1896] on the vulgar view of Henry George that production of outputs by inputs is instantaneous and automatically synchronized, a view that seemed to have been surprisingly condoned by J. B. Clark [7, 1899] and Frank Knight in his many writings of the 1930's, and a view properly questioned in Eugen von Böhm-Bawerk [2, 1906; 3, 1907] and echoed a generation later by Fritz Machlup [13, 1935] and Friedrich von Hayek [9, 1936].

* * *

After this neoclassical digression, the reader may return to the canonical classical system. Whether or not he has sampled the mathematical expositions of §12–19, he should be able to follow the next section's graphical depiction of the canonical classical model's path of dynamic development.

DIAGRAMMATICS OF CLASSICAL GROWTH THEORY

20. Figures 2, 3(a) and 3(b) provide a self-contained derivation of how the classical system is self-propelled into development by capital accumulation and parallel population growth whenever it initially starts from scarcity of capital and labor relative to their long-run equilibrium rates when they barely earn their costs of reproduction.

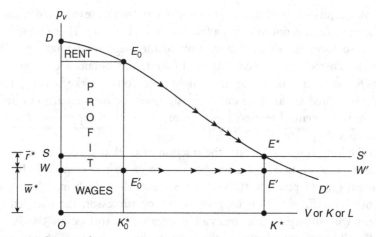

Figure 2. When population supply adjusts virtually instantly, $w(t)$ is always at $\bar{w}^*$ along WW'. With capital (and labor) initially scarce at K_0, rent begins low as shown by the small triangle at E_0: *all* the gain to the composite does goes to profit as a short-term residual, as shown by E_0' being down on WW'. But the excess of $r(t)$ over $\bar{r}^*$ generates accumulation, as shown by the growth arrows at E_0 and E_0'. Gradually, as $E_0 \to E^*$ and $r(t) \to \bar{r}^*$, growth shuts itself off as shown by the shortening of the arrows near the long-run equilibrium E.

For pedagogical simplicity, it is well to begin with the "short-circuited" version of virtually instantaneous population adjustment and the real wage practically always at the subsistence level $\bar{w}^*$. *Figure 2* portrays this archetypical case, essentially embodying the equations of (7) from §16. The legend should be self-explanatory, as the system moves the short-run equilibrium point E_0 down the path of diminishing returns on fixed land: as E_0 approaches E^*, with $w(t)$ always on the WW' level of $\bar{w}^*$ and $r(t)$ therefore falling toward $\bar{r}^*$, the motive for saving shuts itself off and the system eases itself asymptotically into long-run equilibrium with minimal profit and wage rate and maximal land rent.[9]

21. *Figures* 3(a) and 3(b) are interrelated diagrams that handle the more general case. Eschewing the naiveties of the short-circuited pole, they portray the short-term equilibrium in which the transient shortfall of capital and labor leads to both wage and profit being above their ultimate subsistence levels in relative degrees determined by the short-run elasticities of these factors' growth

[9]   If scarcity of land is ignored, the law of diminishing returns is negated and DD' becomes a horizontal line above WW'. This yields the perpetual exponential growth of Marx's *Tableau of Extended Reproduction*, with the growth arrows never shortening and with finite E undefinable.

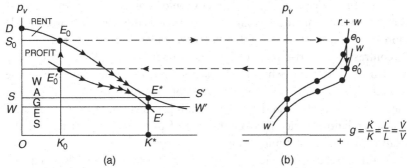

Figure 3. Labor and capital grow in concert from initial E_0. But now competition determines a fractional breakdown of the dose's surplus return between *both* components of the dose, $w(t) - \bar{w}^*$ as well as $r(t) - \bar{r}^*$, at those fractions that just succeed in evoking the same balanced growth in the supplies of the respective factors $L(t)$ and $K(t)$. The $E_0'E'$ locus in 3(a) gives the breakdown of the fruits of transient progress between capitalists and laborers: the faster the relative supply responsiveness of population, the nearer will $E_0'E'$ be to WW' and the greater profit's transient share; the steeper is $E_0'E'$ northwest of E', the greater the transient share of labor in the above-subsistence surplus. (Short-run distribution of total product, of OK_0E_0D, is shown by the rent triangle S_0E_0D; the dose's remaining rectangle $OK_0E_0S_0$ is divided between profit share and wages share by E_0' on the $E_0'E'$ locus.)

3(b) shows exactly how the $E_0'E'$ locus is determined. The locus ww shows the real wage needed to elicit each algebraic growth rate of labor in balance with the composite dose, $g = \dot{K}/K = \dot{L}/L = \dot{V}/V$ (where $\dot{L} = dL/dt$, etc.). The $r + w$ locus shows the p_v composite returns needed for the combined dose to grow, its needed wage rate plus needed profit rate, to induce balanced growth g – with $w(t)$ read from the lower curve and $r(t)$ from the interval between the curves. One begins at the computational cobweb E_0 in 3(a) then moves horizontally to e_0 in 3(b) and down to e_0'. Going back to 3(a) gives appropriate height of E_0' in 3(a) and appropriate short-run distribution of non-rent income between profit and wages, thus filling in at each new time any logical gaps in the "wage-fund" palaver of the classicists.

responses: the auction markets for goods, lands, labor, and capital determine short-term equilibrium factor and goods prices that provide allocation between profits and wages of the composite dose's transient surplus return.

To supplement the legends of *Figures* 3(a) and 3(b), the reader will want to understand what determines the dynamic path $E_0'E'$ in 3(a), the path that summarizes how much goes to above-subsistence wages and how much to what Schumpeter would have called *transient* profits (which, he thought, would soon cease to exist in the absence of technical change and entrepreneurial innovation because $\bar{r}^* = 0$ for Schumpeter).

To test his understanding, the reader should be able to realize that Smith's cheerful rise in real wages would be enhanced if the *ww* curve were made more vertical in 3(b) and the $r + w$ curve were made virtually parallel to it.[10] By contrast, the short-circuited case will be understood as that in which *ww* is virtually horizontal while $r + w$ is not. In every case, the dashed-line cobweb $E_0 e_0 e_0' E_0'$ determines the position of the points on the $E_0'E'$ path of wage-profit allocation and the decelerating growth rate of the classical system as land scarcity invokes the law of diminishing returns and the relapse into long-run equilibrium.

Ricardo's readers should not have been shocked by his third edition discovery that invention of machinery could depress the real wage and lower the population and the total of product in the short and long run. Already in his earlier editions, and quite independently of the *durability* of capital goods, there was present to a truly sophisticated eye the possibility that *DD'* could twist *upward and inward*, the *only* limitation on the *long*-run viability of an invention being that it *raise* the *SED* rent triangle!

FINAL QUALIFICATIONS AND EXTENSIONS

22. The classicists earned for our subject Carlyle's title of the dismal science precisely because their expositions erred in overplaying the law of diminishing returns and underplaying the counterforces of technical change. They lived during the industrial revolution, but scarcely looked out from their libraries to notice the remaking of the world.

Thus, as innovation plucks the *DD'* string outward, it would in all likelihood lift real wages and profit rates above their minima. Before they and the string can dampen down, a new invention plucks again the string. Therefore, a Brownian dance or Schumpeterian fluctuation of real wages and profits at average levels *above* the minima would be the proper and realistic generalization of the notion of gloomy equilibrium. Indeed, if one steps up the rate of innovation enough, an upward trend in the level of E_0'

---

[10] Figures 3(a) and 3(b) in effect solve the simultaneous equations (8.1) and (8.2) for each inherited level of K and its accompanying balanced L. In the pre-balanced stage where one of L or K might be redundant, the diagrams must be reinterpreted. Thus, suppose K/L initially unbalanced above unity. Then only the *ww* curve in 3(b) is relevant: we run from E_0 over to it and short-run E_0' coincides with E_0; V_t grows with L_t and, being redundant, K_t's level is irrelevant. Once L_t rises to K_t, 3(a) and 3(b) apply as shown. To handle the case of initially redundant L_0, the reader should vertically subtract *ww* from $w + r$, labelling the result as *rr*; then, erasing *ww*, he should proceed as in the previous several sentences but with the factors being interchanged in the logically obvious way.

and real wage may be called for as the putative laws of motion of developing capitalism, which could have made economists in Carlyle's eyes the complacent scientists and the apologists for the system.

Just as one example, suppose land-augmenting technical change takes place according to Malthus's *arithmetic* progression. Then if he could analyze correctly his version of the canonical system, he would find that population comes to grow in an *arithmetic* and not in a *geometric* progression [14, 1798]. An amusing irony? Perhaps, but not a joke on Malthus: for, asymptotically, the real wage would then indeed approach his subsistence wage, $w(t) \rightarrow \bar{w}^*$. But, whatever the warrant for geometric progressions in biological reproduction, Malthus never had any plausible reasons behind his gratuitous effusions about arithmetic progressions. If the wrangler had remembered from his Cambridge education three rather than two kinds of progressions, Malthus's impact would have been weakened, but his analysis would have been less special.

23. The present model narrows the classical focus to a single sector. Thereby, one succeeds in freeing their distribution theory from the dreaded complications of value theory. Thereby, one fabricates the Ur-Ricardo model, which determines the system's profit rate from the corn sector alone: having only one sector, it is the corn sector that Ladislaus von Bortkiewicz [5, 1907], Piero Sraffa [30, 1951], Nicholas Kaldor [10, 1956], and others liked to think about; and, contrary to enemies of neoclassicism, there is nothing in the model of a corn-sector-that-determines-its-own-profit-rate which is alien to neoclassicism.

But of course many of the classical problems – as for example the actual share of wages to profits or rent – were recognized by them to depend on many-sector demands. Reducing the Corn-Law tariff on imported food shifted the mix of English production to less land-intensive goods and lowered rent's share. Ricardo knew that in 1815 and 1821: no external margin can logically save his pseudo-labor-theory-of-value from "the complications of value theory and resource scarcities." In my bicentennial appreciation of Smith [28, Samuelson, 1977], I sketched a many-commodity version of the present system, and in my classroom lectures on Ricardo, I show how a 2-primary-factor time-phased system *must* depart from the simplicities of a labor-only technology. It would be easy here to deal with many capital goods of differing durabilities.[11] But it is ludicrous to think that problems that haunt a post-neoclassical writer today – the 1966 Hahn problem of foresight to determine the warrantable allocation among micro-sectors and

---

[11] Thus, we might replace K in (2) by the vector $\mathbf{K} = (K_1, K_2, \dots)$ and dK/dt in (1) by $\sum c_j(dK_j/dt)$, recognizing that depreciation of each K_i occurs at the rate $\delta_i K_i$.

durable goods, reswitching, *etc.* [8, 1966] – were themselves absent from the century of 1750–1850 or were better handled by some lost paradigm of the capitalist writers. Under a powdered wig you find the usual head, like yours and mine, sometimes inflated and sometimes sage, but quite innocent of magic charms and skeleton keys to banish complexity.

24. Much of what has been called history of economic thought deals with questions like, "What did Ricardo mean when he said . . .?" And "Was Smith right and Malthus wrong in alleging . . .?" On this occasion it has not been my purpose to find and quote the pages in which Smith or Marx or Mill did or did not define an exogenous reproduction wage or profit rate, $\bar{w}^*$ and $\bar{r}^*$. Like the Bible, the canon of classical political economy contains passages that seem to assert and to deny the same thing. If, in some mood or for some problem, an ancient writer denies some axiom of what has here been called the canonical classical system, that does not dispose of the problem. It raises the question of what he then intended to provide for the now-missing equation of the new system.

The canonical model is not so realistic in its features or pretty in its logic that any classicist, if he really understood it in all its interrelations and implications, would want to go into a very hot oven to defend it. As you read the letters of debate and agreement between Malthus and Ricardo, the treatises of Smith and Mill, you realize that theirs was not an age where one set out in Whitehead-Rus-sell or even Spinoza purity the structures of their models. Their quarrels lasted because often they were quarrels over misunderstandings and definitions. (I was intrigued a few years ago when Professor Dorfman came from Harvard to my MIT seminar to report on Malthus's theoretical system: it turned out – Say's Law aside – to be isomorphic with my earlier report to the seminar on Ricardo's system, even though Dorfman and I had never compared notes! Yet Ricardo and Malthus thought they had different and irreconcilable views on microeconomics, and most commentators have judged Ricardo the victor in the debate.)

On reflection, I think that the present version of the classical system agrees in behavioral essentials with that understood by John Ramsey M'Culloch, William Nassau Senior, Samuel Bailey, Karl August Dietzel, Francis Y. Edgeworth, Edwin Cannan, Frank W. Taussig, Jacob Viner, and Piero Sraffa. I have checked my relations and behavior equations against those of Nicholas Kaldor [10, 1956], Luigi L. Pasinetti [20, 1960], Mark Blaug [1, 1978], Hans Brems [6, 1960], and Samuelson [22, 1957; 23, 1959; 24, 1959; 25, 1971; 26, 1974; 27, 1977] and believe they all tell essentially the same classical story. Left to the Appendix is a cursory sampling of the semantic quarrels of the classical writers.

LITERARY APPENDIX ON DOCTRINAL DISPUTES AMONG CLASSICISTS

I ought to address myself, even if briefly, to the following queries. "Have you not minimized the basic differences between the classical writers in formulating for them a common canonical model? After all, didn't Ricardo set out to write his *Principles* in considerable degree because he thought Smith in error on important matters?"

The considered answer I would give is this: "Yes, Ricardo differed with Smith; and thought those differences important. But upon detailed examination, we find that their differences do not mainly involve differences in their behavior equations, short-run or long-run, but rather involve their semantic preferences about what names could be given to the same agreed-upon effects. To moderns, it is for the most part a quarrel about nothing substantive, being essentially an irrelevant argument carried out by Ricardo, often with somewhat unaesthetic logic."

I shall illustrate with no less than Ricardo's Chapter 1, Section 1 [21, 1817]: Here Ricardo wishes to relate changes in any good's "value" to changes in its embodied labor content alone; and here he chides Smith for replacing embodied labor content by how many hours of labor a good can command (or, in some Smithian moods, by what need not be quite the same thing, by the amount of corn or means-of-subsistence goods basket that the good in question may trade for or command).

A 3-good version of the canonical model will show Smith and Ricardo in absolute agreement on *all* substantive facts. Corn, ballet, and gold are each producible by land, labor, and possibly out of themselves as needed raw materials or durable goods in a time-phased way. Here are test cases.

Case 1. Land is redundant and rent zero. The profit rate is zero ($\bar{r}^* = 0$). In this initial rude state, each good has a market price in proportion to its labor contents; each good commands precisely those same labor contents. A drop in labor requirements for a good like gold cheapens gold relative to corn and ballet and relative to a day's labor. Gold has dropped in "value," both writers agree. (Note: "money prices" expressed in gold rise for corn, ballet, and a day's labor.)

Case 2. Replace the invention in gold production by a similar one in corn production only. Now only corn has dropped in "value" for Ricardo. Gold and ballet have remained unchanged. The same holds for Smith's labor-command version of value. But now of course Smith's corn-command measure of value must diverge from Smith's labor-command measure: in terms of the former, Smith would say that gold, ballet, and a day's labor have risen in "value" and corn by definition has not changed.

If this were the end of the matter, despite Einstein's shrugging of shoulders, Ricardo's terminology and Smith's here-identical first-version terminology would seem slightly preferable to Smith's second-version terminology. I suspect Smith would agree for this case.

Case 3. But Smith – and Ricardo in Chapter 1, Section 1 – would not expect the matter to end with this new short-run equilibrium. With the real wage now above the (previous) subsistence level, population would grow and in *Figures* 2–3 we would move along $E_0 E'$. With land superabundant and the population adjustment parameter ε in (5) very fast (as suggested by Ricardo's words "in no long time" or "probably at the end of a very few years"), the corn invention would raise the profit rate above zero (actually to 100 percent per period if the labor requirements for corn halved) keeping the corn wage down near $\bar{w}^*$ and making Smith's two versions now agree with each other. But now they differ from Ricardo's version.

And which is semantically more appealing? I believe the jury will say, if *case* 3 is at all the common one in history, then Smith's terminology is more appealing: For Smith, the rise in the prices of gold and ballet in terms of both corn and a day's work (these last are in the same exchange rate as before) represents an increase in their "value." Moreover, Smith's quantitative degree of rise in their "value" does *exactly* match their rise in relative price. By contrast, Ricardo says that gold and ballet are completely unchanged in "value," while corn has halved in "value"; relative to corn's "value," they have exactly doubled in "value" – whereas actually, both men agree that their prices could have increased respectively by 10 percent and 999 percent or by 99 percent and 1 percent or by *any* quantitative degrees, depending on what a 100 percent profit rate does in marking up their competitive prices!

Ricardo's debating gaffe is to chide Smith for departing from concepts appropriate only for a $r = 0 = R$ world, and then in Section 1 himself adopting such departures as the ammunition for his criticisms of Smith.

Case 4. To amplify the point, let's suppose land is scarce and rent no longer zero. For simplicity, posit $\bar{r}^* = 0$ and concentrate on comparing long-run equilibria. Suppose all wages are spent on subsistence corn, which is produced by land and labor. Suppose all rent is spent on a luxury good (say gold), which is produced by labor alone. *Figure* 1, with WW' and SS' coinciding, determines the corn employment level at E (and coinciding E'). Knowing the ratio of the SED rent triangle to the wage rectangle formed by E, we know the ratio of labor employed in gold to that employed in corn. So our 2-good canonical long-run equilibrium is determinate in all details.

Now let a labor-augmenting invention in the corn industry make one laborer be the equivalent to two laborers. After a transient rise in profit and wage rates, $r(t)$ and $w(t)$ settle back to 0 and $\bar{w}^*$ by that determinate change in corn labor that reflects the shifted E intersection. In the end, the prices of corn, a day's labor, and gold are in *exactly the same ratios* as they started out. Both of Smith's verbiages well describe the facts: neither corn nor gold have changed in command over a unit of labor; gold is unchanged in its command over everything else, corn, gold, and a unit of labor.

Ricardo, by contrast, is in a pickle. Gold's embodied labor is unchanged; but corn's embodied labor, measured by *total corn labor/ total corn*, rises if rent's share of corn cost rises and falls if that rent share falls: either case is possible depending on a 1932 elasticity-of-substitution undreamed of by Ricardo or Mill. Who would find it useful to follow Ricardo in saying that corn's "value" has changed when *all* (P_c, P_g, W) ratios are unchanged?

There is one way out for Ricardo – a disastrous one. Suppose Ricardo measures corn's embodied labor content, not by *average* labor content, L_c/Q_c, but by "*marginal* labor content" – measured by labor per corn output on *external* margin land, or on the *internal* land margin's $1/(\partial Q_c/\partial L_c)$. To coin a phrase, this neoclassical version of Ricardo (call it Clark-Ricardo) is a disaster for his debate with Smith *because, using it, Ricardo finds himself here in exact agreement with* the labor-command *doctrine of Smith* that *Section* 1 is attacking![12]

* * *

Other beefs with Smith by Ricardo reduce to similar semantic snarls.[13] We are left with the essential unity of the classical model, the progressions and retrogressions being primarily in the modes of explanation.

---

[12] As Viner [35, 1930, pp. 79–80] pointed out in his famous review of Cannan, a marginal-labor theory of value is isomorphic with a marginal-land theory of value or with a marginal-fertilizer theory of value: when n goods are each producible out of transferable-indifferent labor and transferable-indifferent fertilizer, it is as trivial to say that any competitive price ratio, P_i/P_j, is equal to relative marginal-fertilizer-requirement ratios as to marginal-labor-requirements. It would be anticlimactic if the labor theory of value, from John Locke through Marx, reduced down to this (envelope) triviality.

[13] One such is Ricardo's accusation that Smith makes land rent price determining. After a careful audit, we should agree with the dissenting verdict of Stigler [31, 1952, p. 205]: "...the tenor of Smith's theory of rent, which was not given a coherent statement, was that aggregate rents are a residual, but that the rent of any one use of land is a cost determined

REFERENCES

Blaug, Mark. Economic theory in retrospect. Third edition. London; New York and Melbourne: Cambridge University Press, [1962, 1968] 1978.

von Böhm-Bawerk, Eugen. "Capital and Interest Once More: I. Capital vs. Capital Goods," Quart. J. Econ., Nov. 1906, 21, pp. 1–21.

—"Capital and Interest Once More: II. A Relapse to the Productivity Theory," Quart. J. Econ., Feb. 1907, 21, pp. 247–82.

—"The Nature of Capital: A Rejoinder," Quart. J. Econ., Nov. 1907, pp. 28–47.

von Bortkiewicz, Ladislaus. "On the Correction of Marx's Fundamental Theoretical Construction in the Third Volume of 'Capital,'" Jahr. Nationalökon. Statist., 1907, 89, pp. 319–35; reprinted in English in Karl Marx and the close of his system, by Eugen von Böhm-Bawerk and Böhm-Bawerk's criticism of Marx, by Rudolf Hilferding; with an appendix by L. von Bortkiewicz. Edited by Paul M. Sweezy. New York: Kelley, 1949.

Brems, Hans. "An attempt at a Rigorous Restatement of Ricardo's Long-Run Equilibrium," Canadian J. Econ., Feb. 1960, 26, pp. 74–86.

Clark, John Bates. The distribution of wealth: A theory of wages, interest and profits. New York: Macmillan, 1899.

Hahn, Frank H. "Equilibrium Dynamics with Heterogeneous Capital Goods," Quart. J. Econ., Nov. 1966, 80, pp. 633–46.

von Hayek, Friedrich A. "The Mythology of Capital," Quart. J. Econ., Feb. 1936, 50, pp. 199–228.

Kaldor, Nicholas. "Alternative Theories of Distribution," Rev. Econ. Stud., 1956, 23, pp. 83–100.

Kuhn, Thomas S. The structure of scientific revolutions. Chicago: University of Chicago Press, 1962.

Longfield, Mountifort. Lectures on political economy. Dublin: R. Milliken and Son, 1834.

Machlup, Fritz. "Professor Knight and the 'Period of Production,'" J. Polit. Econ., Oct. 1935, 43(5), pp. 577–624.

by alternative uses of land. Ricardo ignored the multiplicity of uses of land." Another Ricardian non sequitur, Sraffa [30, 1951, p. xxxvii], is his invalid inference that Smith's equating of price to the sum of wages + rent + profit implies that Smith believed that such a price was necessarily higher than in the rude state (when productivity was so low as to make rent zero and the earnable-profit zero). Again, it is the critic, Ricardo, who seems to have nodded.

Professor Stigler points out to me that I have been rather charitable to Smith in attributing to him knowledge of diminishing returns; and less than just to Ricardo in not crediting his Chapter 1 with having succeeded in showing that changes only in wage rates will not affect relative values. I ought to mention that the similarity of Ricardo and Malthus ends when we deal with the macroeconomics of Say's Law. Professor Blaug also doubts that the differences between Ricardo and Smith are usefully dismissed as being merely semantic; in any case, upon review, I find no thought experiments proposed by Ricardo to which he has given a different substantive answer than would Smith's system; outright slips by Smith seem if anything less than those in Ricardo and are of secondary importance in both cases.

Malthus, Thomas R. *An essay on the principle of population* [First Essay on Population].
    London: J. Johnson, 1798.

—*Principles of political economy.* London: J. Murray, 1820.

Marx, Karl. *Capital: A critique of political economy.* Vol. 1, 1867; Vol. 2, 1885; Vol. 3,
    1894.

Mill, John Stuart. *Principles of political economy.* Boston: Little & Brown, 1848.

Modigliani, Franco. "The Life Cycle Hypothesis of Saving, the Demand for Wealth and
    the Supply of Capital," *Social Res.*, June 1966, *33*, pp. 160–217.

Morishima, Michio. *Marx's economics: A dual theory of value and growth.* New York and
    London: Cambridge University Press, 1973.

Pasinetti, Luigi L. "A Mathematical Formulation of the Ricardian System," *Rev. Econ.
    Stud.*, Feb. 1960, 27, pp. 78–98.

Ricardo, David. *On the principles of political economy and taxation.* London: J. Murray,
    1817.

Samuelson, Paul A. "Wages and Interest: A Modern Dissection of Marxian Economic
    Models," *Amer. Econ. Rev.*, Dec. 1957, 47, pp. 884–912; reprinted in *The collected
    scientific papers of Paul A. Samuelson.* Vol. 1. Edited by Joseph E. Stiglitz.
    Cambridge, Mass.: MIT Press, 1965, pp. 341–69.

—"A Modern Treatment of the Ricardian Economy: I. The Pricing of Goods and of
    Labor and Land Services," *Quart. J. Econ.*, Feb. 1959, 73, pp. 1–35; reprinted in *The
    collected scientific papers of Paul A. Samuelson.* Vol. 1. Edited by Joseph E. Stiglitz.
    Cambridge, Mass.: MIT Press, 1965, pp. 373–407.

—"A Modern Treatment of the Ricardian Economy: II. Capital and Interest Aspects of
    the Pricing Process," *Quart. J. Econ.*, May 1959, *73*, pp. 217–31; reprinted in *The
    collected scientific papers of Paul A. Samuelson.* Vol. 1. Edited by Joseph E. Stiglitz.
    Cambridge, Mass.: MIT Press, 1965, pp. 408–22.

—"Understanding the Marxian Notion of Exploitation: A Summary of the So-Called
    Transformation Problem between Marxian Values and Competitive Prices,"
    J. Econ. Lit., June 1971, *9*(2), pp. 399–431; reprinted in *The collected scientific papers
    of Paul A. Samuelson.* Vol. 3. Edited by Robert C. Merton. Cambridge, Mass.: MIT
    Press, 1972, pp. 276–308.

—"Marx as Mathematical Economist: Steady-State and Exponential Growth
    Equilibrium," in *Trade, stability, and macroeconomics: Essays in honor of Lloyd
    A. Metzler.* Edited by George Horwich and Paul Samuelson. New York: Academic
    Press, 1974, pp. 269–307; reprinted in *The collected scientific papers of Paul
    A. Samuelson.* Vol. 4. Edited by Hiroaki Nagatani, and Kate Crowley. Cambridge,
    Mass.: MIT Press, 1977, pp. 231–69.

—"A Modern Theorist's Vindication of Adam Smith," *Amer. Econ. Rev.*, Feb. 1977,
    67(1), pp. 42–49.

—"Correcting the Ricardo Error Spotted in Harry Johnson's Maiden Paper," *Quart.
    J. Econ.*, Nov. 1977, *91*(4), pp. 519–30.

Smith, Adam. *An inquiry into the nature and causes of the wealth of nations.* London: W.
    Strahan and T. Cadell, 1776.

Sraffa, Piero. "Introduction," in *Works and correspondence of David Ricardo.* Vol. 1.
    Cambridge: Cambridge University Press, 1951, pp. xiii–lxii.

Stigler, George J. "The Ricardian Theory of Value and Distribution," *J. Polit. Econ.*, June
    1952, 60, pp. 187–207.

—The scientific uses of scientific biography, with special reference to J. S. Mill. Toronto: University of Toronto Press, 1976, pp. 55–66.

Taussig, Frank W. Wages and capital: An examination of the wages fund doctrine. London and New York: Macmillan, 1896.

Turgot, Anne Robert Jacques. Réflexions sur la formation et la distribution des richesses (1770). Translated as Reflections on the formation and the distribution of riches. New York: Macmillan, 1898.

Viner, Jacob. "Book Review of Edwin Cannan's A Review of Economic Theory," Economica, 1930, 10(28), pp. 74–84.

A Modern Theorist's Vindication of Adam Smith

Inside every classical economist is a modern economist trying to get out. In rereading the *Wealth of Nations*, it seems to me that with a little midwifery sleight of hand, one can extract from Adam Smith a valuable model that vindicates him from criticisms of Ricardo and Marx and from the general supercilious discounting of Smith as an unoriginal theorist who is logically fuzzy and eclectically empty. My general finding, as reported in these brief literary words here today and in a companion mathematical appendix, provides a vindication of Adam Smith and serves, in my mind at least, to raise his stature as an economic theorist, both absolutely and in comparison with his predecessors and successors.

I. Views on Smith

Smith is admired for his eclectic wisdom about developing capitalism, and for his ideological defense of competitive *laissez faire* as against blundering Mercantilist interferences with the market. His analysis of the division of labor, like Allyn Young's analysis of increasing returns in the 1920's, is thought to be seminal for the understanding of change, for the Chamberlinian deviations from perfect competition, and for the young Marx's concept of *alienation* of the overspecialized worker.

But there you have it. As a pure theorist, Adam Smith is written down precisely because of his fuzzy eclecticism. His natural prices and wages are thought to be merely the resultants of long-run supply and demand. His pluralistic decomposition of price and of Net National Product (*NNP*) into components of wages, land rent, and of profit is criticized as emptily tautological. After his good start with the labor theory of value, Smith is

117

thought to have blotted his copybook by introducing *ad hoc* and not-fully-explained deductions from labor's full share by landowners and capitalist owners of stock. Even Smith's accounting decomposition of national income into value added elements of wages, rents and profits has been attacked in *Capital*, Volume 2, as involving vicious-circle reasoning. Too often theorists contrast Adam Smith to his disfavor with his brilliant predecessor, David Hume, and brilliant successor, David Ricardo.

II. The Case for Smith

My reading is otherwise.

1) Smith's value-added accounting is shown to be correct by Leontief-Sraffa modeling.
2) His pluralistic supply-and-demand analysis in terms of all three components of wages, rents, and profits is a valid and valuable anticipation of general equilibrium modeling.
3) His vision of transient growth from invention and capital accumulation, which is brought to an equilibrium end with a low rate of profit and a high total of land rent, is *isomorphic* with the model of Ricardo, Malthus, and Marx. But Smith is less guilty than these three of believing in a rigid subsistence-wage supply of labor in the short and intermediate run; so Smith's transient rise in wage rates is a credit to his model's realism, wherever it deviates in emphasis from its successors.

   As a theorist, I do find things to criticize in Smith. Thus, he seems never to have known how to put net capital formation into his Net National Product concept. His exposition is 1776, not 1876 or 1976, in its vagueness. However, with careful reading, we do infer in the *Wealth of Nations* a complete and valuable theoretical model.

Finally, I omit in this brief paper discussion of pseudo-problems that have monopolized the Smith-Ricardo literature.

Although my axioms are those of the 1776 Adam Smith, my analysis from them utilizes 1976 mathematical methods, including convenient duality theory. Today, heavy mathematics will be eschewed and reference merely made to the accompanying mathematical appendix.

III. Smith's Assumptions

i)   Goods, e.g., food and clothing, are produced in a time-phased way out of land and "doses" of labor-cum-raw-materials.

ii) To arrive at net consumable outputs of goods, e.g., food and clothing, one must subtract from the gross production of each the amounts of that respective good used as input components of the various industry doses.

iii) A ration of subsistence goods per laborer, e.g., m_1 of food and m_2 of clothing, is required to produce and reproduce the population. When the worker's money wage can buy more than the subsistence vector, population grows at a positive percentage rate; when the money wage buys less than subsistence, population declines exponentially; at the subsistence wage, population is constant.

iv) Workers never save and invest. Owners of land and of raw material inputs spend their wealth on food and clothing as they will. So long as the profit rate is above some minimal subsistence rate for saving, which might be zero after allowing for stochastic losses and management expenses, nonworkers do positive saving, which is never aborted. Below that minimal profit rate, nonlaborers decumulate or dissave; at the minimal profit rate, net saving and net accumulation is zero.

v) Perfect competition prevails. Land use is auctioned off for rentals. Free entry and constant returns to scale prevail. Knowledge is, or soon becomes, general.

IV. Smith's Implications

A logician, turning his deductive crank, would deduce the following properties of Smith's system.

1) Suppose it begins in long-run equilibrium. Wages are at the subsistence level. The profit rate is minimal. Depending on the pattern of nonlaborer tastes for food and clothing, land rent will be high or low; land-intensive food price will be high or low relative to clothing price; the size of the population and of the various components of raw material inventories will be high or low depending on nonlaborer tastes; and so will depend the relative distribution of *NNP* between land owners' rent and workers' wages, to say nothing of capitalists' profits if the minimal interest rate is not zero.

Most of this Ricardo missed. Some Malthus caught. Smith denies none of this, but offers little in detail.

2) Now let there be an invention. It will be viable only if, in some industry, it raises one or more of the following: the real wage there, the real rent there, or the profit rate. Except for the singular case where its incidence happens to be solely to raise land rent everywhere, the

invention must transiently raise one, or more probably both, of the profit rate and the real wage rate. This initiates population growth and capital accumulation. We are in Smith's "cheerful" transient state of growth – like England rather than China or India. But ultimately, as in China and Holland, the land fills up; the law of diminishing returns on fixed land operates.

3) The system relapses into Smith's "dull state" of equilibrium with subsistence profit rate, subsistence real wage rate, and *enhanced* land rent. In effect, Smith's system maximizes rent!

4) If inventions keep recurring, the system goes through a Brownian motion in which profit rates and real wage rates average out *above* their subsistence levels, perhaps being trendless.

5) The model captures the general behavior of economic history these last two centuries if only Smith modifies his demographic hypothesis that population explodes whenever the real wage is above an unchanged subsistence level. If the needed ration of subsistence itself grows exponentially in time, then the presumption is that (a) the real wage will oscillate around an upward-rising exponential trend, with the labor force possibly growing slowly; (b) the profit rate will meander, averaging out positive and inducing growing capital inventories; (c) land rent will tend to rise, subject to any land-saving biases in invention and to the subtraction from its rise due to the rise in real wages; (d) once we allow for alternative ways of producing the same things and for any biases in inventions, relative wage and nonwage shares of *NNP* cannot be predicted to show any definite trends; but that does not mean that minor changes contrived in labor supply can necessarily much alter the relative wage share.

These last few propositions sound much like what Simon Kuznets reports for the laws of motion of western economies, even if Ricardo and Marx failed to come as close to them as did the *Wealth of Nations*. Hats off, I say, to Adam Smith.

6) If we add to the above model a declining supply of primary "land" – that is, declining stocks of nonreproducible natural resources, such as rich seams of metal ores and coal and exhausted geologic deposits of oil and gas – we are prepared for the Club of Rome's future.

It becomes a race between invention (spontaneous and induced) and dwindling natural resources per head: the profit rate can be expected to meander in no predictable way, the real wage to grow at a slower rate (or even to suffer a declining trend). Nonwage and nonprofit share, always so important in explaining the great historic fortunes, may possibly rise. Analysis can carry prophecy no further.

V. Verdict

It is serendipitous to be able to announce, not the Scottish verdict *unproven*, but the happy finding that Adam Smith comes through with flying colors from a modern postmortem, provided we conduct it with the modicum of charity due an early pioneer.

Mathematical Appendix

The following equations vindicate Adam Smith from the principal indictments against him, and also reveal the half-untruth present in his INVISIBLE HAND doctrine.

Productivity Assumptions

Smith assumes that any of commodities, $(q_1, \ldots, q_n)$, is produced by its industry out of its labor inputs, $(L_1, \ldots, L_n)$, its land inputs $(T_1, \ldots, T_n)$, and out of produced inputs such as raw materials (or durable equipments) purchased by the various industries: so q_j will require for its production, along with T_j and L_j, also $(q_{1j}, \ldots, q_{nj})$. Smith's production functions embodying known technology can be written as

$$q_j(t+1) = F_j[T_j(t), L_j(t), q_{1j}(t), \ldots, q_{nj}(t)](j = 1, \ldots, n) \qquad (1)$$

Note the time-phasing of production in (1): inputs are needed prior to the appearance of output. In (1), T_j could be a vector of elements representing heterogeneous lands of different grades.

To arrive at net available *consumption* amounts of the ith goods, $[C_i(t)]$, one writes:

$$C_i(t) = q_i(t) - \sum_{j=1}^{n} q_{ij}(t), \ q_{ij}(t) \geq 0 \qquad (2)$$

Whereas a modern neoclassical economist might wish to assume that inputs can be substituted for each other in a smooth way so that $F_j[]$ all have well-defined partial derivatives, a classical economist like Smith usually thought that a variable "dose" of labor-cum-raw-materials could be applied to fixed land more intensively or less intensively. So one rewrites (1) as

$$q_j(t+1) = F_j[T_j(t), V_j(t)] \tag{3}$$

$$V_j(t) = \text{Min}[L_j(t)/a_{0j}, q_{1j}(t)/a_{1j}, \ldots q_{nj}(t)/a_{nj}] \tag{4}$$

The a_{ij}'s are non-negative. When some a is zero, it is as if its argument is absent from the expression Min[ ].

The production functions in equation (3) are postulated to have simple properties once the scale of production goes beyond the initial levels at which the division of labor does not pay. Each $F_j[$] is concave, homogeneous-first-degree, and differentiable:

$$F_j[\lambda T, \lambda V] \equiv \lambda F_j[T, V] \tag{5}$$
$$F_j[T + \Delta T, V + \Delta V] - F_j[T, V] \geq$$
$$\quad F_j[T + 2\Delta T, V + 2\Delta V] - F_j[T + \Delta T, V + \Delta V]$$
$$\partial F_j[T, V]/\partial V > 0, F_j[T, V] - V\partial F_j[T, V]/\partial V \geq 0$$

Finally, Smith even before Malthus and Marx believed that human labor itself had a reproduction cost at that level of *subsistence* (food, clothing, etc.) at which a family could manage to reproduce itself by mortality survival and procreation. The long-run reproduction cost of total labor, $\sum_1^n L_j = L$, is defined per unit of L by the nonzero column vector of needed subsistence: m_1 of q_1, m_2 of q_2, ..., m_n of q_n:

$$\mathbf{m} = [m_i] = \begin{bmatrix} m_1 \\ \vdots \\ m_n \end{bmatrix} \geq 0 \tag{6}$$

If the real wage exceeded the subsistence vector $\mathbf{m}$, L_t would grow; if it fell below $\mathbf{m}$, L_t would decline; at exactly $\mathbf{m}$, Smith's stationary state would prevail. Evaluating the iron ration of subsistence at its market prices, $\sum_1^n P_j m_j$, we compare it with the market wage, W, thereby to determine the rate of population growth. Smith's simplest Malthusian relation, I write as

$$(L_{t+1} - L_t)/L_t = f[1 - \sum_1^n (P_j/W)m_j] \tag{7}$$
$$f[0] = 0, f'[\,] > 0, f[\,] \geq -1$$

Clearly, when the real wage is at the subsistence level **m**, population growth ceases.

Smith's Early "Rude State"

For one page, Smith does have a "labor theory of value," writing (*Wealth of Nations*, Book I, ch. 6):

In that early and rude state of society which precedes both the accumulation of stock ["capital"] and the appropriation of [scarce] land, the proportion between the quantities of labour necessary for acquiring different objects seems to be the only circumstance which can afford any rule for exchanging them for one another ... what is usually the produce of two days' or hours' labour, should be worth double of what is usually the produce of one day's or one hour's labour.. ...

In this state of things, the whole produce of labour belongs to the labourer.. ...

We can make logical, even if not historical and anthropological sense of this, by postulating that land is so abundant as to be redundant and *free*, with the ratio $\sum_1^n T_j / \sum_1^n L_j$ so great as to make land ignorable. To make inventories of raw materials and crude tools ignorable takes a greater stretch of the imagination. I cut the knot by postulating that outputs and inputs are *simultaneous* rather than lagged as in equations (1) and (3).

With land redundant, so that no increase in T_j has any incremental effect on q_j output, one rewrites equations (2) and (3) in the rude state as

$$q_j(t) = \alpha_j V_j(t) = V_j(t), \quad (j = 1, \cdots, n)$$
$$= \text{Min}[L_j(t)/a_{0j}, q_{1j}(t)/a_{1j}, \cdots, q_{nj}(t)/a_{nj}] \tag{8}$$

Here, by proper choice of dimensional units of goods or of doses, we can suppress the $[\alpha_j]$ coefficients.

Indeed, if the rude state is in exact stationary equilibrium, we can ignore all timing designations and define that exact state by the following specializations of (1)–(8):

$$L - \sum_1^n L_j = 0$$
$$q_i - \sum_{j=1}^n q_{ij} - m_i L = 0, \quad (i = 1, \cdots, n) \tag{9}$$

By virtue of equation (3)'s definition of the fixed components of the doses, these relations become

$$L - \sum_1^n a_{0j}q_j = 0$$

$$-m_iL + q_i - \sum_1^n a_{ij}q_j = 0, \ (i = 1, \cdots n) \tag{10}$$

These linear equations can have a positive solution $(L, q_1, \ldots, q_n)$ only if the following technological conditions for the rude state are exactly met:

$$0 = \begin{vmatrix} 1 & -a_{01} \cdots & -a_{0n} \\ -m_1 & 1 - a_{11} \cdots & -a_{1n} \\ \vdots & \vdots & \vdots \\ -m_n & 1 - a_{n1} \cdots & \end{vmatrix} \tag{11}$$

$$= \det[\mathbf{I} - a_{ij} - m_i a_{0j}]$$
$$= \det[\mathbf{I} - \mathbf{a} - \mathbf{m}\mathbf{a_0}]$$

where $\mathbf{a_0}$ is the row vector of *direct labor* requirements, $[a_{0j}]$, $\mathbf{m}$ is the column vector of subsistence requirements per worker, $[m_i]$, and $\mathbf{a}$ is the n-by-n square Leontief matrix of input-output coefficients, $[a_{ij}]$.

We now vindicate Smith's equating the competitive pricing relations of his rude state with their embodied total labor requirements (direct plus indirect). There are of course no further components of the prices of the goods, $[P_1, \ldots, P_n] = [P_j] = \mathbf{P}$, than the wage component involving the money wage, W: land rent is zero, and interest (or profit) is impossible in a world of instantaneous production.

Competition assures

$$\mathbf{P} = [P_j]$$

$$= [Wa_{0j} + \sum_{i=1}^n P_i a_{ij} + 0 + 0] > 0 \tag{12}$$

$$= W[A_{0j}] = \mathbf{W}\mathbf{A_0}$$

where

$$\mathbf{A_0} = [A_{0j}] = \mathbf{a_0}[\mathbf{I} - \mathbf{a}]^{-1} > 0$$

$$= \mathbf{a_0} + \mathbf{a_0}\mathbf{a} + \mathbf{a_0}\mathbf{a}^2 + \ldots, \tag{13}$$

a convergent series.

Positivity and convergence in equation (13) is guaranteed by equation (11) plus the postulate that every good must indirectly, if not directly, require some labor if it is to be a good worth talking about in the rude state.

That the real wage can just buy the iron ration of subsistence was assured by equations (11)–(13), which imply

$$\mathbf{Pm} = W = (\mathbf{A_0m})W, \quad \mathbf{A_0m} = 1 \tag{14}$$

Incidentally, (14) tends to vindicate the empirical usefulness of Smith's notion of "labour command theory of value," as against Ricardo's semantic objections.

Stationarity of the rude state's population now follows from equation (7), which takes the form in the rude state of

$$(L_{t+1} - L_t)/L_t = f[1 - \mathbf{A_0m}] = f[0] = 0 \tag{15}$$

Smith's identification of *net national product* in the rude state with wages only, or with the subsistence consumptions of the workers, is verified:

$$NNP = WL + 0 + 0$$
$$= \sum_1^n P_j C_j = (\mathbf{A_0C})W \tag{16}$$
$$= (\mathbf{A_0m})WL$$

Investment and Malthusian Growth

Smith quickly turns the page on his rude state in which the labor theory of value holds. By the division of labor or otherwise, let some set of the elements of $(\mathbf{a_0}, \mathbf{a}, \mathbf{m})$ decrease. That raises equation (11)'s determinant from zero to positive. That raises the real wage above the subsistence level. That causes population initially to grow at an endogenous positive rate, like $(1 + g)^t$. If we still keep production instantaneous, capital and positive profits cannot yet occur. The workers get all the fruits of the invention, and devote part of that fruit to procreation and longevity. Now

$$\mathbf{Pm} < W, \mathbf{A_0m} < 1, \mathbf{C} \geq \mathbf{mL}$$
$$(L_{t+1} - L_t)/L_t = g = f[1 - \mathbf{A_0m}] > 0 \tag{17}$$
$$L(t) = L(0)(1 + g)^t, q(t) = q(0)(1 + g)^t, \cdots, t \geq 1$$

This initial state of exponential growth, à la Malthus (1798) and von Neumann (1932), must begin to decelerate once land becomes scarce. Eventually, workers elbow each other, trample down fields, and so forth. Land must be rationed by positive rentals, which for Smith were to go to the private appropriators of land, selling their scarce inputs in a competitive market.

As L grows more and more relative to the fixed total of land, $\sum_1^n T_j = T$, positive rent income arises. Depending upon how landowners spend their rent incomes on consumption goods, and workers their surplus wages on goods, an equilibrium will emerge at each level of $(T, L, C_1, \ldots, C_n)$ for all prices $(P_1, \ldots, P_n, W, R)$. Smith's resolution of each P_j into W and R components was essentially correct, despite doubts in Marx (1885). And, even in the absence of profit and differences in time-phasing of production, Smith's solution does contradict the attempt in Ricardo (1817) to measure price ratios in terms of goods' labor content alone.

Equilibrium Restored

At any stage of growth, for the given available technology and land, T, and for any prescribed pattern of feasible total consumption, $(C_1, \ldots, C_n)$, one can solve the planner's efficiency problem of minimizing needed total labor, L:

$$L = M(T; C_1, \cdots, C_n) \quad C_i \geq 0$$

$$= \operatorname{Min} \sum_1^n a_{0j} V_j, \text{ subject to}$$

$$T_i, V_i \sum_1^n a_{ij} V_j - F_i[T_i, V_i] + C_i \leq 0, \tag{18}$$

$$(i = 1, \cdots, n)$$

$$\sum_1^n T_j - T \leq 0, \ V_i \geq 0, T_i \geq 0$$

This is a standard problem in nonlinear programming, as in Kuhn and Tucker (1951). On the assumption that every good needs something of both land and variable factors, the necessary and sufficient conditions for the solution can be written down in terms of equalities involving "dual variables," or Lagrangean multipliers, or "shadow prices," which are interpretable as the non-negative price ratios $[P_1/W, \cdots P_n/W, R/W]$, where R stands for the rental of land. (If T is a column vector of lands, R will be a row vector of rentals.) The unique conditions of equilibrium involve for scalar T,

$$(p_j/W)\partial F_j[T_j/V_j, 1]/\partial V_j$$

$$= a_{0j} + \sum_1^n (P_i/W)a_{ij}$$

$$(P_j/W)\partial F_j[T_j/V_j, 1]/\partial T_j = R/W, \quad (j = 1, \cdots, n)$$

$$\sum_1^n a_{ij}V_j - F_i[T_i, V_i] = C_i, \quad (i = 1, \cdots, n)$$

$$\sum_1^n T_j \leq T, R\left(T - \sum_1^n T_j\right) = 0, T_j > 0$$

(19)

These are $3n + 1$ independent equations that are just sufficient to determine the $3n + 1$ unknowns of the problem: $(V_1, \ldots, V_n; T_1, \ldots, T_n; P_1/W, \ldots, P_n/W, R/W)$. But equations (19), aside from having the planner's optimality interpretation, are precisely the *competitive* equilibrium conditions under Smith's postulated production conditions.

This identifies a valid element in Smith's INVISIBLE HAND doctrine: *self-interest, under perfect conditions of competition, can organize a society's production efficiently.* (But, there need be nothing ethically optimal about the $[C_i]$ specifications and their allocations among the rich and poor, the healthy and the halt!)

We indicate Smith's resolution of the price of every good into its total wage and rent components by deriving from (18) each good's total-land-and-labor requirements. We solve for the respective pairs:

$$L_1^* = M(T_1^*; C_1, 0, \ldots, 0) \leftrightarrow C_1 = \phi_1[T_1^*, L_1^*]$$
$$L_2^* = M(T_2^*; 0, C_2, \ldots, 0) \leftrightarrow C_2 = \phi_2[T_2^*, L_2^*]$$
$$L_n^* = M(T_n^*; 0, 0, \ldots, C_n) \leftrightarrow C_n = \phi_n[T_n^*, L_n^*]$$

(20)

These $\phi_j[]$ functions give the totals of land and labor required, directly *and* indirectly, to produce a net amount of each consumption good. These Smithian functions, never before written down explicitly in quite this way, are concave and first-degree-homogeneous; if the $F_j[]$ functions are smoothly differentiable, as even Ricardo assumes in his arithmetic examples, so too will be the $\phi_j[]$ functions. Hence, as in Shephard (1953), they will have dual unit-cost functions

$$\phi_j^*[R, W] = \text{Min}\{(RT_j + WV_j)/\phi_j[T_j, V_j]\}T_j, V_j$$

(21)

The ϕ_j^* functions have all the concavity, homogeneity, and differentiability properties of the $\phi_j[\,]$ functions.

So, we sustain Smith against the objection that his eclectic breakdown of prices into wage and rent components is a trivial, surface relation. We write down for Smith:

$$P - \phi_j^*[R, W] + 0$$
$$= R\partial\phi_j^*[R, W]/\partial R + W\partial\phi_j^*[R, W]/\partial W \tag{22}$$

These partial equilibrium relations are well-determined by Smith's relations of general equilibrium in equation (19).

Finally, we solve for the new Smithian steady state of zero population growth after diminishing returns has brought the post-invention wage rate down to the subsistence level: we seek the L^* root of

$$1 = M(T; m_1 L + \gamma_1, \ldots, m_n L + \gamma_n) \tag{23}$$

where $(\gamma_1, \ldots, \gamma_n)$ represents landowners' choice of composition of their consumption goods. As Malthus realized, the equilibrium population will be larger or smaller depending upon whether rent collectors tend to spend their incomes on goods of high or low "labor intensity." Thus, their demand for "retainers" will mean greater L^* than will their demand for food or for hunting grounds.

In long-run equilibrium states where (13) holds and the real wage is at the subsistence level, the Physiocractic Land Theory of Value holds, as described in "A Modern Treatment of the Ricardian Economy" (see Chapter IV). Landlords are faced by a linear budget constraint in choosing their y's, namely:

$$\tau_1 \gamma_1 + \ldots + \tau_n \gamma_n = T \tag{24}$$

where the $[\tau_j]$ coefficients involve the total "socially necessary land" involved in each C_j's production, directly and indirectly and after including the land needed to produce the needed labor's subsistence.

Realistic Time-Phasing of Production

Since output is not instantaneously producible from inputs, inventories of raw materials and of subsistence wage goods are needed for steady-state production and for growth. Smith correctly recognized that the rate at which capitalist owners of such capital goods would be willing to save in order to "accumulate" them would set a limit on the system's growth and thereby generate a positive profit rate. With land fixed, new inventions ceasing, and population growing whenever the real wage exceeds subsistence, Smith correctly saw that continued saving and accumulation – contrived by capitalists' consuming less of their current profits than is available to them – must eventually induce a falling trend in the rate of profit. Finally, at a zero profit rate (over and above stochastic average losses) or at some low positive rate below which decumulation will occur, Smith's system reaches its longest-run equilibrium.

Let r^* be Smith's long-run, low positive rate of profit at which capitalists and landowners will spend all their incomes on current consumptions. With land fixed at T, no new inventions and no change in workers' subsistence (m_i), Smith correctly wrote his equilibrium in a tripartite breakdown of national income and each competitive price into wages, rents, and profits. His complete system becomes:

$$F_i[T_i, V_i] - \sum_1^n a_{ij} V_j = m_i L + \gamma_i, \ (i = 1, \ldots, n) \tag{25a}$$

$$P_j \partial F_j[T_j/V_j, 1]/\partial V_j = (Wa_{oj} = \sum_1^n P_i a_{ij})(1 + r^*) \tag{25b}$$

$$P_j \partial F_j[T_j/V_j, 1]/\partial T_j = R(1 + r^*), \ (j = 1, \ldots, n) \tag{25c}$$

$$\sum_1^n a_{ij} V_j = L, \ \sum_1^n T_j \leq T \tag{25d}$$

$$\sum_1^n P_j m_j = W > 0, \ V_j \geq 0, \ T_j \geq 0, \ P_j \geq 0, \ R \geq 0 \tag{25e}$$

For r^* and **m** sufficiently small, and for T and the rations of nonworkers' taste parameters given $[\gamma_i/\gamma_1]$, these are $3n + 3$ equations for the equal number of unknowns: n V's, n T's, n (P/W)'s, γ_1, R/W, L. A meaningful solution is guaranteed to exist by virtue of the postulated properties for $F_j[]$.

Independently of the (γ_i) and (m_i) parameters, there is always a factor-price-frontier tradeoff between the real wage in terms of any good, W/P_j, the real rent, R/P_j, and the profit rate, r^*:

$$W/P_j = -\psi_j[R/P_j; r^*], \ \partial\psi_j/\partial r^* > 0$$
$$\partial\psi_j/\partial(R/P_j) > 0, \ \partial^2\psi_j/\partial(R/P_j)^2 \leq 0 \tag{26}$$

For $r^* = 0$, $\psi_j[\ ; 0]$ is derivable from equating to unity $\phi_j^*[R/P_j, W/P_j)$. For $r^* > 0$ and all inputs used up in each single use, replacing the true $F_j[]$ functions by $(1 + r^*)^{-1} F_j[\ ]$ will give rise to new $\phi_j[\ ]$ and $\phi_j^*[\ ]$ functions exactly as in equations (18) to (22). Then the fundamental factor-price frontiers defined by Smith's system can be defined by

$$\phi_j^*[R/P_j, W/P_j; 1 + r^*] = 1 \qquad (27)$$

For fixed $1 + r^*$, (27) defines convex contours.

With $r^* > 0$, equation (24)'s τ's have to be marked up, but are still constants so long as the m's are constants.

Prior to the system's having settled down into its long-run, time-phased steady state, one can provide for Smith's model an *endogenous* process of growth. Recognize the nonsimultaneous character of (1), and the need for capital inventories implied by such time phasing. So long as the initial rupture from the rude state is so recent that land is still redundant and rent zero, the system can grow in an initial golden age. Its rate of balanced exponential growth and the accompanying intermediate-run rate of interest or profit will provide the endogenous roots at which the supply of saving out of capitalists' profits are just large enough to provide the inventories for widening of capital goods and the advancing of wage goods for the multiplying population. If (7)'s population-growth function f[ ], is given; if (6)'s $[m_i]$ and (23)'s (y_i) for nonlaborers are known; and finally if the fraction of profit that will be saved is a known function of the interest rate $s[r]$ – then there will be an intermediate growth and profit rate, $(g^\dagger, r^\dagger)$, at which golden-age saving will equal golden-age warranted investment. Had Smith been able to write down the full conditions of this transient golden-age equilibrium, he would have anticipated Marx's expanded-reproduction tableaux of *Capital, Vol. II* and would have provided Harrod and Domar with an endogenous natural rate of growth.

Needless to say, once exponential growth runs into the constraint of scarce good land, positive rent will have to be reckoned with and recourse to ever-worse land, or ever-more-crowded best land, will imply a steadily dropping growth rate and a steady fall in the profit or the wage rate (or, most probably in both), as the post-rude *cheerful* state sinks into Smith's long-run *dull* state.

PART IV

DAVID RICARDO

A Modern Treatment of the Ricardian Economy: I. The Pricing of Goods and of Labor and Land Services

Introduction, 133. — In the beginning, 135 — The expanding universe, 137. — Scarcity of land and positive rent, 139. — Residual rent to homogeneous land, 141. — A numerical example, 142. — The case of many goods and homogeneous land, 144. — The Leontief-Ricardo tableau, 147. — Non-substitutability even where substitutability is possible, 149. — Summary and Conclusion, 150. — Appendix: Theory of differential rent, 153.

INTRODUCTION

1. One fool can ask more questions than twelve wise men can answer. And so can one wise man. David Ricardo propounded a number of what we today should call linear programming problems. Except in the simplest cases he was not able to give complete and correct answers. Yet, despite a number of false conjectures, he did intuitively perceive properties of the equilibrium configuration which he probably could not have rigorously proved.

I intend to cast a few of his problems in today's symbolism. To avoid arguments over what Ricardo himself "meant" or understood, I shall describe Ricardo-*like* models. The reader can easily modify my assumptions to correspond more closely to what he regards as Ricardo's. I shall not try to relate systematically modern terminology to Ricardo's, even though a good deal of the apparent novelty of his valid conclusions arises primarily from the special way he used words of many meanings.

This is not intended to be an exercise in piety. Nor a debunking commando raid. If our researches prove that "chimeras" are chimeras – that invariable standards of value and absolute values cannot be accurately defined once Ricardo has left his simplest and singular cases – it is only what David Ricardo himself already realized.[1] What modern theory and

---

[1] See the Editor's Introduction to the Sraffa edition of Ricardo's *Principles*, particularly pp. xl–xlix. All references hereafter to *Principles* will refer to the Sraffa edition. References to other volumes of the Sraffa edition of Ricardo's works will be given as Ricardo, *Works* with the Roman numeral volume number and page reference.

mathematics can add is closure: an assertion of nonexistence can be given definite meaning and proved once and for all.

2. They can also demonstrate what one would have thought Ricardo and other clever economists would have long since discovered, that basic difficulties for a labor theory of value come from the theory of differential rent as much as from problems of the organic composition of capital. By going to an extensive margin, one cannot really "get rid of land as a factor of production and of rent as a determining element of cost and exchange value." For the extensive margin is itself a variable, to be determined like any other equilibrium variable as part of the theorist's explicit task. And a shift – say in the pattern of landlords' consumption – can be expected to change the extensive margin and thus to vary the relative labor costs of the different goods at these margins. Moreover, it can be expected to vary them *in a systematic way,* namely the systematic way predicted by those critics of the one-factor labor theory who seek to replace it by a multi-factor neoclassical theory of economic production and distribution.

The use of mathematics can also produce some amusing conclusions. Thus, a *long-run* Ricardian system involving subsistence wages and *homogeneous* land, can have applied to it the sentence "Labor is the cause and measure of exchangeable value. . .," but with "Labor" struck out and "Land" put in its place. Goods can be shown to exchange in proportion to their mathematically definable "embodied" land content, with land services providing us something like an "invariable standard of value" in terms of which "absolute values" can be measured with perfect accuracy. And all this will hold regardless of inequalities in (i) the organic composition of capital, (ii) the time intensities of different processes, or (iii) the proportions of direct land used in different productive processes.

In a sense the Physiocrats were right after all – if you can make the special long-run econometric assumptions that Ricardo seems often to do!

This significant result is a particular application and a generalization of the "substitutability theorem of one-factor Leontief systems" that Professor Georgescu-Roegen and I separately discovered in 1949.[2]

3. The present paper is divided into two main parts, with an appendix on differential rent sandwiched in between. Except in the appendix, I rarely go beyond school arithmetic and mathematics; but the student of modern

---

[2] See T. Koopmans (ed.), *Activity Analysis of Production and Allocation* (New York: Wiley, 1951), Chap. VII–X. See too the expository RAND monograph, Robert Dorfman, Paul A. Samuelson and Robert M. Solow, *Linear Programming and Economic Analysis* (New York: McGraw-Hill, 1958), Chaps. 9 and 10. Hereafter this book is referred to as *L.P.E.A.*

theory will recognize the underlying skeleton of mathematical economics. Part II is distinguished from the earlier sections by its explicit treatment of the problems of time and capital in the Ricardian system.[3]

IN THE BEGINNING

4. Before good land was scarce or capital goods dreamed of, life was simple and fitted a one-primary-factor theory. Smith, Ricardo, and for that matter the prewar Leontief, would call this single factor "labor." But we can work with any single factor: labor, or land, or a dose of labor-land-shovels, or simply any given total x. If each of n goods – deer, beaver, ..., or $y_1, \ldots, y_n$ – is producible at constant returns to scale in terms of the respective factor input $x_1, \ldots, x_n$ applied to it, our production functions can be written

$$y_1 = \frac{1}{a_1} x_1, y_2 = \frac{1}{a_2} x_2, \ldots, y_n = \frac{1}{a_n} x_n, \tag{1}$$

where the "coefficients of production" $(a_1, \ldots, a_n)$ are all positive.

Our production-possibility (or opportunity cost!) schedule becomes

$$x_1 + \ldots + x_n = a_1 y_1 + \ldots + a_n y_n \leq x \tag{2}$$

for all non-negative x's and y's. Figure I shows the two-good picture.

Technology is here favorable to viable perfect competition in which men trade with each other and with nature at determinate price ratios as follows:

$$p_1 \leq w a_1, p_2 \leq w a_2, \ldots, p_n \leq w a_n, \tag{3}$$

where w is the wage of the single factor x. It is understood that an inequality holding implies that the respective $y_i = 0 = x_i$: i.e., each good's price = factor cost of production whenever a good is produced, but may fall short of it when the industry shuts down. (In Figure I note the broken-line price sloped at the intercepts.)

Thus, if we know y_1 and y_2 are produced and y_3 and y_4 are not, we can from technology alone predict

---

[3] Further material that could have gone into this paper on Ricardo, I found convenient to gather together in a related paper on Marx. See P. A. Samuelson, "Wages and Interest: A Modern Dissection of Marxian Economic Models," *The American Economic Review*, XLVII (Dec. 1957), 884–912.

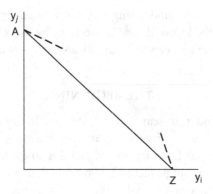

Figure I

$$\frac{p_2}{p_1} = \frac{a_2}{a_1}, \ \frac{p_3}{p_1} \leq \frac{a_3}{a_1}, \frac{p_4}{p_1} \leq \frac{a_4}{a_1}, \ \frac{p_4}{p_3} \gtreqless \frac{a_4}{a_3}.$$

5. Critics and defendants of the labor theory of value have overlooked the following fact: the operational significance of a one-factor hypothesis lies in the powerful predictive value that it gives to *technology alone*. A spy can memorize only the numbers $(a_1, a_2, \ldots, a_n, x)$ and he knows most of what there is to know about such an economy. Most, but not all. Demand considerations, and whatever subjective functions that lie behind them, also are needed to give us the actual breakdown of attainable physical consumption.

Even beyond this, there is a more subtle reliance on demand implied by (3). Both blades of the Marshallian scissors must indeed be cutting. Not until demand (with supply) is brought in to assure $y_i > 0$, can we infer $p_i = wa_i$. To have a full equilibrium solution for $(y_1, \ldots, y_n, x_1, \ldots, x_n, p_1/w, \ldots, p_n/w)$ the classicists would have had to develop a full theory of consumption to supplement their theory of technology. Even to have a determinate theory of $(p_1/w, \ldots, p_n/w)$, they needed an implicit demand theory – as they recognized in regarding "value-in-use" as a *qualitative necessary condition* for market value.

6. Note that in relations (3) the single-factor constant-cost model need assume nothing about the subjective or other supply conditions of the single factor. We could have an inelastic supply of labor x, with all wages being true economic rents and with all relative prices being determined by an opportunity-cost doctrine orthodox enough to delight any Austrian. The possibility of a prescribed total of x shows that a labor-cost doctrine need not have anything to do with psychic disutility or with indifference curves between work and goods.

Philip Wicksteed in his attack[4] on the Marxian labor cost doctrine was therefore perhaps unnecessarily subtle. He could have pointed out the unrealistic technology – for today's USSR or USA and for nineteenth century Europe – of a one-factor economy. This criticism granted, economists' shop talk about value as being derived from utility rather than disutility, or about the need to take demand into account in describing prices, would have been somewhat redundant. Were this technological criticism denied, most of what the modern economist considers significant in a one-factor theory would stand up against Wicksteed's criticisms.

THE EXPANDING UNIVERSE

7. The classical economists did have a "real cost" theory, which in Ricardo's day was still primarily a population theory concerning the reproducibility-at-constant-returns of people. If there were a single necessity corn, y_1, which each unit of labor had to have in amount c_1, then total labor would grow, stand still, or decrease depending upon the difference between actual subsistence per head y_1/x_1 and needed subsistence c_1: i.e.,

$$\frac{1}{x_1}\frac{dx_1}{dt} \gtreqless 0 \text{ depending on whether } \frac{y_1}{x_1} = \frac{1}{a_1} \gtreqless c_1. \tag{4}$$

If $1 - c_1 a_1 < 0$, the population in question will have become extinct. If $1 - c_1 a_1 = 0$, population is in neutral equilibrium.[5]

The case of $1 - c_1 a_1 > 0$ was thought by Malthus to be the most realistic one: in it nature originally provided more than what was needed for life, giving rise to a geometric rate of population growth on a virgin continent. This process would continue indefinitely, were it not for the ultimate limitation on land and the implied operation of the law of diminishing returns.[6]

---

[4] P. H. Wicksteed, *The Common Sense of Political Economy*, Vol. II contains a reprint of his 1884 article, *Das Kapital, A Criticism*. This actually converted Bernard Shaw from Marxism to Jevonism! P. M. Sweezy, *The Theory of Capitalist Development* (New York: Oxford University Press, 1942), pp. 46–47 cogently argues that under the postulated simple conditions supply and demand will agree with the labor theory of value.

[5] The first Leontief system was a closed one and postulated such a vanishing of the matrix $[1 - c_1 a_1]$. W. W. Leontief, *Structure of the American Economy* (New York: Oxford University Press, 1951), p. 47.

[6] The nonspecialist may skip the next section at a first reading.

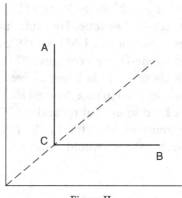

Figure II

8. In terms of linear programming, the system (1)–(4) can be thought to act as if it were trying to maximize the surplus of product over needed cost of reproducing labor: i.e., as if it were to

$$\text{maximize } Z = y_1 - c_1 x_1 \text{ subject to} \tag{5}$$
$$a_1 y_1 - x_1 \leq 0, x_1 \geq 0, y_1 \geq 0.$$

This implies $Z = y_1 - c_1 x_1 \leq x_1 \left(\frac{1}{a_1} - c_1 \right)$; hence ignoring any scarcity of land, the solutions to this problem obviously are

$$
\begin{aligned}
(Z, x_1, y_1) &= (0, 0, 0), & &\text{if } 1 - c_1 a_1 < 0 \\
&= (0, x, a_1 x = x/c_1) \text{ for any } x > 0, & &\text{if } 1 - c_1 a_1 = 0 \tag{6} \\
&= (\infty, \infty, \infty), & &\text{if } 1 - c_1 a_1 > 0.
\end{aligned}
$$

Land ignored, the last case, of course, has no stationary finite solution and represents the exploding Malthusian exponential, which may be moderated into a Verhulst-Pearl logistic or related form only after the limitation of land ceases to be neglectable.

9. Mr. Kaldor[7] has stated that Marx differed essentially from Ricardo in regarding many goods other than "corn" as necessary parts of a minimum standard of living. Actually Ricardo often insisted upon the point that workers required many different goods; and even if he had not, the mathematical picture would be little changed by our introducing such as variety of necessities. We simply stipulate that the worker requires $(c_1, c_2, \ldots, c_n)$ of

[7] Nicholas Kaldor, "Alternative Theories of Distribution," *Review of Economic Studies*, XXIII (1955–56), 87.

the different goods for his subsistence wage. In Figure II, the indifference curve corresponding to the minimum of subsistence is ACB, and goods being non-free, the man will always end up at $C(c_1, \ldots, c_n)$, the corner of the L-shaped indifference curve.

We now can think of a composite good consisting of $(c_1, \ldots, c_n)$ of the n goods. Its labor requirements per unit must then be $c_1a_1 + c_2a_2 + \ldots + c_na_n$, and if population is to be capable of growth (retardation, neutral stability), we must have as our criterion $\Sigma c_j a_j > 1$ (or < 1, or $= 1$). The interesting case is where $1 - \Sigma c_j a_j > 0$, which is the generalization of our earlier one-good condition $1 - c_1a_1 > 0$.[8]

SCARCITY OF LAND AND POSITIVE RENT

10. Exponential growth of men must finally use up finite territory. The labor constraint

$$a_1y_1 + \ldots + a_ny_n \leq x$$

must then be explicitly augmented by a land constraint

$$b_1y_1 + \ldots + b_ny_n \leq L, \tag{7}$$

where b_i represents the minimum positive land required *along with* a_i units of labor to produce one unit of y_i and L is the supply of available homogeneous land.

For L sufficiently large relative to x, this constraint could previously be ignored, since (7)'s inequality would necessarily have held. But when all superfluous L disappears, many things begin to happen.

Competition among laborers will make positive rent for land's services spring up. Goods' costs will now have a non-wage component, with this result: the existence of scarce land has destroyed the simple labor theory of value. (Figure III now contains, in addition to Figure I's labor constraint AB, the new straight line BC depicting equation (7)'s land constraint. The resulting production possibility schedule is ABC, with cost and price ratios

---

[8]   The condition $1 - \sum c_j a_j > 0$ which implies explosion of a closed Malthus v. Neumann system that plows all its superfluous consumption back into itself as invested input, is precisely the 1949 Hawkins-Simon condition for an open statical Leontief system to be capable of positive final consumption and to possess all positive solutions for prices and quantities. See *L.P.E.A.*, p. 215. It would be easy to generalize the above analysis to the case where the base indifference curve allows of substitution – as, e.g., where workers need calories from *any* source.

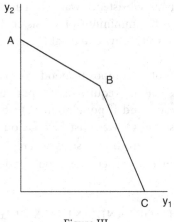

Figure III

of produced goods being anywhere from the slope of *AB* to *BC depending upon the pattern of demand.*[9]

11. When rent on good land is bid up high enough, this will drive laborers to inferior lands if such exist. The postulated existence of many grades of land, of course, permitted Ricardo to phrase a differential theory of rent that compared the productivity of labor on good land with its productivity on free land just at the "extensive margin," the difference being the numerical measure of good land's rent.[10]

However, aside from his extensive-margin theory of rent, Ricardo also had a differential theory of rent based upon the "internal margin." This internal, differential theory is very much in the spirit of the later 1890 neoclassical smooth substitutability theories of J. B. Clark, Wicksteed, and the third-edition Walras. In particular Ricardo did not fall into the trap that caught some of his unwary followers: he did not believe that the existence of a single grade of land would, simply because it made the differential rent

---

[9] Beginning students of economics today learn in their first week that the transformation terms between a labor-intensive and a land-intensive good vary with demand. See P. A. Samuelson, *Economics: An Introductory Analysis* (4th ed.; New York: McGraw-Hill, 1958), pp. 22–23; yet in reading a thousand pages on the labor theory of value, I can remember but one author who comes close to emphasizing that land – and not merely capital – vitiates a simple labor theory and that no tricks with no-rent marginal land can change this. See Lionel Robbins, *Robert Torrens and the Evolution of Classical Economics* (London: Macmillan, 1958), p. 237 *passim.*

[10] In the Appendix on Differential Rent, I investigate the linear programming problems raised by several grades of land, confining the text for the most part to the case of homogeneous land.

measurement between good and marginal land impossible, cause rent to vanish; he knew that scarcity of homogeneous land would create positive rent.

Indeed, even before replying to Say's criticism alleging the non-existence of the extensive margin in contemporaneous Western Europe, Ricardo had insisted that rent could be measured differentially *on every piece* of homogeneous land. In this connection, Ricardo is thinking of varying the doses of labor (and capital, which I temporarily ignore) applied to the same valuable land. The last profitable dose of labor will add to product just what it cost, and so Ricardo speaks of it as the unit of labor "that pays no rent." Thus, in modern terminology, the total of rent is measured by the difference between the product of all labor units and what labor at the intensive margin produces.[11]

RESIDUAL RENT TO HOMOGENEOUS LAND

12. Interestingly enough, if we refuse to let Ricardo have the smooth assumptions of later neoclassical theory, his internal, differential rent formulation fails.[12] In other words, Ricardo's differential method could not handle the simplest of all technological cases, where all land is alike and where a_i and b_i are fixed non-substitutable coefficients. (I omitted labels from Figure II's axes so that it can do double duty and depict the L-shaped isoquants implied here when we deny substitutability.) For in this case,

---

[11] I recall Professor Viner's lectures of a quarter of a century ago in which he pointed out that the extensive and intensive margin is the literary man's substitute for the mathematically rigorous calculus concepts of partial derivatives. Ricardo, without knowing it, is setting up the smooth homogeneous production function $y_i = Q_i(x_i, L_i)$, where $1 = Q_i(a_i, b_i)$ gives the substitutable relations between the labor and land coefficients. Ricardo assumes workers are hired at the given wage up to the point where the last worker is just worth his real wage: i.e., $w/p_i = \partial Q_i / \partial x_i$. Hence residual rent (in goods per acre) = total product/acre minus total wages/acre = $Q_i/L_i - (x_i \partial Q_i / \partial L_i)/L_i$. Euler's theorem implies that this also equals land's marginal physical product, a fact that Wicksteed knew and that J. B. Clark perhaps took too much for granted.

[12] When I speak of Ricardo's rent theory, I really mean the rent theory that Sir Edward West and Malthus independently published in 1815 and that Ricardo later elaborated on. See the Editor's remarks, Ricardo, *Works*, IV, 6–7. I have too little knowledge in these doctrinal matters to make confident assertions; but it is my impression that Ricardo's 1817 *Principles* puts more stress on the quantitative differential aspect of rent involving comparisons of different grades of land than did West and Malthus or than did Ricardo's *An Essay on the Influence of a Low Price of Corn on the Profits of Stock*, which was written in 1815 under the direct stimulus of the Malthus and West writings. At the very beginning of that *Essay* (*Works*, IV, 10), Ricardo quotes a residual-rent formulation of Malthus precisely like that offered in this present section.

when all homogeneous land is used there is no labor "that pays no rent" from which Ricardo can measure differential rent.

None the less this simplest long-run Ricardian model does have a determinate solution, which is intuitively fairly obvious. To see the solution, first consider a corn-labor-land economy. Labor grows in the long run until it is in a determinate ratio to land. (Namely, until there is just enough labor to use up all the land in co-operative production – until $x_1/L_1 = a_1/b_1$.) Now think of this dose of labor-land as producing total corn product. Labor's wage is fixed in corn at the conventional subsistence level c_1. So we know what labor is paid. What's left over is the rent of land. It's as simple as that.[13]

There is a vulgar prejudice against a "residual" theory of distribution. It would be well-taken if directed at a theory that explains wages as what's left over after land gets paid and *simultaneously* explains rent as what's left over after labor gets paid. Such a theory is no theory at all, being one equation for two unknowns. However, there is absolutely nothing unrigorous about a theory that "explains" *one* factor's share as a residual from well-determined other factors' shares. (Incidentally, rent can be simultaneously thought of as a residual or as a marginal product.)

A NUMERICAL EXAMPLE

13. The simple Ricardian economy is completely characterized by its a, b, c technological coefficients and the amount L of its unaugmentable land. Figure IV shows an exact numerical model for the following econometric constants:

$$a_1 = .1 \text{ men per ton of corn}$$
$$b_1 = 50 \text{ acres per ton of corn}$$
$$c_1 = 4 \text{ tons of corn per man}$$
$$L = 1 \text{ million acres.}$$

A million acres needs 2,000 men $(= L/[a_1/b_1])$ to work it. Together they produce 20,000 $(= L/b_1)$ tons of corn, of which 8,000 $(= c_1 2,000)$ tons must be fed as fodder to labor, leaving *produit net* of 12,000 tons in all for land or rent of .012 corn tons per acre.

---

[13] Actually, a dynamic theory of the stability of the long-run equilibrium would recognize oscillations around this level – incidentally in conformity with ecologists' observations of the struggle for biologic survival. Letting the variable factor grow until it hits up against the ceiling of a vanished "reserve army" of unemployed *land*, we might try to construct a "crisis" theory in the later Marxian manner.

The whole area in Figure IV measures gross corn product. The horizontal long-run labor supply curve SS splits this total gross product into the two subrectangles of intermediate wage product and *produit net* or residual rent. The share of wages to total gross product is c_1a_1; the relative share of rent $1 - c_1a_1$. If labor comes to need more corn, c_1 rises and the absolute and relative share of rent must fall. If labor becomes more efficient, a_1 decreases and the absolute and relative shares of rent rise. If land becomes more efficient, b_1 drops and there is an increase in population, wages, and total rent, with relative shares unaffected.

14. That land is the measure and "creator" of all products in the long-run Ricardian system is shown by the fact that doubling L will exactly double the width of all rectangles; halving L will halve the width of all rectangles. Land is the source of wage's gross product, the source of total product, the source of rent's net product. Labor, to be sure, is needed as a co-operating input, but being reproducible within the system it can be regarded simply as "congealed" or "embodied" corn. Even this is an understatement. We shall see that corn itself can be thought of as *congealed or embodied land*, and so labor too can be regarded in the last analysis as embodied land!

When a modern uses words like "embodied," "congealed," "decomposable," he is employing figures of speech for a prosaic mathematical fact. Needless to say no deep philosophical or ethical significance is implied. Beyond the important implication of economic fact and meaningful predictive hypothesis, the present-day economist finds only boring pseudo-questions.

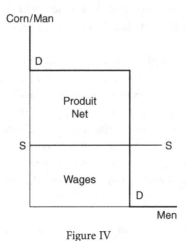

Figure IV

THE CASE OF MANY GOODS AND HOMOGENEOUS LAND

15. The full significance of the "land theory of value" being expounded here can be grasped only after contemplating the many-good case. It would then be a miracle if the direct land and labor requirements, as measured by the a_i/b_i ratios, were the same in every industry. Would not difficulties in the "organic composition" (not of capital but) of land and labor necessarily destroy the invariant relation of price to land content? Would not shifts in landlords' pattern of consumption demand alter the relative costs and prices of goods that are relatively labor or land intensive? And won't such shifts in landlords' demand alter the relative share of wages and rent in the total product? Won't shifts of final demand toward labor-intensive goods raise labor's relative shares, and by lowering rent cause substitutions toward more land-intensive methods?

The answer to every one of these questions is, No. So long as technology and labor's requirements for subsistence, as measured by its $(c_1, c_2, \ldots, c_n)$ coefficients, remain unchanged, *the total of rent* (measured in terms of any single or composite good or in terms of purchaseable labor hours) *must remain exactly the same*! And the terms of trade between any two goods produced must remain unaltered by any shift in the composition of landlord demand. (I say landlord demand because a constant-cost concept of population leaves labor demand no longer free.)

Why these sweeping and possibly paradoxical sounding assertions? Because in this long-run system labor, corn, velvets, deer, beaver, and everything can be decomposed into embodied land – and nothing else! It is nonsense to say that corn is more land-intensive than velvets. For all goods are 100 per cent land intensive when you take into account the indirect land needed to grow the labor foods needed for velvet and corn production.

16. Perhaps Frank Knight, and others, will feel there is a vicious circle here, arguing: "It takes corn to make men, and it takes men (and land) to make corn. Neither corn nor men can be considered antecedent to the other." We need not quarrel with this temporal relationship, nor attempt to argue that a fertile island without men will soon or ever populate itself with people. Still as Leontief has shown, the logical circle is a virtuous one and the unique solution to the problem comes from *solving simultaneously* the algebraic equations relating the variables.[14] This statical

---

[14] Leontief, *op.cit.*, Part II. Marx in *Capital*, Vol. II had already introduced a model of two sectors involving circular interdependence more sophisticated than that of the simple

simultaneous-equation solution can be interpreted to give prices equal to embodied land content, and can be interpreted in terms of a hypothetical multiplier chain going back infinitely in time.

17. The deepest insight into these analytic facts will come from the standard matrix methods of the Leontief input-output system. However, for the nonspecialist I shall first give an elementary algebraic statement of the one-good case, and then an equivalent treatment of the n-good case but using a single composite cost-of-living commodity.

The price of corn p_1 must equal its labor plus rent costs of production. And the wage w must just buy c_1 wants of corn. Depicting rent per acre by r, this gives us two independent equations for (p_1, w, r):

$$
\begin{aligned}
p_1 &= wa_1 + rb_1 \\
w &= p_1 c_1
\end{aligned}
\quad \text{or} \quad
\begin{aligned}
p_1/r &= b_1(1 - c_1 a_1)^{-1} \\
w/r &= c_1 b_1(1 - c_1 a_1)^{-1}.
\end{aligned}
\tag{8}
$$

Clearly the ratios $(p_1/r, w/r)$ are uniquely determined, not the absolute level of prices. Working with ratios to r is equivalent to using land as our *numeraire*, expressing all other prices in terms of embodied land.

18. We can give a symbolic picture in the form of an infinite multiplier[15] of the decomposition of corn's price into its direct land content and into the land needed to produce the corn to produce the labor to produce the corn, etc., back to the "beginning of time." Recalling the converging infinite geometric expansion for any fractional h, $1/(1 - h) = (1 - h)^{-1} = 1 + h + h^2 + \ldots + h^n + \ldots$, we rewrite

$$
\begin{aligned}
\frac{p_1}{r} &= b_1(1 - c_1 a_1)^{-1} = b_1[1 + c_1 a_1 + (c_1 a_1)^2 + \ldots + (c_1 a_1)^n + \ldots] \\
&= b_1 + b_1(c_1 a_1) + b_1(c_1 a_1)^2 + \ldots + b_1(c_1 a_1)^n + \ldots.
\end{aligned}
\tag{9}
$$

Here b_1 is the direct land cost per unit of corn; $b_1 c_1 a_1$ is the direct land cost of the corn needed for the direct labor; and so forth in a series that has a convergent sum by virtue of the Hawkins-Simon-Malthus assumption that $c_1 a_1 < 1$.

---

hierarchical Austrian models in which the stages of production can be uniquely ordered in terms of their "earliness or lateness." Professor Adolph Lowe has called my attention to a neglected discussion of these matters, F. A. Burchardt, "Die Schemata des stationären Kreislaufs bei Böhm-Bawerk und Marx," *Weltwirtschaftliches Archiv*, Kiel, Vol. 34 (1931), pp. 525–64 and Vol. 35 (1932), pp. 116–76. See also the reference in *L.P.E.A.*, p. 234, to Hugh Gaitskell's 1938 notes.

[15] See *L.P.E.A.*, p. 253.

19. Turning to the many-good case, we have equations just like (8) but more numerous.

$$p_1 = wa_1 + rb_1$$
$$p_2 = wa_2 + rb_2$$
$$. \quad . \quad .$$
$$p_n = wa_n + rb_n$$
$$w = p_1c_1 + p_2c_2 + \ldots + p_nc_n. \tag{10}$$

These are $(n+1)$ equations for the $(n+2)$ unknowns $(p_1, \ldots, p_n, w, r)$. Hence, we can solve for the $(n+1)$ price ratios $(p_1/r, \ldots, p_n/r, w, r)$. The simplest way to solve is to multiply the first equation by c_1, the second by c_2, the nth by c_n; then add these all together, getting

$$w = \sum_1^n p_jc_j = w(\sum_1^n c_ja_j) + r(\sum_1^n c_jb_j), \text{ or } \frac{w}{r} = (\sum c_jb_j)(1 - \sum c_ja_j)^{-1}. \tag{11}$$

But this is just like the w/r expression in (8), except that it involves many c's. It can be easily interpreted in terms of a composite market-basket of subsistence, with Σc_ja_j and Σc_jb_j the labor and land requirements of a unit of the composite good.

Knowing w/r, we easily substitute (11) into (10) to get our final solution in terms of land's value alone

$$w/r = (\sum c_jb_j)(1 - \sum c_ja_j)^{-1}$$
$$p_1/r = (\sum c_jb_j)(1 - \sum c_ja_j)^{-1}a_1 + b_1$$
$$. \; . \; . \; . \; . \; . \; . \; .$$
$$p_n/r = (\sum c_jb_j)(1 - \sum c_ja_j)^{-1}a_n + b_n. \tag{12}$$

Our mathematical decomposition is now complete. We can leave to the reader the infinite multiplier expansion of $(1 - \Sigma c_ja_j)^{-1}$ in (12) with its interpretation in terms of direct and indirect land requirements.

20. In concluding this section, I might mention that the price ratios of (12) enable us to write down the production possibility schedule of *produit net*, available for any given L. The straight line in Figure I will still serve, if we reinterpret its axes to refer not to gross production $(y_1, y_2, \ldots)$

but to each of these minus workers' consumptions; or $(Y_1, Y_2, \ldots) = (y_1 - c_1x, y_2 - c_2x, \ldots)$. Also the locus is drawn up with L held constant but with population x changing *mutatis mutandis* whenever landlord demand is shifted toward goods "directly labor intensive." It is the absolute level of rent that is completely fixed when (L, a, b, c) are all given. The absolute level of total wages will vary with population variations induced by changes in the composition of landlord demand; but in the long run, the real wage expressed in terms of our $(c_1, c_2, \ldots)$ composite commodity will be unchanged. Such fixity of the real wage does not in a many-good model imply fixity of labor's total share or relative share of the gross produce.

The new relation corresponding in our land economy to Equation (2)'s simple labor economy is

$$\frac{p_1}{r}Y_1 + \frac{p_2}{r}Y_2 + \ldots + \frac{p_n}{r}Y_n = L, \qquad (13)$$

the (p/r)'s being given by (12).[16]

THE LEONTIEF-RICARDO TABLEAU

21. Labor being an output as well as an input in the classical system, we can summarize the economy by a Leontief matrix that lists in columns each good's input requirements.

LEONTIEF-RICARDO MATRIX

	Outputs					
Inputs	1 corn	2 velvets	...	n zebras	n +1 labor	Landlord consumptions
1 corn	0	0	...	0	c_1	Y_1
2 velvets	0	0	...	0	c_2	Y_2
.	.	.		.	.	.
.	.	.		.	.	.
.	.	.		.	.	.
.	.	.		.	.	.
n zebras	0	0	...	0	c_n	Y_n
$n+1$ labor	a_1	a_2	...	a_n	0	0
land	b_1	b_2	...	b_n	0	

[16] It could easily be shown that each final composition of landlord demand (Y_i) determines a unique amount of x and a unique relative share of wage to rents. The final average share of wages will then depend on how demand patterns weigh the different final goods Y_i. I.e., $x = \alpha_1 Y_1 + \ldots + \alpha_n Y_n$, where the α's depend only on the (a, b, c) coefficients. It follows that wx/rL is a simple rational function of the Y's, which are themselves constrained by (13).

Note that each good requires labor and land, as shown in the last two rows. (Leontief would also add circular requirements of *other goods* as raw materials, but we follow Ricardo and put in zeros.) Labor requires goods as shown by the $(c_1, \ldots, c_n)$ column; for luxuries, $c_i = 0$. Land is below the line because in the "open Leontief system" it is unproducible, being a primary factor. Landlord consumption is also exogenous and is to the right of the line.[17]

22. Now we can rewrite in matrix form the cost of production equations (10),

$$[p_1, \ldots, p_n, w] = [p_1, \ldots, p_n, w] \begin{bmatrix} 0 & \cdots & 0 & c_1 \\ 0 & \cdots & 0 & c_2 \\ \cdot & & \cdot & \cdot \\ \cdot & & \cdot & \cdot \\ \cdot & & \cdot & \cdot \\ 0 & \cdots & 0 & c_n \\ a_1 & \cdots & a_n & 0 \end{bmatrix} + r[b_1, \ldots, b_n, 0]$$

$$(14)$$

Letting A be the indicated $(n+1) \cdot (n+1)$ matrix, $B = [b_1, \ldots, b_n, 0]$ and $P = [p_1/r, \ldots, p_n/r, w/r]$ we can rewrite (14) in matrix terms as

$$P = PA + B$$
$$P = B[I - A]^{-1} = B[I + A + A^2 + \ldots] \qquad (15)$$
$$= B + BA + BA^2 + \ldots.$$

The last multiplier chain (of Gaitskell type) has the advantage of giving labor's price as well as goods' prices in terms of direct and indirect needed land. All such prices are determined by the full land costs of (12) or (14). Also, the gross outputs $[y_1, \ldots, y_n, x]$ can by similar algebra be written as the following column vector

$$[I - A]^{-1}Y = Y + AY + A^2Y + \ldots \qquad (16)$$

which is the so-called Leontief-Cornfield infinite multiplier chain of input requirements.

---

[17] The next section can be skipped by the nonspecialist.

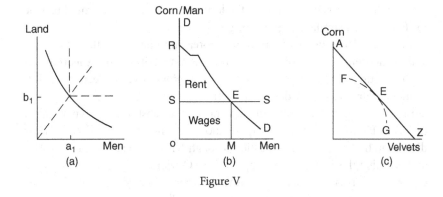

Figure V

NON-SUBSTITUTABILITY EVEN WHERE
SUBSTITUTABILITY IS POSSIBLE

23. We can now leave the simple case of fixed (a_i, b_i) input coefficients. As mentioned, Ricardo himself varies the inputs applied to a unit of land in the later neoclassical manner. I can now apply the "substitutability theorem" to show that *even though there are possibilities for substitution, the long-run one-factor Ricardo system need experience no substitutions.*

This already cited theorem has been proved by Georgescu-Roegen, Koopmans, Arrow, and myself and need not here be repeated.[18] It will be enough to indicate its implication in the corn-labor-land case. Figure Va shows the fixed-coefficient L-shaped isoquants of Figure II replaced by solid isoquants admitting of *alternative* (a_1, b_1) combinations. Figure Vb shows the long-run SS labor supply curve determining a unique real wage: the residue for rent is given by the triangle SER, total wages by $OMES$, and total product by $OMER$.

Note that Ricardo's differential formula for rent measured from the intensive margin E is now directly valid, and gives us the SER area. Note too that land now becomes scarce and expensive long before labor reaches its subsistence size.[19] The long-run constancy of the real wage because of the horizontal SS is crucial. It means that in Figure Va we shall always be at the same slope of the isoquant and hence we must remain at the point (a_1, b_1)

---

[18] See L.P.E.A., pp. 224–26, 248–52.

[19] In such a world of smooth substitution it might be harder to devise a plausible "crisis" theory dependent on a reserve army of land suddenly disappearing. Cf. the earlier footnote on a crisis theory.

with no observed substitutions in the long run; and the same would be true for (a_2,b_2) on a similar diagram for good 2.

24. Figure Vc adds insight into the far-reaching nature of the "substitutability theorem" – or more exactly, the "non-substitutability theorem." A simple argument can show why the transformation curve between two goods cannot be curved as in the dotted *FEG* curve, but must instead be a straight line as in *AEZ* or Figure I. For by giving up our right to substitute and remaining at (a_1,b_1) in Figure Va, we can always deduce from the earlier fixed-coefficients discussion that a straight-line relation through *E* is feasible: let us call this *AEZ* and note that this is simply the graph of (13). Obviously, if every frontier point of the transformation curve has a feasible straight line going through it, the transformation schedule must be a straight line.[20]

To conclude: in a one-factor world there is never any leverage for substitution; a rise in rents raises the cost of labor and of all potentially substitutable factors. (We shall later see that, with the long-run interest rate unchanged, a rise in rents also raises proportionately the price of every machine and every other input.)

25. Of course, one obvious qualification is in order. Ricardo and Smith would probably have admitted that the relative prices of joint products – of venison and deer skin, for example – would have to be determined by a demand theory and not from labor or land costs alone. One wonders why they did not worry more about this "jointness," which every student of Walrasian equilibrium knows to be an intrinsic part of the actual pricing relations among diverse factors and goods.[21]

SUMMARY AND CONCLUSION

26. We have seen that a simple labor theory of value is a valid general equilibrium formulation in the special case where land and capital are assumed to be ignorable. The importance of such a classical theory is not in its emphasis upon real costs and psychic disutility – there need not be such an emphasis; nor is its importance in catering to the metaphysician's desire for an "absolute" standard of value. Rather is the simple labor theory of importance because it *permits of a wide class of predictions concerning*

---

[20] That the curve cannot be concave from above already is implied by the classical law of constant returns to scale and addibility of separate productions.

[21] When we come to speak of fixed capital, joint products *must* be in the picture: a new machine produces corn *and* old machines. Hence, a needed condition for the usual substitutability theorem will be denied. The theorem will be saved, though, when we generalize it to cover cases of joint intermediate products that are never used by two separate industries.

price behavior from a knowledge of technology alone. This does not deny that demand conditions operate as well as production conditions. They, of course, do. But many of the technical predictions of the theory have a wide range of validity independently of sweeping changes in demand conditions. To be sure, if we insist upon a full description of the system, we must even in this simplest classical case invoke the full equations of general equilibrium.

27. Students of the classical theory have always recognized that the presence of capital and time created real difficulties for a simple labor theory of value. But, along with Ricardo, they have been under the illusion that land and rent could be avoided as a genuine difficulty by going to the external margin where labor works with free no-rent land and thus provides all the costs of commodity production. This is definitely an illusion; and it would indeed be remarkable if by introducing the complication of lands of many different grades, Ricardo and the classicists could simplify the equilibrium problem rather than complicating it.

Actually, raising the problem of many grades of land at once raises an equilibrium problem that Ricardo never explicitly faced up to. Although he was one of the formulators of the theory of comparative cost designed to explain the international division of labor (which was itself an early example of modern linear programming!), Ricardo did not recognize that an exactly similar problem was raised for the domestic division of labor: on which land of which grade will corn rather than potatoes be raised – and so forth? I am relegating to the Appendix the discussion of this important problem which, as far as I know, has been virtually overlooked by all writers since Ricardo's time with the sole exception of the later cited paper of Ragnar Frisch.[22]

---

[22] Figure III and its accompanying footnote demonstrated the inadmissibility of a simple labor theory once homogeneous land came into the picture. The device of going to the internal margin and concentrating on the outputs produced by the last increments of labor which pay no rent fails to work for the following mathematical reason: our cost of production for such a last unit becomes $p_i = w(\partial Q_i/\partial x_i)$. But the expressions in parentheses are now not hard technological constants or parameters; instead they are varying unknowns of the problem whose values have to be determined by the general equilibrium pattern of supply and demand. Professor Viner, in his 1930 *Economica* review of Edwin Cannan's, *A Review of Economic Theory* partially defends Ricardo's labor theory of value by use of the above marginal identity. This review is reprinted in J. Viner, *The Long View and the Short* (Glencoe, Ill.: Free Press, 1958), pp. 400 – 1. But, as Viner knows, a similar identity holds for land and shovels, and no one is interested in such a verbalistic shovel theory of value – particularly since the "constants" in it are economic variables whose new values we must determine every time demand shifts. (I wish I had given this answer on Viner's final examination a quarter of a century ago!)

28. Having demolished labor as an absolute standard of value, we can turn Ricardo upside down and find in his simplest long-run model a "land theory of value." This physiocratic interpretation of the Ricardian system comes from the special assumption that labor is reproducible – like any other good – at constant costs. Were there then but one homogeneous grade of land, we could in the manner of the Leontief system decompose the costs of every good – luxuries, wage goods, and even that intermediate good called labor itself – into its direct and indirect land content.

The substitutability theorem of modern input-output guarantees that even though technological substitutions are possible in such a one-primary-factor economy, they in fact never need be made. All other factors being the indirect product of land, there is never any leverage possible for relative-price change and substitution.

True, this decomposition into embodied land involves an infinite-chain multiplier; but its sum is definitely convergent, as can be shown by simple algebra or matrix methods familiar to students of input-output. Or, if we like we can avoid the multiplier chain completely, instead solving simultaneous equations for all prices in terms of land alone.

Land, being the only primary (i.e., nonproducible) item in this simplest model, has imputed to it – either as a residual or as a marginal product – all the net product of the system. As Ricardo well knew, it is scarcity and bottlenecks that give rise to value.

As the Physiocrats and classicists were aware, this central importance of land would have vast implications for public policy and taxation.

After the appendix on differential rent, Part II will grapple explicitly with the complications introduced by capital goods and time into the simplest Ricardian system. Provided we are willing to go along with the extreme classical assumption that in the long run the minimum interest rate is determined by an infinitely elastic supply schedule that is like the long-run supply schedule of labor, we shall find that an extension of the substitutability theorem will apply and that a decompilation of all value magnitudes into land alone will still be possible.

As the Appendix shows, the same variability holds in the case of the extensive margin. Thus, in the simplest case where there are two grades of land, a change in the composition of landlord demand in the direction of the good which uses relatively much of the good land will finally lead to recourse to the second grade of land. At that new extensive margin, we are on a new straight-line segment – like *BC* rather than *AB* in Figure III. So no predictability of prices independently of demand is possible in the extensive margin case either.

APPENDIX: THEORY OF DIFFERENTIAL RENT

Introduction

1. In the body of this paper I have shown that scarce land – even of one grade and in the absence of interest complications – destroys the possibility of a labor theory of value. Instead, under the special Ricardian longest-run assumptions, a single grade of land would itself provide a simple "land theory of value," based upon all prices equal to mathematically definable "embodied land."

In this Appendix, I examine the complications raised by the existence of many grades of land. The resulting theory is even more damaging to a labor theory of value, and in fact destroys my own simple "land theory of value." Though the theory of differential rent is straightforward, I have not been able to find a rigorous treatment of it in the old or new literature.[23] And when we examine its main outlines, we see how illusory is Ricardo's belief that an extensive margin enabled him to "get rid" of rent and land as complications and how odd it is that this fact was not long ago pointed out in the strongest terms by economists.

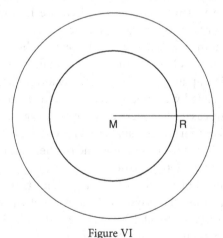

Figure VI

---

[23] Since completing this Appendix, I have had pointed out to me by Paul Rosenstein-Rodan, a pioneering discussion of this problem, Ragnar Frisch, "Einige Punkte einer Preistheorie mit Boden und Arbeit als Produktionsfaktoren," *Zeitschrift für Nationalökonomie*, III (Sept. 25, 1931), 62–163.

Frisch, fifteen years before the development of linear programming, had properly formulated this problem, discovered many aspects of its solution, and rigorously analyzed the few-goods few-lands fixed-coefficient case, and outlined important aspects of the general problem. As Schumpeter would have said, "A remarkable performance!"

One-Good Case of Corn

2. Figure VI uses Thünen-like concentric circles to depict smooth differences in land quality (but ignores the transportation costs upon which Thünen based his location theory). The most fertile land is at the center M. The first unit of labor (I ignore capital in this Appendix for simplicity of exposition) will be applied to M. Then additional land will be applied in widening circles around M.

If all the land around M were equally fertile, labor would at first be applied at the same density around M in widening circles. Of course, doubling total labor x will not double the radius of the circle: it will double the area; and since area is proportional to the square of the radius, doubling x will increase the radius MN by about 40 per cent. (Recall $\sqrt{2} = 1.4 + .$) Only after top-fertile land became scarce would land cease to be free factor and begin to command positive market rent.

If we assume that land's fertility drops continuously after leaving the center M, then the fact that labor applied at M begins to yield diminishing marginal products implies that labor will spread in concentric circles around M. Fertile land at M will from the beginning yield positive rent. At the frontier of the widening concentric circle we face no-rent external-marginal land; labor working there pays no rent.

A modern economist would say that labor anywhere inside the circle receives the same pay as labor at the external margin, and that the competitive market will impute to inside land exactly its marginal product if that magnitude is definable by a smooth constant-returns-to-scale production function. But in any case, the modern economist can agree with Ricardo that the rent on good land must *also* equal the difference between total product produced there and what the labor *there* (and on the frontier!) has to be paid under competitive wage determination.

3. Only a minority of writers have noticed that there is an ambiguity in the usual formulation that says: Good land's rent equals the difference between what labor (and "capital") produce on it and what "they" would produce at the external margin. It is forgotten that if one man and one plow till one good acre, there is no particular reason to think that one man and one plow will also be tilling an acre of frontier no-rent land. One man might be tilling five acres of such land, or one-fifth of an acre; and he might find it most economical to use two plows and one drill in doing so. In short, there is a good deal of "implicit theorizing" in the classical account of how factors are to be allocated and compared on different lands, with Adam Smith's

Invisible Hand being relied on to provide the determining equations that the conscientious economic scientist ought explicitly to provide.

Since I have agreed to ignore the complications due to use of capital goods, I can sidestep the plow-drill problem for now. But we must face up to the question of how we optimally combine labor with land.

4. First, what do we mean by saying that land declines in fertility as we move on the radius away from the center M? Do we mean that less corn will in fact be produced *per acre* at each outlying point than will be produced per acre at M? No; not necessarily. It could well happen that the poor land *toward* the frontier *has* to be cultivated more *intensively* and in such a way as to give us more corn y_1 per acre.

To study this problem write down the constant-returns-to-scale production function relating corn output at R to labor and land there. It is convenient to relate output per acre, called $y_1(R)$, to labor per acre, called $x_1(R)$ and to total number of land acres devoted to corn at R_1 called $L_1(R)$. Then

$$y_1(R) = \frac{f_1[x_1(R)L_1(R), L_1(R); R]}{L_1(R)}$$

$$= f_1[x_1(R), 1; R], \tag{1A}$$

where the marginal physical productivity of labor and land are given by the partial derivatives $\partial f_1 / \partial x_1(R)$ and $\partial f_1 / \partial L_1(R)$ respectively and where f_1 is a homogeneous function of the first degree in terms of its labor and land inputs.

To say that the quality of land decreases as the radius R increases is to say that labor's *beginning* average or marginal productivity, $\partial f_1[0, 1; R] / \partial x_1(R)$, is a diminishing function of R: hence land at larger R will be used only after diminishing returns has reduced labor's marginal productivity on land at smaller R.

We can proceed to relate the technical coefficients, a_1 and b_1, defined in the text as the needed inputs of labor and land per unit of corn output, to the production function. Now a_1 and b_1 become functions of R, $a_1(R)$ and $b_1(R)$, which are connected by the relations:

$$b_1(R) = \frac{1}{y_1(R)}, a_1(R) = \frac{x_1(R)}{y_1(R)}$$

$$1 = f_1[a_1(R), b_1(R); R]. \tag{2A}$$

This last relation will look like the cornered isoquants of the text's Figure II if we have fixed coefficients, or like the smoother isoquants of Figure Va if we have variable coefficients.

The requirement coefficient $a_1(R)$ is simply the reciprocal of labor's average productivity; and if we assume zero labor produces zero output, average and marginal productivities are equal when labor is initially applied. Hence, the initial $a_1(R)$ is the reciprocal of $\partial f_1[0, 1; R]/\partial x_1(R)$ and we can replace our definition of the criterion for a decline in land's quality by the following equivalent one: To say land declines in quality with R is to say that the initial needed amount of labor per unit of output, $a_1(R)$, is a rising function of R.

5. At first one is tempted to think of land at the frontier as being used in a very extensive rather than intensive way. That this is not universally true is shown by working through the case of fixed coefficients, where $a_1(R)$ and $b_1(R)$ are technically given. How then will labor and output be determined at each R? I.e., what will the equilibrium profile of $y_1(R)$ be for each available total labor x?

For each given x, labor will be applied up to a variable frontier R^* that is determined by solving the implicit equation:

$$2\pi \int_0^{R^*} a_1(R)y_1(R)RdR = 2\pi \int_0^{R^*} \frac{a_1(R)}{b_1(R)} RdR = x, \qquad (3A)$$

which is a single equation solvable for the unknown R^* in terms of x. (The 2π and RdR factors in the integrals come from the geometric relation between circular area and radius: i.e., from the analytical facts $\int_0^{2\pi} d\theta = 2\pi$, $dA = RdRd\theta$.) For $R > R^*$, production will be zero with $y_1(R) \equiv 0 \equiv x_1(R)$.

All this is no accident but follows from the solution of the following mathematical problem: Pick that non-negative $y_1(R)$ function which maximizes total output

$$y_1 = 2\pi \int_0^\infty y_1(R) \, RdR, \text{ subject to}$$

$$2\pi \int_0^\infty a_1(R)y_1(R) \, RdR \leqq x \qquad (4A)$$

$$y_1(R) \leqq \frac{1}{b_1(R)}.$$

For $a_1(R)$, a rising function, the optimal solution will necessarily entail $y_1(R)$'s vanishing beyond the cut-off point R^* of (3A).

Now what is the resulting intensity of cultivation? Measured in men/acre it is given by $a_1(R)/b_1(R)$. If $b_1(R)$ rises more slowly with R than $a_1(R)$ – as certainly can happen – then $a_1(R)/b_1(R)$ will increase with R and we see that frontier land will be more intensively tilled by labor. (E.g., suppose bad land is very weedy and requires much manual stooping.)

6. The variable-coefficient case, which Ricardo thought more realistic when considering varying doses applied to land, is a little more complicated. The mathematical problem (4A) still holds; but now $a_1(R)$ and $b_1(R)$ are not technologically given but are to be determined by the solution to the maximum problem, subject only to the production-function relation connecting them in (2A).

Intuitively, the economist realizes that in the smooth case where marginal productivities $\partial f_1/\partial x_1(R)$ exist, our solution must satisfy (3A) and (2A) and also equality of labor's marginal productivity everywhere that labor is used.

To see all this we have to set up the calculus of variations problem.

Maximize $y_1 = y_1(x) = 2\pi\int_0^\infty f_1[x_1(R), 1; R]RdR$ subject to

$$2\pi \int_0^\infty x_1(R)RdR \leq x, x_1(R) \geq 0. \tag{5A}$$

By use of a Lagrange multiplier $\lambda = w/p_1$, we derive the conditions of equilibrium

$$\frac{\partial f_1[x_1(R), 1; R]}{\partial x_1(R)} = w/p_1, \ R \leq R^*$$
$$< w/p_1, \ R > R^*$$
$$\frac{w}{p_1} = \frac{\partial f_1[0, 1; R^*]}{\partial x_1(R)} = \frac{dy_1(x)}{dx} \tag{6A}$$
$$2\pi \int_0^{R^*} x_1(R)\, RdR = x$$

with the economic laws of returns giving us the Legendre condition $\partial^2 f_1/\partial x_1^2 < 0$ and the Jacobi and Weierstrass conditions sufficient to assure a true maximum.[24]

At each R we can define a unique land rent $r(R)$ satisfying

---

[24] Cf. G. A. Bliss, *Lectures on the Calculus of Variations* (University of Chicago Press, 1946).

$$\frac{r(R)}{p_1} = \frac{\partial f_1[x_1(R), 1; R]}{\partial L_1(R)} = \frac{1}{b_1(R)} - \frac{a_1(R)}{b_1(R)} \frac{w}{p_1}, \quad R \leq R^*$$

$$\frac{r(R)}{p_1} \equiv 0, R \geq R^*.$$

(7A)

For R just below R^*, rent will necessarily decline with R; but well inside the frontier, there is the possibility that rent could at times rise with R.

As kind of a "dual problem" to (5A), we could derive the conditions (7A) as the solution to the *minimum* problem

Subject to $$\frac{r(R)}{p_1} \geq \frac{1}{b_1(R)} - \frac{a_1(R)}{b_1(R)} \frac{w}{p_1} \qquad R \geq 0$$
$$1 = f_1[a_1(R), b_1(R); R]$$

pick non-negative $r(R)/p_1$ and w/p_1 to minimize

$$y_1^* = 2\pi \int_0^\infty \frac{r(R)}{p_1} R dR + \frac{w}{p_1} x$$

(8A)

$$= y_1(x).$$

Let us summarize the resulting equilibrium of the corn-labor-land economy. An external observer who merely recorded the total of corn y_1 produced for each total of labor x would see a marginal product curve $dy_1(x)/dx$ such as mn in Figure VII. This is indistinguishable from the case

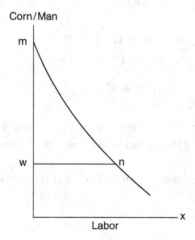

Figure VII

of homogeneous land. The only generalization possible is that the absolute total of rent – measured in corn by the residual triangle *mnw* – always goes up as total labor *x* grows. But nothing at all can be predicted about labor's relative share, whether it will be a small or large fraction of the total or how it will change with extra labor. The writings of the classical economists are replete with false statements on these delicate questions of relative shares.

Of course, if the supply of labor is determined by a horizontal long-run *SS* curve through *wn* in the Ricardian fashion, we have a complete theory. Or alternative supply conditions could be postulated.

RENTS IN THE MULTI-GOOD, MULTI-LAND ECONOMY

7. We now must consider the case of more than one good, where $y_1, y_2 \ldots$ are to be produced. For each point R on a radius in Figure VI, we are now given a production function for each different good, as in (1A). Such as production function will for the ith good give us the possible relations between $a_i(R)$ and $b_i(R)$, just as in (2A). In all we have

$$y_i(R) = f_i[x_i(R), 1; R] \qquad (i = 1, 2, \ldots)$$
$$1 = f_i[a_i(R), b_i(R); R]. \tag{9A}$$

What pattern of cultivation will now follow for each given total of labor *x*? It could happen that the production functions for $i = 1$ and $i = 2$ differ only

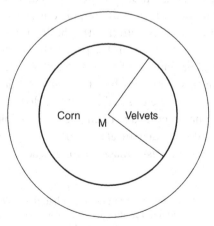

Figure VIII

in scale. In this singular case, corn and velvets would be produced *indifferently anywhere* in the circle of cultivation. Figure VIII shows the pie-wedge possibilities; but local polka dots of corn and velvets would be as good. The reason for the indifference is that corn and velvet, once scales have been rectified, are essentially the same good with a production possibility curve for each x being a negatively-sloped straight line.

The pie-wedge case of Figure VIII has the merit that both goods can be said to be producible at the external margin, with their price ratios being determinable from their external-margin wage costs alone.

8. But we must face up to the fact that it is terribly unrealistic to suppose that all qualities of land are *equally* good or bad in the production of *every* good. Sandy land good for cucumbers is terrible for rice. To each scarcity of labor and each pattern of commodity demand, there will be an elaborate set of comparative advantage conditions needed to determine the optimal geometric pattern of cultivation.

David Ricardo is rightly given great credit for his origination of the theory of comparative cost in international trade. I find it therefore a little paradoxical that he failed to see how within a region – where labor is fully mobile and lands have differential qualities – there arises a difficult economic problem of resource allocation. Not only did he leave the equilibrium conditions implicit, but he quite failed to see that the new set-up is fatal to his "embodied labor" theories.

For now with two or more lands having different comparative advantages for two or more goods, the production possibility between y_1 and y_2 – say corn and velvets – will be concave to the origin as in Figure Vc's broken curve *FEG*. Having dropped the assumption of homogeneous land, and even if still adhering to Ricardo's long-run assumptions of constant reproduction cost of labor, we no longer can end up with the straight line transformation curve – of Figures I and Vc. Each change in the pattern of landlord demand must change the relative labor contents of corn and velvets at the external margins (if such can be found), and presumably at all other locations as well both in physical and value terms. The classical attempt to deduce and predict price ratios from labor alone becomes a mathematical impossibility.[25]

I propose to give the mathematical solution to the many-land case, not merely to buttress the criticism made of long-dead Ricardo, but for the

---

[25] The same criticism holds also for Marx, but he at least had the grace to assume away land rent explicitly thereby avoiding Ricardo's logical error and being guilty only of the misdemeanor of unrealism. To explain actual production – under capitalism or communism, between nations or sub-regions – the Marxian theory must become neoclassical!

constructive reason that modern location theories are greatly in need of further theoretical development.

LINEAR PROGRAMMING FORMULATION

9. I first consider the case of m finite grades of land, in fixed amounts $[L(1), L(2), \ldots, L(j), \ldots, L(m)]$. After that the case of an infinity of grades can be heuristically summarized. As before I begin with the simple case where $a_i(j)$ and $b_i(j)$ are fixed, technologically-given coefficients for each industry on each land.

To deduce the production possibility locus of $(y_1, y_2, \ldots, y_n)$ for each available x, it is most convenient to think of specifying the outputs (y_i) and then to seek to minimize the needed total labor x, subject to the prescribed technology. This gives us the following linear programming problem: Subject to

$$y_1(1) + y_1(2) + \ldots + y_1(m) \geq y_1$$
$$y_2(1) + y_2(2) + \ldots + y_2(m) \geq y_2$$

$$y_n(1) + y_n(2) + \ldots + y_n(m) \geq y_n,$$
$$\text{all } y_i(j) \geq 0$$
$$b_1(1)y_1(1) + b_2(1)y_2(1) + \ldots + b_n(1)y_n(1) \geq L(1)$$
$$b_1(2)y_1(2) + b_2(2)y_2(2) + \ldots + b_n(2)y_n(2) \geq L(2)$$

$$b_1(m)y_1(m) + b_2(m)y_2(m) + \ldots + b_n(m)y_n(m) \leq L(m),$$
minimize

$$x = \sum_{i=1}^{n}\sum_{j=1}^{m} a_i(j)y_i(j)$$
$$= X[y_1, \ldots, y_n; L(1), \ldots, L(m)]. \tag{10A}$$

Provided the specified outputs are not more than the specified lands can produce, this will be a proper linear programming problem with a determinate solution assured. The resulting optimal pattern of production $[y_i(j)]$ can be converted into the optimal pattern of labor allocation $[x_i(j)] = [a_i(j)y_i(j)]$. Many of the grades of land, such as $L(k)$ say, may not be used at all or may be used incompletely: in that case the inequality $\sum y_i(k) < L(k)$ will hold, and such land will be redundant with its rent $r(k) = 0$. If a grade of land is used some, it may have to be used for only one good or it may have to be used for more than one good. (If $m < n$, more than one good will have to be produced by *some* grade of land, the exact geographical pattern being indifferent. Recognizing transport costs hitherto ignored will get rid of many of the inessential geographical indeterminacies.)

10. Now exactly how are prices p_i/w and land rents expressed in wage units $r(j)$ determined? Ricardo would probably have recognized the cost-of-production inequalities

$$\frac{p_i}{w} \leqq a_i(j) + r(j)b_i(j) \qquad (i = 1, \ldots n; j = 1, \ldots m), \qquad (11A)$$

with an inequality for any i and j implying that nothing of the ith good is to be produced on the jth land. But he could not from these have deduced prices and rents, since there is an infinity of possible solutions.

Of course, if he could have found for any good a no-rent land on which it was produced, he would then know its price. And then he could infer, residually or "differentially," the rent of any other land where it was also produced. Moreover, he could also infer the prices of any other good produced on lands whose rents he had thus deduced. Proceeding in this chain-like way (along a "mathematical tree") he could hope to determine still other land rents, namely those on which were also produced the further goods whose prices had just been inferred, etc., etc.

I say Ricardo could have done all this. But I don't recall that he ever did explicitly do so or fully realized the complicated nature of the problem that was to be solved. Moreover, even had he been able to pursue the above complicated reasonings, he would still not be out of the woods. For there could easily remain goods and lands which are never related by an indirect chain to any of the goods and lands whose prices and rents have been determined. To see this, we have only to consider the simple case where *no* lands actually used turn out to have zero rents. The Ricardian differential method based upon an extensive margin then breaks down completely.

To be sure, as we already have seen, Ricardo thought of coefficients as being variable on each intra-marginal unit of land: hence, he claimed to determine such land's rent by a differential measurement between what all labor applied to it produces and what the last unit of labor (the one at the internal margin that "pays no rent") produces; this is precisely what we should today call the land's marginal physical product valued at output's market price. But the simplest case of all, the case of fixed coefficients, Ricardo could apparently not solve by such methods.[26]

---

[26] A reader might wonder whether Ricardo's comparative advantage analysis applied within a country (*Principles*, p. 136 footnote) might not be used to solve this problem. It cannot. Working out the comparative advantage of $L(j)$ and $L(k)$ in corn and velvets by comparing $b_1(j)/b_2(j)$ and $b_1(k)/b_2(k)$ gives no valid clue to the optimal pattern, nor would $a_1(j)/a_2(j)$ and $a_1(k)/a_2(k)$ comparisons.

11. Is the failure intrinsic? No, it is not. The modern technique of linear programming gives us the optimal solution in a straight-forward manner. The challenge of Cairnes – What economic truth was ever derived or ever will be derived by the mathematical method – has been answered hundreds of times in subsequent years. Here is a further striking case where a literary problem, old in Cairnes's time, could not be rigorously solved until the development a decade ago of the "duality theorem" of linear programming. Of course, could we confront Cairnes with this fulfillment of his challenge, he would probably dismiss the whole problem as a trivial one and besides, *after* he had grasped its solution, he might regard it as obvious. There are some competitions you just can't win!

12. The definitive solution for the ratios of prices, rents, and wage comes from solving a maximum problem in linear programming that is the so-called "dual" to the minimum problem of (10A). Until this decade, no economist of literary or mathematical persuasion realized that just as the ideal competitive system acts so as to get as much outputs with as little inputs as is possible, so does it act as if it were trying to maximize the factor return to the minimized input. This sounds obvious, when stated, but its meaning is not at all obvious and to fail to realize this is to convict one's self of superficiality.

Specifically, subject to the *nm* price inequalities of (11A)

$$\frac{p_i}{w} - r(j)b_i(j) \leqq a_i(j) \qquad (i = 1, \ldots, n; j = 1, \ldots, m),$$

we are to pick non-negative $[p_1/w, \ldots, p_n/w; r(1), \ldots, r(m)]$ to

$$(12A) \quad \text{maximize } x^* = \frac{p_1}{w}y_1 + \frac{p_2}{w}y_2 + \ldots + \frac{p_n}{w}y_n - r(1)L(1)$$
$$- r(2)L(2) - \ldots - r(m)L(m).$$

The duality theorem tells us that the maximal $x^* = X[y_1, \ldots, y_n; L(1), \ldots, L(m)]$ must be the same in magnitude as the minimized labor of the original problem. We can regard x^* as a maximized total wage return, measured in labor hours; or multiplying through by w, as maximized total wage return in any wage units; or dividing through by p_i/w, as the real wage return measured in the ith good as *numeraire*. Lest anyone think the formulation gives any comfort to those who hanker for a labor theory of value, I must point out that instead of minimizing labor we could have minimized any grade of good land and formulated our dual problem in such terms.

I should add that the formulation (12A) provides a solution to the over-and-under determinacy problem raised in 1932 concerning the Walras-Cassel fixed-coefficients production equations.[27]

---

[27] See *L.P.E.A.*, Chap. 13.

13. From the $x = X[y_1, \ldots, L(m)]$ function of our original problem (10A) alone, we can define prices and rents without the dual formulation. It can be mathematically shown that

$$\frac{\partial X(y_1, \ldots; \ldots L(m))}{\partial y_i} = \frac{p_i}{w} \quad (i = 1, \ldots, n)$$

$$-\frac{\partial X(y_1, \ldots; \ldots L(m))}{\partial L(j)} = \frac{r(j)}{w} \quad (j = 1, \ldots, m). \tag{13A}$$

Total rent

$$= \sum_1^m \frac{r(j)}{w} L(j) = -X[y_1, \ldots; \ldots L(m)] + \sum_1^m y_i \frac{\partial X[y_1, \ldots; \ldots, L(m)]}{\partial y_i},$$

where Euler's theorem on homogeneous functions of the first degree has become applicable to $X[y_1, \ldots; \ldots, L(m)]$ by virtue of our constant-returns-to-scale assumptions.

Again, with or without Ricardian assumptions of long-run constant real wages, the relative shares of total wages and rent will be dependent on the pattern of consumption demand. And it is no longer true that an increase in labor must always increase the absolute total of rent: only if all y_i are increased in proportion can we be sure that absolute land rent then rises, and even here the *relative* distribution of income can move in either direction or stand still.

14. The time has come to consider the variable-coefficient case favored both by Ricardo and later neoclassical economists. The minimum problem (10A) still stands, but the a's and b's are no longer given constants, being instead related by the mn production relations

$$1 = f_i[a_i(j), b_i(j); j] \quad (i = 1, \ldots, n; j = 1, \ldots, m). \tag{14A}$$

Unless each production function admits of but a finite number of alternative activities, such a minimum problem is no longer strictly a linear programming problem; but it will have a determinate solution.

In the infinite-activity case where the production functions everywhere have second partial derivatives, the full conditions of equilibrium can be defined in terms of marginal productivity inequalities. Combining the theory of nonlinear programming[28] with the spirit of neoclassical economics, we can

---

[28] See *L.P.E.A.*, Chap. 8.

reformulate the augmented (10A) and (12A) problem in terms of a saddle-point requirement. Thus, the "labor" expression

$$\Phi = \sum_{i=1}^{n}\sum_{j=1}^{m}x_i(j) + \sum_{i=1}^{n}\frac{p_i}{w}\left\{y_i - \sum_{j=1}^{m}f_i[x_i(j), L_i(j); j]\right\}$$

$$+ \sum_{i=1}^{m}\frac{r(j)}{w}\left\{\sum_{i=1}^{n}L_i(j) - L(j)\right\}$$

$$(15A)$$

must be at a *minimum* with respect to the output-input variables $[x_i(j), L_i(j)]$ and at a *maximum* with respect to the price-rent variables $[p_i/w, r(j)/w]$.

This implies firstly that the bracket expressions are all nonpositive; and that, if a particular bracket expression is not zero, its price or rent coefficient must be zero and must correspond to a free output or input.

Secondly, the saddlepoint condition implies the following marginal productivity conditions, derived from differentiating Φ:

$$1 \geqq \frac{p_i}{w}\frac{\partial f_i[x_i(j), L_i(j); j]}{\partial x_i(j)}$$

$$(i = 1, \ldots, n; j = 1, \ldots m) \qquad (16A)$$

$$\frac{r(j)}{w} \geqq \frac{p_i}{w}\frac{\partial f_i[x_i(j), L_i(j); j]}{\partial L_i(j)},$$

it being understood that an inequality rather than equality implies in each case that the output or input in question is zero. The classical laws of diminishing returns will guarantee the convexity needed to assure genuine maximum and minimum conditions.

Ricardo's intensive-margin differential measurement of rent using the last unit of labor that pays no rent does point in the direction of the correct conditions (16A). But we see how much implicit theorizing there remains in his formulation.

15. We can dispense with the assumption that marginal productivities $\partial f_i/\partial x_i(j)$ and $\partial f_i/L_i(j)$ exist everywhere. In fact an interesting case is provided by the assumption that each industry has only a finite number of different $[a_i(j), b_i(j)]$ possibilities on each land. (Of course, "mixtures" of these provide an infinite gradation of possibilities.) Such a case is easily converted into a standard linear programming problem by defining nonnegative activity levels $[y_i(j)'; y_i(j)''; \ldots]$ corresponding to each possible $[a_i(j)'; b_i(j)'; a_i(j)'', b_i(j)''; \ldots]$ technical method. Then the conditions of (10A),

$\sum\limits_{j} y_i(j) \geqq y_i, \sum\limits_{i} b_i(j) y_i(j) \leqq L(j), \sum\limits_{i} \sum\limits_{j} a_i(j) y_i(j)$ a minimum, now simply become

Subject to

$$\sum_{j} y_i(j)' + \sum_{j} y_i(j)'' + \ldots \geqq y_i \ (i = 1, \ldots, n)$$

$$\sum_{i} b_i(j)' y_i(j)' + \sum_{i} b_i(j)'' y_i(j)'' + \ldots \leqq L(j), (j = 1, \ldots, m)$$

pick non-negative variables $[y_i(j)', y_i(j)'', \ldots]$ to minimize

$$x = \sum_{i} \sum_{j} a_i(j)' y_i(j)' + \sum_{i} \sum_{j} a_i(j)'' y_i(j)'' + \ldots, \qquad (17A)$$

a standard linear programming problem.[29]

In the limit as the number of alternative activities becomes infinite, we can approach as close as we like to the smooth neoclassical marginal productivities.

17. The theory of rent will be complete if I sketch the corresponding treatment when land takes on a continuum of different fertilities. Our discussion can be quite brief because the assumed circular patterns now become quite artificial: a point M where corn is most efficiently produced is not likely also to be the point where velvets are first to be produced; so relations that depend on a radius R are no longer worthy of detailed mathematical analysis.

I shall go directly to the smooth variable-coefficient case. The formulation (15A) suggests how we should generalize the one-good continuum formulation (5A). Now let (u, v) be generalized space co-ordinates, with each point of space giving a "density" production function for each good.

Now we set up a saddlepoint labor expression like Φ of (15A), but replacing $\sum_1^m$ everywhere by a double integral over the (u, v) space, $\iint \ldots du dv$. The conditions of equilibrium will, disregarding all transport costs, everywhere be

---

[29] Alternatively in (10A), we can regard n as greater than the number of distinct goods by the number of alternative ways of producing actual goods. So the condition $\Sigma y_i(j) \geq y_i$ can now be added for all y_i produced by different methods but really representing the same goods. Subject then to the new conditions, we solve the problem in the (10A) form, interpreting the result in terms of optimal methods to be used. It may be noted that no industry ever has to use more than two different methods on any one spot at any one time.

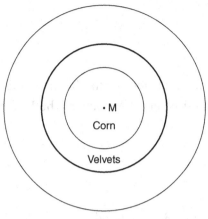

Figure IX

$$\frac{p_i}{w}\frac{\partial f_i[\quad ; u, v]}{\partial x_i} \leqq 1 \qquad (i = 1, \ldots, n)$$

$$\frac{p_i}{w}\frac{\partial f_i[\quad ; u, v]}{\partial L_i} \leqq \frac{r(u, v)}{w},$$

(18A)

it being understood that an inequality for an i at some point means that nothing of good i is produced there.

Thünen-like circles of production are shown in Figure IX. Presumably certain lands will be definitely better for some goods than for others – depending on the changing pattern of demand.

The only significant difference between the case of finite and infinite land varieties is the likelihood that the finite case will produce corners in the $X(y_1, \ldots, y_n)$ function. In either case, in terms of suitably generalized partial derivatives, total rent is given by $-X + \sum y_i \partial X / \partial y_i$, a function rising as all y's rise in proportion but with few other predictable properties.

Massachusetts Institute of Technology

A Modern Treatment of the Ricardian Economy:
II. Capital and Interest Aspects of the Pricing Process

Back to the beginning, 168. – Time and interest, 170. – Failure of the labor theory, 171. – A simple corn economy, 173. – The special timeless case, 173. – The extreme Torrens-Ricardo case, 174. – Land scarcity and falling interest, 176. – A long-run, constant floor for interest, 178. – The land theory restated, 179. – A final word, 181.

BACK TO THE BEGINNING

28. Part I has neglected the role of time in the productive process. To this I now turn.

Both Smith and Ricardo speak in parables when they refer to an earlier golden age when land rent and interest can be neglected. There never was such a golden age in human history; but we are entitled to think of this device as an ancient form of the method of successive approximations, in which one first assumes very simple models before introducing various complications into them.

The way we got rid of the complication of land rent at the beginning of Part I is really different from the way we might hope to get rid of the complication of interest. In Part I we began by assuming that good land is so superabundant that its rent is free and can be neglected. Certainly one can imagine a Europe peopled by so few cavemen as to make this a logical possibility. But can we imagine an early age in which all production relationships take place in an instant, so that time is perfectly ignorable? I do not think we can. Production operations must always have taken place over a period of time.

An alternative formulation would be to assume that our early system is "time saturated." By this I mean that so much accumulation had taken place in the system's past as to have driven the interest rate down to zero or to a negligible level. It is then still true that outputs become available after inputs in time; but the market place is supposed to evaluate these time differences as if they were unimportant. What about this interpretation? I do not think that any classical economist would have been such a utopian antediluvian as to have imagined that ever in the golden past capital was superabundant in the same sense as land might have been superabundant. (Recall that Smith uses the words "*before* stock had accumulated.") And certainly such a model would not provide a convenient springboard for the study of the effects of accumulation in lowering the interest rate.

We must instead, I think, imagine a golden age which was not very golden – one in which life was short and brutish, in very part because of the extreme shortage of capital. In such a world we might still hope to be able to neglect interest at a first approximation provided the interest rate were so high as to force the system into using very short-lived projects exclusively. (Alternatively, we may turn back the clock of technology and envisage a system with only very short-lived processes available to it.) If all the delay periods in the system are sufficiently short – say of the magnitude of a day rather than a year – then even if the interest rate is quite high expressed as a rate per annum, interest per day and the relative share of interest in the total may be so small as to be at first neglectable. And so if we persist with the assumption of free land, the simple labor theory of value may serve as a good approximation, as in Figure I of Part I.

29. When, however, we leave the realm of parables and nursery tales, the phenomenon of interest or profit[1] does raise its head and we must take it explicitly into account.

As accumulation lowers the interest rate, time-consuming processes which previously had not paid will now become worthwhile. This the classical economists, along with any observers of technology, would presumably have recognized[2] even if they did not explicitly foresee a Böhm-Bawerkian

---

[1] Profit in the real world consists (1) partly of implicit wages, paid for the services provided by the entrepreneur himself (including management services); (2) partly of monopoly returns to "contrived scarcities," and imperfectly competitive situations; (3) partly of the *ex ante* and *ex post* rewards to uncertainty bearing; and (4) partly of the "surplus" residual or rents paid to factors in inelastic supply. Assuming perfect competition and sidestepping the important problems connected with uncertainty, we need not distinguish implicit factor returns from explicit factor returns and we can strictly identify the profit rate with the pure interest rate.

[2] That Ricardo was aware of substitution possibilities induced by changes in factor costs is shown by passages like the following: "Now if the wages of labour rise 10 per cent . . ., he will no longer hesitate, but will at once purchase the machine. . ." David Ricardo, *Works,*

model in which some dimension of time intensity can be continuously varied so as to increase the outputs of primary inputs. Still another way that more time consuming processes become relevant is through the process of irreversible technological change and invention, even though the older economists were not so meticulous as moderns in separating out reversible, induced changes from irreversible changes of exogenous or induced type.

TIME AND INTEREST

30. We now no longer ignore the fact that labor and land do not instantaneously produce outputs. Ricardo, following Smith and the Physiocrats, thinks of each worker (and each acre, if land is scarce) as engaged in moving raw materials towards completion – "adding value" we would say today. But the worker needs finished consumption goods today and ordinarily does not want to be paid out of the *ultimate* finished fruits of his today's labor. The employer "advances" to the worker finished consumption goods; such a primitive "wage fund" theory regards these advances as "capital" and supposes wages today to be limited by the magnitude of the available finished wage goods "destined" to be paid out as wages. The men (and acres) receive today less than their tomorrow's fruits. The capitalist or entrepreneur receives the difference as profit or interest on the money value of the capital he has advanced.

In brief, employers hire current men and acres and now pay them money wages and rents. These factors push the employer's inventory of unfinished goods towards completion, and when the goods are finished the employer sells them. Under free entry and absence of uncertainty, competition ensures that the employer earns the market rate of interest (per annum or per day) on the value of his goods in process as determined in the auction markets for unfinished or finished goods. Per year or per day the money flow of society's final product (finished consumption goods plus net capital formation) exceeds the sum of wages (and rents) by the interest return of capitalists.[3]

31. Some may say that workers (and landlords) are "exploited" by the "interest discounting" of their ("ultimate") productivity entailed by the

Sraffa ed., I, 61. Any who attribute to Ricardo a fixed-proportions model do him an injustice.

[3] If land is not free, its rent can also be regarded as the interest return on land's capitalized market value. Though one saver can "invest" in land by buying part of the limited supply from some seller, society cannot create more of the inelastically-supplied original and indestructible land. Operationally, it would be hard to separate improvements in land that are like other capital projects from the original supply of land.

lapse of time between inputs and outputs. Others may say that workers are free to be paid in their current unfinished products without any discount; but such unfinished products, when the workers now try to sell them, would be found to have a market price lower than the price of finished goods – lower by exactly the amount of interest that the workers could earn on their sale proceeds in the time between now and completion.[4] Such people argue that there is no "exploitation" here, no more than in the case of a Kansas landlord who gets the full Kansas value of his land's marginal product, which naturally involves a discounting of the full Chicago value for the transport cost across space.

There is no need here to go into the welfare economics of the problem. Those who approve or disapprove both recognize (1) that a positive market rate of interest coupled with the fact (2) that it takes months to change grape juice to wine means that interest receivers will share in the gross or net output of the economy. Of course, if the interest rate were lower, if corn grew faster, if nature were kinder, if brains were better and muscles harder – in short if pies were bigger and others' shares less, the world and things would be different!

32. The above section deals only with circulating capital: i.e., with productive processes in which labor transforms one material into another. Ricardo was also familiar with the kind of fixed capital represented by a machine. Fixed capital working with labor and materials produces new materials *and* also produces as a by-product (slightly older) fixed capital. Such is the modern distinction between fixed and circulating capital. There is no implication, as Ricardo at first may have thought, that the durability of fixed capital is necessarily greater than that of circulating capital: wine or redwood trees may be circulating capital while a brief candle may be fixed capital. Both circulating and fixed capital, which are not to be confused with Marx's variable and constant capital, create insuperable difficulties for an exact labor theory of value – as Ricardo well knew.

FAILURE OF THE LABOR THEORY

33. The simplest model to show that relative exchange values cannot be predicted from the labor theory of value alone is the following. Let there be two goods as before, y_1 and y_2. Let each require a_1 and a_2 of labor per unit;

---

[4] For simplicity I here neglect possible needed later factor inputs; these can be taken account of in an obvious manner. See also my "Wages and Interest: A Modern Dissection of Marxian Economic Models", *American Economic Review*, XLVII (Dec. 1957), 884–912.

and let the land requirements b_1 and b_2 be neglectable because land is so
abundant as to be free. But now assume, as Jevons later was to do, that
inputs in the two industries produce their outputs exactly θ_1 and θ_2 periods
later, respectively.

Then if i is the interest rate per period, the steady-state cost of production
equations for prices become

$$p_1 = wa_1(1+i)^{\theta_1} \quad p_2 = wa_2(1+i)^{\theta_2}, \tag{17}$$

with

$$\frac{p_2}{p_1} = \frac{a_2}{a_1}(1+i)^{\theta_2-\theta_1}. \tag{18}$$

From the embodied labor coefficients a_i alone, we can no longer predict
unchanging relative prices – except in the singular cases where the time
intensities of the industries are exactly equal, $\theta_1 = \theta_2$; or where the interest
rate i is literally zero.

When he came to write his *Principles*, Ricardo realized this. But instead of
cutting his losses,[5] he continued to toy with standards of durability that
involved one year periods or that represented the social average. And he was
even under the illusion[6] that he was making great improvements on Adam
Smith's pragmatic doctrine that price equals the sum of all costs of production. (To have done that he would have had to anticipate Leon Walras's
doctrine of general equilibrium, which made sure that it had enough
equations to determine *all* the constituents of price.)

34. In (18) a change in the profit rate will vary the price ratios between
goods of different durability. This change in the interest rate is associated
with what Ricardo[7] calls an opposite change in "wages," meaning by this not
as one might at first think, money wages, but rather real wages. (This effect
can be seen from regarding the first equation in (17) as determining the
price of corn, the sole wage good: then the real wage $w/p_1 = 1/a_1(1+i)^{\theta_1}$,
an inverse function of the interest rate i.)

Ricardo is again wrong to think that he can neglect effects of these
changes on rent by going to the external margin where no rent is paid. A
change in the interest rate or real wage can be presumed to change the
location of the extensive margin. Because he insufficiently realized this,

---

[5]   As he was tempted to do in his famous 1820 letter to McCulloch, *Works*, I, xxxix, xl.
[6]   *Works*, I, xxxvi, xxxvii.
[7]   *Works*, I, xxxviii, 53, 56–63, 66.

Ricardo repeatedly set up too sharp an opposition between wages and interest, not sufficiently realizing that the problem is really a three-factor one.

A SIMPLE CORN ECONOMY

35. We have been using the interest rate before explicitly introducing the conditions needed to determine it. The time has come to try to come to grips with this problem. Rather than beginning with the complex case of many goods, I shall first follow the example of West and Ricardo and concentrate on the one-good example of corn. How does the fact that there must be a passage of time between inputs and outputs affect wages, rent, interest, and the distribution of income? Insight is provided by the simplest example where corn, y_1, appears one period ($\theta_1 = 1$) after the application of labor, x_1, and homogeneous land L_1.

As in Sections 7–17 of Part I of this paper, all the technological facts are summarized by the (a_1, b_1) technical coefficients giving the needed amounts of labor and land per unit of corn. (These coefficients may be taken as technically given, or we may wish to assume the variable-coefficient case in which more a_1 may be substituted smoothly for less b_1.) We can complete the system by specifying c_1, the number of units of corn needed by each man to insure that the labor supply will be exactly reproduced.

We saw that $1 - c_1 a_1 < 0$ would imply that population becomes extinct. The interesting case is where land is still free and $1 - c_1 a_1 > 0$. Statically, this implies a "contradiction." Corn cannot sell for its labor cost simultaneously with labor selling for its corn cost, since $1 - c_1 a_1 > 0$ implies the incompatibility of the two cost-of-production equations

$$p_1 = a_1 w \text{ and } w = c_1 p_1. \tag{19}$$

Which relation must give? Actually, both of them must be made non-statical to take account of the dynamic dating implicit in the problem.

THE SPECIAL TIMELESS CASE

36. If corn output were producible instantaneously but periods of human gestation were nine months and periods of infancy were measured in decades, then undoubtedly under competition the first equation would be valid and the one to be jettisoned would be the second equation: so long as land continued superabundant, the Ricardo-Malthus subsistence real wage

would be irrelevant to the higher actual market real wage. Workers could earn "surplus rent over subsistence" or surplus quasi-rent. Surplus rent on what? On their temporary scarcity! Biological factors and the height of the real wage above subsistence would determine the geometric rate of population and output growth.

But what about the long run? So long as land remains abundant, no matter how long the run this state of affairs with real wage equal to $1/a_1$ could continue forever. (West, better perhaps than Ricardo, realized that in America wages had remained and were remaining higher than subsistence.) What has to give in (19) is the assumption of equilibrium or stationariness of population, no other contradiction occurring. Let us be clear about this: with land free and production instantaneous, there is no possibility of exploiting labor or depriving men of their full product; they need only move to the frontier. Only by withholding from labor something it needs for production can you get it to share with you the total produce. And then *whose* produce it is that is being shared becomes a welfare-economics or semantic question.[8]

THE EXTREME TORRENS-RICARDO CASE

38. It is unrealistic to get around (19)'s contradiction by making corn production instantaneous. Instead of holding the first equation and dropping the second, Ricardo followed Torrens in tending to neglect the long time period it would take for population to bring the real wage back to the conventional-subsistence level. This is in accordance with his tendency to treat long-run relations as if they held in the shorter run and also represents a one-sided resolution of (19)'s contradiction.

However unrealistic is such a practice, it does provide us with an instructive, extreme case. Now the second equation of (19) is assumed to hold instantaneously, but the lag in time between labor input and corn output is

---

[8] We have already seen how the ultimate scarcity of homogeneous or heterogeneous land and the law of diminishing returns would, in a zero-interest or timeless system, cause population to grow until the new a_1 coefficient at the external (or speaking loosely, at the intensive) margin will be such as to just satisfy $1 - c_1 a_1 = 0$. Hence, at such margins (19)'s costs of production of corn and of people are consistent. *Men on the margin* then do work twelve hours per day, and twelve hours per day is just enough to produce *their* subsistence. Men on good land, or the hypothetical first men applied to good land, will in working twelve hours produce their own subsistence and, let's say, an equal amount of produce for landlords. To say that such men produce in six hours *their own* subsistence and work six hours producing *surplus value* for the landlord is always my privilege: but little insight into the laws of motion of the system or its distribution is provided by such a formulation.

explicitly introduced. Still keeping land superabundant with rent free and keeping $\theta_1 = 1$, we now write (19) as

$$p_1 = w_1 a_1(1 + i), \; w_1 = c_1 p_1; \; \text{or } 1 + i = \frac{1}{c_1 a_1}. \tag{20}$$

The rate of interest is now determinable from the (a_1, c_1) coefficients alone!

This is what Ricardo had in mind already in 1813, before the Malthus-West rent theory of 1814 had been published. Ricardo believed that only the limitation on land could explain a falling rate of profit: for if one could always tack on new islands to the existing England, accumulation would spend itself in expanding the scale of population and production with no law of diminishing returns ever coming into play. Neither West nor Ricardo would have believed in Marx's falling rate of profit – on the basis of Marx's usual willingness to ignore rent and to postulate an inexhaustible reserve army of the unemployed.

39. Though Ricardo had many children, one often wonders whether he knew the biological facts of life, so content is he with the assumption that labor will *soon* adjust to its long-run horizontal wage at the subsistence level. Actually, it is unrealistic and inconsistent to make either one of the equations in (19) hold as if it referred to a timeless adjustment. As in equation (4) of Part I, any discrepancy in the equalities of (19) will act as an "error signal" to set up certain dynamic adjustment processes both in the creation of people and of goods: thus, the percentage rate of population growth might be a rising function of the discrepancy of the real wage and the subsistence level; and each greater profit discrepancy between market price and labor cost alone might be expected to give rise to a greater rate of capital accumulation.

I shall not stop to write down a specific model of these dynamic processes. But the general outline of the results is reasonably clear and can be related to the discussion in my cited paper on Marx.

First, it would probably be most natural to assume that some accumulation is going on. This is spending itself in population increase – in a widening of capital. The real wage is above the subsistence-reproduction level by enough to coax out the described rate of endogenous labor increase. The interest rate is positive but less than the $1/a_1 c_1$ level appropriate to instantaneous population growth, the remainder being what has been referred to as the quasi-rent to labor's temporary (but recurring) scarcity.

The above process *could* go along in a geometric or exponential steady state, with only scale expanding and with unchanging wage and profit rates.

But Ricardo is wrong to think that in the absence of land shortage the profit rate cannot permanently possibly fall. It can. Provided the propensity to save out of interest income is sufficiently large relative to the requirements for extensive growth of the system, there may actually be a deepening of capital. Capitalists will be trying to save more than mere growth in scale is using; this means they will be bidding among themselves for existing labor, thereby raising the real wage, and undermining the profit rate, and in all probability finding that more roundabout processes now pay. This drop in the profit rate could go on forever. But it is unlikely, so the classicists thought, to bring the profit rate down below a critical equilibrium level. This asymptotic equilibrium level for i will be reached when interest has fallen low enough to reduce the incomes of savers enough to call forth from them a pace of accumulation no larger than can be absorbed in mere duplication of population and scale.[9]

LAND SCARCITY AND FALLING INTEREST

40. For Ricardo and West a dynamic model which neglects scarcity of land is like a whodunit without a corpse. How does the using up of all the available best land affect the pattern of development? We have seen that as more and more men work on the best land their marginal returns decline; this can be expressed by saying that some kind of an intensive marginal a_1 coefficient goes up, which is the reason why recourse may also be had to poorer qualities of land; and if lands are of continuous grades of quality, we can also concentrate on the extensive marginal a_1, which corresponds to the high labor requirements on that piece of land which is just worth cultivating when you have to pay no rent for it at all.

With a_1 no longer a constant but now a variable over an indefinite range, Ricardo no longer has a determinate formula for the interest rate in terms of technological coefficients alone. (The matter is even worse if large θ_1's can be substituted for smaller a_1's at the margin.) But he correctly felt that the process of accumulation would entail a steadily falling profit rate and higher rent as land became more intensively cultivated and commanded higher rents. As we have seen he rather exaggerated the speed with which real wages would revert to their conventional-subsistence level, and we can cling

[9] The critical level might be reached from below, with i rising as accumulation belatedly catches up with population increase. The critical steady state might be at a profit rate so low as to kill off all accumulation and growth. Indeed once scarce land is taken into account, most classical economists would expect accumulation to lead eventually to an interest rate at the floor determined by capital's long-run "subsistence" level of supply, as we shall see.

to the Smith notion that, depending upon how fast accumulation is causing the system to advance, real wages will remain somewhat above the subsistence level.

For intramarginal and marginal lands respectively, we can write down the formulas

$$p_1 = (wa'_1 + rb'_1)(1+i)^{\theta'_1}, \quad p_1 = wa''_1(1+i)^{\theta''_1} \tag{21}$$

But even if we knew the real wage to be $1/c_1$, these are not sufficient equations to determine the interest rate, there being a suitable a_1'' to satisfy the last equation for *any* interest rate. Again, we face the fact that the external and internal margins vary in direct response to drops in the interest rate – as Ricardo well realized.

41. The classical economists never did write down an explicit model to determine in each moving short run the level of interest and of the other variables of the system. We cannot criticize them too harshly for this in that the neoclassical economists also – save in very special cases – failed to write down explicit models which determined rigorously the time shape of interest and other variables. These failures seem due to the intrinsic difficulty of getting into two- or few-dimensional diagrams the complexity of the real world's vectors of diverse capital goods and time processes.

Most of the classicists spoke vaguely of some kind of a capital stock or wage fund. By analogy with what happens when you increase the quantity of something so apparently concrete as land or labor, they felt that accumulation of more of this capital stuff would bring down its price – the profit or interest rate. Qualitatively, these vague notions do, I think, lead to the correct insights into the dynamics of a developing, competitive system. But we must not be under any illusion that such notions go far beyond the language of parable.[10]

However, the problem of the storyteller must not be confused with the action of the market place. In the real world engineers combine inputs over time to produce outputs. And merchants and consumers buy and sell securities and goods in various markets. Were it not for imperfections of competition – whose intrinsic difficulties for the analyst are tied up with the *uncertainty of the future* – we could write down in great detail the full set of

---

[10] Jevons, Böhm-Bawerk, Wicksell and others carried the parable farther. See also Robert Dorfman, Paul A. Samuelson, and Robert M. Solow, *Linear Programming and Economic Analysis* (New York: McGraw-Hill, 1958), Chaps. 11, 12; and P. A. Samuelson and R. M. Solow, "A Complete Capital Model Involving Heterogeneous Capital Goods," this *Journal*, LXX (Nov. 1956), 537–62.

equations for all the diverse micro-processes that are going on. We would talk of the interest rate for each period along with a host of other inter-temporal price ratios. We might also talk of capital asset values, as determined in competitive market places, and as might be added by the recording statistician. But no market would directly hinge on such a defined capital aggregate, and our rigorous theory of interest and general equilibrium could eschew completely the use of any homogeneous aggregate of capital. Thus, we could hope to sidestep completely the index number problem that every social aggregate, including Capital with a capital C, is known to involve intrinsically.

A LONG-RUN, CONSTANT FLOOR FOR INTEREST

42. One of the reasons the classical economists had so weak a theory for short-run interest and wages was that they had so strong a long-run theory. If you believed, as Ricardo somehow did, that wages would soon settle down to their floor as determined by a long-run horizontal schedule of supply, what was the point in elaborating a theory to explain the ephemeral deviations from this level? The same, but to lesser degree, might be said of the long-run level of interest. Ricardo is not so explicit as John Stuart Mill and other classicists, but he does at times come close to the notion of a horizontal long-run supply curve for interest like that for wages. Thus, he says

"Long indeed before this period [of zero interest rate], the very low rate of profits will have arrested all accumulation . . .

"I have already said, that long before this state . . ., there would be no motive for accumulation; for no one accumulates but with a view to make accumulation productive. . . . *The farmer and manufacturer can no more live without profit, than the labourer without wages.* Their motive for accumulation . . . will cease altogether when their profits are so low as not to afford them an adequate compensation for their trouble, and the risk which they must necessarily encounter in employing their capital productively."[11]

43. For the purpose, therefore, of seeing how my land theory of value can be extended to a Ricardian system involving time, I shall interpret the system as literally having a long-run *SS* schedule for interest like the one shown in Figure IV for wages. Above that critical interest rate accumulation will be

[11] *Works,* I, 120, 122; my italics. The last sentence might possibly be interpreted as being compatible with a zero interest rate, once we allow for wages of management and *ex post* losses. It might also open the door to an equilibrium with Keynesian stagnation rather than full employment.

taking place; below it, decumulation will be taking place so as to restore it; at it, there will be a stationary equilibrium.

We have then in addition to our (a,b,c) coefficients one new important constant – the long-run interest rate. Let us label this $i = d$. And we must now turn back from a simple one-good economy involving corn alone to a many-good model. The total of homogeneous land, L, is also taken as a given.

THE LAND THEORY RESTATED

44. Under the postulated conditions, it then follows that my "Ricardian land theory of value" remains intact in the long run.

1. All long-run magnitudes remain directly proportional to the supply of land L.
2. The prices of all goods produced (final and intermediate) and the wage rate all remain in determinate ratio to the rent rate r, *independently of the quantitative pattern of consumption demand.*
3. While the absolute level of total rent or *produit net* depends only on the a,b,c,d coefficients independently of the composition of consumption demand, the absolute and relative sizes of the gross returns to wages and interest will depend upon the quantitative pattern of landlord and capitalist consumption demand.

45. To see all this I suggest we consider a three-good example. Let y_1 (corn) and y_2 (velvets) involve only circulating capital in their production; but follow Ricardo in letting y_2 have, say, twice the time interval that y_1 has between first application of land and labor and ultimate product. (I.e., $\theta_2 = 2\theta_1 = 2$.) Finally, let y_3 (gold) require in addition to labor and land (and one time interval for their action to take effect) also fixed capital in the form of a machine (and one time interval for its co-operative action with land and labor to take effect).

This simple three-good case presents all the complicating difficulties that rightly bothered Ricardo. It involves circulating capital of different degrees of durability. And it involves fixed as well as circulating capital. (Indeed, since the third industry uses new and old machines, we really have a fourth industry that produces machines.)

I now proceed to write down the cost-of-production relations of this system, in order of their simplicity.

$$\text{(i) } w = p_1 c_1$$
$$\text{(ii) } p_1 = (wa_1 + rb_1)(1 + d)$$
$$\text{(iii) } p_2 = (wa_2 + rb_2)(1 + d)^2$$
$$\text{(iv) } p_0 = (wa_0 + rb_0)(1 + d) \tag{22}$$
$$\text{(v) } p_3 + e_3 p_0' = (wa_3 + rb_3 + p_0 f_3)(1 + d)$$
$$\text{(vi) } p_3 \;\; = (wa_3' + rb_3' + p_0' g_3')(1 + d)$$

The first equation is Ricardo's long-run corn theory of the real wage. The second gives corn's cost of production, as in (17). Before going any farther, we can solve equations (i) and (ii) by simple substitution to determine in terms of the given (a, b, c, d) coefficients the corn level of rent, or corn's price in terms of rent. I leave this to the reader.

Now consider the first three equations alone. By themselves they are enough conditions to enable us to solve for $(w/r, p_1/r, p_2/r)$ in terms of the (a, b, c, d) coefficients alone.

The last three equations are more complicated because they involve the use of fixed capital. Thus, they introduce the unknown price of a new machine, p_0, as determined in (iv) by its cost of production. More complicated is (v), which gives the cost of the third good, gold's p_3; but now it takes f_3 units of the new machine along with labor and land to make gold; and as a by-product, so to speak, the process also leaves us with e_3 old machines, each worth an unknown price p_0'. The last equation gives the same p_3 for gold produced with old machines.

In all we have six equations to determine the six unknowns $(w/r, p_1/r, p_2/r, p_0/r, p_0'/r, p_3/r)$; and provided that (generalized) Hawkins-Simon conditions are satisfied, these will determine unique positive solutions. What is important to emphasize is that *if the primary factors returns (r,d) are given us, the resulting pattern of prices is quite independent of the mix of consumption demand.* Equations (22) make this quite clear in the case of fixed (a, b, c, e, f, θ) coefficients. But even if there were a finite, or infinite, set of substitutable processes in (ii)–(vi), a change in consumers' demand for corn, velvets, or gold would not make any new substitutions profitable.

46. A sketchy proof is given in P. A. Samuelson, "Prices of Factors and Goods In General Equilibrium,"[12] But it needs to be modified to take account of the joint production inherent in (v). Ordinarily, jointness of production will rule out the "substitutability theorem." Thus, if people

[12] *Review of Economic Studies*, XXI (1953–54), 19.

wanted to consume old machines directly, as well as use them to produce gold, a shift in tastes towards such old machines would tend to raise the price p_0', and probably to lower p_3. Mathematically, new (a, b, e, f) coefficients would be substituted. Or if these were fixed, the last equation would become an inequality once it became too expensive to use old machines to produce gold; but in the production of gold with new machines, it is gold which, so to speak, now becomes the by-product to the production of such valued old machines that are now highly in demand. However, when we rule out the possibility that machines are anything but intermediate goods, each belonging solely to one consumers good industry, the substitutability theorem is saved.

Recall Section 25's qualification concerning joint consumer goods, venison and deer skin. Similarly, if corn stalks were used in gold production, or if old gold machines were used to produce velvets, the substitutability theorem would be lost. For it to be valid, all jointness must be *within* each vertically integrated single consumer good.

47. *Net product* for society would be proportional to land L. Since there is no accumulation, net product would equal the gross value of all consumers goods minus the goods consumed by laborers and by interest receivers. Why define net product so? In post-Ricardian language, because there is no consumer's or producer's surplus enjoyed by laborers or capitalists, their returns just being enough to cover their costs.

The equation for net product would be

$$\frac{p_1}{r} Y_1 + \frac{p_2}{r} Y_2 + \frac{p_3}{r} Y_3 = L \tag{23}$$

where the p's come from (22).

While the total value of net product is unaffected by changes in the mix of (Y_i) demand, the total of wages and of interest-bearing capital will definitely depend on that mix. Thus, if landlords (or capitalists) want more labor-intensive goods, the short-run rise in wages will be wiped out by a permanent increase in population, with the typical man ending up no better off than before. Likewise, if final demand moves towards capital-intensive goods, the total interest return and capital value will permanently rise but the return per dollar, d, will stay the same by hypothesis.

A FINAL WORD

49. After examining Ricardo-like models, what feeling are we left with? Were the classical economists fools? Were they gods? What were they?

I for one am left with mixed feelings. Ricardo's logical skills have been, I think, somewhat exaggerated.[13] But they were very considerable. He would have made a most excellent modern economist! Despite though the high native abilities of the ancients, we have advanced a long way ahead of their discussions. Poor as our knowledge and insights are, they are way ahead of those of our predecessors.

In particular we are more humble. They declared so many things to be necessarily so that we today recognize as not having to be so. This is, in a sense, a step backward. How exciting to be able to assert definitely that invention of a machine cannot do this and must do that! But, alas, dull as it may be, the modern theorist must face the facts of life – the infinite multiplicity of patterns that can emerge in actuality. Good, advanced theory must be the antidote for overly-simple, intuitive theory.

[13] If Ricardo has been overrated, Smith has in our day perhaps been underrated. I mean as a theorist.

Mathematical Vindication of Ricardo on Machinery

Ricardo is shown to be right that machinery can hurt wages and reduce output. A dramatic robot example reveals Wicksell's error in believing that Pareto optimality calls for no drop in total output from a viable invention. Under Ricardo's axiom that labor supply adjusts to keep wages at the subsistence level, he can correctly deduce on a market-clearing basis a rise in his net product (rent plus interest), while the greater drop in population and total wages results in a reduction in his gross product (rent plus interest plus wages).

The chapter on machinery that Ricardo added to the third edition of his *Principles* (1821) has generally been suspect among his contemporary economists and his posterity. I regard this suspicion as unjustified and consider it the best single chapter in this overpraised work.

Presented here is a simple classical scenario in which the invention of a robot machine does, as he said was possible, reduce the demand for labor permanently, reduce the total of wages, reduce what Ricardo defines to be the gross product, and cause the population to decline. Moreover, the scenario takes place along the lines of his arithmetic example. The behavior equations underlying my model are precisely those that have been used by Pasinetti (1960) and Samuelson (1959a, 1959b, 1978) to model the Ricardian system: rent as a residual and not explicitly as a Clarkian marginal product, wage-fund elements, market-clearing full employment, a single-good (corn) model, or a many-good model.

Since the literature has been in doubt on the logical possibility of what Ricardo contended, it is appropriate that I should fabricate an over-dramatic example of the starkest type that provides an instance vindicating Ricardo's reasoning. I have done this by using robots that decimate human labor in a corn-only world. The reader will realize that, once the Ricardian contention is demonstrated to be logically feasible, with trifling ingenuity I can manufacture ad lib examples of it in elaborated multicommodity cases that simulate realistic scenarios in economic history.

ASSUMPTIONS

The labor supply, L_t, remains constant when the real corn wage is at the subsistence level of $\bar{w}$: by dimensional license this can be a corn wage per worker of unity. When the actual wage is above the subsistence rate, population grows; when it is below, population declines:

$$L_{t+1} - L_t = a(w_t - 1), \tag{1}$$

where a may be a positive constant or any function of (w_t, L_t) that is positive.

Initially corn is produced by labor working on fixed available acreages of land, assumed to tail off in quality continuously so that there are always observable external margin zero-rent acreages just worth cultivating. The competitive wage rate for *all* workers, w_t, equals the corn product produced on the external margin by a worker there but discounted at the market rate of interest r_t because workers get paid at the beginning of the production periods while corn output becomes available at the end.

Mathematically, as is well known,

$$Q_{t+1} = f(L_t), \ f' > 0 > f'', \tag{2}$$

$$\text{Wage rate} \ = \bar{w}_t = \frac{f'(L_t)}{1 + r_t}, \tag{3}$$

$$\text{Rent} \ = f(L_t) - w_t(1 + r_t)L_t, \tag{4}$$

where Q is corn output; L is labor input; w is the real wage rate, $\bar{w} = 1$ being its subsistence level; r is the interest rate; f is the production function giving total Q for each level of L spread competitively among the diverse acres; and the derivative $f'(L)$ is what a worker produces of corn at the no-rent margin.

In initial long-run equilibrium, when t subscripts are ignored because all variables are stationary, for each long-run $\bar{r}$, we have

$$f'(L) = 1 + \bar{r}, L = 100 \text{ (say)},$$
$$Q = f(L) = f(100) = 220 \text{ (say)},$$
$$\text{Wages} = \bar{w}L = 100,$$
$$\text{Rent} = f(L) - \bar{w}(1 + \bar{r})L = 220 - (1 + \bar{r})100 \qquad (5)$$
$$= 220 - 120 \text{ (say)} = 100,$$
$$\bar{r} = .20 \text{ (a 20 percent interest rate per period)},$$
$$\text{Interest} = \bar{r}(\bar{w}L) = .2(100) = 20.$$

Of the 220 of gross corn output, Ricardo counts the $100 + 2$ consumed by property owners (landowners' 100 and capitalists' 20) as net output. He treats the 100 of subsistence corn for humans as fodder, a necessary cost of producing the net product. Net output for him equals Rent plus Interest and falls short of gross output, which includes Wages; Kuznets-Haig national income is Ricardo's gross product.

It would not matter if I introduced an invention of robot machines into a growing Ricardian system rather than into an initial long-run equilibrium. But it is useful to show that Ricardo's argument does *not* need to depend at all on short-run frictions or transitional technological unemployments. (Also, the initial interest rate could as well be zero as 20 percent if property owners continued to save positively at any secure positive rate of interest. The reader may replace $\bar{r} = 0.2$ by $\bar{r} = 0.0$ in the fashion of Schumpeter and Kalecki-Marx.)

Now let there be invention of a robot machine that lasts one period and can do exactly the work of one man. Let one new machine be producible by exactly the labor-land resources that produce $1 - \epsilon$ units of corn. This instance in which a machine is definitely cheaper than a man provides the starkest case for Ricardo's logic.

After the invention, we rewrite (2) to take account of the number of machines, writing for gross product (in terms of the corn numeraire)

$$Q_{t+1} + (1 - \epsilon)K_{t+1} = f(L_t + K_t). \qquad (2')$$

How (3) and (4) must be rewritten will soon be seen.

At the old pricing equilibrium, even without any new desire to save, after the invention it will pay to divert some of the resources being used to produce corn to the task of producing some new robots – a switch from the wage fund to fixed capital, just as Ricardo's example called for. If $1 - \epsilon$ is little less than unity, the new profit rate will be little different from that of the previous equilibrium; but ever so little a difference will motivate the described shift of some resources away from corn production. (So we see that those writers who tried to criticize Ricardo's arithmetic example on the ground that it presumed no realistic rise in the profit rate from the innovation were beside the mark: the rise in r can be large or little.)

As soon as the diversion of resources away from corn reduces its total output, on the reasonable assumption that property owners do not massively abstain from corn consumption to finance the robot capital formation, there will be less left over in the wage fund than before: now fewer than 100 corn bids for the existing population of 100. So the market-clearing real wage falls at least temporarily below the subsistence level. Ricardo's equation (1) dictates a falling off of population – as he says, a redundant population.

It is well that the wage falls since otherwise the higher interest rate occasioned by the invention could not be earned on the corn advanced to an unchanged number of workers. Marx properly criticized Ricardo for the calm way he faced the Malthusian destruction of people and the abortion of natural fertility. But it is Ricardo's story, and we must let him tell it his own way. As the stock of robots gets built up, the wage fund shrinks and necessarily shrinks fast enough to match the declining population and to keep the wage rate below the population maintenance level.

The land will come to be cultivated even more intensively than before, but more and more of it is used to replace robots and to provide increments to the stock of robots. And more and more of the acres are being tilled by robots rather than by people.

LONG-RUN EQUILIBRIUM

Before I sketch the dynamic path of transition, let me describe the terminal equilibrium after all adjustments to the robot invention have been made.

For simplicity, I follow Ricardo's assumption that there is always some long-run effective interest rate at which it just pays to keep capital intact and save zero net. Let this $\bar{r}$ be as before: 20 percent in my example, perhaps 0 percent in the reader's variant of it.

THEOREM. In the new equilibrium, *all* labor will have been rendered redundant. Human labor will have died out. The stock of robots will necessarily be so large as to extend the margin of cultivation to worse lands than in the original equilibrium; Ricardo's net product, his Rent plus Interest that property owners spend in the new steady state on their corn consumption, will be higher after the invention than ex ante as long as $\bar{r}$ is sufficiently small. The Kuznets national product, Wages + Interest + Rent, will (as Ricardo claimed and as Wicksell denied to be possible) have fallen in any situation in which the labor saving is not too extreme (in the sense that $1 - \epsilon$ is not too minuscule).

When we recognize products other than corn, Ricardo recognizes that less of the labor supply will have to be reduced, especially when property owners spend their enhanced income on personal service (retainers etc.); but still, for ϵ not too large, his gross product does fall.

The conditions of postinvention equilibrium for the stock of robot machines K, the labor supply L, and the output of corn Q are

$$Q + (1 - \epsilon)K = f(K + 0), \tag{6a}$$

$$f'(K + 0) = (1 + \bar{r})(1 - \epsilon) < 1 + \bar{r}, \tag{6b}$$

$$\bar{w} = 1 > \frac{f'(K + 0)}{1 + \bar{r}} = 1 - \epsilon. \tag{6c}$$

Because the wage that a worker would earn on the external margin, which is the same as the "net rental" an equivalent robot earns there, is seen in (6c) to be *always* below the subsistence wage, no farm workers at all can survive! Therefore,

$$L = 0, \tag{6d}$$

$$f'(K) < f'(100), \tag{6e}$$

from (6b)

$$K > 100 = \text{previous } L, \tag{6f}$$

$$\text{Rent in corn} = f(K) - Kf'(K)$$
$$> f(100) - 100f'(100) = \text{previous rent.} \tag{6g}$$

A more triumphant vindication of Ricardo could hardly be possible, and this within his own concepts and in the longest-run equilibrium.[1]

---

[1] One must never go overboard in praising the uneven Ricardo. As Stephen Leacock would say, Ricardo was away from school the day they taught the difference between necessary and sufficient conditions. It is not required that gross product be reduced by an invention if the demand for labor is to be hurt by that invention, but his way of seeing this last possibility was by way of the former possibility. For large ϵ the rent alone can exceed the preinvention gross product, and yet this case of *increased* gross product is most quickly harmful to labor! Also, for $\bar{r} > 0$, Ricardo erred if he thought that every viable invention *must* increase his net product.

GRAPHICAL VINDICATION

Figure 1 is the standard Ricardo diagram of Kaldor (1956), Samuelson (1978), and many others. Though it resembles a Clark marginal product diagram, it needs only the classical concept of external margin land. The new element here is that robots are zero before the invention, and it is deduced that labor must be zero after the system adjusts to the new robot equilibrium. If robots had not been such perfect human substitutes, the reduction of population would of course have been less extreme. The graphs are seen to corroborate perfectly the mathematics of the previous section.

Ricardo's fervor for laissez-faire made him balk at endorsing restrictions on technical innovations to help labor – as *his* logic required. One straw he grasped for was the possibility that the enhanced total of property incomes might get spent in part on more menial servants, so the new total L might not be so bad. The diagrams can handle this. Suppose one-tenth of the property income area, $DEGO$ and $D'E'G'O$ as the case may be, gets spent on labor servants; then form out of that area a rectangle with the Os height of unity and add it to these diagram's respective gross output areas to get correct total gross output.

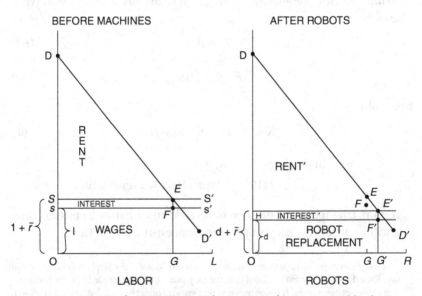

Figure 1. Note that Rent′ > Rent because $G' > G$, Interest′ > Interest, and land is more intensively cultivated in the postinvention equilibrium. Note that population has been made extinct then. New gross output $DE'F's$ will be below old $DEGO$ whenever E' is near to E – in vindication of Ricardo vis-à-vis Wicksell (OS' is $1 - \epsilon$ times the length of OS; Os' is $1 - \epsilon$ times Os).

Similarly, Ricardo argued that more might get saved after property incomes are swelled by invention. Figure 1*b* already shows such an effect, but it could be enhanced it we made the new $\bar{r}$ lower than before, with the logical possibility that more servants would survive in the robot epoch than had previously found a living tilling corn. Of course, this ultimate induced rise in the demand for labor might be offset in the intermediate run by the stipulated adverse substitution effects of robots for farm labor – as Ricardo hinted.

Needless to say, the doctrine is wrong which claims that all inventions that shift resources from circulating capital to fixed capital – to durable machines at the expense of "wage funds" – *must* reduce the demand for labor. New diagrams can depict widened wage rectangles in Ricardian diagrams such as these that portray inventions of durable machines that are less robot-like.

Had Ricardo lived long enough to prepare a fourth edition, perhaps he would have changed his mind to eliminate his evident error in believing that more saving *must* be favorable to the demand for labor. Rapid saving will, in the polar robot model, speed up the euthanasia and genocide of human labor and accelerate the rise in land rent. While such saving raises Ricardo's net product, it can decimate his gross product – whatever Wicksell's confusion.

TRANSITIONS

A determinate dynamic path of reaction to the robot invention might be worked out by any reader using the canonical classical model of Samuelson (1978).[2] This could be done in a market-clearing context: as long as people still exist, they accept the lowered real wage rates that the auction market metes out. Alternatively, it would be realistic in 1820 to assume that people

---

[2] Equation (3) applies after the invention as long as the transition involves positive L. Equation (4) also applies at all times. After the invention that brings robots into existence, we have the following relations, which are the dynamic versions of (6b) and (6c):

$$1 + r_t = \frac{f'(K_t + L_t)}{1 - \epsilon},\tag{6b'}$$

$$w_t = 1 - \epsilon\tag{6c'}$$

for $L_t > 0$, from (6b') and (3). To eqq. (1), (3), (6b'), and (6c'), we need to add a dynamic supply of saving by property owners to have a determinate path to Ricardo's long-term steady state. Note that labor is indeed hurt by the invention even when we and Ricardo obey Say's law and rule out nonclearing of any market.

lose jobs (at least temporarily). The usual charge against Ricardo criticizes him for chronically neglecting short-run frictions that are realistic. So it is a twist that critics, who found unpalatable his Chapter 31 conclusion that machines can hurt workers and wages, commonly had to discount his new chapter with the accusation that he needs to depend on techno- logical unemployment and other fleeting frictions for his pessimistic results.

Where is there warrant for this in his Chapter 31 text? At most one of its sentences even mentions people losing jobs (and later getting new ones). Once I steeped myself in the odd classical subsistence wage supply-of-labor mentality, I made perfectly good sense out of the sentences in this chapter while never departing from market-clearing methodology that would satisfy a devotee of the Lucas school of rational expectations.

DISCUSSION

A few remarks are in order. Ricardo's laissez-faire fervor made him think that a continuous stream of inventions has to be more favorable to labor than a single discontinuous one. There is little warrant for this, as the present mode of analysis can demonstrate. It is more forgivable that Ricardo in 1821 should have erred in this regard than that the host of commentators since then have fallen into this shallow trap.

Chapter 31 is often criticized for what I regard as its excellences. In it Ricardo admits that he cannot free his theory of distribution of income from dependence on how consumers choose to spend their incomes. (Example: Peace makes population redundant as the labor-intensive demands of the military are replaced by normal demands. This sensible result led John Stuart Mill to his fuss concerning the demand for commodities not being the demand for labor – a result not so much wrong as overdramatized by Mill.)

In Chapter 31 Ricardo makes it clear that he does not assume fixed proportions between labor and capital good(s). In this chapter he antici- pates the induced factor-biased inventing that we associate with Marx, Hicks, Fellner, Charles Kennedy, von Weizsäcker and Samuelson, Dandrakis and Phelps, and many others: if accumulation raises the real wage and lowers the interest rate, the speed of the trend, Ricardo perceives, can be lowered by the encouragement it gives to the invention of labor- saving, capital-using techniques. In Chapter 31 Ricardo discovers what he has elsewhere gratuitously denied: that an improvement abroad can hurt Britain under free trade (or, as needs to be said today, that an improvement in Japan can hurt the American living standard).

I for one find Chapter 31 a refreshing change from the sterilities and nonoptimalities of Ricardo's opening chapters and hope to have presented some evidence to support this unfashionable opinion.[3]

REFERENCES

Hicks, John R. *A Theory of Economic History*. Oxford: Clarendon, 1969.

Kaldor, Nicholas. "Alternative Theories of Distribution." *Rev. Econ. Studies* 23, no. 2 (1956): 83–100.

Pasinetti, Luigi L. "A Mathematical Reformulation of the Ricardian System." *Rev. Econ. Studies* 27 (February 1960): 78–98.

Ricardo, David. *On the Principles of Political Economy and Taxation*. 3d ed. London: Murray, 1821. In *The Works and Correspondence of David Ricardo*, vol. 1, edited by Piero Sraffa. Cambridge: Cambridge University Press (for Royal Econ. Soc.), 1951.

Samuelson, Paul A. "A Modern Treatment of the Ricardian Economy: I. The Pricing of Goods and of Labor and Land Services." *Q.J.E.* 73 (February 1959): 1–35. *(a)* Reprinted in *Collected Scientific Papers of Paul A. Samuelson*, vol. 1. Cambridge, Mass.: MIT Press, 1965.

—"A Modern Treatment of the Ricardian Economy: II. Capital and Interest Aspects of the Pricing Process." *Q.J.E.* 73 (May 1959): 217–31. *(b)* Reprinted in *Collected Scientific Papers of Paul A. Samuelson*, vol. 1. Cambridge, Mass.: MIT Press, 1965.

—"The Canonical Classical Model of Political Economy." *J. Econ. Literature* 16 (December 1978): 1415–34. Reprinted in *Collected Scientific Papers of Paul A. Samuelson*, vol. 5. Cambridge, Mass.: MIT Press, 1986.

—"Ricardo Was Right." *Scandinavian J. Econ.* (in press).

Wicksell, Knut. "Ricardo on Machinery and the Present Unemployment." *Econ. J.* 91 (March 1981): 200–205. [Rejected by *Econ. J.* in 1923.]

—*Lectures on Political Economy*. London: Routledge, 1934.

---

[3] Elsewhere (in Samuelson, in press) I focus on the erroneous conclusions concerning Ricardo on machinery by Wicksell ([1923] 1981, 1934), who led many an excellent economist down the garden path. Logic aside, Wicksell seems to me more plausible in believing that, on the whole, inventions happen to raise real wages than Ricardo is in believing that they are likely to be hurtful (or than Hicks [1969] is in hypothesizing a harmful bias in the first decades of the nineteenth century).

JOHANN HEINRICH VON THÜNEN

Thünen at Two Hundred

1983 is a year of centennials: the death of Karl Marx, the births of Maynard Keynes and Josef Schumpeter. But also, running exactly a century before Schumpeter's life clock (1883–1950) was that of Johann Heinrich von Thünen (1783–1850), the economist who met a payroll and, in recording and analyzing his Junker estate accounts, not only created *marginalism* and *managerial economics*, but also elaborated one of the first models of *general equilibrium* and did so in terms of realistic *econometric* parameters.

Thünen was a loner with a one-track mind. By 1803 – still a minor! – he had already glimpsed the equilibrium of his *Isolated State*: a town surrounded by a homogeneous plain, trading city goods for the rural fruits of labor and land; and with the inner rings nearest the town specializing on the goods dearer to transport, while the farther out low-rent-generating acres are growing the goods cheaper to transport.

Knowing Adam Smith, Thünen arrived at his own model determining wages and rents before David Ricardo (or Edward West or Robert Malthus). But publishing only in German, and in several installments of a lengthy and intricate book, Thünen's work of genius is primarily admired by the public at a distance while serving as an occult mine for hundreds of German dissertation writers to sift over and sniff at.

Among geographers and location theorists, Thünen is a founding God. What John Bates Clark did at the end of the nineteenth century in formulating a theory of distributive shares, in terms of the marginal productivities of factors

I have benefited from suggestions by Ronald Jones and Edwin Burmeister, and from editorial assistance by Aase Huggins. Partial support from the Sloan Foundation is gratefully acknowledged.

of production, Thünen had already done in the 1842 and 1850 installments to his original 1826 *The Isolated State*. Since J. B. Clark (like his son John Maurice Clark) was notorious for never reading anybody and having to work out his ideas for himself, and since to this day a full translation of Thünen into English is lacking, we undoubtedly face here another example of Robert K. Merton's doubletons of independent scientific discovery.[1] Only Alfred Marshall among the modern greats "professed" to be much influenced by Thünen: and Schumpeter is probably right to insinuate the quoted verb, since Marshall's sanctimonious acknowledgement provides a self-serving downplaying of Marshall's more important borrowing from Augustin A. Cournot.[2]

Whatever his neglect, Thünen would merit first-rank fame in the annals of economic theory if he had written no more than the following brief lines:

The significance of capital we have measured by the increase in the product of the labor of a man which results from an increase in the capital with which he works. Here labor is a constant, capital a varying magnitude.

When, on the other hand, we consider capital as remaining constant and the number of workers as varying, we realize in a large business that the significance of labor and the share of labor in the product is determined by the increase in the product which results from the addition of another laborer [Thünen, *Der Isolierte Staat*, 1930 ed., p. 584; trans. in Douglas, 1934, pp. 36–37].

With these lines, the primitive implicit marginalism involved in classical Ricardian rent theory graduates into neoclassical marginal productivity.

Before proceeding to substantive analysis of Thünen's system, let me mention that two clouds have always hung over his name. The first, and less important one, was connected with Eugen von Böhm-Bawerk's need to clear the way for his own positive theory of capital and interest by annihilating all earlier theories (and theorists) of the subject. Thünen is indicted and convicted by Böhm as holding a "productivity theory of interest": in allegedly *merely assuming* that capital projects exist that do yield a saving of labor greater than the labor needed to produce the capital goods themselves, Thünen is accused by Böhm of the logical fallacy of *petitio principii* – he is begging the question that needs to be faced and resolved. However, as Böhm's admirer Knut Wicksell had to point out, the scientist has no choice but to beg every such question in the sense that ultimately a Newton must accept how it is that apples do fall; and that

---

[1]   Again in the Merton manner, Clark's 1889 break-through had simultaneous quasi-independent marginal-productivity discoveries on the part of such diverse scholars as Stuart Wood, Philip Wicksteed, Vilfredo Pareto, Enrico Barone, Léon Walras, Knut Wicksell, and Alfred Marshall. On the sociology and history of science, see Robert K. Merton (1973).

[2]   For Clark on Thünen, see J. B. Clark (1914, pp. 321–24). For Marshall's testimony, see Arthur C. Pigou (1925, pp. 359–60) and J. A. Schumpeter (1954, pp. 465–68).

it is not in the power of an Einstein to deduce why Mercury must lag in the way that telescopes confirm it does and that the truth of general relativity theory would entail. (Böhm's own "third cause of interest," the alleged and merely assumed superior technical productivity of time-involving processes, is ultimately just as question begging and inescapably so.)[3]

The other reason for Thünen's disrepute in certain quarters is Thünen's own fault. He spent years and gallons of ink on his weird doctrine of the natural wage, and I use the adjective "weird" advisedly. One of my purposes in an appendix is to show that critics have been both too harsh and too kind to Thünen on the topic of his natural wage. When historians of thought parrot the phrase that Thünen was the first to apply the differential calculus to political economy, they could add that Thünen was also one of the first to misapply it to our subject. In this paper's text I confine myself mostly to Thünen's timeless land-and-labor model, a magnificent edifice and one that still can benefit from modern treatment.

Here are a few suggestions to a reader in a filial mood wishing to salute Thünen's bicentennial. Arthur H. Leigh (1946) provides the best modern survey of Thünen's capital theory and natural wage labyrinth. Horst C. Rechtenwald (1973) gives a photograph and abridgments from Leigh, along with an evaluation by Edgar Salin (1958). Erich Schneider (1934) provides a good biographical account. Mark Blaug (1962, 1968) overlaps with Schumpeter (1954, pp. 465–68). An abridged translation of *The Isolated State*, with some biography and emphasis on geographers' location theory, is provided by Peter Hall, ed. (1966). For the economics treasures in Part Two, Section 1 of *The Isolated State*, see the translation provided in Bernard W. Dempsey (1960, pp. 187–367). But read with caution the extensive defenses of Thünen's natural wage. Hall (1966, p. xii) recommends as a definitive commentary on Thünen's theory of agricultural location that in German by Asmus Petersen (1944). Martin Beckmann and Thomas Marschak (1955) give a brief look at Thünen's system from a modern viewpoint.

THÜNEN'S RINGS

Someone, somewhere, must surely have provided an exact and complete version of Thünen's space model. Here is my stripped-down version.

---

[3] Cf. E. von Böhm-Bawerk (1884, 1889). None of this is to deny that there are arbitrarinesses in Thünen's program to measure capital in terms of stored-up labor. One purpose of my Appendix is to clean up Thünen's capital model so that it is logically consistent and complete.

All labor is alike, free to move either to country or town. All land is alike except for distance from town. All people (laborers or landowners), wherever they permanently reside, have identical (homothetic) tastes at all income levels, involving a city-produced good (cloth) and two country-produced goods (vegetables dear to transport, and grain cheap to transport).

I ignore the fact that the city good might require for its production raw materials from the countryside. To keep all capital out of this Act 1, I assume cloth is produced instantaneously by labor alone at constant returns to scale.[4] Each farm good has its smooth first-degree-homogeneous production function that is concave in its labor and land inputs. (In short, neoclassical conditions obtain: the law of diminishing returns; constant returns to scale; well-defined limit ratios for [Δoutput/Δland, Δoutput/Δlabor], and so forth.) The case of fixed coefficients, where marginal products are not defined, will also be discussed in an example. Three possibilities are of interest: both farm goods have the same labor/land intensities; grain is the more land/labor intensive of the two goods at all wage/rent ratios; grain is the less land/labor intensive in the above sense.

The simplest version of Thünen's rings of specialization is then supposed to follow:

1. Immediately around the town comes a circle where only hard-to-transport vegetables can bid successfully for the limited nearby acres of land.
2. Outside of this first ring comes an annulus in which easier-to-ship grain is grown. (With more farm goods, Thünen envisages more distinct zones of specialization. Also, for him, the same product may have to be produced farther out by a different and more "land intensive" method.)
3. At the farthest extremity of cultivation comes the endogenously determined *external margin*, where land rent has fallen to zero because the cost of transporting town cloth outward and farm products inward has lowered farm-goods' prices relative to prices for city-goods and has reduced the economical density of labor to land. Beyond this frontier land is a free good.

Some questions remain open to this day:

---

[4] It is agreed that a town is a town because certain activities involve, at least for a range, *increasing* returns to scale, specialization, and the division of labor. I assume the town is large enough so that all internal and external economies of scale in cloth production have been exhausted, after which all variations in cloth output involve proportional variations in town labor input, and market competition can be treated as if it were perfect.

(a) Are vegetables shipped outward as well as inward, in exchange for the grain needed by residents of the first circle? Could the grain received from this outward trade ever be for barter with city workers for first-circle residents' cloth needs?

(b) Can people in a zone of specialization produce also some of the other goods they desire for their own consumption? Must they?

(c) So long as the rural good that is cheapest to transport is also most labor-intensive, and therefore most sparing in its requirement for limited nearby land, the pattern of specialization zones is quite intuitive. But suppose the good dear to transport is also the good that is most land/labor-intensive, can it still usurp the inner position where land is so scarce?

(d) Can it really be universally true that the labor/land intensity drops with distance from the city? As in the case just mentioned, when the farm good cheapest to transport happens to be most labor intensive, couldn't we encounter higher labor/land intensity in the farther-out ring than prevails in the circle nearest to town?

Rigorous proofs are seen not to be superfluous luxuries. They are indispensable for true understanding and for answering long-open questions.

THE ONE-FARM-GOOD CASE

To tune up our analytical engines, start with the simplest case of essentially cloth and grain only. (If vegetables had the same transport cost and production function as grain, the two-farm-good model would degenerate essentially into the present one-farm-good case.)

Intuition tells us:

1. A preassigned labor supply will divide itself, at the direction of competition's Invisible Hand, between town labor, L_0, and labor smeared out over the plain in a density relative to land that diminishes along radial spokes emanating from the city.

2. Town labor receives in wages all of the town cloth product, its real wage in cloth being set by the technical productivity constant in the cloth-labor production function.

3. Town labor spends part of its real income on cloth. Part it barters for grain, paying the delivered-price of grain (the price in terms of cloth at the town center of the Thünen circles), as set by the auction market to balance supply and demand involving town and rural exports.

4. Remember all rural labor, in close to town or far out, must get the same
real wage in utility terms – which must also equal town labor's utility
wage. People migrate from low to high utility-wage places, thereby
bidding down wages at the latter places, bidding up wages at the
former, and achieving stationary equilibrium only when real-utility
wage equalization has been attained.

5. Of course, equality of real wage, near and far from town, does not
mean that workers at the two places enjoy equal real wage rates in both
grain and in cloth. Actually, neither of these can be equal along
different circumferences. At far circumferences, real wage rates in
cloth are low because of transport-cost-losses in moving cloth and
grain; but out there real wage rates in grain must be compensatingly
high as a condition of equilibrium under labor mobility. Labor thins
out there until, by the law of diminishing-returns acting in reverse, its
grain wage-product has risen enough to keep labor contented in utility
terms. (As Thünen knew, if some people liked country life or country
goods more than others did, people would sort themselves out to
where they most want to be and it would not be meaningful to say
wage rates are equal everywhere; what is meaningful is that auction
markets bid up and down the delivered price ratios between grain and
cloth, until labor's location is endogenously determined and all markets clear. I ignore all differences in tastes.)

6. Land is not mobile. Its rent far from town, measured in either grain or
cloth, can and will stay permanently lower than the real rents of similar
acres that are located nearer town. The rent rate (in grain) of land r
radial miles from town, $y(r)$ is determinate as soon as the labor/land
intensity at that place r, $L(r)$, is known. Both $y(r)$ and $L(r)$ fall off with
distance r and do so in accordance with simultaneous equations.
Today, thanks essentially to Thünen, J. B. Clark, and Philip
H. Wicksteed (1894), we know that the real rent rate at any place is
the same whether determined as a Ricardian residual or as a neoclassical marginal productivity. At the outer perimeter of cultivation,
land rent has dropped to zero (the condition that defines endogenously the external margin of cultivation).

Where do landowners live and consume in this scenario? One
possibility, perhaps in Thünen's mind and convenient for me to
stick with here, is that rent collectors are permanently rooted on the
acres they own. (A second possibility would be that of absentee ownership, where all rents earned on land are paid in kind there but are
exchanged for consumption goods in town. A third possibility, which

also calls out for future examination, is to make landowner's location an endogenous variable to be determined by their own utility maximization as footloose rentiers.)

7. Now that I've supplied technology and tastes, my model will be complete when I've specified the exact nature of transport costs to move grain and cloth (and vegetables when we return to multiple farm products). Thünen devotes much thought to realistic transport technology for his time and region. Often this involves an element of cost that is constant for each mile a particular good travels. Thus, from an F.O.B. price intercept, the delivered C.I.F. price would rise linearly.

My transport-cost functions are made even simpler in this first stripped-down version. Samuelson (1954) introduced the "iceberg" model to obviate in trade models the need to handle new industries whenever positive transport costs are met. By serendipity, Thünen himself had already noted the case where grain is moved by oxen, who must eat some of that grain while moving it a mile – so that some fraction of the grain moved can be conceived of as melting away in the iceberg fashion as the necessary cost of moving it a unit distance.

My iceberg assumption entails that

a) Price of town cloth delivered r miles from town, $P_0(r)$, must rise like $P_0^0 e^{a_0 r}$, where P_0^0 is the F.O.B. price of cloth in town and a_0 is the percent of melting of cloth per mile of transport. (On convenient semi-log diagrams, $P_0(r)$ rises linearly from its in-town intercept; and, it will be seen, $P_1(r)$ falls linearly.)

b) If price of grain delivered in the city is P_1^0, then it becomes cheaper as we move out r distance into the plain. Its price at $r, P_1(r)$, decays away like $P_1^0 e^{-a_1 r}$, where a_1 is the melting coefficient for grain. All this presupposes that cloth is in fact moving outward in positive amounts between 0 and r; and that grain is moving inward in positive amounts between r and 0.[5]

Figure 1 plots the town-good and country-good case, giving only a quarter arc of the perfect circles. Town is at the circles' center in 1(a). The outer circumference is at the boundary of purposeful cultivation, R miles from town. To depict the declining labor density of cultivation along each radius, the circles are drawn more closely bunched together near town. By

---

[5] Actually, my version has need only for *relative* prices not absolute prices: for $[P_i(r)/P_j(r)$, $W(r)/P_i(r)$, $y_1(r)]$. If you could imagine a transport-free gold numeraire you might use it to express fictional absolute prices – a harmless and redundant convention.

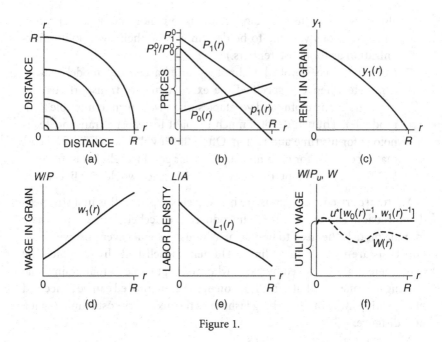

Figure 1.

radial symmetry, along any one intermediate circumference, r and $[W(r)/P_0(r), W(r)/P_1(r), y_1(r)]$ are everywhere the same, as will be total production and aggregate consumptions of resident laborers and land-owners, $[q_1(r), c_0(r), c_1(r)]$.

Figures 1(b)–1(f) show the equilibrium variation with distance from town of the different variables. The intercept depicting in 1(b) the grain-cloth price ratio in town, $(P_1/P_0)^0$ as shown by the bracket, plays a key role in generating *all* the other relations once technology and transport-cost parameters are known.

In 1(b), the exponential decay of the grain-to-cloth price ratio follows from my "iceberg" assumption, as an outward flow of "melting" cloth and an inward flow of "melting" grain have their terms of trade set to agree with no-arbitrage-profit conditions. (The diagram is semi-log to make the exponential curves graph as straight lines.)

In 1(c) the grain rent rate drops with r as less and less laborers are able to earn the common utility wage on each acre of land.

In 1(d) is shown the rise in grain wage needed to compensate the workers for the higher relative cost of town goods when the latter must be carted far from town (and exchanged for the grain that is destined to be expensively carted into town).

In 1(e) is shown how sharply labor/land density must drop off as the grain wage rises and the grain rent falls.

Finally, 1(f)'s solid line shows the horizontal pattern of wage utility, $u^*(r)$. The broken curve shows the nominal wage at each point r: whether it rises or falls as we leave town depends on whether the fraction of income that people spend on cloth relative to what they spend on grain is at each r greater than a_1/a_0; when cloth is preponderantly important, the nominal wage, $W(r)$, must rise to compensate for the rise in $P_1(r)/P_0(r)$; etc. The bracketed intercept for u^* is one of our two basic endogenous unknowns, along with the bracketed $(P_1/P_0)^0$ in 1(b).

Important remark: We have here a set of simultaneous equations, whose solution yields our determinate equilibrium. If $(P_1/P_0)^0$ is initially set too high in 1(b), then the town level of wage-earners' utility would be too low. That means too many workers would be able to live in the country earning the initial level of town utility. The external boundary would be too far away for true equilibrium: so much grain would be grown over the swollen acreage as to inundate town with grain, leading to erosion of the too-high initial $(P_1/P_0)^0$ ratio.

The reader can show how too low an initial $(P_1/P_0)^0$ would lead to too-high common utility, to too-few rural workers and too-small acreage and grain production, and thus to a subsequent bidding up of $(P_1/P_0)^0$. All the related diagrams will be permanently compatible only after the system finds, by trial and error of competition, the correct equilibrium level for $(P_1/P_0)^0$.

MATHEMATICAL DERIVATION

An *indirect utility* function conveniently handles the demand functions for the town and farm goods, defined for people in terms of the prices they face at their given location, (P_0, P_1), and their total income, Y:

$$u^*[P_0/Y, P_1/Y] = Yu^*[P_0, P_1], \tag{1}$$

where we embody the assumption that all consumers have identical, homothetic tastes. The amounts they demand of the respective goods, $[C_0, C_1]$ are known from modern duality theory to be given by

$$C_i = V_i[P_0/Y, P_1/Y] = Y\, V_i[P_0, P_1], (i = 0, 1) \tag{2}$$

where

$$V_i[P_0/Y, P_1/Y] = -\partial \log_e u^*[P_0/Y, P_1/Y]/\partial(P_i/Y). \qquad (3)$$

The production functions for cloth and grain are given respectively by

$$Q_0 = f_0 L_0 \qquad (4)$$

$$Q_1 = A_1 f_1[L_1/A_1], \quad f_1'[\ ] > 0 > f_1''[\ ] \qquad (5)$$

where L_0 is town labor and (L_1, A_1) are labor and acres of land used for grain production. If we write the density of labor to land at any radial distance r from town as $L_1(r)$ and the density of grain grown there as $q_1(r)$, (5) takes on the normalized form

$$q_1(r) = f_1[L_1(r)]. \qquad (6)$$

The area of a circle with radius R is given by

$$\int_0^R dr[\int_0^{2\pi} rd\theta] = \int_0^R 2\pi r dr = \pi R^2. \qquad (7)$$

Therefore, the total of labor applied to the farm farm good, spread around the countryside out to the frontier R and with the labor/land density of $L_1(r)$, is given by

$$2\pi \int_0^R L_1(r)r dr = L_1 = L - L_0. \qquad (8)$$

Here L is the total of labor supply preassigned by Thünen, and which is to be endogenously divided between town and the various acres of the countryside.

The real wages are given respectively by the marginal products

$$W/P_0 = w_0(0) = f_0, \qquad (9)$$

$$W/P_1 = w_1(r) = f_1'[L_1(r)],$$
$$L_1(r) > 0, 0 < r \leqq R < \infty. \qquad (10)$$

In town there is no rent. (With Thünen we neglect site-value scarcity within a city. Our town is an idealized point.) The rural rent, expressed in grain, is given by

$$y_1(r) = f_1[L_1(r)] - L_1(r)w_1(r),$$
$$0 < r \leqq R. \qquad (11)$$

With Thünen we make the realistic assumption that at some low-enough positive labor density, λ_1, further abundance of land would add nothing to total product.

By definition of R as the external margin, it is the root that makes the following expression zero

$$y_1(R) = 0 = f_1[L_1(R)] - L_1(R)f_1'[L_1(R)] \equiv f_1[\lambda_1] - \lambda_1 f_1'[\lambda_1]. \quad (12)$$

For all values of $L_1(r)$ satisfying the following

$$0 < L_1(r) < \lambda_1 < \infty, \quad (13)$$

land rent will be positive.

It remains only to write down how the price ratio of grain to cloth must fall as we make the r distance to town greater. Spatial arbitrage ensures that for every r, where that grain destined for town is auctioned off for what it will bring locally in terms of cloth of town origin, we must have

$$P_1/P_0 = p_1(r) = p_1(0)e^{-a_0 r}e^{-a_1 r}, 0 \leq r \leq R. \quad (14)$$

From (9), (10), and (14), we deduce the real-wage relation

$$
\begin{aligned}
w_0(r) &= p_1(r)w_1(r) \\
&= p_1(0)e^{-a_0 r}e^{-a_1 r}f'[L_1(r)].
\end{aligned} \quad (15)
$$

Knowing both real wage rates in terms of $p_1(0)$, we can write down the real wage rate in utility at each point in space and equate them all to town workers' utility wage:

$$
\begin{aligned}
u^*[w_0(0)^{-1}, w_1(0)^{-1}] &= f_0 u^*[1, p_1(0)] \\
&= u^*[w_0(r)^{-1}, w_1(r)^{-1}] \\
&= w_1(r)u^*[p_1(r)^{-1}, 1] \\
&= w_1(r)u^*[p_1(0)^{-1}e^{a_0 r}e^{a_1 r}, 1].
\end{aligned} \quad (16)
$$

This tells us how fast the grain real wage must rise with distance from town

$$w_1(r) = f_0 u^*[1, p_1(0)]/u^*[p_1(0)^{-1}e^{a_0 r}e^{a_1 r}, 1]. \quad (17)$$

From (17) and (10) we deduce how fast labor density must fall as we move away from town. For each value of $p_1(0)$, we put $f_1'[L_1(R)]$ on (17)'s left-hand side and solve the resulting implicit relation for its $L_1(r)$ root. When r is large enough to make the calculated $L_1(r)$ root small enough to equal (13)'s λ_1, we have found the limiting R of profitable land cultivation.

We still lack the final basic relation needed to solve for the $p_1(0)$ parameter. We can provide this for Thünen if, borrowing a leaf from the modern book of international trade theory, we require balance-of-trade equilibrium between (i) what town workers will want to buy of delivered grain (spending their $f_0 L_0$ wage income and facing the delivered price ratio, $p_1(0)$ in town) and (ii) the grain that will get to town after rural laborers and landowners have decided how much of the grain that they produce they will want to devote to exports (a decision made in terms of total grain income at each place and in view of the price ratio for the two goods that prevails at that place).

The demand functions of (2), combined with our transport-cost designations, enable us to write down the final balance-of-trade relation as follows:

$$
\begin{aligned}
&[L - \int_0^R 2\pi r L_1(r)\,dr]\, V_1[1, p_1(0)] f_0 \\
&= \int_0^R 2\pi r f_1[L_1(r)]\{1 - V_1[1/p_1(r), 1]\} e^{-a_1 r}\,dr.
\end{aligned}
\tag{18}
$$

Our previous discussion has established that every function that appears in (18) is determined once $p_1(0)$ is known. So (18) is itself essentially one implicit equation in the one unknown variable $p_1(0)$. That it will have a unique positive root under our postulated conditions can be demonstrated by modern analytical tools. Thünen's intuition is confirmed – a nice 200th birthday offering!

Remark: With each additional farm good, we have the additional requirement that its physical supply voluntarily brought to town must match the amount of it that will be voluntarily bought in town. The way that lands at each r distance from town are allocated to the productions of different farm goods are new unknowns, solvable so as to maximize land rent at each place. The spatial price and real-wage patterns are, as before, determined by spatial arbitrage conditions and by the labor mobility that equalizes utility wages. When Thünen perceived what spatial pricing and specialization patterns are admissible under competition, he was anticipating the methods and results of Kuhn-Tucker nonlinear programming (P. A. Samuelson, 1959, Appendix).

EXAMPLES

Suppose all people spend half their incomes on town-produced cloth and half on rural-produced grain. Negating neoclassical smoothness of the production function for grain, let 1 of grain require f_1^{-1} units of labor input and 1 of land input.

The indirect utility function and demand functions are given by

$$u^* = \tfrac{1}{2}I/(P_0 P_1)^{1/2} = \tfrac{1}{2}(w_0 w_1)^{1/2} \tag{19}$$

$$c_0 = \tfrac{1}{2}I/P_0, c_1 = \tfrac{1}{2}I/P_1. \tag{20}$$

The production functions are given by

$$\begin{aligned} Q_0 &= f_0 L_0 = f_0(L - L_1) \\ &= f_0[L - \int_0^R 2\pi r L_1(r)dr] \end{aligned} \tag{21}$$

$$q_1(r) = \mathrm{Min}[f_1 L_1(r), 1]. \tag{22}$$

Between town and the frontier where $r = R$, we have

$$\begin{aligned} q_1(r) &\equiv 1, L_1(r) \equiv f_1^{-1} \\ q_1(r)/L_1(r) &\equiv f_1. \end{aligned} \tag{23}$$

Now that our $f_1[L_1(r)]$ lacks a defined derivative at $L_1(r)$ of f_1^{-1}, we have lost our marginal productivity definition of the real wage in grain. We know that $w_1(r)$ cannot exceed f_1; how much it falls short of f_1 determines the magnitude of land rent, $y_1(r)$.

Fortunately, for each value of the $p_1(0)$ parameter, there can be only one spatial pattern of the real grain wage that will give workers everywhere the same utility wage as in town. Our determining relations are, from (16),

$$\begin{aligned} (u^*)^2 &= w_0(0)w_1(0) = f_0^2 p_1(0)^{-1} \\ &= w_0(r)w_1(r) = w_1(r)^2 p_1(r) \\ &= w_1(r)^2 p_1(0)e^{-a_0 r}e^{-a_1 r} \end{aligned} \tag{24}$$

$$\begin{aligned} w_1(r) &= f_0 e^{(1/2)a_0 r} e^{(1/2)a_1 r}/p_1(0) \\ f_1 &= w_1(R) \\ &= f_0 e^{(1/2)a_0 R} e^{(1/2)a_1 R} p_1(0)^{-1} \end{aligned} \tag{25}$$

$$R^* = 2(a_0 + a_1)^{-1}\log_e[p_1(0)f_1/f_0]. \tag{26}$$

The basic balance of payments relation of (18) then becomes

$$\tfrac{1}{2}f_0[1 - \int_0^{R^*} 2\pi r f_1 dr]/p_1(0) = \tfrac{1}{2}\int_0^{R^*} 2\pi r[1 - \tfrac{1}{2}]e^{-a_1 r}dr. \tag{27}$$

We solve this for

$$p_1(0) = \frac{f_0[L - \pi(R^*)^2]}{\int_0^{R^*} \pi r e^{-a_1 r} dr}$$

$$(28)$$

$$= a_1^2 \frac{f_0[L - \pi(R^*)^2]}{\pi[1 - e^{-a_1 R^*} - a_1 R^* e^{-a_1 R^*}]}.$$

With $p_1(0)$ known, $[p_1(r), w_0(r), w_1(r), y_1(r), c_0(r), c_1(r), L_1(r), L_0, C_0(0),$ $C_1(0)]$ and all relevant unknowns can be solved for.

The reader can replace $\text{Min}[f_1 L_1(r), 1]$ by the CES function $[f_1^{-1} L_1(r)^{-1} + 1^{-1}]^{-1}$ and solve the resulting example, making use of the marginal productivity relation (10) now that $q_1(r)/f_1[L_1(r)]$ is open to an infinity of choices. (Remark: If labor's marginal product goes to infinity as its density to land goes to zero, show that "iceberg" transport costs entail that $R = \infty$ and land's rent never quite disappears; the Cobb-Douglas choice for $f_1[L_1(r)]$ of $L_1(r)^{1/2}$, or the CES choice of $[L_1(r)^{1/4} + 1]^4$, will illustrate.)

TWO OR MORE FARM GOODS

One sees how any number of farm goods are to be handled in the Thünen model. The present impressionistic sketch can stay with the case of two farm goods. In addition to L_0 devoted to production in town of cloth, Q_0, we have a pair of farm goods: $L_1(r)$ is the density of labor applied to production of vegetables, a commodity expensive to transport because its $e^{a_1 r}$ is high; $L_2(r)$ is the density of labor applied to production of grain, an easily transported good with $e^{a_2} < e^{a_1}$.

When we go beyond Thünen's simplest picture of separate zones, each of which specializes on a single good – and we cannot avoid doing so – we shall need to determine the fractions of the land at each place in the given zone that are devoted to the respective farm goods.[6] I write these fractions as:

---

[6] A small conceptual problem arises when more than one good is produced at points that are all the same r distance from town. How is the land corresponding to an element of circular area to be allocated to the different productions? To ensure that no unnecessary rural cross-shipments be introduced, I imagine space covered by a fine network of hexagonal fields. In every local region, however small, the relative number of hexagons devoted to each good is made to agree with the desired production ratios. Thünen, as a realistic observer, never pushed the assumption of constant returns to scale to its logical limit as I am doing; he thought of actual Prussian farms.

This is a place to mention the element of jointness of production that is entailed by cultivation systems that follow rotation of different crops so as to enhance land's steady-state productivity. I duck all joint products here and do so with a better conscience because

$$[g_1(r), g_2(r)] \geq 0, g_1(r) + g_2(r) = 1. \tag{29}$$

We have as many production functions and marginal productivity relations as there are farm goods:

$$q_i(r) = f_i[L_i(r)], \quad (i = 1, 2) \tag{6'}$$

$$w_i(r) = f_i'[L_i(r)], f_i'[\ ] > 0 > f_i''[\ ]. \tag{10'}$$

In the demand relations of (1)–(3), we flesh out $u^*[P_0, P_1]$ and $V_i[P_0, P_1]$ to become $u^*[P_0, P_1, P_2]$ and $V_i[P_0, P_1, P_2]$ – and so forth for goods $(0, 1, \ldots, n)$. Our total labor supply in (8) now becomes

$$L = L_0 + \sum_{1}^{2} \int_0^R 2\pi g_j(r) L_j(r) r dr. \tag{8'}$$

Now our spatial-arbitrage price gradients become more complicated. It being assumed that town laborers require something of every farm good and all country folk require some positive amount of cloth, there must be an innermost circle within which every farm good is travelling toward town and is exchangeable at each radius point for outmoving cloth. Call the radius of this innermost circle $\underline{R}$, with $\underline{R}$ not greater than the R of the external margin. Inside this inner circle, (14) generalizes easily to

$$P_j/P_0 = p_j(r) = p_j(0)e^{-a_0 r}e^{-a_j r}$$
$$0 \leq r \leq \underline{R} < R\,(j = 1, 2). \tag{14'}$$

Similar relations would hold for all of n goods, whatever n might be.

Suppose that Thünen was right in believing, outside an inner circle that exports vegetables to town, there is an outer annulus that exports to town only grain. Then throughout this outer zone, (14') does assuredly apply for $j = 2$, corresponding to grain. It, however, need not apply for perishable vegetables. What does obtain? Only the spatial arbitrage inequality applies:

$$P_1/P_0 = p_1(r) \geq p_1(0)e^{-a_0 r}e^{-a_1 r}, \quad \underline{R} \leq r \leq R. \tag{14''}$$

If the strong inequality obtains in (14''), it cannot be the case that vegetables are being shipped from $\underline{R} + h$ inward to $\underline{R}$ where they would be exchangeable for cloth. Although $p_1(\underline{R} + h)$ can exceed

---

of the tactic of leaving to the Appendix discussions of time phasing (of which crop rotation would be one special case).

$$p_1(\underline{R})e^{-a_0 h}e^{-a_1 h},$$

it cannot exceed this by more than a limit set by its transport cost relative to cloth's transport cost. Spatial arbitrage requires that

$$e^{-a_0 h}e^{-a_1 h} \lesseqgtr \frac{p_1(\underline{R}+h)}{p_1(\underline{R})} \lesseqgtr e^{-a_0 h}e^{a_1 h}. \tag{30}$$

Were the left-hand strong inequality to hold, vegetables would be just capable of being shipped inward from $\underline{R}+h$ to $\underline{R}$; were the right-hand strong inequality to hold, both vegetables and cloth could be shipped outward for exchange with grain there.

In the important singular case where grains and vegetables have technologies that involve the same labor/land intensities – so that the $f_i[L]$ are the same $f[L]$ function in (6') – it can be deduced that outward export of vegetables is quite forbidden. (If this outrages readers' intuition, which suggests to them that each zone might profitably specialize completely and exchange products to mutual advantage, remember that constant returns to scale does not afford the Smith-Young advantages to specialization that we intuitively expect in many real-life situations.)

At $r = \underline{R}$, by definition of $\underline{R}$ as the watershed between the zones from which town consumers get their vegetables and their grain, the ratio $p_2(\underline{R})/p_1(\underline{R})$ is precisely unity – the critical and invariant cost ratio of the two farm goods. Nearer in than $\underline{R}$, the vegetables have risen more in price than the grain because of the postulated difference in accruing transport costs. So, inside the inner ring, vegetables displace grain in profitability.

Unwary readers think to reverse this argument as one moves outward from $\underline{R}$. But this begs the question of the proper flow of goods and does so by proffering a false answer. Beyond $\underline{R}$ communities have the option of growing their own vegetables, and were they to exercise this option no transport costs would accrue on them.

Competition's Invisible Hand will contrive that people out there import cloth in barter for grain exports, while being self-sufficient in vegetables. This is a provable theorem, not a probability.[7]

---

[7] If I knew Thünen's text better, I could judge whether this is an old finding. As a realist, Thünen knew about farmers growing their own vegetables: but that could merely reflect his correct apprehension that kitchen gardens are a natural *joint* product, a phenomenon ruled out here. In the same way, I would have to refuse full marks to a student who thought he was proving the present theorem by pointing to the realistic fact that vegetables would spoil completely before they could be shipped very far out beyond $\underline{R}$: in the present iceberg

Thus, $p_2(r)$ falls exponentially all the way to the external margin. However, with similar labor/land intensities for the two goods, $p_1(r)$ falls at its exponential rate only to the $\underline{R}$ watershed. Beyond that, $p_1(\underline{R} + h)/p_2(\underline{R} + h)$ stabilizes at the cost ratio of unity, with $p_1(\underline{R} + h)$ falling between $\underline{R}$ and R only at grain's slower exponential rate.

In this singular case of equal factor intensities, it is indeed the case that the overall rural labor/land ratio, no matter how demand-tastes parcel out the $[g_1(\underline{R} + h), g_2(\underline{R} + h)]$ fractions, will fall uniformly as the distance from town grows. (With fixed coefficients, that of course couldn't be true – even though land rent would still fall steadily. With a few different techniques to choose from out of a book of Robinsonian blue prints, as one moves out of town the labor/land ratio will discontinuously travel down steps, alternating between steps and their riders. A nice example of such a finite-number of activities model is provided by Thünen's assertion of the three-field system as paying only on land far enough from town to bear low rent-wage ratios.)

GEOGRAPHICAL SUMMARY OF TWO-FARM-GOOD CASE

Figure 2 provides almost full verification of Thünen's specialization rings in the case where the farm goods have the same factor intensities.

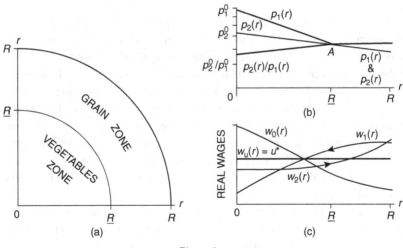

Figure 2.

model, some would get through and thus we are back to having to distinguish between a *quantitative* and a *qualitative* necessity.

The inner zone of 2(a) grows only vegetables, some of which are exported to town in exchange for cloth. The outer zone exports grain to town, but also grows vegetables for worker and landowner consumption.

In the semi-log diagram of 2(b), the price of vegetables (in cloth) at first falls faster as we move outward from town than does the price of grain. This reflects the latter's relative cheapness to transport. Beyond A, where r is at $\underline{R}$, the watershed between the zones, only grain moves to town. Everywhere in the outer-zone the price ratio between vegetables and grain stays at its unit relative costs of production. Hence, despite vegetables' dearness for transport, its price now drops relative to cloth's at the same gentle rate that grain's transport costs entail. (The prices follow straight lines on semi-log charts.) In 2(c), the real wage rate in cloth falls steadily. To compensate, the real wage rates in the farm goods have to rise. The real wage in utility is thus able to be the same everywhere. With the real wage rates of farm-goods rising, real land rents must correspondingly fall. Reading Thünen's text closely, we can only with charity attribute to him comprehension of the post-1953 factor-price-frontier concept. Like David Ricardo, he glimpsed this tradeoff frontier from a considerable distance and through some haze.

FACTOR INTENSITY COMPLICATIONS

I have left to the end the intricate question of whether a good that is most expensive to transport, if it were sufficiently land-intensive, could find itself priced out of the town's innermost neighborhood by virtue of the natural scarcity of such near-to-town land. Peter Hall writes: "It is necessary to stress this [intensity] point because . . . in the German literature . . . there has been the most fundamental confusion about it" (1966, pp. xxx–xxxii). He goes on to quote reprovingly H. Weighman's assertion that "the central feature of the Thünen system is that intensity of cultivation rises towards the market"; and Theodor Brinkmann's similar contention: "Zones near to the market are locations of specifically intensive types of land use."

By contrast, Hall insists that ". . . the pattern of location which Thünen describes . . . in no way follows any simple rule of intensity . . . Thus in the second ring . . . there is forestry, a very extensive [low labor/land] activity . . . And in the sixth or outermost ring we find a whole series of intensive cash crops such as oil-seeds, hops, tobacco and flax" (p. xxx). Hall, warning against oversimple definitions of "intensity," concludes with the flat claim: ". . . the general rule will be that the site nearest to the [town] market will be appropriated by that product which experiences the greatest cost reduction nearer the market, or in other words, the greatest cost increase away from the market" (p. xxxii).

In my iceberg model, where all costs are unambiguously defined, such a general rule, if it is to have any content, must presumably be interpreted to assert: vegetables, whose cost gradient is steepest as one moves away from town, must outbid grain for acres nearest to town *even if vegetables are much more land/labor intensive.* Hall (1966, p. xxxii, n. 2) associates A. Petersen with this viewpoint of his.

My investigation of the point bears out that Hall is right in asserting that nearest to town, no matter how land-sparing the good cheap to transport is, it will be outbid by the good dearer to transport (and no matter how land intensive that good is.) But it would be wrong to assert the truly general rule that *the exports cheap to transport always arise farther out than the exports dear to transport.*

To provide a counter example to the most general rule, while at the same time putting to a severe and successful test Hall's assertion about the acres nearest to town being usurped by the good dearest to transport, I employ the following strong model.

Vegetables, dear to transport, are producible by land alone. Grain, cheap to transport, requires both labor and land and is unequivocally less land/labor intensive than vegetables. (Thus, let 1 of grain output require as inputs 1 of labor and 1 of land.)

We shall discover that equilibrium for this model involves four zones:

Paradoxically, the far hinterlands grow vegetables only, even though that is the good dearest to transport.

As Hall claims, the innermost zone also grows vegetables only, even though this is a good that is anything but sparing in its use of scarce nearby acres.

All town imports of grain come from the next nearest second zone. That zone also grows the vegetables that its laborers and landowners consume.

Then comes a third zone that grows grain destined for home use and to be shipped outward in exchange for vegetables and inward in exchange for cloth. (Some regions in the third zone might also grow their own vegetables, one supposes.)

As already mentioned, stretching forever without limit, comes the model's final zone of vegetable production.[8]

---

[8] Any violence done to the reader's intuition by this final result can be attributed to my polar model's strict assumptions: iceberg transport costs; literally zero labor required for good 1;

Why are all acres very far out used for vegetables? If no labor will go there – and footnote 8 shows that a high enough price of cloth will make workers refuse to go far out – those acres might as well produce what it is that they can produce. The total vegetables, produced over the infinite plain, would be infinite; but after transport cost, only a finite amount will get through to any inner radius.

Why can't innermost acres be used exclusively for grain? Suppose that were so, from $r = 0$ out to $r = \hat{R}$, a watershed where both goods can first be produced. At $\hat{R}$, vegetables are just beginning to pay. If, for the first time, they are beginning to pay it must be (for constant utility wages) because $p_1(\hat{R})/p_2(\hat{R})$ has risen relative to where it had been inside the first zone. But, being dearer to transport, its relative price has to have fallen. And so we have our needed logical contradiction from our false supposition, and we can rule out the supposition.

Why can't both goods be produced in the innermost zone? This also would lead to a contradiction: it would not permit real utility wages to stay the same and arbitrage-proof price gradients to prevail.

In the third and fourth zones, grain and cloth are moving outward and meeting vegetables moving inward. So $p_1(r)$ must resume falling with the same exponential gradient as in the first zone. Likewise $p_1(r)/p_2(r)$ must now fall with a gradient set by $e^{-a_1} e^{+a_2}$. How $p_2(r)$ behaves depends upon $e^{a_2} e^{-a_0}$; if cloth is cheaper to transport than grain, $e^{a_0} < e^{a_2}$, then $p_2(r)$ will rise; if $a_2 < a_0$, then $p_2(r)$ is ultimately falling.

CONCLUDING REFLECTIONS AND SOLUTIONS

Thünen's system is seen to be a grand one, and one grandly worked out by him. Hall's claim for it as "the world's first economic model" is a pardonable exaggeration (1966, p. xxi).

Thünen's model has in it elements of all of the following systems:

1. The Ricardo-Torrens theory of comparative advantage.

fixed coefficients for good 2. In actual life, delivered cloth could become so expensive for workers far enough out that, realistically, no cheapness of the farm goods could induce them to live out there. That would define a *finite* external margin (which is ruled out by my extreme assumption that vegetables require land only). Far out landowners have rent per acre that yields ever lower utility. Therefore, we might suppose that each ekes out a living by owning ever more acres. Since the model requires zero work of the landowners, this is no problem. But the mind does rather boggle at the prospect of an indivisible human being straddling over ever more expansive acres and doing all consuming on them.

2. The Malthus-West-Ricardo theory of rent.
3. The Heckscher-Ohlin and Stolper-Samuelson theory of factors-and-goods pricing.
4. The Marx-Dimitriev-Leontief-Sraffa system of input-output.[9]

Moreover, Thünen has correctly perceived how his versions of those models operate under competition. Not only has he understood their positivistic features but, in addition, he has anticipated the Allyn Young, Frank Knight, and Dennis Robertson demonstration that charging competitive land rents is what leads to normative social efficiency (albeit possibly great inequalities and inequities).

Thus, Thünen would understand at once a demonstration by a modern economist that it would be wrong to allocate workers homesteads on which they alone are to work – wrong, even if the size of their acres was made lower near to town in order to achieve ethical equity. As each homesteader sought to acquire more land, or to hire more workers, preventing them from doing so would lead to deadweight loss. I think Thünen would also soon understand the point that an egalitarian society would want to distribute its land rents in *lump sum* transfer payments, the size of which payments would have to be geared to the worker's location, with transfer of goods being in the Pareto-efficient patterns that competitive spatial arbitrage would dictate.

It would be a mistake to think of Thünen's theory as applying to the frontier's wage. His is a complete theory of distribution. Moreover, he avoids the curse of general equilibrium models, in which all that can be said is that everything depends on everything else. His comparative statics is beautifully simple.

An increase in labor supply will raise land rent, extending the circle of cultivation. It will lower real wage rates.[10] (A higher supply of capital – as in

---

[9] To eliminate any vestige of time-phasing, I have ignored Thünen's insistence that town products use farm goods as raw materials and farm products use town products as inputs.

    A part of Thünen's capital theory is his own assumption that rural production does require town products as inputs, and vice-versa for town production. This accelerates the drop in rent with distance from town and accentuates the thinning out of factor intensities on far-out acres. If Thünen's capital good, K, is producible by labor and itself without need for land inputs, I'd expect K to be produced in town and everywhere that it is used, thereby eliminating deadweight cross-haulage.

[10] As Thünen realized, when there is enough total labor, a second, third, . . ., and nth town will become viable. So, if the plain were really infinite in acreage, the longest-run returns to labor would be constant rather than diminishing. In each short run, when the number of towns is temporarily fixed, more L means more rent; but when a new town is formed and attracts labor away from settled to virgin lands, rents decline to a base level that corresponds to a hexagonal network of towns. With the earth a finite globe, all of whose good

my Appendix rehabilitation of Thünen's capital theory – will tend to raise both wages and rents unless some particular pattern of substitutability between separate pairs of the three factors happens to obtain. Thus, if capital goods are robots, produced in town and serving as close substitutes for labor, an increase in their supply will be much like a higher-supply of L and will raise rents while lowering wages.)

A decrease in transport costs will also widen the circle of cultivation. But it will lower land rents and raise real wage rates.

By coincidence, Thünen anticipated contemporaneous as well as later theoretical discoveries. It is not surprising that his independent researches went beyond the findings of the mainstream of economics. Here is but one example.

Ricardian trade theory traditionally assumes zero factor mobility between countries or regions and 100 percent commodity mobility between countries or regions. Thünen's model works out the opposite case. Within a region, labor moves freely (on immobile land); goods move only at a cost. Where labor will locate was not a question that traditional trade theory considered, but Thünen did.

* * *

Modern geographers claim Thünen. That is their right. But economists like me, who are not all that taken with location theory, hail Thünen as more than a location theorist. His theory is a theory of general equilibrium.

Thünen belongs in the Pantheon with Léon Walras, John Stuart Mill, and Adam Smith. As Schumpeter would say, it is the inner ring of Valhalla they occupy.

APPENDIX: THÜNEN'S NATURAL WAGE AND HIS CAPITAL THEORY

Thünen who spent much of the last twenty years of life perfecting his "Natural wage," found his handiwork so good that he had its formula put on his gravestone.

His natural wage is the geometric mean of the Subsistence wage rate and the worker's Average Product: in his notation,

$$w^* = \sqrt{ap}.$$

In his 1934 Chicago lectures Paul Douglas, himself a do-gooder but already hooked on a marginal-product theory of wages, explained this

---

acres ultimately get settled, still further L must imply lower real wage ceteris paribus as land scarcity invokes the law of diminishing returns.

natural wage as more the product of Thünen's warm heart than his cool intellect – a partial atonement on his part for the sad, hard fact that an extra worker brings down the earnings of charter-member workers even though these work as hard as before and are as deserving (P. H. Douglas, 1934, pp. 34–37). As a beginning student, I regarded this natural wage as a naive Aristotelean golden mean between the least that labor could be paid in the steady state and the most. Half a century later I can discern only a superficial resemblance between Thünen's formula and John Nash's threat-bargaining theory.

Actually, as the reader of Schumpter (1954, pp. 465–67) or of Arthur H. Leigh (1946, 1968) will know, Thünen deduced his natural wage from a (rather odd) maximum problem, finding that wage as the root of a first-derivative equation. Almost universally Thünen has been hooted at for his natural wage.[11] One cannot say that posterity has been biased against him: in my reading of the evidence, commentators have been both too hard and too soft on him; but the fact remains that a scrupulously just autopsy will find that Thünen's natural wage lacks both positivistic verisimilitude and normative optimality.

For the present purpose I reviewed a dozen commentaries on the derivation of the natural wage, but singly or all together they do not quite provide the needed fair and complete post-mortem.

SCHUMPETER'S VERSION

Thünen, like Ricardo, is under the illusion that he can get rid of the complication of land and its rent by focussing on the external margin with zero rent. Grain is produced there by labor, and also by "capital" in Thünen's special sense of past labor stored up.

Schumpeter's scenario for Thünen is perhaps the simplest one. In effect, Schumpeter (1954, pp. 465–68) poses a Jevons-Wicksell point-input and point-output model. Labor at time t produces grain at time $t + \theta$ in the future. Call grain output p and labor-inputs' wages w. (These can be measured in numeraire of grain or anything else.) Profit or total interest is $p - w$. The rate of interest, earned on each unit of wage outlay and

---

[11] Bernard W. Dempsey (1960) is an exception. At the same time that we owe him gratitude for providing an English translation of Thünen's Volume II, Father Dempsey's defenses of the natural wage is subject to the same objections as are directed here against Thünen's own derivations.

expressed as a percentage return for a time period equal to the lag θ, is $(p - w)/w$ and is called z.

Thünen envisages workers who can own capital; or, what is the same thing, capitalists who may also work for wages. It is rather odd, for the last century or this one, to regard workers' wages as the prime source of saving. If the interest rate z is positive, there must be positive profits earned on past accumulations and it would be strange for Thünen not to regard such incomes as also a source of saving. Thünen in effect turns Marx and Kalecki upside down and makes wages rather than profits the source of saving. Accordingly, I shall keep the story uncluttered by assuming that all non-wage income gets consumed: current saving, y, comes for each of society's identical workers from the surplus of their w wages over a postulated subsistence level of consumption, $a : y = w - a$. (Remark: Malthus, Ricardo, and Marx meant by "subsistence wage" the rate workers had to get to maintain and reproduce their supply of labor. Thünen's "subsistence wage" is to be understood mostly as equalling what consumers spend on consumption out of their wage income – beyond their property income that, in my model, they also spend on consumption. Leigh and others have denied that a is a recognizable constant; I see no reason not to give Thünen all the rope he needs, so that we can assay the logic of his conceptions.)

During and since World War II, economists have learned that experts in operations analysis often devote much hard and clever effort in maximizing some maximands that are not sensible goals for policy. Thünen offers a similar case. Posterity has scoffed at his assumption that society will, or ought to, want to maximize the current return earned on current saving.

Thünen says:

$$\text{Maximize } z \times y = [(p - w)/w][w - a]. \tag{A1}$$

That is Thünen's major felony. It is a crime against normative economics, and against the positivistic economics of competitive behavior under laissez faire.

He compounds this felony by a major misdemeanor, which is a crime against logic. In Thünen's maximization, and with Schumpeter blowing no public whistle, a and p are both held constant at prescribed levels; only w is to be varied, and it is allegedly at our disposal to vary w arbitrarily.

There is no logical objection to regarding consumption out of wages as being frozen at a. (Only the facts are against the relevance of this.) But, as we shall see, it runs counter to the logic of Thünen's own model, to believe that what changes w won't also change p.

Mathematically, Thünen carries out an absurd purpose:

Subject to $p = \bar{p}$ and $a = \bar{a}$, $w \geq 0$,

$$\text{Max}_{w} \, \Phi(w) = \text{Max}_{w} \left[\frac{p - w}{w} (w - a) \right],$$

$$= \Phi(w^*) \tag{A2}$$

$$w^* = +\sqrt{ap}. \tag{A3}$$

Here w^* is the root of

$$0 = \Phi'(w) = (d/dw)[(p - w)w^{-1}(w - a)]$$

$$= -1 + (ap)w^{-2} \tag{A4}$$

$$\Phi''(w) < 0 \text{ for } w > 0.$$

Thünen, who knew that a tree growing on rent-free land ought to be cut at an age when its percentage instantaneous biological growth rate of saleable lumber is just as big as the interest rate at which money grows, ought to understand the following proper analysis of the Wicksell-Jevons model that Schumpeter should have squared his exposition with.

Grain output at $t + \theta$, $Q(t + \theta)$, is produced by labor input at $t, L(t)$:

$$Q(t + \theta) = f(\theta)L(t) > 0, f' > 0 > f''. \tag{A5}$$

If W/P_Q is the grain real wage rate and r is the instantaneous rate of interest, then competition implies for (A5) in the steady state:

$$f'(\theta)/f(\theta) = r, \, dr/d\theta < 0$$

$$f(\theta)e^{-r\theta} = W/P_Q, \, d(W/P_Q)/d\theta > 0 \tag{A6}$$

$$r = \rho(W/P_Q), \, dr/d(W/P_Q) < 0.$$

The last of these relations, the modern factor-price-frontier, Thünen and Ricardo only occasionally perceived.

What is the earnings flow from current saving of (W/P_Q) minus a? On an instantaneous rate basis, Thünen's zy becomes

$$r \times [(W/P_Q) - a] = \frac{f'(\theta)}{f(\theta)} [f(\theta)exp\{-f'(\theta)f(\theta)^{-1}\} - a]. \qquad (A7)$$

This is a monstrous maximand. But if it is to be maximized, Thünen should differentiate every one of its terms with respect to θ. (Or, expressing θ as a function of either one of r or W/P_Q, he will get the same result by differentiating *all* expressions by the chosen independent variable.)

In no case will the correct solution involve a geometric mean of Thünen's tombstone type. Specifically, it will *not* be anywhere near the case that

$$W/P_Q = +\sqrt{af(\theta)}.$$

There is no reason why (A7)'s maximand should even have a maximum. As we'll see, Thünen's criterion can call for an indefinitely large θ.

It is a case of what might be called the Sentimental Fallacy to think that a society, not now in the golden-rule state of maximal per-capita consumption, can by an act of will (or of capital expropriation by edict), attain that zero-interest nirvana. It is a mathematical theorem that neither Peking nor Manchester can go from a non-golden-rule technological steady state to a golden-rule steady state without experiencing sacrifice of current consumption in favor of (higher) future consumption. Starting from present θ, not equal to a larger θ^* that corresponds to maximum Thünen ry, our feasible current ry is less than that maximum, which itself may not be reachable for less than a century of $w - a$ thrift.

In short, there is no reason to want to go to Thünen's goal, and every reason to realize that you can't now be there anyway.

VINDICATING THÜNEN'S LOGIC ON CAPITAL

Schumpeter's scenario is only one such. I want to move to Thünen's own model, which involves a permanent-lived durable good (a "leet" or machine) that is produced instantaneously out of labor alone. (If a short lag occurred between input of labor and output of the machine, footnote 13 will show that this involves no essential complications.) Despite Leigh's reproving comments, I find Thünen's sure-footed treatment in 1850 of this case as highly commendable. He has anticipated correctly one instance of the modern Solow-Uzawa two-sector flow model of capital.

Let K be the stock of capital (of "leets"), measured in physical terms. The total labor supply of L is held constant. L is divided between the new machine industry, L_K, where it works alone; and the grain industry, L_Q where it works with K to produce grain. The production functions are:

$$dK/dt \text{ or } \dot{K} = bL_K = b(L - L_Q) \tag{A8}$$

$$Q = F[K, L_Q]$$

$$= L_Q f[K/L_Q], \; f' > 0 > f''. \tag{A9}$$

Combining (A8) and (A9), we have society's production-possibility frontier that is valid both in steady states and in general:

$$Q = F[K, L - b^{-1}\dot{K}]. \tag{A10}$$

The interest rate, r, and the real wage in grain, W/P_Q, are given respectively by

$$r = \partial\dot{K}/\partial K = \frac{\text{rent in grain of capital goods}}{\text{cost in grain capital goods}} \tag{A11}$$

$$= \frac{F_1[K, L - b^{-1}\dot{K}]}{F_2[K, L - b^{-1}\dot{K}]b^{-1}}.$$

The wage rate is given by marginal productivity:

$$W/P_Q = F_2[K, L - b^{-1}\dot{K}]. \tag{A12}$$

Here, $F_i[K, L_Q]$ stands for $\partial F/\partial K$ and $\partial F/\partial L_Q$ respectively. Thünen deserves highest marks for getting all this right.[12]

Since the right-hand sides of (A11) and (A12) depend only on the single parameter $K/(L - b^{-1}\dot{K})$, r and W/P_Q are connected by the factor-price-frontier trade-off:

---

[12] See Arthur H. Leigh (1968, Vol. 16, p. 19, first complete paragraph): what I call $(K/L, F_1, F_2)$ Leigh writes as $(q, \alpha, w = p - \alpha q)$. My maximand in (A14) Leigh writes as $[\alpha(p - \alpha q)^{-1}(p - \alpha q - a)]$. What Thünen should not be permitted to do is to differentiate this expression with respect to α without making p and q change as my (A14) and earlier relations show they must. Doing it right completely negates Thünen's derivation that $p - \alpha q$ or w will equal $+\sqrt{ap}$.

$$r = \rho(W/P_Q), dr/d(W/P_Q) < 0. \tag{A13}$$

Having vindicated Thünen's capital model,[13] we must indict him for mistreating it. If Thünen insists on maximizing $r[(W/P_Q) - a]$ – which happens to maximize the *grain* value of earnings on current saving and not their value in wage units or leets units! – he should do so recognizing all the interdependences between r and W/P_Q that his own model calls for:

$$\underset{K/L_Q}{\text{Max}} \left[\frac{F_1[K/L_Q, 1]}{F_2[K/L_Q, 1]b^{-1}} (F_2[K/L_Q, 1] - a) \right]. \tag{A14}$$

The resulting maximizing $(W/P_Q)^*$ – if it exists, and it need not – has absolutely no relation to Thünen's geometric mean:

$$(W/P_Q)^* \neq \sqrt{aF[K/L, 1]}. \tag{A15}$$

THE RAMSEY-SOLOW SANTA CLAUS CASE

Enough can be too much. However, the one-sector model of Frank P. Ramsey (1928) and Robert M. Solow (1956) is so simple as to permit a wrapup of the issues.

Here, with proper choice of units,

---

[13] Leigh, along with earlier critics of Thünen, is concerned whether circularity vitiates Thünen's capital-theory formulation. Here is how one vindicates Thünen in a discrete-period model. We write for him

$$K(t+1) - K(t) + \delta K(t) = bL_K(t)$$

where δ is the rate of (exponential) depreciation. Combine this with

$$\begin{aligned} Q(t+1) &= K[K(t), L_Q(t)] \\ &= F[K(t), L - L_K(t)] \\ &= F[K(t), L - b^{-1}K(t+1) + b^{-1}(1-\delta)K(t)]. \end{aligned}$$

Then the interest rate z and real grain wage become

$$z = \frac{F_1[K(t)/L_Q(t), 1]}{F_2[K(t)/L_Q(t), 1]b^{-1}} - \delta$$

$$W/P_Q = F_2[K(t)/L_Q(t), 1]/(1+z).$$

Any circular interdependence constitutes virtuous and not vicious circularity. QED.

Incidentally, the charge by Erich Carrell, discussed in Hall (1966, p. xxii, n.l), that there is some inconsistency or circularity in Thünen's space model is completely rebutted in my present version of Thünen's model.

$$Q + \dot{K} = F[K, L] = Lf[K/L], f' > 0 > f''$$
$$r = F_1[K/L, 1] \tag{A16}$$

$$W/P_Q = F_2[K/L, 1] = W/P_{\dot{K}},$$
$$p = F[K/L, 1],$$
$$r = \rho(W/P_Q), \rho' < 0. \tag{A16}$$

If people are all alike, we can set L equal to unity. If what they save, y, is always $(W/P_Q) - a$, then the system's evolution over all time must from (A16) satisfy

$$\dot{K} = F[K, 1] - KF_1[K, 1] - a. \tag{A17}$$

Thünen's maximand, ry, is precisely the system's instantaneous growth rate

$$\dot{F} = \dot{K} \, \partial F[K, 1]/\partial K = r\dot{K} = F_1[K, 1](F[K, 1] - KF_1[K, 1] - a)$$
$$= r(F[K, 1] - Kr - a). \tag{A18}$$

His bizarre saving stipulation, when taken literally as I have done, makes the system overshoot the golden-rule state once it gets there. His is a cancerous mode of behavior. It is an instance of the Sentimental Fallacy to believe that we can alter any system's growth rate *after* we have committed it to having its consumption frozen at a constant profit income, and with existing $K(t)$ given to us as a heritage of the long past. Still we can humor Thünen and ask on his behalf the meaningful question: For what K — what K/L — does his system achieve *its* fastest growth rate? To answer this, we seek the maximum of Thünen's ry:

$$\underset{K}{\text{Max}}[r(w - a)] = \underset{K}{\text{Max}} \dot{F}$$
$$= \underset{K}{\text{Max}}(F_1[K, 1]F[K, 1] - KF_1[K, 1]^2 - aF_1[K, 1]). \tag{A19}$$

The answer is a surprising one. Possibly no such maximum exists. Thus, if $F[K,1]$ were Cobb-Douglas, of the Wicksell type $K^{1/2}$, $\dot{F}$ like F will grow forever, obeying

$$\dot{F} = \frac{1}{2}[1 - aK^{-1/2}] > 0, K > a^2. \tag{A20}$$

The system has no inflection point, no Thünen maximum point, since

$$\dot{F} > 0, \; \tfrac{1}{4}a < K < \infty. \tag{A21}$$

If $f[K,1]$ were quadratic, the system would also grow cancerously. Once it reaches Thünen's inflection point, it will not tarry there. Nor should it. But, alas, once it reaches the golden-rule bliss point, it will overshoot disastrously – as all its capital formation is wasted or even worse can become harmful.

The Ramsey-Solow model shows us that a wage equal to Thünen's geometric mean between a and labor's average product could well be a rotten wage, worse than the competitive marginal-product wage. Thus, for $F[K,L]$ a Cobb-Douglas function, the marginal-product wage $F[K,L]$ becomes as $(K, L) \to \infty$ an *infinite multiple* of Thünen's $\sqrt{ap}$. If the elasticity of substitution is less than unity, as $K/L \to \infty$ the competitive wage becomes all of the average product, p, and this approaches an infinite markup on $\sqrt{ap}$. If the elasticity of substitution is always above unity – a dubious possibility – Thünen's $\sqrt{ap}$ would eventually grant the workers an infinite multiple of their rising competitive wage.[14]

FINAL REFLECTIONS

1. Conceptual difficulties in Thünen's theory of distribution between labor, land, and capital have been shown to be capable of being cleared up while still his essential vision is preserved.

   At 200 we hail Thünen more admiringly than was possible at 100 or at the time of his death.

2. Posterity has been right to criticize Thünen's arbitrary maximand of current earnings on current saving out of wages. Where posterity has

---

[14] I have had to free myself of the 1934 impression that the natural wage is something necessarily in excess of the marginal-productivity wage. I believe Thünen regarded it as exceeding the marginal-productivity wage that laissez faire would bring about spontaneously, probably regarding it rather to be equal to the marginal-productivity wage that property-owning workers can and should contrive for themselves. Such an interpretation is a disquieting one, for it implies that Thünen did not understand that his own system, given its short-run labor supply and stock of capital (even if a growing one), will determine only one present-day marginal-productivity real wage.

When contemplating capital and labor, Thünen treats the two factors symmetrically. The return on each is interchangeably treated as a residual or as a marginal product; thus, Thünen presents a heuristic proof of Euler's Theorem along the lines of Joan Robinson (1934) or Paul Samuelson (1972). I don't recall that he treated land in a labor-land context other than as a residual. He sensed that even with zero transport costs, if land were limited relative to labor, it would bear rent even if all acres were alike. We see that it was no exaggeration, in Samuelson (1983), to hail Johann Heinrich von Thünen as one of the great microeconomists of all time, a peer of Augustin Cournot and the often over-rated David Ricardo.

nodded is in failing to realize that Thünen fell victim to the Sentimental Fallacy in specifying the wrong technological constraints within which his maximizing was to take place.

3. Curiously, just as technical change was ushering in a century of rising agricultural real wage rates in Europe – a trend that would have been even more favorable were it not for New World competition (an element that does not really belong to Thünen's most abstract isolated state) – Thünen succumbed to pessimism over laissez-faire wage trends and labored away on his utopian alternative.

How did so deep and subtle a mind get mired in the doctrine of the natural wage? Who can say? I venture the hypothesis that it was because Thünen was an autodidact – a lone scholar without colleagues, students, readers, or critics within his own lifetime – that his generous impulse to reform the world drove him to a grandiloquent recipe for the world.

Having taken measure of the chaff and the kernel of his analysis, posterity can cherish his heritage.

REFERENCES

Beckmann, Martin J. and Marschak, Thomas. "An Activity Analysis Approach to Location Theory," *Kyklos*, 1955, 8 (fasc. 2), pp. 125–41.

Blaug, Mark. *Economic theory in retrospect*. Homewood, IL: Richard D. Irwin, [1962] 1968, Ch. 8.

Böhm-Bawerk, Eugen von. *Capital and interest*. Vols. I-III, South Holland, IL: Libertarian Press, [1884, 1889], 1959.

Clark, John B. *Distribution of wealth*. NY: Macmillan, [1899] 1944.

Dempsey, Bernard W. *The frontier wage: With the text of the second part of the Isolated State*. Chicago: Loyola University Press, 1960.

Douglas, Paul H. *Theory of wages*. NY: Macmillan, 1934.

Hall, Peter, ed. *Von Thünen's isolated state*. London: Pergamon Press, 1966.

Leigh, Arthur H. "Von Thünen's Theory of Distribution and the Advent of Marginal Analysis," *J. Polit. Econ.*, Dec. 1946, 54, pp. 481–502.

—"J. H. Von Thünen," in *International encyclopedia of the social sciences*. NY: Macmillan and Free Press, 1968, pp. 16–20.

Merton, Robert K. *The sociology of science*. Chicago: University of Chicago Press, 1973.

Petersen, Asmus. *Thünen's Isolierte Statt: Die Landwirtschaft als Glied der Volkswirtschaft*. Berlin: Parez, 1944.

Pigou, Arthur C., ed. *Memorials of Alfred Marshall*. London: Macmillan, 1925.

Ramsey, Frank P. "A Mathematical Theory of Saving," *Econ. J.*, Dec. 1928, 38, pp. 543–59.

Recktenwald, Horst C., ed. *Political economy: A historical perspective*. London: Collier-Macmillan, 1973, pp. 135–56.

Robinson, Joan. "Euler's Theorem and the Problem of Distribution," *Econ. J.*, Sept. 1934, 44, pp. 398–414.

226   *V. Johann Heinrich von Thünen*

Salin, Edgar. "Johann Heinrich von Thünen in seiner Zeit," *Zeitschrift für Agrargeschichte und Agrarsoziologie: Sonderheft: Johann Heinrich von Thünen*, 6, 1958, abridged.

Samuelson, Paul A. "The Transfer Problem and Transport Cost, II: Analysis of Effects of Trade Impediments," *Econ. J.*, June 1954, 64, pp. 264–89.

—"A Modern Treatment of the Ricardian Economy: I. The Pricing of Goods and of Labor and Land Services," *Quart. J. Econ.*, Feb. 1959, 73(1), pp. 1–35.

—"A Quantum-Theory Model of Economics: Is the Coordinating Entrepreneur Just Worth His Profit?" *Essays in honour of Paul Rosenstein-Rodan.* Eds.: Jagdish Bhagwati and Richard S. Eckaus. London: Allen and Unwin, 1972, Ch. 18. See corrected version in *Collected scientific papers of Paul A. Samuelson.* Vol. 4. Eds.: Hiroaki Nagatani and Kathleen Crowley. Cambridge, MA: MIT Press, 1977, Ch. 214.

—"1983: Marx, Keynes and Schumpeter," speech given at Eastern Economic Association, March 10, 1983; *Eastern Econ. Assoc. J.*, forthcoming.

Schneider, Erich. "Johann Heinrich von Thünen," *Econometrica*, Jan. 1934, 2, pp. 1–12.

Schumpeter, Josef A. *History of economic analysis.* NY: Oxford University Press, 1954.

Solow, Robert M. "A Contribution to the Theory of Economic Growth," *Quart. J. Econ.*, Feb. 1956, 70, pp. 65–94.

Thünen, Johann H. von. *Der Isolierte Staat in Beziehung auf Landwirtschaft und Nationalökonomie.* Third ed. Ed.: Heinrich Waentig, Jena: Gustav Fischer, 1930. See Peter Hall and Bernard W. Dempsey for English translations.

Wicksteed, Philip H. *Coordination of the laws of distribution.* London: 1894. Reissued in *London School of Economics Scarce Tracts*, No. 12. London: 1932.

PART VI

KARL MARX

Wages and Interest: A Modern Dissection of Marxian Economic Models

Modern economic analysis can throw light on the ancient problems of Ricardo and Marx. Neither of these gave a logically complete description of factor and goods pricing in the simplest case where land is free and where labor and intermediate capital goods applied today produce output after one period of time according to a constant-returns-to-scale production function. I propose to analyze such a simple economy, and then compare it with their formulations.

Just as the utilitarian Bentham was called "Paley without hell-fire," Marx can be classified by the modern theorist as "Ricardo without diminishing returns." The present treatment is part of a longer study of Ricardo-like systems. It makes no attempt to do justice to the many noneconomic and imperfect-competition aspects of Marx's thought, but takes seriously his belief that he was baring the inner workings of competitive capitalism.

Technological Assumptions. Assume two industries. Industry I produces homogeneous physical machines or raw materials called K (for physical capital). Industry II produces homogeneous consumption goods called Y. Production in both industries requires homogeneous labor $L_1 + L_2 = L$ and physical capital $K_1 + K_2 = K$ today, with output appearing one period later. Or:

$$K^{t+1} = F(L_1^t, K_1^t) \quad L_1^t + L_2^t \leqq L^t$$

$$Y^{t+1} = f(L_2^t, K_2^t) \quad K_1^t + K_2^t \leqq K^t, \tag{1}$$

where the inequalities reflect the fact that one input may be redundant in supply.

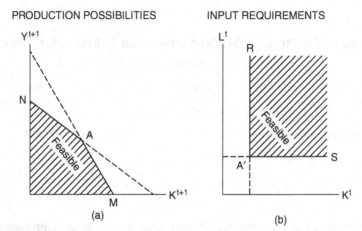

PRODUCTION POSSIBILITIES   INPUT REQUIREMENTS

(a)   (b)

Figure 1. *NAM* shows goods producible with given inputs. *RA'S* shows inputs needed to produce specified outputs.

Marx is supposed to have thought the production functions F and f in (1) to be of the fixed-coefficient type rather than of the smooth J. B. Clark type. So in this case we can[1] replace the functions of (1) by the logically equivalent relations:

$$L_1^t \leqq a_1 K^{t+1} \quad K_1^t \leqq b_1 K^{t+1}$$

$$L_2^t \leqq a_2 Y^{t+1} \quad K_2^t \leqq b_2 Y^{t+1},$$

where (a_1, b_1, a_2, b_2) are the positive technical production coefficients characterizing the fixed-proportion constant-returns-to-scale production functions.

The system's production possibilities can be summarized by

$$a_1 K^{t+1} + a_2 Y^{t+1} \leqq L^t$$
$$b_1 K^{t+1} + b_2 Y^{t+1} \leqq K^t. \qquad (2)$$

These relations are portrayed in Figures 1a and 1b. In Figure 1a, the straight lines correspond to the two equations of (2) with inputs L^t and K^t given. The corner A of the production-possibility locus will move northwest or southeast when one of the inputs is increased. Figure 1b shows the equations of

---

[1] For this and other facts about linear programming and modern economic theory, see R. Dorfman, R. M. Solow, and P. A. Samuelson, *Linear Programming and Economic Analysis* (New York, 1957), particularly Ch. 11. It is shown there that the functions F and f can be written in the form:

Minimum of $(L_i^t/a_i, K_i^t/b_i)$.

(2), but with outputs K^{t+1} and Y^{t+1} specified: if an output rises, the corner A' of society's input-requirement locus $RA'S$ will move northeast.

The relative prices of outputs K^{t+1} and Y^{t+1}, $(p_2/p_1)^{t+1}$, must equal the absolute slope of the NAM locus at the production point actually observed. The relative prices of inputs L^t and K^t, $(w/p_t)^t$, where w is the wage of labor, can be any nonnegative number because the corner A' in Figure 1b can have a straight line of any slope tangent to it.

I. Stationary Conditions

Simple Reproduction. Under stationary conditions, or slowly changing conditions, the capital stock K^t will accommodate itself to the supply of labor L^t, which is assumed to be fixed, so that we shall be at a corner A rather than at a point on NA or AM where one of the inputs would be redundant and therefore free. Hence, p_1, w, and p_2 will all be strictly positive. These prices, or their ratios, need not be constant through time but may be slowly changing – probably in a rather predictable way.

The model of "simple reproduction," in which all variables repeat themselves over time, is the natural starting place for an exact analysis. In this case we replace (2) by:

$$L^t = L^{t+1} = \cdots = L$$
$$K^t = K^{t+1} = \cdots = K$$
$$Y^t = Y^{t+1} = \cdots = Y$$

$$a_1 K + a_2 Y = L$$
$$b_1 K + b_2 Y = K; \tag{3}$$

or solving, by:

$$Y = \frac{1 - b_1}{a_2(1 - b_1) + a_1 b_2} L$$

$$K = \frac{b_2}{a_2(1 - b_1) + a_1 b_2} L \tag{4}$$

where labor supply L^t is taken as given at the L level. Being the only factor nonaugmentable in the long run, labor plays a pivotal role: all other magnitudes are proportional to it. The national product NP can be expressed in labor units simply as L; in consumption-good units NP is given by Y in the first equation of (4). Production of K goes into gross product; but K being an intermediate good needed to produce final consumption goods, it is not included in stationary NP.[2]

Prices, Wages, Interest. Though prices and wages are constant under repetitive stationary conditions, this does not mean that production is timeless or that intermediate products just now produced by labor and machines will exchange one for one against themselves when "ripened" one period from now – or one for one against finished goods produced today from last period's inputs. The fundamental factor relating unripened product today to ripened product one period from now is the market interest rate r (or what Ricardo and Marx would call the rate of profit, a pure percentage per period).

If the interest rate were $r = .05$ per period, then 100 finished units of Y (or of K) would today trade in the competitive market for 105 unfinished units of Y (or of K) just produced by current labor and capital goods. Free competition among producers, investors, owners of labor, and owners of capital goods will insure the following unit cost-of-production equations:

$$p_1 = (wa_1 + p_1b_1)(1 + r)$$
$$p_2 = (wa_2 + p_1b_2)(1 + r). \tag{5}$$

The first of these equations is directly solvable for p_1/w; and substituting the result into the second, we get the following explicit solution to (5) in terms of $(a_1, b_1; a_2, b_2; r)$:

$$\frac{p_1}{w} = \frac{a_1(1 + r)}{1 - b_1(1 + r)}$$
$$\frac{p_2}{w} = \frac{a_2(1 + r)[1 - b_1(1 + r)] + a_1(1 + r)b_2(1 + r)}{1 - b_1(1 + r)}. \tag{6}$$

The reciprocal of the last of these is the real wage expressed in terms of consumption goods. If interest were zero, this expression would equal the full productivity of labor in producing consumption goods, as given in the

---

[2] Ricardo made quite different assumptions about L. He assumed a Malthus-like subsistence wage level at which any number of workers would be produced and reproduced. Such subsistence wages he treated as intermediate product – like hay being fed to horses or coal to furnaces; hence Ricardo's net product would be mine minus wages. Marx assumed actual L used to be less than available L because of the existence of a "reserve army of the unemployed." He would interpret L in (4) then as actual L and would have to add this magnitude as a further unknown variable of the system. A new equation is then needed. The Marxian literature relates the size of the reserve army to labor-saving innovations, depressions, and migration but does not appear to contain a determinate quantitative equation to explain why it is as large as it is, why it is not larger than it is.

first equation of (4). But of course (4) refers only to steady states of output and input, paying no attention to the time lag between inputs and outputs. Only under special, and unrealistic, market assumptions can the competitive supply and demand relations be expected to ignore these timing relations: if supply and demand among investors and consumers yields a positive r, then workers will receive their "discounted" productivity. This means many things to many writers: exploitation to some, to others merely that workers (and machine-owners) receive their full *undiscounted* productivities in terms of the intermediate product that they *now* produce. Because of the workers' supply and demand for ripe and unripe products, and the corresponding supply and demand of those who own consumption or capital goods, the market rate of interest r is what it is. And being what it is, costs and prices and incomes are what they are.

Note too that the price ratio between any two goods, such as $p_2/w \div p_1/w$ in (6), or between either of these and any third good, will *not* be proportional to their embodied labor contents as given in the first equation of (4) and the corresponding equation derivable for K in terms of L_1 alone.[3] Exchange values would precisely be given by such labor contents if interest or profit were zero. (Remember we have also conveniently banished all land rents from existence.) This mathematical fact will not be of comfort to one looking for a labor theory of value as a base point for a theory of labor exploitation; the proportionality of market price to labor content applies validly only when surplus value is zero and not worth talking about!

When interest is positive, a change in its magnitude will change all relative prices, a hard fact that Ricardo never could square with his desire to find an absolute measure of value based upon labor. And even had Marx lived to write a fourth or fortieth volume of *Capital*, he could not have altered this arithmetic obstacle to the relevance of his labor theory of value.

The Tableau Économique. For each stationary state based on L and r, we can combine the prices of (6) and the quantities of (4) to get the Quesnay-Marx-Leontief money-flow matrix. Of course, we must reverse the Marxian emphasis, beginning with market exchange values rather than labor values

---

[3] If we write $\Delta K = K^{t+1} - K^t$ as the net production of physical capital, over and above what is used up as intermediate product in production ("depreciation"), then the steady-state production-possibility equation of final goods producible for each L may be shown to be given by:

$$a_1(1 - b_1)^{-1}\Delta K + [a_2 + a_1(1 + b_1)^{-1}b_2]Y = L.$$

because that is what the market that determines people's incomes and goods' prices begins (and ends!) with. We get:

$$p_1 K = (wL_1 + p_1 K_1)(1 + r)$$
$$p_2 Y = (wL_2 + p_1 K_2)(1 + r). \tag{7}$$

Write $p_1 K_1$ as the Marxian "constant capital" C_1, wL_1 as "variable capital" V_1, and the difference between Industry-I receipts and the sum of these as "surplus value" S_1. Define C_2, V_2, S_2 for the second industry likewise. Then by definition (7) can be rewritten:

$$p_1 K = C_1 + V_1 + S_1$$
$$p_2 Y = C_2 + V_2 + S_2. \tag{8}$$

Such a relation would be valid even if positive accumulation were taking place, with $\Delta K = K^{t+1} - K^t > O$, and (7)'s $K = K_1 + K_2 + \Delta K$. If simple reproduction is assumed, with $K = K_1 + K_2$, then it is easy to derive the Marxian condition for simple reproduction.[4]

$$C_2 = V_1 + S_1 \tag{9}$$

However, the supposition made in *Capital*, Vol. I, of equal rates of surplus value in different industries, $S_1/V_1 = S_2/V_2$, is seen to be generally untrue. By (6)–(8), we find:

$$\frac{S_1}{V_1} = \frac{r(wa_1 + p_1 b_1)}{wa_1} = r + r\frac{p_1}{w}\frac{b_1}{a_1} = \frac{r}{1 - b_1(1 + r)}$$
$$\frac{S_2}{V_2} = \frac{r(wa_2 + p_1 b_2)}{wa_2} = r + r\frac{p_1}{w}\frac{b_2}{a_2} = \frac{S_1}{V_1} + r\frac{p_1}{w}\left(\frac{b_2}{a_2} - \frac{b_1}{a_1}\right). \tag{10}$$

It would be a fortuitous selection of $(a_1, b_1; a_2, b_2)$ – namely that for which $b_1/a_1 = b_2/a_2$ – that would make these equal when both are not zero. However, the situation is a little better than Marx's critics have realized: for if the "organic composition of capital" happened to be the same for different industries at one interest rate, then it would have to be the same for all values of r.

Table I shows the simple reproduction model in the Leontief tableau form of input-output money flows. Each industry is listed in rows and in columns. Thus, the column of Industry I gives the dollar production costs it

---

[4]   P. M. Sweezy, *The Theory of Capitalist Development* (New York, 1942), p. 77. This seems by all odds the best book on Marxian economics.

Table I. – *Simple Reproduction, Leontief-Style*

Industries	I	II	Final Products	Gross Product Totals
I	p_1K_1	p_1K_2	0	Σ
II	0	0	p_2Y^*	Σ^*
Value Added $\Big\{$ Wages	wL_1	wL_2		Σ $\Big\}\Sigma^*$
Interest	$r(wL_1 + p_1K_1)$	$r(wL_2 + p_1K_2)$		Σ
Gross Costs	Σ	Σ^*	Σ^*	$\Sigma\Sigma$

pays out. The row indicates where Industry I sells its products. Above and to the left of the broken lines are the intermediate-goods flows; then on the right comes the value of final output, and below come the value-added cost items (excluding, of course, all depreciation). The starred quantities represent national product, as final commodity flow or equivalent factor costs. The sums of rows or columns are indicated by Σ, and the $\Sigma\Sigma$ checks the identity of all the table items to the gross sum of column sums and to the gross sum of row sums. As a condition of stationariness, $\Delta K = 0$ in row I's third column: hence (9)'s identity between p_1K_2 and the value-added items of column I.

To be stressed is the fact that our table is limited by more than the tautological accounting identities: having committed ourselves to equations (1)–(6), we must make each entry in the table directly proportional to total labor L, with a proportionality coefficient that is an easily determined function of $(a_1, b_1; a_2, b_2; r)$ and nothing else. I leave the working out of such coefficients to the reader, since they are important only for Marx's special two-industry circular model. Later we shall see how the coefficients vary for each percentage rate of growth of the system.

A Digression on the "Transformation" Problem. Marx seems never to have quite mastered the purely technological implications of his simplest models. It is idle to speculate whether his Volume II analysis of circular flows might not have been more fruitful if he had not misled himself by Volume I's attempted labor theory. After all, we don't expect in 1860 to find 1960 models. But later scholars surely would have made progress faster in this field if they had subjected the labor theory to careful analysis rather than spent so much time in what must seem to a critic as sterile apologetics.

One honest attempt to analyze the relations between exchange values and labor values beyond the unsatisfactory state left by the posthumous Volume

III is associated with the names of Bortkiewicz, Sweezy, and Winternitz.[5] Yet the present *exact* analysis of this model suggests that this so-called "transformation problem" is rather pointless. Equations (6)–(7) determine all market magnitudes in terms of $(a_1, b_1; a_2, b_2; r; L)$. Using the definitions implicit in (8), we can then evaluate all the Marxian expressions as functions of these same variables. Logically this transformation goes from exchange values to Marxian-defined values – not vice versa! This is because exchange values are solidly based on equations (5)–(6), as Ricardo, Smith, and all modern economists would agree. There is no similar solid ground to be found in the Marxian labor theory of value; a model based on equal rates of surplus value is like a made-up nursery tale, of no particular relevance to the ascertainable facts of the simple competitive model (nor to the facts, for that matter, of the Chamberlin monopolistic competition models or the models of developing and oscillating capitalism).

Many Marxians have thought it a virtue of the labor theory of value that it "explains its deviations" from the market-price theory. If so it shares this virtue with every theory, however nonsensical: for truth always equals "error plus a deviation"; and while I should prefer to say that Euclid's geometry explains the deviations between it and my daughter's geometry rather than vice versa, I would not go to the guillotine over such a semantic issue. A quite different defence of the Volume I detour is the historical argument that prices *once* were in accord with Volume I's labor theory, but just as Volume III evolved from Volume I so did the capitalistic system outgrow the simple labor theory: ontogeny repeating phylogeny may be accurate biology, but a respect for the facts of history and anthropology stands in the way of this hypothesis. There is finally Marx's own view that the labor theory of Volume I is needed to "determine" or "explain" the *aggregate* of surplus value, with the bourgeois theories of Volume III having the mundane task of settling the details of how the determined aggregate is to be *allocated* among the different industries. Actually, in the competitive Marxian model

[5] See Sweezy, *op. cit.*, Ch. 7 for discussion and references. Also, L. von Bortkiewicz, "On the Correction of Marx's Fundamental Theoretical Construction in the Third Volume of *Capital*," transl. by Sweezy from the July 1907 *Jahrbücher für Nationalökonomie und Statistik* and given as an appendix in Sweezy's English edition of Böhm-Bawerk's critique of Marx and Hilferding's rejoinder: *Karl Marx and the Close of His System* (New York, 194) J. Winternitz, "Value and Price: A Solution of the so-called Transformation Problem," *Econ. Jour.*, June 1948, LVIII, 276–80. R. L. Meek, *Studies in the Labour Theory of Value* (London, 1956), pp. 189–200, discusses this problem and gives reference to later *Econ. Jour.* writings.

defined by equations (1) and the following, there can be no prior determination of the aggregate: the whole is the sum of its (admittedly nonindependent) parts and all the pricing relations are simultaneously determined.[6]

I have not the space to deal with the defensive argument that Volume I's labor theory is a (needed or unneeded?) simplifying first approximation. Modern science and economics abound with simplifying first approximations, but one readily admits their inferiority to second approximations and drops them when challenged. Moreover, to my mind, the only legitimate first approximation would be that of Smith and Ricardo in which the labor theory is first introduced with zero surplus value or profits (as in Ricardian comparative advantage examples) but is then to be dropped as unrealistic. Volume I's first approximation of equal positive rates of surplus value, S_i/V_i, is not a simplifying assumption but rather – to the extent it contradicts equal profits rates $S_i/(V_i + C_i)$ – a complicating detour. Marxolaters, to use Shaw's term, should heed the basic economic precept valid in all societies: Cut your losses!

II. Incompatibility of Falling Profit and Falling Real Wage

Falling Real Wage or Falling Rate of Profit? We now have the equipment to answer an unresolved problem of the Marxian literature. Is there a

---

[6] Maurice Dobb, *On Economic Theory and Socialism* (London, 1955), Chapter 17, deals with the transformation problem. Dobb, as does Sweezy, seems to feel that Bortkiewicz came to criticize Marx but in effect ended up justifying him by showing that labor's wage was determined after a "deduction" and by arguing as follows: "If . . . the rate of profit in no way depends on the condition of production of those goods which do not enter into real wages, then origin of profit must clearly be sought in the wage-relationships and not in the ability of capital to increase production." (L. von Bortkiewicz, "Value and Price in the Marxian System," English transl. in *International Economic Papers No. 2* [1952], p. 33). I do not see that the Bortkiewicz "deduction" or "withholding" theory of wages differs essentially from the conventional "discounted" productivity theories here analyzed and subscribed to by Taussig, Wicksell, Böhm-Bawerk, and non-Austrians. Adding a nonwage-good sector with its new (a, b) coefficients and adhering to horizontal labor-supply conditions which fix the real wage, we may find it true that all three industries can come into stationary equilibrium and with r determinable from (6) or (11) quite independently of the new (a, b) coefficients. But how does this make anyone prefer Volume I to Volume III or to any modern bourgeois theory?

Without going into the social relations of the past or future, any economist can see these implications of competitive market prices.(He can also see that the (b_1, b_2) coefficients reflecting the productivity of capital *do* affect r; and he can envisage a case where Industry III alone, by virtue of having $a_3 = 0$ and $b_3 < 1$ will determine its own-rate of profit by itself, and he will realize that if this new r differs from that of (11) what must give is not bourgeois economic theory or the capitalistic institutional economy but rather the assumption of stationary relative prices!)

law of the declining rate of profit as time goes on? Ricardo and Sir Edward West in 1815 showed that the answer is, Definitely yes, if you assume Malthusian reproduction of labor matches the capital accumulation that is applied to scarce land. The law of diminishing returns applied to land then guarantees that profit, or interest, should fall.

Marx, having in most of his work ruled out such rising rent considerations, explicitly rejects this explanation of falling profits. Moreover, Marx was like Malthus and older economists in not bothering to distinguish between technological changes and changes within a given production function. This does not mean that for him a postulated secular econometric law meant that literally what it prophesied would indeed happen; for, like Malthus and others, he often spoke of "tendencies", and in such a way that we hardly know how to decide when he was wrong – and hence when he was right!

From a tautology relating the profit rate r to society's rate of surplus value $\Sigma S / \Sigma V$ and its organic composition of capital $\Sigma C / \Sigma V$, Marx deduced the tautology that higher values of the latter, the former being held constant, would necessarily mean that r falls. Sweezy, Joan Robinson, and most analysts of Marx have rightly, I think, criticized this arbitrary *ceteris paribus* type of argument. The rate of surplus value is a purely derived concept about which little can be said in advance until we already know what is happening to the (a, b) technological coefficients and the supply-demand relations for labor and interest loans. Instead therefore we must tackle directly the question of what accumulation will tend to do to r, basing ourselves on the actual behavior equations of competitive capitalism.

First though, we should note a contradiction in Marx's thinking that analysts have pointed out. Along with the "law of the falling rate of profit," Marxian economists often speak of the "law of the falling (or constant) real wage of labor." Some Marxians have even thought that the important fruit of *Capital*'s peculiar definitions has been this law of the "immiseration" of the working classes, with the rich getting richer the poor poorer, and with nothing to be done about it until capitalism becomes so senile and cycle-ridden as to lead inevitably to a revolutionary transformation into socialism or communism. The facts of economic history have, of course, not dealt kindly with this law. And Marx himself did not adhere to it at all times. But he perhaps didn't fully realize the inconsistency of his two inevitable laws. As Joan Robinson points out: "Marx can only demonstrate a falling tendency in profits by abandoning his argument that real wages tend to be constant."[7] Our model is well-designed to show this.

Specifically, with specified (a, b) coefficients if attempts to accumulate did succeed in bringing profit r down to a lower plateau, the real wage would have to be higher – and by a quantitative amount to be predicted from our second formula of (6), namely

$$\frac{w}{p_2} = \frac{1 - b_1(1 + r)}{a_2(1 + r)[1 - b_1(1 + r)] + a_1(1 + r)b_2(1 + r)}. \qquad (11)$$

This rational function grows as the interest or profit rate falls, reaching its maximum when r reaches its zero level.

A Theorem about Technological Change under Perfect Competition. This wage-profit relation is derived, not from the orthodox model involving smooth marginal productivities, but from the simplest fixed-coefficients model that Marx seems often to have had in mind.[8] It does rest though on fixed technology as given by the (a, b) coefficients. Since Marx admits technological change into his system, doesn't *my* argument that falling r with given (a, b) coefficients implies rising real wage w/p_2 become irrelevant? In the competitive model, I believe not completely.

For technological change is itself subject to *some* laws. A technical improvement must be an improvement or it will not be introduced in a

---

[7] Joan Robinson, *An Essay on Marxian Economics* (London, 1942), p. 42. Also, Sweezy, *op. cit.*, Ch. 6.

[8] J. Robinson, *op. cit.*, p. 43 demonstrates the orthodox case, making implicit use of a smooth two-factor homogeneous production function. Her next page's numerical example, suggesting that with a fixed real wage r *might* fall, is inconsistent with such a model, no matter how "very sharply" the marginal productivity of capital is assumed to fall; forgotten is the fact that when increased capital to labor leaves the real wage constant, decreased labor to capital *must* leave the profit rate constant too; actually, for all changes within a smooth or unsmooth homogeneous production function, Δ(real wage) equals $-\lambda\Delta$(profit rate), where λ is an intermediate positive capital/labor ratio.

Recently William Fellner, "Marxian Hypotheses and Observable Trends under Capitalism: A 'Modernized' Interpretation," *Econ. Jour.*, Mar. 1957, LXVII, 16–25, argues that a two-factor, homogeneous production function, zero-monopoly world can have its real-wage marginal productivity and its profit marginal productivity simultaneously fall – provided a sufficiently labor-saving invention has intervened. Fellner's conclusion is inconsistent with my theorem: competition would keep the invention he envisages from ever becoming exclusively dominant. The rest of Fellner's excellent paper is quite unaffected by his pp. 20–21 discussion of this point, which in any case no longer represents his opinion on the subject. Since writing this paper, I note H. D. Dickinson, "The Falling Rate of Profit in Marxian Economics," *Rev. Econ. Stud.*, Feb. 1957, XXIV, 120–31, deals with a similar topic, attempting to use the Marxian C, V, S, categories. The sharp contrast with the present treatment is worthy of note.

perfect-competition market economy: Marx cannot repeal the valid part of Adam Smith's law of the Invisible Hand, for its validity depends only on the existence of numerous avaricious competitors. To illustrate, imagine an old set of coefficients $(a_1, b_1; a_2, b_2; r)$ and a new possible set $(a_1', b_1'; a_2', b_2'; r')$. Then if $r' < r$ and if the new technology will actually win its way in a competitive market over the old, I assert the theorem that *the new steady-state real wage $(w/p_2)'$ must be greater than the old real wage.*[9]

This is straightforwardly provable by the mathematics of linear programming. It will become intuitively clear if one considers the special Ricardian case where $b_1 = 0$ and no circular complications can arise from the fact that it takes machines (K_1) to make machines (K). Remember that in a perfectly competitive market it really doesn't matter who hires whom: so have labor hire "capital," paying the new market interest rate $r' < r$; then labor could always use the old technology and paying less than r get better than the old real wage. If labor does not do this, it must be because it can now do even better than better.[10]

If my result or my argument seems paradoxical, remember that perfect competition – like Christianity – will be found to be very paradoxical if ever it is universally tried. And remember too that Marx has made the unrealistic assumption that everything except labor is reproducible in the long run. If he had abandoned his labor-theory-of-value concepts and from the beginning built on the patent fact that natural resources too are productive (in the unemotive sense that if the U.S.A. or U.S.S.R. didn't have them, its product would be less), then the possibility of having profit and wages both fall would have to be admitted. He would also have been in a better position to explain why some people are very rich indeed and why some countries are more prosperous than others.

---

[9] Rewriting (11) as $w/p_2 = \Phi(r; a, b)$, and now letting (a,b) be variable as a result of technological change, the competitive Invisible Hand can be proved to select (a,b) so that $w/p_2 = \Phi(r) = $ maximum of $\Phi(r; a, b)$ with respect to (a,b). Similarly, $r = \Phi^{-1}(w/p_2) = $ maximum of $\Phi^{-1}(w/p_2; a, b)$ with respect to (a,b). Always $\Phi'(r) < 0$. I believe this to be a new theorem. Of course, it is a prosaic mathematical fact not a Dr. Pangloss teleology.

[10] The argument holds even if capitalists do all the hiring, provided only that workers go where they get highest w and competing capitalists do what gives highest profits. If $b_1 > 0$, the argument needs some amplification because workers have to hire some of the old-type K_1 to carry through the old-type activities and for quite a while the rents of the K's might be adverse to labor; also we could not be sure of being able to settle down to a steady state in two periods when $b_1 > 0$. The stated theorem remains valid though. (Note that with $b_1 > 0$, there *must* have been other ways of producing or getting K, else the system could never have gotten started and could never recreate any K if it were all bombed out – or if, like passenger pigeons or dodo birds, K once became extinct.)

Causality and History. Faced with two contradictory dogmas, what are we to do? Decide that the capitalistic system is doomed to contradiction, and that when the irresistible force meets the immovable object there will ensue an inconceivable disturbance – with communism peeking up through the revolution's ruins? This is the "pathetic fallacy" – in which the observer inputes to Nature his mental states – with a vengeance.

Instead, of course, we jettison one (at least!) of the dogmas. Which one? I nominate the law of the declining (or constant) real wage for the junk pile, and note with interest that modern Marxians increasingly turn to that part of the sacred writings more consistent with last century's tremendous rise in workers' real wage rates.[11]

It would be unsafe to predict an actual secular decline in interest or profit rates in that most economists – notably Schumpeter and Irving Fisher – have emphasized how technological change may raise sagging interest rates, just as plucking a violin string restores its dissipating energies. Moreover, interest rates have historically oscillated in such a way as to lead many economists to the view that there is a fundamental law of constancy of the interest rate. (Taussig, *e.g.*, tried to frame a theory of a horizontal savings schedule to explain this alleged constancy.)

None the less it is of some import to know what would be the effect of attempts to accumulate capital at a rate greater than labor supply increases, *on the assumption of unchanged technology.* For such an inquiry can throw light on the tendencies upon which technological changes of a labor-saving, capital-saving, or neutral character have to be superimposed. Within the framework of my simple two-sector fixed-coefficients model, the resulting analysis will be seen to be at least a little like the despised wage-fund doctrines of Smith, McCulloch, and the Mills.

III. Steady Growth

The Expanded-Reproduction Model. Apparently Marx did not have the time to perfect his "expanded reproduction" model in which investment and growth take place. Modern techniques make such analysis a simple task. I retain the fixed-proportions assumption and take up the natural case where, instead of being geared to a stationary level, the economic system is geared to steady growth. This necessarily means steady geometric or exponential growth at uniform percentage rates: no other time-path is

---

[11] See for example, discussion of this topic in *Econ. Rev.* (Tokyo), Jan. 1957, VIII, particularly 21–25.

possible if many variables and their rates of change are to remain in constant proportions. Such a geometric progression has the further property that relative contemporaneous prices and relative intertemporal prices can be constant along it.

Our production conditions (1) and (2) remain applicable. So do our cost-of-production conditions (5)–(6). But now our simple-reproduction equations (3)–(4) must be replaced by their equivalent relations corresponding to each percentage rate of growth m per period. Now:

$$
\begin{aligned}
K^{t+1} &= (1+m)K^t = \cdots = (1+m)^t K^o \\
L^{t+1} &= (1+m)L^t = \cdots = (1+m)^t L^o \\
a_1(1+m)K^t &+ a_2 Y^{t+1} = L^t \\
b_1(1+m)K^t &+ b_2 Y^{t+1} = K^t,
\end{aligned}
\tag{12}
$$

where I have substituted for K^{t+1} its indicated value in terms of K^t and have omitted all inequalities by virtue of the assumption that the system is geared to its rate of growth with no excess capacities of men or machines. Just as we solved the static (3) for (4), we can solve the last two equations of (12) explicitly to get

$$
\begin{aligned}
Y^{t+1} &= \frac{1 - b_1(1+m)}{a_2[1 - b_1(1+m)] + a_1 b_2(1+m)} \\
K^t &= \frac{b_2}{a_2[1 - b_1(1+m)] + a_1 b_2(1+m)}.
\end{aligned}
\tag{13}
$$

The first of these coefficients has a slight similarity to the expression for the real wage in (11) or (6). In (11) and (6) the positive interest factor r acted to blow up, so to speak, every input requirement a_i or b_i into $a_i(1+r)$ and $b_i(1+r)$. Here the positive growth rate m acts to blow up b_1 and a_1 into $b_1(1+m)$ and $a_1(1+m)$, but b_2 and a_2 are quite unaffected.[12]

Table II presents the moving equilibrium. Except for $p_1 \Delta K$, which is equal to $mp_1(K_1 + K_2)$, it looks like the earlier Table I. National product is now given by fewer starred sums Σ^*, and this must equal the sum of all the value-added items. No longer does the condition for simple reproduction, $p_1 K_2 = wL_1 + r(wL_1 + p_1 K_1)$ as in (9), hold. Also the precise dollar magnitudes are now definitely weighted toward more importance to Industry I, since we now spend more of our available final incomes on capital growth:

---

[12] In the closed von Neumann model of dynamic equilibrium, characterized by constant-returns-to-scale and everything plowed back into the system, m and r turn out to be identical. This is not such a system and the possible relations are $m \gtrless r$.

Table II. – *Steady-Growth Expanded-Reproduction, Leontief-Style*

Industries	I	II	Final Products	Gross Product Totals
I	p_1K_1	p_1K_2	$p_1\Delta K$	Σ
II	0	0	p_2Y	Σ
Value Added { Wages	wL_1	wL_2		Σ } Σ^*
Value Added { Interest	$r(wL_1 + p_1K_1)$	$r(wL_2 + p_1K_2)$		Σ }
Gross Costs	Σ	Σ	Σ^*	$\Sigma\Sigma$

the exact quantitative magnitudes are given by functions of the $(a_1, b_1; a_2, b_2; r; m)$ coefficients and are easily computed from equations (6) and (13).

In the next period our tableau would look like that of this period, but with all magnitudes blown up by the common factor $(1 + m)$; and so forth with each succeeding period. Hence, such a steady-growth progression *could* go on forever if only the same behavior rules continue to prevail. (The only restriction on the possible rate of growth is that $1 - b_1(1 + m) > 0$ or $0 \leq m < (1 - b_1)/b_1$ so that all indicated ratios shall exist and keep all our variables positive. A similar restriction $1 - b_1(1 + r) > 0$ had to hold for r. Otherwise production of capital goods K could never have paid.)

I have said nothing about the saving habits of wage or interest earners that would give rise to the analyzed growth rate m. Certainly if each group saved a constant proportion of its income at all times, say σ_w for workers and σ_r for interest receivers, we could solve for the only "warranted rate of growth" m that is compatible with these properties. (Of course, to assume that L^t is always available at the resulting geometric rate is tantamount to postulating a "natural rate of growth" equal to whatever warranted rate results.)[13]

The solution for m in terms of σ_w and σ_r is more complicated than one might at first think. Obviously, the distribution of income depends upon the interest rate r, postulated to go along with the given $(a_1, b_1; a_2, b_2)$ technical coefficients. Call the fractions of income going to wages and interest k_w and $k_r = 1 - k_w$. Then the community's average propensity to save must be

$$\sigma = k_w\sigma_w + k_r\sigma_r = k_w(\sigma_w - \sigma_r) + \sigma_r;$$

[13] These terminologies will be recognized as those of the modern Harrod-Domar growth models.

and we see that this will be the higher the higher is the income of the relatively more thrifty interest receivers.

What we may not realize is that the distribution of income coefficients, besides being functions of the interest rate r, are also functions of the unknown m growth rate as well; indeed the ratio of total capital asset value to income, the so-called "accelerator" coefficient β, which is needed along with σ to define the warranted rate of growth, is itself a function of m (as well as of r). So the equation defining the warranted rate of growth:

$$m = \frac{\sigma}{\beta} \quad \text{or} \quad \beta m - \sigma = 0$$

must, even for given (a, b) coefficients, be written in the implicit-equation form:

$$m = \frac{\sigma(r; m)}{\beta(r; m)}, \quad \text{or} \quad \beta(r, m)m - \sigma(r, m) = 0. \tag{14}$$

Why do the accelerator and the distribution-of-income coefficients depend on m as well as on r? First, because the relative share of wages will differ generally in Industries I and II, and each different growth rate gives a different relative importance to the capital-goods and consumption industries. Our equations permit us to compute the exact effects for each $(a_1, b_1; a_2, b_2; r; m)$ coefficients. Second, and related to the above, each different r will change the dollar (or consumption-good or labor-hour) total of asset value to which the yield r is applied. The equation:

$$
\begin{aligned}
\text{Total interest return} &= r \, (\text{total asset value}) \\
&= r(wL_1 + wL_2 + p_1K_1 + p_1K_2) \tag{15} \\
&= r[A(a_1, b_1; \; a_2, b_2; \; r; \; m)wL],
\end{aligned}
$$

where A is a function determinable from our earlier equations and where the bracketed expression represents total asset value.

Our whole problem then has a determinate solution quite free of any of the dilemmas of "capital metaphysics." All is grounded in hard technological fact and hard competitive-market fact: there are circular relations between interest and asset value, but they are virtuous circles not vicious ones.[14]

---

[14] The case where profit receivers have $\sigma_r = 1$ and workers have $\sigma_w = 0$, however econometrically unrealistic, is a special case of the above analysis. Were $\sigma_w > \sigma_r$, the logic of the

IV. Changing Factor Proportions and Prices

The Law of the Rising Rate of Profit. So long as labor and the system are geared to grow at the same rate, there is no need for profit or interest to change. But if labor grows at a faster percentage rate than does "capital," our equilibrium conditions become inconsistent. Something has to give. What?

One definite possibility is for labor to become redundant and – if it has no reservation price or real cost of staying fit to work – its wage will have to fall. Fall how far? Adhering to the extreme assumption of fixed-coefficient production functions as given in (1) and what follows, we recognize that the real wage becomes literally zero. Kill off one of the now superfluous man-hours and you have outputs unchanged: so the competitive market will impute a zero wage to all man-hours. Mathematically, the inequality will now hold in the first relation of (2); and since all subsequent equations were based on the equality in this relationship, all must now be replaced by new relations. *E.g.*, cost-of-production now requires:

$$p_1^{t+1} = b_1 p_1^t (1 + r^t) + a_1 0$$
$$p_2^{t+1} = b_2 p_1^t (1 + r^t) + a_2 0 \tag{16}$$

and if prices are to be constant through time with $p_i^{t+1} = p_i^t$, we must have

$$1 + r = \frac{1}{b_1}$$
$$\frac{p_2}{p_1} = b_2 (1 + r) = \frac{b_2}{b_1}. \tag{17}$$

These show that the interest rate, which is now interpretable as the own-rate and net-reproductive-rate of machines, must, so long as any of them are being produced, be determinable by technology alone quite independently of all time preferences; and that the terms of trade between consumer goods and machines now depends only on technology, and more specifically only on machine requirements as given by the *b*'s with the *a* requirements of free labor now being irrelevant.

---

system would be little changed. Of course, with $\sigma_w = \sigma_r$, the distribution of income would become irrelevant and the analysis slightly simplified. Also, in the singular case earlier mentioned, where $a_1/b_1 = a_2/b_2$ and labor-values are proportional to prices, k_w and k_r are independent of *m* and the analysis becomes even more simple; but to assume away differences in the organic composition of capital is to ignore one relevant factor in the distribution of income.

We can now reckon the national product from the first equation of (12). The following must all hold:

$$b_1 K^{t+1} + b_2 Y^{t+1} = K^t$$

$$b_1 \Delta K + b_2 Y^{t+1} = (1 - b_1) K^t$$

$$\frac{b_1}{1 - b_1} \Delta K + \frac{b_2}{1 - b_1} Y^{t+1} = 1 \cdot K^t \qquad (18)$$

$$\frac{p_1}{p_2} \Delta K + 1 \cdot Y^{t+1} = r\left(\frac{p_1}{p_2} K^t\right).$$

The next-to-the-last of these shows the total value of final products expressed in machine *numeraire* units. The last equation shows on the left side the total value of final products expressed in consumer-good *numeraire* units. The right side, which was derived by using the relations (17), shows that the national product is equal from the cost side to interest on value of machines alone. This is natural enough since wages are zero and must have a zero share of total income.[15]

In this case where capital goods have ceased growing as fast as labor, the rate of profit has risen to become all of the product. So bizarre a result came from the bizarre assumption of fixed coefficients. If there were many alternative techniques, a faster growth of labor than capital would imply rising interest or profit rates and falling real wages, but not a zero wage with profits getting all.[16]

Even in the extreme case of fixed-proportions technology, a zero wage is one possibility: indeed a quite likely one. But it is not the only possibility. As long as the organic compositions of the two industries differ, by shifting demand toward that industry with relatively high labor requirements – as measured by higher a_i/b_i – we could put off the evil day of labor redundancy and zero wage. There is no Invisible Hand, though, which inevitably leads the system to this demand shift: the reduction in the relative price of the

---

[15] If capitalists saved all, with $\sigma_r = 1$, and if they received all the income, with $k_r = 1$, then the system's actual rate of growth would be $m = r = (1 - b_1)^{-1}$, which would prevail so long as available labor grew even more rapidly and stayed freely available. It would involve a certain amount of implicit theorizing to argue that this actually would happen in a model in which laborer's-consumption was tied to subsistence and had already been included by convention in the b (rather than a) coefficients; but such a mode of arguing would not be logically wrong, however unrealistic these econometric assumptions might be regarded.

[16] The simplest neoclassical model is one where $Y + (dK/dt) = Q(K, L)$, Q being a homogeneous function of the first degree with partial derivatives ("marginal productivities") Q_L and Q_K. The diminishing-returns condition $\partial^2 Q/\partial L^2 = Q_{LL} < 0$ implies that a rising trend in L/K entails a rising trend in $r = Q_K$ and a falling trend in $w = Q_L$.

labor-intensive good need not coax out much more physical demand for it. In any case, if labor really grows at a faster geometric rate than capital, labor must inevitably become more plentiful relative to capital than either industry could employ and must ultimately become free.

How Profits Fall. The case where capital grows more rapidly than labor is perhaps more true to Western life. In order to see what happens when people try to accumulate faster than the labor supply, consider the special instance where labor is completely stationary and yet savers would like to accumulate. This special case, where the natural rate of growth of the system is given by $m = 0$, does not differ in its qualitative features from any case where m is positive but less than the warranted percentage rate at which capitalists would like to have the system grow.

The Marxian model with fixed coefficients presents some quite pathological features. For if the attempt to accumulate were to cause physical machines K to grow relative to fixed labor L, the machines would become redundant in supply and their rents would fall immediately to zero.[17] The most obvious case in which this would have to happen instantaneously is that in which the organic compositions of capital are equal: $b_1/a_1 = b_2/a_2 = b/a$. The instant K/L exceeded b/a, K would become free, with $(p_1/w)^t = 0 = (p_1/p_2)^t$. We should then have:

$$p_2^{t+1} = w^t a_2(1 + r^t). \tag{19}$$

No production of future K would take place unless it covered its production costs; so only so much would take place as could match the b/a machine-labor ratio. Industry I would therefore contract so as no longer to produce K^{t+1} in excess of La/b. Industry II would temporarily produce more consumption goods: whether these would end up consumed by workers or

---

[17] There is the possibility, mentioned in the last section, that shifts in product-demand-mix toward the industry using more of the excessively-supplied factor might absorb its extra supply – at least for a while. Thus the cheapening of the machine-intensive good might meet a sufficiently elastic demand for that good to keep both factors nonredundant. But note that this shift could not carry us back to the stationary-state simple-reproduction configuration of Table I with the same price ratios and interest rate prevailing and the same zero net investment prevailing, because our hypothesis is that people are no longer content to refrain from saving in that situation. And growth of K at ever so small an exponential rate faster than labor's growth rate would inevitably make it a free good in finite time.

In this pathological model labor might collusively wipe out all K rents by producing one redundant unit of K. But only temporarily. Production of K will subsequently contract. In this model, collusion of all owners of K could limit its supply and wipe out wages. However, if any one unit of K escaped from the cartel, it and collusive labor could eventually reproduce any needed K *outside* the cartel.

capitalists would depend on the interest rate and price configuration prevailing at the end of the next period.

A similar but slightly more complicated analysis would handle the case where $b_1/a_1 \neq b_2/a_2$. In every case should the attempt to save cause a disproportionate temporary growth in K, K would become free. This does not imply euthanasia of the capitalist class, not even temporarily. For as (19) shows, interest would still be received on "advances" to workers. Machines are only one type of capital asset. Goods in process are another.[18]

Had the attempt to save forced K rents to zero, it could only be the result of a miscalculation: competitive future prices could not have been correctly quoted in the market place. To be sure, competitive capitalists have no crystal ball picturing the exact future and mistakes have often been made. But once K had become free, it could never stay free and continue to be produced. Curtailment of its production by Industry I would undoubtedly take place. One could even try to construct a cobweb-like business cycle theory of intermittent over- and underproduction of capital goods; certainly, though, a two-sector fixed-coefficients model has such special features as to make the result rather unrealistic.

What then is the equilibrium time-path that is consistent with stationary L and attempts to accumulate? The fixed-coefficient Marxian model makes all "real" accumulation quite impossible: there can be *no* technical "deepening of capital" in it. Does this mean that the profit rate r cannot fall? No. Why should it mean this? If I wish to save, for my old age or to enhance my power, why should I be led to desist from trying to do so by the consideration that the system is incapable of using new investment? Rather will I continue to try to save, to try to buy up existing assets.

Thus, suppose I earn income from K rents, or from interest return on goods in process, or from selling goods for more than I paid in wages and rent in producing them, or for that matter merely from my wages. Then instead of spending all this income on current consumption goods Y, I may *try* to hire labor or machines for next period's production, giving up so to speak my consumption allotment to owners of those factors.

Now what is it which guarantees that there will be owners of such factors willing to hire them out in the amount that investors wish to employ them? Of course, it is the competitive pricing mechanism that causes all markets to

---

[18] Such intermediate goods are probably a better description of capital than the old view of capital as the historic, now gone, food that was advanced to workers. The latter double-counts if we add it to the former; by itself, the latter undercounts in that interest is also earned on outlays for factors other than labor.

be cleared.[18a] Crudely, you can say that the interest rate r^t falls enough to eliminate any excess in the value of what people want to save and invest over the value of factors available to them; contrariwise, if the wish to save and invest is lagging, the present factor prices p_1^t and w^t will be depressed relative to future goods' prices p_1^{t+1} and p_2^t and the competitive rate of interest (or of profit) will be bid up very high. It is crude to speak of the interest rate r^t as alone providing equilibration: actually it is the whole pattern of present and future prices $(p_1^t, p_2^t, w^t; p_1^{t+1}, p_2^{t+1}, w^{t+1})$.

In the special case where the urge to accumulate is modest and steady, the profit rate r^t could be steadily falling as a result of this process, but at so slow a rate as to permit relative prices $(p_1/w)^t$ and $(p_2/w)^t$ to remain practically constant over time.[19] Then our cost-of-production equations (5)–(6) would still be valid but are to be written with a slowly falling r^t in them. The steady attempt to accumulate leads to no physical accumulation of K or anything else; rather it causes an upward valuation of existing input prices relative to output prices, which is the same thing as a reduction in the profit rate r^t. Some savers may now succeed in hiring additional inputs $(K_1^t, K_2^t, L_1^t, L_2^t)$ but, if they do, it is because other capitalists become content at the new interest rate and price pattern to hire less. If all capitalists are exactly alike, they merely bid up factor prices and bid down profit rates.

What has all this attempted accumulation done to real wages? With lower r^t in equations (5)–(6), and in particular in the last line of (6), we see that less is being "discounted" from labor's ("gross") productivity. Real wages have been rising. If, at the lower interest rate, net accumulation should now cease, the real wage going to the unchanged labor supply will not fall back to its previous level but will stay at the higher plateau forever.

Each capitalist in trying to save and increase his own profits ends up killing off the total of profits in favor of the workers. This extreme phenomenon results from the extreme assumption of fixed-coefficients with implied zero marginal-productivity to all further machines or changes in the roundaboutness of production. Yet something of what happens in this case will also hold in a more realistic case of multiple production techniques. As attempted saving lowers interest rates it lowers the discounting of real wages; but in the more neoclassical case, employers will not lose all that workers gain, the

---

[18a] See later sections for some qualifying remarks concerning "effective demand."

[19] I make a point of considering a slow change in r^t because the actual interest change in each period will cause changes in (p_2/p_1) and (p_2/w) and create revaluations and money windfalls. With relative prices changing, we no longer have equality of "own-interest-rates" and (5)–(6) need obvious modifications. By assuming $(r^{t+1} - r^t)$ always very small, we make these revaluation-effects small and ignorable.

difference coming from the extra product producible from "deepening of capital" (*i.e.*, producible from the new complex of physical capital goods brought into existence by the pricing changes induced by the attempt to save).[20]

All this makes clear that the technical (a, b) coefficients and the competitive cost-of-production equations are insufficient to determine all our variables: we need further equations of supply and demand, as *e.g.* ordinal utility conditions showing how workers and interest receivers allocate their consumption expenditures among different goods. But even the latter consumption demand equations are not enough: the rate of interest r^t would still not be determined.[21] We need saving-investment propensities, and propensities to hold and add to earning assets to complete the system.

The next sections show the wage-fundlike character of this competitive process.

V. Wage-Fund Notions

Perhaps the expression "wage fund" should be avoided altogether as conjuring up too many ghosts and as being too hopelessly ambiguous. Sometimes the wage fund meant merely sums of money "destined" for wage payments, whatever the word "destined" is supposed to mean. Sometimes it meant inventories of finished consumption goods "destined" for workers, and to some writers supposedly consisting of different consumption items than more elegant capitalists would deign to consume. Sometimes it meant a numerator of "all capital," which in some ill-described fashion got divided by the denominator of population number to give as an arithmetic quotient the real wage per capita. Finally in F. W. Taussig's resurrection, *Wages and Capital* (1896), the wage-fund doctrine merely becomes a reminder that production does take time and that men do not consume unfinished goods, with the implication of a certain short-run inexpansibility in the consumption goods available to the community (to nonworkers as well as workers).[22]

---

[20] See Figures 2b and 2c for elucidation of the many-techniques case.

[21] If labor is assumed always to be on a horizontal long-run supply schedule at a "subsistence real wage w/p_2," then (6) or (11) would alone determine r. But prescribing employment L leaves r and w/p_2 still to be determined.

[22] In its most rigid form, the wage-fund doctrine implied that unionized or ununionized workers face a short-run aggregate demand schedule of exactly unitary elasticity. This neglects the short-run possibility of using up finished-goods inventories faster than the usual rate, and tells nothing about the longer-run demand elasticity, which could be on either side of unity. In its weakest form, it suggests that the demand for labor is not perfectly inelastic and that the demand curve's rightward and upward shift induced by accumulation *may* be slowed down by concerted measures to raise present wage levels at the expense of thrifty capitalists.

In connection with the present two-sector model, it is superficial to split consumption Y^t into two parts, Y^* "destined" for workers and Y^{**} destined for capitalists, and then to write down the trivial identities:

$$(1 - \sigma_w)w^t L^t = p_2^t(Y^t - Y^{**}) = p_2^t Y^*$$
$$\left(\frac{w}{p_2}\right)^t = \frac{(Y^t - Y^{**})/(1 - \sigma_w)}{L^t} \tag{20}$$

Except possible for L^t, none of the right-hand variables are given constants. In the shortest run itself, when we are realistic enough to introduce inventories into our model, we see that not even total consumption Y^t is unilaterally given. And suppose it were: still, in anything but the shortest run, decisions could be made to cause it to change.

What does need emphasizing is the fact that in every run the supply-demand decisions of workers, of old capitalists, of new investors are needed to give us determinate equations for our set of present and future prices $(p_1^t, p_2^t, w^t, p_1^{t+1}, p_2^{t+1}, r^t, \ldots$ etc.). Taussig was quite right in pointing out that the Malthus red herring of a (very-long-run) horizontal supply schedule of labor at the "[conventional] subsistence level" kept Ricardo, J. S. Mill, and most of the Classicals – but not the aging Malthus! – from perceiving how undetermined and implicit was their theory of current wage determination and pricing. Marx's reserve army is in some ways an even redder herring that deflects attention from the missing supply-demand relations.

Here I shall simply sketch in a superficial way the process determining wages, surplus values or interest, and goods pricing. We start out with a given K^t owned by its owners, with a given L^t perhaps to be taken as a demographic parameter. Today's Y^t we suppose to be given by past decisions, and we overlook changes in short-term inventories of consumer goods. The system has a history of prices and wages. This period's market must determine decisions on how much of $(K_1^t, L_1^t, K_2^t, L_2^t)$ are to be hired to produce next period's (K^{t+1}, Y^{t+1}). The competitive market does this through determining now $(p_1^t, p_2^t, w^t; r^t)$. Simultaneously a set of notions about future prices (p_1^{t+1}, p_2^{t+1}) are formed and in terms of these relative prices, employers make decisions. If goods were homogeneous, undoubtedly a futures market would spring up to register and resolve differences of expectations about future prices; but if this did not happen, our theory would still be valid after certain easy alterations.

The "profits" of employers are, retroactively reckoned, determined by comparing $p_1^t K^t$ and $p_2^t Y^t$ with their past wage and machine costs. The profits resulting from today's decisions will similarly be known in the next period. In tranquil times, the *ex ante* hopes for profit and *ex post* realized profits will not differ too much; but differences that do develop will be noted in the market and will influence later decisions in the obvious direction.

"Net or excess demands" for $(Y^t, K^t; K^t_1, L^t_1, K^t_2, L^t_2)$ will be determinate interdependent functions of $(w^t, p^t_1, p^t_2; p^{t+1}_1, p^{t+1}_2; r^t; \dots$ etc.$)$. Our number of independent equations is equal to the number of unknowns, with only price ratios being determinable until we specify enough about the supply and demand conditions for a circulating medium (*e.g.*, given gold coins; or minable gold; or paper currency issued by the State according to specified behavior rules; or stipulated banking practices).

My fixed-coefficient Marxian model, in the absence of technical innovations altering the (a, b) coefficients, would probably be characterized by attempted accumulation whenever r^t is high. As we have seen, this would cause r^t to be falling; with no physical deepening of capital possible, capitalists would lose in income what workers gain, which might slow up the accumulation process and which later could even cause it to cease. (If we assume that interest and profit rates are quite high, we can perhaps avoid some of the effective-demand problems that arise from the temptation to hoard money when interest rates are very low.)

Where alternative (a, b) techniques exist, lower r^t will induce adaptations in technique. These adaptations can be expected usually to slow down the drop in total interest income. Does this mean that the real wage will grow less rapidly? If lower r^t induces irreversible (a, b) changes of a so-called "labor-saving" type, the rise in real wage could indeed be slowed down or even be wiped out; and if this were to happen, the fall in r^t would have been converted into a subsequent rise in r^t, interest rising more than the drop in total wages. However, any change to a new (a, b), which now pays only because r^t is lower, will produce a higher real wage for each r^t than would the old (a, b); but if the demand for "capital" is sufficiently elastic or sufficiently little inelastic, induced technical changes might slow up the rate of fall of r^t so much as to cause the real wage to rise more slowly than it would under a single technique. I suspect, but cannot prove conclusively, that a Marxian who takes seriously the fixed-coefficient single-technique case is selecting the very model in which improvement of labor's share of the total income would be easiest within the framework of an unchanged-technology capitalism.

Life's Libretto: One Technique or Many? The case of a single fixed-coefficient technique is a very peculiar one indeed. Increase labor by epsilon and its share of the product may go from 100 per cent to zero! The later neoclassical economists would consider this as the extreme case of a marginal product curve for labor that is infinitely steep over a wide range:

confront so steep a curve with a coinciding infinitely-steep supply curve of labor, and you have indeed created an indeterminate equilibrium wage with all the scope for collective bargaining and class power struggles that you could want.

Perhaps Karl Marx really had such a technology in mind. Perhaps not. It may be reasonable to believe that Marx, like Ricardo and other early writers, and unlike modern neoclassicists, never explicitly thought about what properties of the production function (a concept not yet explicitly defined or named) he wished to posit. It would be reading into him things that he would not recognize to claim a smooth production function with infinite substitution possibilities. On the other hand, he speaks again and again of alternative techniques. While many of these clearly depict technological change in the production function rather than movement within one function, the fact that the old methods are still known along with the new shows that Marx and Ricardo definitely envisage the existence of more than one technique. (Both Ricardo and Marx write of technical changes induced by price changes and adapted to changed price ratios; neither rules out the possibility that if the old price ratios were restored, the old technique might again become more economical.)

Whether or not Marx would resent being interpreted as a believer in a fixed-coefficient single-technique world, I should resent on behalf of the real world any such description. Go into any machine plant, pick up any engineering catalogue, study the books of physics and the histories of industrial processes, and you will see the variety of different ways of doing anything. If fixed Leontief coefficients (a_i, b_i) had characterized the world, it could never have got started. If the world has changed, the old processes are still remembered. Changing prices will induce accommodating changes in techniques. Perhaps the bookish economist will reply, "Foul! You are bringing in nonstatical, nonreversible changes." To this the realistic observer of the world will shrug his shoulders and answer, "So much the worse for a statical one-technique theory, or for that matter for any statical theory of production: but if we are to approximate reality by quasi-statical tools, the more realistic production function to use is one with numerous alternative techniques, quite different in their input combinations and intensities."

We must not be put off by the bogey-man query: "Do you think that God created the earth with smooth Wicksteed homogeneous production functions involving a few aggregative factors, Socially Necessary Labor, Efficiency-unit Land, and Catch-all Dollar Capital?" To deny such a belief is not to confirm a belief in fixed-coefficients. A more realistic interpretation of actuality will recognize the existence of a large, perhaps finite, number of alternative techniques. The modern theory of linear programming permits the economist to handle these analytically; but even if we ivory-tower observers could not easily handle the analysis of many techniques, it would be another case of the Pathetic Fallacy to think that the actors in the real world will desist from making jig-saw puzzle substitutions because we economists can't easily analyze them.

John Jay Chapman once said that a visitor to this world would find its people behaving more like the people in a Verdi opera than in an Emerson essay. So if a visitor from Mars insisted upon a grandiose simplification of the economic system – instead of using the less dramatic methods of Walras, Chamberlin, and Keynes – I think he'd be safer in positing an aggregative production function of the Clark-Wicksteed type than one of the Leontief-Walras type.[23]

VI. The Reserve Army of the Unemployed

I shall conclude my dissection by investigating whether the existence of a reserve army of the unemployed can do the powerful things Marxians have claimed for it. Can it lower real wages to subsistence? Can it lower real wages below the marginal product of the last man when all the unemployed are put to work? Can it lower real wages below the marginal product of the first man of the reserve army when put to work?

Such questions must not be answered in simple terms. First, we shall have to specify exactly what monetary assumptions we are making; what institutional assumptions with respect to unionism, labor mobility, interpersonal differentials in skills and zealousness; what microeconomic assumptions about the mix of demand; etc. I shall not attempt to deal with these intricacies but will for the sake of the argument walk along the road with the simple Marxian aggregative models, making drastically simplifying assumptions.

Thus I assume two industries: Industry I producing capital goods and Industry II producing consumption goods. I go along with the simplifying assumption that machines and chocolates are produced with the same organic compositions of labor and capital goods; and that all capital is used up in one period so that the Marxian "constant capital" concept is easiest to handle. I assume the unemployed workers are as zealous and able as the employed. I

---

[23] I speak here of the first-edition Walras. In his second-edition *Éléments*, Walras had the system select among a number of different techniques to minimize costs; and in his third edition, he considered the infinite-substitution homogeneous production function case. Leontief, it must be said, never meant that his fixed coefficients be applied to gross aggregates.

assume away monopsony and monopoly to see where cruel competition will lead.

How do the unemployed depress real wages? If the unemployed are away at a distance and unable to offer their services, they will have no effect on money or real wages. It is by offering to work for less, and only by so doing, that they can depress money wages. The employer cannot get his workers to accept a cut merely by talking about the threat of replacing them by the unemployed; he will get the cut only if experience has taught the workers that this is not an empty threat. If men out of work do offer to work for less, the money wage cannot remain stationary in a perfectly competitive labor market. The money wage will fall and continue to fall until no more excluded men bid it down. I stress these banalities because so much Marxian literature seems to regard the mere *existence* of the unemployed (or of the "disguised unemployed") as itself a reason for competitive wages to fall. The natural question to ask then is this: "What is the effect on wages after the unemployed have been employed? How much have they depressed money and real wages?" Today, thanks to Keynes and others, we know that this is a complicated question. Falling money wages need not mean falling real wages if prices are made to fall as much. Indeed, waiving favorable Pigou-Keynes effects resulting from increased real balances induced by the price-wage decline, we can construct models of hyperdeflation in which money wages push down prices indefinitely with unemployment never disappearing and real wages not necessarily changing. Had Marx used a reserve army of the unemployed as a reason for falling *money* wages, one could better understand the logic of his system.

To isolate the effects the unemployed have on real as against money wages, let's make the unrealistic supposition that they can bargain institutionally in terms of real wages – in terms of consumer goods or Ricardian corn. Then under the equal-organic-composition assumptions of our two-sector model, the "aggregative demand curve for labor in terms of wage goods" would be given by the discounted-marginal-physical-product curve of labor for either industry, the consumer-goods curve being exactly the same as the discounted-marginal-product curve in the capital goods industry once we have scaled the products so that they are 1-to-1 producible with the same labor and machine inputs.[24]

---

[24] The reader may make his own effective-demand assumptions to make this compatible with his theory of income determination. Thus, a good Keynesian will probably prefer to assume that aggressive government fiscal policy operates to offset any incipient deflationary or inflationary gaps threatened at full employment by nonintersecting saving and investment schedules. Some may give an active offsetting role to the central bank. Still others may be unaware or may deny that a problem could arise.

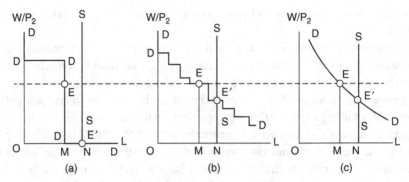

Figure 2. In every case *DD* is "aggregate real demand for labor," *SS* is total labor force available for work, *MN* is the "reserve army of the unemployed," and E' the real wage when reserve army has disappeared.

Figures 2a, 2b, and 2c show the resulting aggregative real demand for labor in the single-technique case, the many-technique case, and the infinitely-many-techniques neoclassical case. In every case, the unemployed reserve army of *NM* is made about 10 per cent of the labor force. Depending upon the technical elasticity of the marginal-product curve, the reserve army could reduce real wages by different amounts – but in Figures 2b and 2c wages can be reduced only by the reserve army's shrinking in size. The wage level E' in the three diagrams represents the lowest that real wages could fall when the reserve army had done its worst and become indistinguishable from the army of the employed. Would any competent observer of U.S.A., U.K., or U.S.S.R. technology believe that 10 per cent more men could not in any way be employed without making the last man incapable of adding much to product?[25]

The question is not whether in the shortest run, before employers knew they were to employ more and had made the necessary adjustments, marginal products might not fall greatly. Of course, they might fall. To get me to hire more workers in the next minute or day might require a great reduction in real wages. But let this happen for a few days or for months and years. Spurred by the ridiculously low real wages, employers will make needed adjustments and if we insist upon letting the real wage fall to absorb the unemployed in the long run, the equilibrium long-run

---

[25] Writing in the 1860's, Marx could with some excuse think that real wages might fall to a subsistence level. A Marxian acquainted with the statistics of real wages in modern Western economies has no such excuse.

wage will be at E' along the long-run marginal product curve *after* adjustments are made.[26]

I conclude from this way of looking at the problem that the strongest competition among the unemployed, the employed, and the employers will – when it has done its worst and depressed real wages enough to wipe out the unemployed – fail in modern western societies to depress real wages to anything like the subsistence level, instead bringing it down at worst to the (quite high) discounted marginal product of labor at the level of employment equal to 100 per cent of the available labor force. Such a wage-floor is not only very high in the most advanced capitalistic society, but the bulk of the statistical evidence of economic history and the qualitative evidence concerning scientific invention and capital formation suggest as well that this wage-floor is advancing dynamically from year to year, decade to decade, at a rate that doubles perhaps about every 30 years.

VII. Some Conclusions

I have dealt with Karl Marx the economist, not Marx the philosopher of history and revolution. A minor Post-Ricardian, Marx was an autodidact cut off in his lifetime from competent criticism and stimulus. In applying to the models of Ricardo and Marx modern tools of analysis, I hope we are violating no rules of etiquette and in no way trying to suggest we are cleverer than they were!

What then is the verdict of the present dissection? Our post-mortem suggests the following conclusions:

1. Marx did do original work in analyzing patterns of circular interdependency among industries. Such work gains few converts and is not very helpful in promoting revolution or counterreactions. But like all

---

[26] A simple set of mathematical equations describing the content of Fig. 2c would be:

$$Y + (dK/dt) = Q(L, K), \quad dK/dt = \sigma_w(LQ_L) + \sigma_r(KQ_K),$$

with government expenditure or aggressive central bank policy assuring that (dK/dt) is always such as to take up the resources not required for consumption. With fixed K, we can compute the reduction in real wage resulting from ΔL of the unemployed becoming employed, as follows: new real wage $= w + \Delta w = \partial Q(L + \Delta L, K)/\partial L$, and with $\Delta w/w$ equal to $[Q_{LL}L/Q](\Delta L/L)$, where the bracketed expression is the "reciprocal of the elasticity" of the marginal product curve at some intermediate point. Note that for given K and L, w is here quite independent of σ_w and σ_r. If we drop Marx's equal-organic-composition-of-capital assumption, this will no longer be true and the analysis has to be expanded.

pioneering effort it deserves the commendation of later craftsmen, and it deserves further development. There is half-truth in Schumpeter's adaptation of Clemenceau: "Marxian economics is too hard to be left to the Marxians." Only half, because the present paper is seen to involve little worse than school algebra and to be well within the frontier of modern economic theory.

2. Marx's labor theory of value of *Capital*, Volume I, does appear to have been a detour and an unnecessary one for the understanding of the behavior of competitive capitalism. The admittedly important analysis of imperfect of monopolistic competition is helped little or none at all by the "surplus-value" approach. That Böhm-Bawerk, Wicksteed, and Pareto were essentially right in their critiques of Marx seems borne out by the present investigation of the Marxian model.

3. I have concentrated, however, not on the problem raised for the pricing of many different goods by the unnecessary Marx-Ricardo labor-value assumptions. Instead I have concentrated on the more-neglected implications for relative goods-factor pricing of the Marxian surplus-value notations and notions. The present logical analysis suggests that the Marxian notions do not achieve the desired goal of "explaining the laws of motion or of development of the capitalistic system."

If it were true that the rich get richer the poor poorer, the distribution of income more skewed against labor and in favor of profit,[27] the two-sector models here analyzed would provide no particular hint of this. Indeed, writing in 1860 and being aware of the Industrial Revolution going on, an economist who took those models seriously should have (i) expected technological change to lower the (a,b) coefficients, (ii) should have expected the odds to favor a strong increase in real wages, the only exception arising from an extreme "bias" of inventions toward the extreme labor-saving type

---

[27] We know little about the secular trends of the inequality of the personal distribution of income, as measured by Pareto's coefficient or by Gini's parameter describing the Lorenz curve. Pareto himself thought he had established a natural law of constancy of income inequality, independent of all public policies and institutional frameworks. The empirical basis for this generalization was never very impressive. The bulk of the available evidence, in fact, suggests that as capitalism has developed the Pareto coefficient has moved towards greater equality: whereas underdeveloped countries did, and do, show Pareto coefficients around 1.3, we find in developed countries Pareto coefficients of 2.0 for income before taxes and 2.2 after taxes. See J. Tinbergen, "On the Theory of Income Distribution," *Weltwirtschaftliches Archiv*, 1956, LXXVII, 156–57. Modern economics has no grandiose explanations to offer, but it can contribute to an analysis of the relevant forces at work.

(a phenomenon *not* particularly suggested by the pre-1860 data known to financial journalists or men-of-affairs, nor particularly suggested by any a priori reasonings about the model or about the nature of technology).

I blame no one for failing to foresee the trends in the century after his death. But one can be forgiven for insisting upon the established fact that real wages in Germany, England, and America did rise more or less proportionately with total product from 1857 to 1957. To have been judged lucky by economic historians, Marx should have phrased a theory to explain the approximate constancy of wage's relative share of the national product, not the secular decline of this relative share. His actual models, we have seen, were perhaps better than he: for gifted with hindsight, we see that they contain in them no tendency for real wages to fall or to lag particularly behind the growth of output.

Nor do such models throw much light on the secular trends in the degree of imperfection of competition or on the propensity of the system to oscillate or stagnate. But all that is another story.

Marx as Mathematical Economist

Steady-State and Exponential Growth Equilibrium

INTRODUCTION

What do Marx and Metzler and Markov have in common? The German radical in London exile, the small-town Kansas boy, and the Petersburg aristocrat all worked with matrices of nonnegative elements.

So important are these in varied branches of science that we could speak of Marx–Leontief–Sraffa input–output matrices; of Metzler–Keynes–Chipman–Goodwin–Machlup–Johnson many-country multiplier matrices; of Metzler–Hicks–Mosak–Arrow–Hurwicz gross-substitutes matrices; of Markov–Frechet–Feller–Champernowne–Solow transition-probability matrices; and in pure mathematics itself, of Perron–Frobenius–Minkowski matrices a, with nonnegative elements, and the related $(I - a)^{-1}$ matrices with either positive or nonnegative elements. Or, divorcing them from any one application, we could call them Morishima–Solow–Dosso–McKenzie–Kemp matrices, after writers who explicated their general properties and applications. I am sure that I have omitted some important names and some important fields of application.[1]

Just when the New Left seems beginning to lose interest in the mature Marxism of *Das Kapital* – in favor of the *Grundrisse* and early philosophical writings of the Young Marx (alienation and all that) – the Leontief–Sraffa analytical literature is beginning to pay deserved homage to Marx's seminal contribution to the study of "simple reproduction" and "extended reproduction."

Tongue somewhat in cheek, I once referred to Karl Marx as ". . .from the viewpoint of pure economic theory. . .a minor Post-Ricardian. . .a not uninteresting precursor of Leontief's input–output of circular independence. . ."

---

[1] I vaguely recall that these matrices arose a century ago in connection with electric network theory.

[1]. This is a bit less fulsome than Professor Morishima's recent evaluation: ". . .economists are in the wrong. . .in undervaluing Marx, who should in my opinion be ranked as high as Walras in the history of mathematical economics."[2] I do not know where Professor Morishima's tongue was when his quill penned these lines, but one can hope that the truth will eventually be found within these valid bounds!

Ignoring the fact that Marx is an important ideological figure, I propose in this essay to explore the nature of Marx's key analytical contribution to economic theory – one that links him directly with Leontief and modern Harrod–Robinson–Solow growth theory, and links him indirectly with Keynes, Metzler, Hicks, and the rest.

I. Two Claims to Fame

I agree with Morishima (and I think, with Joan Robinson and Nicholas Kaldor) that Marx's volume II models of simple and extended reproduction have in them the important germ of general equilibrium, static and dynamic. If Schumpeter reckoned Quesnay, by virtue of his *Tableau Économique*, among the four greatest economists of all time,[3] Marx's advance on Quesnay's *Tableau* should win him a place inside the Pantheon.

One's respect for Friedrich Engels as an editor goes up when one wades through Marx's Volume II, made up as it was of incomplete, overlapping, and tedious manuscripts and notes written at different times. However, by going three-quarters of the way through the book and singling out the tableau of simple reproduction found there (Tableau 1), one can claim immortal fame for Marx. This was presumably arrived at by Marx in the 1860's.

Before reviewing the meaning of the symbols, we may consolidate Marx's right to fame by adding his tableau of extended reproduction (Tableau 2), taken almost from the book's end. This seems to come from the 1870's; and from the internal evidence of Marx's expositions, one senses that he had not mastered the intricacies of the extended reproduction case in quite the way he had that of simple reproduction.[4]

---

[2] Morishima [2]. I salute this valuable work, and respect its differences of conclusions from my own. The quotation is from p. 1.

[3] After Walras, and along with Cournot and either Smith or Marshall (from his 1935–1936 Harvard lectures; I cannot remember which one of the last two).

[4] These tableaux are taken, in trivially modified notations, from Volume II, Part III, Chapter XX, Section 11 (p. 459 of the 1909 Kerr edition), Chapter XXI, Section III (pp. 598 and 599). We might have been able to avoid some sterile disputes over Marx's "transformation"

Tableau 1 *Simple Reproduction*

Department I, Capital goods:	4000 of c_1 + **1000** of v_1 + **1000** of s_1 = 6000 total
Department II, Consumption goods:	**2000** of c_2 + 500 of v_2 + 500 of s_2 = 3000 total

Tableau 2 *Expanding Reproduction (at 10% Rate per Period)*

Present period
I: 4400 of c_1 + 1100 of v_1 + 1100 of s_1 = 6600
II: 1600 of c_2 + 800 of v_2 + 800 of s_2 = 3200

Next period
I: 4840 of c_1 + 1210 of v_1 + 1210 of s_1 = 7260 = $\left(1 + \frac{1}{10}\right)6600$
II: 1760 of c_2 + 880 of v_2 + 880 of s_2 = 3520 = $\left(1 + \frac{1}{10}\right)3200$

II. Simple Reproduction

We may quickly explain Marx's terminology. Society is split into two industries or departments:

Department I, which produces a capital good – to keep notions simple, suppose it to be a raw material such as coal.

Department II, which produces a consumption good – corn for simplicity, to be consumed by workers for their needed sustenance and reproduction and by capitalists for their luxurious spending of surplus value or profit.

It will simplify exposition *not* to regard each department as the consolidation of several different capital-goods and consumption-goods industries. Though it would not be hard to replace coal by a durable machine, we avoid all problems of depreciation and periods of turnover by sticking with a raw material (such as coal) consumed completely in each production use.

of his notions of "values" into his Volume III discussion of bourgeois prices if Marx had carried through a straightforward conversion of his p. 459 simple reproduction example, with its equal-organic composition or direct-labor intensity property, into the following alternative to his quoted p. 598 examples, recorded here for future reference.

Tableau 1*

I: 4400 of c_1 + 1100 of v_1 + 1100 of s_1 = 6600
II: 1600 of c_2 + 400 of v_2 + 400 of s_2 = 2400

This preserves the technology and initial labor supply of his simple reproduction example, but displays balanced growth of 10% per period. Thus in the following period 4400 would be replaced by 4400(1 + 0.1), and all entries would be amplified by the same (1 + 0.1) factor.

Technically, corn is produced by labor and by coal. There is no great novelty here. But coal is produced by labor and by *itself* – a great leap out of what came to be known as the Ricardo–Austrian world (with "triangular hierarchy" of earlier and later stages of production) and into the Leontief-Sraffa world of circularly interdependent input–output.

A. Explanation of Symbols

The v_1 and v_2 in Tableau I represent the 1000 and 500 of direct wage costs – "variable capitals" in standard Marx terminology. The c_1 and c_2 represent the 4000 and 2000 of raw material costs for coal – "constant capitals."

Marx assumes that "surplus" or capitalists' profit happens to be equal to the wage cost in each industry. As we would say, half of *all* values added goes to property and half to labor, with Net National Product happening to be distributed in equal shares.[5]

B. Equal Rates of Surplus Value and of Profit

Because of the happy accident that this first example of Marx chances to involve equal"organic compositions of capital" in all departments (i.e., equal

---

[5] Incidentally, Marx's long quibble with Adam Smith over Smith's assertion that "...the price of every commodity finally dissolves into one or another of these...parts (wages, profit, ...)" which "...are the final...sources of all income as well as exchange value" is refuted after all by Marx's own analysis! When Smith resolves price into $\sum(s+v)$, he obviously is referring to summed value added, even being quoted by Marx on p. 427 to say: "The value which laborers add to the material resolves itself...," Marx nodded, and failed to point out that Net National Product = 3000 of Department II's final corn; and *not* the gross total 6000 + 3000 of I and II together, since Smith would have agreed with Marx that it would involve double counting in the labor needed to produce corn's needed net coal *along* with that of coal itself. (I return to this dispute in footnote 12.)

Modern economists, Smith, and Marx would today agree that Net National Product equals both the sum of values added and the flow of *final* products:

$$\text{NNP} = \sum_1^x (v_j + s_j) = \sum_1^2 \{(c_j + v_j + s_j) - c_j\}.$$

Ricardo, the Physiocrats, and other classical economists would, in certain moods, regard subsistence wages as a cost not unlike that involved for coal; hence, they would subtract from NNP labor-subsistence costs, $\sum v_1$, to get Neat Product, *Produit Net*, or Net-Net National Product:

$$\text{NNNP} = \sum_1^2 s_j = \sum \left(\{(c_j + v_j + s_j) - c_j\} - \sum v_j \right).$$

Fortunately, Marx's vendetta with Smith and his predecessors led him, in this case, to the pure gold of simple and extended reproduction.

fractions of total cost in the form of direct wages, or equal v_i/c_i), we can luckily have equality in all industries of *both* the rates of surplus value s_i/v_i and the usual bourgeois rates of profit or interest $s_i/(c_i + v_i)$ – at 100% and 20%, respectively. That is, in Tableau 1,

$$1000/1000 = s_1/v_1 = 1.00 = \text{uniform } s/v = s_2/v_2 = 500/500 \quad \text{(1a)}$$

$$
\begin{aligned}
1000/(4000 + 1000) &= s_1/(c_1 + v_1) \\
&= 0.20 = \text{uniform } s/(c + v) \\
&= s_2/(c_2 + v_2) = 500/(2000 + 500).
\end{aligned}
\quad \text{(1b)}
$$

C. Zero Saving

The wage half of NNP, $\sum v_i$, goes to buy half of Department II's corn output for needed real-wage subsistence. Since there is no accumulation in simple reproduction, capitalists spend all their incomes, $\sum s_i$, on the other half of the corn, performing zero net saving. Hence,

$$\sum_1^2 (v_i + s_i) = c_2 + v_2 + s_2. \quad \text{(2)}$$

It follows then, by arithmetic tautology, that the total of coal used up in all industries, $\sum c_i$, must just equal all of Department 1's coal production. Or (2) implies

$$\sum_1^2 c_i = c_1 + v_1 + s_1, \quad \text{(3)}$$

since by definition

$$\sum_1^2 (v_i + s_i) + \sum_1^2 c_i \equiv \sum_1^2 (c_i + v_i + s_i). \quad \text{(4)}$$

Marx clearly sees, and somewhat belabors, a further implication of either (2) or (3): namely, simple reproduction requires

$$c_2 = v_1 + s_1. \quad \text{(5)}$$

That is why in Tableau 1 I wrote these numbers in boldface, so that the reader could see their equivalence. Since the sum of the first column equals the sum of the first row's terms, striking out the upper-left-hand element shared in common by the row and column, $4000 = c_1$, gives us this equivalence.

D. Changing the Rate of "Exploitation"

Suppose that, by some mechanism (not well explained by Marx), workers are now to get a lower subsistence wage. Then there must result a higher rate of surplus value and of profit – even if technology remains unchanged.

Thus, suppose the same laborers can now be made to work for wages low enough to give them only 1200 rather than 1500 of the producible corn. Then we must now have a rate of surplus value of 150% rather than 100%. Similarly, with *fully* as much insight, we can say that the rate of profit must now be 25% rather than 20%. To see this, calculate

$$(3000 - 1200)/1200 = 1.50 > 1.00 = 1500/1500$$
$$(3000 - 1200)/(6000 + 1200) = 0.25 > 0.20 = 1500/(6000 + 1500).$$

In this special case of equal organic compositions of capital, the price ratio of a ton of coal relative to a bushel of corn will be unaffected by a change in the profit rate. If, instead, corn were more labor intensive than coal (as in Marx's Tableau 2, where $v_2/c_2 > v_1/c_1$), a rise in the rate of profit would raise the market price of coal relative to that of corn. But in no case could a change in the real wage and a rise in (the equalized-across-industries) rate of surplus value alter in any way the ratio of corn's Volume I "value" to coal's "value". This ratio will still remain equal to the ratio of embodied total labor contents ("direct" and "indirect") of the two goods.

I recall no evidence that Marx ever knew how to calculate the infinite-term matrix series that decomposes each good into its total labor content – namely, the matrix series

$$a_0 + a_0 a + a_0 a^2 + \ldots$$

where a_0 is the row vector of direct labor requirements and a is the square matrix of input–output coefficients. (See footnote 12 that comments further on his quarrel with Adam Smith.)

However, he could in principle have calculated the total labor requirement of the simple reproduction 3000 corn by replacing *all* $(v_i + s_i)$ by a new equivalent $(v_i^* + 0)$. Then $\sum(v_i^* + 0)$ is the total labor cost of the corn.

And to get the total labor cost of each unit of *net* coal, or of the 6000 −
4000 = 2000 *net* coal, he had only to reckon the $v_1^* + 0$ total.

E. The Three-Sector Model

I leave mathematical analysis of simple reproduction until after extended
reproduction is discussed. But, in concluding the zero-growth case, we may
notice that Marx could treat capitalists' consumption of luxury corn as a
separate luxury Department III. Now Tableau 1 takes the form given in
Tableau 3.

Tableau 3

I:	$4000 \text{ of } c_1 + 1000 \text{ of } v_1 + 1000 \text{ of } s_1 = 6000$	Capital goods
II:	$1000 \text{ of } c_2 + 250 \text{ of } v_2 + 250 \text{ of } s_2 = 1500$	Subsistence goods
III:	$1000 \text{ of } c_3 + 250 \text{ of } v_3 + 250 \text{ of } s_3 = 1500$	Luxury goods

This is a familiar three-sector model in the Marxian literature. And for it
we have obvious equalities between respective rows and columns:

$$c_1 + c_2 + c_3 = c_1 + v_1 + s_1$$
$$v_1 + v_2 + v_3 = c_2 + v_2 + s_2 \tag{6}$$
$$s_1 + s_2 + s_3 = c_3 + v_3 + s_3.$$

And, corresponding to (5), we have the equivalent three-sector relation

$$c_2 + c_3 = v_1 + s_1 \tag{5'}$$

with numerous similar implications of (6). Note that any two of (6)'s three
relations implies the remaining third one, as well as implying (5').

F. Changed Pattern of Luxury Consumptions

What if capitalists chose to spend one-third of their incomes on coal, and
only two-thirds rather than three-thirds on corn? At least in this simple
case, Marx could probably arrive at the correct new form of the two-sector
model of simple reproduction (Tableau 4). No longer is $c_2 = v_1 + s_1$, now
that Department I is providing *more* coal than the system *uses up as
intermediate* $\sum c_j$.

Tableau 4 *Simple Reproduction ($\frac{1}{3}$ Luxury Spending on Coal, $\frac{2}{3}$ on Corn, Zero Saving)*

I: 4400 of c_1 + 1100 of v_1 + 1100 of s_1 = 6600
II: 1600 of c_2 + 400 of v_2 + 400 of s_2 = 2400

Note that Tableau 4 is in fact identical to footnote 4's extended reproduction variant of Marx's first simple reproduction tableau (Tableau 1), namely, the footnote's Tableau 1*. That is why I decided to pick this numerical amount of luxury coal consumption – to prepare the way for exponential growth equilibrium.

III. Balanced Expanding Reproduction

A gap of years separated Marx's writing on simple and extended reproduction. Perhaps this explains why he did not proceed directly from his original simple reproduction example of Tableau 1 to Tableau 1*, its new equilibrium configuration when capitalists accumulate part of their incomes to finance golden-age exponential growth of all parts of the system, including the labor supply.

Thus, let capitalists save half their $\sum s_j$ incomes. With a uniform profit rate assumed to remain at 20%, we know from modern Kalecki–Robinson–Kaldor tautologies that a balanced growth rate of 10% per period is then implied.[6] If coal production is, like everything else, to rise at this rate, our new tableau must have coal output available for next period, $c_1 + v_1 + s_1$, equal to $\frac{11}{10}$ of the total used up, $\sum c_j$, of this period. With the same initial labor supply of Tableau 1, we have our new Tableau 1* (which is not in *Das Kapital*).

To explain the interrelations of Tableau 1*, note that the half of 1500 of $\sum s_j$ saved comes to 750; this total of net saving is exactly enough to match the increment of capital between the two periods. Thus, we have the saving-investment identity

---

[6] In Marx's own extended reproduction case (Tableau 2), this tautology would not be available – since, with unequal organic compositions of capital and insistence on uniform rates of surplus value, we encounter unequal rates of profit and inapplicability of the tautology. See Morishima [2, Chapter 12] on the "dynamic" transformation problem, for demonstration of the greater complexity of the relationship between the rates of growth, saving, and uniform surplus value, in comparison with the first two and the rate of uniform profit.

$$0.5\sum s_j = 750 = S = I = \{6600 \text{ of coal produced} - 600 \text{ of coal used up}\}$$
$$+ \{1650 \text{ of new corn-wage outlay}$$
$$-1500 \text{ of old corn-wage outlay}\}$$
$$= \{600\} + \{150\} = 750. \text{ Q.E.D.}$$

Tableau 1* *Extended Reproduction (10% Growth Rate; 0.5 Saving Rate Out of Profits)*

First period
I: 4400 of c_1 + 1100 of v_1 + 1100 of s_1 = 6600
II: 1600 of c_2 + 400 of v_2 + 400 of s_2 = 2400
     6000   1500   1500   = 9000

Next period
I: 4800 of c_1 + 1210 of v_1 + 1210 of s_1 = 7260 = 6600(1 + 0.1)
II: 1760 of c_2 + 440 of v_2 + 440 of s_2 = 2640 = 2400(1 + 0.1)
     6000   1650   1650   = 9900 = 9000(1 + 0.1)
Etc.

A three-sector rearrangement of Tableau 1* can illuminate how $\sum v_j, \sum s_j$, and $\sum c_j$ get "spent" (see Tableau 1**).

Note that in this rearrangement[7] the sum of the columns do match the sum of the respective rows. Again verify that the two final columns of "values added" and the final two rows of "flow of *final* products (consumption + net capital formation)" do each equal Net National Product or National Income. I see no reason to doubt that both Adam Smith and Marx could agree on this.

A. Comparative Exponential-Growth States

When we "go" from the simple reproduction of Tableau 1 to the extended reproduction of Tableau 1**, we are not describing an actual transition process that takes place in the real world. All we are doing is comparing (a) an equilibrium system that has always been, and will always be, in no-

[7] If corn and coal have unequal organic composition, in any model with uniform profit rates, the aggregation in Department III** of diverse (c_1, v_1, s_i) magnitudes would make the resulting totals sensitive to the weightings of the various subaggregates. By contrast, using Volume I's regime of equalized rates of surplus value would leave the breakdown between aggregate v_3 and s_3 invariant; moreover, a mere change in the rate of surplus value would not affect the relative size of c_3 to $v_3 + s_3$. This simplification of analysis is not matched by real-world simplification.

†All page references to Marx's *Capital* are to the 1909 Kerr edition.

Tableau 1** *Extended Reproduction (10% Growth Rate; 0.5 Saving Rate of Profits)*

I**: 4000 of c_1 + 1000 of v_1 + 1000 of s_1 = 6000 of "nonfinal" coal

II**: 1000 of c_2 + 250 of v_2 + 250 of s_2 = 1500 of "subsistence" corn wages

$$
\text{III**}:b \left.\begin{array}{l} a \\ \\ c \end{array}\right\} : \quad
\begin{array}{l} 500 \\ 400 \text{ of } c_3 + 100 \\ 100 \end{array}
\left.\begin{array}{l} 125 \\ 100 \\ 25 \end{array}\right\} \text{of } v_3 +
\begin{array}{l} 125 \\ 100 \\ 25 \end{array}
\left.\begin{array}{l} \\ 100 \\ \end{array}\right\} \text{of } s_3 = 1500 =
\left\{\begin{array}{l} 750 \text{ of luxury corn consumption} \\ 600 \text{ of new coal inventory} \\ 150 \text{ of new corn inventory for wage "advances"} \end{array}\right.
$$

growth balance with (b) an equilibrium system that has always been, and
will always be, in 10%-growth balance. Marx seems to understand this, as
suggested by his shrewd observation (p. 572):† "It is further assumed that
production on an enlarged scale has actually been in process previously."

Yet in some of Marx's attempts to compute a valid extended reproduction
Tableau, he begins with a no-growth configuration and goes through an
algorithm designed to end him with a balanced-growth equilibrium.
Morishima [2, pp. 117–122] nicely clears up the steps in Marx's algorithm.
As Morishima observes (p. 118):

Marx then introduced his very peculiar investment [saving] function, such that (i)
capitalists of Department I devoted a constant proportion of their surplus value to
accumulation ...[whereas] (iii) capitalists of Department II adjusted their investment [behavior] so as to maintain the balance between the supply and demand for
capital goods.

Morishima shows that Marx's algorithm, whatever you or I may think of its
illogical split in capitalists' behavior, does converge in two periods to an
admissible configuration of true balanced growth. And (on p. 120)
Morishima contrasts this exact two-period convergence of Marx with the
disappointingly slow rate of convergence to balanced-growth golden-age
states of neoclassical growth models.

Such a pejorative comparison seems odd. Marx presumably is not purporting to describe a real-life transition. The algorithm does not take place
in the capitalist marketplace, but rather at Marx's desk in the British
Museum. There are an infinite number of alternative unrealistic algorithms
that could also be conjured up. For that matter, once we permit ourselves
unrealistic saving behavior, why not pick on one of the infinite number of
alternative models each with the property of converging in *one* step from
simple reproduction.[8]

This would be an arbitrary scenario, but neither more nor less arbitrary
than Marx's suggested algorithm.

---

[8]   Thus, start with Tableau 1. Let the 6000 of coal be diverted, not 4000 to Department I and
2000 to Department II, but 4400 to I and 600 to II. And let all capitalists still save nothing
for this initial period. Then Tableau 1 goes in one step to the first state of Tableau 1*; and
forever after all capitalists can save half their incomes and have the system grow at 10% per
period bringing 10% more labor into the system in each period. When organic compositions are unequal, one of course cannot keep, in the one-stage transition to the expanding
model, both the labor total and the coal-input total the same as in the steady state. "Putty-
clay" models, as against "putty–putty" models, become even more complicated.

IV. A Digression on Morishima's Alternative to Marx

Morishima [2, pp. 122–126] proposes to replace Marx's admittedly "unnatural" behavior equations by what he hopes will be more reasonable assumptions about saving behavior. He ends with the matrix difference equations for the two departments' values, $y(t)$, of the form $y(t) = My(t + 1)$, where M is a positive matrix with characteristic roots less than unity in absolute value. [The coefficients of M depend on the (a_0, a) technical coefficients, and on the consumption propensities of the classes: if the technology satisfies Hawkins–Simon conditions for productivity of a net surplus above subsistence requirements, and if the percent saved from profits cannot exceed unity, M should be well behaved.] As is well known from the work of Jorgenson [3] Solow [4], Morishima [5], Dorfman–Samuelson–Solow [6], and others, such a "backward-defined" difference equation must be damped moving *backward* in time, and anti-damped or explosive as we follow it forward in time. One wonders then why Professor Morishima wishes to propose it as the "fundamental equation of the theory of reproduction."

Actually, it is expecting too much of a pioneer like Marx that he should solve adequately the non-steady state behavior of a system. This problem taxes modern ingenuity. Indeed, we have here the indeterminacy of the famous Hahn problem, on which Hahn [7], Stiglitz [8], Shell [8, 9], Samuelson [10], Burmeister [11], and many others have written much in the last decade. Whatever the ultimate solution of the Hahn problem – i.e., the problem of how a *heterogeneous*-capital *many*-sector model can be expected to develop under competition when *overall* saving propensities are *alone* given – the Morishima proposal seems not to constitute a "self-warranting" permanent time solution. His variant of what Dorfman–Samuelson–Solow [6] called a "Leontief trajectory" (defined as a path that *insists on the equalities*, and rules out the feasible inequalities, of the dynamic relations) will necessarily become self-contradictory, generating negative physical quantities and ultimately in effect recognizing bankruptcy.

To see that static equalities cannot hold on a consistent self-warranting solution, consider the easier case of a Ramsey-planned Marxian system that acts to maximize, say, $\sum_0^\infty (1 + \rho)^{-t} \log x_t \, y_t$, where x_t and y_t are per capita corn and coal consumptions, ρ is a planner rate of time preference equal to $(1 + \text{profit rate of } 20\%)/(1 + \text{growth rate of } 10\%)$, available labor supply grows at 10% per period, Marx's implicit technology prevails, and we begin with prescribed initial stocks of corn and coal appropriate to an outmoded simple reproduction state. Then it can be shown that the system will asymptotically change itself optimally into the extended reproduction configuration proportional to Tableaux like my earlier Tableaux 2 or 4. In the transition, the dual variables of price will *not* have the steady state values that the system both begins and ends with and which Marx and Morishima seem implicitly to use. One sees heuristically (the Furuya–Inada theorem generalized) that, if there is a self-warranting (perfect-futures market!) path consistent with strictly constant fractions of profit saved, it must asymptotically approach the golden-age state and not explode away from it in the Morishima manner. [For certain special utility functions, such as $U = \log x_t y_t$ or $(x_t y_t)^y / y$, constant average saving propensities may hold.]

I dare not state arguments as heuristic as these except with the greatest diffidence and absence of self-confidence.

V. Marx as Advancer of Mainstream-Economics Analytical Technique

First, let us observe that there is nothing "radical" or "leftish" about these tableaux – even for the mid-nineteenth century. On the contrary, they could be used to convey a 1931 Hayek message[9] that the Douglas Social Credit cranks are wrong in believing that there is a necessary flaw in the circulation system that must lead to underconsumption and unemployment. Indeed, in some moods, Engels and Marx wrote with scorn of Rodbertus's naive underconsumptionist views. And, after the turn of the century, Tugan–Baronowsky or a Domar could use these compound-interest models of Marx to refute a crude Luxemburg–Hobson thesis of *necessary*-and-*inevitable* eventual underconsumption in a closed capitalistic system.[10]

Second, careful examination of Marx's analysis will show that, despite his frequently reiterated belief that he is correcting this or that contemporary vulgar economist or earlier bourgeois writer, there is no sense in which these tableaux, properly understood, *refute* earlier mainstream writers. Merely

[9] See, for example, Hayek [12], where the easier Austrian case is shown to have identity between total value added and flow of final product.

[10] Not too much should be read into this last sentence. We must remember that the Harrod–Domar "warranted rate of growth" that Marx is anticipating need not be equal to the "natural rate of growth of the labor supply" in a realistic not-necessarily-Marxist model of actual population and labor-price growth. We must remember too the "instability" or knife-edge property of the warranted rate in a fixed-coefficient technology. And, finally, we must remember the possible indeterminacy of the Hahn problem of heterogeneous-capital's dynamic behavior when only *aggregate* saving propensities are hypothesized.

one case in point is the one already mentioned, in which Marx thought he was correcting Smith's erroneous belief[10a] that wages and profit (rent being ignored) form the "components" of price; but, as seen, once the straightforward differentiation between gross and net totals is respected, Marx's own analysis serves to confirm Smith's formulation. Indeed Marx deserves high praise for demonstrating this formulation in the important and novel "non-Austrian" case of circular interdependence. In summary, Marx's tableaux of simple and extended reproduction constitute an important extension and generalization – to the case of circular interdependence – of the orthodox techniques of equilibrium analysis employed by Smith, Ricardo, or Mill.

VI. Living in Marx's Skin: Numerical Examples Generalized

It is a somewhat odd feeling to immerse one's self in the numerical-example world of an earlier writer like Marx. Perhaps only by doing so can one infer how he arrived at his insights, and recognize the limitations of his perceptions. Nor will it do, when you are reading the gropings, backslidings, and discoverings of a Kepler, to become irritated and wish to clap him on the shoulder and say – from the vantage point of post-Newtonian celestial mechanics – "Why can't you see this and that?"

A. Possible Class of Numerical Tables of Simple Reproduction

One expects pioneering work to be somewhat rough. Elegance can come later after genius encounters diminishing returns in new insights. Having no students, no colleagues, and no readers, Marx understandably wanders a bit in his derivations. Let us stand back and see the general rules that one can follow to generate *any* tableau of simple reproduction and of extended reproduction.

It simplifies things to begin by combining all value-added terms: work with two $(v_i + s_i)$ terms rather than four such terms; call them $d_i = v_i + s_i$ for short. So long as we stick with Marx's value formulation, where d_i is always broken up into the same proportional fraction, only the (c_i, d_i) totals need be considered.

[10a] In private correspondence, Professor William Baumol has expressed the view that Marx's only, or main, difference with Smith's view of price as equal to wages plus profits was that this was only a superficial surface relation (as indeed it is). Baumol may be right; but the reader should review the thousands of words on Smith in Volume II and decide whether that is *all* Marx finds wrong with Smith's view.

Not any four positive numbers $\begin{bmatrix} c_1 & d_1 \\ c_2 & d_2 \end{bmatrix}$ can provide a tableau of simple reproduction. Only those with column sums equal to respective row sums can serve. This makes the off-diagonal elements equal, $c_2 = d_1$, and leaves us with only three arbitrary degrees of freedom. Since mere scale does not matter, we are free to set column 2's total value added or NNP equal to unity, leaving us with only two degrees of freedom. We may select the two elements of the main diagonal arbitrarily: thus every admissible tableau comes from picking for d_2 an arbitrary fraction, and for c_1 an arbitrary positive number.

Suppose we consider the narrower case of equal organic compositions of capital, not for its realism but because the simplicities of algebra that Marx employed turn out to be legitimate for it. Then we have only one degree of freedom left, since the rows (or columns) must be proportional. Instead of the general simple reproduction case

$$\begin{bmatrix} c_1 & 1 - d_2 \\ 1 - d_2 & d_2 \end{bmatrix},$$

we have

$$\begin{bmatrix} (1 - d_2)^2/d_2 & 1 - d_2 \\ 1 - d_2 & d_2 \end{bmatrix},$$

as for example, $\begin{bmatrix} 4/3 & 2/3 \\ 2/3 & 1/3 \end{bmatrix}$, that corresponds to Marx's Tableau 1 (p. 262).

As we will see, for fixed technology, it will not be the case that the (c_i, d_i) preserve the same magnitudes when the real subsistence wage changes, changing the uniform rate of profit with it. Only in the equal-organic-composition case will this be true – for the reason that only in such a case will equalized-profit-rates be compatible with the alternative of equalized-rate-of-surplus-value model (in which it must be always true that the c_i and d_i break-downs are invariant to changes in the real wage).

B. Possible Tableaux of Extended Reproduction

Actually, a square array of *any* four positive numbers is admissible to define such a growth tableau, since no longer do respective column and row sums have to correspond. The ratio $(c_1 + d_1)/(c_1 + c_2)$ defines a growth rate,

$1 + g$, whether it be greater or less than unity. However, since scale does not matter, we have only three degrees of freedom once we fix column 2's NNP or total value added at unity. Two arbitrary elements of the first column plus an arbitary fraction for one element of the second column define an admissible extended reproduction tableau. For example,

$$\begin{bmatrix} c_1 & 1 - d_2 \\ c_2 & d_2 \end{bmatrix} \text{ or } \begin{bmatrix} c_1 & 1 - d_2 \\ (1 - d_2 - c_1 g)/(1 + g) & d_2 \end{bmatrix},$$

as in Tableau 2's $\begin{bmatrix} 22/19 & 11/19 \\ 8/19 & 8/19 \end{bmatrix}$.

Turn now to the singular case of equal organic compositions of capital, where a change in the profit rate within fixed technology leaves invariant the expanded reproduction (c_i, d_i) tableau for a given balanced-growth rate (it being understood that the saving ratio changes appropriately and scale is immaterial). Since now the columns and rows must be proportional, we lose one of our three degrees of freedom. Now instead of the general case of three arbitrary elements, such as (g, c_1, d_2) only (g, d_2) are assignable: e.g.,

$$\begin{bmatrix} (1 - d_2)^2/(g + d_2) & (1 - d_2) \\ (1 - d_2)d_2/(g + d_2) & d_2 \end{bmatrix},$$

as in $\begin{bmatrix} 44/30 & 22/30 \\ 16/30 & 8/30 \end{bmatrix}$ of Tableau 1*, that corresponds to Marx's Tableau 1 modified to grow at 10% per period.

VII. Handling Marx's Underlying Technology

As far as I have been able to discover, Marx apparently never pierced below the veil of his pound, franc, or labor-hour tableaux to their underlying technology. This was not so much fetishism on his part, as that the implied problem may not have occurred to him or may have seemed to him to be too hard algebraically. That it was probably not the latter reason is suggested by the fact that it apparently never occurred to him to master even that one case where the algebra would have been easy to handle – namely, the Ricardo–Austrian case where the coal that labor needs to produce corn is itself producible by labor *alone*. Let us shift to this simple case for expository clarity.

A. The "Triangular" Ricardo-Austrian Hierarchy

Let us suppose 1 labor in Department I produces 1 coal. And, in Department II, $\frac{1}{2}$ labor plus $\frac{1}{2}$ corn produces 1 corn. Then coal and corn each have total labor requirements (direct plus indirect) of 1.

B. Bourgeois Pricing Regime

Using capital letters (C_i, V_i, S_i) for equalized-profit-rate regimes, the correct simple reproduction tableaux at zero profit, 100%, and 200% profitrates are given in Tableau 5. Note that the D_i/C_i or $(V_i + S_i)/C_i$ ratios are quite different depending on the real corn wage and corresponding profit rates e.g., for the 100 and 200% profit rates of Tableau 5, we find $(0.5 + 1.5)/1 \neq (0.5 + 4.0)/1.5$.

A word of explanation of these tableaux may help. For simple reproduction, one-half of society's labor – the total of which can be taken as unity – must go to produce coal, all of which is used with the other half of labor to produce consumed corn. Nothing is saved out of profits (whose share of NNP depends on the posited rate of profit). This is the technocratic bedrock at the base of all examples.

At 100% profit rate, the 0.5 of labor used to produce 0.5 of coal gets marked up by 100%. So 0.5 coal costs 1.0 in all. Hence, the cost of corn is the sum of this 1.0 of coal plus 0.5 of labor, all marked up by 100%, until corn ends costing 3.0 in all. Likewise a 200% profit markup on all $(C_i + V_i)$ outlays at every stage would lead to Department II's corn receipts of 6.0 in all.

To distinguish actual capitalistic pricing at uniform profit rates in all departments from Marx's Volume I regime of values reckoned at uniform rates of surplus value in all departments (i.e., uniform markups on direct labor alone), I have used capital letters, $C_i + V_i + S_i = C_i + V_i + R(C_i + V_i)$

Tableau 5

Profit Rate	
0%	0 of $C_1 + 0.5$ of $V_1 + 0$ of $S_1 = 0.5$
	0.5 of $C_2 + 0.5$ of $V_2 + 0$ of $S_2 = 1$
100%	0 of $C_1 + 0.5$ of $V_1 + (1.0)(0 + 0.5)$ of $S_1 = 1.0$
	1 of $C_2 + 0.5$ of $V_2 + (1.0)(1 + 0.5)$ of $S_2 = 3$
200%	0 of $C_1 + 0.5$ of $V_1 + (2.0)(0.5 + 0)$ of $S_1 = 1.5$
	1.5 of $C_2 + 0.5$ of $V_2 + (2.0)(1.5 + 0.5)$ of $S_2 = 6$

against Marxian lower case letters, $c_i + v_i + s_i = c_i + v_i + r(v_i)$. A uniform rate of profit is written as R; a uniform rate of surplus value is written as r.

C. "Values" Regime

The "values" regimes alternative to the above "prices" regimes produce the corresponding three tableaux (given in Tableau 6) which at $r = 0, 2.0$, and 5.0, respectively, provide the comparable subsistence real wage in corn terms that was provided by $R = 0, 1.0$, and 2.0, respectively. If you calculate the three $(c_i, d_i = v_i + s_i)$ numbers for these three quite different distributions of incomes between laborers and capitalists, you find them all exactly the same except for inessential scale, each being proportional to $\begin{bmatrix} 0 & 1/2 \\ 1/2 & 1/2 \end{bmatrix}$. That is definitely not at all the case for the (C_i, D_i) numbers of realistic competitive pricings, which are respectively proportional to

$$\begin{bmatrix} 0 & \frac{1}{2} \\ \frac{1}{2} & \frac{1}{2} \end{bmatrix}, \quad \begin{bmatrix} 0 & \frac{1}{3} \\ \frac{1}{3} & \frac{2}{3} \\ & \frac{1}{3} \end{bmatrix}, \quad \begin{bmatrix} 0 & \frac{1}{4} \\ \frac{1}{4} & \frac{3}{4} \end{bmatrix}.$$

Tableau 6

0%	0 of c_1 + 0.5 of v_1 + 0 of s_1 = 0.5
	0.5 of c_2 + 0.5 of v_2 + 0 of s_2 = 1
200%	0 of c_1 + 0.5 of v_1 + (2.0)0.5 of s_1 = 1.5
	1.5 of c_2 + 0.5 of v_2 + (2.0)0.5 of s_2 = 3
500%	0 of c_1 + 0.5 of v_1 + (5.0)0.5 of s_1 = 3
	3.0 of c_2 + 0.5 of v_2 + (5.0)0.5 of s_2 = 6

D. Extended Reproduction Alternatives

Now, in parallel, I show the way the tableaux must look at the same balanced growth rate of 100% per period in the alternative prices and values regimes. All have to be generated by the same technology, in which $\frac{2}{3}$ of society's labor goes to Department I to produce twice as much coal as was produced in the previous period for use in this period's Department II corn production.

To these same physical labor-coal-corn magnitudes, I apply the respective "prices" and "values" appropriate to the stipulated (R or r) rates, (0% or 0%), (100% or 200%), and (200% or 500%). This gives the first-period tableaux (Tableau 7) each with $1 + g = 1 + 1.0$, so that in the subsequent period each tableau will have all of its elements *double*.

Tableau 7

R	
0%	0 of $C_1 + \frac{2}{3}$ of $V_1 + 0$ of $S_1 = \frac{2}{3}$
	$\frac{1}{3}$ of $C_2 + \frac{1}{3}$ of $V_2 + 0$ of $S_2 = \frac{2}{3}$
100%	0 of $C_1 + \frac{2}{3}$ of $V_1 + (1.0)\frac{2}{3}$ of $S_1 = \frac{4}{3}$
	$\frac{2}{3}$ of $C_2 + \frac{1}{3}$ of $V_2 + 1.0(\frac{2}{3} + \frac{1}{3})$ of $S_2 = \frac{6}{3}$
200%	0 of $C_1 + \frac{2}{3}$ of $V_1 + 2.0(0 + \frac{2}{3})$ of $S_1 = \frac{6}{3}$
	$\frac{3}{3}$ of $C_2 + \frac{1}{3}$ of $V_2 + 2.0(\frac{3}{3} + \frac{1}{3})$ of $S_2 = \frac{12}{3}$

r	
0%	0 of $c_1 + \frac{2}{3}$ of $v_1 + 0$ of $S_1 = \frac{2}{3}$
	$\frac{1}{3}$ of $c_2 + \frac{1}{3}$ of $v_2 + 0$ of $S_2 = \frac{2}{3}$
200%	0 of $c_1 + \frac{2}{3}$ of $v_1 + (2.0)\frac{2}{3}$ of $s_1 = \frac{6}{3}$
	$\frac{3}{3}$ of $c_2 + \frac{1}{3}$ of $v_2 + (2.0)\frac{1}{3}$ of $s_2 = \frac{6}{3}$
500%	0 of $c_1 + \frac{2}{3}$ of $v_1 + (5.0)\frac{2}{3}$ of $s_1 = \frac{12}{3}$
	$\frac{6}{3}$ of $c_2 + \frac{1}{3}$ of $v_2 + (5.0)(\frac{1}{3})$ of $s_2 = \frac{12}{3}$

The substantial differences between the Tableau 5 price regimes and the Tableau 6 value regimes are obvious. The greater algebraic simplicity of the market-unrealistic right-hand-side tableaux is also apparent. All three of the right-hand value tableaux are, except for scale,[11] identical in everything but the three uniform fractional allocations of the d_i of value added between wages and surplus, v_i and s_i.

VIII. Indeterminacy of Wage and Distributive Shares?

Suppose any of the preceding elementary relationships not fully understood by Marx were explained to him. What difference would it make to his

[11] These scale changes arise from my choice of normalizing the elements of the tableaux by conveniently stating the V_i and v_i elements in terms of actual labor-hour allocations.

Weltanschauung and fundamental vision about capitalist development? Quite possibly none of importance.

A. Roots of the Polemic against Smith's View of Price or Wages-Plus-Profits

Marx might concede that some of his strictures against Smith's formulation of price as composed of wage-plus-profit components would have to be withdrawn or reworded.[12] But I think his animus against Smith's "explanation" of price as wage-cost-plus-profit goes deeper. Putting things this way, he might legitimately have felt, tends to *justify* the state of affairs in which capitalists get much of what might otherwise go to labor.

Marx is here revealing more than a value judgment against unearned property incomes. He seems also to be stressing that there is nothing inevitable, nothing determined by lasting economic principle, in an existing share of profit in price formation. There is an implicit prediction by Marx that, by power or otherwise, labor could *alter* the status quo of high profits and low wages.

But there is also more here than a value judgment, and a hortatory call to action on the part of the proletariat. There is, I think, a perception by Marx that NNP $= \sum v + \sum s$ (or price equals the sum of wages and surplus) is,

---

[12] In Volume II, Part III, Chapter XIX, Section II, 3, fourth paragraph of the section, pp. 431–432, Marx comes close to admitting that Smith is correct in decomposing price into all the values added, $v + s$, of all the earlier stages – provided we stay in a Ricardo–Austrian triangular hierarchy of production (where everything can be "ultimately" produced out of labor above). But he denies that this will work in the case of circular interdependence, where without initial raw materials production can never get off the ground: so, in effect, he is missing the fact that the multiplier chain already referred to, $a_0(I + a + \cdots + a^r + \cdots)$, is a *convergent* infinite series. Had he constructed the tableaux of Section VII and compared them with his general case, he would still have avoided all error and realized that *final* product, or NNP, can be taxonomically split up into its $V_i + S_i$ or $v_i + s_i$ components (*pace* Sraffa [30]). The cited passage where Marx comes near to clearing up his own confusion bears quoting:

> Smith...admits...that the price of corn does not only consist of v plus s, but contains also the price of the means of production consumed in the production of corn.... But, says he, the prices of all these means of production likewise resolve themselves into v plus s.... He forgets, however,...that they also contain the prices of the means of production consumed in their production. He refers us from one line of production to another, and from that to a third. The contention that the entire price of commodities resolves itself "immediately" or "ultimately" into v plus s would not be a specious subterfuge in the sole [!] case that the product...[depends ultimately on] products...which are themselves produced by the investment of mere variable capital, by a mere investment in labor-power [i.e., what I here dub the Ricardo–Austrian hierarchy of non-circularly-dependent production] [Volume II, p. 431].

by itself, an indeterminate system. The economic system of his predecessors, he feels, lacks the conditions needed to determine whether 4 is $2 + 2$, or $1 + 3$, or $4 + 0$.

B. Marx's Anticipation of Robinsonian Critique?

This perception strikes a resonant response in our own age. Joan Robinson, building on Sraffa's work and her own earlier writings, says as much: Microeconomists lack an equation to determine the profit rate and profit share.[13] Theirs is an *indeterminate system* – once microeconomists' fanciful marginal-productivity conditions are denied by virtue of (a) heterogeneity of capital goods, and (b) fixity of input proportions in nonsmooth production functions.[14]

From the side of Böhm-Fisher time preference, the missing equation for the steady state profit rate might be sought; but to do so would not be to incur the pleasure and approval of the Cambridge–Italian school, or of Karl Marx.

I do not wish to pronounce any opinion at this time on whether Marx was insightful or obtuse in regarding the profit component of price and NNP as being undetermined by mainstream bourgeois political economy. I merely wish to advance the by hypothesis that we understand much of Marx's *Weltanschauung* if we employ this interpretive hypothesis. And we

---

[13] Of course, one might supply the missing link from a Kalecki–Kaldor–Robinson Pasinetti long-run tautology of macroeconomic theory. But that is another story, and not one easily found in Smith, Ricardo, Marshall, or Walras – or, for that matter, in Marx.

[14] In order to achieve clarity on exact differences of opinion between different modern schools, it would be well to ignore smooth neoclassical production functions in any Department. But one might still stipulate, as being realistic or interesting, that in Tableaux 1 or 2, there are many alternative ways of producing coal and corn out of labor and raw materials. Thus, in Department I, along with (a_{01}, a_{11}) coefficients of $\frac{2}{3}$ coal needed to produce 1 of coal, along with say $\frac{1}{3}$ labor, we might have the alternative technical options $\left(\frac{1}{3}, \frac{2}{3}\right)$, $\left(\sqrt{2}/3, \sqrt{2}/3\right)$, $\left(\frac{1}{30}, \frac{20}{3}\right)$ and $\left(\frac{20}{3} \text{ and } \frac{1}{30}\right)$. And, at the same time, we might have in Department II, a half-dozen equally varied technical options: i.e., varied "pages" in Joan Robinson's book of technical blueprints.

As a matter of logical clarity, it would be useful to know whether those who dislike Cobb–Douglas and other simplified Clarkian production functions would agree or disagree with the proposition that this sheaf-of-varied-option cases produces pretty much the same results as would two Clarkian functions of coal and labor inputs for Departments I and II. Thus, a Ramsey planner with low time preference in $\sum (1 + \lambda)^{-t} V[c_t]$ would give up corn consumption in the present in order to build up coal stocks for greater future efficiency in producing corn, etc., etc. – much as in the Clarkian case. If this is not a bone of contention, its conclusion perhaps need not be – namely, that in the Marxian system, the inherited stock of coal per capita (or the amount accumulated at the expense of current consuming) will be an important factor bearing on whether it is likely to involve a high or low trend for the profit rate.

understand better why he was attracted to a subsistence-wage hypothesis (however far-fetched, empirically and analytically, such an hypothesis appeared to his critics).

IX. The Number One Issue in Appraising Karl Marx's Theoretical Innovations

I leave to the Appendix the Leontief-Sraffa-Metzler elucidation of Marx's models of simple and extended reproduction. But we must not let a preoccupation with Marx as a *mathematical* economist divert us from trying to form a just opinion of how novel and fundamental was what he and Engels and Lenin regarded as his most innovative and insightful contribution to political economy – namely, Marx's way of handling "surplus value."

What Marx claimed as most originally his is also precisely that which mainstream economists have been most unanimous in rejecting. It is precisely Marx's models in Volume I and Volume II of equalized-rates-of-positive-surplus-value-markups-on-direct-wages-alone that have seemed bizarre to most non-Marxian economists. "Reactionaries" like Pareto or "liberals" like Wicksteed, as well as pedants like Böhm-Bawerk, are only the most dramatic examples of the near-universal rejection by non-Marxian political economists of these Volume I and Volume II paradigms as (a) gratuitously unrealistic, (b) an unnecessary *detour* from which Marx in Volume III had to beat a return, even though a return he was too stubborn or too unperceptive or too unscientific to admit.

This, I think, has been the Number One issue in the debates about Marxian economics throughout the years of my professional life as an economist and indeed both before and after the 1894 posthumous appearance of *Capital's* Volume III.

Failure to recognize and focus on this clearly defined question seems to me to account for a good deal of the confusion and cross-talk in pro-Marxian and anti-Marxian economics debate. What is less important, some of the misinterpretation of my own Marxian analyses (commented on in footnote 24 in the Appendix) seem to me to stem from a failure to realize that it was this issue that has motivated my own exploration in understanding, appraising, and developing Marxian analyses. And it is on this key issue that two such different people as Joan Robinson and I have been so singularly in agreement.

The issue, to repeat, is this:

What are the merits or disadvantages of hypothesizing models of (a) uniform s_t/v_t markups, alongside of, or as against, models of (b) uniform $S_t/(C_t + V_t)$ markups?

What, if any, are the advantages of equalized-rates-of-surplus-value regimes, in comparison with the regimes of Marx's predecessors, contemporaries, and successors, which stipulate that competitive arbitrage enforces equalized-rates-of-profit by industries? What valid insights come from a macroeconomic ratio, $\sum s_j / \sum v_j$ or $\sum S_j / \sum V_j$, that are not already (better?) contained in a $\sum S_j / \sum (C_j + V_j)$ ratio?

To guide the reader in more rapid understanding of my argument, let me state at once that I have arrived at a definite view as to how this Number One question should be answered. On the basis of much reflection and analysis of the problem, and after a valiant attempt to read every Marxian and non-Marxian argument that bears on the issue, here is my own opinion.

Save as only an admitted first approximation, justifiable for dramatic emphasis and hortatory persuasiveness or defended because of its obvious greater simplicity of algebraic structure, the paradigm of equalized-rates-of-surplus-values is an unnecessary detour from the alternative paradigm of equalized-rate-of-profit that Marx and mainstream economists inherited from Ricardo and earlier writers. This digressing Marxian alternative paradigm not only lacks empirical realism as applied to competitive arbitrage governing capital flows among industries and competitive price relations of different goods and services, but also it is a detour and a digression to the would-be student of monopolistic and imperfect competition, to the would-be student of socialism, to the would-be student of the modern mixed economy and its laws of motion, to the would-be student of the historic laws of motion of historic capitalism (including, be it stressed, of earlier golden or nongolden ages of pre-commodity exchanges among artisans and farmers).

Specifically, logical analysis – like that here, and enumerated at greater length in my 1971 discussion [13][15] of the Marxian "transformation problem" – will *refute* the more sophisticated notion[16] that, although the equal-rates-of-profit behavior equations are indeed more valid *microeconomically* (to parcel out the

---

[15] See also refs. [14] and [15], and my two replies [16, 17]. See also Samuelson [18] which carries further the Weizsäcker-Samuelson demonstration that, even in a planned socialist society, uniform $R^* = S_j (C_j + V_j)$, rather than $r^* = s_j / v_j$, would be needed for efficient dynamic asymptotes. My earlier articles on Marx and Ricardo are also relevant [19–22]. The elements of Marxian analysis are given in my *Economics* [23].

[16] This point, which I argue is not valid, is perhaps most clearly made by Meek [24]. In ref. [13], p. 417], my parody tries to make the point that the macroeconomic total of profit does not (repeat not) require or benefit from any s/v analysis. The present chapter spells out my arguments for this thesis. I have tried to appraise impartially Meek's thesis [24, p. 95]: "For, according to him [Marx], the profit which the capitalists receive in each branch of industry must be conceived of as accruing to them by virtue of a sort of a redivision of the aggregate surplus value produced over the economy as a whole." And my findings are as adverse to this as they are to Marx's contention (Volume I, Chapter IX, Section 1, p. 239, n. 2): "We shall see, in Book III, that the rate of profit is no mystery, so soon as we know the laws of surplus-value. If we reverse the process, we cannot comprehend either the one or the other." A careful search of Marx's earlier and later writings does not produce any evidence that he was able to make good on this claim in the eyes of a competent analyst who understands all the issues – pro-Marxian and anti-Marxian. A referee has also made this point. Baumol [25] has made a similiar claim for Marx, and in [31] I have assayed to refute the cogency of the line of argument Baumol attributes to Marx.

macroeconomic total of surplus among the different subaggregate departments), nonetheless the insights of the s/v or $\sum s/\sum v$ Marxian paradigm are crucial (or at least "useful") in "explaining" and "understanding" how the total of social product gets divided into paid labor and the exploiter's surplus in the years of developing capitalism. To repeat, there is no validity to this doctrine of surplus-value-paradigm-needed-macroeconomically-to-determine-the-rate-of-profit-that-microeconomically-partitions-out-the-surplus.

This is not the place to provide a comprehensive analysis of the pros and cons of these issues, as discussed by Marx, Hilferding, Dobb, Sweezy, Mandel, Meek, and many others. What is appropriate in this discussion of Marx as mathematical economist is to take notice of writings of Bortkiewicz, Sraffa, Robinson, Okishio,[17] Bródy,[18] Johansen,[19] and, most of all, Morishima.

From the standpoint of this Number One question I have scrutinized each page of Morishima's *Marx's Economics: A Dual Theory of Growth* [2], and each equation and footnote. My resulting judgment is that there is no reason given there that leads me to want to weaken the above view on the Number One question.[20]

---

[17] Okishio [26]. If I had known of the article earlier, I would have referred to it in the bibliography of my 1971 paper. Its views essentially coincide with my own (although I do not think its attempt to resolve differences in labor qualities into differences in producible education does justice to the empirical complexity of realistic "primary" factors).

[18] Bródy [27] provides a valuable and original analysis of Marx along general Leontief lines.

[19] To my 1971 bibliography should now be added the article by Johansen [28].

[20] Volume I's discussion can make this clear. Since in that volume, Marx talks repeatedly of successive stages of production, such as the spinning of yarn and the weaving of it into cloth, he is evidently already in what Leontief, Sraffa, and Böhm would dub a more-than-one-department world. But, even without the mathematics given in the Appendix, we can easily jot down a truly one-department-model – to see whether I am right in denying that S/V reveals some insight that conventional $S/(C+V)$ analysis deceptively conceals.

Suppose to produce 1 corn at the end of a period, it takes at the beginning of the period, $a_0 = \frac{1}{2}$ of labor along with $\frac{1}{2}$ of corn as raw material or seed. Then if labor can be reproduced instantly for less than 1 corn, an exploitative positive rate of profit is deducible. Thus, if subsistence corn per unit of L is $m = \frac{1}{3}$ corn, the competent reader can verify that R is 50%. He can verify that half the gross product goes for raw materials. Of the remaining half of Net National Product, one-third goes to labor and two-thirds goes to profit receivers (to consume now in simple reproduction cases; or, in extended reproduction cases, to consume a fixed fraction and plow back into extensive growth of the system the remaining fraction saved).

We have full insight into the problem, by mainstream economic concepts that are Ricardian (i.e., pre-Marxian), Millian (i.e., contemporaneous with Marx), Wicksellian, or Sraffian (i.e., post-Marxian). We know: At any profit rate R higher than R^*, workers will get too low a real wage to reproduce themselves; at any profit rate lower than R^*, there would be opportunity for infinite-sure-thing arbitrage – in which I borrow to buy corn, pay workers with it, and use it as raw material, then sell the product at a return greater than what I have to pay as interest, and without risk, make as much as I like. So we see, from capitalist pricing and accounting and avaricious arbitrage exactly how and why exploitation takes place.

I have discussed elsewhere the views of others of these writers. Specifically, I wish to iterate that my view on these matters is quite divorced from the disputes over the inadequacies of neoclassicism. I would be quite content to call my position on this Number One question Sraffian, or Robinsonian, or

If we want to write down a $C + V + S = C + V + R^*(C + V)$ tableau, here is how it would read for each unit of steady state labor:

1 of corn as raw material $+ \frac{1}{3}$ of corn as subsistence wage $+ 0.5(1+\frac{1}{3})$ of corn profit
   $=2$ of corn produced gross (of which the 1 of NNP is seen to be divided up into $\frac{1}{3}$ for labor and $\frac{2}{3}$ for exploiter).

Thus, we know all there is to know both in pecuniary and physical terms.

Now, is there any *new insight* possible from concentrating on the ratio of surplus to wages alone, S/V? Since with only one department there cannot be differing organic compositions of capital, we know from the beginning that the surplus-value innovations of Volume I must give us exactly the same answer as mainstream economics. So, was that trip really necessary? Or somehow desirable? Surely, on reflection, one will see that in this case, where it does no harm and requires no transformation algorithm, it also does not one iota of extra good. One might as usefully squander one's time in considering still a third regime in which we concentrate on S/C ratios.

To be sure, one can describe the same degenerate 1-department tableau by saying that the rate of surplus value is 200%: i.e., $r^* = 2.00$. Admittedly, a 200% rate *sounds* more exploitative than a 50% rate. But that is only for illiterates, since (as Marx clearly points out) the 200% of S/V is the same absolute loot for the exploiter merely expressed as a fraction of the smaller base V, rather than the base $(C + V)$.

But have we not added the vital fact that "living labor" is the true source of all product and *a fortiori* exploitative profits? No; conventional analysis tells us that without labor, there is no product at all. And it tells us that, without beginning-of-the-period raw material, there is also no product. That is not an apologetic for profit; it is a technical fact: mainstream economics fully recognizes that, if the m minimum of subsistence goes up, R^* will fall; and if the workers – by power or eduction – insist on an m up to 1, they can get all the NNP and bring R^* to zero. But, you may say, there may be strong political reasons why workers will not succeed in doing this or will be prevented from organizing to raise m and their real wage. You may be right. But you will be equally right or wrong or insightful in terms of R^* analysis as in parallel r^* analysis. And further, you will be able with R to understand the Sraffa dated-labor resolution, à la Adam Smith, of price into wages and profit in all the (infinite but converging) earlier stages of production – namely

$$p = a_0(1 + R^*) + a_0 a(1 + R^*)^2 + \cdots + a_0 a^{t-1}(1 + R^*)^t + \cdots$$
$$= a_0(1 + R^*)/[1 - a(1 + R^*)]$$

which Marx, throughout all his jousting with Adam Smith, was never able to get straight when $R > 0$. [Indeed, this makes one wonder whether he actually ever was able to rigorously perceive that, for $R^* = 0$, price does indeed equal total embodied labor content (direct plus indirect).] Now try to make that same correct resolution in the surplus-value rregime, with its gratuitous neglect of compound interest, and its quite unmerited belief that only the last-stage's direct labor contributes to profit. Tell that to a capitalist who hires a worker to plant a 10-year rather than a 5-year tree. On these workers' "live labor," will the exploiters'profit end up the same? Of course not.

Ricardian, or Passinettian, or Leontiefian. (For example, in a regime of values, with uniform rates of surplus value, the realistic possibility of reswitching could not logically occur: The technique that minimizes "values" at $r = 0$ will minimize them for all r's – a shortcoming of the "values" model.)

X. Final Summing Up

The preceding analysis does demonstrate that Karl Marx deserves an honored place among economic pioneers of steady state and balanced growth equilibrium. What is valid in this seminal contribution is in no sense contrary to mainstream economics of Marx's predecessors, contemporaries, or successors. Even if we end with the view that Marx was not so much a mathematical economist as "merely" a great economist, this recognition of his analytical abilities in no sense diminishes our appreciation of him as an original and creative shaper of the science of political economy. In science, your ultimate grade depends on the best performance you achieve, and not on your worst or even average performance.

I leave to the Appendix the more rigorous summarizing of these models, and discussion of Morishima's criticism of my Marxian writings.

APPENDIX

1. Technical Coefficients of Production

Let X_{ij} be the amount of the ith good used as input for the industry producing the jth nonnegative output, X_j; let L_j be the direct labor used by the jth industry. All these are nonnegative. Then $a = [a_{ij}] = [X_{ij}/X_j]$ represents the nonnegative Marx–Markov–Metzler–Leontief matrix, and $a_0 = [L_j/X_j]$ represents the row vector of direct labor requirements.

2. Examples

Some possible cases are the following.

$$\begin{bmatrix} a_0 \\ \cdots \\ a \end{bmatrix} = \begin{bmatrix} 1 & 1 \\ \cdots & \cdots \\ 0 & 0 \\ 0 & 0 \end{bmatrix}, \text{ Smith's deer–beaver case;} \quad (2.1)$$

$$\begin{bmatrix} a_0 \\ \cdots \\ a \end{bmatrix} = \begin{bmatrix} 1 & \frac{1}{2} \\ \cdots & \cdots \\ 0 & \frac{1}{2} \\ 0 & 0 \end{bmatrix},$$ the Ricardo–Austrian coal – corn case of my six tableaux;

$$\begin{bmatrix} a_0 \\ \cdots \\ a \end{bmatrix} = \begin{bmatrix} \alpha & \beta \\ \cdots & \cdots \\ 1-\alpha & 1-\beta \\ 0 & 0 \end{bmatrix},$$ Marx's tableaux of corn–coal :

$\alpha = \beta$ as in Tableau 1, (2.3)

$\alpha < \beta$ as in Tableau 2;

$$\begin{bmatrix} a_0 \\ \cdots \\ a \end{bmatrix} = \begin{bmatrix} 1-\alpha_1-\beta_1 & 1-\alpha_2-\beta_2 \\ \cdots & \cdots \\ \alpha_1 & \alpha_2 \\ \beta_1 & \beta_2 \end{bmatrix},$$ the general two - department case.

(2.4)

In every case, I have followed the convention of selecting units so that "total" labor requirements ("direct" plus "indirect") are unity.

3. Admissible Cases

In case (2.4) we could have $1 - \alpha_2 - \beta_2 = 0$; but in order that every good require, directly or indirectly, some labor input, we could *not* then also have either α_2 or $1 - \alpha_1 - \beta_1$ zero. Sraffa chooses to require that there exist at least one good (a basic) that is directly or indirectly required by all goods (including itself). But there seems no reason to rule out cases (2.1) and (2.2).

The simplest case to talk about is where a_0 and a have strictly positive elements: $a_0 > 0$, $a > 0$. But it is almost as simple if nonnegative a is "indecomposable" and at least one element of a_0 is positive. (Indecomposability is verified when $(1 + a + \cdots + a^{n-1})$ is strictly positive.) Ricardo and Marx often adjoined to "necessary" goods a set of "luxury" goods, i.e., goods which are not themselves needed as inputs for the necessary goods. This gives

$$
\begin{bmatrix} a_0 \\ \cdots \\ a \end{bmatrix} = \begin{bmatrix} a_{0,I} & a_{0,II} \\ \cdots & \cdots \\ a_{I,I} & a_{I,II} \\ 0 & a_{II,II} \end{bmatrix}.
$$

Here $a_{I,I}$ must be nonnegative and indecomposable and at least one element of $a_{0,I}$ must be positive. Columns of $a_{I,II}$ must have a positive element. The subscript I refers to necessary goods; the subscript II, to "luxury" goods (which must be understood to be able to include a wage-subsistence good such as corn).

4. General Time-Phased System

These input-output relations are the steady state plateaux of the actual time-phased technology and allocation relations.

$$
X_j(t+1) = F_j[L_j(t), X_{1j}(t), \ldots, X_{nj}(t)] \quad (j = 1, \ldots, n) \tag{4.1}
$$

$$
= \text{Min}[L_j(t)/a_{0j}, X_{1j}^{(t)}/a_{1j}, X_{nj}^{(t)}/a_{nj}] \tag{4.1'}
$$

$$
X_j(t) = X_{j1}(t) + \cdots + X_{jn}(t) + B_j(t) \tag{4.2}
$$

where $B_j(t)$ is the nonnegative "final consumption" in the tth period of the jth good. (Whenever an a_{ij} is zero rather than positive, we can follow the convention of disregarding its X_{ij}/a_{ij} term.)

In (4.1) we can have *any* continuous production function (not necessarily possessing well-defined partial derivatives of marginal productivity). Only joint production and externalities are ruled out.

However, much of the Marx and Leontief literature chooses to concentrate on the single-fixed-technology case shown in (4.1'). It is well to notice that in (4.1') any pattern of nonnegative a's and a_0's are permitted, provided only that every good requires directly or indirectly some positive labor. In short, the so-called Hawkins-Simon conditions – that are necessary and sufficient if something of every good is to be producible for *steady* net consumption – need *not* be stipulated to hold in general. (It is worth pointing out that the belated discovery of the H–S conditions came out of Hawkins' study of a dynamic *Marxian* system!)

5. Steady State Plateaux

For steady states, we equate variables at all times:

$$X_j(t) = X_j(t+1) = \cdots = X_j$$
$$X_{ij}(t) = X_{ij}(t+1) = \cdots = X_{ij}$$
$$L_j(t) = L_j(t+1) = \cdots = L_j$$
$$B_j(t) = B_j(t+1) = \cdots = B_j.$$

(5.1)

If the consumption $[B_j]$ are to be capable of taking on all-positive values, we must be able to satisfy the steady state form of (4.1') and (4.2).

$$L_1 + \cdots + L_n = L > 0, \qquad X_{ij} \geqq 0$$
$$X_i - (X_{i1} + \cdots + X_{in}) = B_i > 0 \qquad (i = 1, \ldots, n)$$

(5.2)

$$a_{01}X_1 + \cdots + a_{0n}X_n = L > 0$$
$$X_i - (a_{i1}X_1 + \cdots + a_{in}X_n) - B_i > 0 \qquad (i = 1, \ldots, n)$$

(5.2')

or, in matrix terms,

$$\begin{bmatrix} a_0 \\ \cdots \\ I - a \end{bmatrix} X = \begin{bmatrix} L \\ \cdots \\ B \end{bmatrix} > 0.$$

(5.3')

6. Hawkins-Simon Conditions for Positive Steady State Consumptions

Suppose nonnegative a can be rearranged by renumbering of corresponding rows and columns into the partitioned form

$$\begin{bmatrix} A_{0,I} & A_{0,II} & \cdots & A_{0,N} \\ \cdots\cdots\cdots\cdots\cdots\cdots\cdots \\ A_{I,I} & A_{I,II} & \cdots & A_{I,N} \\ 0 & A_{II,II} & \cdots & A_{II,N} \\ \cdots\cdots\cdots\cdots\cdots\cdots\cdots \\ 0 & 0 & \cdots & A_{N,N} \end{bmatrix}$$

(6.1)

where each diagonal $A_{I,I}, \ldots, A_{N,N}$ matrix is indecomposable, except possibly the last, but where elements above this diagonal can be zero (provided, of course, that every indecomposable set is tied directly or indirectly to a positive A_0 element). [Examples would be (2.4) with (β_1, α_2) the only vanishing elements; or with β_1 and $1 - \alpha_2 - \beta_2$ the only vanishing elements.]

Then the Hawkins-Simon conditions say: "It is necessary and sufficient for producible steady state production of any one consumption good (and of all such) that every principal-minor subsystem of $I - a$ (and of $I - A_{J,J}$) have a positive determinant."

Our examples (2.1)–(2.4), because of their normalized-to-unity form automatically satisfy the H–S conditions for a "steady state surplus economy." This is so because the condition

$$\sum_{j=1}^{n} a_{ij} < 1 \ (i = 1, \ldots n) \tag{6.2}$$

is a sufficient condition for H-S. It is of course not necessary, since changing units of goods can always destroy it; but H-S holds, if and only if, for *some* choice of units, *every* diagonal matrix in (6.1) can be made to have its row sums satisfy

$$a_{0i} = 1 - \sum_{j} a_{ij} \geqq 0 \tag{6.3}$$

with the strong inequality holding for at least one of its columns. Clearly, (6.2) is an overly strong case of (6.3).

7. Subsistence-Wage Theory of Labor's Cost of Reproduction

We must now introduce the Marx-like notion that labor itself has a cost of production and reproduction. If $L(t+1)$ satisfied equations like those satisfied by $X_j(t + 1)$ in (4.1), we would have a von Neumann system in which labor could be treated like any other "nonprimary" input. But Marx never quite articulated that case.

Marx failed to develop in detail his subsistence-wage process. Perhaps the simplest version is to assume that, from the reserve army of unemployed or the countryside, the system can always get the $L(t) = \sum_{j=1}^{n} L_j(t)$ it needs *now* at the beginning of the period's production process. It gets each such unit of $L(t)$ by providing it with the column vector of subsistence-goods requirements $[m_i]$, where one or more of these nonnegative elements is strictly positive. (In the typical Marxian model, when workers consume different goods from those used as inputs, the only positive m_i elements belong to rows of A_{NN} in (6.1) that consist exclusively of zeros. If capitalists' luxury consumption item are different from those of workers' subsistence consumption, there may be still other rows of A_{NN} in which the elements are zero.[21] But the results would be essentially similar if m_i were positive for *all i*).

8. Technocratic Subsistence-Wage Model

Without using Marx's "value" concepts or (as yet) those of bourgeois prices, I review the familiar Leontief-Sraffa technocratic formulation of a steady state, where workers get subsistence wage consumption mL, or M for short, and capitalists get the rest, $B - M$. We have, from (5.3'):

$$X = aX + B = (I - a)^{-1}B$$
$$a_0 X = a_0(I - a)^{-1}B = L > 0 \qquad (8.1)$$
$$a_0(I - a)^{-1}(B - M) = L - a_0(I - a)^{-1}mL.$$

Here the row vector $a_0(I - a)^{-1}$ represents the total technocratic labor requirements (direct plus indirect) required in the steady state to produce unit amounts of the respective goods. If $B - M = 0$, so that the system is just producing needed wage subsistence, and "exploitation" were zero, goods might actually be priced (relative to the wage) at these undiluted-labor-theory-of-value $a_0(I - a)^{-1}$ levels.

9. Coefficient of "Exploitation"

We could for any system calculate as a measure of exploiters' "share" in social production:

$$\rho \overset{\text{def}}{=} a_0(I - a)^{-1}(B - M)/a_0(I - a)^{-1}M \geqq 0. \qquad (9.1)$$

[21] By Seton's 1957 device of "feeding coefficients," we could handle subsistence wages by adding to each original a_{ij} the new requirement $a_{0j}m_i$. Or, in the case where a unit of work in each jth industry requires a different amount of subsistence to be paid at the beginning of the period, namely, m_{ij}, we add to a_{ij} the term $a_{0j}m_{ij} = k_{ij}$. Here I shall not make m_i depend on j, and shall not employ the feeding-coefficient notation even through it has its advantages. Thus, let $[a_{ij} + k_{ij}]$ be indecomposable. Then positive principal minors of $[I - a_{ij} - k_{ij}]$ is the *strengthened* Hawkins–Simon condition that guarantees not merely the producibility of positive B, but also that enough be producible to leave something over for employers' positive profit. In our notation, this is equivalent to $a_0[I - a]^{-1}m < 1$, so that $a_0(1 + R)[I - a(1 + R)]^{-1}m = 1$ have a positive R root for the profit rate. The reader of Morishima will note that there is no need no *duplicate* this condition by an *equivalent* requirement that $a_0(1 + r)[I - a]^{-1}m = 1$ have a positive r root for the "rate of surplus value." This last adds (and subtracts) nothing to the analysis of realistic competitive equilibrium. (For simplicity, I posit length of working day constant.)

(This is sometimes given the Marxian name, ratio of "unpaid" to "paid" labor.) Under the rude undiluted labor theory of value, we would have ρ and $B - M$ zero rather than positive. This ρ coefficient has the pleasant property that changes in capitalists' tastes among different $B - M$ consumption will not affect the magnitude of ρ. However, as we should expect, changes in the consumption of subsistence m or M requirements, like changes in any a_{0j} or a_{ij}, will change ρ. For example, reducing any one m_i, or any one a_{0j} needed for some m's production, will necessarily raise ρ.

10. Exploitation Pricing

To verify that there is never an advantage, save to those of limited algebraic ability, in *ever* considering Marx's regime of equalized-positive-rates-of-surplus value, I proceed on conventional bourgeois Ricardo-Sraffa-Leontief lines. For each uniform profit rate R, the row vector of prices (relative to the wage numéraire), written as $P[1 + R]$, will consist of monotone-increasing functions of R, $P_j[1 + R]$, satisfying competitive-arbitrage steady state pricing

$$P_j[1 + R] = \left\{ a_{0j} + \sum_{i=1}^{n} P_i[1 + R]a_{ij} \right\}(1 + R) \quad (j = 1, \ldots, n). \quad (10.1)$$

In matrix terms

$$\begin{aligned} P[1 + R] &= a_0(1 + R) + P[1 + R]a(1 + R) \\ &= a_0(1 + R)[I - a(1 + R)]^{-1} > 0. \end{aligned} \quad (10.1')$$

11. Effect of Varying Level for Exploitative Profit Rate on Relative Prices

Generally, as R increases from 0 to its maximum value at which $[I - a(1 + R)]^{-1}$ remains finite, $R = R_{\max} \leqq \infty$, the $P_j[1 + R]$ prices will grow at *unequal* percentage rates. Hence, the ratio $P_{1+j}[1 + R]/P_1[1 + R]$ can rise, or can fall, or in general can both rise and then later fall. However, Marx realized that in the case he called "equal organic composition of capital," such price ratios could never change. We may express this in the following propositions.

Marx-Sraffa Theorem If, and only if,

$$a_{0j}(1+R)/P_j[1+R] \equiv a_{01}(1+R)/P_1[1+R] \quad (j=2,\ldots,n) \qquad (11.1)$$

for *some* nonnegative R, will this identity be true for *all* admissible R. And, in that case, for an observed equilibrium profit rate, $R = R^*$:

$$P_j[1+R^*] \equiv P_j[1](1+\rho) \qquad (11.2)$$

where ρ is the exploitation coefficient of Section 9, which can be defined, as we will see in the next section, once the subsistence-requirement vector is known, as a unique function of the $R = R^*$ profit rate that is implied by the condition of a real wage rate at the subsistence level.

12. Defining the Subsistence-Theory's Equilibrium Profit Rate

The equilibrium profit rate is defined as the unique $R = R^*$ level at which

$$P[1+R]m = 1 \qquad (12.1)$$

where

$$1/P[1+R]m = \mathbf{W}[R] \qquad (12.2)$$

defines the "factor-price tradeoff frontier" linking the real wage and the profit rate. Because $P_j'[1+R] > 0$, necessarily $W'[R] < 0$.

13. "Exploitative Rate" Greater than Profit Rate

An easy Marx-like tautology is that, for equilibrium R positive

$$\rho > R \qquad (13.1)$$

provided only that some one positive intermediate input a_{ij} is needed to produce the subsistence-wage basket.[22]

---

[22] To see this, define the monotone-increasing function

$$g[R_1] = a_0[I - a(1+R_1)]^{-1}m = P[1+R_2]m/(1+R_2).$$

By definition of R^* and ρ^*

$$1 = P[1+R^*]m = g[R^*](1+R^*) = P[1](1+\rho^*)m = g[0](1+\rho^*).$$

For $R^* > 0$, $g[R^*] > g[0]$ and hence $r^* > R^*$, the final proof that the defined exploitation rate ρ exceeds the profit rate numerically. This tautology has no empirical content (and no empirical relevance or insight).

14. The Equal-Organic Case of Constant Relative Prices

When all $a_{0j}(1 + R)/P_j[1 + R]$ have uniform values $\alpha[R]$, as in (11.1), each price takes on the special simple form of (11.2):

$$P_j[1 + R] = (1 + \rho[R])P_j[1] \qquad (14.1)$$

where the monotone function $\rho[R]$ is defined in terms of $\alpha[0] = \alpha$ by

$$\rho[R] = R/[1 - (1 - \alpha)(1 + R)] > R, \qquad 0 < R \leq R_{max} = \alpha/(1 - \alpha) \qquad (14.2)$$

This follows from easy substitution into (10.1). As a convenient check, we note that the exploitation rate ρ corresponding to the positive subsistence-equilibrium profit rate R^* is given as

$$\rho = \rho[R^*] = (L - P[1]M)/P[1]M = (P[1]m)^{-1} - 1 \qquad (14.3)$$

15. Simple Reproduction Tableau

L is given. It produces steady state gross outputs (X_i), which, at the equilibrium profit rate R^* sell at $P_j[1 + R^*]$. The revenues of each jth industry $P_j[1 + R^*]X_j$ are equal to costs of production defined by

$$P_j[1 + R^*]X_j = \{a_{0j}X_j\} + \left\{ \sum_{i=1}^{n} P_i[1 + R^*]a_{ij}X_j \right\}$$
$$+ R^* \left\{ a_{0j}X_j + \sum_{i=1}^{n} P_i[1 + R^*]a_{ij}X_j \right\}$$
$$(j = 1, \ldots, n). \qquad (15.1)$$

This can be rearranged into my text's $C + V + S$ arrangement:

$$\left\{ \sum_{i=1}^{n} P_i[1 + R^*]a_{ij}X_j \right\}$$
$$+ \{a_{0j}X_j\} + R^* \left\{ \sum_{i=1}^{n} P_i[1 + R^*]a_{ij}X_j + a_{0j}X_j \right\}$$
$$\equiv \{C_j\} + \{V_j\} + R^*\{C_j + V_j\} = C_j + V_j + S_j \qquad (j = 1, \ldots, n).$$
$$(15.1')$$

The prime cause of stumbling (and sterility) in the usual $C + V + S$ analysis is the failure to relate these magnitudes to the underlying technology, and the related failure to breakdown C_j into its price and quantity factors. These capital letters, note, represent the bourgeois pricing regime in which

$$S_1/(C_1 + V_1) = S_2/(C_2 + V_2) = \ldots = R^* \qquad (15.2)$$

where R^* is the equilibrium profit rate.

In matrix terms, by the usual transposition of the row vectors of (15.1′), we get the simple reproduction tableau,

$$P[1 + R^*]aX + a_0X + R^*\{P[1 + R^*]aX + a_0X\} = P[1 + R^*]X \quad (15.1'')$$

where the composition of X is determined by the $B - M$ selected by the capitalists subject to the simple reproduction no-saving condition

$$P[1 + R^*](B - M) = \sum_{j=1}^{n} S_j. \qquad (15.3)$$

Except for the usual transposition of row and column, we then have the well-defined tableau of simple reproduction[23]

$$P[1 + R^*]a(I - a)^{-1}B + a_0(I - a)^{-1}B$$
$$+ R^*\{(P[1 + R^*]a + a_0)(I - a)^{-1}B\}$$
$$= P[1 + R^*]X. \qquad (15.4)$$

[23] I have qualms about calling ρ by the commonly met Marxian expression "the ratio of 'unpaid labor' [which workers perform for the exploiting employers' ultimate benefit] to 'paid labor' [which workers do for themselves]." This expression tempts one to think that ρ is an indicator of "profit share in NNP ÷ labor share in NNP." But, in a general competitive regime, such an identification is not valid. Actually, a shift in employers' tastes toward consumption goods with low $a_{0j}/P_j[1]$ will raise profit's NNP share to its upper limit; conversely, a shift to high $a_{0j}/P_j[1]$ will depress it to its lower limit; yet ρ itself remains constant between these limits independently of how, at the fixed profit rate R^*, capitalists select their luxury consumption. Although

$$\text{Min}[S_j/V_j] \leqq \rho \leqq \text{Max}[S_j/V_j].$$

it will generally not be the case that, "in the aggregate,"

$$\rho = \sum_j S_j / \sum_j V_j.$$

Only for the uninteresting lowercase "values" definition of s_j/v_j will each of these equal ρ. But my defined ρ never has need for any $s_1/v_1 = s_2/v_2$ concepts.

16. Extended Reproduction

Now, what about the case of extended reproduction, with growth rate $g = (\text{Saving rate out of profits})/R^*$? Then we must have dynamically

$$aX(t + 1) \leqq X(t) - B(t), \qquad a_0X(t + 1) \leqq L(t). \qquad (16.1)$$

For $L(t) \equiv L_0(1 + g)^t$ and *all* variables growing in proportion

$$X(t) = (1 + g)^t X, \qquad B(t) = (1 + g)^t B, \quad M(t) = (1 + g)^t m L_0. \quad (16.2)$$

Then (16.1) becomes

$$a(1 + g)X = X - B, \qquad a_0(1 + g)X = L_0. \qquad (16.3)$$

Evidently (16.3) relating the coefficients of the $(1 + g)^t$ expression is just like (5.3), but with all (a_0, a) coefficients blown up by $(1 + g)$ to allow for "widening" of capital goods.

As before, $B(t)$ gets split up into $M(t)$ and capitalists' expenditures for consumption, an amount determined by that part of their profit income which they do not invest. But as final product, we now have added to consumption B the vector of net capital formation gX.

Applying prices $P[1 + R^*]$ to (16.3), we get the extended reproduction tableau for the system at time $t = 0$, namely,

$$\left\{ \sum_{i=1}^{n} P_i[1 + R^*]a_{ij}X_j \right\}$$
$$+ \{a_{0j}X_j\} + R^* \left\{ \sum_{i=1}^{n} P_i[1 + R^*]a_{ij}X_j + a_{0j}X_j \right\}$$
$$= P_j[1 + R^*]X_j + \sum_{i=1}^{n} P_i[1 + R^*]a_{ij}gX_j \quad (j = 1, \ldots, n). \qquad (16.4)$$

The last term on the right, involving gX_j, represents net capital formation needed for widening of capital.

The left-hand side of (16.4) can be rewritten in the familiar form

$$C_j + V_j + R^*\{C_j + V_j\} \qquad (i = 1, \ldots, n)$$

of the extended reproduction tableaux – as in my text's equal-profit-rate tableaux.

17. The Alternative "Values" Regime of Marx

Now we must jettison Sections 10–16. ("Erase and replace." Or "Consider a
dual accounting system.") I have argued that there is no good reason for a
person well versed in algebra and logic to waste a moment on this alternative regime. (It is not a "dual" regime in the usual sense of dual – as for
example Peter's game strategy as compared to Paul's dual strategy; or the
primal linear programming maximum problem and its *dual* minimum
problem; or the conjugate variables of coordinates and *dual* momenta in
mechanics; or the point–line dualities of projective geometries; or the
production function and its *dual* minimum unit cost of production; or
optimal-control variables and their Pontryagin *dual* shadow prices; or of
the duality theorem relating $P[1]X$ from (10.1) to $a_0(I - a)X^{-1}X$ of (8.1)
and also discussed in Morishima's first chapter.

Still, this final section may be useful to those of us who wish, if only for
antiquarian reasons, to be clear on the logical differences between the
concepts involved in Marx's detour and those involved in a regime of
ruthless competition.

The same subsistence wage defines, in the "values" regime, not "prices"
written in capital letters, P, but "values," written as $(p_1, \ldots, p_n) = p$. It is
understood that, as a useful convention, these prices are expressed in wage-
numéraire units. They are defined in terms of a parameter r, the rate of
equalized markups on direct wages alone and are written as $P_j[1 + r]$.
Alternatively to the behavior equation of arbitrage in (10.1), we now
arbitrarily postulate with Marx

$$P_j[1 + r] = a_{oj} + \sum_{i=1}^{n} p_i[1 + r]a_{ij} + ra_{oj} \qquad (j = 1, \ldots, n) \qquad (17.1)$$

In matrix terms this gives

$$p[1 + r] = a_0 + p[1 + r]a + ra_0 = a_0(I - a)^{-1}(1 + r)$$
$$= p[1](1 + r) = P[1](1 + r). \qquad (17.2)$$

Note that, for $r = 0$ and no exploitation, we do not get something *better*
than our bourgeois $P[1]$ of embodied labors. Actually, we get the *identical*
technocratic total labor requirements (direct plus indirect) of the undiluted
labor theory of value, namely, $p[1] \equiv P[1]$. However, once workers do not
get all the product, it is false in logic and in history (century by century) that

there was ever a time when (17.2) could have been expected to prevail under the unequal organic composition of capital.

The equilibrium rate of surplus value, $r = r^*$, set by the minimum subsistence postulate of each laborer's consumption being m, is determined as the unique root of

$$p[1 + r]m = 1 = p[1]m(1 + r), \ r^* = (p[1]m)^{-1} - 1. \tag{17.3}$$

It is an easy exercise, along the lines of footnote 22, to prove that the technocratically defined exploitative coefficient, ρ of (4.1), must equal r^*:

$$r^* = \rho = P[1](B - mL)/P[1]mL = p[1](B - mL)/p[1]mL. \tag{17.4}$$

When we apply the X terms of (5.3') or (16.3) to (17.2), we get the simple reproduction or extended reproduction tableaux of Marx's "values" regimes (as in Volume II of *Capital*). Thus, in matrix terms

$$\{c\} + \{v\} + \{s\} = \{c\} + \{v\} + r\{v\} = \{p[1 + r^*]aX\} + \{a_0X\} + r\{a_0X\} \tag{17.5}$$

as in my text's simple and extended reproduction "values" tableaux.

Of course, by the stated Marx-Sraffa theorem, if $a_{0j}/P_j[1]$ are the same α for all industries, the two alternative regimes coincide, with

$$p_j[1 + \rho[R]] \equiv P_j[1 + R] \ (j = 1, \ldots, n)$$

and where $\rho[R]$ is defined as in (14.2).

In general, the "transformation problem" consists of the procedure that relates r^* to R^* taking into account the common subsistence-wage basket imposed on the alternative regimes. (Morishima uses the name "dynamic transformation problem" for discussion that relates "the saving rate out of profit" to "the saving rate out of surplus values," at a common growth rate imposed on the alternative regimes.)

How can one describe the greater algebraic simplicity of the values regime in comparison with the prices regime? Chiefly in three aspects:

$$\frac{p_j[1 + r]}{p_1[1 + r]} \equiv \frac{P_j[1](1 + r)}{P_1[1](1 + r)} = \frac{p_j[1]}{p_1[1]} \ \text{for all } r. \tag{17.6}$$

No similar relation holds for general $P_j[1 + R]/P_1[1 + r]$.

Instead of having to solve an nth degree polynomial for the subsistence-wage profit rate R^*, as in (12.1), in (17.3) we need solve only a *linear* equation

$$1 = (p[1]m)(1 + r) \tag{17.7'}$$

for r^*!

Finally, suppose we have a reproduction tableau

$$c + v + s$$

for one real wage and r^*. Suppose there is now a change in r^*, but (for some odd reason) the capitalists spend on consumption goods in the same proportion that the workers spend. (Neither Marxians nor non-Marxians vouch for realism in this.) Then, by dropping our no-longer-useful convention of measuring always in wage-numéraire units, we can immediately write down the new reproduction tableau as equal to, or proportional to,

$$\{c'\} + \{v'\} + \{s'\} = \{c\} + \{\beta(v + s)\} + \{(1 + \beta)(v + s)\}.$$

That is, we simply repartition the total $v + s$ of each industry into new proportionate parts as between wages and surplus, leaving their c and $v + s$ unchanged. This simplicity explains how Marx could consider a variety of cases without having to know how to handle his tableaux in detail.

Have I omitted an advantage for "values" when it comes to aggregating into more manageable subaggregates? Yes, deliberately. For I perceive no such advantages in the $p[1 + r]$ or $p[1]$ weights over the $P[1 + R^*]$ or $P[1 + R]$ weights. Since R, empirically, is poorly approximated by the biased value of $R = 0$, the $p[\cdot]$ values weights are unnecessarily biased. Apparently, Professor Morishima and I have not reached agreement on this point, since his case for values seems in significant part to hinge on this dubious aggregation question. (I like his generalization of the Marx–Sraffa theorem, but I think it is *better* stated in $P_j[1 + R]$ terms.)

Have I omitted an advantage for the $s_1/v_1 = s_2/v_2$ values regime when it comes to computing "employment multipliers" in the $L = \sum A_{0j}B_j = a_0(I - a)^{-1}B$ relation for societies' net-production-possibility frontier?[24] Yes, deliberately. For, *all* we need is $P[1] = a_0(I - a)^{-1}$ concepts of the *bourgeois* analysis for the $R^* = 0$ case.

---

[24] I owe to an unpublished review by von Weizsäcker [29] a similar point. Also for the point that $P_j[1]$, $p_j[1]$, or $P_j[1 + r]$ weights are worse than $P_j[1 + R]$ weights would be for some positive R provides a more realistic approximation than $R = 0$. Arguing that $P_j[1]$ weights are more fixed than $P_j[1 + R]$ weights when R is changing is like arguing that a frozen weather vane is less capricious than one which is changed by the wind!

18. Conclusion

I append in a terse footnote my elucidation of positions that Morishima has taken explicit exception to.[25] But I believe that this Appendix could be

---

[25] The Morishima index has 16 references to me by name. Some, like those referring to pp. 29, 56, 140, 181, and 185 contain citations that represent no disagreements. Those on pp. 70 and 78 point out that the equal-internal-organic-composition of capitals case of Section VII of my 1971 *JEL* paper [13] is, for more-than-two department systems, a sufficient but not necessary condition – to which I gladly agree and authorize the reader to go through an "erase-and-replace" algorithm: *erase* the section's first word "The" and *replace* it by "A." And I agree that this singular case is not empirically realistic or even admissible for those Marx models in which wage goods are not used for production and other goods are: I never thought otherwise. All that I wished to do was show that Marx's algorithm need not always be wrong; but that *even* where it is not, his claim that we need "value" systems to reveal active exploitation processes is completely unfounded, *logically* and *empirically*, macroeconomically and microeconomically. [Although Morishima thinks that the issue of these two pages are relevant to his criticisms on other pages, I believe that once misunderstandings of my arguments are cleared away, such issues as whether $C_j + V_j = c_j + v_j$ (or, for Morishima's notation, $C_j^p + V_j^p = C^j + V^j$) are quite irrelevant and uninteresting.]

On p. 129 Morishima argues that Marx would have rejected the Neumann–Malthus model of Section IV of my *JEL* paper. That is no point against me (even *if* one argues that the logic of the passages Morishima quotes are relevant and cogent to the issue). I tried to fill the lacunae in Marx's models with possible realistic demographic and migration patterns. And, as a special limiting case of that model, I was able to generate exactly his exploitation conditions and to do it without departing from bourgeois competitive conditions.

On p. 115, Morishima somehow thinks that Dorfman–Samuelson–Solow (1958) [6] fall into the error of believing that competition requires profit to be zero. On pp. 224, 227, and 229 of Chapter 9 of ref. [6] where $P[1] = a_0 + P[1]a$, the authors are obviously dealing with the statical, instantaneous, or time-satiated Leontief system – as the chapter's beginning warns in its early statement: "Subsequent chapters will deal with dynamic models involving time and stock of capital, and also more general models. . .of Leon Walras and J. B. Clark," I, for one, regret that we did not explicitly deal with the special steady state case $P[1 + R] = \{a_0 + P[1 + R]\}(1 + R)$ in the book, but the very fact that all three of us in those same years were writing papers with $R > 0$ should have prevented any such odd interpretation of our view of the real competitive world. (In the same 1958 year, my *QJE* papers on Ricardo appeared [21, 22] with pre-Sraffa models of exactly this type, with or without joint production.) Making a Marx versus no-Marx issue on this is straining.

Most of the rest of the references – as for example, on pp. 39, 46–47, 59–61, 72, 74, and 85 – involve the same set of misunderstandings, in which I (either alone, or in the good company of Marx, or of Paul Sweezy or Joan Robinson) am supposed to have made misleading assertions. Here is a typical sentence of mine, quoted no less than three times (pp. 47, 59, 74): "Volume I's first approximation of equal positive rates of surplus value, S_j/V_j, is not a simplifying assumption but rather – to the extent it contradicts equal profit rates $S_i/(V_i + C_i)$ – a complicating detour." That sentence, the reader can confirm in context, purports to say precisely this:

If, as generally holds, $C_i/(C_i + V_i) \neq C_j/(C_j + V_j)$, where these refer to an actual competitive system, then the $S_i/(C_i + V_i) = S_j/(C_j + V_j)$ real-world arbitrage equivalences imply $S_i/V_i \neq S_j/V_j$, except as an unuseful first approximation; and any alternative model or expanded to show that there is never macroeconomic or microeconomic advantage in rate-of-surplus-value analysis.

ACKNOWLEDGMENTS

I owe thanks to the National Scitence Foundation for financial aid, and to Norma Wasser for editorial assistance. I have also benefited from helpful comments by Professor Edward Ames of Stony Brook.

REFERENCES

[1] Samuelson, P. A., "Economists and the History of Ideas (Presidential Address)," *American Economic Review* 52 (March 1962), 1–18, reproduced as Chapter 113 in my *Collected Scientific Papers*, Volume II. Cambridge, Massachusetts: MIT Press, 1966. The quotation appears on p. 12 of the former, or p. 1510 of the latter.

[2] Morishima, M., *Marx's Economics; A Dual Theory of Growth*. London and New York: Cambridge University Press, 1973.

[3] Jorgenson, D. W., "Stability of a Dynamic Input-Output System," *Review of Economic Studies* 28 (February 1961), 105–116.

accounting regime, where by definition uniform s_i/v_i rates are postulated and equal $s_i/(v_i + c_i)$ rates denied, represents an unuseful detour.

Now that is what is said. It could be right or wrong; the reader must weigh my many arguments, here and elsewhere, on this; and he may read the Morishima book line for line for light it throws on this Number One question.

But now see what interpretations are put on the quotation. It is supposed to overlook that $C_i + V_i \equiv c_i + v_i$ equivalences may not hold [and why should they?]. It is supposed to fail to see that $s_i/v_i = s_j/v_j$ is no logical contradiction to $S_i/V_i \neq S_j/V_j$. Perhaps when different writers use different letters for similar things, such misinterpretations are unavoidable. But no one who reads this paper and Morishima's book need be left with the view that we disagree on all the things his text thought we did.

Morishima's transformation algorithm is isomorphic to that of Seton [32] (and for that matter 1907 Bortkiewicz). So is mine. So *if* mine is [and it is] an "erase and replace algorithm," so must be his. To speak of a "dual accounting system" is to be isomorphic with what my *JEL* paper [13] said. If one reads the remaining dissents with quoted positions of mine, they are generally of the type, "Samuelson doesn't recognize that Marx is trying to reveal the deceptiveness of capitalist accounting in terms of price," to explain and uncover the divergences between what is written here as $P_j[1 + R]$'s and $p_j[1 + r]$'s or $p_j[1]$'s, or $(P_j[1 + R]m)^{-1}$ and $(P_j[1]m)^{-1}$, to illuminate exploitation, to show how profit has its source in living labor, etc. Of course I recognize that Marx was trying to do that (he said so repeatedly), and thought he had. But why should Morishima and I believe that he had *succeeded* in such a useful program? That is the Number One question, and I could not find a single theorem in the Morishima book that predisposes one toward a favorable verdict on the question. (This includes the more-than-one proposition awarded the adjective "fundamental.")

Space does not here permit the more detailed evaluation of Morishima's criticisms that one could make, nor the explicit singling out for praise of his many novel contributions.

[4] Solow, R. M., "Competitive Valuation in a Dynamic Input-Output System," *Econometrica* 27 (January 1959), 30–53.

[5] Morishima, M., "Prices, Interest and Profits in a Dynamic Leontief System," *Econometrica* 26 (July 1958), 358–380; *Equilibrium, Stability and Growth.* London and New York: Oxford University Press, 1964.

[6] Dorfman, R., Samuelson, P., and Solow, R., *Linear Programming and Economic Analysis*, Chapter 11, pp. 283–300. New York: McGraw-Hill, 1959.

[7] Hahn, F. H., "Equilibrium Dynamics with Heterogeneous Capital Goods," *Quarterly Journal of Economics* 80 (November 1966), 633–646.

[8] Shell, K., and Stiglitz, J. E., "The Allocation of Investment in a Dynamic Economy," *Quarterly Journal of Economics* 8 (1967), 592–609.

[9] Caton, C., and Shell, K., "An Exercise in the Theory of Heterogeneous Capital Accumulation," *Review of Economic Studies* 38 (January 1971), 13–22.

[10] Samuelson, P. A., "Indeterminacy of Development in a Heterogeneous-Capital Model with Constant Saving Propensity," in *Essays in the Theory of Optimal Growth* (K. Shell, ed.). Cambridge, Massachusetts: MIT Press, 1967.

[11] Burmeister, E., Caton, C., Dobell, A. R., and Ross, S., "The 'Saddlepoint Property' and the Structure of Dynamic Heterogeneous Capital Good Models," *Econometrica* 39 (January 1973).

[12] Hayek, F. A., "The 'Paradox' of Saving," *Economica* 11 (May 1931), 125–169.

[13] Samuelson, P. A., "Understanding the Marxian Notion of Exploitation: A Summary of the So-Called Transformation Problem between Marxian Values and Competitive Prices," *Journal of Economic Literature* 9 (June 1971), 399–431. Reproduced as Chapter 153, pp. 276–308, of my *Collected Scientific Papers* (hereafter *CSP*), Volume III. Cambridge, Massachusetts: MIT Press, 1972).

[14] Samuelson, P. A., "The 'Transformation' from Marxian 'Value' to 'Competitive' Prices: A Process of Replacement and Rejection," *Proceedings of the National Academy of Sciences* 67 (September 1970), 423–425 (*CSP*, Volume III, Chapter 152, pp. 268–275).

[15] Samuelson, P. A., and von Weizsäcker, C. C., "A New Labor Theory of Value of Rational Planning through Use of the Bourgeois Profit Rate," *Proceedings of the National Academy of Sciences* 68 (June 1971), 1192–1194 (*CSP*, Volume III, Chapter 155, pp. 312–136).

[16] Samuelson, P. A., "The Economics of Marx: An Ecumerical Reply," *Journal of Economic Theory* 10 (March 1972), 51–56.

[17] Samuelson, P. A., "Samuelson's 'Reply on Marxian Matters'," *Journal of Economic Theory* 11 (March 1973), 64–67.

[18] Samuelson, P. A., "The Optimality of Profit-Inducing Prices under Ideal Planning," *Proceedings of the National Academy of Sciences* 70, No. 7 (July 1973), 2109–2111.

[19] Samuelson, P. A., "Wages and Interest: A Modern Dissection of Marxian Economic Models," *American Economic Review* 47 (December 1957), 884–912 (*CSP*, Volume I, Chapter 29, pp. 341–369).

[20] Samuelson, P. A., "Reply," *American Economic Review* 50 (September 1960), 719–721 (*CSP*, Volume I, Chapter 30, pp. 370–372).

[21] Samuelson, P. A., "A Modern Treatment of the Ricardian Economy: I. The Pricing of Goods and of Labor and Land Services," *Quarterly Journal of Economics* 73 (February 1959), 1–35 (*CSP*, Volume I, Chapter 31, pp. 373–407).

[22] Samuelson, P. A., "A Modern Treatment of the Ricardian Economy: II. Capital and Interest Aspects of the Pricing Process," *Quarterly Journal of Economics* 73 (May 1959), pp. 217–231 (*CSP*, Volume 1, Chapter 32, pp. 408–422).

[23] Samuelson, P. A., *Economics*, 9th ed., Chapter 42 Appendix. New York: McGraw-Hill, 1973.

[24] Meek, R., "Some Notes on the Transformation Problem," *Economic Journal* 66 (March 1956), 94–107 (reprinted in Meek, R., *Economics and Ideology and Other Essays*, pp. 143–157. London: Chapman and Hall, 1967.

[25] Baumol, W., "Values versus Prices, What Marx 'Really' Meant," *Journal of Economic Literature* 11 (December 1973).

[26] Okishio, N., "A Mathematical Note on Marxian Theorems," *Weltwirtschaftliches Archiv* 2 (1963), 297–298.

[27] Bródy, A., *Proportion, Prices and Planning: A Mathematical Restatement of the Labor Theory of Value*. Budapest: Akadémie Kiadó, and Amsterdam: North-Holland *Publ.*, 1970.

[28] Johansen, L., "Labour Theory of Value and Marginal Utilities," *Economics of Planning* 3 No. 2 (September 1963).

[29] von Weizsäcker, C. C., "Morishima on Marx" (Working Paper No. 7, Institute of Mathematical Economics, University of Bielefeld), 1972.

[30] Sraffa, P., *Production of Commodities by Means of Commodities*, Appendix D, 3, 94. London and New York: Cambridge University Press, 1960.

[31] Samuelson, P. A., "Insight and Detour in the Theory of Exploitation: A Reply to Baumol," *Journal of Economic Literature* 11 (March 1974).

[32] Seton, F., "The 'Transformation Problem'," *Review of Economic Studies* 25 (June 1957), 149–160.

PART VII

POST-"CLASSICAL" POLITICAL ECONOMY

What Classical and Neoclassical Monetary Theory Really Was[*]

Qu'était au juste la théorie monétaire classique et néo-classique? L'article présente le point de vue d'un de ceux qui ont contribué à la théorie monétaire classique et néo-classique. Comme l'auteur à cru pendant les années 1932 à 1937, cette théorie (jamais formulée d'une façon formelle sous forme d'un systéme d'équations) supposait, sans en contester le bien-fondé, qu'en longue période le volume monétaire n'avait aucune importance une fois que l'économie considérée était devenu une économie monétaire. Toutefois, la théorie n'allait pas jusqu'à prétendre qu'une économie monétaire et une économie de troc fussent identiques même si l'on supposait des goûts, des connaissances techniques et des quantités de facteurs de production identiques.

Certains tenants ont aussi postulé que ces facteurs réels affectaient les prix et les niveaux de production relatifs, alors que le volume monétaire affectait le niveau absolu des prix. Il y avait ainsi deux dichotomies au lieu d'une, mais la seconde dichotomie n'a jamais été prise tellement au sérieux par qui que ce soit. Elle constituait plûtot une simplification provisoire. L'essentiel de la formulation présente est d'inclure la monnaie dans la fonction d'utilité, puis de considérer la fonction comme jouissant de la propriété d'homogénéité suivant laquelle un doublement de tous les prix et de la monnaie n'avantage personne. Par conséquent, lorsque chacun pèse la commodité de détenir de la monnaie en comparaison de son coût en intérêt, sa fonction de demande pour les biens est indépendante du niveau absolu des prix, mais sa demande pour la monnaie est proportionnelle aux augmentations balancées de tous les prix.

Quoi qu'il en soit, les deux dichotomies sont légitimes pourvu que les modéles sousjacents soient définis en conséquence. L'auteur présente ensuite un modéle qui démontre le bien-fondé d'une dichotomie entre « les éléments réels » et « l'élément monétaire qui ne détermine que le niveau absolu des prix ». L'auteur prétend que les meilleurs auteurs néo-classiques avaient intuitivement ce modéle en tête, même s'ils ne l'ont jamais explicité ou publié. L'auteur termine son article par une discussion des contributions de Lange, Patinkin, et Archibald et Lipsey.

To know your own country you must have travelled abroad. To understand modern economics it is good to have lived long enough to have escaped

---

[*] I owe thanks to the National Science Foundation.

competent instruction in its mysteries. When Archibald and Lipsey try to draw for Patinkin a picture of what a "classical" monetary theorist believed in, they are pretty much in the position of a man who, looking for a jackass, must say to himself, "If I were a jackass, where would I go?"

Mine is the great advantage of having once been a jackass. From 2 January 1932 until an indeterminate date in 1937, I was a classical monetary theorist. I do not have to look for the tracks of the jackass embalmed in old journals and monographs. I merely have to lie down on the couch and recall in tranquillity, upon that inward eye which is the bliss of solitude, what it was that I believed between the ages of 17 and 22. This puts me in the same advantageous position that Pio Nono enjoyed at the time when the infallibility of the Pope was being enunciated. He could say, incontrovertibly, "Before I was Pope, I believed he was infallible. Now that I am Pope, I can *feel* it."

Essentially, we believed that in the longest run and in ideal models the amount of money did not matter. Money could be "neutral" and in many conditions the hypothesis that it was could provide a good first or last approximation to the facts. To be sure, Hume, Fisher, and Hawtrey had taught us that under dynamic conditions, an increase in money might lead to "money illusion" and might cause substantive changes – e.g., a shift to debtor-entrepreneurs and away from creditor-rentiers, a forced-saving shift to investment and away from consumption, a lessening of unemployment, a rise in wholesale prices relative to sticky retail prices and wage rates, *et cetera*.

But all this was at a second level of approximation, representing relatively transient aberrations. Moreover, this tended to be taught in applied courses on business cycles, money and finance, and economic history rather than in courses on pure theory. In a real sense there *was* a dichotomy in our minds; we were schizophrenics. From 9 to 9:50 a.m. we presented a simple quantity theory of neutral money. There were then barely ten minutes to clear our palates for the 10 to 10:50 discussion of how an engineered increase in M would help the economy. In mid-America in the mid-1930s, we neoclassical economists tended to be mild inflationists, jackasses crying in the wilderness and resting our case essentially on sticky prices and costs, and on expectations.

Returning to the 9 o'clock hour, we thought that *real* outputs and inputs and price ratios depended essentially in the longest run on real factors, such as tastes, technology, and endowments. The stock of money we called M (or, to take account of chequable bank deposits, we worked in effect with a velocity-weighted average of M and M'; however, a banking system with fixed reserve and other ratios would yield M' proportional to M, so M alone would usually suffice). An increase in M – usually we called it a doubling on the ground that after God created unity he created the second integer – would cause a proportional increase in *all* prices (tea, salt, female labour, land rent, share or bond prices) and values (expenditure on tea or land, share dividends, interest income, taxes). You will hardly believe it, but few economists in those days tried to write down formal equations for what they were thinking. Had we been asked to choose which kinds of equation system epitomized our thinking, I believe at first blush we would have specified:

A. Write down a system of real equations involving *real* outputs and inputs, and *ratios* of prices (values), and depending essentially on real tastes, technologies, market structures, and endowments. Its properties are invariant to change in the stock of money M.

B. Then append a fixed-supply-of-M equation that pins down (or up) the absolute price level, determining the scale factor that was essentially indeterminate in set A. This could be a quantity equation of exchange – $MV = PQ$ – or some other non-homogeneous equation. More accurately, while A involves homogeneity of degree zero in *all Ps*, B involves homogeneity of degree 1 of *Ps* in terms of M.

I have purposely left the above paragraphs vague. For I doubt that the typical good classical monetary theorist had more definite notions about the *mathematics* of his system.

Moreover, I must leave room for an essential strand in our thinking. Our expositions always began with barter and worked our fundamental pricing in barter models. But then we, sensibly, pointed out the *real* inconvenience of barter and the real convenience of an abstract unit of money. Here we made explicit and tacit reference to the real facts of brokerage or transaction charges, of uncertainties of income and outgo, and so on. In short, we did have a primitive inventory theory of money holding, but we were careful to note that true money – unlike pearls, paintings, wine, and coffee – is held only for the *ultimate exchange* work it can do, which depends upon the scale of *all Ps* in a special homogeneous way.

So there was another dichotomy in our minds, a very legitimate one. We had, so to speak, *qualitative* and *quantitative* theories of money. According to our qualitative theory, money was not neutral; it made a big difference. Pity the country that was still dependent upon barter, for it would have an inefficient economic system. But once this qualitative advantage had been realized by the adoption of market structures using M, the *quantitative* level of M was of no particular significance (except for indicated transient states and uninteresting resource problems involved in gold mining or mint printing). We liked the image of John Stuart Mill that money is the *lubricant* of industry and commerce. As even women drivers know, lubrication is important. But M is quantitatively a special lubricant: a drop will do as well as a poolful. So an even better image was the post-Mill one: money is like a catalyst in a chemical reaction, which makes the reaction go faster and better, but which, like the oil in the widow's cruse, is never used up. To push the analogy beyond endurance, only an iota of catalyst is needed for the process.

What I have just said makes it unmistakably clear that a classical monetary theorist would not go the stake for the belief that the real set of equations A are independent of M, depending essentially only on price ratios as in barter. If time were short on a quiz, I might carelessly write down such an approximation. But if asked specifically the question "Is Set A really independent of M?" I and my classmates would certainly answer "No" and we would cite the qualitative aspects mentioned earlier.

In a moment we shall see that this considered qualitative view requires that M *enter quantitatively in Set A in certain specified homogeneous ways.* But first let us investigate how those of us who were mathematically inclined would have handled the Set A and Set B problem. The economists interested in mathematics tended to be specialists in value theory. They had a big job just to describe the real relations of A, whether under barter or otherwise. They wanted to simplify their expositions, to sidestep extraneous complication. Hence, many would have followed the practice (which I seem to connect with Cassel's name, at least) of writing Set A purely in barter terms, and essentially giving enough equations to determine real quantities and price ratios – as follows:

$$\text{A}' \; f_i(Q_1, \ldots, Q_n, P_1, \ldots, P_n) = 0 \; (i = 1, 2, \ldots, 2n)$$

where there are n inputs or outputs, with n prices. However, the f_i functions are made to be homogeneous of degree zero in all the Ps, and, luckily, the $2n$ functions f_i are required to involve one of them as being dependent on the other, thus avoiding an overdetermination of the $2n$ functions. This homogeneity and dependence postulate enables us to write A' in the equivalent form:

$$\text{A}' \; f_i(Q_1, \ldots, Q_n, \lambda P_1, \ldots, \lambda P_n)_\lambda \equiv 0 \; (i = 1, 2, \ldots, 2n),$$

This formulation does not contain price ratios explicitly. But since λ is arbitrary, it can be set equal to $1/P_1$ to give us price ratios, $P_i/_1$. Or if you have an interest in some kind of average of prices, say

$\pi(P_1,\ldots,P_n) = \pi(P)$, where π is a homogeneous function of degree one, you can rewrite A' in terms of ratios $P_i/\pi(P)$ alone, by suitable choice of λ. Hence, Set A' involves $2n-1$ independent functions which hopefully determine a unique (or multiple) solution to the $2n-1$ real variables $(Q_1,\ldots,Q_n,\ P_2/P_1,\ldots P_n/P_1)$. With the special structure of A', we are now free to add any non-homogeneous B' we like, of the following types:

$$P_1 = 1, \text{ good 1 being taken as numéraire, or}$$

B' $\quad P_1 + P_2 = 3.1416,$ or

$$P_1 + P_2 + \ldots + P_n = 1, \text{or}$$

$$P_1[Q_1{}^* + (P_2{}^*/P_1)Q_2{}^* + \ldots + (P_n{}^*/P_1)Q_n0] = \bar{M}, \text{ Fisher's Constant,}$$

$\quad$ where $Q_i{}^*, (P_i/P_i)^*$ are solutions of A'.

Of course, the last of these looks like the Fisher-Marshall formulation of the "quantity equation of exchange." But, since some Q_i are inputs, my way of writing it recognizes the realistic fact that money is needed to pay factors as well as to move goods.[1]

I do not defend this special A', B' formulation. I am sure it was often used. And even today, if I am behind in my lectures, I resort to it in courses on pure theory. But we should admit that it is imperfect. And we should insist that the classical writers, when they did full justice to their own views, did not believe that this formulation was more than a provisional simplification.

What is a minimal formulation of (A, B) that does do full justice? I am sure that I personally, from 1937 on at least, had a correct vision of the proper version. It is as if to understand Gary, Indiana, I had to travel to Paris. I began to understand neoclassical economics only after Keynes' *General Theory* shook me up. But I am sure that I was only learning to articulate what was intuitively felt by such ancients as Ricardo, Mill, Marshall, Wicksell, and Cannan. I regret that I did not then write down a formal set of equations. I did discuss the present issue at the Econometric Society meetings of 1940, of which only an incomplete abstract appeared, and also at its 1949 meetings, where W. B. Hickman, Leontief and others spoke; and there are fragmentary similar remarks in half a dozen of my

---

[1] An equation like the last one could be split into two equations without altering the meaning:

$$B'_1 \ 1/FC\textstyle\sum_{j=1}^{n}(P_j/M)Q_j^r = 1$$

$B'_2\ M = M$, a prescribed total. The important thing to note is that B'_1, even if it looks a little like some A' equations, is completely decomposable from the set A'.

writings of twenty years ago. The nub of the matter is contained in my 1947 specification[2] that the utility function contain in it, along with physical quantities of good consumed, the stock of M and all money Ps, being homogeneous of degree zero in $(M, P_1, \ldots, P_n)$ in recognition of money's peculiar "neutral" quantitative properties.

Frankly, I was repelled by the abstract level at which Oskar Lange, Hicks, and others carried on their discussion of Say's Law, staying at the level of equation counting and homogeneity reckoning, without entering into the concrete character of the models. And this was one of the few continuing controversies of economics from which I steadfastly abstained.

For the rest of this discussion, what I propose to do is to get off the couch and go to the blackboard and write down an organized picture of what we jackasses implicitly believed back in the bad old days.

THE WAY THINGS ARE

I abstract heroically. We are all exactly alike. We live forever, We are perfect competitors and all-but-perfect soothsayers. Our inelastic labour supply is fully employed, working with inelastically supplied Ricardian land and (possibly heterogeneous) capital goods. We have built-in Pigou-Böhm rates of subjective time preference, discounting each next-year's independent utility by the constant factor $1/(l + \rho)$, $\rho > 0$. We are in long-run equilibrium without technical change or population growth: the stock of capital goods has been depressed to the point where all own-interest-rates yielded by production are equal to r, the market rate of interest; in turn, r is equal to the subjective interest rate ρ, this being the condition for our propensity to consume being 100 per cent of income, with zero net capital formation.

We equally own land, and such capital goods as machinery and material stocks. We own, but legally cannot sell, our future stream of labour earnings. We hold cash balances, because we are *not* perfect soothsayers when it comes to the uncertainty of the timing of our in-and-out-payments, which can be assumed to follow certain probability laws in the background; this lack of synchronization of payments plus the indivisible costs of transactions (brokerage charges, need for journal entries, spread between bid and ask when earning assets are converted into or out of cash, etc.) requires us to hold money. To keep down inessential complications, while not omitting Hamlet from the scenario, I am neglecting the need for cash balances for corporations; it is as if consumer families alone need cash balances for their final consumption purchases, whereas in real life cash is needed at every vertical stage of the production process. Later we can allow our holdings of earning assets – titles to land and machines – to economize on our need for M balances, just as does the prospect of getting wage increases.

Our system is assumed to come into long-run equilibrium. This equilibrium can be deduced to be unique if we add to our extreme symmetry assumptions the conventional strong convexity assumptions of neoclassical theorizing – constant returns to scale with smooth diminishing returns to proportions, quasi-concave ordinal utility functions that guarantee diminishing marginal rates of substitution, and so on.

We should be able to *prove rigorously* what is probably intuitively obvious – doubling all M will exactly double *all* long-run prices and values, and this change in the absolute price level will have absolutely no effect on real output-inputs, on price ratios or terms of trade, on interest rate and factor shares generally.

For this system, it is not merely the case that tautological quantity equations of exchange can be written down. Less trivially, a simple "quantity theory of prices and money" holds exactly for the long-run equilibrium model. Although Patinkin has doubts about the propriety of the concept, I think our meaning was unambiguous – and unobjectionable – when we used to say that the "demand curve for money" (traced out by shifts in the vertical supply curve of M) plotted in a diagram containing, on the x axis, M and, on the Y axis, the "value of money," (as measured by the reciprocal of *any* absolute money price $1/P_i$ or any average price level) would be a rectangular hyperbola with a geometrical Marshallian elasticity of exactly minus one.

To prove this I write down the simplest possible set of equations. These do split up into two parts, showing that there is a legitimate "dichotomy" between "real elements" and "monetary elements which determine only the absolute level of prices." Call these two parts A and B. Now this legitimate dichotomy will not be identical with the over-simple dichotomy of A' and B' mentioned earlier. If Patinkin insists upon the difference, I am in complete agreement with him. If he should prefer not to call the (A, B) split a dichotomy, that semantic issue is not worth arguing about so long as enough words are used to describe exactly what the (A, B) split is, and how it differs from the (A', B') split. If Patinkin insists on saying that my A equations do have in them a "real balance effect," I see no harm in that – even though, as will be seen, my formulation of A need involve no use of an average price index, and hence no need to work with a "deflated M" that might be called a real balance. Peculiarly in the abstract neoclassical model with its long-run strong homogeneity properties, all Ps move together in strict proportion when M alone changes and hence no index-number approximations are needed. By the same token, they do absolutely no harm: Patinkin is entitled to use any number of average price concepts and real-balance concepts he wishes. If Patinkin wishes to say that the principal neoclassical writers (other than Walras) had failed to *publish* a clear and unambiguous account of the (A, B) equation such as I am doing here, I would agree, and would adduce the worth and novelty of Patinkin's own book and contributions. On the other hand, the present report on my recollections claims that the best neoclassical writers did *perceive* at the intuitive level the intrinsic content of the (A, B) dichotomy which I am about to present. All the more we should regret that no one fully set down these intuitions thirty years ago!

Now what about Archibald and Lipsey?[3] I want to avoid semantic questions as to what is meant by real-balance effects being operative. If they claim that the (A', B') dichotomy does justice to the tacit neoclassical models of 1930, I think they are wrong. If they think an (A', B') dichotomy does justice to a reasonably realistic long-run model of a monetary economy, I think they are also wrong. Whether, as a *tour de force*, some special, flukey (A', B') model might be found to give a representation of some monetary economy is a possibility that I should hate to deny in the abstract; but I should be surprised if this issue turned out to be an interesting one to linger on or to debate. For what a casual opinion is worth, it is my impression that Patinkin's general position – which I interpret to be essentially identical to my (A, B) dichotomy *and* to the tacit neoclassical theory of my youth – is left impregnable to recent attacks on it. There is one, and only one, legitimate dichotomy in neoclassical monetary theory.

Abjuring further doctrinal discussion, I proceed now to the equations of my simplest system.

STRUCTURE OF THE MODEL

1. Production Relations

To keep down inessentials, let land, T, real capital, K (assumed homogeneous merely as a preliminary to letting K stand for a vector of heterogeneous capital goods), and labour, L, produce real output which, because of

---

[3] Don patinkin, in his *Money, Interest, and Prices* (New York, 1966), summarizes his pathbreaking writings on money over the last twenty years. For a critique of aspects of its first (1954) edition, see Archibald and Lipsey (*Review of Economic Studies*, XX) and articles in subsequent numbers of that journal.

similarity of production factors in all sectors, can be split up into the linear sum of different physical consumption goods $\pi_1 q_1 + \ldots + \pi_n q_n$ and net capital formation $\dot{K}(= dK/dt)$, namely: $\dot{K} + \pi_1 q_1 + \pi_2 q_2 + \ldots + \pi_m q_m = f(K, \bar{L}, \bar{T})$ where F is a production function of the Ramsey-Solow type, homogeneous of first degree, and where the π_i are constants, representing marginal costs of the ith goods relative to machines. From this function, we can deduce all factor prices and commodity prices relative to the price of the capital good P_K, namely:

$A_{I,1}$ $\quad \dfrac{P_i}{P_K} = \pi_i \ (i = 1, 2, \ldots, n)$

$A_{I,2}$ $\quad \dfrac{W}{P_K} = \dfrac{\partial F(K, \bar{L}, \bar{T})}{\partial L}$, the marginal productivity wage,

$\quad\quad \dfrac{R}{P_K} = \dfrac{\partial F(K, \bar{L}, \bar{T})}{\partial T}$, the marginal productivity rent,

$\quad\quad r = \dfrac{\partial F(K, \bar{L}, \bar{T})}{\partial K}$, the marginal productivity interest rate.

Bars are put over L and T because their supplies are assumed to be fixed. To determine the unknown stock of capital K we need:

$\quad r = \rho$, the subjective time preference parameter;[4]

A_{II} $\quad \dot{K} = 0$, the implied steady-state long-run equilibrium condition;

$\quad r = R/P_T$, the implicit capitalization equation for the price of land.

Hence, $\rho = \partial F(\bar{K}, \bar{L}, T)/\partial K$ henceforth gives us our fixed $\bar{K}$.

The above relationships determine for the representative man the wage and interest income (inclusive of land rentals expressed as interest on land values) which he can spend on the $(q_1, q_2, \ldots, q_n)$ goods and on holding of M cash balances which bear no interest and thus cost their opportunity costs in terms of interest forgone (or, to a net borrower, the interest on borrowings). What motive is there for holding any M? As I pointed out in *Foundations*, one can put M into the utility function, along with other things, as a real convenience in a world of stochastic uncertainty and indivisible transaction charges.[5]

---

[4]   In unpublished memos and lectures, using a Ramsey maximum analysis I have shown how the long-run steady-state condition where $r = \rho$ is approached so that K(or $K^{t+1} - K^t$) is zero. The steady-state analysis of $U (q: M, \ldots)$ here is shorthand for the perpetual stream $\sum_0^\infty U(q^t; M^{t+1}, \ldots)/(1+p)^t$, etc. My colleague, Professor Miguel Sidrouski, has independently arrived at such dynamic formulations.

[5]   This is not the only way of introducing the real convenience of cash balances. An even better way would be to let U depend only on the time stream of qs, and then to show that holding an

If, however, one does put M directly into U, one must remember the crucial fact that M differs from every other good (such as tea) in that it is not really wanted for its own sake but only for the ultimate exchanges it will make possible. So along with M, we must always put all Ps into U, so that U is homogeneous of degree zero in the set of monetary variables $(M, P_1, \ldots, P_m)$, with the result that $(\lambda M, \lambda P_1, \ldots, \lambda P_m)$ leads to the same U for all λ.

In *Foundations*, I wrote such a U function:

$$U(q_1, q_2, \ldots, q_n; M, P_1, P_2, \ldots, P_n)_\lambda \equiv U(q_1, \ldots, q_m; \lambda M, \lambda P_1, \ldots, \lambda P_n),$$

where Ps are prices in terms of money. Here I want merely to add a little further cheap generality. The convenience of a given M depends not only on Ps, but also upon the earning assets you hold and on your wage prospects. It is not that we will add to M the earning-asset total EA, which equals $P_T \bar{T} + P_K \bar{K}$. Nor shall we add EA after giving the latter some fractional weight to take account of brokerage and other costs of liquidating assets into cash in an uncertain world. Rather, we include such new variables in U to the right of the semicolon to get:

$$U(q_1, \ldots, q_n; M, EA, W\bar{L}, P_1, \ldots, P_n) = U(q; x) = U(q; \lambda x).$$

That is, increasing all Ps, including those of each acre of land and machine and of hourly work along with M, will not make one better off. Thus U ends up homogeneous of degree zero in M and *all* prices $(M, P_K, P_T, W, P_1, \ldots P_n)$ by postulate.

Now, subject to the long-run budget equation indicated below, the representative man maximizes his utility:

$$U(q_1, \ldots, q_n; M, P_K \bar{K} + P_T \bar{T}, W\bar{L}, P_1, \ldots, P_n)$$

subject to

$$\operatorname*{Max}_{\{q_1, \ldots, q_n, M\}} \quad P_1 q_1 + \cdots + P_n q_n = W\bar{L} + r \,(\text{Total Wealth} - M)$$

or

$$P_1 q_1 + \ldots + P_n q_n + rM = W\bar{L} + r\,(TW)$$

$$= W\bar{L} + r\,(P_K \bar{K} + P_T \bar{T} + M^*),$$

where each representative man has Total Wealth defined as:

inventory of M does contribute to a more stable and greatly preferable stream of consumptions. The present oversimplified version suffices to give the correct general picture.

Total Wealth (in money value) $= EA +$ Money Endowment

$$= P_K \bar{K} + P_T \bar{T} + M^*,$$

where M^* is the money created in the past by gold mining or by government.

The maximizing optimality conditions give the demand for all q_1 and for M in terms of the variables prescribed for the individual, namely:

$$(P_1, \ldots, P_n, W, P_K, P_T; r, \bar{K}, \bar{L}, \bar{T}).$$

The optimality equations can be cast in the form:

$$\frac{\partial U/\partial q_1}{P_1} = \cdots = \frac{\partial U/\partial q_n}{P_n} = \frac{\partial U/\partial M}{r}$$

or

$(A_{III,1})$
$$\frac{\partial U/\partial M}{\sum_1^n q_j \dfrac{\partial U}{\partial q_i} + M \dfrac{\partial U}{\partial M}} = \frac{r}{W\bar{L} + r(P_K \bar{K} + P_T \bar{T} + M^*)}$$

$(A_{III,2})$
$$\frac{\partial U/\partial q_i}{\sum_1^n q_j \dfrac{\partial U}{\partial q_j} + M \dfrac{\partial U}{\partial M}} = \frac{P_i}{W\bar{L} + r(P_K \bar{K} + P_T \bar{T} + M^*)}$$

$$(i = 1, 2, \ldots, n).$$

But for society as a whole (and hence for the representative man who, even if he does not know it, represents 1/Nth of the total in our symmetrical situation) total money demanded, M, must end up equalling total money endowment, M^*:

$(A_{III,3})$ $M = M^*.$

An important comment is in order.[6] Although $A_{III,3}$ holds for society as a whole, being essentially a definition of demand-for-money equilibrium, each representative man (one of thousands of such men) can*not* act in the belief that his budget equation has the form:

$$P_1 q_1 + \cdots + P_n q_n + rM = W\bar{L} + r(P_K \bar{K}_t P_T \bar{T} + M),$$

---

[6]   The next few paragraphs can be skipped without harm.

even though substituting $A_{III,3}$ into the earlier budget equation would yield this result. What is true for all is not true for each. Each man thinks of his cash balance as costing him forgone interest and as buying himself convenience. But for the community as a whole, the total M^* is there and is quite costless to use. Forgetting gold mining and the historical expenditure of resources for the creating of M^*, the existing M^* is, so to speak, a free good from society's viewpoint. Moreover, its *effective* amount can, from the community's viewpoint, be indefinitely augmented by the simple device of having a lower absolute level of *all* money prices. To see this in still another way, with fixed labour L and land T and capital K big enough to give the interest rates equal to the psychological rate ρ, the community can consume on the production possibility equation:

$$P_1 q_1 + \ldots P_n q_n = F(\bar{K}, \bar{L}, T) = W\bar{L} + r(P_K K + P_T \bar{T})$$

and to *each* side of this could be added rM of any size without affecting this true physical menu.

Evidently we have here an instance of a lack of optimality of laissez-faire: there is a kind of fictitious internal diseconomy from holding more cash balances, as things look to the individual. Yet if all were made to hold larger cash balances, which they turned over more slowly, the resulting lowering of absolute price would end up making everybody better off. Better off in what sense? In the sense of having a higher U, which comes from having to make fewer trips to the bank, fewer trips to the brokers, smaller printing and other costs of transactions whose only purpose is to provide cash when you have been holding too little cash.

From society's viewpoint, the optimum occurs when people are satiated with cash and have:

$$\partial U / \partial M = 0 \text{ instead of } r \times \text{(positive constant)} > 0.$$

But this will not come about under laissez-faire, with stable prices.[7]

Now let us return from this digression on social cost to our equations of equilibrium. Set A consists of the A_I equations relating to production and implied pricing relations, and of the A_{II} equations relating to long-run equilibrium of zero saving and investment, where technological and subjective interest rates are equal and provide capitalized values for land and

---

[7] See P. Samuelson, "D. H. Robertson, "*Quarterly Journal of Economics*, LXXVII, 4 (Nov. 1963), 517–36, esp. 535 where reference is made to earlier discussions by E. Phelps, H. G. Johnson, and R. A. Mundell. This article is reproduced in Joseph E. Stiglitz, ed., *The Collected Scientific Papers of Paul A. Samuelson* (Cambridge, Mass., 1966).

other assets. Finally, A_{III} are the demand conditions for the consumer, but generalized beyond the barter world to include explicitly the qualitative convenience of money *and to take into account the peculiar homogeneity properties of money resulting from the fact that its usefulness is in proportion to the scale of prices.* Though the exact form of A_{III} is novel, its logic is that implied by intuitive classical theories of money.

All of equations A have been cast in the form of involving ratios of prices, values, and M^* only (to put A_{III} in this form, multiply M into the numerators on each side). That means they are homogeneous functions of degree zero in all Ps, and M^* or M, being capable of being written in the general form:

$$A \qquad G_i\left(q_1, \ldots, q_n, K, \bar{L}, \bar{T}, r; \frac{P_K}{M}, \frac{W}{M}, \frac{R}{M}, \frac{P_1}{M}, \ldots, \frac{P_n}{M}, \frac{TW}{M}\right) = 0$$

where all the magnitudes to the left of the semicolon are "real" and all those to the right are *ratios* of a price or a value to the quantity of money. If a price ratio like P_i/P_j appears in an equation and no M, we can rewrite the ratio as $(P_i/M)/(P_j/M)$.

To the set A, we now append a decomposable single equation to fix the supply of money:

B M or $M^* = \bar{M}$, an exogenous supply.

This single equation is not homogeneous of degree zero in Ps and M and therefore it does pin down the absolute scale of all Ps and values in direct proportion to the quantity of M. Why? Because Set A consists of as many independent equations as there are unknown real quantities and ratios. Let us check this. Omitting fixed $(\bar{L}, \bar{T})$, we count $n + 2 + n + 5$ unknowns in G_i when we ignore both $\dot{K}$ and the $\dot{K} = 0$ equation. We count $n + 3$ equations in A_I, 2 equations in A_{II}, and $n + 2$ *equations* in A_{III}. Thus $2n + 7 = 2n + 7$. Another way of looking at the matter is this: A_I and A_{II} determine all Ps as proportional to P_K. Then for fixed P_K and M^*, A_{III} determines all qs and M, the latter doubling when P_K and M^* double.

Summarizing, Set A determines all real quantities and all prices and values in ratio to the stock of M^*. Then equation B determines $M^* = M$ and hence the absolute level of all prices in proportion to $\bar{M}$.

Where in A or B is the quantity theory's "equation of exchange" to be found? Certainly not in B. If anywhere, an $MV = PQ$ equation must be found in A. Where? Certainly not in A_I or A_{II}. In A_{III}, equation $A_{III,1}$ deals with the relative marginal utility of the cash balance. By itself, it is not an $M = PQ/V$

equation. Only after all the A_{III} equations are solved, can we express M in a function that is proportional to any (and all) P_i :

$$M = P_i \psi_i(\ldots)$$

where the ψ functions depend on a great variety of real magnitudes.

This suggests to me that the late Arthur Marget was wrong in considering it a fault of Walras that, after the second edition of his *Elements*, he dropped a simple $MV = PQ$ equation. Classical and neoclassical monetary theory is much better than a crude quantity theory, although it can report similar results from special ideal experiments. In particular, correct neoclassical theory does not lead to the narrow anti-Keynesian view of those Chicago economists who allege that velocity of circulation is not a function of interest rates.

HOW M GETS ALLOCATED

Symmetry plays an important role in the model given here. With every man exactly alike, it does not matter where or how we introduce new money into the system; for it gets divided among people in exactly the same proportions as previous M. We classical writers were aware that the strict (A, B) dichotomy held only when every unit's M (say $M^1, M^2, \ldots$) stayed proportional to total $\bar{M} = \Sigma M^k$. But being careless fellows, we often forgot to warn that this was only a first approximation to more complicated incidents of gold inflations and business cycle expansions.

Can this rock-bottom simplicity be retained if we relax this extreme symmetry assumption (which renders the problem almost a Robinson Crusoe one)? Providing all income elasticities, including that for M, are (near) unity, it never matters (much) how things are divided among people. Collective indifference curves of the Robinson Crusoe type then work for all society. The simple structure of A_{III} is preserved and the uniqueness of equilibrium is assured. Again, it matters not how the new M is introduced into the system.

Finally, there was an even more interesting third assumption implicit and explicit in the classical mind. It was a belief in unique long-run equilibrium independent of initial conditions. I shall call it the "ergodic hypothesis" by analogy to the use of this term in statistical mechanics. Remember that the classical economists were fatalists (a synonym for "believers in equilibrium"!). Harriet Martineau, who made fairy tales out of economics (unlike modern economists who make economics out of fairy tales), believed that if the state redivided income each morning, by night the rich would again be sleeping in their comfortable beds and the poor under the bridges. (I think she thought this a cogent argument against egalitarian taxes.)

Now, Paul Samuelson, aged 20 a hundred years later, was not Harriet Martineau or even David Ricardo; but as an equilibrium theorist he naturally tended to think of models in which things settle down to a unique position independently of initial conditions. Technically speaking, we theorists hoped not to introduce *hysteresis* phenomena into our model, as the Bible does when it says "We pass this way only once" and, in so saying, takes the subject out of the realm of science into the realm of genuine history. Specifically, we did not build into the Walrasian system the Christian names of particular individuals, because we thought that the general distribution of income between social classes, not being critically sensitive to initial conditions, would emerge in a determinate way from our equilibrium analysis.

Like Martineau, we envisaged an oversimplified model with the following ergodic property: no matter how we start the distribution of money among person – M^1, M^2, ... – after a sufficiently long time it will become distributed among them in a unique ergodic state (rich men presumably having more and poor men less). I shall not spell out here a realistic dynamic model but content myself with a simple example.

Half the people are men, half women. Each has a probability propensity to spend three-quarters of its today's money on its own products and one-quarter on the other sex's. We thus have a Markov transitional probability matrix of the form

$$
A = \begin{bmatrix} \dfrac{3}{4} & \dfrac{1}{4} \\ \dfrac{1}{4} & \dfrac{3}{4} \end{bmatrix} = \begin{bmatrix} \dfrac{1}{2}+\dfrac{a}{2} & \dfrac{1}{2}-\dfrac{a}{2} \\ \dfrac{1}{2}-\dfrac{a}{2} & \dfrac{1}{2}+\dfrac{a}{2} \end{bmatrix}
$$

with $a = \frac{1}{2}$ and

$$
A^t = \begin{bmatrix} \dfrac{1}{2}+\dfrac{a^t}{2} & \dfrac{1}{2}-\dfrac{a^t}{2} \\ \dfrac{1}{2}-\dfrac{a^t}{2} & \dfrac{1}{2}+\dfrac{a^t}{2} \end{bmatrix}
$$

$$
\lim_{t \to \infty} A^t = \begin{bmatrix} \dfrac{1}{2} & \dfrac{1}{2} \\ \dfrac{1}{2} & \dfrac{1}{2} \end{bmatrix}, \text{ the ergodic state.}
$$

Suppose we start out with men and women each having M of ($100, $100). Now introduce a new $100 to women only. Our transitional sequent in dollars will then be ($200, $100), ($175, $125), ($162½, $137½), ($156½, $143¾), ((151⁹/₁₆, 148⁷/₁₆), ... with the obvious limiting ergodic state 150, 150) since the divergence from this state is being halved at each step. Such an ergodic system will have the special homogeneity properties needed for the (A,B) dichotomy.[8]

None of this denies the fact that the leading neoclassical economists often recognized cases and models in which it does make a difference, both in the short and the long run, how the new money is introduced and distributed throughout the system. One of the weaknesses of a crude quantity theory is that it treats M created by open-market purchases by the central bank as if this were the same as M left over from last century's (or last minute's) mining. A change in M, accompanied by an opposite change in a near-M substitute like government short-term bonds, is *not* shown in my Set A.

Indeed, when all men are alike and live for ever, we have too simple a model to take account of the interesting effect upon the system of permanent interest-bearing public debt which we as taxpayers know we will not have to pay off or service beyond our lifetimes.[9]

---

[8] Let me warn that this discussion in terms of a Markov probability matrix is meant to be only indicative. The temporal sequence of decisions to exchange money for goods and services and goods for money, with all that is implied for the distribution among units of the stock of M at any time, is more complicated than this. In our most idealized models, we assumed that, whatever the complexity of the process, after enough time had elapsed the M would get distributed in a unique ergodic way. This does not beg the question, since there are models in which this is a theorem. In our more realistic moods, we tacitly used models involving *hysteresis*: Spain would never be the same after Columbus; Scarlett O'Hara would be permanently affected by the Confederate inflation, just as Hugo Stinnis was by the 1920–23 German inflation. Obviously, in such models all real variables do not end up unchanged as a result of certain unbalanced introductions of new M into the system. In that sense realistic equations do not seem to have the homogeneity properties in $(M, P, ...)$ of my Set A; but if we were to write in A the variables $(M^1, M^2, ...)$ and not merely their sum $\sum M^k$, it is still possible that homogeneity properties would hold – so that doubling *all* M^k together would be consistent with doubling all Ps. But this is too delicate a question to attempt in brief compass here.

[9] My *Economics* (6th ed., New York, 1964), 342, shows that $(M, \text{public debt})$ and $(\lambda M, \lambda \text{public debt})$ play the role in more complicated systems that (M) and (λM) play in the simple classical system given here. Crude quantity theorists should take note of this distinction, which Franco Modigliani has also insisted on.

EPILOGUE

With the positive content of traditional monetary theory now written down concretely for us to see, kick, and kick at, a few comments on some controversies of the last twenty years may be in order.

Oskar Lange began one line of reasoning on price flexibility in 1939 which culminated in his 1944 Cowles book, *Price Flexibility and Employment.*[10] Hicks' *Value and Capital,*[11] with its attempt to treat bonds and money just as some extra $n + 1$ and $n + 2$ goods along with n goods like tea and salt, had, I fear, a bad influence on Lange. It led to his suppressing possible differences between stocks and flows, to attempts to identify or contrast Say's Law with various formalisms of Walrasian analysis (such as the budget equation), and to discussion in the abstract of functions of many variables possessing or not possessing certain abstract homogeneity properties. There are many interesting points raised in Lange's book, and several analytical contributions to nonmonetary economic theory. But only about a dozen pages grapple with the key problem of money (e.g., pp. 5 – 19), and these stay at a formalistic level that never deals with the peculiar properties and problems of cash balances. I do not say that this approach of Lange's cannot be used to arrive at valid results, but in fact it remained rather sterile for twenty years.

I had thought that Don Patinkin's work from 1947 on, culminating in his classic *Money, Interest, and Prices* was much influenced by the Lange approach, and I thought this a pity. But, on rereading the book, I am not sure. What Patinkin and Lange have in common is a considerable dependence upon the *Value and Capital* device of lumping money in as an extra good. This approach has not kept Patinkin from arriving at a synthesis consistent with what I believe was the best of neoclassical theory, or from going beyond anything previously appearing in the literature. But it may help to account for his attributing error to earlier thinkers when a more sympathetic reading might absolve them from error. When we become accustomed to approaching a problem in a certain way and using a certain nomenclature, we must not confuse the failure to use this same language and approach with substantive error. Still, beyond that, Patinkin scores many legitimate points: monetary economists had better intuitions than they were able to articulate. Thus I suspect that my (A,B) dichotomy is really very similar to what Cassel had in mind, but the only form in which he could

[10] (New York, 1944).
[11] (Oxford, 1939).

render it mathematically was (A', B'), which is inadequate (as Patinkin insists, though perhaps not for all the reasons he insists on). In what sense can one say that a man believes one thing when he says something else? In this non-operational sense: if one could subpoena Cassel, show him the two systems and the defects in one, and then ask him which fits in best with his over-all intuitions. I believe he would pick (A,B) and not his own (A', B').[12] I might add that Cassel is not Walras; and it seems to me that Walras comes off better on Patinkin's own account than he is given credit for.

Some will interpret Archibald and Lipsey as defending an (A', B') dichotomy against Patinkin's rejection of that dichotomy. If that is their primary intention – and I am not sure that it is – I fear I must side with Patinkin. Logically, one can set up (A', B'), as I did here and as Cassel did. But I think it is bad economics to believe in such a model. *All* its good features are in the (A,B) dichotomy and none of its bad ones.

On the other hand, there is certainly much more in Archibald and Lipsey than a defence of (A', B') and this important part of their paper seems to me to be quite within the spirit of Patinkin's analysis and my own. Here, however, I shall comment on the two different dichotomies.

I begin with (A', B').

A' $F_i(q, P)_\lambda \equiv F_i(q, \lambda P)$ $(i = 2, \ldots 2n)$

B' $P_1 = 1$ or $\sum_{j-1}^{n} q_j^k P_j = \overline{V}M, M = \bar{M}.$

Suppose that we can solve n of the A' equation to eliminate the qs, ending up with the independent homogeneous functions

A' $f_i(P)_\lambda \equiv f_i(\lambda P) \equiv f_i(1, P_2/P_1, \ldots, P_2/P_1)$ $(i = 2, \ldots, n-1)$

B' $\sum q_j^*(P_j/M) = \bar{V}, M = \bar{M}.$

Although f_i involve actually money Ps, it is not logically or empirically mandatory to interpret them as "excess-demand" functions which drive up (or down) the *money* Ps. Some students of Hicks, Lange, and Patinkin fall into this presupposition. Logically, there *could* be dynamic adjustments of

---

[12] Needless to say, the test is not whether Aristotle, apprised of Newton's improvements over Aristotle, would afterwards acquiesce in them; the test is whether in Aristotle's writings there are non-integrated Newtonian elements. If so, we credit him only with non-integrated intuitions.

price ratios – as e.g. P_i/P_1 or P_i/P_j, either of which could be written as $(P_i/M)/(P_j/M)$ – of the type

a′ $\quad [d(P_i/P_1)]/dt = k_i f_i(1, P_2/P_1, \ldots, P_n/P_1) \ (i = 2, \ldots, n)$

b′ $\quad [d(P_1/M)]/dt = k_M\left[\bar{M} - \sum(P_j/P_1)(P_1/M)Q_j^*(1/V)\right]k_j, k_m > 0,$

where the ks are positive speed constants of adjustment and where the q^* and V may be functions of relative Ms. Such a system could dynamically determine *relative* prices within a decomposable real set A′ and then determine the absolute price level in Set B. Note that no version of Walras' Law relates B′ to A′ or b′ to a′. Walras' Law in the form that merely reflects the Budget Equation of each consumer is expressed in the functional dependence of the $f_1(1, P_2/P_1, \ldots)$ function (which we can ignore) on the rest – namely

$$f_1(1, P_2/P_1, \ldots) \equiv -\sum_2^n (P_j/P_1)f_j(1, P_2/P_1, \ldots).$$

If (a′, b′) is dynamically stable, $P_i/M \to$ constant is in agreement with the long-run quantity theory.[13]

---

[13] A short-run quantity theory need not hold. Doubling M this minute or this week need not double this week's prices. But there is a sense in which homogeneity holds in *every* run. Suppose as a *fait accompli* we are all made to wake up with every dollar of M *exactly* doubled and every P (present *and* future) exactly doubled. If nought else has changed, we recognize this to be indeed a new equilibrium. And if the time-profile of equilibrium is unique, how can we have any other time-profile of prices? At the root of this paradox is the assumption of perfectly balanced changes in M, perfect foresight, and the postulate of uniqueness of equilibrium. All this is a far cry from interpreting the stream of contemporary history.

A Modern Post-Mortem on Böhm's Capital Theory: Its Vital Normative Flaw Shared by Pre-Sraffian Mainstream Capital Theory

The Nobel Prize of Piero Sraffa and Joan Robinson that Stockholm never awarded might have pleased at least one of them. Its citation would have included: "Their investigations uncovered a fatal normative flaw in Böhm-Bawerkian and modern mainstream capital theory."

Just prior to Alfred Marshall's 1890 ascendancy as leading world economist, Eugen von Böhm-Bawerk (1851–1914) perhaps wore that crown thanks to his three-volume treatise on the history and fundamentals of interest theories. Böhm (1884, 1889, 1909, 1912) somewhat independently followed in the footsteps of Stanley Jevons (1871) and himself strongly stimulated Knut Wicksell (1893), Irving Fisher (1906, 1907, 1930), and Friedrich Hayek (1931, 1941). Pugnacious and somewhat incoherent, Böhm and his disciples battled cogently the competing school of John Bates Clark (1899) and Frank Knight (1934, 1935a, 1935b), which idealized a permanent *scalar* capital alleged to be virtually permanent and with a marginal productivity determining its interest rate in much the same way that primary labor's marginal productivity determines its real wage rate and primary land's marginal productivity determines its real rent rate(s). The Clark-Knight paradigm – and, for that matter, Frank Ramsey's 1928 mathematical clone – shares the Böhm-Hayek vital normative flaw.

Great pioneers are great because their novel insights are great. They need not have fully understood their own innovations; that can be left for later crafts-persons to do.

Thus, Joan Robinson (1956) attributes what she called the bamboozling apologetics for capitalists' interest rate to the swindle of an aggregate *scalar* Kapital – "leets" in her contemptuous lingo, which is simply "steel" spelled backwards. Sraffa (1960) more importantly associated the faults of neoclassical capital theory with its gratuitous assumption that technology admits of an infinite-continuum of substitutable alternative techniques such as are needed for the existence of marginal productivities in the form of partial derivatives of the form $\partial(\text{output})/\partial(\text{factor input})$. As my exposition will reveal, the fatal flaw in question can exist even when a scalar "leets" is the sole producible input; it can exist even when precise neoclassical marginal products *do exist* and do serve to pin down unequivocally the distribution of incomes between propertyless workers and affluent capitalists. The statues of Piero and Joan belong in the pantheon of neoclassicism itself.

When I uncover wherein Böhm went wrong more than a century ago, that is not a humdrum exercise in ancient history. Hayek's *Pure Theory of Capital* of 1941 – a work on which he spent most of his thirties and which does correct some of Böhm's gratuitous flaws – does *not* escape my present indictment. And indeed, when I reread some early editions of my own *Economics* textbook, my pen longs to strike out certain over-simplifying sentences in the capital theory section.

Following the present introduction, Section I describes the time-phased circulating capital much used by Böhm and also contemplated by Jevons, Wicksell, and the 1931 macro model of Hayek's *Prices and Production*.[1]

Section II, by use of discrete alternative techniques which are innocent of neoclassical margins so unacceptable to Sraffa, explicates how Smith's Invisible Hand of perfect competition cares not a fig to assure that *a lower stationary-state interest rate will necessarily raise society's steady-state level of consumable product.* (An Invisible Hand does assure *"intertemporal" Pareto-optimality* but *this* is quite another thing.)

Section III concludes with a brief enumeration of just what properties of the Irving Fisher general theory of interest do and do not survive this modern post mortem. Only some of Joan Robinson's rebuttals of mainstream orthodoxy possess cogent validity. An Appendix uses some modern mathematical notations to explicate various of Böhm's scenarios.

---

[1] The latter had an initial excessive vogue and, even before its eclipse by Keynes' *General Theory*, fell into deserved disfame as a diagnosis of the Great Depression. Hayek himself thought to repair the reputation of his business-cycles paradigms by perfecting the over-simplifications of his period-of-production apparatus adapted from Böhm. However, after ten years of unstinting effort, his best shot at a complete capital theory still missed the bull's eye of how to prescribe for the 1929–1935 macro pathologies, and indeed, those elements of validity in his original 1929–1931 business cycle analysis can be formulated without particular reference to *Austrian* time-phasing models of production.

I. BÖHM'S PRODUCTIVITY SLANT

Böhm-Bawerk and Wicksell emphasized the important insight that in the holy trinity of land, labor and capital, capital is not so much a third factor like labor and land but rather involves various time-phasings of labor and land inputs. By contrast, J. B. Clark and his school envisaged scenarios in which a producible aggregate factor of production, Kapital, did serve in a completely parallel fashion to primary labor and land. Almost precisely the way labor earns its wage and land earns its rent, so, too, does Clarkian Kapital earn its marginal productivity interest rate.

To beginners in crude neoclassical economics:

$$\text{output } Q = F(\text{labor, land, capital}) = F(L, A, K) \qquad (1a)$$

$$= \text{Consumption} + \text{Net Capital Formation} \qquad (1b)$$

$$\text{wage } = w = \partial Q/\partial L, \text{ rent} = R = \partial Q/\partial A, \text{ interest } = i = \partial Q/\partial K$$
$$(1c)$$

$$\text{Net National Income} = wL + RA + iK. \qquad (1d)$$

Böhm (1906, 1907), Hayek (1936), and Machlup (1935) over thirty years prevailed against the view of Clark (1907) and Knight (1935a) that such capital is virtually (!) permanent, insisting cogently that its permanence and its algebraic growth will depend on motivated consumption decisions about dissaving and saving of income receivers and asset owners. Additionally, in the last half of the twentieth century, Joan Robinson and Piero Sraffa rightly queried the reality and relevance of the above notion of a *single aggregate metric* of real Kapital *à la* Clark. But also they cogently queried the universality of the Austrian circulating capital models that Böhm, Jevons, and Wicksell nominated from the viewpoint of time-phasing of labor and land. In the present critique I shall concentrate mostly on Böhm's favored circulating-capital model, but all of my points pro and con will apply to the Clark and other mainstream scenarios.

Aristotle, the two Biblical Testaments and the Medieval Schoolmen, in their moral antipathy to a positive interest rate, focused on *consumer loans* between the borrowing poor and the lending rich. Böhm's final synthesis does not overlook subjective decisions about time spending on consumption. Of his well-known three causes for interest, Böhm's *second cause* involved asymmetric time preference for present consumption versus future consumption: whether rationally or irrationally, most people would (other things equal) prefer the pair ($2000 now, $1000 later) to ($1000 now, $2000 later); even animals in Darwin's jungle bolt down their recent kill, storing away only some of it in order to somewhat smooth their cycles of feedings.

Böhm's *first cause* of positive interest – first not in importance but only in how he listed things that day – recognized that if in the future I will be richer than I am today, I can afford to pay a positive interest premium to borrow and thereby make my consumption stream more smooth. (In a modern society where one can expect to live a long time in a retirement without earning power, Böhm's logic might rationalize a *negative* real interest rate!) Nassau Senior (1836) before Böhm, as well as Frank Fetter (1914) and the younger Irving Fisher (1906, 1907) after him, share Böhm's reputation for linking positive interest rate to subjective time-preference aspects of inter-temporal consumer loans and borrowings.

However, Böhm's greatest fame in the Bismarckian era, when Marxist and social-democratic ideologies were burgeoning, came from his stringent critiques of the socialists' notion that it is *exploitation* that accounts for positive interest and profit rates under competitive capitalism. In rebuttal, Böhm offered his important *third cause* for interest, namely the brute technological fact that more "time-intensive," more "round-about," and more "capital-intensive" processes (somehow measured) allegedly do create extra consumable harvests from the same totals of labor and natural resources. Just as the laborer was worthy of his hire, the capitalists who accumulated more capital and thereby lowered the interest rate would, Böhm believed, at the same time raise (a) society's producible steady-state output and (b) the competitive total of laborer's wage and land's rent.

By contrast with the Clarkian technology of Equation (1) Jevons-Böhm-Wicksell's simplest technology says "point output now" is a function of "point input of labor θ time earlier":

$$q(t) = L(t - \theta)\phi(\theta); \phi'(\theta) \geq 0, \phi''(\theta) < 0 \quad \text{or} \quad \phi''(\theta)/\phi'(\theta) < 0 \quad (2a)$$

$$= L(t - \theta)\sqrt{\theta}, \text{ for example.} \quad (2b)$$

This relates the period of production, θ, as being *inverse* in equilibrium to the instantaneous force of interest r, namely

$$\phi'(\theta^*)/\phi(\theta^*) = r^*, d\theta^*/dr^* < 0. \quad (2c)$$

Only at lower rates of r^* can competition permit more θ^* to be used. And, just as in the Clark case of Equation (1), always with a lower interest rate there comes *larger* steady-state *output* from any specified plateau of $L(t)$ labor.

Böhm, less mathematical than Jevons or Wicksell, wished to be more generally realistic than Equation (2)'s Jevons model in which trees planted by labor on redundantly free land grow more lumber merely from passage of time; or, as in the case of fine wine, the mere passage of time results in more (hedonic) output. Böhm focuses on an Austrian model in which labor on redundant land produces wheat in an earliest stage of production, then wheat and second-stage labor produces flour, and then finally bread gets produced by flour and third-stage labor. I call this Austrian, but even primitive 1817 Ricardo could have handled this simple scenario in which no good is 1960-Sraffa "basic," none needing directly or indirectly some of itself as input; no Leontief-Sraffa simultaneous-equations matrices enter into this Böhm-Ricardo non-Marxian world.

Here in modern notations is the typical Böhm-Hayek technology of labor-wheat-flour-bread:

Q now is a function of (labor one period back, labor two periods back, . . ., labor T periods back), or

$$Q_t = Q = f(L_{t-1}, \ldots, L_{t-T}), T \geq 1; \tag{3a}$$

$$\partial Q/\partial L_{t-\tau} \geq 0, \tau = 1, 2, \ldots, T \tag{3b}$$

$$\partial^2 Q/(\partial L_{t-1})^2 < 0, \text{dim. returns with } f \text{ } concave \tag{3c}$$

$$f \text{ to be first degree homogeneous: } con. \text{ } ret. \text{ } to \text{ } scale. \tag{3d}$$

The neoclassical (*non*-Sraffian) version of this production function assumes that genuine marginal productivities of direct and indirect labor inputs can be defined to provide stationary-state equilibrium pairs of (real wage, interest rate). And if a scarce homogeneous land is in the picture, marginal productivities do pin down admissible, viable steady-state triplets of distribution, namely (W/P_{bread} of wage, i of interest, R/P_{bread} for rent). Like Böhm, I'll mostly ignore land purely for brevity (a cardinal sin in studying Sraffa's David Ricardo!). See Frank W. Taussig, *Wages and Capital*, 1896.

Here are the neoclassical Taussig (1896) discounted marginal productivities for Böhm's Equation (3a) technology

$$W/P_Q = \frac{\partial f(L_{t-1},\ldots,L_{t-T})/\partial L_{t-\tau}}{(1+i)^\tau}, \tau = 1,\ldots,T \geq 1. \qquad (3e)$$

These Equation (3) relations do serve to define a necessarily *inverse* relation between steady-state $(i^*, [W/P_Q]^*)$. They come from competition-imposed minimum-cost inclusive of interest (with zero excess profit rate over and above the safe interest rate that is included in cost):

$$\underset{L_\tau}{\text{Min}} \left[f(L_1,\ldots,L_T) - (W/P_Q)\sum_{\tau=1}^{T} L_\tau(1+i)^\tau \right] \qquad (4a)$$
$$= f(L_1^*,\ldots,L_T^*) - (W/P_Q)\sum_{1}^{T} L_\tau^*(1+i)^\tau$$

$$P_Q Q^* = W \sum_{1}^{T} L_\tau^*(1+i)^\tau : \text{no excess profit} \qquad (4b)$$

From Equation (4) we can prove that, rent aside, invariably a rise in either one of the real wage or the interest rate must lower the other:

THEOREM 1: *In the general Böhm circulating capital model of Equations (3) above, there is invariably a negative-sloped tradeoff between stationary-state wage and interest:*

$$d[W/P_Q]/d_i = -\sum_{1}^{T} \tau L_\tau^*(1+i)^{\tau-1} / \sum_{1}^{T} L_\tau^*(1+i)^\tau = -(+)/(+) < 0. \text{ QED.}$$
$$(5)$$

Even in Sraffa's 1960 world without "genuine *marginal* products," this *inverse* tradeoff also holds regardless of Wicksell effects or double reswitchings.

When within the same known (landless) technologies the interest rate is permanently lowered, there will assuredly be filtered down to workers an increase in their real competitive wage rate. This rebuts Marx's laws of (under capitalism) a simultaneous Declining Rate of Profit and an Immiseration of the Wage Earner. This is one gloom too many.[2] Joan

---

[2] When land is in the picture along with labor and time-phasing, within unchanged technical knowledge both wage and interest could rise (or fall) together, provided rent is

Robinson's first edition of her 1942 book on Marxism missed this Marx error; even after it was called to her attention in correspondence, she must have forgotten to correct her revised text. Morever, Robinson, like Henry George, Bernard Shaw, and Vladimir I. Lenin, did not believe that any genuine productivity of capital that raised wages – or added to total social steady-state per capita output – could justify the owners of land or of produced inputs collecting rent and interest returns from them: society, if necessary by political expropriation, could collect those proceeds from property and divvy them back amongst the proletariat. While in hiding between the 1917 February revolution and the 1917 October revolution, Lenin wrote down the view that capitalism's assets already in existence neither deserved nor needed capitalistic returns. Lenin never remotely glimpsed Hayek's point about the crucial role of *information* in keeping a running economy running.

Between 1942 and 1956 Robinson, with the prompting of her fellow don Ruth Cohen, began to doubt that a lowering of the interest rate necessarily had to raise total output. See Robinson (1956, pp. 109–10) on "the Ruth Cohen *curiosum*," an in-joke occasioned by Piero's refusal to take credit for any of Joan's purported analyses.[3]

By 1956, fifteen years after Robinson's first study of Marx, she began cogently to separate – as I believe Böhm and Hayek never did – Equation (5)'s (correct) inverse tradeoff between i and w from the different stationary-state tradeoff between i and consumption per capita. Her doubt that this too was a valid inverse relation, even with neglectable land, was arrived at independently of Sraffa's published classic (1960), whose contents for reasons that anal Isaac Newton would understand, Piero was not willing to divulge to Joan.

One cannot match a proof like that of Equation (5) by finding a valid proof for the stationary state conjecture

moving compensatingly in the other direction. After new viable technologies are discovered, one or all of the three could rise simultaneously; never could all be lowered by technical change in convex-constant-returns-to-scale scenarios Böhm and his contemporaries, along with Smith, never quite mastered these properties of Pareto-Optimality.

[3] By 1956, Sraffa's *Production of Commodities by Means of Commodities* (1960) was nearing completion of its matrix algebra. Although his final text never crisply proves any theorem about "double reswitching" and more general reversals of sign in the (real wage, consumption) steady-state tradeoffs, his understanding of this can be confidently inferred. In the next section my primitive numerical examples will demonstrate the point (and do so in the absence of any double reswitching and also in the presence of Böhm-Clark neoclassicism).

$$d(C/L)^*/di^* \le 0. \tag{6}$$

Why not? Because, as the next section will illustrate with numerical examples, such a conjecture is simply not true! In the neighborhood of $i^* = 0$, the golden-rule stationary state of Joseph Schumpeter, James Meade, Griffith Evans, Maurice Allais, Edmund Phelps, Robert Solow, and Christian von Weizsäcker, Equation (6) must indeed be *locally* true. But in the domain of positive i^* (even in the absence of double-reswitching), the inequality of Equation (6) can be reversed any number of times.

I cannot remember any words in Böhm glimpsing this truth. Even Hayek, Böhm's crown prince and magisterial heir writes as late as 1941: "so long as there are possibilities of increasing the product by investing for a longer period, only such prolongations will be chosen as will actually give a greater product. The rather obvious reasons [sic] for this we shall consider later" (1941, p. 60).

II. KEY NUMERICAL EXAMPLES

Austrian novices and Nassau Senior's readers trumpet (in my paraphrase): "Time itself is productive. Roundaboutness can be substituted for labor. The price of time is the interest rate. Aristotle, the Bible, the Koran, and St. Thomas Aquinas are wrong: competitive interest rate is not exploitation. The capitalist gets and needs to get the reward of positive interest rate. And to assuage him for his pains of (a) *waiting* to consume and (b) *abstaining* from eroding his capital by consuming more now rather than replacing the capital already in existence, he is properly being given part of the extra social product that *his* activity makes possible. It is a good bargain for the laborer: his wage product is fructified by what the capitalist provides *as the real wage rate always rises when thrift and accumulation succeed in lowering the interest rate.*"

But suppose time itself is not productive. Suppose the technical choices were between seven of labor two periods back and ten of labor three periods back. Incautious writings of Böhm's contemporaries declare, Humpty Dumpty-like: that is impossible; it contradicts a valid (*a priori?*) law of returns that more time means more product for the same total labor; read Jevons, read Böhm.

This is not cogent argumentation, as Hayek understands (1941, p. 60). In a timeless world more labor on the same acreage of land does usually raise output. But too much L/A can come to lower Q. However, under free competition, no equilibrium will occur in a rent-collecting market in which firms will pay a positive wage to hire workers who lower their production. All Böhm needs to say is this: If ten of labor three periods back does indeed bring less product now than seven of labor two periods back does, then at a positive market interest rate, the latter will surely be out-competed by the former and never be used.

However, this defense does not validate an inverse $(i, C/L)$ tradeoff in Equation (6) above. Adam Smith's Invisible Hand does ensure Equation (5) above but cares nought for Equation (6). This is why books entitled *Economics in One Lesson* must evoke from us the advice: "Go back for the second lesson."

Böhm was understandably tempted to say things like: "Among the *viable competitive* time-phasing techniques, the technological law holds: Using more time, more roundaboutness, more complexity – when a lower interest rate motivates that competitively – must surely bring society a higher output from the same steady-state primary inputs of labor and land. Adam Smith's Invisible Hand must [sic] surely ensure that."

Even if Sraffa were wrong in his empirical critique about the relevance of "genuine margins," even if $f(L_{t-1}, L_{t-2}, L_{t-3})$ had smooth partial derivatives that served fully, along with other supply-and-demand manifestations of tastes and time preferences, to solve the riddle of *laissez-faire* distribution of incomes – a task 1960 Sraffa never even tackles or gives hints about – I can give functional examples for $f(L_{t-1}, L_{t-2}, L_{t-3})$ which would negate the truth of Equation (6). However, in my dialogue with Sraffians, out of *noblesse oblige* I let them choose their weapons. By three well-chosen numerical examples, which Fisher (1907) might easily have fabricated, I side with Sraffians to show how and why there can be no universal measure of "depth or duration of time-phased produced inputs" that can serve as simple apologetics for mainstream theories of interest. Unequivocal "capital deepening" just cannot be defined.

Here are three specified, assumed-known alternative techniques: A, B, and C. They are amplified examples from my "Summing Up" (1966) on double reswitching.

To produce 1 of bread now:

A needs 7 of labor 2 periods back; or
B needs 6 of labor 1 period back and 2 of labor 3 periods back; or
C needs 6 of labor 1 period back and 1.68 of labor 2 periods back.

Which is most "roundabout?" Böhm could calculate for each simple "average periods of production": μ_A or μ_B or μ_C.

$$\mu_A = 2 \text{ periods} > \mu_B = 1.5 \text{ periods} > \mu_C = 1.22 + \text{ periods}. \quad (7)$$

This nominates that at zero i and lowest positive interest rates, A will be solely competitive-viable; at intermediate interest rates, B will be competitively dominant; and at highest interest rates, C will be solely viable. And actually this guess happens not to be wrong, as the following inequalities verify:

$$(P_Q/W)_A < (P_Q/W)_B < (P_Q/W)_C \text{ for } 0 \le i < .5 : A \text{ beats B and C} \quad (8a)$$

$$(P_Q/W)_B < (P_Q/W)_A, \ (P_Q/W)_B < (P_Q/W)_C \text{ for}$$

$$.5 < i < .8 : B \text{ beats A or C} \quad (8b)$$

$$(P_Q/W)_C < (P_Q/W)_B, \ (P_Q/W)_C < (P_Q/W)_A \text{ for}$$

$$.8 < i < \infty : C \text{ beats B or A}. \quad (8c)$$

Figure 1 plots, at its upper level, for each interest rate the costs of production for A, B, and C respectively. And then at its lower level, it plots against i the implied competitive-viable $(C/L, i)$ locus. Böhm ought to be astonished by the switch point S_{BC}, where a rise in i^* above .8 is seen to actually *raise* $(C/L)^*$!

By contrast, Figure 2 portrays the conventional over-simplified scenario of Böhm, Clark, and other neoclassical stalwarts. Here there are no reversals, no corners, and no discontinuous jumps. (If Ricardo ever had a lost 1815 manuscript, in which i^* was determinable from a single agricultural sector employing but one self-produced factor input, Figure 2 could capture its over-simplified story.)

Finally, Figure 3 portrays the generic case of what it is that a convex technology can generate. Any number of ups and downs can occur for the $(C/L, i)$ tradeoff locus – provided only that C/L can nowhere ever rise to exceed the golden-rule $(C/L)^*$ corresponding to zero i^*.

What misled earlier apologists were the one-capital-good leets model, the simplistic Jevons-Wicksell ripening with time model, and also Böhm's special $T = 2$ case where $Q_t = f(L_{t-1}, L_{t-2})$ happens to apply. As soon as (α) there are more than two Böhm states, or (β) there are more than one Clark capital goods, or (γ) there is intrinsic joint production in a one-leets model, then it follows that one can encounter the numerous ups and downs portrayed in the general Figure 3 picture.

In summary:

THEOREM 2: *Unlike the uniform inverse tradeoff of (w, i) in Theorem 1 above, it is always possible that:*

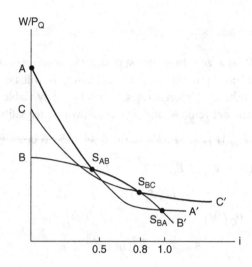

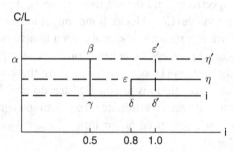

Figure 1. The switch point S_{AB}, which is at $\beta\delta$, agrees with classical and neoclassical pretentions. But S_{BC} and $\varepsilon\delta$ are valid Sraffa-Robinson rebuttals. (If Technique C were not feasible, $\alpha\beta\gamma\delta\varepsilon\eta$ would replace $\alpha\beta\gamma\delta\varepsilon\eta$, and we would be in "double-switching": normal S_{AB} and Sraffian S_{BA}!).

I. A rise in stationary-state i^* can accompany an increase in the plateau of per capita consumption.

II. However, near to the golden-rule technology of maximal $(C/L)^*$ at $i^* = 0$, any admissible tradeoff must nearby be (if anything) an inverse one. Indeed, never at any non-zero i can there be a higher $(C/L)^*$ than that which prevails at $i^* = 0$ – for if such existed it would already have dominated competitively at $i^* = 0$. QED.

III. These stated properties hold for continuum-differentiable technologies that possess partial derivatives of the $\partial output/\partial input$ type as well as holding for von Neumann-Sraffa discrete technologies (of the A, B, C type).

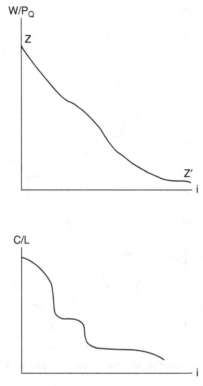

Figure 2. Over-simple classical and neoclassical picture: two inverse tradeoffs.

In the A, B, and C example here, there is no double-switching involved. (However, if I had omitted the C optional technique, understanding readers could then find that the new black minimum-cost envelope, instead of being αβγδεη as shown, would be αβγδ′ε′η′: this would be my (1966) double-switching example, in which at the highest interest rates competitive equilibrium will revert back to the zero-i* golden-rule marginal technique.)

IV. Whatever competition renders viable can be proved to be Pareto-Intertemporally-Optimal.

The simplest proof for Theorem 2 is to produce actual counter examples to a uniform inverse tradeoff: A, B and C do that for Sraffa-like technologies. For Clark-like smooth technology, see the Liviatan-Samuelson (1969) specified joint-output neoclassical function. Or, alternatively, one can come as close as you like to A, B, and C situation by approximating them by smooth-neoclassical functions that are differentiable. For Böhm's $f(L_1, L_2, L_3)$

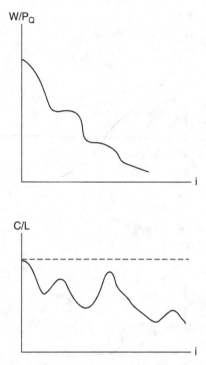

Figure 3. General possibility in non-joint production cases.

neoclassical case, after you solve for C/L as a function of i, the expression resulting for $d(C^*/L^*)/di^*$ will *not* be found to be negative just because f's technology is convex. QED.

III. CONCLUDING REFLECTIONS

Böhm-Bawerk and his contemporaries were products of their own time. A later age finds it easy to notice gaps and incoherences in their expositions. Such a critique is cheap and only too easy. Fairness and objectivity oblige us to stress the hits and not the misses of our predecessors. Were Isaac Newton reborn today at the age of eighteen, in a short time he could master what is known by our best physicists and mathematicians; and not long afterwards his own work would move out ahead on a par with the subject's greatest present-day leaders.

So it would be with Böhm or Clark and – I dare to add – with a young Sraffa reborn at age eighteen in 2005. "Render unto Caesar what is Caesar's." Yes, and I have done just that with the important normative insight that traces to Sraffa and to Robinson. One truth does not, however, invalidate a further truth. "Render unto Caesar *only that which is Caesar's due.*" "Render unto Sraffa and the post-Sraffians only that which is their (logical and empirical) due."

Both Böhm and Fisher rightly attributed crucial importance for the rate of interest to (1) the size of society's *vector* elements of capital goods (inclusive of human capital: knowledge, education, and training) relative to the supply of raw genetic labor and the supplies of nature's resources; and (2) a society's degree of real affluence and its rate of progress do depend on the known effective techniques of input–output technology – its fundamental pure science, basic applied sciences, industrial know-how, managerial prowess. These are sources of the high productivity that gives society the ability to produce for its members a high rather than low material real income. An economy's inventory of produced inputs is both complex and simple. Maintaining and improving upon congeries of productive inputs is an indispensable part of economic progress. All such time-phased processes will not evolve automatically: cave-people rose and fell in material well-being; eons passed without much cumulative change; great diversity of performance characterized geographically separated societies. Attempts to generalize simple family's or related-families' habit formation to large-group polities – *à la* utopian experimental cults or in the Lenin-Stalin and Mao pattern have not hitherto succeeded in organizing production with approximate Pareto-Optimality efficiency features. Gradual evolution toward near *laissez-faire* market mechanism responding to individual's self-interest, history suggests and advanced economic theory second guesses, will incur areas of market failure and will generate and perpetuate considerable degrees of economic and political inequalities. Just as there is no asymptotic communist utopia, neither is an asymptotic *laissez-faire* utopia.

Böhm and Wicksell and Cassel and Wieser and Clark and Walras and Hayek and other economists before and after Sraffa, all must face what the role of *intertemporal pricing* must be in organizing technologies that are *irreducibly time-phasing*. When Joan Robinson and I discussed these matters face to face, I used to get nowhere with her by babbling about supply and demand. She already had seen through that tommy-rot. Things went better if I could keep the focus on Mao's China. "Could Mao's 1970 China now, *sans* trade, produce a U.S. per capita standard of living for her near-billion population?"

"Of course not. She can't convert her few steam trains into diesels and electric-fed railways. Her workers can use only few and primitive tools. Their medical care is fragmentary, their years of education limited by China's previous despotism."

"Joan, by what steps can a People's Society move into the golden-rule plenty available to a 1970 America, or Britain or Spain?"

"First they should build the higher-yield bridges, roads, and machines. Then, later, deferred and delayed projects can be ranked in their turns."

Trite stuff, you will say? That is my point. Learned Aristotle couldn't handle such trite stuff. And neither could the physicist-statistician P. C. Mahalanobis who had Premier Nehru's ear in the decades just following India's liberation from the British Empire.

Am I arguing on the basis of this present article that modern students should read 1960 Sraffa rather than 1888 Böhm-Bawerk? Not that. I have Sraffa's 100 pages before me. In them we can learn how a whole range of (real wage, interest rate) unique tradeoffs can be generated in a technology with a given total of homogeneous labor and with a specified sustainable vector of produced inputs (if such a vector of inventories were somehow supplied to the society in question). Is the interest rate zero and per capita output maximal? It could be, but Sraffa knows it usually isn't. Is the interest rate maximal and the real wage literally zero? It could be, if we don't wish to worry about how a population maintains itself with so lean a diet. Had the editor of David Ricardo wished to, by adding a dozen pages to his 100 he could have told the reader what three-way tradeoffs would be competitively possible for (real wage, real land rent, interest rate) for a given technology with a specified array of techniques and with each specified homogeneous (labor total, land total). Now almost nothing would be unique in his equilibrium for each interest rate. And Ricardo would find few hints toward a solution of what he considered the basic economist's problem: How to understand the distribution of social income between wage workers, land owners, and other rentier capitalists.

On Mondays, Wednesdays, and Fridays I used to provide for Sraffa a Pigou-Fisher-Ramsey supplement to make determinate a change from one stationary state to another endogenous steady state. On Tuesdays and Thursdays I would toy with Modigliani lifecycle savings hypotheses to augment and complete the Sraffian technological relations. Experiments with Massachussetts Institute of Technology seminarians disillusioned me with Kaldorian exponential-growth micro-models, so on weekends I rested.

Risking some redundancy, I conclude here by appending to Theorems 1 and 2 the following:

THEOREM 3: *If a Sraffa system begins with a non-zero interest rate and finds itself in a non-Golden Rule stationary state of per capita consumptions, and if it is dynamically possible for it by a specifiable time-profile of savings and dissavings to move into a feasible Golden-Rule state, then somewhere along the transition path there will have to be some sacrificing of current consumption(s) in return for a perpetual future increment of consumption(s).*

Joan Robinson would not like to have to believe in this. But if we could explain it to Nassau and Böhm, they would find something in my paper to like.

MATHEMATICAL APPENDIX

1. Böhm liked to approximate the three alternatives in Section II's text, all of which can be written as a simple formula of the $f(L_1, L_2, L_3)$ type, by

$$f(L_1, L_2, L_3) \approx (L_1 + L_2 + L_3)F(\text{average time period of production})$$

$$\equiv \left(\sum_1^3 L_\tau\right) F\left(\frac{(1)L_1 + (2)L_2 + (3)L_3}{L_1 + L_2 + L_3}\right) \equiv LF(\mu), F' > 0 > F''. \quad (A1)$$

Fisher pointed out how arbitrary it was to use this *weighted arithmetic mean,* μ, instead of an infinity of other *general means* such as *geometric* mean of the τ_s, *harmonic* mean, etc. Since there is no interest rate at all in Böhm's μ, it fails to discriminate on how relevant chosen μ's might change at different positive interest rates. Böhm, and more recently Robert Dorfman (2001), rebuke Fisher cogently for being dismissive of the arithmetic mean when i is very near to zero. There, where i^2 can be ignored as negligible, *compound* interest expressions like $(1 + t)^2$ or $(1 + i)^\tau$ can be replaced by their *simple* interest form of $1 + 2i$ or $1 + \tau i$; and then μ can be shown to have relevance.

2. Here I present for Böhm a twenty-first century vindication. Ignoring land's rent, we write down free-entry competition's arbitrage which equates price to minimum cost, inclusive of the ruling interest rate. Competition's visible hand now serves to approximate

$$\underset{\mu}{\text{Max}}[LF(\mu) - (W/P_Q)L(1 + i\mu)] \quad (A2a)$$

$$= L^*F(\mu^*) - (W/P_Q)L^*(1 + i\mu^*) \quad (A2b)$$

$$= 0 \text{ under free entry competition.} \quad (A2c)$$

At Equation (A2) necessarily the maximal conditions prevail:

$$0 = [\partial/\partial L][LF(\mu) - (W/P_Q)L(1 + i\mu)] \qquad \text{(A2d)}$$

$$0 = [\partial/\partial \mu][LF(\mu) - (W/P_Q)L(1 + i\mu)]. \qquad \text{(A2e)}$$

Rearranging terms gives the simple-interest version of Taussig's (1896) discounted marginal productivities,

$$W/P_A = F(\mu^*)/(1 + i\mu^*) \qquad \text{(A3a)}$$

$$i = F'(\mu^*)/(W/P_Q) = [F'(\mu^*)/F(\mu^*)](1 + i\mu^*). \qquad \text{(A3b)}$$

Note the close resemblance of Equation (A3b) with my text's Equation (2c), which is Jevons' famous $r = \phi'(\theta)/\phi(\theta)$.

3. This article's main purpose is to discover and explicate a basic normative flaw in Böhm's capital theory. That does not exclude my now identifying a logical flaw in it *á la* Newton combined with a Baconian flaw concerning empirical inference and confirmation. Böhm's approximation, $Q = (\sum_1^T L_\tau)F(\mu)$ gratuitously slips in the Humpty Dumpty-ism that the iso-Q contours for $f(L_1, \ldots, L_T)$ are straight lines for $T = 2$, three dimensional planes for $T = 3$ and (for $T > 3$) flat hyper-planes – instead of being contours strictly-convex to the origin. It is no extenuation to reply that only near to $i = 0$ is this assumed to be true. Technology is technology. It does not dance around at the author's whim of the moment. Böhm's error involves the hoary selection phenomenon that traps neophytes into believing that noses do evolve in order to fit spectacles, as fingers do to fit forks.

The case $T = 3$ will suffice to make the point. By dimensional convention we may set $L_1 + L_2 + L_3 = 1$ (remember *constant scale* returns). Then Böhm's postulated approximation becomes

$$Q = (1) \times F(L_1 + 2L_2 + 3L_3), \quad \frac{\partial Q/\partial L_3}{\partial Q/\partial L_1} = 3 > \frac{\partial Q/\partial L_2}{\partial Q/\partial L_1} = 2 > 1. \quad \text{(A4)}$$

At what engineering lab did these alleged bizarre facts get observed or confirmed?

The same logical slip can be contrived even when Böhm eschews *any* approximation. At *every* positive interest rate, what will be observed in competitive neoclassical arbitrage is – from rearranging Equation (A3) above –

$$\frac{\partial Q/\partial L_3}{\partial Q/\partial L_1} = (1 + i)^2 > 1. \qquad \text{(A5)}$$

Does that mean that nature's technology is biased by an Austrian deity to make early L_3's inherently more productive, unit for unit, than late L_1's? Not at all. Both for the first symmetric Cobb-Douglas counter-example in Equation (A6) below, and for the second antithesis of Böhm's third law, as well as for the final possibility that confirms Böhm's insistence, the Böhm extra productivity will locally hold at the competition-selected equilibrium. (Scarce sugar in Iceland has three times the relative marginal utility that it has in Cuba because at Iceland's higher sugar price, consumers can buy so little of it.) Never confuse supply and demand as the Böhm school here did. Below are three obvious Cobb-Douglas neoclassical f's that all make the point.

$$Q' = L_1^{1/2}L_2^{1/2}, \; Q'' = L_1^8 L_2^2, \; Q''' = L_1^1 L_2^9. \tag{A6}$$

Even Hayek's 1941 language seems to allege that without Böhm's productivity-time-*asymmetry*, there could not be a positive interest rate. Let him try the $L_1^8 L_2^2$ case to refute any such contention. Depending upon Pigouvian time preference or Modigliani life-cycle scenario in which the interest rate clears the market for the dissavings of retired workers and the savings of prime-age workers, i^* can be high positive or low positive. Only in the absurd *linear* neoclassical technology where

$$Q_{t+1} = C_{t+1} + (K_{t+1} - K) = aL_t + bK_t; a > 0, \; b > 0 \tag{A7a}$$

could technology *alone* (!) determine

$$0 < i^* = b. \tag{A7b}$$

Even for Equation (A7b), a possible outcome is no stationary-state plateau of Kapital being possible, at the same time that

$$i(t) \neq b \tag{A7c}$$

in the rational-expectations transitional dynamics.

When I tried to use Böhm's $LF(\mu)$ approximation in Equation (3)'s generic case, after having provided for him *his* needed general equilibrium, his scenario generated contradictions to all of $(L_1 L_2 L_3)$ being positive. Fisher was thus not completely captious when he caviled at Böhm's glorification of the arithmetic-mean period of production.

Final remark: a typical $f(L_1, L_2)$ such as the Cobb-Douglas $\sqrt{L_1 L_2}$ or $L_1^2 L_2^8$ cannot be approximated well by *any* F in $(L_1 + L_2) \times F([L_1 + 2L_2]/[L_1 + L_2])$.

4. Mathematically adept readers can prove Theorem 2 for Böhm's general smooth $f(L_1, L_2, L_3)$ case by solving

$$a_1 + a_2 + a_3 = 1 \tag{A8a}$$

$$1 + i = \frac{\partial f(a_1, a_2, a_3)/\partial a_2}{\partial f(a_1, a_2, a_3)/\partial a_1} = \frac{\partial f(a_1, a_2, a_3)/\partial a_3}{\partial f(a_1, a_2, a_3)/\partial a_2} \tag{A8b}$$

$$w(1 + i) = \partial f(a_1, a_2, a_3)/\partial a_1. \tag{A8c}$$

These are four equations binding five unknowns: $(a_1\, a_2\, a_3; 1 + i, w)$. Knowing any one of $(w, 1 + i)$ can be shown to determine the other, in an inverse relationship $d(1 + i)/dw < 0$. Knowing each $1 + i$ enables us to know the other four equilibrium values; and from them we can determine

$$C/\sum_1^3 L_\tau = f(a_1^*, a_2^*, a_3^*). \tag{A9}$$

But the sign of $d(C/\sum_1^3 L_\tau)^*/d(1 + r^*)$ cannot be shown to be necessarily negative from convex technology's negative-semi-definite 3-by-3 matrix $[\partial^2 f/\partial a_i \partial a_j]$. I owe to Sraffa and post-Sraffians my own recognition of this at-first-surprising truth.

A similar proof of Theorem 2 can be given for the Clark-Ramsey multi-capital good case described by

$$C = \phi(L; K_1, \ldots, K_n; \dot{K}_1, \ldots, \dot{K}_n), \partial\phi/\partial K_i > 0 > \partial\phi/\partial\dot{K}_i \tag{A10a}$$

$$\lambda C = \phi(\lambda L; \ldots, \lambda K_j, \ldots; \ldots \lambda \dot{K}_j, \ldots), \phi \text{ concave.} \tag{A10b}$$

Write

$$\partial\phi(x_0; x_1, \ldots, x_n; x_{n+1}, \ldots, x_{2n})/\partial x_i \text{ as } \phi_i, i = 0, 1, \ldots, n. \tag{A11}$$

Then classical returns assumes that the $2n + 1$ matrix $[\partial^2\phi/\partial x_i \partial x_j]$ is of rank $2n$ and is negative semi-definite.

To determine the (w, r) tradeoff and the $(C/L, r)$ tradeoff in this continuous-time, smoothly differentiable technology, we have the relations

$$w = \phi_0() \tag{A12a}$$

$$r = -\frac{\phi_i()}{\phi_{n+1}()}, i = 1, \ldots, n \tag{A12b}$$

$$C/L = \phi(). \tag{A12c}$$

Even though dw/dr is negative as in Theorem 1, it would not follow from convexity of the technology that $d(C/L)^*/dr^*$ must be negative away from $r^* = 0$.

REFERENCES

Böhm-Bawerk, Eugen von. 1884. *Kapital und Kapitalzins. Erste Abteilung: Geschichte und Kritik der Kapitalzins-Theorien*. Innsbruck: Wagner. Translated by G. D. Huncke, and H. Sennholz as *Capital and Interest, Vol. I*, 4th edition. South Holland, IL: Libertarian Press, 1959.

Böhm-Bawerk, Eugen von. 1889. *Kapital und Kapitalzins. Zweite Abteilung: Positive Theorie des Kapitales*. Innsbruck: Wagner. Third edition in two volumes, 1909 and 1912. Translated as *The Positive Theory of Capital*. London: Macmillan, 1891. Translated as *Capital and Interest, Vols. II and III*, 4th edition. South Holland, IL: Libertarian Press, 1959.

Böhm-Bawerk, Eugen von.1906. "Capital and Interest Once More: I. Capital vs. Capital Goods. II. A Relapse to the Productivity Theory." *Quarterly Journal of Economics*, 21: 1–21, 247–82.

Böhm-Bawerk, Eugen von.1907. "The Nature of Capital: A Rejoinder." *Quarterly Journal of Economics*, 22: 28–47.

Clark, John Bates. 1899. *The Distribution of Wealth: A Theory of Wages, Interest and Profits*. New York: Macmillan.

Dorfman, Robert. 2001. "Modernizing Böhm-Bawerk's Theory of Interest." *Journal of the History of Economic Thought* 23: 37–54.

Fetter, Frank. 1914. "Interest Theories, Old and New." *American Economic Review* 4: 68–92.

Fisher, Irving. 1906. *The Nature of Capital and Income*. New York: Macmillan.

Fisher, Irving. 1907. *The Rate of Interest*. New York: Macmillan.

Fisher, Irving. 1930. *The Theory of Interest*. New York: Macmillan.

Hayek, Friedrich. 1931. *Prices and Production*. London: Macmillan.

Hayek, Friedrich. 1936. "The Mythology of Capital." *Quarterly Journal of Economics* 50: 199–228.

Hayek, Friedrich. 1941. *The Pure Theory of Capital*. London: Macmillan.

Hayek, Friedrich. 1945. "The Use of Knowledge In Society." *American Economic Review* 35: 519–30. Reprinted in *Individualism and Economic Order*. London: Routledge & Kegan Paul, 1949.

Jevons, W. Stanley. 1871. *The Theory of Political Economy*. London and New York: Macmillan.

Knight, Frank. 1934. "Capital, Time and the Interest Rate." *Economica, N. S.* 1: 257–86.

Knight, Frank. 1935a. "Professor Hayek and the Theory of Investment." *Economic Journal* 45: 77–94.

Knight, Frank. 1935b. "Professor Knight and the 'Period of Production': Comment [and] a Final Word." *Journal of Political Economy* 43: 625–27, 808.

Lenin, Vladimir Ilyich. 1917. "The State and Revolution." In *Collected Works*, 45 volumes. Translation of the fourth largest Russian edition, 1960–70. Moscow: Progress Publishers.

Liviatan, Nissan and Paul A. Samuelson. 1969. "Notes on Turnpikes: Stable and Unstable." *Journal of Economic Theory* 1: 454–75. Reproduced as Chapter 141 in *The Collected Scientific Papers of Paul A. Samuelson*, vol. 3. Cambridge, MA: The MIT Press, 1972.

Machlup, Fritz, 1935. "Professor Knight and the 'Period of Production'." *Journal of Political Economy* 43: 577–624.

Marshall, Alfred. 1890. *Principles of Economics*. London: Macmillan.

Ramsey, Frank. 1928. "A Mathematical Theory of Saving." *Economic Journal* 38: 543–49.

Robinson, Joan. 1942. *An Essay on Marxian Economics*. London: Macmillan.

Robinson, Joan. 1956. *The Accumulation of Capital*. London: Macmillan.

Samuelson, Paul A. 1948, 1951, 1955, 1958, 1961, 1964, 1967. *Economics*. New York: McGraw-Hill.

Samuelson, Paul A. 1966. "A Summing Up." *Quarterly Journal of Economics* 80: 568–83. Reproduced as Chapter 148 in *The Collected Scientific Papers of Paul A. Samuelson*, vol. 3. Cambridge, MA: The MIT Press, 1972.

Samuelson, Paul A. 1975. "Steady-State and Transient Relations: A Reply on Reswitching." *The Quarterly Journal of Economics* 89: 40–47. Reproduced as Chapter 216 in *The Collected Scientific Papers of Paul A. Samuelson*, vol. 4. Cambridge, MA: The MIT Press, 1977.

Samuelson, Paul A. 1976. "Interest Rate Determinations and Oversimplifying Parables: A Summing Up." In M. Brown, K. Sato, and P. Zarembka, eds., *Essays in Modern Capital Theory*. Amsterdam: North Holland Publishing Co. Reproduced as Chapter 215 in *The Collected Scientific Papers of Paul A. Samuelson*, vol. 4, 1977.

Samuelson, Paul A. 1999. "The Special Thing I Learned from Sraffa." In G. Mongiovi and F. Petri, eds., *Value, Distribution and Capital, Essays in Honour of Pierangelo Garegnani*. London and New York: Routledge.

Senior, Nassau. 1836. *An Outline of the Science of Political Economy*. New York: Farrar & Rinehart, 1939; Kelley reprint, 1965.

Sraffa, Piero. 1960. *Production of Commodities by Means of Commodities: Prelude to a Critique of Economic Theory*. Cambridge: Cambridge University Press.

Taussig, Frank. 1896. *Wages and Capital*. New York: D. Appleton.

Wicksell, K. 1893. *Über Wert Kapital and Rente nach neueren national-ökonomischen Theorien*. Jena: Fischer. Translated as *Value, Capital, and Rent*. London: Allen & Unwin, 1954.

PART VIII

RETROSPECTIVES ON EARLY MODERN
ECONOMISTS

Schumpeter as an Economic Theorist

SCHUMPETER was a universalist in economics. Mention a field in the subject of political economy, and you will find his name already established there: economic theory, macroeconomic business cycles, methodology, econometrics, Marxian economics, economic history, *Dogmengeschichte* – the list is only countably finite.

In a discipline that is undergoing dynamic development and being swept by gales of creative destruction, it is lucky if a scholar of age 67 is even remembered or curtsied to. Yet, at the time of this death, a citation index shows that Joseph Schumpeter was the scholar most often cited in the whole field of economics. As he himself might put it, 'This is a remarkable performance.' It is one that ought to have brought him satisfaction and fulfilment. But his was an enterpreneurial nature whose appetite for scientific achievement grew by what it fed upon.

The Wagnerian hero does not strive to be a Jack-of-all-trades and Schumpeter, 1 venture to suspect, would have traded his Popeship for a Keynesian revolution. Moreover, often we want what it is that we are not. A beautiful woman wishes to be clever, a sage to be an Olympic athlete. Norbert Wiener would trade ten mathematical theorems and three lemmas for one biological discovery. I have retold Schumpeter's story about his three wishes in life – to be the greatest lover in Austria, the best horseman in Europe, and the greatest economist in the world – and his regret of having failed to fulfil the second wish. It is not a joke that Joseph Schumpeter aspired to scholarly greatness, however lighthearted his tone and amusing his stories. As with Sigmund Freud and Abraham Lincoln, from the time of puberty there was a little clock in Schumpeter's breast ticking with the impulse for scholarly fame. Before I knew of Robert J. Merton's sociology of scientists, before I had myself articulated that the coin we scholars work for is our own applause, the example of my old Harvard teacher taught me this not-really-dirty little secret about the motives that run scientists.

Yes, Schumpeter may have envied a Keynes. Or a Ricardo, who changed the course of one of intellectual history's rivers. But we know that Schumpeter also had a certain condescension and contempt towards the economist who comprised his scientific birthright for a mess of populist pottage. And it is sad that Schumpeter's great 1942 *Capitalism, Socialism and Democracy* did not have greater worth in its author's own eyes.

I suspect that, in Schumpeter's heart of hearts, the scholar he admired most was the economic theorist, Ragnar Frisch. To have innovated in the many corridors of pure theory as Frisch had done – and then himself to surpass such magnificent performance by creating his own Newtonian *Principia* – that might have brought fulfilment to Joseph Schumpeter's insatiable soul.

NIHIL NISI?

As the centenary of Joseph Schumpeter's birth looms close, we are in a orgy of discussions of him and his works. To prepare for this symposium, to contribute a chapter to Professor Heertje's symposium volume, *Schumpeter's Vision Capitalism, Socialism and Democracy after 40 Years*, and to clarify my own thinking on the economic future at century's end for the Mexico City World Economic Congress, I have found myself preoccupied with Schumpeter's thought and person. It is a pleasant orgy, and a rewarding one. But it is boring to say the same thing twice and to have to engage in elegant variation merely to avoid exact repetition.

Already I have written much on Schumpeter. For his sixtieth *Festschrift* in the 1943 *Review of Economics and Statistics*, I wrote to clarify the logic and taxonomy of statics and dynamics. At the same time I both defended the *logic* of the *possibility* of zero interest rate in the stationary state and, as much as was meet in a scholar's own *Festschrift*, queried the importance of Schumpeter's dogma on that point. Shortly after Schumpeter's death in January 1950, I contributed a chapter to Seymour Harris's 1951 memorial volume, *Joseph Schumpeter: Social Scientist*, and returned there to the subject of his own interest theory.

I was honoured to have my memoir on 'Schumpeter as a teacher and economic theorist' appear along with the excellent essays by Arthur Smithies, Gottfried Haberler, Wolfgang Stolper, Paul Sweezy, Herbert von Beckerath, Arthur Marget, Erich Schneider, and others. As I re-read my words, I feel they catch much of what that remarkable man was. Still a problem of decorum does arise, a delicate question of whether and how to apply the doctrine of *de morituri nihil nisi bonum*. Should one's pen write of a beloved teacher that he was a 'showman' (or, a bit of a poseur)? What warts – beloved warts – should be airbrushed out of the photograph?

Within the family one speaks freely of Mama's engaging foibles, Brother's accident-proneness, Aunt Sophie's tone-deafness. But that does not mean that you should sell your Grandfather for a wisecrack. For a reserved and dignified scholar like Frank Taussig, the eulogist encounters few problems. With an engaging extrovert like Schumpeter, who loved to *épater* the bourgeoisie, aristocracy, priesthood, proletariat and the universal set, how acute the problem has to be for biographers. As Paul Sweezy used to say, 'You hate to hear outsiders criticize Schumpie; but within the inner circle, you find much to criticize.'

Moses Outside the Promised Land

There is an element of anticlimax in my assignment for today – to talk about Schumpeter as an economic theorist. Since Schumpeter's most theoretical work was his first German book of 1908 – *Das Wesen und Hauptinhault der theoretischen Nationalökonomie* – my inadequate mastery of German disqualifies me for the assigned task. Also, though much of the world regarded Schumpeter as the very essence of an economic theorist, he regarded himself as in a sense a theorist *manqué*. When singing the praises of more exact methods in our beloved science of economics, Schumpeter claimed he was entitled to do so with a better right since his own work was primarily not in the airy heights of mathematical theory. He would have loved to team up, later in life with someone like Nicholas Georgescu-Roegen, to write a profound treatise on modern economic theory. After that he could toss off his mathematical logic, complete his sociology, and in well-earned old age write his novel.

If it was not given to Moses to enter into the Promised Land, it is understandable that he should have tended to exhalt the promise of that fair country. So with Schumpeter. His schemata of three interacting cycles – the intermediate Juglar wave, superimposed on the shorter Kitchen cycle and the longer Kondratieff cycle – seemed less commanded by the facts of economic history than by Schumpeter's fascination with the mysteries of harmonic analysis. If a Ragnar Frisch came up with a new inflection-point technique for identifying cyclical phases, Schumpeter's admiration for Newtonian dynamics made him a favourable consumer to buy his theories. Chamberlin and Robinson, through their geometrical novelties, gained

Schumpeter's support for their new theories of imperfect competition. Leon Walras's comprehensive equations of general equilibrium represented the pinnacle of economics for Schumpeter. Böhm-Bawerk's tortured numerical examples tended to be put to a discount, perhaps because they were the sort of thing Schumpeter himself could so easily do. My own early work in *revealed preference*, Schumpeter, if anything, overvalued, because it brought into economics some of the elegance and economy of the most exact sciences and of mathematical logic itself.

Eclectic Methodologist

Young Schumpeter was a stormy petrel. He did not mind giving offence. He was not a good Austrian, in that he whored after mathematical economics, praised American and English economics, and questioned some of the established verities of Böhm-Bawerk. All this is in character.

One might then expect Schumpeter to take an extreme position in the debate between the German Historical School and the theorists of Austria and England. Perhaps to thumb his nose at his teachers, Schumpeter might have been expected to embrace Marxism; or to speak up for empiricism; or to denounce all grubbing in the facts. But it was not so. From the beginning his methodology took the eclectic road of good sense. In his view, inductive facts need to interact with simplifying theories whose logical implications are rigorously deduced with the help of advanced mathematics; probability techniques must be applied to interpret that which is ephemeral and singular in the empirical data from that which is persistent. Ricardo and Menger have merit. But so do Schmoller and List. Even Karl Marx, especially for his *chutzpah* in attempting to devise a dynamic theory for all aspects of the social universe, deserves praise.

Before there was a Vienna Circle, Schumpeter and Pareto embraced a separation of positivist science from normative aspiration. Before Tom Kuhn entered kindergarten, Schumpeter emphasized: It takes a theory to kill a theory; no dirty single fact can do so and, given our need to have a systematic way of thinking about complicated reality, our present theories will hold their place even in the face of cascades of *ad hoc* discordant observations.

At the same time that Schumpeter hailed the new, he warned against the Whig historians' propensity to criticize the historic great because they did not wear present-day beards and cravats and did not know all we have since learned. Each generation is entitled to its own mistakes, which if made by a Newton or Ricardo can be of interest in their own right. (I would add that this does not absolve us from the responsibility of naming as mistakes that which is mistaken.)

This core of good sense – unlike Schumpeter, I can never identify good sense with *common sense* – sometimes got concealed under Schumpeter's patronizing affectation of omniscience. It is not quite the case that Schumpeter's posthumous *History of Economic Doctrines* (1954) contains the lines, 'I shall not weary the reader with discussions of the 83 economists whose views dominated Rome from 100 B. C. to 53 A. D., for the reason that she or he will know much more about them than I do.' But somewhat similar passages do occur, and experience shows that readers will make an error if they think that Schumpeter is dropping names of authorities he has not tackled. The erudition he parades was erudition – *his* erudition.

PREVIEW

Since I was Schumpeter's student and friend for the last fifth of his life, I shall begin by recording some of my memories from his lectures and oral discourses. My account accords him less than full credit since what is memorable in a scholar is what is unexpected. The countless doctrines that he early appreciated at their correct worth are lost to memory, and one hardly remembers his judgements on people that merely agree with the conventional wisdom.

Then, in the last part of this paper, I stop chattering about theorists and Schumpeter's theoretical views. I actually do some economic theorizing, applying standard modern tools to Schumpeter's own paradigm of the interest rate. Although what I do here seems never to have been done in its entirety, it does not really have to be done. I show in the end that my extended analysis, using the standard neoclassical model of Solow, leads precisely to the conclusions and emphases arrived at briefly by Gottfried Haberler, Schumpeter's affable younger colleague. My elaborate Ramsey dynamics only corroborate what Haberler's (1951) simple Fisherine diagram showed. Nonetheless, as we approach the Schumpeter centennial year, a little excess of attention to his analysis can be forgiven.

Personal Likes

I can recall some of the theorists Schumpeter especially admired. He adored his brilliant young colleague Wassily Leontief. He had great respect for Leontief's teacher at Berlin, L. von Bortkiewicz, honouring his Herculean labours in trying to keep clean the Augean stables of economics, but regretting that more of von Bortkiewicz's energies did not go into creative innovations all his own. On the other hand, the corrosive common-sensical criticisms of an Edwin Cannan, Schumpeter rather underrated, being turned off by Cannan's antipathy to anything fancy and by his overconclusive simplifications. Knut Wicksell, Schumpeter beatified. But Wicksell's more highly publicized rival, Gustav Cassel, Schumpeter despised as a plagiarist, saying: 'Cassel is 10 per cent Walras and 90 per cent water.' He did faint-praise Cassel's textbook, as exactly what was needed on the Continent at the time. (I think Cassel, for all his personal faults, pretensions, and over-simplifications is now underrated as an original analyst.)

Before the world took much notice of American economists, Schumpeter singled out J. B. Clark for attention and respect. He found Irving Fisher amusing for his solemn do-goodism and health faddisms, but that never diminished his reverence for Fisher's theoretical innovations in value theory and interest determination. Schumpeter studied carefully the works of Carver, Fetter (who took him to his first and probably only football game), Walker, H. L. More, Allyn Young, Davenport, and Wesley Mitchell. Frank Taussig was an uncle figure with whom Joseph Schumpeter did not joke. As widowers, each twice bereft, they shared Taussig's massive Scott Road house in the 1932–37 years before Schumpeter married the economic historian Elizabeth (Boody) Firuski.

Frank Knight, Jacob Viner, Henry Schultz, J. M. Clark – leaders of American economics when I began my studies – Schumpeter went for whole lecture hours without much discussing. (In the autumn of 1935 I apparently became something of a joke because I so often talked about Frank Knight, whose intellect dominated the Chicago barnyard where I began my studies.) Harold Hotelling, Frisch, Tinbergen,[1] R. G. D. Allen, Hicks, Bowley, Divisia, Amoroso, Barone, Georgescu-Roegen, A. P. Lerner, Chamberlin, R. F. Kahn, Joan Robinson, von Stackelberg, Zeuthen, Lange, and Wald were mathematical economists whom Schumpeter applauded. The new and exciting *Review of Economic Studies* he recommended to his Ec

---

[1] I have commented elsewhere on Schumpeter's rapturous amazement that business cycles – his Kondratieffs and Juglars – might be produced by Frisch and Tinbergen using imaginary numbers involving $\sqrt{(-1)} = i$. He could understand sin t as a cycle; and that $d^2y/dt^2 = -y$ had the oscillatory solution $y(t) = y(0)\cos t + y'(0)\sin t$. But that its solution could be generated by the oscillations of $ae^{it} + be^{-it}$ smacked to him of delicious black magic. Had he understood why $(e^{it} - e^{-it})/2i$ can be short for sin t, the mysticism would have vanished, as it would if he had realized that the complex number $5 + 3i$ can be regarded as a way to depict the coordinates $(5, 3)$ of a vector that obeys certain natural laws of addition and multiplication: then only real numbers would be needed to handle the real numbers of pig-iron and price data.

11 classes. He spoke of the brilliant Pierro Sraffa, whom he had met when the latter was young, leading me to draw the false inference that Sraffa was a bit of a lazy dilettante because of his inherited wealth.

Although Schumpeter recognized that the 1924–33 'cost controversy' was mostly a catching-up of the Marshallians to 1838 Cournot, Schumpeter overvalued the lasting importance of that controversy. It is I think indicative of a certain uneasiness in his own handling of the tools of mathematical economics that, to his final hour, Schumpeter believed he could justify against the criticism of Viner's draftsman, Y. K. Wong, Viner's contention that the long-run cost curve should go through the *bottoms* of the U-shaped short-run curves. Schumpeter conceded that Wong (and, later, Harrod) were correct in the *two-dimensional* picture of the envelope. But in three dimensions – output, unit cost, planned scale of plant(?) – Schumpeter professed he could find normative significance in bottom-of-the-U points. I cannot reproduce his argument because I have always found it hard to formulate and remember false arguments.[2]

Aside from this erroneous identification of the minimum-unit-cost point with efficiency optimization, I can recall another Napoleonic claim of Schumpeter that I should have written down in my lecture notes because I could never reconstruct the steps of his alleged syllogism. After correctly informing his Harvard Ec 11 students that truly joint costs can never be allocated meaningfully between joint products, Schumpeter went on to say: 'Nevertheless, when recently I sat down with [some forgotten expert] over drinks, I showed how it could be done by means of an infinite series . . . [? in which the costs that wool does not bear are initially attributed to mutton, after which . . ., and so on until all costs are in the end fully and uniquely allocated]. . . .' I hope St Peter confronted Joseph with the case, $TC = \min[\text{mutton},\text{wool}/2]$, and asked for its meaningful series-expansion imputation into $f(\text{mutton}) + g(\text{wool})$.

Alfred Marshall's *Principle of Economics* was the admitted classic of the 1890–1930 period. It was typical of Schumpeter's love for theory that he

---

[2] Schumpeter's own Bonn student, Erich Schneider, had provided, in the same 1931 volume of the *Zeitschrift für Nationalökonomie* that carried Viner's famous cost article, a graph involving *total* cost curves demonstrating the envelope tangencies that Wong properly insisted on. I may retell the story that, as late as 1935, Viner insisted to his Chicago class: 'Although Wong is mathematically right, I can draw the envelope curve through the bottoms of the U's.' My cheeky rebuke as a nineteen year old was, 'Yes Professor Viner, you can, with a *thick* pencil!' As a twenty-five year old, I realized that I might better have added: 'Or, of course, if your U-shaped short-run curves are V-shaped, with *cornered* minima, and provided the economies of plant enlargement aren't too rapid.'

rejected Marshall's view that the reader could skip the footnotes and appendixes. If time were short, Schumpeter advised, read them and skip the *text*!

Schumpeter's older Harvard colleague, Edwin Bidwell Wilson, mathematical physicist and last student of J. Willard Gibbs, devoted part of his 1936–37 seminar to Marshall's Mathematical Appendix. I was then struck by how patchy these notes are and how hard it was for us economists to answer Wilson's proper questions about them. I came to realize that Marshall, despite his reputation as a synthesizer, was in fact primarily a *miniaturist* who lacked the energy and will to shape a coherent masterwork in analytical economics. It went against the grain to admit that Schumpeter was right in elevating Leon Walras above Marshall and the rest as the Newton of economics who discovered the system of the world in his paradigm of general equilibrium. All the more credit is due the youthful Schumpeter, since after 1900 the moon of Pareto was serving to eclipse the sun of Walras. All hats off to Pareto, but as Lagrange lamented in eulogizing Newton, there is alas only one system of the economic world to discover and Walras had already done that when Pareto was still a schoolboy.

Marshall, having managed to bury Jevons, kept Francis Edgeworth in the shade for four decades. Schumpeter accorded Edgeworth his due. 'If you don't write books, and merely squander your genius in articles, you won't command your true value in the markets of scholarship,' Schumpeter used to say. He therefore rejoiced when the Royal Economic Society brought out Edgeworth's collected papers in three large books. The cases of Einstein and Frank Ramsey (the latter's three immortal contributions to economics appeared in separate articles) suggest that Schumpeter's emphasis on books can be refuted – at least by a genius. Still, Edgeworth's own important innovations in statistics – which, despite their obscurity of exposition, anticipated much of R. A. Fisher's maximum likelihood and went beyond Karl Pearson's large-sample asymptotics – were never part of one unified book and have failed to receive the credit they deserve. In any case Schumpeter practised what he preached. He was usually engaged on an ambitious book. And, although he published articles every year, he resisted temptation to make small contributions to economic science.

Maturity and Youth

Schumpeter stayed alive as a theorist. That means he improved in his understanding, sloughing off old skins or covering them up with new. That also means that he is sometimes a bit inconsistent in his expositions of any one date. I was struck in reading his last years' work on welfare economics: in some places he betrays clear understanding of Pareto optimality; in other places he accepts L. Robbins' view that economists have virtually nought to say in this domain; in no one place does he provide a unified grasp of the subject's final status. All this is merely to say that Schumpeter was human. Even Pareto, who innovated in replacing one cardinal measure of utility by any numberings of the indifference contours that preserve ordinal rankings, often forgot about his own innovations and reverted back in his definitions of complementarity to operations on the cardinal utility he had already thrown out into the trash.

Progression in Schumpeter's thought offers special problems. Schumpeter had respect for the past. To tamper with Smith's 1776 text in the light of 1913 scientific findings he would have considered foolish. Schumpeter's own youthful classics are part of the past. What right does J. A. S. have in 1934 to second-guess the thought of J. A. S. of 1912? For better or worse, a classic should be left to stand. Besides, Mertonian study of the sociology of science suggests that you will retain a higher ranking in the history of a scholarly discipline if you stand your ground. Never complain and never explain. Newton's warts are part of his picture and to use an airbrush to shade them out is to distort the portrait and rob it of interest.

For the rest of this survey of Schumpeter as a theorist, I am going to stop talking about him as a connoisseur of theory and patron of theorists. I am going to discuss in a theoretical way one of Schumpeter's own most famous – you might say most notorious – theories. I refer to Schumpeter's paradigm of a zero rate of interest in equilibrium when innovational development is ruled out. If this view is correct, it is only as a result of innovation that society accords any income to people who do not work for wages or receive rents for the land resources they own. A bourgeois class that receives permanent net income from its ownership of machines, factories and inventories continues to exist only to the extent that innovations do not flag.

Many of my comments will have to be critical. All of them might have been written in, say, 1934 when Schumpeter was 51 and his theory was at least a quarter of a century old. Since Schumpeter rarely discussed his own theories, and nowhere repudiated them, one's pen tends to write almost angrily: 'Do you mean to say in 1934 that ...?' Yet the argument is really with a 1912 text. I find no useful way to evade this problem. So I must ask the reader to realize that what seems like strong criticism is not really that of a student directed against his beloved friend and benefactor, but rather is a pungent verdict by a later generation on the preliminary scientific findings of an earlier generation.

T. S. Eliot was told, 'We know more than the classics.' Much as this message pained him, if it is scientists we are talking about, Eliot must accept this fact. But even scientists must recognize the epsilon of truth in Eliot's rejoinder: 'Yes, and it is the classics that we know.' The greatest of scientists was honest in saying that he took off from the shoulders of giants. I can be as objective in weighing the merits and demerits of Schumpeter's 1912 paradigm because it was Joseph Schumpeter who taught me how to administer justice.

EVALUATING SCHUMPETER'S ZERO-INTEREST-RATE DOCTRINE

The Ramsey (1928) and Solow (1956) one-sector paradigm can illustrate Schumpeter's contentions. It was this I had in mind in earlier expositions (Samuelson, 1943, 1951). In view of Schumpeter's youthful admiration for J. B. Clark, my modelling is a fair one.

Technology

Output, $Q(t)$, is the sum of consumption, $C(t)$, and net investment: $C(t) + K'(t)$. It is produced by a first-degree-homogeneous, concave, smooth neoclassical production function whose variables are land, labour, and a homogeneous stock of capital ('leets' in Joan Robinson's sardonic lingo), $[T, L, K(t)]$:

$$Q(t) = C(t) + K'(t) = F[T, L, K(t)] = Tf[L/T, K(t)/T] \tag{1}$$

where $f[L, K]$ is a smooth, strictly concave function.

It suffices to consider land and labour as 'primary' factors not producible within the system, instead being given in constant amounts, $[T, L]$, which by appropriate definition of units could each be taken to be unity. With the understanding that labour supply is fixed, $f[L, K]$ can be written as $f[K]$, with $f''[K] < 0$.

Competitive Imputation

In the absence of uncertainty and technical change, [real wage rate, interest or profit rate, rent] are given respectively by the competitive marginal-productivity relations:

$$w(t) = \partial f[L, K(t)]/\partial L, \ L \equiv 1 \equiv T \tag{2a}$$

$$r(t) = [\partial K'/\partial K] = \partial f[L, K(t)]/\partial K, \ L \equiv 1$$
$$= f'[K] \tag{2b}$$

$$R(t) = Q(t) - w(t)L - r(t)K(t)$$
$$= \partial F[T, L, K(t)]/\partial T, \ [T, L] \equiv [1, 1] \tag{2c}$$

Golden-Rule State

Schumpeter's theory of a zero rate of interest in the circular-flow equilibrium posits that, for given primary factors of $[T, L]$, there is a *finite* golden-rule K^s, a Schumpeter point such that

$$0 = r^s = f'[K^s] \tag{3}$$

Before Ramsey, Meade, Allais, Phelps, von Weizsäcker, and other analysts of the 'golden-rule state of maximal per capita consumption', Schumpeter recognized that his zero-interest-rate equilibrium would maximize the aggregate steady-state real consumption of fixed-supply primary factors of production. The competitive breakdown of this aggregate between wages and rent would depend on technology and endowment of land relative to labour, w and Q/L being the greater the greater is the T/L ratio.

Falling Rate of Interest

In the absence of innovation, if $K(0)$ begins below K^s, Schumpeter may be presumed to be supposing that positive accumulation of $K'(t)$ will always be forthcoming and will soon bring the interest rate down to zero:

$$\lim_{t \to \infty} = [K(t), r(t), Q(t)] = [K^s, 0, \text{maximal } Q] \tag{4}$$

And then equilibrium will persist happily ever afterwards forever.

If $K(0)$ begins above K^s, a possibility I do not remember Schumpeter having recognized, $r(0)$ begins negative and decumulation brings it up to zero.

Innovational Development

But now let us introduce the possibility of gales of creative self-destruction. A parameter of technological improvement, $\theta(t)$, is put in the production function:

$$f[L, K(t); \theta] \quad \text{with} \quad \partial f[L, K(t); \theta(t)] / \partial [\theta(t)] > 0 \qquad (5)$$

$\theta(t)$ increases as t increases. The increases in θ may be jerky; or they may be quasi-periodic; or they could be near to random. In any case, so long as such innovations are going on, the competitive interest will be perturbed above [3] zero by development.

For land and labour fixed, output will grow for two reasons: first, improved technology will raise product directly; secondly, the induced rise of the interest rate above zero will in Schumpeter's scenario cause capital to grow.

A Schumpeter Cycle

I can even construct a regular cycle of Schumpeterian developmental evolution. Thus, assume that $\theta'(t)$ is a positive periodic function of time:

$$\theta'(t) \equiv \theta'(t + \tau)$$

Or let technical advance be almost periodic. Or let it be bunchy in time like an autocorrelated error function. Or, even if technical change is purely random (as white as the driven snow of 'white noise'), the economic system will then show quasi-realistic autocorrelated fluctuations in the fashion of the Wicksell–Frisch rocking horse subject to random impulsive shocks.

The reader can verify this in the case of a quadratic production function, and where we postulate that $K'(t)$ accumulates at a rate proportional to the deviation of r from 0. This gives, after appropriate choice of units,

$$f[K; \theta] = \theta(t)K(t) - \tfrac{1}{2}K(t)^2 \qquad (6)$$

$$r = \theta - K \qquad (7)$$

$$K'(t) = \alpha r(t), \quad \alpha > 0 \qquad (8)$$

Then, if $\theta'(t)$ is sinusoidal with period τ, it can be shown that investment becomes ultimately sinusoidal with the same period (but with a lag). Profits,

---

[3] Only in preparing this paper did I notice what Schumpeter did not emphasize: namely, technical change can *lower* the interest rate rather than raise it; e.g. when $\partial^2 f[L, K; \theta] / \partial \theta \partial K < 0$ and the prior zero interest rate turns negative as innovation makes the stock of leets become redundant.

growth of output, and other variables will display behaviour a bit like that observed by the National Bureau of Economic Research.

Summary

Seventy years after Schumpeter glimpsed his basic model, I have produced this instance to show that it involves no *logical* contradictions. We observe a system that evolves cyclically, displaying a rising trend of real wage and output and cyclical fluctuations in the profit rate around a flat long-run trend.

Note, however, that Schumpeter had no real need to put into his system that which economists have found to be most novel and shocking in Schumpeter. I refer to the *zero* rate of interest. How Böhm-Bawerk must have smarted at that saucy conception of Schumpeter. And we all know how vehemently Frank Knight rejected in the 1930s the very notion of a zero rate of interest.

My point is a simple one. Suppose Schumpeter had believed in a *positive* rate of subjective time preference *à la* Böhm, Irving Fisher, Pigou, Cassel, and other orthodox neoclassical writers. Call it ρ, and let it be positive (as when Pigou's representative Englishman is born with a psychological rate of subjective time preference of 4 per cent: $\rho = 0.04$).

Schumpeter's model of cyclical development would have been little different with a positive rather than a zero floor for the interest rate! Output would still grow cyclically, while real wage and interest rates would still vary in the same quasi-cycles.

To see this, replace the proportionality of accumulation to the interest rate by its proportionality to the deviation of the interest rate above the time preference rate:

$$K'(t) = \alpha[r(t) - \rho] \qquad (9)$$

Then $\rho > 0$ merely gives a positive asymptote to which the interest rate may descend in the absence of innovation, rather than a zero asymptote. It is still fits and starts of innovation that create dynamic development and cycles. The scenario for the economy is still essentially a cheerful one, even if golden-rule perfection is not being attained or even aimed at.

Simplifications

Though my model is in the sense just described even more general than Schumpeter's 1912 schemata, it quite fails to catch some qualitative properties of the Schumpeterian scenarios. My transient positive profit is merely the competitive interest rate generated as innovation makes every item of capital more productive. My profit is temporary, but it is a phenomenon of perfect competition equilibrium.

Schumpeter's innovators, by contrast, are *temporary monopolists*. Their transient profits come because rivals are not yet able to do what they can do. To understand them you need to read pages in Chamberlin on imperfect competition, or in Cournot and Marshall on monopoly.[4] As knowledge and methods are gradually imitated by rivals, oligopoly will atrophy and degenerate into competitive imputation. So to speak, I have aped with changes in *quantity* of K and its productivity what Schumpeter contrives by changes in *quality* of market structure and entrepreneurial power. Keeping this qualification in mind, we are pleased to see how much of the Schumpeterian epic this dynamic Clark–Solow model can capture.

Imperfect Competition Theory

This qualification also explains why Schumpeter should have always had so keen an interest in the analysis of imperfect competition. His laudatory views on Joan Robinson and Edward Chamberlin reflect this.

John Kenneth Galbraith's giant corporations fit well into the modified version of Schumpeter's model that he arrived at in his final years. But unlike Galbraith, Schumpeter insisted that these giants were constitutional monarchs, who reigned only so long as they desisted from trying to rule. 'What have you done for us lately?' is the question ever put to the Fortune-500 companies. Those with disappointing replies are evicted from the choice rooms of capitalism's hotel: those suites are always full, but with a changing roster of guests, each of whom must earn his place in every epoch.

The *countervailing power* that runs Schumpeter's jungle is the competition of giant seller against giant seller. And even a pygmy can challenge a giant, and hope to become a giant.

When I look at the great fortunes amassed since World War II, I understand them through Schumpeter's spectacles. David Packard or

---

[4]   Schumpeter early admired Cournot's 1838 analysis of monopoly, duopoly, and oligopoly. It was Schumpeter who edited the last symposium in which Wicksell participated, which dealt critically with A. L. Bowley's duopoly analysis. Illustrative of Schumpeter's felt need to believe in the stability of capitalism and, by extension, to rule out instability of bilateral monopoly, was the ambivalent doctrine on duopoly that Schumpeter maintained from 1925 to his death in 1950. He believed that the Cournot determinate solution is the correct one, except when it is not! – and then the collusive joint-profit-maximization solution of Wicksell is the correct and determinate solution. I am still amazed that such feckless eclecticism could satisfy him. Was it a case of the heart superseding the head?

Edwin Land or Sheikh Yamani have each become as rich as Rockefeller. The Marxian paradigm of the falling rate of profit or rising organic competition of capital throws no light on the Pareto distribution of incomes and their genie coefficient of concentration. The strictly competitive model of Hicks, Solow, and J. B. Clark, as well as the Kaldorian and Kaleckian widow's cruses, equally withhold insight on the trends and causes of income inequality.

Progression in Schumpeter's View?

I am not sure that I can document what I have described as a change in Schumpeter's view on innovators and on the welfare economics of oligopoly that took place between the autumn of 1935 when I first attended his Harvard lectures and his mature thought in his final years. In 1935 he believed Du Pont could not long hold its innovational lead. General Electric, General Motors, IBM, and AT&T all had limited life expectancy as producers of enterpreneurial profit – which is essentially the only source of profit he then gave diplomatic recognition to.

By 1950 Schumpeter was prepared to concede that a bureaucratic corporation might be able to continue to innovate. Moreover, the *statical* deadweight loss transiently arising from the Fortune-500 innovational oligopoly power, Schumpeter came to believe, was more than compensated for by the consumers' surplus they created from their dynamic innovations. Their monopolists' Danegeld was a bargain in Schumpeter's recalculation.

Schumpeter's final logic ought to have predisposed him to accord to Hayek the final victory over Lerner and Lange in the debate over whether a socialist state could play the game of parametric pricing. To find new *cost* technologies and husband scarce knowledge as it is forever newly arriving, the letter of Walrasian equations achievable by Lerner–Lange auctioneers and bureaucrats serves as nothing compared to what Hayek's real-life speculators and profit receivers are led by the invisible hand of market competition to contribute. I do not remember Schumpeter as pronouncing on this point, but on my reading it should be congenial to his *Weltanschauung.*

How Vital Is Money Creation?

The present model is unrelievedly microeconomic in its ignoring of money supply and nominal spending behaviour. It thus fails to do justice to what was considered important in Schumpeter's model, namely his insistence that innovational development be financed by money *creation*, which in turn leads to unanticipated inflation that cuts the real consumption people can purchase with their previous nominal incomes, thereby procuring the 'forced saving' that offsets the incremental innovational investment. Dennis Robertson and other writers of the 1920s on forced saving were thus anticipated by Schumpeter. Even though many orthodox economists were shocked by Schumpeter's notion that inflation could advance progress, Viner and Hayek have shown that forced-saving notions occur as early as 1803 in Henry Thornton. Keynes's *General Theory*, preoccupied with the *ex post* identity of saving with investment, needlessly denied the importance of forced saving; similarly the recent school of rational expectationists do well to insist that inflation foreseen is less effective than unexpected inflation in releasing resources from consumption for investment.

We can add money to the Solow–Ramsey model. Whether we do or do not, it confirms doubt that there *has* to be money creation for capitalism to work in its characteristic way. When the banking system keeps aggregate money inelastic in supply, innovational investment can still pull resources out of the old circular flow by competing with older kinds of investment and reinvestment for the limited quota of funds (and, in essence, resources). A disciple of Schumpeter has no need to insist upon the same degree of business–cycle overshoot relative to innovation under different policy regimes.

QUALIFICATION AND EXTENSION

Approach Towards Zero Interest Rate

My equations (1)–(4) demonstrate that Schumpeter's paradigm of an interest rate that is zero in innovationless equilibrium is not a logically impossible one. That does not mean that Schumpeter himself ever provided an adequate demonstration of this fact, and does not answer the question of whether he understood how to reply to the legitimate queries on the matter. Also, for a thing to be logically possible does not mean that it is necessarily *likely* or probably *relevant*.

There are also models, as simple as the Clark–Solow model that I have just analysed, in which the interest rate only *asymptotically* goes to zero but never quite reaches there. Frank Knight exaggerated the necessity or likelihood of such models in the 1930s, but that is no reason to refuse them careful analysis.

Thus, instead of having output attain a maximum at a *finite* stock of capital, at $K^s < \infty$, suppose $f[\bar{L}, K] \equiv f[K]$ only approaches its upper bound at $K = \infty$. Then

$$\lim_{K \to \infty} f[K] = B < \infty$$

$$f'[K] > 0, \quad 0 < K < \infty$$

$$\lim_{K \to \infty} f'[K] = 0, \quad \lim_{K \to \infty} \int_{\epsilon}^{k} f'[x] \, dx < \infty \tag{10}$$

Any constant-elasticity-of-substitution (CES) function, with Hicksian σ less than unity, will have this property. An easy CES example is the 'harmonic mean':

$$F[T, K, L] = (aT^{-1} + bK^{-1} + cL^{-1})^{-1} \tag{11}$$

This really alters Schumpeter's vision of cyclical evolution very little. True, net investment never quite ceases after innovation ceases. But it does trickle away to an ignorable infinitesimal. And quasi-periodic or even white-noise perturbations in innovation (i.e. in $\theta'(t)$ above) will still produce a quasi-regular pattern of cyclical evolution.

Therefore, even if we take the view of Schumpeter's fair-minded critic, Gottfried Haberler – namely, that it is hard to conceive of *zero* net productivity of capital being quite reached – Schumpeter's theoretical system remains intact in its important logical properties.

Unbounded Output

Knight went farther than Haberler. For him, $f'[K]$ falls very slowly indeed. That is Knight's empirical allegation, and for which he gives a bag of uneven arguments. (It is as if Knight believes σ is virtually infinite; or that $T(t)$ and $L(t)$ are not exogenously given as 'primary factors' but are, in the von Neumann fashion, themselves producible and produced at constant returns to scale *within* the economic system. Then, as Kaldor cogently noted in his critique of Knight, the innovationless system could approach positive exponential growth and an asymptote of positive interest rate would be possible.)

Whatever the slowness at which the interest rate would drop, Knight seems to assert the further view that $f'[K]$ cannot fall so fast with K as to make $f[K]$ bounded. As with the Cobb–Douglas function, where $\sigma \equiv 1$ and relative factor shares are constant,

$$\lim_{K \to \infty} f[K] = \infty, \quad \lim_{K \to \infty} f'[K] = 0 \tag{12}$$

Again, a lawyer for Schumpeter can make good a defence for the view that this need not change his vision. Thus, if utility in a Ramsey integral attains an upper bound at finite consumption levels, investment will peter out in the absence of innovation.[5]

Now, however, there is no guarantee that pure profit falls towards zero in the absence of development. Nor is there even guarantee that the *fractional share* of profit falls towards zero. Schumpeter's startling doctrine of euthanasia of the rentier, which differs from Keynes's *General Theory* version in that Schumpeter's leads to no lasting unemployment problem and happily splashes workers and landowners with real income, now could be invalidated. My lament over this would be limited, since in any case there is no likelihood that innovation will cease (and perhaps no great reason to expect it to fall substantially). Why agitate oneself about a quarrel over contrafactual asymptotes?

Logical Confusions?

Even if technology could permit the interest rate to become zero, Schumpeter never spelled out correctly why and exactly how this would come about. This may have been only inadvertence. But my reading of his 1912 classic (and later discussions) raises doubt that Schumpeter perceived the problem correctly. Schumpeter seems to have had a vague notion that, in the absence of development, the interest rate *logically* could have no equilibrium other than zero.

If he held such a view, he was in error. I have used the Clark–Solow model to show that $r(t)$ going to zero is a *logically possible* case. That same model can serve to show that a zero interest rate is not *logically necessary*. It is a puzzle that Schumpeter did not perceive this and concede it.

My example of a subjective rate of time preference of $\rho > 0$ has already made the point. True, Schumpeter might have the empirical hunch that $\rho = 0$. But if that were the basis for his notion of a zero interest rate, in his polemics with Böhm-Bawerk he might have been expected to marshal the factual evidence for so unconventional a view. Instead his arguments,

---

[5] However, now that $U(C) \le U(f[K^s])$, with $f'[K^s] = r^* > 0$, as $t \to \infty$, we find $r(t) \to r^* > 0$. Also, as $\theta(t) \to \infty$, utility satiation will be achieved and the behaviour equations of the truly affluent society would have to be altered beyond recognition by traditional economists. If $U(\infty) = B < \infty$, and $f[K]$ is Cobb–Douglas, Ramsey's optimized integral could still be convergent, and Schumpeterian evolution would still involve an interest rate that falls towards zero except when innovation transiently elevates it.

inconclusive as they may seem to a careful reader, appear to be theoretical in character. (Later I review some of the 1912 points.)

Suppose Böhm were to put this question to Schumpeter: 'If the physical net productivity of capital never falls below a positive constant, do you still insist that the equilibrium real rate of interest would be zero?'

It is unflattering to say so, but I fear that Schumpeter would still have answered 'yes'. Somehow, he thought, the present K input that produced the postulated future fruits would have imputed to itself so much value as to make its subsequent net yield zero. But, as I see it, no finite value for K could do that. And, unlike the case of land, which I shall deal with presently, there is no reason for an infinity to rear its head in the model's depiction of K. (I return below to Schumpeter's 1912 exposition on this issue.)

Infinite Capitalization of Land

Permanent productive land will have an infinite value when the interest rate is zero:

$$P_T T / r = \infty \text{ if } r = 0 > P_T T \tag{13}$$

This would shock many critics of Schumpeter. Blunt Edwin Cannan dismissed the problem of proving that the rate of interest must be positive, taking it for granted that there has to exist a (finite) ratio between the stock value of a flow.

Suppose Schumpeter conceived of a Robinson Crusoe who lived forever. Or, better, conceived of a Swiss Family Robinson that as a clan will live forever and that empirically is free of systematic time preference. Then there is nothing absurd about land's having a value higher than any multiple of its annual net rent. Two acres of land will be worth twice one acre; but no acres will ever be permanently sold for finite annual incomes.

We think land's value must be finite because we think of each person as dying. We expect that people do not attach as much importance to their remote heirs as they do to their own old age and to their immediate children and grandchildren. Empirically, we introduce the elements of subjective time preference that seem realistic and which are inconsistent with Schumpeter's idealized scenario.

We then face a model of overlapping generations and the Modigliani life-cycle model for wealth and saving applies. As I showed in my A. P. Lerner *Festschrift* contribution, with permanent land in the picture, a Turgot–Modigliani paradigm will yield a positive interest rate that is just large enough to make the amount of wealth that people will want to hold (out of their savings and inheritances) equal to society's valuation of all earning assets. At r too low, land and leets will be worth more than people want to continue to own; as people try to sell assets and spend proceeds on increments of consumption, asset prices will drop and r will return towards equilibrium r^*. At r above r^*, people of all ages will not be able to hold on the average as much as they need to plan to hold to fulfil their expected retirement consumption needs; they will try to save more, bidding up asset values, enhancing the stock of K leets and lowering the $f'[K]$ yield back down to r^*.

So, realistically, a positive interest rate seems indicated for Schumpeter's circular-flow equilibrium. Nonetheless, since the logical issue has been debated, in the next section I shall use Ramsey's 1927 model of optimal saving to vindicate Schumpeter's *logic* of a zero interest rate.

A RAMSEY MODEL FOR SCHUMPETER

To the Clark–Solow capital technology, I add a concave utility function for Schumpeter's society. The undiscounted integral of this utility integrand, extended over the *infinite* future, is to be maximized. Thus, we have

$$\max \int_0^\infty U(c)dt = {}^{\max}_{K(t)} \int_0^\infty U(f[K] - K')dt$$

$$K(0) = K^0 < K^s, \quad f'[K^s] = 0 > f''[K], \quad f[K^s] \geq f[K] \qquad (14)$$

$$U'(C) > 0 > U''(C), \quad U(f[K^s]) = U(B) \geq U(f[K])$$

As is well known, $K(t)$ will grow by positive accumulation from initial K^0 gradually towards the golden-rule Schumpeter turnpike K^s. This means that the interest rate falls asymptotically towards zero, doing so at the optimal rate given by the Ramsey–Keynes 'energy integral':

$$U(B) = U(f[K] - K') + K'U'(f[K] - K') \qquad (15)$$

This first-order differential equation in K has, from each initial K^0, a solution that asymptotically approaches Schumpeter's zero-interest golden-rule state. By standard mathematical methods that I need not review here, the following asymptotic limits can be shown to hold – in close agreement with the heuristic relations (1)–(4) presented earlier:

$$\lim_{t \to \infty} \left\{ K(t), K'(t), r(t), \frac{K'(t)}{r(t)}, \frac{K'(t)}{K^s - K(t)} \right\} = \{K^s, 0, 0, \alpha, \beta\} \qquad (16)$$

$$\alpha = \left\{ \frac{U'(f[K^s])}{U''(f[K^s])f''[K^s]} \right\}^{1/2}, \quad \beta = \left\{ \frac{f''[K^s]U'(f[K^s])}{U''(f[K^s])} \right\}^{1/2} \quad (17)$$

The integral of present-discounted value of land, calculated along the system's path to equilibrium, will diverge to infinity as the interest rate decays exponentially to zero. But that is only as it should be in a system where decision-making is made on an infinite-lifetime basis.

Corrections

This concrete Schumpeter model permits us to correct any possible mis-apprehensions. Thus, suppose $r(t)$ or $f'[K(t)]$ can never fall below a positive number $\bar{r}$. Then with utility unsatiable, $U'[C] > 0$, Ramsey's integral will be infinite and no Schumpeter circular-flow equilibrium becomes possible. Böhm would then be right to reject any contention of a zero equilibrium rate of interest.

Also, suppose we realistically attach to Schumpeter's people finite life-times. And suppose that their bequeathing motivations are realistically limited: some of their Modigliani life-cycle wealth they want to leave to children and grandchildren, but they definitely fail to give like consideration to consumption by their descendants a million years from now. Then my earlier remarks about a Turgot–Modigliani model apply to negate a zero rate of interest.

Derailings

There would be some interest in dissecting Schumpeter's own 1912 expo-sitions, to trace where his logic nods, what are his idiosyncratic definitions and views of empirical reality, and how he entraps himself in his own rhetoric. I have not the time to do this adequately. With diffidence, I mention a few of the highlights.

First, Schumpeter glimpses the golden-rule maximizing property of the zero-interest configuration. Thus Schumpeter (1912, p. 35) observes that a person who departs from the zero-interest state ' . . . would discover in due course that he had obtained a smaller total satisfaction than he might have done.' This is at least a vague perception that $U(f[K])$ is at its maximum when K is at the K^s where $f'[K^s] = 0$. And it reflects a glimpse of the truth that $\int_0^\infty U(f[K^s] - K')dt$ is larger if $K(t) \equiv K^s$ than for any other $K(t)$ path emanating from $K(0) = K^s$.

Second, Schumpeter out-Smiths Adam Smith. He thinks that rational circular-flow competition most assuredly *achieves* the optimum glimpsed above. Only irrational 'children and primitive men', who are ignorable, will fail to be led by the invisible hand of competition to the golden-rule state. This is logically quite unwarranted, except if there is gratuitously slipped into the premises of the argument that all decision bodies live foreever and happen to perceive complete time-symmetry in their esteemings of future consumptions in 1912, 2012, and 9999 ... 912! There is no sign that the logical issues have been thought through and sorted out from the empirical plausibilities.

Third, it can be shown that, when we specify a zero interest rate, the resulting competitive-arbitrage conditions of steady-state pricing will permit the total value of society's consumption to be decomposed into the factor-returns of labour and land (the 'primary' non-reproducible inputs). Smith asserted this (and, when the interest rate is not zero, showed how the interest return on non-primary inputs must be included as a third return). Marx, worried about the infinite regress when it takes iron to produce coal and coal to produce iron, grappled with this truth over tens of thousands of words. Schumpeter blithely asserts this truth. Since Dimitriev's 1898 Russian essay, students of Leontief and Sraffa are in a position to demonstrate that it is indeed truth.

Fourth, Schumpeter erroneously thinks that the zero-interest-rate *premise* needed for the theorem's conclusion is itself a *guaranteed* property of innovationless circular-flow competition. He errs. Competitive arbitrage has no intrinsic tendency of its own to compete interest out of existence. All it does is equalize between every effort the market-sustainable interest rate. Schumpeter (1912, p. 29ff.) gratuitously asserts that *all* final values are imputed back to land rent[6] and labour wages *alone* – a truth only true on the stipulation of zero interest rate. To deduce zero interest from a syllogism

---

[6] Schumpeter on p. 166 of the 1934 English version of 1912 *The Theory of Economic Development* – my few page references will always be to this source – rejects by logic any view of Böhm that, if the interest rate is zero, the rent yield of land must evaporate: for, on an infinite base a zero yield can form a finite product: $0 \times \infty$ can equal a finite positive number. But this formality fails to meet our *empirical* rejection of infinite value for land. Our senses tell us that people do not live forever; they do buy and sell land *in the circular flow* at predictable ages and at predictable finite 'number of years' purchase'. The young Schumpeter somehow doped himself into identifying innovationless competitive equilibrium with clans that live forever!

that is valid only if you have already stipulated a zero interest rate is the height of self-deception. At best Schumpeter's comments only serve to show that there is a *self-consistency* about the golden-rule state (even though, we remind him, that is only *one of an infinity* of self-consistent steady states!).

Fifth, Schumpeter falls into the attractive fallacy of automatic synchronization that entrapped J. B. Clark, Frank Knight, and Henry George. Böhm-Bawerk's turn-of-the-century polemics against Clark had to be replicated in the 1930s by Hayek's polemics against Knight to refute this fallacy. In the steady-state circular flow, the same inputs are followed by the same outputs. An observer sees simultaneously an input and an output: ergo, he is tempted to cry blunderingly that there is no time lag between inputs and outputs and no tempting temporary gain in consumption to be had by departing from the circular flow. In truth the steady state only stays steady because people choose not to fail to do that which keeps it steady.

A Lionel Robbins is wrong to assert that a zero interest rate robs people of the incentive to stay in it: our Ramsey paradigm demonstrates that Robbins is wrong.[7] But a Robbins is right to insist that staying in a steady state does require that it continues to be the more attractive of the multiplicity of choices open to you in every new period of the process.

Sixth, Schumpeter does not reconcile his doctrine that *all* value is decomposable into land rent and labour wages with a *possible* technological case: 100 rice ripen into 110 rice in one year's time without need for any labour or scarce land. (You may say, 'Surely, land is needed, eventually if not now.' Do not say it. Let Schumpeter accept the challenge and observe what he does with the rope Böhm and we give to him.)

Schumpeter's answer might start out in terms of these words (which I put into his mouth). 'With more rice next year, the price of each grain falls. Thus, 110 then sell for the total of marks 100 now will sell for. So 100 marks today still get you 100 marks tomorrow. The rate of interest is zero *sans* innovations. Q. E. D.' Around p. 170, Schumpeter (1912) repeatedly makes the point that (*when* the interest rate is truly zero) the greater magnitude of the forest is *already* imputed back in value to the saplings: so these foreseen changes in time only conserve the already calculated value of the process. Without labour and land, zero Kuznet product is being produced and it is correctly decomposable into zero real rent and zero real wages.

---

[7]   Robbins (1930) may however be considered to have more of a point in connection with the issue of *whether a decentralized pricing mechanism can sustain the golden-rule state* with each producer's integrals of present-discounted-value being *finite*. See Samuelson (1943, 1951, 1971), Whitaker (1972), and McCrae (1947).

But this is pure self-deception. Real rice *is* being produced net. Kuznets can measure it. You can eat 10 rice every year and still not impair your circular-flow income. With land redundant and labour not needed, Kuznets measures national income of zero in terms of primary-factors' income. To this he adds permanent real interest income of 10 rice per year. No hocus-pocus of backward imputation – of forest to sapling, or rice grain to rice grain – evades the naive fact of productive interest.

Empirically, Schumpeter may deny to Böhm that there always exists positive technical productivity of capital at the margin. But *logically* he must throw in the towel: when 100 rice as input yields 110 rice output at the end of the year, *no* steady-state (real!, 'own'!) rate of interest can obtain other than 10% per year. A zero equilibrium rate becomes a contradiction (and settling down of the system to a steady state may no longer occur).

Seventh, and this will be my final point as patience ebbs, although Schumpeter correctly perceives the need to keep our thinking straight on the difference between (1) our being in a steady state, and (2) the process of getting into a steady state, Schumpeter himself often makes errors of logic in *denying that the differences between a magnitude in two adjacent alternative steady states may themselves be relevant for understanding what are the market pricings in each of these alternative steady states.* For a Leets model, the ratio $(f[K^2] - f[K^1])/(K^2 - K^1)$ involves only (alternative) steady-state magnitudes. But it has good relevance to the r^2 or the r^1 that you would measure in each such steady state! And, in the Leets model, it has considerable relevance to the optimal path of development that a socialist planner would aim for in maximizing the social utility over time of the ongoing society. One can hardly criticize a 1912 genius for occasional failures in understanding these subtleties. But respect for truth compels one to note in dissecting that genius's work wherein the pathologies originated.

Schumpeter à la Sraffa

My earlier 'leets' model of Solow-Ramsey type can help make clear the error in believing that competitive arbitrage makes it a requirement of steady-state circular flow that the profit rate be zero.

I replace continuous time by discrete time: $K(t)$ by $K_t, t = 0, 1, 2, \ldots; K'(t) = dK(t)/dt$ by $K_{t+1} - K_t$. For convenience I replace the net-product function $f[K_t]$ by the gross-product function $g[K_t] \equiv f[K_t] + K_t$. To avoid Sraffian joint products, I assume leets are used up in one use as input: we have 100 per cent depreciation and a working capital model.

Now (1) and (2b) take the form

$$C_{t+1} + K_{t+1} = g[K_t], \quad g''[K] < 0 \tag{18}$$

$$1 + r_t = \partial K_{t+1}/\partial K_t = g'[K_t], \quad g'[K^s] = 0 + 1 \tag{19}$$

In steady-state equilibrium, we have

$$(C_{t+1}, K_{t+1}, r_{t+1}) \equiv (C_t, K_t, r_t) \equiv (C, K, r) \tag{20}$$

Prices of consumption and leets are the same, P. The steady-state wage rate and rent rate are W and V. The interest rate per period is r.

The Leontief–Sraffa conditions of price equal to competitive unit costs – which could also be called the Ricardo-Dimitriev-Smith conditions – are as follows for the consumption-good sector and the leets sector:

$$PC = (WL_C + VT_C + PK_C)(1 + r) \tag{21a}$$

$$P(K_K + K_C) = (WL_K + VT_K + PK_K)(1 + r) \tag{21b}$$

where $L = L_C + L_K, T = T_C + T_K, K = K_C + K_K$. Remember that the Ramsey–Solow 'one-sector' model involves both industries with the same technique:

$$(L_C + T_C + K_C)/C \equiv (L_K, T_K, K_K)/(K_C + K_K), \quad L_C + L_K = L \tag{21c}$$

Schumpeter's pivotal error of imputation is to think that competitive arbitrate requires that $(1 + r)$ be $(1 + 0)$ in (21a) and (21b). We know better. We know that $1 + 0$ is only one of an infinity of arbitrage-proof equilibria. One must look to the behaviour equations of saving-investing, and not those of competition or to the definition of circular flow, to find conditions determining the relevant choice of $1 + r$ from the admissible set.

In Part I of Sraffa's (1960) classic, the six ratios in (21c) are taken as technically given. The unknowns of $(W/P, V/P, r)$ become determinate only if three further equations are specified from outside (21)–(23). However, here (21c)'s ratios are not exogenously prescribed, but instead are specified to satisfy the neoclassical production function:

$$K_{t+1} = G[T_t, L_t, K_t], \quad K = G[T, L, K] \tag{22a}$$

$$1 = G[T_K/K, L_K/K, K_K/K] \tag{22b}$$

No competitive steady state could survive if the technique used could be replaced by a known technique that could produce a surplus profit beyond the interest rate $1+r$. Therefore, we adjoin to (21a)–(21c) the following two marginal-productivity relations:

$$1 + r = G'[K] = \partial G[T, L, K]/\partial K \tag{21d}$$

$$W/P = (1 + r)^{-1}\partial G[T, L, K]/\partial L \tag{21e}$$

Along with these there is a third such marginal-productivity relation for land. But it is redundant, being implied by the formula for residual rent already implied in (21a)–(21e).

Schumpeter missed the discount factor $(1 + r)^{-1}$ in (21e)'s Wicksell–Taussig discounted-marginal-product relation. And in (21d)'s Jevons–Wicksell relation, Schumpeter failed to mention that $1+r$ need *not* be $1+0$. That need obtain only in the special case where K is always guaranteed to have grown to reach K^s after innovation ceases. This is a possible case, but not an inevitable one, and certainly not so probable a case as Schumpeter's quill proclaimed it to be.

We still lack in relations (18)–(22) one final relation to make steady-state r and all our variables determinate. Schumpeter, implicitly thinking of perpetual-life actors with 'neutral' subjective time preference, supplies the missing equation by having $K(t)$ accumulate to the golden-rule level of K^s. Pigou and Fisher postulated a subjective rate of time preference, ρ, that sets the asymptote for $r(t)$. Classical economists (Smith, Ricardo) similarly closed their long-run system by having $r(t)$ fall to ρ while population grows or shrinks when $W(t)/P(t)$ differs from some postulated subsistence-wage level, $\bar{W}$. Marxians, usually ignoring land as if it were redundant, get their missing equation by similarly specifying a $\bar{W}$ level at which labour supply is reproduced from the reserve army of the unemployed.

FINALE

As I re-read my words, they strike me as overly critical and insufficiently appreciative. Joseph Schumpeter will not stay dead and exalted. His memory is so vivid, his thought so lively, that one finds oneself arguing with unseemly vigour as if he were a mere mortal.

This is not the first time I felt an urge to go back and paint in more favourable brush strokes, not for the purpose of eulogizing but simply to redress the balance properly. Thus, at Mexico City I had to say explicitly that Schumpeter was anti-Hitler and anti-Nazi, because some who read my remarks about his belief that market capitalism would not prevail unless politically imposed mistakenly equated his distrust of Stalin with sympathy for Hitler. When evaluating *Capitalism, Socialism and Democracy* (1942), and finding in the end reasons to doubt Schumpeter's belief that capitalism's *success* would be its undoing, I had to state explicitly, lest I be misunderstood, that it is a great book.

Here, in closing, I must make a similar disclaimer. My failure to agree that a zero interest rate is the inevitable equilibrium when innovation does not occur, and my discussion of some limitations in Schumpeter's mathematical expertise, in no sense lessens his claim to have been one of the few most important economic theorists of the twentieth century. His fame is secure.

ACKNOWLEDGEMENT

I owe thanks to the National Science Foundation for financial aid, and to Kate Crowley and Aase Huggins for editorial assistance.

REFERENCES

Haberler, G. (1951) Schumpeter's theory of interest. In *Schumpeter: Social Scientist* (Ed.) S. Harris, Cambridge, MA: Harvard University Press.

Heertje, A. (Ed.) (1981) *Schumpeter's Vision: Capitalism, Socialism and Democracy after 40 years*. New York: Praeger.

Kaldor, N. (1960) *Essays on Economic Stability and Growth*. London: Duckworth.

Kaldor, N. (1960) *Essays on Value and Distribution*. London: Duckworth.

Kaldor, N. (1964) *Essays on Economic Policy*. 2 volumes, London: Duckworth.

Macrae, C. D. (1974) Equilibrium, efficiency, and the golden rule. *Quarterly Journal of Economics*, 88, 143–8.

Ramsey, F. (1928) A mathematical theory of savings. *Economic Journal*, 38, 543–59.

Robbins, L. (1930) On a certain ambiguity in the conception of stationary equilibrium. *Economic Journal*, 40, 194–214.

Samuelson, P. A. (1943) Dynamics, statics, and the stationary states. *Review of Economics and Statistics*, 25, Essays in Honor of Joseph Schumpeter. Reprinted (1966) in *The Collected Scientific Papers of Paul A. Samuelson*, Vol. 2. Cambridge, MA: MIT Press.

Samuelson, P. A. (1951) Schumpeter as a teacher and economic theorist. In *Joseph Schumpeter: Social Scientist* (Ed.) Harris, S. Cambridge, MA: Harvard University Press. And (1951) *Review of Economics and Statistics*, 33, 98–103. Reprinted (1966) in *The Collected Scientific Papers of Paul A. Samuelson*, Vol. , Chap. 116. Cambridge, MA: MIT Press.

Samuelson, P. A. (1979) Land and the rate of interest. In *Theory for Economic Efficiency: Essays in Honor of Abba P. Lerner* (Eds.) Greenfield, Levenson, Hamovitch and Rotwein. Cambridge, MA: MIT Press.

Schumpeter, J. A. (1908) *Das Wesen und Hauptinhalt der theoretischen Nationalökonomie (Nature and Main Content of Theoretical Economics)*. Leipzig: Verlag von Duncker und Humblot.

Schumpeter, J. A. (1912) *Theorie der wirtschaftlichen Entwicklung*. Leipzig. English translation (1934) *Theory of Economic Development, An Inquiry into Profits, Capitalism, Credit, Interest and the Business Cycle (Harvard Economic Studies,* Vol. XLVI). Cambridge, MA: Harvard University Press.

Schumpeter, J. A. (1942) *Capitalism, Socialism and Democracy.* New York: Harper & Row.

Schumpeter, J. A. (1954) *History of Economic Doctrines.* Oxford: Oxford University Press.

Solow, R. M. (1956) A contribution to the theory of economic growth. *Quarterly Journal of Economics,* 70, 65–94.

Sraffa, P. (1960) *Production of Commodities by Means of Commodities.* Cambridge: Cambridge University Press.

Whitaker, J. K. (1972) Private wealth as an obstacle to Pareto optimality. *Review of Economics and Statistics,* 39, 325–29.

D. H. Robertson (1890–1963)

"Everyone deserves justice – even Cambridge mathematicians." So wrote that eccentric genius of electricity and mathematical operators, Oliver Heaviside, with the evident implication that it would have to be meted out to them in eye-droppers. Cambridge economists, God bless them, also deserve justice; and since they cannot always be counted on to pour it on each other in buckets, it is up to us barbarians to join in the rituals.

Dennis Robertson dead? It is like having one of the fixed stars disappear. To those of my generation, Robertson was always there. In a scholarly field, age is measured not from birth but from the time of first notable publication, which explains I suppose the astonishing fact that Robertson 3was actually younger than, say Alvin Hansen, and others who came to economics after transitional detours. Robertson's notable book, *A Study of Industrial Fluctuation* (1915),[1] was written before the first war and is very nearly contemporaneous with the classic *Business Cycles* (1913)[2] of Wesley Mitchell. The book was written in good part when Robertson was but twenty-two years of age and in the third year of his economic study! Such precocity is hard to match. It reminds one again of the incredible ability of talented youth to master in a season all that the past has established, and then to push the flag forward another furlong. Galois in mathematics, Ramsey in philosophy, and Abba Lerner (who after months of part-time study at the London School was writing articles of classical stature), all belong in this same remarkable category of precociousness.

---

[1] London, P. S. King.
[2] Berkeley, University of California Press.

THE STYLE THAT IS THE MAN

Dennis Robertson is well remembered for his quotations from *Alice in Wonderland*. Robertson not only gathered harvest, he produced it. He had the rare vice of being a charming writer. He would sneak up on the unwary reader and gain his acquiescence by a siren song. The man could almost make you believe in such absurd things as cardinal utility. What others had to steal by the bludgeon of matrix calculus, he deftly purloined by the stiletto of wit.

There was, of course, one exception. (There *always* is an exception – save for special cases, such as Alfred Marshall's uncanny ability to avoid lapsing into humor.) *Banking Policy and The Price Level* (1926),[3] which many would regard as Robertson's greatest work, is almost unreadable. Professor John Williams used to be able to say without shame that he had never finished reading it, because every few years, when conscience drove him to the effort, he always got to the same page 40 at which the frailty of the flesh took over. Hoping to benefit by his example, I tried as a student to read it backward but not with greater success: at page 103 minus 40, I too conked out. If we should ever meet in the Pullman club-car an explorer who began his climb at page 40, the three of us might be able to gauge the book's greatness. Fortunately, in several books and articles, Robertson splashed us with the essence of his 1926 contribution to the subject of forced saving and lacking (long and short; direct and indirect; spontaneous and induced; applied and abortive). The book's elementary mathematics is not presented gracefully, which is a pity since Robertson can justly claim to have been an originator of the period analysis (i.e., dynamic difference equations and the qualitative analysis of market "days"), which became in the 1930's so useful a tool in the hands of Lundberg, Hicks, J. M. Clark, Metzler, and others. He also made claim – with more than an epsilon of justification – to having been an originator of the geometric progressions that Harrod, Domar, and others have made so famous in the golden age we live in.

If being English were a quantity instead of a quality, Robertson would merit a high cardinal score. First, he was the son of a clergyman headmaster. (Pigou's father was an army officer, Keynes's a don, Marshall's a cashier in the Bank of England.) Robertson proceeded to Eton and apparently belonged to that happy few of public school men who were both (1) literate enough to record memories and (2) possessed of pleasant memories to record. He

---

[3]   London, P. S. King.

went up to Trinity and remained in Cambridge virtually all his life. The time he might have spent in learning how to read Spiethoff's German writings on business cycles was better spent on the classics, at which he excelled; and his inability to understand what $e=2.718\ldots$ meant, he wore throughout his life as a badge of honor. From Robertson's writings I had always thought that he must have been among the last of Marshall's protegés, and was surprised to learn from him how few and casual his personal contacts were with the retired Marshall. Pigou, Marshall's emissary on earth, was his teacher, along with Keynes and Walter Layton. Needless to say Robertson mopped up every honor in sight, including those in amateur dramatics.

Although an ardent pacifist, when the war came Robertson signed up at once. He was awarded the Military Cross, and according to rumor, came close to receiving the Victoria Cross. The man who in his bath first said, "Eureka: there does exist something I shall call the Establishment," might well have been thinking of Dennis Robertson when inspiration struck. The only deviation from the Edwardian pattern is the fact that he was mercifully spared in battle.

BEFORE THE BREAK

And so he returned to Cambridge to live happily ever after and pick up his economic studies. There followed in the 1920's what I fancy was the happiest decade of his scholarly life: working closely with Keynes in a mutually productive relationship, Robertson formulated most of his lasting contributions to monetary theory; he also found time to make a number of worthwhile points about economic theory and international finance. Besides his 1926 monograph, he wrote the first two editions (1922, 1928) of the justly famous handbook on *Money*[4] in the Cambridge series of Keynes, and also *The Control of Industry* handbook.[5] (My own earliest introduction to economic theory came from Sir Hubert Henderson's handbook, *Supply and Demand*;[6] my earliest introduction to money from the 1928 Robertson *Money*. I often think I should have quit while I was ahead. Certainly I was well-qualified to run the Bank of England or solve minor Treasury crises.) *Economic Fragments* (1931),[7] the first of his self-selected anthologies, records the theoretical work of that period.

[4] London, Nisbet.
[5] London: Nisbet, 1923.
[6] London: Nisbet, 1922.
[7] London, P. S. King.

Biography refuses to stay on the nonfiction shelf. At about the end of the decade came Robertson's break with Keynes (or vice versa). The timing is curious. One would not have been too surprised if the revolutionary accomplishments and pretensions of the 1936 *General Theory*[8] had precipitated a rift between them: but it is hard today to imagine anyone's getting aroused over the anticlimactic 1930 *Treatise on Money*[9] – except perhaps for its digs at $MV = PQ$. Perhaps the friction between the two men was quite independent of scholarship: one really does not want to know, except as personal information illuminates scholarly issues. In any case a new note enters into Robertson's writing which was to remain until the end – a querulous note of protest over the pretensions and correctness of so-called new ideas and a somewhat repetitious defense of earlier wisdom. I do not mention this for the reason that full candor is mandatory in an obituary notice. I mention it because it is there, recognized by foe, friend and Robertson himself, and it may put readers off unduly. This Robertsonian querulousness was not, I conclude on reflection, sterile. Many of Robertson's points, had they come from within the Keynesian camp, would have been recognized as valuable contributions. One of the attributes that make the *General Theory* a great book is this uncanny ability to convert its critics (many of them, anyway) into fruitful reformulations – Pigou being a prime example.

LIFE AT THE TOP

Dennis Robertson reached the height of his fame in the mid-1930's, when he was in his mid-forties. Thus, in Haberler's first edition of *Prosperity and Depression*[10], Keynes, Pigou, Hayek and Robertson receive by far the most index references. This fame was also symbolized by Harvard's picking him out of all the world's economists to receive an honorary degree at the time of its 1936 Tercentenary Celebration. Except in one respect, the choice was an excellent one. Robertson was urbane and cultured. He gave a nice speech, in which he pointed out the difference between cycles and secular stagnation; he warned against doing too little, and warned even more against doing too much. One suspects his hosts appreciated the latter message, for those who live in Newcastle invariably love to import people whom they expect will bring them coals. As a student at Harvard in the days before Hansen, I can testify that the coals of caution concerning doing too much about

---

[8] New York, Harcourt Brace.
[9] New York, Harcourt Brace.
[10] Geneva: League of Nations, 1937.

unemployment were not scarce goods in 1936 Cambridge. In those days of 15 per cent unemployment, there was coal doled out in each class, every hour on the hour; there were coals piled up in Holyoke House, where wisdom reigned before Littauer was built.

The scandal was not with the man who was there, who had after all been invited to the party. What constituted the scandal in Cambridge, Massachusetts in the fall of 1936 was the man who was not there. The fact that every reader will know his name confirms the justness of my diagnosis, which I may add did not have to be formulated with the wisdom of hindsight.

Robertson's one departure from Cambridge took place in the late 1930's. The pull of a professorship at the London School of Economics must have been a powerful one indeed to draw so attached a Trinity don away from his familiar rooms and walks, from his beloved music and contacts with young people. Probably the push from an environment grown hostile was more powerful still.

THE EVER AFTER

The war broke out. Robertson served his government well. And after the war he returned to the Marshall chair of political economy in Cambridge.

To understand Robertson's polemical writings in this final period, one would have to understand Cambridge. And no outsider can do that. Suffice it to say that the reader of his works is merely eavesdropping on an ancient argument that only Cambridge students could witness in full. The whole spectacle does not, an outsider fears, reflect great credit on anyone. It has been acted out a hundred times in continental universities. Yet who is to say that an adversary procedure does not have a constructive role in the long-run history of a science?

Finally, in the years of his retirement, Sir Dennis again became a controversial figure in connection with the Cohen Council on Prices, Productivity and Incomes. Now the issue of personality and doctrine becomes submerged by deeper ideological and political divergences. Will a slow-growing, somewhat open, economy like the United Kingdom benefit from contractionary restraint on aggregate demand so as to engineer (at least temporarily) enough labor and capacity slack to moderate the upward trend of wage and entrepreneurial costs? While it is hard to judge wherein lies the proper balance between expansionary and restrictionist policies, it is easy to guess how an economist with Robertson's background and lifetime writings would react to such an issue. Had he not been one who insisted from the beginning that much of the business cycle was an inevitable and even a good thing? Had he not through thick and thin favored a policy of having the price level decline as technical productivity rises? Had he not always warned against "forced saving?" Against doing too much? Against a belief in the complete impotence of orthodox monetary policy (and also against a belief in its omnipotence)? It was inevitable that he should have come out strongly for restrictionism. And inevitable that he should have been criticized bitterly for doing so. I say this while eschewing all judgment on the merits or demerits of his case. Suffice it to say that there are many, in his country and mine, who argue that the only cure for a bad Phillips Curve (implying upward price drift before near-to-full employment) is a deliberate investment by the community in temporary deflation. Once again, for good or ill, Dennis Robertson had been a leader in formulating a key economic issue.

SOME ROBERTSONIAN CONTRIBUTIONS

Turning away from matters of personality, I should like to mention a few of Dennis Robertson's lasting contributions to economics.

1. *Exogenous investment as an important source of fluctuations.* In *A Study of Industrial Fluctuation* Robertson cultivated a field too much neglected in the Anglo-Saxon literature. At a time when monetary theories of the Hawtrey type were challenged only by Pigou's emphasis on cumulative psychological factors, Robertson did well to emphasize real factors in the business cycle, such as innovation and capital intensity. On the continent, where Spiethoff, Schumpeter, and Cassel were stressing such factors, his contribution would perhaps not have had so much *Grenznutzen*. Time permits us to filter out Robertson's overemphasis on factors such as agriculture, which experience shows has no simple relationship to business cycles.

All his life Robertson was predisposed to regard fluctuations in activity as in some important degree desirable, a view which I cannot think subsequent experience has fully endorsed. On the other hand, this same stubborn insistence kept Robertson from being the darling of the libertarians: they never liked his skepticism, as expressed to the Macmillan Committee and elsewhere, that monetary policy could succeed in curing a slump; nor would most of them approve of his early emphasis, long before the *General Theory*, on fiscal policy as a partial substitute for the inadequacies of Hawtreyan monetary policy.

2. *Overinvestment aspects of a turn-down.* While never stooping to Hayekian extremes, Robertson always cherished the belief that there is in some sense "a shortage of saving" associated with the underinvestment that leads to a cycle down turn. I am not the one to do this notion justice, having lived in a generation taught every nonsensical variant of what remains a fairly incoherent and mystical doctrine. Certainly it is true that in many expansion periods, prices rise and the labor market gets tight; capital formation takes place under the influence of animal spirits and the profits associated with boom; interest rates tighten naturally and central banks can be counted on to countenance and encourage this tightening. Such a boom may have to run ever faster to stand still. Profits begin to erode as capital accumulates and mistakes become apparent. Like a tulip mania or a stock market bubble, the process lives on its own acceleration: the bubble, for reasons no one has ever been able to codify, will eventually prick itself. Or we can prick it. Or we can feed it some of the things it needs to keep going a little longer. But not all the angles in heaven know how to stretch out this kind of expansion indefinitely. Now let the financial and real bubble burst. If quick compensatory action is taken that is strong enough to resuscitate the mania, we are still on the tiger-ride that cannot last. How long then should we wait before preventing the recession that follows from snowballing into a secondary depression? These are real problems in a subset of upswings, but in what degree do they vindicate an overinvestment-undersaving theory of the peak? An increase in consumption expenditure would seem the least controversial policy in such an early recession; this Robertson perceived in his gentle renunciation of Hayekian deflationism, which Lionel Robbins had marshalled all his talents of persuasion to advocate in *The Great Depression* (1934).[11]

3. *The synthesizer and critic.* Although Robertson once referred to his "natural indolence" as the cause for not having written large tomes, he was in fact a hard and meticulous worker all his life.[12] Here is but one example. At sixty he read through one of my less appetizing articles, and wrote, "Do you not, on page 10, want to add 'not' in the sentence on line 3?" Like Oscar

---

[11] New York, Macmillan.

[12] Aside from the books already mentioned, the following collections of essays and lectures testify to his industry: *Economic Essays and Addresses* (with A. C. Pigou) (London: P. S. King, 1931); *Essays in Monetary Theory* (London, P. S. King, 1940); *Utility and All That* (New York: Macmillan, 1952); *Britain in the World Economy* (London: Allen and Unwin, 1954); *Economic Commentaries* (London: Staples Press, 1956); *Lectures on Economic Principles* (London: Staples Press, 1957–59); *Growth, Wages, Money; The Marshall Lectures for 1960* (London: Cambridge University Press, 1961).

Wilde, who spent all morning putting in a comma and all afternoon taking it out, I passed a morning deciding that Robertson was right and an afternoon in wondering whether he had been.

He embodied the results of his reading in periodic surveys of monetary theory, the interest rate, price theory of the firm, utility and all such. These served a purpose and met a need, one must admit even while disagreeing with some of his formulations. In rereading Robertson's many collections of essays, I felt anew what a shame it was that his many criticisms of Keynesian writings from 1936 to the mid-1950's had not come from *within* that tradition.

Thus, he rightly pointed out that the equality of saving and investment was by many early Keynesians treated simultaneously as (i) an identity and (ii) as an equality achieved by movement of income to an equilibrium level. And he was also right in asserting that neither (a) $S \equiv I$, nor (b) the fact that investment-induced income increments will "generate" extra saving, can ensure against price inflation. He was right in questioning Keynes's insistence that the multiplier held instantaneously, and (with Haberler) in pointing out the tautological nature of the identity $\Delta Y / \Delta I \equiv 1/(1 - \Delta C / \Delta Y)$, derived from $\Delta Y \equiv \Delta C + \Delta I$ or $Y \equiv C + I$. (But I fear he was wrong in suggesting that the world could be the same after Richard Kahn's 1931 multiplier article, that no useful empirical hypothesis could be made about $\partial C / \partial Y$ and the shifts in schedules of C as a function of Y, and that the doctrine of forced saving was not in need of careful qualification in a world of considerable unemployment. When Robertson later referred to Hicks's *Trade Cycle*[13] as a brilliant book, he was thereby conceding that the *General Theory* was a classic.)

Particular credit should be given to Robertson for his fruitful contributions to the post-1936 discussion of interest rates. He often made better Keynesian sense – and good sense – than did some of the writings by those labeled with the epithet Keynesian.

4. *Inequality of investment and lagged Robertsonian saving.* The resistance to Keynes's 1936 definitions of saving and investment as equivalent was given temporary appeasement by Robertson's supplying more dynamic definitions. This led to schizophrenia of the type reported by my colleague, Professor Ralph E. Freeman. "From ten to eleven I teach the equality of saving and investment from an elementary text, and have barely ten minutes between classes to adjust myself to teach their Robertsonian inequality from a money-and-banking text." (Actually, most desires for a neo-Wicksellian

[13] Oxford: Clarendon Press, 1950.

inequality of saving and investment were not correctly met by the special Robertsonian period definitions.) Robertson himself never conceded to Hawtrey and Keynes that he was merely uttering a tautology in asserting that income will rise (or fall) when observed investment exceeds (or runs short of) Robertsonian saving, which is defined as the difference between last period's income and this period's consumption. Yet $S_t \equiv Y_{t-1} - C_t$, $I_t \equiv Y_t - C_t$, does *tautologically* imply $Y_t - Y_{t-1} \equiv I_t - S_t$, with no refutable causation being necessarily implied. Robertson never seems to have realized the difference between such a tautology and the dynamic causal sequence involving an hypothesized consumption function $c(Y_{t-1})$, $Y_t \equiv C_t + I_t = c(Y_{t-1}) + I_t$. This last has the testable hypothesis $C_t = c(Y_{t-1})$; it also displays the test criterion for income change $Y_t - Y_{t-1} = I_t - [Y_{t-1} - c(Y_{t-1})] = I_t - [s(Y_{t-1})]$, where the expression in brackets is now Robertsonian saving, $s(Y_{t-1})$, a specific hypothesized *behavior equation* – e.g., with the refutable property $0 < ds(Y_{t-1})/dY_{t-1} < 1$. The above is a particular dynamic model, one actually given earlier by J. M. Clark in *The Economics of Planning Public Works* (1935);[14] Erik Lundberg, Lloyd Metzler, Richard Goodwin and many others showed it to be but one model; the criticism of so simple a model, made by Arthur F. Burns, in his well-read piece, "The Keynesian Thinking of Our Times," could itself be rewritten, without change in substance, so as to appear from within the Keynesian schools as a constructive criticism of the inadequacy of ultra simple models and the need for even more post-1936 elaboration.

5. *Eclectic insights.* When Robertson argued in effect, that a speculative demand for money would (i) arise merely from a willingness to pay a premium to hold safe cash in preference to risk-containing assets, and (ii) all this independently of any one-sided expectation that interest rates would soon harden and produce capital losses, he may have thought he was being anti-Keynesian. And so may some Keynesians of the late 1930's. History knows better. This is actually a superior statement of Keynesian liquidity preference.

A different case is provided in his disagreement with the view of someone like Joan Robinson, that an increase in thriftiness will lower interest, r, through its reducing income, Y. He argued that it could, even with unchanged total money M, lower interest directly. Now it is easy to imagine a man on his way to buy bread stopping at the broker's office and bidding down the yield on bonds. Hurrah for Marshall. But what happens to the

[14] Washington, Government Printing Office.

bread piled up on bakers' shelves? To the former bondholder now with cash to invest? It was characteristic of Robertson that he resisted setting up a definite and *determinate macroeconomic system* either of dynamic or static type. The simplest Keynes system $Y - c(Y) \equiv s(Y) = I(r)$, $r = L(M, Y)$ may not be realistic in transitional states (nor better than a crude approximation to stationary equilibrium). But you can look at it, examine its deficiencies, even bomb it. What hostages has Robertson given to fortune – i.e., to testable science? Actually, in the absence of the Pigou effect – which, to my surprise, I have not been able to isolate in all the Robertson pre-1940 literature – Robertson too will come in the end to the conclusion that a lowering of the $c(Y)$ relationship will reduce income. When people save more, income will fall unless there is an easing of interest rate and credit great enough to expand investment in full compensation. Does Robertson really want $r = L(M, Y)$ to be replaced by $r = L(M, Y, s(Y))$ in the steady state, which can certainly be done easily if the facts call for such an alteration of the Keynesian building blocks? Again, when we are reminded that Marshall pointed out how an easing of interest rates *now* may sometimes trigger off a boom that will raise it *later*, are we to conclude that this is an exception to the proposition that creation of more M tends to depress r? If so, a drink now could tend to send me to church tomorrow.

6. *The transfer problem.* To illustrate Robertson's versatility, he and Pigou seem to have been the first to realize that when Germany pays reparation to England, the Marshallian offer curves of *both* countries shift. In simplified modern terms, he is suggesting that the endowment point in an Edgeworth-Meade box diagram be moved northeast to the benefit of the receiver and the detriment of the payer. In 1932 Pigou gave his all-but-definitive treatment of the transfer problem under barter conditions and in 1952–54 I brought to completion the Robertson-Pigou resolution of the issues debated by Keynes, Ohlin, Taussig, Viner, and earlier writers.[15] Robertson supported the ortho-dox view that the payer's terms-of-trade would deteriorate by claiming that a country has a greater income elasticity for its own-produced goods than for its imported goods. I showed subsequently that, in the absence of all trans-port costs and tariff impediments, this is an inadmissible hypothesis and no presumption about terms-of-trade are possible; and that, in the presence of such "frictions," all presumptions become very complicated indeed.

7. *Those four crucial fractions.* Once discussing the waves of fashion in economics – such things as the period of production, elasticity of

---

[15] Essentially this last paper was submitted by name for publication in early 1937 but rejected.

substitution, the twenty-six ways of measuring consumer's surplus, the Ricardo effect, and other 365 – day wonders that sweep and resweep our science – I jokingly said to Robertson: "I don't suppose that even *you* remember your four crucial fractions." I was wrong. He took them very seriously up until the end, as I have been reminded in rereading his lifework: Robertson thought that the great depression and other basic trends might be related to a nonequilibrium development of *the desire of the public to hold in bank money exactly as much as would be consistent with the fraction of circulating capital that the banks would need and be willing to finance in business loans!*

This analysis has two claims to historical interest. First, Robertson was able to point out in his 1953 Harvard-Princeton paper, "Thoughts on Meeting Some Important Persons,"[16] that this 1926 strain of analysis has some valid claims to have foreshadowed the Harrod-Domar type of equilibria.

Second, Robertson used his model to refute the ancient, but endemic, "real-bills" doctrine, which alleges that so long as money elastically expands and contracts in response to the desires of manufacturers and merchants for "sound, productive loans," money will manage itself in an optimal manner. This old notion underlay one of the important quarrels between the Banking School and Currency School more than a century ago, between the Qualitative and Quantitative theories of credit debated at Columbia thirty years ago, and it represented a faulty premise underlying our original Federal Reserve System of 1913.[17]

Robertson believed that his was a sufficient (and necessary) vindication of orthodox economic tradition, going back at least to Henry Thornton (1803), against its Banking School and practical-man critics. According to Robertson's exposition, it would be practically a miracle if *the velocity of turnover of money* were to be geared just properly with what might be called the (velocity of) *turnover of the average item of circulating capital,* so as to lead to price stability under laissez-faire banking. A summary, and appraisal, of his view seems long overdue. I use his notation for the most part.

First, simplify Robertson and assume all capital goods are circulating capital or goods-in-process, C. Let annual income be R. Then the now-familiar capital output is a crucial fraction C/R. (These variables can be

---

[16] This *Journal*, LXVIII (May 1954); reprinted in *Economic Commentaries, op. cit.*
[17] See Lloyd Mints, *A History of Banking Theory in Great Britain and the United States* (Chicago: University of Chicago Press, 1945).

measured in real or deflated terms; or, on the admissible simplifying assumption that the same price level, P, applies to all goods, we find PC/PR gives exactly the same ratio. Usually the capital output ratio is measured in calendar years and exceeds unity rather than being a fraction; but Robertson was thinking only of circulating capital, and in any case we can call 2.5 an honorary fraction.)

Second, simplify Robertson and assume *all* capital assets are financed by bank intermediaries and not by firms or families directly. Bank loans finance all capital assets. (Firm's assets of goods-in-process are matched by their loan liabilities. Banks' assets of loans receivable are matched by their deposit liabilities. Families have as assets their checkable bank deposits, which are matched by their net worth.)

Third, all money is bank-deposit money, M. By good Marshall-Fisher reasoning the average stock of money people will (want to) hold is a crucial fraction K, which is, of course, the reciprocal of the velocity of circulation of money and is measured in fractions of a year.

In this trivial system, since balance sheets must balance and by hypothesis all capital assets are bank financed, the total of money, M, equals the total value of capital, PC (or just C if Robertson assumes the price level is at its base of unity). By school algebra, we can write the equations

$$M \equiv PC$$

$$M \equiv \{K\}(PR) \quad PC \equiv \left\{\frac{PC}{PR}\right\}PR$$

$$\therefore \{K\} \equiv \left\{\frac{PC}{PR}\right\}.$$

These are Robertson's *two* crucial fractions – two and not four because I have assumed that banks lend *only* on circulating capital and that circulating capital is financed *only* by the banks.

If I understand Robertson (a simplifying supposition), he believes the left side and the right side are quite independent of each other in causation and motivation: K is determined by institutional spending habits – how often we get paid, how near we are to a bank, and all the Fisher-Marshall considerations that determine the income velocity of circulation of M. On the other hand, the capital output ratio is a quasi-technical constant changing only if innovation or something else raises or lowers the average period of production. We have two quasi-constants which must (i) "instantaneously" always be equal or (ii) must "end up in equilibrium" equal. Will they? Won't they? Must they? If they don't – or if they try not to – what will follow from this "contradiction?"

All this is very non-neoclassical. It is very non-Robertsonish. Politics aside, it is like the 1936 Keynes and unlike the 1820 Say or James Mill. It is even like Marx with his everlasting contradictions. It is like Balogh or others who think that a dollar shortage (or glut) is not, of itself, an absurd notion. Since Robertson has commented on Lerner, Kalecki, Robinson, Kahn and others concerning Keynesian identities and behavior equations, their comments on his exposition would seem in season.

As I have written his system, it cannot even be used to controvert the "real bills" doctrine. For suppose producers became optimistic and asked for more loans, and thereby expanded M, say doubling it. Then if prices were to double, the identity of bank loans and firm's capital goods will persist; hence we seem to have no protection against over-issue of M even when the two crucial fractions are always equal. And, cannot the same equality hold in transitions when we have positive dM/dt and not necessarily matching changes in R, or in PR, or for that matter in P itself?

One suspects that Robertson sometimes wants to regard the left- and right-hand sides of the identity as "intended" or "*ex ante*" or "sustainable" or "scheduled" magnitudes, and to let their difference $\left[\{K\} - \left\{ \frac{PC}{PR} \right\} \right]$ act as some kind of an "error-signal" in making *something* change. If so, and if that "something" is the price level P, do we have a Wicksell-like theory of secular price change? Or is the adjustment taking place in real output R, so that we have a theory of the great depression? Suppose we do adopt this general kind of interpretation, say for P, and write out

$$ -\frac{dP}{dt} \text{ is proportional to } \left[\{K\} - \left\{ \frac{PC}{PR} \right\} \right] $$

does our "inflationary gap" finally "close itself" by virtue of the fact that the right-hand quasi-constants are to be regarded as gradually melting into adjusting functions of the price level? (I must interject the query: "Why in the world should a *balanced* higher-level of prices change spending habits or technical periods of production?")

But one must not brow-beat Robertson for my simplified version of his model. Let's see whether his two other crucial fractions clarify the difficulties.

In real life a fraction of all firms' capital may be financed and owned directly by families: let $1-b$ be that fraction, with $b(PC)$ being the amount of circulating capital actually financed by bank loans.

In real life, some of bank assets will go for other purposes than circulating capital (e.g., government securities, durable-goods financed by term-loans or even by renewable 90-day promissory notes, it being understood that such capital goods are to be designated by a letter different from C). So, to bring in the last of the four crucial fractions, let $aM = a(KPR)$ be the fraction of total bank assets or liabilities that are used for circulating capital financing.

Now our simple algebra turns what was a two-fraction equivalence into a four-fraction equivalence

$$aM \equiv b(PC)$$

$$aK(PR) \equiv b\frac{PC}{PR}PR$$

$$\boxed{\{a\}\{K\} \equiv \{b\}\left\{\frac{PC}{PR}\right\}}$$

Here then are Robertson's four crucial fractions of *Money*.[18]

Is the Robertson Equivalence a balance sheet identity? A definitional identity by virtue of definitions of a and b? Are the two sides quasi-constants, determined by quite different motivational and institutional forces? Are all four fractions such independent quasi-constants? Is some kind of an *ex ante* discrepancy $|aK - b\frac{PC}{PR}|$ conceivable; and is its intended-sustainable magnitude a function of some economic variables like P or R or short-term interest rate or differential 'twixt short- and long-term interest rate? Is the mere fact that a/b is not unity Robertson's principal weapon in refuting the erroneous real-bill doctrine; and, if so, did he on reflection, stand by such an argument? I wish someone had asked Robertson these and other questions.

How a man uses a concept often throws light on what he thinks he means by it. Robertson at times seems to have had in mind something like the following application. In the 1920's the capital output ratio was perhaps shrinking for technical reasons as firms seemed to require less inventories for the same sales. So banks, the principal source of finance for inventories, might begin to have trouble in finding enough loan outlets to keep the community's supply of (checkable) M growing at, say, the 1 per cent rate needed to balance population growth and the resulting output growth. This

---

[18] 1928 and 1948 editions, pp. 105–7, 182. There is the trivial difference that I have written the last one as the now familiar capital/output ratio rather than in his symbolism $\frac{1}{2}D$, D being the Jevons-Wicksell range of the period of production.

might put undue downward pressure on the price level and lead to deflationary conditions of a slump.

Coming from a commentator writing in 1928 or 1930, this train of thought makes some logical sense and would appear to have some measure of empirical importance. But can one honestly say much more for it? If a and b and K do not spontaneously match the change in the capital output ratio, why wouldn't banks threatened with excess reserves underbid direct financers of circulating capital and increase b by changing their interest and availability requirements? Why wouldn't banks lower their a by making term-loans? (Robertson could claim to have foreseen this trend by his theory, and to have warned against the institutional and legal lags.) Why not help banks lower their a by providing them with government securities to hold? For a capitalistic system to let itself suffer from a fatal Robertsonian contradiction because it is unwilling to use such traditional methods of public debt management would seem laughable in 1963, and paradoxical even in 1928.

I owe it to Robertson's memory to try to interpret his crucial fractions. But I am not sure I have succeeded in doing so correctly.

8. *Should prices fall with progress?* It was long a matter of debate whether the growth in real output due to technical progress and population should result in (i) stable prices, (ii) falling prices, or (iii) rising prices. Implied in each of these patterns is a corresponding trend in money wage rates.

It is not always clear just what the terms of the debate are. Is the issue purely a *normative* one, with all the widows and *rentiers* naturally favoring a falling price level in opposition to the interests of equity speculators and active entrepreneurs or workers? Indeed if only self-interest is involved why shouldn't an advocate for pensioners advocate a fall in prices much *greater* than the technical cheapening of production? Usually as the issue has been debated, something more than *self-interest* is involved: According to reasonable ethical welfare functions, which price trend is fairer, *more equitable*? Finally, to bring the issue still more within the area of nonsubjective analysis, there is near the surface a feeling that one or another of these patterns is more "natural," in the quasi-objective sense of giving rise to less difficulties, distortions, and dead-weight loss. These are all very slippery notions and it does not help a great deal to repose the problem in terms of which pattern is "more neutral," in the sense of duplicating more closely the putative (optimal?) pattern that would be achieved in a hypothetical world of perfect barter where money could not "distort" things.

From an early date, Dennis Robertson favored a pattern of steady money wages, with the fruits of progress going "even-handedly" to all consumers through a steady fall in the price level. He considered such writers as Haberler, Hayek, and Lord Robbins as his allies, in opposition to the plain man who thought stable prices natural and such pre-Keynesians as Hume and Harrod; and Robertson certainly disagreed with more recent writers, like the late Sumner Slichter, who believed gently-rising prices to be the optimal feasible. In what was probably Robertson's last economic writing, his excellent *Memorandum Submitted to the Canadian Royal Commission on Banking and Finance* on July 28, 1962[19], he reiterated his scientific view of the matter. While agreeing that political expediency might make stable prices a necessary compromise, he stated that the "more scientific view" called for falling prices, quoting with approval a letter to the *Times* of January 11, 1962 by the Archbishop of Wales:

To a simple fellow like myself it seems that the lower prices which increased productivity makes possible would benefit everybody, but I recognize that there must be a flaw in my thinking, for increased productivity has not brought – and does not seem likely to bring – lower prices. Presumably there is good reason for this. Will someone explain?

"Nobody did," Robertson added dryly.

In my own *Memorandum Submitted to the Canadian Royal Commission on Banking and Finance* of October 19, 1962, I took mild issue with Robertson's statement on scientific grounds and I refer the specialist to my rebuttal. The problem is important enough to merit discussion here.

To sum up my Canadian testimony on this point, I argued that a steady foreseeable trend of productivity accompanied by any one of the three patterns of price trend would, as long as the price trend was itself steady, foreseeable and foreseen, result in essentially the same real division of product between labor wages and interest returns to property. Employing good classical Thornton-Marshall-Wicksell-Fisher-Sraffa-Keynes reasoning, the equilibrium money rate of interest r_m would equal the real-natural-own rates of interest r_q plus an algebraic built-in factor $(dP/P)/dt$. E.g.,

$$.06 = r_q = r_m - \frac{dP/P}{dt} = .06 - 0 = .09 - .03 = .02 - (-.04),$$

giving essentially the same 6 per cent interest on profit returns in real terms, under steady, rising and falling price trends. In my idealized model, only once-and-for-all unforeseen inflation achieves appreciable real effects. Reason tells us this. Hume realized it. When Professor Earl Hamilton and

---

[19] Now available in the Princeton series *Essays in International Finance*, No. **42, May 1963**.

others produced contrary evidence for the price revolution of post-Columbus centuries, this seemed odd; but reason cannot quarrel with bullets and facts. Yet cross-sectional experience with chronic inflations in underdeveloped and other lands gives much corroboration to my theory. And now, I believe, further historical research is at least somewhat negating Professor Hamilton's provisional hypotheses. I have before me the report of a large insurance company which earns more than 5 per cent on its new investments: I have no doubt that, if Robertsonian policy pushed the consumer's price index steadily downward by 2 per cent per annum, that company's annuitants would not be earning their current 5 per cent. Actually, if we now agree to bring in practical nonidealized considerations, my strong thesis will have to be qualified: but most economists will think these new elements of expediency will tell more against Robertson's "scientific" claim for falling prices than against his antagonists' claim.

To be specific consider[20] a Model T Solow system (where technical change does not have to be "embodied" in qualitatively new capital equipment). In this miracle country, equidistant from Germany, Japan and France but alas farther away from the United States and United Kingdom, labor grows at 1 per cent per year; versatile physical capital grows at 5 per cent; technical progress proceeds at 3 per cent per annum. The time-dependent production function was measured by Solow to be of the following Cobb-Douglas form

$$Q = e^{.03t} L^{3/4} C^{1/4}, L(t) = e^{.01t}, C(t) = e^{.05t}$$
$$= e^{.03t} e^{.01t\,3/4} e^{.05t\,1/4} = e^{.05t}.$$

Thus, total output grows at 5 per cent in all; and because of the constant-relative-shares property of the Cobb-Douglas function, so must total wages and total interest (or profit). Since labor numbers grow at 1 per cent, the per capita real wage grows at 4 per cent; since total capital grows at 5 per cent, the interest rate (or the net rent per unit of capital good) remains constant. Although Kaldor would consider this country unrealistic, it would portray his stylized features of capitalism: constant capital output ratio, constant relative shares, constant profit rate, and even a constant saving income ratio. If we wickedly gave one of his students the data of the country without giving him its name, he could be forgiven for thinking that Kaldorism would "explain" its properties, although we sadists know better.

---

[20] The remainder of this section may be skipped.

Now Robertson, if I understand him, would not insist on the price level's dropping by 5 per cent. In his Quantity Equation, $M = KPQ$, he would want M to grow at least as fast as the population increase, or by 1 per cent per year. Prices should then fall by $5 - 1 = 4$ per cent per year; as a check, note that this would indeed correspond to a constant money wage rate and a rising real wage rate of 4 per cent per annum attained through lower prices of goods. Also, the money price of machines is falling at 4 per cent per annum, and the money rate of interest is 4 per cent less than the real rate of interest, since capitalists can also buy all goods 4 per cent more cheaply each year. While people, or at least Archbishops, take it for granted that the 3 per cent fruits of technical progress – which are sent, so to speak, freely from heaven – should be splashed indiscriminately on all consumers (including workers, capitalists and consumers of capital formation), Robertson does not tell us why the fruits of deepening of capital, from a rising C/L ratio, should be splashed in this indiscriminate way.

Actually in such a crude or refined neoclassical model, any growth pattern for prices – such as $P(t) = e^{.03t}$ à la Slichter, or $e^{.0t}$ à la the plain man, or $e^{-.04t}$ à la Robertson[21] – is optimal provided only that the wage rate and other pecuniary parameters are at the appropriate levels – $w(t) = e^{-.03t}e^{.04t}$ or $e^{.0t}e^{.04t}$ or $e^{-.04t}e^{.04t}$, respectively.

After returning from Ottawa, I noted one flaw in my own argument of price-trend neutrality. If the M used as a medium of exchange bears no interest – a monstrous assumption in an idealized model and, as our banks now are learning in an era when Treasury bills give yields of more than $2\frac{1}{2}$ per cent – the cash-to-income ratio K will be greatest (least) if prices are falling (rising). This is because the opportunity cost of holding sterile money for transaction purposes is greatest when prices are rising and the *money* rate of interest, r_m, is highest. Why impose this (minor) deadweight loss on mankind?[22] This does seem a small point in Robertson's favor; but it does also raise a nice question concerning Pareto-optimality of laissez-faire. Do we have here a case of the fallacy of composition, where each man cuts down on his cash balance because of the extra interest income he can get by so

---

[21] If money is storable, it is hard to see how the money rate of interest can be made negative: so a price decline exceeding in absolute value the real rate of interest would be impossible to achieve, meaning that in all cases where $r_q < |-.04|$, as is quite possible, Robertson's scientific pattern will be simply unachievable. Pathology illuminates normalcy!

[22] I have benefited from talk on this point with Professor Edmund Phelps, who was at M.I.T. in exile from Yale last year. See also Harry G. Johnson, "Equilibrium under Fixed Exchanges," *American Economic Review* LII (May 1963), 113; Robert Mundell, "Inflation And Real Interest," *Journal of Political Economy*, LXXI (June 1963), 280–83.

economizing? But when all persons act in this self-serving way, does society really economize on anything real or does it simply end up with a higher nominal price level? To appreciate the point about Pareto-optimality, suppose by collusive agreement we all hold *on the average* twice the cash balance dictated by *ceteris paribus* selfish maximizing. Then we save shoe leather on trips to the broker or savings banker. Doesn't *everybody* end up better off, with less deadweight loss?

* * * *

In leaving this problem of the optimal trend of the price level, I have to warn that I have been discussing it in abstract terms. Realistically, there is much to be said for pay-as-you-go social security, constant-purchasing-power bonds to be made available to the public in limited amounts for various long-term saving purposes, and other devices to compensate the aged who have been irreversibly hurt by wartime or other inflation. Such escalation need not be of a magnitude to make inflation appreciably greater or more explosive.

CONCLUSION

Among the Iroquois it was the custom to do the newly dead more than justice, indicting them so to speak for the offense of virtue and leaving for a later tribunal judgment on the charge. I fear I have done Dennis Robertson less than justice. And perhaps it could not be otherwise, coming from one near to incorporating in himself all that Robertson deplored in modern economics: an addict of mathematics and neat models, a debunker of Alfred Marshall (not in the manner of economists like Joan Robinson who regard him as the best of a bad neoclassical lot, but as one of the new barbarians who deem him third to Walras and Wicksell), a zealot for full employment and critic of inequality, Robertson's friend and yet even more the friend of his antagonists – in short a silly-clever economist at an age when one should know better.

Let my tribute to him stand, then, as an underestimate.

PART IX

REVOLUTIONS IN TWENTIETH-CENTURY ECONOMICS

Lord Keynes and the General Theory

THE death of Lord Keynes will undoubtedly afford the occasion for numerous attempts to appraise the character of the man and his contribution to economic thought. The personal details of his life and antecedents will very properly receive extensive notice elsewhere.

It is perhaps not too soon to venture upon a brief and tentative appraisal of Keynes's lasting impact upon the development of modern economic analysis. And it is all the more fitting to do so now that his major work has just completed the first decade of its very long life.

THE IMPACT OF THE GENERAL THEORY

I have always considered it a priceless advantage to have been born as an economist prior to 1936 and to have received a thorough grounding in classical economics. It is quite impossible for modern students to realize the full effect of what has been advisably called "The Keynesian Revolution"[1] upon those of us brought up in the orthodox tradition. What beginners today often regard as trite and obvious was to us puzzling, novel, and heretical.

To have been born as an economist before 1936 was a boon – yes. But not to have been born too long before!

"Bliss was it in that dawn to be alive,
But to be young was very heaven!"

---

[1] I owe much in what follows to discussions with my former student, Dr. Lawrence R. Klein, whose rewarding study shortly to be published by The Macmillan Company bears the above title.

The *General Theory* caught most economists under the age of 35 with the unexpected virulence of a disease first attacking and decimating an isolated tribe of South Sea islanders. Economists beyond 50 turned out to be quite immune to the ailment. With time, most economists in-between began to run the fever, often without knowing or admitting their condition.

I must confess that my own first reaction to the *General Theory* was not all like that of Keats on first looking into Chapman's Homer. No silent watcher, I, upon a peak in Darien. My rebellion against its pretensions would have been complete except for an uneasy realization that I did not at all understand what it was about. And I think I am giving away no secrets when I solemnly aver – upon the basis of vivid personal recollection – that no one else in Cambridge, Massachusetts, really knew what it was about for some 12 to 18 months after its publication. Indeed, until the appearance of the mathematical models of Meade, Lange, Hicks, and Harrod there is reason to believe that Keynes himself did not truly understand his own analysis.

Fashion always plays an important role in economic science; new concepts become the *mode* and then are *passè*. A cynic might even be tempted to speculate as to whether academic discussion is itself equilibrating: whether assertion, reply, and rejoinder do not represent an oscillating divergent series, in which – to quote Frank Knight's characterization of sociology – "bad talk drives out good."

In this case, gradually and against heavy resistance, the realization grew that the new analysis of *effective demand* associated with the *General Theory* was not to prove such a passing fad, that here indeed was part of "the wave of the future." This impression was confirmed by the rapidity with which English economists, other than those at Cambridge, took up the new Gospel: e.g., Harrod, Meade, and others at Oxford; and still more surprisingly, the young blades at the *London School* like Kaldor, Lerner, and Hicks, who threw off their Hayekian garments and joined in the swim.

In this country it was pretty much the same story. Obviously, exactly the same words cannot be used to describe the analysis of income determination of, say, Lange, Hart, Harris, Ellis, Hansen, Bissell, Haberler, Slichter, J. M. Clark, or myself. And yet the Keynesian taint is unmistakably there upon every one of us. (I hasten to add – as who does not? – that I am not myself a Keynesian, although some of my best friends are.)

Instead of burning out like a fad, today ten years after its birth the *General Theory* is still gaining adherents and appears to be in business to stay. Many economists who are most vehement in criticism of the specific Keynesian policies – which must always be carefully distinguished from the scientific analysis associated with his name – will never again be the same after passing through his hands.[2]

It has been wisely said that only in terms of a modern theory of effective demand can one understand and defend the so-called "classical" theory of unemployment. It is perhaps not without additional significance in appraising the long-run prospects of the Keynesian theories that no individual who has once embraced the modern analysis has – as far as I am aware – later returned to the older theories. And in universities where graduate students are exposed to the old and new income analysis, I am told that it is often only too clear which way the wind blows.

Finally, and perhaps most important from the long-run standpoint, the Keynesian analysis has begun to filter down into the elementary textbooks; and as everybody knows once an idea gets into these, however bad it may be, it becomes practically immortal.

THE GENERAL THEORY ITSELF

Thus far, I have been discussing the new doctrines without regard to their content or merits, as if they were a religion and nothing else. True, we find a Gospel, Scriptures, a Prophet, Disciples, Apostles, Epigoni, and even a Duality; and if there is no Apostolic Succession, there is at least an Apostolic Benediction. But by now the joke has worn thin, and is in any case irrelevant.

The modern saving-investment theory of income determination did not directly displace the old latent belief in Say's Law of Markets (according to which only "frictions" could give rise to unemployment and overproduction). Events of the years following 1929 destroyed the previous economic synthesis. The economists' belief in the orthodox synthesis was not overthrown, but had simply atrophied: it was not as though one's soul had faced a showdown as to the existence of the Deity and that faith was unthroned, or even that one had awakened in the morning to find that belief had flown away in the night; rather it was realized with a sense of belated recognition that one no longer had faith, that one had been living without faith for a long time, and that what after all was the difference?

The nature of the world did not suddenly change one black October day in 1929 so that a new theory became mandatory. Even in their day, the older

---

[2] For a striking example of the effect of the Keynesian analysis upon a great classical thinker, compare the fructiferous recent writings of Professor Pigou with his earlier *Theory of Unemployment*.

theories were incomplete and inadequate: in 1815, in 1844, 1893, and 1920. I venture to believe that the 18th and 19th centuries take on a new aspect when looked back upon from the modern perspective; that a new dimension has been added to the rereading of the Mercantilists, Thornton, Malthus, Ricardo, Tooke, David Wells, Marshall, and Wicksell.

Of course, the Great Depression of the Thirties was not the first to reveal the untenability of the classical synthesis. The classical philosophy always had its ups and downs along with the great swings of business activity. Each time it had come back. But now for the first time, it was confronted by a competing system – a well-reasoned body of thought containing among other things as many equations as unknowns. In short, like itself, a synthesis; and one which could swallow the classical system as a special case.

A new *system*, that is what requires emphasis. Classical economics could withstand isolated criticism. Theorists can always resist facts; for facts are hard to establish and are always changing anyway, and *ceteris paribus* can be made to absorb a good deal of punishment. Inevitably, at the earliest opportunity, the mind slips back into the old grooves of thought since analysis is utterly impossible without a frame of reference, a way of thinking about things, or in short a theory.[3]

Herein lies the secret of the *General Theory*. It is a badly written book, poorly organized; any layman who, beguiled by the author's previous reputation, bought the book was cheated of his 5 shillings. It is not well suited for classroom use.[4] It is arrogant, bad-tempered, polemical, and not overly-generous in its acknowledgments. It abounds in mares' nests and confusions: involuntary unemployment, wage units, the equality of savings and investment, the timing of the multiplier, interactions of marginal efficiency upon the rate of interest, forced savings, own rates of interest, and many others. In it the Keynesian system stands out indistinctly, as if the author were hardly aware of its existence or cognizant of its properties; and certainly he is at his worst when expounding its relations to its predecessors. Flashes of insight and intuition intersperse tedious algebra. An awkward definition suddenly gives way to an unforgettable cadenza. When it finally is

---

[3] This tendency holds true of everybody, including the businessman and the politician, the only difference being that practical men think in terms of highly simplified (and often contradictory) theories. It even holds true of a literary economist who would tremble at the sight of a mathematical symbol.

[4] The dual and confused theory of Keynes and his followers concerning the "equality of savings and investment" unfortunately ruled out the possibility of a pedagogically clear exposition of the theory in terms of schedules of savings and investment determining income.

mastered, we find its analysis to be obvious and at the same time new. In short, it is a work of genius.

It is not unlikely that future historians of economic thought will conclude that the very obscurity and polemical character of the *General Theory* ultimately served to maximize its long-run influence. Possibly such an analyst will place it in the first rank of theoretical classics along with the work of Smith, Cournot, and Walras. Certainly, these four books together encompass most of what is vital in the field of economic theory; and only the first is by any standards easy reading or even accessible to the intelligent layman.

In any case, it bears repeating that the *General Theory* is an obscure book so that would-be anti-Keynesians must assume their position largely on credit unless they are willing to put in a great deal of work and run the risk of seduction in the process. The *General Theory* resembles the random notes over a period of years of a gifted man who in his youth gained the whip hand over his publishers by virtue of the acclaim and fortune resulting from the success of his *Economic Consequences of the Peace*.

Like Joyce's *Finnegan's Wake*, the *General Theory* is much in need of a companion volume providing a "skeleton key" and guide to its contents: warning the young and innocent away from Book I (especially the difficult Chapter 3) and on to Books III, IV, and VI. Certainly in its present state, the book does not get itself read from one year to another even by the sympathetic teacher and scholar.

Too much regret should not be attached to the fact that all hope must now be abandoned of an improved second edition, since it is the first edition which would in any case have assumed the stature of a classic. We may still paste into our copies of the *General Theory* certain subsequent Keynesian additions, most particularly, the famous chapter in *How to pay for the War* which first outlined the modern theory of the inflationary process.

This last item helps to dispose of the fallacious belief that Keynesian economics is good "depression economics" and only that. Actually, the Keynesian system is indispensable to an understanding of conditions of overeffective demand and secular exhilaration; so much so that one anti-Keynesian has argued in print that *only* in times of a great war boom do such concepts as the marginal propensity to consume have validity. Perhaps, therefore, it would be more nearly correct to aver the reverse: that certain economists are Keynesian fellow travellers only in boom times, falling off the band wagon in depression.

If space permitted, it would be instructive to contrast the analysis of inflation during the Napoleonic and First World War periods with that of the recent War and correlate this with Keynes's influence. Thus, the "inflationary gap" concept,[5] recently so popular, seems to have been first used around the Spring of 1941 in a speech by the British Chancellor of Exchequer, a speech thought to have been the product of Keynes himself.

No author can complete a survey of Keynesian economics without indulging in that favorite indoor guessing game: Wherein lies the essential contribution of the *General Theory* and its distinguishing characteristic from the classical writings? Some consider its novelty to lie in the treatment of the *demand for money*, in its liquidity-preference emphasis. Others single out the treatment of *expectations*.

I cannot agree. According to recent trends of thought, the interest rate is less important than Keynes himself believed; therefore, *liquidity preference* (which itself explains part of the lack of importance of the interest rate, but only part) cannot be of such crucial significance. As for expectations, the *General Theory* is brilliant in calling attention to their importance and in suggesting many of the central features of uncertainty and speculation. It paves the way for a theory of expectations, but it hardly provides one.

I myself believe the broad significance of the *General Theory* to be in the fact that it provides a relatively realistic, complete system for analyzing the level of effective demand and its fluctuations. More narrowly, I conceive the heart of its contribution to be in that subset of its equations which relate to the propensity to consume and to saving in relation to offsets-to-saving. In addition to linking saving explicitly to income, there is an equally important denial of the implicit "classical" axiom that motivated investment is *indefinitely expansible or contractable*, so that whatever people *try* to save will always be fully invested. It is not important whether we deny this by reason of expectations, interest-rate rigidity, investment inelasticity with respect to over-all price changes and the interest rate, capital or investment satiation, secular factors of a technological and political nature, or what have you. But it is vital for business-cycle analysis that we do assume definite amounts of investment which are highly variable over time in response to a myriad of exogenous and endogenous factors, *and which are not automatically equilibrated to full-employment saving levels by any internal efficacious economic process.*

---

[5] This "neo-Austrian" demand analysis of inflation has, if anything, been overdone in the present writer's opinion; there is reason to suspect that the relaxations of price controls during a period of *insufficient* general demand might still be followed by a considerable, self-sustaining rise in prices.

With respect to the level of total purchasing power and employment, Keynes denies that there is an *Invisible Hand* channeling the self-centered action of each individual to the social optimum. This is the sum and substance of his heresy. Again and again through his writings there is to be found the figure of speech that what is needed are certain "rules of the road" and governmental actions, which will benefit everybody but which nobody by himself is motivated to establish or follow. Left to themselves during depression, people will try to save and only end up lowering society's level of capital formation and saving; during an inflation, apparent self-interest leads everyone to action which only aggravates the malignant upward spiral.

Such a philosophy is profoundly capitalistic in its nature. Its policies are offered "as the only practical means of avoiding the destruction of existing economic forms in their entirety and as the condition of the successful functioning of individual initiative."

From a perusal of Keynes's writing, I can find no evidence that words like these resemble the opportunistic lip-service paid in much recent social legislation to individual freedom and private enterprise. The following quotations show how far from a radical was this urbane and cosmopolitan provincial English liberal:

How can I accept [the communistic] doctrine which sets up as its bible, above and beyond criticism, an obsolete economic textbook which I know to be not only scientifically erroneous but without interest or application for the modern world? How can I adopt a creed which, preferring the mud to the fish, exalts the boorish proletariat above the bourgeois and intelligentsia who, with all their faults, are the quality of life and surely carry the seeds of all human advancement. Even if we need a religion, how can we find it in the turbid rubbish of the Red bookshops? It is hard for an educated, decent, intelligent son of Western Europe to find his ideals here, unless he has first suffered some strange and horrid process of conversion which has changed all his values. . . .

So, now that the deeds are done and there is no going back, I should like to give Russia her chance; to help and not to hinder. For how much rather, even after allowing for everything, if I were a Russian, would I contribute my quota of activity to Soviet Russia than to Tsarist Russia.[6]

Nothing that I can find in Keynes's later writings shows any significant changes in his underlying philosophy. As a result of the Great Depression, he becomes increasingly impatient with what he regards as the stupidity of businessmen who do not realize how much their views toward reform harm their own true long-run interests. But that is all.

[6] J. M. Keynes, *Essays in Persuasion*, 1932, pp. 300 and 311.

With respect to international cooperation and autonomy of national policies, Keynes did undergo some changes in belief. The depression accentuated his post-World-War-I pessimism concerning the advisability of England or any other country's leaving itself to the mercy of the international gold standard. But in the last half dozen years, he began to pin his hopes on intelligent, concerted, multilateral cooperation, with, however, the important proviso that each nation should rarely be forced to adjust her economy by *deflationary* means.

PORTRAIT OF THE SCIENTIST

There is no danger that historians of thought will fail to devote attention to all the matters already discussed. Science, like capital, grows by accretion and each scientist's offering at the altar blooms forever. The personal characteristics of the scientist can only be captured while memories are still fresh; and only then, in all honesty, are they of maximum interest and relevance.

In my opinion, nothing in Keynes's previous life or work really quite prepares us for the *General Theory*. In many ways his career may serve as a model and prescription for a youth who aspires to be an economist. First, he was born into an able academic family which breathed in an atmosphere of economics; his father was a distinguished scholar, but not so brilliant as to overshadow and stunt his son's growth.

He early became interested in the philosophical basis of probability theory, thus establishing his reputation young in the technical fields of mathematics and logic. The *Indian Currency and Finance* book and assiduous service as Assistant Editor and Editor of the *Economic Journal* certified to his "solidity" and scholarly craftsmanship. His early reviews in the *Economic Journal* of Fisher, Hobson, Mises, and of Bagehot's collected works gave hints of the brilliance of his later literary style. The hiatus of the next few years in his scientific output is adequately explained by his service in the Treasury during the First World War.

The first extreme departure from an academic career comes, of course, with the Byronic success of the *Economic Consequences of the Peace*, which made him a world celebrity whose very visits to the Continent did not go unnoticed on the foreign exchange markets. As successful head of an insurance company and Bursar of King's College, he met the practical men of affairs on their own ground and won the reputation of being an economist who knew how to make money. All this was capped by a solid two-volume *Treatise on Money*, replete with historical accounts of the

Mycenean monetary system, and the rest. Being a patron of the ballet and theater, a member of the "Bloomsbury Set" of Virginia Woolf and Lytton Strachey, a Governor of the Bank of England, and peer of the realm simply put the finishing gilt on his portrait.

Why then do I say that the *General Theory* still comes as a surprise? Because in all of these there is a sequence and pattern, and no one step occasions real astonishment. The *General Theory*, however, is a mutant notwithstanding Keynes's own expressed belief that it represents a "natural evolution" in his own line of thought. Let me turn, therefore, to his intellectual development.

As far back as in his 1911 review of Irving Fisher's *Purchasing Power of Money*,[7] Keynes expresses dissatisfaction with a mechanical Quantity Theory of money, but we have no evidence that he would have replaced it with anything more novel than a Cambridge cash-balance approach, amplified by a more detailed treatment of the discount rate. All this, as he would be the first to insist, was very much in the Marshallian oral tradition, and represents a view not very different from that of, say, Hawtrey.

Early in life he keenly realized the obstacles to deflation in a modern capitalistic country and the grief which this process entailed. In consequence of this intuition he came out roundly against going back to the prewar gold parity. Others held the same view: Rist in France, Cassel in Sweden, *et al*. He was not alone in his insistence, from the present fashionable point of view vastly exaggerated, that central-bank discount policy might stabilize business activity; again, compare the position of Gustav Cassel. Despite the auspicious sentence concerning savings and investment in its preface, the *Tract on Monetary Reform* on its analytical side goes little beyond a quantity-theory explanation of inflation; while its policy proposals for a nationally-managed currency and fluctuating exchange are only distinguished for their political novelty and persuasiveness.

In all of these, there is a consistency of pattern. And in retrospect it is only fair to say that he was on the whole right. Yet this brief account does not present the whole story. In many places, he was wrong. Perhaps a pamphleteer should be judged shot-gun rather than rifle fashion, by his absolute hits regardless of misses; still one must note that even when most wrong, he is often most confident and sure of himself.

---

[7] *Economic Journal*, Vol. 21, September, 1911, pp. 392–398. This is a charactertistically "unfair" and unfavorable review, to be compared with Marshall's review of Jevons, which Keynes's biography of Marshall tries weakly to justify.

The *Economic Consequences of the Peace* proceeds from beginning to end on a single premise which history has proved to be false or debatable. Again, he unleased with a flourish the Malthusian bogey of overpopulation at a time when England and the Western European world were undergoing a population revolution in the opposite direction. In his controversy with Sir William Beveridge on the terms of trade between industry and agriculture, besides being wrong in principle and interpretation, he revealed his characteristic weakness for presenting a few hasty, but suggestive, statistics. If it can be said that he was right in his reparations-transfer controversy with Ohlin, it is in part for the wrong reasons – reasons which in terms of his later system are seen to be classical as compared to the arguments of Ohlin. Again, at different times he has presented arguments to demonstrate that foreign investment is (1) deflationary, and (2) stimulating to the home economy, without appearing on either occasion to be aware of the opposing arguments.

None of these are of vital importance, but they help to give the flavor of the man. He has been at once soundboard, amplifier, and initiator of contemporary viewpoints, whose strength and weakness lay in his intuition, audaciousness, and changeability. Current quips concerning the latter trait are rather exaggerated, but they are not without provocation. It is quite in keeping with this portrait to be reminded that in the early '20's, before he had an inkling of the *General Theory*, or even the *Treatise*, he scolded Edwin Cannan in no uncertain terms for not recognizing the importance and novelty of modern beliefs as compared to old-fashioned – I might almost have said "classical" – theories.

Where a scientist is concerned it is not inappropriate, even in a eulogy, to replace the ordinary dictum *nihil nisi bonum* by the criterion *nihil nisi verum*. In all candor, therefore, it is necessary to point out certain limitations – one might almost say weaknesses were they not so intrinsically linked with his genius – in Keynes's thought.

Perhaps because he was exposed to economics too young, or perhaps because he arrived at maturity in the stultifying backwash of Marshall's influence upon economic theory – for whatever reason, Keynes seems never to have had any genuine interest in pure economic theory. It is remarkable that so active a brain would have failed to make any contribution to value theory; and yet except for his discussion of index numbers in Volume I of the *Treatise* and for a few remarks concerning "user cost," which are novel at best only in terminology and emphasis, he seems to have left no mark on pure value theory.[8]

Just as there is internal evidence in the *Treatise on Probability* that he early tired of somewhat frustrating basic philosophic speculation, so he seems to have early tired of theory. He gladly "exchanged the tormenting exercises of the foundations of thought and of psychology, where the mind tries to catch its own tail, for the delightful paths of our own most agreeable branch of the moral sciences, in which theory and fact, intuitive imagination and practical judgment, are blended in a manner comfortable to the human intellect."[9]

In view of his basic antipathy to economic theory, it is all the more wonder therefore that he was able to write a biography of Alfred Marshall, which Professor Schumpeter has termed not only one of the best treatments of a Master by a Pupil but one of the best biographies ever written.[10] Never were two temperaments more different than that of the two men, and we can be sure that the repressed Victorianism and "popish" personal mannerisms which Keynes found so worthy of reverence in a Master and Father would have been hardly tolerable in a contemporary.

From Marshall's early influence, no doubt, stems Keynes's antipathy toward the use of mathematical symbols, an antipathy which already appears, surprisingly considering its technical subject, in the early pages of the *Treatise on Probability*. In view of the fact that mathematical economists were later to make some of the most important contributions to Keynesian economics, his comments on them in the *General Theory* and in the Marshall and Edgeworth biographies merit rereading.[11]

Moreover, there is reason to believe that Keynes's thinking remained fuzzy on one important analytical matter throughout all his days: the

---

[8] Indeed only in connection with Frank P. Ramsey's "A Mathematical Theory of Saving" (*Economic Journal*, Vol. 38, December, 1928, pp. 542–559) does he show interest in an esoteric theoretical problem; there he gave a rather intricate interpretation in words of a calculus-of-variations differential-equation condition of equilibrium. His reasoning is all the more brilliant – and I say this seriously! – because it is mathematically unrigorous, if not wrong. The importance which Keynes attached to this article is actually exaggerated and can be accounted for only in terms of his paternal feeling toward Ramsey, and his own participation in the solution of the problem.

[9] *Essays in Biography*, pp. 249–250.

[10] Keynes's discussion of Marshall's monetary theory is much better than his treatment of Marshall's contribution to theory.

[11] Keynes's critical review of Tinbergen's econometric business-cycle study for the League of Nations reveals that Keynes did not really have the necessary technical knowledge to understand what he was criticizing. How else are we to interpret such remarks as his assertion that a linear system can never develop oscillations?

relationship between "identity" and functional (or equilibrium-schedule) equality; between "virtual" and observable movements; between causality and concomitance; between tautology and hypothesis. Somewhere, I believe in the 1923 *Tract*, he already falls into the same analytic confusion with respect to the identity of supply and demand for foreign exchange which was later to be his stumbling-block with respect to the identity of saving and investment.

Perhaps he was always too busy with the affairs of the world to be able to devote sufficient time for repeated thinking through of certain basic problems. Certainly he was too busy to verify references ("a vain pursuit"). His famous remark that he never learned anything from reading German which he didn't already know would be greeted with incredulity in almost any other science than economics.[12] What he really meant was that his was one of those original minds which never accepts a thing as true and important unless he has already thought it through for himself. Despite his very considerable erudition in certain aspects of the history of thought, there was probably never a more ahistorical scholar than Keynes.

Finally, to fill in the last little touch in this incomplete portrait of an engaging spirit, I should like to present a characteristic quotation from Keynes:

In writing a book of this kind the author must, if he is to put his point of view clearly, pretend sometimes to a little more conviction than he feels. He must give his own argument a chance, so to speak, nor be too ready to depress its vitality with a wet cloud of doubt.

Is this from the *General Theory*? No. From the *Treatise on Money* or the *Tract*? No, no. Even when writing on so technical a subject as probability, the essential make-up of the man comes through so that no literary detective can fail to spot his spoor.

THE ROAD TO THE GENERAL THEORY

It was not unnatural for such a man as I have described to wish as he approached fifty to bring together, perhaps as a crowning life work, his intuitions concerning money. Thus the *Treatise* was born. Much of the first volume is substantial and creditable, though hardly exciting. But the

[12] Around 1911–1915, he was the principal reviewer of German books for *E.J.*; also he must have read – at least he claimed to have – innumerable German works on probability. That he could not speak German with any fluency is well attested by those who heard him once open an English lecture to a German audience with a brief apology in German.

Fundamental Equations which he and the world considered the really novel contribution of the *Treatise* are nothing but a detour and blind alley.

The second volume is most valuable of all, but it is so because of the intuitions there expressed concerning bullishness, bearishness, etc. and even these might have been prevented from coming into being by too literal an attempt to squeeze them into the mold of the Fundamental Equations. Fortunately, Keynes was not sufficiently systematic to carry out such a program.

Before the *Treatise* was completed, its author had already tired of it. Sir Isaac Newton held up publication of his theory for twenty years because of a small discrepancy in numerical calculation. Darwin hoarded his theories for decades in order to collect ever more facts. Not so with our hero: let the presses roll and throw off the grievous weight of a book unborn! Especially since a world falling to pieces is ripe to drop Pollyanna and take up with Cassandra on the rebound.

Perhaps not being systematic proved his salvation. A long line of heretics testifies that he is not the first to have tried to weld intuition into a satisfactory, unified theory; not the first to have shot his bolt and failed. But few have escaped from the attempt with their intuitions intact and unmarred. In an inexact subject like economics, concepts are not (psychologically) neutral. Decisions based upon ignorance of the equiprobability of the unknown are not invariant under transformation of coordinates or translation of concepts. Simply to define a concept is to reify it, to breathe life in it, to create a predisposition in favor of its constancy; *vide* the falling rate of profit and the organic composition of capital, the velocity of circulation of money, the propensity to consume, and the discrepancy between saving and investment.

The danger may be illustrated by a particular instance. Shrewd Edwin Cannan in characteristic salty prose throughout the first World War "protested."[13] At first his insights were sharp and incisive, his judgments on the whole correct. But in the summer of 1917, to "escape from an almost unbearable personal sorrow," he undertook to set forth a *systematic* exposition of the theory of money. The transformation of Cinderella's coach at the stroke of twelve is not more sudden than the change in the quality of his thought. Here, I am not so much interested in the fact that his voice becomes shrill, his policies on the whole in retrospect bad – as in the fact that his intuitions were perverted and blunted by his analysis, almost in an

---

[13] E. Cannan, *An Economist's Protest*, 1927.

irrecoverable way! Not so with Keynes. His constitution was able to throw off the *Treatise* and its Fundamental Equations.

While Keynes did much for the Great Depression, it is no less true that the Great Depression did much for him. It provided challenge, drama, experimental confirmation. He entered it the sort of man who might be expected to embrace the *General Theory* if it were explained to him. From the previous record, one cannot say more. Before it was over, he had emerged with the prize in hand, the system of thought for which he will be remembered.

Right now I do not intend to speculate in detail on the thought-process leading up to this work, but only to throw out a few hints. In the 1929 pamphlet, *Can Lloyd George Do It?*, written with H. D. Henderson, Keynes set up important hypotheses concerning the effects of public works and investment. It remained for R. F. Kahn, that elusive figure who hides in the preface of Cambridge books, to provide the substantiation in his justly famous 1931 *Economic Journal* article, "The Relation of Home Investment to Unemployment." Quite naturally the "multiplier" comes in for most attention; which is in a way too bad since the concept often seems like nothing but a cheap-Jack way of getting something for nothing and appears to carry with it a spurious numerical accuracy.

But behind lies the vitally important consumption function: giving the propensity to consume in terms of income; or looked at from the opposite side, specifying the propensity to save. With investment given, as a constant or in the schedule sense, we are in a position to set up the simplest determinate system of underemployment equilibrium – by a "Keynesian savings-investment-income cross" not formally different from the "Marshallian supply-demand-price cross."

Immediately everything falls into place: the recognition that the *attempt* to save may lower income and actual *realized* saving; the fact that a net autonomous increase in investment, foreign balance, government expenditure, consumption will result in increased income *greater* than itself, etc., etc.

Other milestones on the road to Damascus, in addition to the Lloyd George pamphlet and the Kahn article, were Keynes's testimony before the Macmillan committee[14] and his University of Chicago Harris Foundation

---

[14] Young economists who disbelieve in the novelty of the Keynesian analysis on the ground that no sensible person could ever have thought differently might with profit read Hawtrey's testimony before the Macmillan Committee, contrasting it with the Kahn article and comparing it with Tooke's famous demonstration in his *History of Prices*, Volume I, that government war expenditures as such cannot possibly cause inflation – *because what*

lectures on unemployment in the summer of 1931. In these lectures, Keynes has not quite liberated himself from the terminology of the *Treatise* (*vide* his emphasis on "profits"); but the notion of the level of income as being in equilibrium at a low level because of the necessity for savings to be equated to a depressed level of investment is worked out in detail.

From here[15] to the *Means to Prosperity* (1933) is but a step; and from the latter to the *General Theory* but another step. From hindsight and from the standpoint of policy recommendations, each such step is small and in a sense inevitable; but from the standpoint of having stumbled upon and formulated a new system of analysis, each represents a tremendous stride.

But now I shall have to desist. My panegyric must come to an end with two conflicting quotations from the protean Lord Keynes between which the Jury must decide:

In the long run we are all dead.

... the ideas of economists and political philosophers, both when they are right and when they are wrong, are more powerful than is commonly understood. Indeed, the world is ruled by little else. Practical men, who believe themselves to be quite exempt from any intellectual influences, are usually the slaves of some defunct economist. Madmen in authority, who hear voices in the air, are distilling their frenzy from some academic scribbler of a few years back. I am sure that the power of vested interests is vastly exaggerated compared with the gradual encroachment of ideas ... soon or late, it is ideas, not vested interests, which are dangerous for good or evil.

---

the government spends would have been spent anyway, except to the extent of "new money" created.

[15] I should like at this point to pass a clue on to the future historian of economic thought. What was happening in Cambridge in the months between Mrs. Robinson's patient elucidation of an aspect of the *Treatise* entitled "A Parable on Savings and Investment," *Economica*, Vol. 13, February, 1933, pp. 75–84, and her publication of "The Theory of Money and the Value of Output," *Review of Economic Studies*, Vol. 1, October, 1933, pp. 22–26? Could it be that Mrs. Robinson was let in on a little secret in between?

The Monopolistic Competition Revolution

SOME SOCIOLOGY OF KNOWLEDGE

No historian of science would be surprised to learn that Edward Chamberlin and Joan Robinson[1] had written in the same year separate books that break definitively with the assumptions of perfect competition. Newton and Leibniz both discovered the calculus because that subject was then in the air, waiting to be discovered. Similarly, 1933, the year of *The Theory of Monopolistic Competition* and of *The Economics of Imperfect Competition*, followed a decade of intense discussion concerning the nature of competition, the so-called "cost controversy" initiated by Clapham's famous complaint about the "empty boxes" of economic theory.

Many of the great names of the day were involved in that controversy: Allyn Young, Knight, J. M. Clark, Dennis Robertson, Robbins, Viner, Shove, Harrod, Schumpeter, Yntema, Hotelling, Sraffa, Pigou, J. Robinson, Kahn, and many others.[2] In retrospect I judge it to have been rather a sterile debate, as will appear from what follows. But experience with the history of science amply testifies that the journey between two points is not a straight

Grateful acknowledgement is made to the Carnegie Corporation for granting me a reflective year, to Harvard University for providing the fulcrum on which to place my lever, and to Mrs. F. Skidmore for research assistance.

[1] E. H. Chamberlin, *The Theory of Monopolistic Competition*, Harvard University Press, Cambridge, Mass., first edition, 1933; eighth edition, 1962; J. Robinson, *Economics of Imperfect Competition*, Macmillan, London, 1933.

[2] For a sampling, see G. J. Stigler and K. E. Boulding, eds., *Reading in Price Theory*, Irwin, Homewood, Ill., 1952, which contains articles by J. H. Clapham (1922), A. C. Pigou (1922), D. H. Robertson (1924), F. H. Knight (1924), P. Sraffa (1926), and J. Viner (1931); cf. also J. M. Clark, *Economics of Overhead Costs*, University of Chicago Press, Chicago, 1923. Aside from preparing the way for theories of monopolistic and imperfect competition, the cost controversy did result in a better understanding of competitive theory.

line. Having made detours and been caught in *culs-de-sac*, a subject must make progress by the negative act of dumping ballast.

The keen historian of science will not be surprised, either, to learn that simultaneous discoveries that appear to be substantially similar turn out, on careful examination, to be substantively different. In our own field of economics, it is customary to bracket Jevons, Menger, and Walras as independent discoverers of the subjective theory of value and of utility; but with the hindsight of a century we see that Walras's formulation of general equilibrium quite overshadows the brilliant work of his contemporaries and he might have been spared the pain of discovery that Jevons had beaten him to what both thought was the important Pole.

With cogency and pertinacity, Chamberlin has always insisted on differentiating his product from that of Mrs. Robinson. Posterity will agree. But in its typical wayward manner, posterity will amalgamate into an optimal package what it conceives to be the best of the various systems. Thus, when Chamberlin tells us that his work did not find its inspiration in the cost controversy, we find strong corroboration in the historical documents denoting his journey along the road to Damascus, from 1921 through 1927 and beyond, as well as in the structure and texture of his 1933 classic. But, again, as the sociologist of science knows, there is a feedback reaction between the readers of a seminal work and its author. Most of Chamberlin's readers, in America as well as in England, were exercised by the cost controversy. Allyn Young, Chamberlin's thesis supervisor and teacher of Frank Knight, who in turn taught Chamberlin, was an important participant in the controversy. Although we have abundant evidence, after 1933 as well as before, that Edward Chamberlin was a lone-wolf scholar with infinite capacity for formulating and pushing a problem to solution in his own way, still, no man is an island unto himself. If A has any sort of communication with B who has any communication with C, ..., there is no way to rule out mutual interaction between A and Z even if they have never met or had any direct contact.

As an illustration of mutual dependence, consider Mrs. Robinson and J. M. Clark's *Economics of Overhead Costs*. There is no reason to think she had ever heard of this stimulating 1923 book. But if Robertson, Pigou, Shove, Austin Robinson, Kahn, or any other member of the Cambridge set had ever read the work, then some degree of influence cannot be ruled out by the historian of science even though he can never hope to measure its degree. Or consider Sraffa's December 1926 article. Without doubting that an April 1927 thesis could have been written completely independently of it, we are still not surprised that Chamberlin's 1933 book should take notice of the great similarity between the *Weltanschauung* of Sraffa's final part with the perfected theory of monopolistic competition. In rereading Sraffa for the present essay, I was struck by, and marked, certain lines that seemed to me to be in the Chamberlin spirit; and it was, therefore, with interest that I subsequently noted some of them quoted at the beginning of Chamberlin's book.

A final illustration of the virtual impossibility of ruling out truly independent simultaneous scientific discovery can be taken from the combined field of international trade and welfare economics. At the London School of Economics in the 1930's, brilliant young economists such as Lerner, Hicks, and Kaldor worked out graphical models of international exchange and what we would today call Pareto-optimality necessary conditions for welfare. References to Vilfredo Pareto will be sought in vain, even though his books were known to the more widely-read members of that circle. The reason? Pareto is an obscure enough writer, the subject is a sufficiently subtle one, and the men involved are sufficiently creative and self-stimulating for me to think that Pareto's influence was at best subconscious. But a quite different influencing is that which I would associate with the name of Viner. In January 1931, Viner gave a public lecture at L.S.E. on international trade, in which he married Haberler's production-possibility frontier to consumer indifference curves. Everyone, including the lecturer, may have forgotten the very fact that the lecture was given. But nothing can change the fact that independent rediscovery of this bit of analysis became impossible in that environment after that date. Even if only Victor Edelberg understood Viner...[3]

THE THEORETICAL SHORTCOMINGS OF PERFECT COMPETITION

My purpose in this essay is not to isolate the peculiar contributions to price theory made by Edward Chamberlin. He has done that job superlatively well and we can take it for granted. Indeed the time has come when we may permit ourselves to use the terms monopolistic competition and imperfect competition interchangeably, emancipating them from their first associations with the different conceptions of Chamberlin and Mrs. Robinson, and

---

[3] That the compensation principle as applied to losers from free trade should have been enunciated in the late 1930's using the same kind of example that Viner had used earlier shows a similar indirect influence of Viner on the London School, but it would take a more tedious detective operation to trace through its unconscious contacts. See J. Viner, *Studies in the Theory of International Trade*, Harper, New York, 1937, p. 521.

using them as convenient names for the best current models of price theory.[4]

My purpose here is to discuss some of the *theoretical* reasons why perfect competition provides an empirically inadequate model of the real world. This forces us to work with some versions of monopolistic or imperfect competition. Chicago economists can continue to shout until they are blue in the face that there is no elegant alternative to the theory of perfect competition.[5] If not, the proper moral is, "So much the worse for elegance"

---

[4] Admittedly, impure competition might be a better name than imperfect competition, in consideration of Chamberlin's point that denying perfect knowledge can still leave the firm a pure competitor facing a price at which it can sell all it wishes; but impure competition sounds dirty, just as monopolistic competition sounds evil, and so we find convenience in the label *imperfect competition*.

[5] G. J. Stigler, *Five Lectures on Economic Problems*, Macmillan, London, 1950, in particular Lecture 2, "Monopolistic Competition in Retrospect"; M. Friedman, *Essays in Positive Economics*, University of Chicago Press, Chicago, 1953, Ch. 1; E. H. Chamberlin, *Toward a More General Theory of Value*, Oxford University Press, New York, 1957, Ch. 15; G. C. Archibald, "Chamberlin *versus* Chicago," *Review of Economic Studies*, XXIX (1961), pp. 2–28; G. J. Stigler, "Archibald *versus* Chicago," *Review of Economic Studies*, XXX (1963), pp. 63–64; M. Friedman, "More on Archibald *versus* Chicago," *Review of Economic Studies*, XXX (1963), pp. 65–67; G. C. Archibald, "Reply to Chicago," *Review of Economic Studies* XXX (1963), pp. 68–71. First, I must emphasize that, despite some ambiguity in Chamberlin's own writing, the symmetric large group of Chamberlin must not be taken to be the content of the words "monopolistic competition" or even to constitute the significant content of the theoretical revolution. Second, although I personally emphasized in my *Foundations of Economic Analysis*, Harvard University Press, Cambridge, Mass., 1947, the importance of the empirically testable implications of second-order maximization inequalities, I must dissociate myself from Archibald's criticism of the Chicago criticism, which consists of Archibald's demonstration that the Chamberlin theory has few unambiguously signed implications of my *Foundations* type. If the real world displays the variety of behavior that the Chamberlin-Robinson models permit – and I believe the Chicago writers are simply wrong in denying that these important empirical deviations exist – then reality will falsify *many* of the important qualitative and quantitative *predictions* of the competitive model. Hence, by the pragmatic test of prediction adequacy, the perfect-competition model fails to be an adequate approximation. When Friedman claims (*Essays*, pp. 36–37) that a tax will have the type of incidence on the cigarette industry that it would on a competitive industry, he is at most showing that *some* predictions of the latter theory are adequate. To the degree that other predictions are falsified – consumer price approximately equal to marginal cost, advertising cost equal to zero – the competitive model fails the pragmatic predictive test.

The fact that the Chamberlin-Robinson model is "empty," in the sense of ruling out few empirical configurations and being capable of providing only formalistic descriptions, is not the slightest reason for abandoning it in favor of a "full" model of the competitive type *if reality is similarly* "empty" and "non-full." In 1960, elementary particle theory was similarly "empty" and Newtonian mechanics similarly "full"; but only an idiot would have tried in 1960 to use Newton's model to describe high-energy physics. To reach retro-actively into the urn of monopoly to explain advertising expense and into that of the competitive model to explain some case of tax incidence is to advance not a step, and, as the rather than, "Economists of the world, unite in proclaiming that the Emperor has almost no clothes, and in pretending that the model of perfect competition does a good enough job in fitting the real world." More than once I shall have to report that we theorists, quite removed from Cook County, have retrogressed in the last quarter of a century, taking the coward's way of avoiding the important questions thrown up by the real economic world and fobbing off in their place nice answers to less interesting easy questions.

EXORCIZING THE MARSHALLIAN INCUBUS

The ambiguities of Alfred Marshall paralyzed the best brains in the Anglo-Saxon branch of our profession for three decades. By 1930 the profession had just about reattained the understanding of the pure theory of monopoly that Cournot had achieved in 1838; and it had yet to reattain the understanding of the theory of competitive general equilibrium that Walras had achieved by 1878 or 1896.

Although Marshall was a great economist, we must remember in appraising his originality that he knew well the work of Mill, Cournot, Dupuit, and Mangoldt. Even if we accept at face value his claim that he owed little or nothing to such contemporaries as Jevons and Walras – and I for one think the only appropriate answer to that claim is: the more fool he – we must realize that there was precious little in the theory of partial equilibrium under perfect competition to be developed by anyone unlucky enough to have been born as an economist *after* Cournot, Mill, Dupuit, and Mangoldt.[6]

wastes of free entry under imperfectly competitive conditions cannot be predicted by any blend of items selected from each urn, illustrates the indispensability of the 1933 revolution. Cf. R. L. Bishop, "Monopolistic Competition after Thirty Years: the Impact on General Theory," *American Economic Review, Papers and Proceedings,* LIV (1964), pp. 33–43.

As a final instance, consider the notion that many business firms set price on some kind of a "full-cost mark-up" over some kind of cost (R. L. Hall and C. J. Hitch, "Price Theory and Business Behavior," *Oxford Economic Papers,* II (1939), pp. 12–45). It might be argued that this is an empty formulation, because, depending on alternative estimates of demand elasticity and alternative specifications of entry of rivals, this model can lead to price above marginal cost to any percentage degree. Granted, but by what logic does that permit anyone to replace the vacuum by asserting the competitive outcome of P equals one times M.C., or P equals one-plus-epsilon times M.C.?

[6] Testifying to the cogency of my a *priori* reasoning on this point is the fact that both Fleeming Jenkin (1870) and Auspitz and Lieben (1889) developed partial-equilibrium theory in all of its fundamentals before Marshall's 1890 *Principles of Economics*; neither could have been helped in this regard by Marshall's 1879 tract, *The Pure Theory of*

Unfortunately, because of his unwillingness to make sharp distinctions between perfect and less-than-perfect competition, Marshall managed to set back the clock both on competitive theory and on the theory of monopoly. Edgeworth was almost an exact contemporary of Marshall, but seems to have been scared to death of that eminent Victorian. The profound researches of Edgeworth on bilateral monopoly and various forms of oligopoly received little attention from the Marshallian tradition. And it was not until 1934 with the work of von Stackelberg, and indeed 1944 with the *Theory of Games* of von Neumann and Morgenstern, that the modern literature reattained the depth of Edgeworth's analysis.[7]

Let us make no mistake about it. The theory of simple monopoly is child's play. That grown men argued seriously in 1930 about who had first used or named the curve that we now call "marginal revenue" is a joke. Cournot had settled all that a century earlier and in a completely modern manner, so that the reader who picks up the English translation of his book and has to guess at the date of its authorship merely on the basis of an understanding of the cost-controversy literature ought to guess 1927 or 1933. Chamberlin always used to insist that the essence of his contribution to the subject had nothing particularly to do with the rediscovery and naming of the simple marginal curves. We can readily agree with him. Whether it is correct to go on and say, as some have said, that Mrs. Robinson's book differs from his in that hers is primarily a book on monopoly, I find a more difficult question to answer. To a considerable extent her book is that, and we feel that the reviewer of it had a small point when he said that the time spent in reading her work might with better profit be spent on studying Irving Fisher's little

---

Domestic and International Values, which deals hardly at all with partial equilibrium and deserves high praise thereby.

[7] H. von Stackelberg, *Marktform und Gleichgewicht*, Springer, Berlin, 1934; W. Fellner, *Competition Among the Few*, Knopf, New York, 1949; J. von Neumann and O. Morgenstern, *Theory of Games and Economic Behavior*, Princeton University Press, Princeton, New Jersey, 1944. Chamberlin's Chapter 23 and Appendix A provide a valuable but far-from-adequate history and analysis of the problems of bilateral monopoly, duopoly, and general game-theoretic problems. In particular the 1929 notion that Edgeworth was principally to be known for his "oscillatory" solution to duopoly is a sad understatement. By 1897 Edgeworth already had a full appreciation of the game-theoretic indeterminacy: his Arctic explorers already trace out 1934 von Stackelberg solutions and much else. F. Y. Edgeworth, *Papers Relating to Political Economy*, Royal Economic Society, London, 1925. Indeed, in his *Mathematical Psychics*, Paul, London, 1881, pp. 35–39, 139–148, Edgeworth had already anticipated the modern concept of the "core" of a game, in its relation to large numbers of sellers. See also footnote 17 below.

textbook on the infinitesimal calculus.[8] For it is true that simple monopoly theory consists of little other than elementary calculus, in which ordinary and partial derivatives are to be set equal to zero whereas higher derivatives are required to be nonpositive. Marshall was so enamored of his silly little unitary-elasticity hyperbolas that he omitted a straightforward treatment of simple monopoly, leaving room in the first third of this century for quasi-independent rediscovery by literary economists of these rudiments.

RETROGRESSION IN MONOPOLY THEORY

But where Marshall threw off two generations of scholars was in his insistence on having his cake and eating it too. He would try to treat at the same time cases of less-than-perfect and of perfect competition. He would try to achieve a spurious verisimilitude by talking about vague biological dynamics, and by failing to distinguish between reversible and irreversible developments. He would insist on confusing the issue of external economies and diseconomies – which played an important role in the work of such pre-Marshallian writers as Henry Sidgwick – with the entirely separable (and separate!) issue of varying laws of returns. Marshall was so afraid of being unrealistic that he merely ends up being fuzzy and confusing – and confused.

Although harsh, these are my well-considered judgments on the matter, and I mention them only because no one can understand the history of the subject if he does not realize that much of the work from 1920 to 1933 was merely the negative task of getting Marshall out of the way. I shall not document these opinions but shall merely give single examples of what I have in mind.

First, that part of simple monopoly theory which consists of neat theorems – such as that a lump-sum tax or a tax on net profits will have no effect on monopoly output, whereas a tax on gross revenues or on output will lower output and raise prices – was well known to any reader of Cournot and involves little more than the calculus of a single variable.

Second, which of us has not been brought up short in his reading of Marshall when suddenly, in the midst of what was thought to be a discussion of "competition," it turns out that some entrepreneur fails to do something because of his "fear of spoiling the market," a sure sign of some

---

[8] A. J. Nichol, "Robinson's Economics of Imperfect Competition," *Journal of Political Economy*, XLII (1934), pp. 257–259. Actually, when Mrs. Robinson comes to discuss a world of monopolies and other issues, she does go far beyond simple monopoly theory.

kind of imperfection of competition? Such aberrations as these, to which I point in horror, are taken by some modern writers as signs of Marshall's genius and erudite wisdom about the facts of life. "It's all in Marshall," they say, failing to add, "All the words of economics are in Webster's dictionary or in the fingertips of monkeys in the British Museum." But just as it takes more than monkeys to find the Michaelangelo statues that lurk in any old cube of marble, so it takes more than can be learned in Marshall to isolate the good sense that is embalmed therein. Marshall's crime is to pretend to handle imperfect competition with tools only applicable to perfect competition.

Third, Marshall was a victim of what the modern Freudians call self-hate. He was a good chess player who was ashamed of playing chess, a good analytical economist who was ashamed of analysis. He well understood Cournot's insistence that the marginal cost curve must not be falling for any maximizing pure competitor, but balked at simple acceptance of the fact. All of his prattle about the biological method in economics – and the last decades' genuine progress in biology through the techniques of physics has confirmed my dictum of 20 years ago that talk of a unique biological method does mostly represent prattle – cannot change this fact: any price taker who can sell more at the going price than he is now selling and who has falling marginal cost will not be in equilibrium. Talk of birds and bees, giant trees in the forest, and declining entrepreneurial dynasties is all very well, but why blink at such an elementary point?

Fourth, this leads to the further confusion by Marshall of *external* effects with increasing *returns* phenomena. Because Marshall (*Principles*, Book V, Ch. XIII, pp. 467–470) made an elementary mistake in his graphical reckoning of consumers' surplus, forgetting to take into account producers' surplus – an odd omission for a chap who always insisted correctly that there are two blades in the scissors of supply and demand – he came up with what seems like an exciting policy theorem: *Tax to contract increasing cost industries; subsidize to expand decreasing cost industries.*

As we congratulate ourselves that commonsense economics has for once produced fruit, we are brought up short by the realization that this is quite wrong. It merely sounds like a couple of other things that are right. Increasing returns industries are likely to be somehow monopolized, and a monopoly markup of price over marginal cost does create a *prima facie* case for public expansion of that industry. Futhermore, under increasing returns, marginal cost is below average cost; and hence marginal cost pricing would require a state subsidy. But wait: it was a *competitive* decreasing cost industry we were talking about, a contradiction in terms if the increasing returns are *internal* to the firm. So Marshallians hasten to say that it must be, of course, decreasing cost due to *external economies* that was meant, and which ought to be subsidized. Subsidizing external economies is indeed correct but, unfortunately for the false theorem of Marshall, external economies ought to be subsidized even when they occur in industries strongly subject to increasing cost; and external diseconomies require penalty even when they occur in decreasing cost industries. The point is that Marshall was simply wrong in focusing on the effect of external diseconomies and economies on the trend of industry *unit* costs. It took Pigou years to extricate his welfare economics from their Marshallian origins and misconceptions.[9]

RETROGRESSION IN PERFECT COMPETITION THEORY

At the same time that Marshall was doing a disservice to the theory of monopoly and less-than-perfect competition, he was inadvertently delaying the understanding of general equilibrium. (I might have written Walrasian general equilibrium but there is only one general equilibrium, whatever its name.) Ironically, it was not until after World War II that economists generally began to think in terms of general equilibrium. As will be seen in a moment, this represents an advance in logical clarity but something of a retreat in terms of realistic appraisal of actual imperfectly competitive market structures.

If there is a proper understanding of general equilibrium, it is possible to attain for the first time an understanding of partial equilibrium. The studies by Chamberlin and the contemporaries involved in the cost controversy had, along with the task of developing an analysis of monopolistic or imperfect competition, the task of developing for the first time a proper analysis of the relationship between firms and industry. This task, neglected by Marshall, was not needed by Walras for his ideal model of general

[9] Allyn Young in his original review of Pigou's 1912 *Wealth and Welfare* pointed out Pigou's error in thinking that the upward bidding of rents in an industry whose output expands represents anything other than a transfer item that ought to be allowed to take place. Later Knight and Robertson made the same point and Pigou finally capitulated. For an historical recapitulation and summary, see H. S. Ellis and W. Fellner, "External Economies and Diseconomies," *American Economic Review*, XXXIII (1943), pp. 493–511, reprinted in Stigler and Boulding eds., *op. cit.*, pp. 242–263. My generally critical view of Marshall is not universally shared, but a trend is discernible, and it is significant that Marshall's remaining defenders among theorists tend to be those satisfied with perfect competition as an approximation to reality.

equilibrium. For, as we shall see, perfect competition proceeds most smoothly when the extreme assumption of *constant returns to scale* is firmly adhered to. And yet it is precisely under strict constant returns to scale that the theory of the firm evaporates.

If scale does not matter it is immaterial where we draw the boundaries of the firm or whether we draw them at all. So to speak, the proportions of labor and fertilizer to land are determined at the same ratio everywhere on the homogeneous Iowa plain; and it is industry demand that sets the total output to be produced with these factor proportions. Or as Wicksell so well put the matter, under constant returns to scale and statical conditions of certainty, it is immaterial which factor hires which. Like Topsy, they all spontaneously come together under Darwinian competition in the proper amounts, with any deviations lacking survival value. Labor as much hires capital goods and land as capital hires labor and land. (As we shall see, the situation is a little changed if strict constant returns to scale is relaxed in favor of replicable quanta of least-unit-cost combinations.)

This euthanasia of the concept of the firm under most-perfect competition – which is actually an odd way of putting the matter since what need never exist cannot very well be said to wither away – paradoxically bothered writers of the 1920's and 1930's. Writers like Kaldor and Hicks seemed to agree with Schumpeter that pushing perfect competition to its extreme assumptions led ultimately to the blowup of perfect competition. Thus a constant unit cost curve coinciding with a horizontal firm demand curve would make each pure competitor's output quite indeterminate. (The mathematical economists encountered the same phenomenon in the shape of a singular Hessian matrix associated with homogeneous functions and semidefinite quadratic forms.) My example of the Iowa plain shows that this concern over the firm's indeterminacy was misplaced, for the reason that it is inessential under strict constant returns just how industry's (determinate!) output is allocated among firms. These writers erred in supposing that with every firm in neutral equilibrium, there would be no penalty to having one expand indefinitely until it "monopolized" the industry. Actually, as pointed out elsewhere,[10] even if a firm has 99 or 100 percent of the output, it has under the stipulated returns condition *zero* long-run monopoly power: the net long-run demand curve to it is derived by subtracting from the industry curve the horizontal supply curve of actual and *potential* suppliers, leaving it with a horizontal long-run personal demand

[10] P. A. Samuelson, *Foundations of Economic Analysis*, Harvard University Press, Cambridge, Mass., 1947, pp. 78–79.

curve; like a constitutional monarch, it is left to reign only so long as it does not rule.[11]

THE REVOLUTION BECKONS

The empty boxes that Clapham should have been asking to be filled in the 1920's were thus not the Marshallian categories of increasing, constant, and diminishing cost under competition. The empty boxes were those of market description and classification, involving all the possible patterns of oligopoly, monopoly, duopoly, differentiation of products with numbers large and numbers small, and so forth. But Chamberlin had not yet created this new theoretical vision of the economic world.

Piero Sraffa's justly famous 1926 article takes on a new light in terms of this analysis of the Marshallian influence. Truly reversible decreasing cost industries associated with external economies are perhaps a *curiosum*. If a competitive industry is small, and to the degree that it uses no specialized factors in intensities different from that of the bulk of the rest of industry, it does tend to fall in the category of *constant* costs. We can agree with Sraffa on this.

But this constant cost case is of no intrinsic difference for policy or other purposes from the case that Sraffa needlessly plays down – the case in which the industry uses some factors of special advantage to it alone or in which it uses the various factors of production of society in proportions significantly different from the rest of industry. In this case, and particularly where we add the realistic consideration that almost any product you can name is something of a joint product produced along with and in partial competition with certain by-products, increases in demand for the products of the industry *will* result in increasing costs and relative prices. Such cases create absolutely no complications for general equilibrium, even though Sraffa may be right in thinking they do for partial equilibrium (in which case, so much the worse for partial equilibrium analysis, Marshallian or otherwise!). The point needing emphasis for Sraffa's readers is that *these* phenomena

---

[11] Even within the constant returns technology, we shall see that there are possible advantages (and no disadvantages!) to be derived from having the owners of any unique factor of production, e.g., land suitable for mulberry growing, form a coalition that exploits its monopoly power. We should not wonder that the calculating self-interest on which Adam Smith relies to move the Invisible Hand of perfect competition should motivate people to utilize the ballot box of democracy to institute crop control and other public programs interfering with perfect competition. To a psychologist, Bentham's individualism and Webb's Fabianism are one in motive and appeal.

and complications do not themselves create a need for monopolistic competition theory. Where that theory is needed is in handling genuine empirical deviations from perfect competition. Mere interdependence of essentially competitive industries should have led Sraffa merely to a plea for abandonment of Marshallian partial-equilibrium models in favor of Walrasian general-equilibrium models.

Today, as a result of quite other historical influences and developments, general-equilibrium thinking has swept the field of analytical economics. A modern theorist would say that the box diagram analysis of optimal allocation of inputs among industries is just the tool to handle this standard instance of increasing cost. The production possibility frontier, or so-called opportunity cost transformation frontier, captures the essence of the phenomena. But remember that this frontier was first introduced, and then in connection with Haberler's analysis of international trade, only in 1930. It was *after* the 1930's that Stolper and Samuelson, Joan Robinson, and Viner clarified the increasing cost case by considering it in its general-equilibrium context by use of the factor box diagram or equivalent verbal reasonings.[12]

Fortunately, Sraffa's failure to realize that the Walrasian model would supply many of the deficiencies of the Marshallian partial equilibrium served the useful function of pushing him down the road toward Chamberlinian monopolistic competition theory. Because of realistic market conditions that standard theory had been forced to gloss over, ignore, or deny, economics was long overdue for a movement in that direction. If anyone doubts that Sraffa, Mrs. Robinson, and Chamberlin had a useful task to perform, let him only compare the contribution to the cost controversy by Dennis Robertson in 1924 (Stigler and Boulding, *op. cit.*, pp. 143–149) with the Sraffa contribution of 1926. Robertson was one of the world's leading economists, a Marshallian expert if ever there was one, and at the

---

[12] See W. F. Stolper and P. A. Samuelson, "Protection and Real Wages," *Review of Economic Studies*, IX (1941), pp. 58–74, reprinted in H. S. Ellis and L. A. Metzler, eds., *Readings in the Theory of International Trade*, Irwin, Homewood, Ill., 1949; J. Robinson, "Rising Supply Price," *Economica*, VIII (1941), pp. 1–8, reprinted in Stigler and Boulding, *Readings in Price Theory*, pp. 233–241; J. Viner, Supplement to 1931 *Zeitschrift für Nationalökonomie*, appearing in *Readings in Price Theory*, pp. 198–232. For Haberler's first paper using the frontier, see G. Haberler, "Die Theorie der komparativen Kosten und ihre Auswertung für die Begründung des Freihandels," *Weltwirtschaftliches Archiv*, XXXII (1930), which gave rise to the well-known expository articles by A. P. Lerner in the 1932 and 1934 *Economica* and by W. W. Leontief in the 1934 *Quarterly Journal of Economics*. Irving Fisher had used a transformation curve in connection with the trade-off between present and future consumption early in this century; Frederic Benham and R. F. Harrod had anticipated in the 1930's a number of the critical relationships involved in the factor-price box diagrams.

prime of his scholarly life. Yet he still enmeshed himself in mystical falling cost curves of a competitive industry, conjuring up group identities that have no existence, and failed completely to relate the behavior of the trees to that of the forest. Robertson's realistic instinct was right – costs do *not* behave as if generated by constant-returns-to-scale production functions – but he failed to follow through and drop the incompatible assumption of perfect competition, thereby forcing himself into logical contradiction and ambiguity. In Sraffa's world of monopolies, each with its own market but checked by overlapping substitutes, we are clearly on the way to Robert Triffin's 1940 *Monopolistic Competition and General Equilibrium Theory*, and hence on the way to *The Theory of Monopolistic Competition*.

THE BREAKDOWN OF PERFECT COMPETITION

Perfect competition theory had to be jettisoned in favor of some alternative theory, primarily in the decreasing cost case. J. M. Clark sensed this and gave as title to his too-little appreciated classic of the 1920's, *The Economics of Overhead Costs*. This is a good title, but it would be a better one still if it had been named *The Economics of Increasing Returns*. Returns rather than costs are the relevant phenomena because costs can depend on pecuniary changes in factor prices that have no distorting effects on competitive equilibrium.

It is hardly an exaggeration to assert:

Increasing returns is the prime case of deviations from perfect competition.

Its corollary is this:

Universal constant returns to scale (in every thing, including the effective acquisition and communication of knowledge) is practically certain to convert laissez-faire *or free enterprise into perfect competition.*

I must not overstate my case. Let me digress to recognize that there are other causes of monopolistic imperfection than deviations from constant returns.

(i) There are of course patents, trademarks, and other government created or "institutional" monopolies. But notice even here that the King does not give the princely gift of being permitted to compete with a million other farmers for a living; his franchise often, though not always, refers to an industry with some monopoly feature to begin with.

(ii) Then there are self-serving scarcities of knowledge. I ought to share my profitable secrets on how to produce competitive corn more efficiently with other farmers, but why should I? It might eventually depress the price of corn, and inhibit me from expanding the scale of my profitable operations. In a utopian world, one man need not give up his fertilizer to another because in doing so he is deprived of its use; but when one man gives up knowledge to another he is still left with as much useful knowledge for himself, and an optimally running society would ensure that this external economy be extended beyond the point that the private pecuniary calculus would motivate. Still, we must not confuse the issue by classifying any departure from the optimum due to externalities as itself necessarily coming under the heading of monopolistic competition.

(iii) The old-fashioned notion of *contrived* scarcity, as distinguished from *natural* scarcity, deserves mention.[13] Reformers used to speak of the "land monopoly," meaning no more than that land is scarce, and earns very high incomes for the few people who happen to own much of it. Fabians like Shaw and Webb also used such terms, and extended this concept of monopoly to all private property (at the same time making what we would call the Austrian assumption that all factors of production can be regarded as being fairly inelastic in supply to society and hence can be viewed as "rent-earning"). Often they joined with Marxians in regarding human labor as being exploited in the sense of getting less than 100 percent of the national product, having to give up too large a fraction to undeserving owners of property.[14]

Of course to modern theorists such usage of the nomenclature of *monopoly* is only confusing. All the phenomena of exploitation described are completely compatible with the most pure competition. The Duke of Liverpool may earn tens of millions of pounds a year by renting his vast acres of land in perfectly competitive markets. The demand curve for his factors of production could conceivably be

---

[13] See the chapter on profit in any of the recent editions of P. A. Samuelson, *Economics*, McGraw-Hill, New York, 1964.

[14] In the 1930's, Oskar Lange urged Marxists to look at the problem of exploitation in this way and not to waste time on the orthodox Marxian labor theory of value. O. Lange, "Marxian Economics and Modern Economic Theory," *Review of Economic Studies*, II (1935), pp. 189–201. For essentially the same, view, see J. Robinson, *An Essay on Marxian Economics*, Macmillan, London, 1942. For a diagnosis of property income that neglects the identification made by such reformers of nonland property with land property, see G. J. Stigler, "Bernard Shaw, Sidney Webb, and the Theory of Fabian Socialism," *Proceedings of the American Philosophical Society*, CIII (1959), pp. 469–475.

perfectly horizontal and still he would not be receiving from society according to his needs. The most simplified J. B. Clark model of perfectly competitive equilibrium would be subject to all of the reformers' criticisms.

Monopolistic or imperfect competition enters in genuinely only when the owner of a factor of production perceives that he faces a derived demand curve for his factor whose slope is appreciably negative. It then pays him to withhold some of his supply lest the last bit affect adversely the terms of trade of the whole supply. This means merely that he always equates marginal revenue product, which deviates from value of marginal product, to his marginal disutility; and the resulting discrepancy leads to a deviation from Pareto-optimality, with the consequence that it would be possible to find a movement that would make each and every person better off. Whatever ethical criticism may be made of the perfectly competitive imputation of rents to the so-called land monopoly, that configuration is assuredly Pareto-optimal. So to speak, what the exploited lose in material terms, the exploiters gain.[15]

(iv) This instance of monopolistic competition, associated with the ownership under one direction of a unique productive factor, can certainly

---

[15] The ancient antipathy toward interest and usury represents a beautiful mingling of elements of imperfect competition and ethical abhorrence of purely competitive imputations. The Bible, Aristotle, the Medieval Schoolmen, and the man in the street abhor usury for any or all of the following reasons. (1) The man who borrows is usually poorer and in greater distress than the man who lends. (We should for the same reason criticize the purchase of bread for cash by a low-income consumer from a prosperous baker.) (2) The curse of the poor is their ignorance and, ignorant or not, many debtors have traditionally had to borrow in monopolistically competitive markets. (3) A man may be tempted to borrow even though society and he himself in retrospect or in tranquil contemplation may deem the full consequences of such actions personally and socially harmful. (In the same way *laissez-faire* could lead to opium, cigarette, and unaesthetic-auto-mobile purchases, which some or all of the electorate might deem better prohibited by self-imposed democratic fiat, unanimous or of lesser majority. There would be more such legislation but for the realization that many such fiats are practically unenforceable and end up doing more harm than good. This does not affect the principle.) (4) Simple failure to see through the monetary veil covering the true production and time-phasing-of-consumption implications of money borrowing. (I have in mind here a statement we would consider ridiculous if not attributed to Aristotle: money is barren, hence interest *verboten*. One who believes it legitimate to pay rabbits for the borrowing of gravid rabbits, or pay twenty-years-purchase for permanently fertile land, ought not to cavil at the same operations performed with the device of money.) See Thomas F. Divine, *Interest, an Historical and Analytical Study in Economics and Modern Ethics*, Marquette, Milwaukee, 1959, for a Jesuit's view, which seems to argue that, today, interest transactions should be regarded as legitimate if arising in truly competitive markets.

persist even in the presence of universal constant returns to scale. When is such concentration of decision making to be expected? If we think in oversimplified terms of social output as being produced by the few broad categories of homogeneous land, homogeneous labor, and the capital goods ultimately producible out of these primary factors, and if these primary factors are under the dispersed ownership of millions of different individuals, then contrived scarcity would seem out of the question. Each small factor owner faces a derived demand curve of virtually infinite elasticity: there is no discrepancy between marginal revenue and price to cause deadweight loss.

But even here the competitive configuration is vulnerable. Unless we invoke a significant real cost to the formation of collusive communications, pushing the theory of games to its logical limits will lead to the following paradox. Let everyone in the system act like a pure competitor except the owners of one factor, say the owners of homogeneous land. Now let two small land owners collude, acting tacitly or explicitly in common. Ending up still small relative to the whole, they will reap no advantage, but it is important to realize there will be no *dis*advantage in their colluding – and this can be said about the colluding of 100,000 land owners or 90 or even 100 percent of all land owners. With respect to incipient collusion, then, the *laissez-faire* system is under a kind of neutral equilibrium even in universal constant returns to scale. But when millions of land owners act in concert, they do face a tilted demand curve and benefit by taking into account the discrepancy between their marginal and average revenues. This can be summarized.

THEOREM. *Even under universal constant returns to scale, the competitive configuration is unstable with respect to (costless) collusion of owners of factors of production.*

It will be said that the above result depends critically on assuming away all costs of organizing and policing collusions. And so it does. Realistically, there are always some costs to organizing concerted action – the basic costs of communication and persuasion, and the important costs of overcoming or adjusting to antitrust and common-law prohibitions against such collusions. Perhaps we are lucky that people are so dispersed, perverse, cantankerous, and deaf to communication, for otherwise our world of not-very-workable competition could be far more imperfectly competitive indeed. That is the moral of the story of the Tower of Babel. Easy communication can add to knowledge; it can also add to deadweight loss!

Anyone who had tried to coordinate two people on the dance floor or eleven people on the playing field will appreciate how difficult it is to coordinate hundreds of millions of producers. There is safety in numbers. (And we shall see that it is the deviations from constant returns to scale that seriously deprive society of that safety.) It is precisely here, though, that the competitive configuration becomes vulnerable to a new threat – *the use of government itself to coerce collusive action*. A million farmers cannot persuade each other to withhold wheat from the market, but – speaking luridly – the pistol in the hands of the U.S. marshal and the threat of bars of the Leavenworth penitentiary work miraculously toward orderly marketing.

It was Gunnar Myrdal, in his 1950 Manchester lectures[16], who stressed the fundamental fact that the same self-interest on which economists rely to keep atomistic competitors minimizing costs and maximizing profits can be expected in a modern democracy to lead to class legislation that is destructive of *laissez-faire* and competitive equilibrium. How could it be otherwise? You breed me a race of individualistic Benthamites, and after a century of democratic development I have to confront you with a race of Fabian interventionists. It will be said that coercion is involved. Precisely.[17]

Thus far I have been talking about an idealized aggregative model with only a few homogeneous categories of inputs. From the standpoint of coercion by government, this homogeneity or symmetry of factor owners is a boon, making the attractiveness of a common rule

---

[16] G. Myrdal, "The Trend towards Economic Planning," *Manchester School of Economic and Social Studies*, XIX (1951), pp. 1–42.

[17] A question in the theory of games poses itself. In the absence of government coercion, once all n owners formed a monopolistic collusion, could not one of them hope to benefit by breaking away and refusing to withhold part of his supply? More specifically, is such a collusion therefore unstable and can we prove that, as $n \to \infty$, perfect competition is immune to the collusions I have been talking about? Yes, in the following formal sense: let land be equally divided among n identical landlords, and let there be m identical propertyless laborers. Modern game theory, following Edgeworth, defines the "core" of the resulting game as the set of final imputations with the property that they are immune to being upset by some new coalitions among a subset of the $m + n$ participants. Then it is a theorem that as n and m both go to infinity, the core of the game shrinks to the purely competitive imputation. Cf. G. Debreu and H. Scarf, "A Limit Theorem on the Core of an Economy," *International Economic Review*, IV (1963), pp. 235–246, where references to the work of R. J. Aumann, M. Shubik, and H. Scarf are given. I have benefited from oral conversation with Professor Scarf.

and its enforcement all the easier. But in real life, factors of production are not homogeneous. No two acres of land, no two pairs of hands, are really alike. When we put away our telescope and look at economic reality with a microscope we see that the occurrence of contrived scarcities becomes locally almost universal.

Here is a strong example. Withholding one of two one-hundred-acre Iowa corn farms will not increase the pecuniary marginal product gained from the other. But suppose we divide any one such farm into a consecutively numbered checkerboard of one-inch squares. Give me ownership of all the odd-numbered squares and my identical twin ownership of the even. We have now created for ourselves a fine problem in bilateral monopoly, and it is a problem that, despite all the brave symbolism of game theory, is indeterminate in its solution. Without my plot, my twin's land is useless. Conceivably I might contrive my scarcity so as to get up to 100 percent of the joint pecuniary product. Conceivably he might get up to 100 percent or any figure in between. Ultimately, there is no way to tell. Because we happen to be identical twins, a facile mind will come up with the principle of insufficient reason and suggest a 50 percent split or even an imputation based on the toss of a fair coin. But why need that be the outcome? He needs me, I need him. If stubborn enough, either one can inflict total damage on the other and on both.

Of course many will say that the farm ought to be cultivated as an organic whole regardless of the ultimate distribution of the thereby maximized product. And actually a court of equity would probably so rule. Indeed, our jurisprudence evolves traditions and principles that serve to rule out transparently obvious deadweight loss. I could devise a contract to bequeath every other square of a checkered farm to one of my two sons; but I would have to be explicit in drawing up such a will and my executor might have difficulty in proving that I was of sound mind while doing so. In the absence of unmistakable specification, the prudent court will act to ensure that the whole plot of land can be "prudently" used.

Let us be clear, though, that the rational self-interest of each of two free wills does not necessitate that there will emerge, even in the most idealized game-theoretic situation, a Pareto-optimal solution that maximizes the sum of the two opponents' profits, *in advance of and without regard to how that maximized profit is to be divided up among them*. Except by fiat of the economic analyst or by his tautologically redefining what constitutes "nonrational" behavior, we cannot rule out a non-Pareto-optimal outcome. We can rule it out only by Humpty-Dumptyism.

This microscopic prevalence of contrived scarcity and indeterminate bilateral monopoly is obvious, because I have selected a transparently obvious case of artificially numbered checkerboard plots of land. It is not so obvious, but it is true, that a similar problem is ubiquitous in real life at the microscopic level. If my secretary has been trained to my ways and I have been trained to hers, there is a range of indeterminacy to the imputation of our joint product. Without her I can find some kind of a substitute but not necessarily, per dollar of cost, a close substitute. On the other hand, were I to turn tomorrow to a career in plumbing, her considerable investment in mastering the vocabulary of my peculiar kind of economics might become totally valueless. If I were poised on the margin of indifference it might pay her to make me side payments to tempt me to eschew a career with the monkey wrench.

Again, this is a fanciful example. But as Gerald Shove of Cambridge used to insist, actual commercial life is at one level more like a jig-saw puzzle than like an equilibrium of homogeneous substances. This Shovian insight is well known to every personnel director and real-estate agent.[18]

(v) Probability or uncertainty phenomena are another breeder of bigness and possible monopolistic imperfections. This can be considered an alternative to "increasing returns" as a cause of monopoly; or, if we wish to alter our terminology, stochastic phenomena can be said to be a cause of increasing returns and decreasing costs. What is involved here is the fact, basic to the "law of large numbers" and the "central limit" theorems of statistics, that the sum of two identical independent variates does not have twice the standard deviation of each but only 40 percent more than each. Since $\sqrt{2} = 1.4+$, we see that a $\sqrt{N}$ law is involved for total cost or $1/\sqrt{N}$ for average costs; this implies for

---

[18] Some readers have interpreted R. H. Coase, "The Problem of Social Cost," *Journal of Law and Economics*, III (1960), pp. 1–44, as having shown how *laissez-faire* pricing can solve the problem of "externalities" and "public goods" harmoniously. The above analysis shows that a problem of pricing two or more inputs that can be used in common is not solved by reducing it to a determinate maximized total whose allocation among the parts is an indeterminate problem in multilateral monopoly. It should come as news to no economist or game theorist that duopoly, oligopoly, bilateral and multilateral monopoly are indeterminate in their solution.

returns, instead of a homogeneous function of degree one, a homogeneous function of degree two.

Thus if two power grids are side by side it always pays to convert them in order to take advantage of noncoincidence of peak loads. General Motors can borrow at a lower interest rate as a result of its being able to cancel Pontiac variations against those of Oldsmobile and Chevrolet – a fact that should give pause to those critics of government who feel it is somehow unfair or inefficient for it to borrow large sums at low interest rates to allocate among diverse public projects. Indeed, in a world of stochastic risk, where technology itself can be made to follow constant returns to scale, the ultimate state would seem to be one in which all enterprise is owned by one large mutual fund, with maximum diversification of risk enjoyed by its security owners. If this seems like a Leviathan monopoly, we can alternatively think of it as benevolent-government ownership, under the control of all of us as citizens.

It is important to realize that reduction of relative risk takes place only to the degree that the contingent events pooled are *not* perfectly positively correlated. Thus the tendency toward merger and monopoly is not so harmful if it is merely a case of pooling *independent* risks: if Tri-Continental Investment Company owns both a Montana ranch and a Florida Ford agency, it pools risks without creating monopoly power itself. However, in real life the fact that largeness permits reduced riskiness is only too likely to reinforce *other* increasing returns factors making for bigness *and* imperfection of competition.

Before turning to increasing returns proper, the Hamlet of the drama involving imperfect competition, I ought to point out some interaction between stochastic uncertainty and quasi-geometrical deviation from constant returns.

Consider the case of oil drilling. A homogeneous field is best drilled by wells located in hexagons with an optimal grid distance between wells. Under *laissez-faire* this does not happen: I drill at the boundary of my property to "rob" my neighbor, and he does the same to rob me. Here then is a case of an "external diseconomy." But when we analyze the reasons for it, we see that drilling oil on two acres of land involves essentially a joint productive phenomenon, not intrinsically different from joint production of wool and mutton. But joint production is not itself a sufficient condition to kill off perfect competition. Farming, our most competitive industry, always involves joint production. I have heard of sheep farmers, but never of separate wool and separate mutton farmers. As long as the joint production of sheep (i.e., wool-*cum*-mutton) can be replicated at constant returns, competition remains perfect among multiproduct firms.

The same *almost* applies to an oil field (or to an orchard, which needs bees to cross-fertilize it but which may find its bees flying off to fertilize some other orchard). As one firm grows in size to encompass many oil wells, it is a geometric fact that the ratio of its perimeter declines relative to its area. Hence, with each firm very large, the oil field will be exploited mostly by optimal hexagons: the joint production phenomena will be mostly internalized and the external diseconomy held down to a minimum. Even if you own a county in Texas, you still have negligible monopoly power in the oil markets of the world.

But here is where uncertainty enters in. No one can know in advance how much oil will be found in any region of Texas. Even the largest oil companies will prefer to buy up only part of any new region, in order to diversify their risks. Hence uncertainty phenomena help, under *laissez-faire*, to pulverize the optimal size arrangements that ought to prevail.

We are back to the fact that perfect knowledge is not producible and capable of being optimally allocated according to first-degree homogeneous production functions. Impurity of competition is a mighty breeder of imperfection of knowledge and foresight – as every small-town banker knows, and for which he is grateful.

Before returning to increasing returns, we may digress to discuss some geometric instances in which imperfect competition could produce inefficiencies not present in either (a) perfect competition, or (b) "perfect" monopoly. (The impatient reader may skip the next section at a first reading.)

WASTES OF FREEDOM UNDER IMPERFECT SPATIAL COMPETITION

To illustrate that free enterprise can lead to greater inefficiency than either monopoly or ideal planning or a perfectly competitive configuration, I take a spatial example like that of Chamberlin's Appendix C. Rival stores or plants locate on a circle along which customers are distributed evenly. The farther goods must be transported the greater the real costs. Furthermore, true cost is assumed to increase more than proportionally with distance: hence, for two units each to go two miles is better than for one to go three miles and one to go one mile.

Figure 5–1 shows the pattern that would be optimal if there are $n = 1, 2, 3,$ 4, 5, 6, 7, 8 stores or factories. They should, of course, be symmetrically

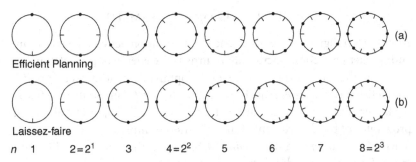

Efficient Planning

Laissez-faire

n 1 $2=2^1$ 3 $4=2^2$ 5   6   7 $8=2^3$

Figure 5-1. The symmetric, efficient pattern of planning is duplicated where $n = 2^m$, $m = 0, 1, 2, 3, \ldots, \ldots$; but, in the remaining half of the instances where $n{\neq}2^m$, the pattern compares unfavorably with the oligopoly pattern that results when each new man finds it most profitable to settle halfway between the most separated – but neighboring – established centers.

placed to minimize cost, as in the upper circles of Figure 5–1a. The halfway point between centers is the watershed between markets, and the median person in each market encounters a distance to the center of half of the market length.

By contrast the lower row of circles, Figure 5–1b, shows what will happen under higgledy-piggledy *laissez-faire*. A single monopoly has the same pattern as that utopian planning. A second seller then moves to the antipodal point, again producing the same pattern as ideal planning. But for $n = 3$, there is asymmetry and waste: the third man can do no better, in the short run when the others are located, than toss a coin and go halfway between the existing two sellers. Now one quarter of the customers get their distances reduced, the rest are left with unchanged distances, and the maximum distance traveled by any customer is $0.5\pi R$: this contrasts with the efficient pattern that cuts the maximum distance a consumer must travel from $0.5\pi R$ to $0.33\pi R$, or by one third.

Paradoxically, oligopoly leads again to the ideal when $n = 4$; similarly, for $n = 8$ and generally for $n = 2^m$, where m denotes an integer. But between 2^m and $(2^m)2$, no matter how large n (and m) become, we are half the time in the unbalanced, asymmetric, inefficient pattern. No wonder cities need planning: the random walk of history does not know where it is heading, and its past wandering prejudices the efficiency of each new increment. Inefficient reality is not a blend of efficient monopoly and Pareto-optimal competition.[19]

[19] If society moves permanently from $n = 2$ to $n = 3$, the seller at 6 o'clock might well ultimately move toward 4, drawing the middle seller half as far in the same direction. But under dynamic growth, in passing through the efficient 1, 2, 4, 8, $\ldots$, 2^m, points, the firms

THE PARADOX OF ADAM SMITH

After the last digression, let us go back to the relation between laws of return and market perfection. Increasing returns is the enemy of perfect competition. And therefore it is the enemy of the optimality conditions that perfect competition can ensure. How ironic it thus is that Adam Smith, the founding father of the doctrine of the beneficent Invisible Hand, should also be the progenitor of the doctrine that "specialization is limited by the extent of the market." A *leitmotiv* in the *Wealth of Nations* is the concept of *division of labor*. Even if Smith did not realize it, we dwarfs who can stand on his gigantic shoulders should:

As long as the specialization is still *being limited by the division of labor, competition cannot be working perfectly.*

To this consideration should be added another. We have seen that constant returns to scale is the condition most perfectly constituted to produce perfect competition. But it is precisely the conditions of deviation from constant returns to scale that are the essence of the division of labor.

I must not overstate the case. There are certain kinds of specialization and division of labor that are compatible with constant returns: Ricardian comparative advantage in international trade gives us an example; the Heckscher-Ohlin analysis of international trade in terms of differences in *relative* factor endowments is another. But, and this is the point, the kind of division of labor that is limited, or could be limited, by the extent of the market is precisely the kind that is nonexistent under constant returns to scale.[20]

need have no incentive to avoid spending half the time in unbalanced states. Similarly, in two-dimensional space, an initial pattern of squares gives a less efficient grid than hexagons. Given stationary conditions, squares might get transformed into hexagons; but given *laissez-faire* growth, each new man has a short-run advantage in placing himself inside the largest market left, so that increased numbers lead to another grid of smaller squares or diamonds – still not efficient hexagons.

[20] Ohlin's now classic *Interregional and International Trade*, Harvard University Press, Cambridge, Mass., 1933, shows this same dualism. The Heckscher-Ohlin relative-factor-endowment theory is quite different from the other Ohlin theory, which in effect attributes trade to the advantages of specializing to reap the advantages of large-scale operations. In this second theory, Ohlin is being Smithian and plunging us into a Chamberlin universe. In his first theory, Ohlin is generalizing Ricardo. It is worthy of note that Smith, the great critic of mercantilistic protectionism, did not present so sophisticated a monetary mechanism of trade-balance equalization as did his friend and predecessor, David Hume; nor does he anticipate the conclusive Ricardo-Torrens arithmetic of comparative advantage. What does he give us free traders besides commonsense – I mean rhetoric? Merely the parable and symbol of the Invisible Hand, a metatheorem at best – and one not understood until the present generation of economists.

NUMBER GROWTH AND PERFECTION OF COMPETITION

Because I have repeatedly related perfection of competition to strict constant returns, I have by logical implication been relating imperfection of competition to deviations from constant returns. This requires me, in an essay glorifying the Chamberlinian revolution, to take sides in a long-standing controversy between Chamberlin and Kaldor. Kaldor[21] long maintained that much of market imperfection would disappear if all production functions obeyed strict constant returns to scale – that is, if they were strictly homogeneous of degree one. This Chamberlin has always denied. Wording the issue as I have carefully done, my verdict must be for Kaldor in this matter – but with the warning that Chamberlin is instinctively right in his concern that we must not extrapolate new significances into such a verdict.

Logically, our syllogisms can be set out as follows.

THEOREM: *In the absence of institutional elements of monopoly, production functions that are universally of strict first-degree homogeneity lead under laissez-faire to perfect (or pure) competition no matter how "differentiated" are the products consumers demand.*

COROLLARY: *In the absence of institutional elements of monopoly, imperfection of competition presupposes some deviations from constancy of returns. The terribly important welfare and market problem of differentiation of product arises only because of these deviations (which are inevitable in the real world, because at small enough output, first-degree homogeneity is an empirical absurdity). All degrees of sourness of cider could be produced and enjoyed under constant returns. But as soon as we abandon this strong returns case, product differentiation becomes an acute problem and one with "public good" aspects.*[22]

I don't see why any Chamberlinian should deny the literal truth of my carefully worded propositions. They do not say (i) imperfect competition is unimportant; (ii) product differentiation is irrational; or (iii) the use of the word "indivisibility" is mandatory or helpful in describing (or

---

[21] See N. Kaldor, "Market Imperfection and Excess Capacity," *Economica*, II (1935), pp. 33–50, reprinted in G. Stigler and K. Boulding, eds., *Readings in Price Theory*, pp. 384–403; and *Theory of Monopolistic Competition*, particularly Appendix G and Chapter IX.

[22] P. A. Samuelson, "The Pure Theory of Public Expenditure," *Review of Economics and Statistics*, XXXVI (1954), pp. 387–389; "Diagrammatic Exposition of Public Expenditure," *Review of Economics and Statistics*, XXXVII (1955), pp. 350–356; "Aspects of Public Expenditure Theories," *Review of Economics and Statistics*, XL (1958), pp. 332–338.

"explaining"!) unit cost curves that decline in some short or long period. My propositions do not imply, but I admit they do tempt one to accept, the extrapolation that says:

CONJECTURE: *As the size of the market grows relative to the size of the minimum scale at which unit costs are at their lowest, the system approaches the perfectly competitive equilibrium.*

This last conjecture Chamberlin has stoutly denied on a variety of grounds. Thus, assuming zero costs and a homogeneous product, he points out (in Appendix G) that for any number of sellers – whether $N = 1$ or some large number – firm equilibrium is at the point of maximum gross (and net) revenue where elasticity of demand $E_N = -1$. Hence as $N\to\infty$, $E_N = -1 \neq -\infty$. We can grant Chamberlin this, and sidestep the issue of whether, in calculating a typical firm's E_N as $p(\sum q_j)/p'(\sum q_j)q_i$, we should hold $p(q_1 + \cdots + q_N)$ constant as we take the limit $N\to\infty$, or hold q_1 constant. But Chamberlin's is an empty victory, once we introduce ever-so-little positive marginal cost for each firm. Thus, if every firm has constant M.C. equal to $m > 0$, the equilibrium condition $p + q_i p' = m$ leads, as $N\to\infty$, to $E_N = -\infty$, the competitive result. Geometrically, how can free entry result in tangency of a downward sloping firm demand curve to a horizontal non-U-shaped cost curve? The answer is, only when $N = \infty$ and the firm's demand has its intercept touching but not crossing the horizontal cost curve. Although, as $N\to\infty$, $q_i = Q/N\to 0$, we find industry $Q = Nq_i\to Q^*$ the root of the competitive equilibrium M.C. $= m = p(Q)$.[23]

Chamberlin cannot seem to admit the logic of Kaldor's result because his imagination will simply not let him envisage anything so unrealistic as strict constant returns to scale. His subconscious keeps reminding him that at very small scales such an assumption is empirically preposterous. Granting

---

[23] I must defend Chamberlin from having, in his Chapter 5 large-group case, become enmeshed in Zeno's Paradox, in which an infinite number of infinitesimals are wrongly summed to zero rather than a positive finite case. Stigler (*op. cit.*, pp. 15–17) wrongly treats such a symmetric case of heterogeneous substitutes as *logically* self-contradictory; questions of realism aside, Stigler simply has not used his mathematical imagination strongly enough. Let $q_i = D^i(p_1,\ldots,p_n,\ldots) = D(p_i, p_1 \ldots,)$, a function symmetric in the (p_j) variables where $j\neq i$. Suppose $\partial q_i/\partial p_i = -A$, independently of n and $\partial q_i/\partial p_j = -B/(n-1)$ for $j\neq i$. Then the effect of a change in p_i on any p_j does indeed go to zero as $n\to\infty$. The effect, however, on the sum of the *increasing* (!) number of such other price changes does add up to a finite positive number, namely $B/(2A - B)$. But the resulting effect of *all* such changes on q_i, which is what is relevant for testing the legitimacy of Chamberlin's *ceteris paribus* dd curve, nevertheless does go to zero as Chamberlin says, being equal to $B^2/(2A - B)(N - 1)$.

that the point is a purely logical one, reminiscent of Scholastic quarrels over how many angels can stand on the point of a pin, we must insist that under the ideal conditions postulated, each consumer could have produced to his own order any differentiated product at minimum cost, and hence Chamberlin ought to concede absence of the slightest monopolistic imperfections.

QUANTUM-THEORY ECONOMICS AND ASYMPTOTIC HOMOGENEITY

The "new math" has infected mathematical economics. Inequalities, convex sets, and the theories of cones have made modern formulations more elegant and easier. Unfortunately, if we look at modern treatises[24] we find that often they score easy victories and represent a retrogression where realism in dealing with market imperfections is concerned. Thus the nice necessary and sufficient conditions for a maximum in linear programming, or in more general Kuhn-Tucker concave programming, come after ruling out increasing returns and varying returns phenomena – in which things often get worse before they get better, and for which there is a formidable search problem for the *maximum maximorum* among a large number of local maxima.

Because the convexity conditions of the modern formulations of competition are rarely met in real life, I propose in this section to state and prove some asymptotic theorems according to which we approach, in the limit as replicable numbers become indefinitely large, an approximation to the convexity conditions needed for competition.

Whether or not we care to use the terminology of "indivisibilities," we can agree with Chamberlin that, at the smallest scales of production, unit cost curves are falling; hence, production functions, $Q = F(V_1, \ldots, V_n)$, act at small enough scales as if they possessed homogeneity of greater than degree one, as measured locally by the scale elasticity coefficient $R = \sum_1^n V_j(\partial F/\partial V_j)/F$. In principle there is no reason why this stage should not prevail forever, with the unit cost function $c(Q) = C(Q)/Q$, forever having a negative slope. In some such cases, as where $R \leq 1 - \varepsilon$ always, no matter how great the demand grows for the homogeneous product a regime of perfect competition can never be attained.

---

[24] For example, R. Dorfman, P. A. Samuelson, and R. Solow, *Linear Programming and Economic Analysis*, McGraw-Hill, New York, 1958; G. Debreu, *Theory of Value*, Wiley, New York, 1959.

Suppose, however, that there is a level c' of unit cost below which $c(Q)$ can never fall. Then asymptotically, $c(Q)$ must approach as a limit the horizontal curve $c(Q) \equiv c^*$; and along with unit cost, marginal cost $c'(Q) = C(Q) + QC'(Q)$ must approach the same horizontal asymptote, c^*. Asymptotically, a near approach to perfect competition is then possible, with $R \to 1$, the constant returns case suitable for perfect competition.

A third of a century ago M. F. W. Joseph[25] indicated how U-shaped cost curves, belonging to replicable plants or (under free entry) to replicable firms, lead asymptotically to *horizontal* unit cost curves for the industry and multiplant firms. After elucidating this analysis, I shall show that the possibility of replication leads to "asymptotic-first-degree-homogeneity" of the production function.

Figure 5–2a constructs the lower-envelope unit cost curve attainable from 1, 2, ..., N, ... replicable plants. The basic curve 1–1 is shown U-shaped in Figures 5–2a and 5–2b. The curve 2–2 shows U-shaped unit costs when output is divided *equally* among 2 plants; similarly in 3–3, output is divided equally among 3 plants. Geometrically, 2–2 is the same as the 1–1 curve but with the horizontal scale doubled; 3–3 is the same as 1–1 curve but with the horizontal scale tripled; and so forth. To keep unit, and hence total, costs as low as possible, follow 1–1 to its intersection point with 2–2, marked 12, corresponding to Q_{12}; then follow 2–2 until it intersects with 3–3 at 23; and so forth.

Thus we generate the scalloped or curved heavy curve. But, as is shown in the enlarged horizontal scale of Figure 5–2b, depicting what happens in each and every identical plant, the height of the switch points $(12; 23; 34; \ldots; N; N + 1)$ moves east and south to the level of minimum unit costs, $c^* = c(q^*)$. Asymptotically, the heavy envelope approaches the horizontal level c', and the sharpness of its corners becomes less and less. Within each of the identical plants, when N becomes so large that its difference with $N + 1$ becomes of negligible relative importance, each of the identical plants has its outputs remaining ever closer to the optimum scale q', corresponding to the bottom of the U.

To pave the way for asymptotic homogeneity, I present briefly the mathematics of the Joseph analysis.

Let $c(q) = C(q)/q =$ unit cost of 1 replicable plant; $c(q^*) < c(q), q \neq q^*$. Then unit costs when N plants are being used equally are given by

[25] M. F. W. Joseph, "A Discontinuous Cost Curve and the Tendency to Increasing Returns," *Economic Journal*, XLIII (1938), pp. 390–398.

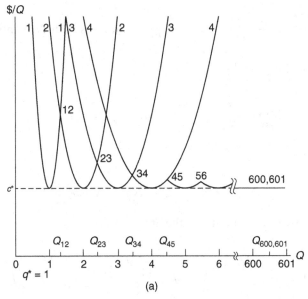

Figure 5-2a. The heavy lower envelope goes along 1–1 to its 12 intersection with 2–2, to its 23 intersection with 3–3, ..., until asymptotically it is the horizontal line at the $c^* = c(q^*) = \text{Min } c(q)$ level.

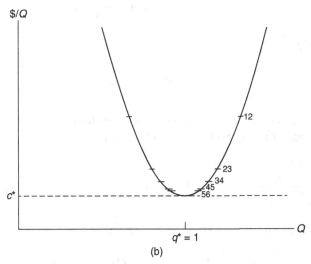

Figure 5-2b. Each of the identical plants cuts back its output when one new plant is brought in. The rearrangements, from the right of q^* to the left, become smaller and smaller as the switch points (12; 23; ...) approach the (q^*, c^*) bottom-of-the-U as a limit.

$$\frac{NC(Q/N)}{Q} = \frac{C(Q/N)}{Q/N} = c\left(\frac{Q}{N}\right) = \text{unit costs with } N \text{ plants} \quad (5\text{-}1)$$

The envelope is given by

$$\operatorname*{Min}_{(N)} c\left(\frac{Q}{N}\right) = \Phi(Q) \geq \operatorname*{Min}_{(q)} c(q) = c(q^*) = c^* \quad (5\text{-}2)$$

Obviously,

$$\Phi(Q) = c^* \text{ for } Q = Nq^*, \quad N \text{ integral} \quad (5\text{-}3)$$

The successive switchpoints are the unique roots of

$$c\left(\frac{Q_{12}}{1}\right) = c\left(\frac{Q_{12}}{2}\right), c\left(\frac{Q_{23}}{2}\right) = c\left(\frac{Q_{23}}{3}\right), \dots, c\left(\frac{Q_{N,N+1}}{N}\right)$$
$$= c\left(\frac{Q_{N,N+1}}{N+1}\right) \quad (5\text{-}4)$$

Asymptotically, if $c''(q^*) > 0$, it can be shown that

$$Q_{N,N+1} \approx Nq^*\left(1 + \frac{1}{2N+1}\right) \quad (5\text{-}5)$$

Necessarily

$$\lim_{N \to \infty} \Phi(Q) = c^* \quad (5\text{-}6)$$

which is the Joseph theorem on asymptotic constant costs.
Now consider a replicable production function

$$Q = F(V_1, V_2, \dots, V_n)$$
$$= F\left(V_1, \frac{V_2}{V_1}V_1, \dots, \frac{V_n}{V_1}V_1\right) = F(V_1, v_2 V_1, \dots, v_n V_1) = F(V_1) \quad (5\text{-}7)$$

For fixed factor rations, $(V_2/V_1, \dots, V_n/V_1)$, let

$$\operatorname*{Max}_{[V_1]} \frac{F(V_1)}{V_1} = \frac{F(V_1^*)}{V_1^*} = f^*(v_2, \dots, v_n) \quad (5\text{-}8)$$

THEOREM OF ASYMPTOTIC HOMOGENEITY: *The maximum output obtainable from optimally replicated production processes is given by*:

$$\underset{[N]}{\text{Max}} NF\left(\frac{V_1}{N}, \frac{V_2}{N}, \ldots, \frac{V_n}{N}\right) = \underset{[N]}{\text{Max }} NF\left(\frac{V_1}{N}\right)$$
$$= \psi(V_1, V_2, \ldots, V_n) = \psi(V_1) \geq f^* V_1,$$

with equality sign[26] *holding for* $V_1 = NV_1^*$; *and* (5-9)

$$\underset{\substack{V_1 \to \infty \\ V_i/V_1}}{\lim} = v_i \left[\frac{\psi(V_1, \ldots, V_n)}{V_1 f^*(V_2/V_1, \ldots, V_n/V_1)}\right] = 1. \qquad (5\text{-}9)$$

This is an important formalization of the Smithian dictum that widening the extent of the market will, after it can result in no further extension of the division of labor and exploitation of increasing returns, create conditions suitable for workably perfect competition.

One way to apply this is to hold technology of an industry constant, and also factor prices to it, while widening the demand curve for its homogeneous product (where there is such a thing!).

Thus, let

$$\sum q = Q = M \cdot D(p), \quad M \text{ being a parameter of widening} \qquad (5\text{-}10)$$

Then, as $M \to \infty$, the industry and firm equilibrium will approach that of perfect competition.

An alternative application of the asymptotic theorem comes from holding industry demand constant, $\sum q = Q = D(p)$ but imagining a technological change that reduces q^*, the bottom-of-the-U scale. Thus, write $c(q/\lambda q^*)$, and let $\lambda \to 0$ to attain perfect competition.

These asymptotic theorems must be used with great caution. Often they merely say, "If the world were different (in range and density,. . .) from what

---

[26] In the cases I have considered, the minimal asymptote is actually realized in the quantum states $(q^*, 2q^*, \ldots, Nq^*, \ldots)$, or $(V_1^*, 2V_1^*, \ldots, NV_1^*, \ldots)$. It is easy to construct cases in which this does not happen. Thus, consider two distinct elements of cost $[c_1(q), \Phi(q); c_2(q), \Phi_2(q)]$. If q_1^* and q_2^* are incommensurable numbers, like $(1, \sqrt{2},)$ their sum $\Phi_1(q) + \Phi_2(q)$ will still have the asymptotic property of approaching $c_1^* + c_2^*$, but $\Phi_1(q) + \Phi_2(q) > c_1(q) + c_2(q)$ for all finite q. Even if q_1^* and q_2^* are commensurable, but like 100 and 101 have a least common multiple that is very large (namely 10,100), then only for $q^* = (10, 100, 20, 200, \ldots N\, 10, 100)$, truly gigantic scales, will the minimum c^* be fully achieved. For the auto industry to be perfectly competitive, it must attain the optimum scale of that component with largest minimal scale.

it is, competition might be more perfect than it now is."[27] On the other hand, Bain, Sylos-Labini, and Modigliani have rightly emphasized that the conditions for replication and entry are important in determining and limiting the degree of imperfection of competition.[28]

THE PROLIFERATION OF DIFFERENTIATION

We now have the equipment to analyze and appraise Chamberlin's contention that proliferation of numbers alone need not lead to perfection of competition. No one will dispute his contention that merely doubling the areas containing, say, imperfectly competing barber shops need not reduce monopolistic elements. But of course it is an increase, in some sense, of the

---

[27] But where applicable, the asymptotic theorems are crucial. Thus most of the "successful solutions" to the public goods problem referred to in footnote 22 come in cases – like those where traffic is heavy enough to require numerous parallel roads, in which marginal cost pricing will just recover full cost – in which sufficient replication is possible.

[28] J. S. Bain, *Barriers to New Competition*, Harvard University Press, Cambridge, Mass., 1956; P. Sylos-Labini, *Oligopoly and Technical Progress*, Harvard University Press, Cambridge, Mass., 1962; F. Modigliani, "New Developments on the Oligopoly Front," *Journal of Political Economy*, LXVI (1958), pp. 215–252. This asymptotic theorem is relevant to the discussion of M. J. Farrell, "The Convexity Assumption in the Theory of Competitive Markets," *Journal of Political Economy*, LXVII (1959), pp. 377–391, with later contributions by F. Bator, T. C. Koopmans, S. Reiter, and M. J. Farrell in the 1961 *Journal of Political Economy*.

In (5–2) and my theorem it is important that N be integral. If N is unrealistically treated as any real number, (5–2) becomes $\Phi(Q) \equiv c^* Q$, since $\text{Min } c(Q/N) = c(q^*)$ is attained by setting $N = Q/q^*$, even where the latter ratio is not integral. This gives us our asymptotic result from the beginning! But, as Solomon knew when he ironically ordered the baby to be divided into halves for division between rival mothers, babies and plants come in integral numbers and it makes no sense to speak of $\sqrt{2}$ babies or even p/q babies where p and q are integers, $q \neq 1$.

I recall discussion by my old teacher, Paul Douglas, of a dubious demonstration by Wicksell that all production functions must be homogeneous of degree $R = 1$. For if R were greater than 1, we would have one single firm – an empirical absurdity. And if R were less than 1, we would have an infinite number of firms, each producing an infinitesimal – also, an empirical absurdity. Ergo, $R \equiv 1$! Actually, if $R > 1$ always, in the limit you could produce output with vanishingly small inputs per unit – perhaps an absurdity, but no man has ever been to the horizon to report back on its plentitude. And, if $R < 1$ always, with no integral or quantum restrictions on inputs, the expression $Nf(V^1/N, \ldots, V_n/N) \rightarrow \infty$ as $N \rightarrow \infty$, so you could get an *infinite* output from an iota of inputs – a neat trick if you can bring it off. The absurdity is in thinking that all functions can be divided into three categories: those with R *always* equal to, greater than, or less than unity. Given such an absurd Hobson's choice, perhaps $R = 1$ would win. But who needs accept such a specified choice, when R can be a variable magnitude, varying with scale for each set of proportions and going through the U-shaped pattern of this section.

density of numbers that everybody recognizes to be the relevant situation that needs to be appraised.

Chamberlin (Appendix G, p. 288) is willing to meet head on the case where numbers, and hence density, increase along a spatial line. He indicates, rightly, that if the sellers double and each remains sovereign in his halved market area, there is no presumed increase in each seller's elasticity of demand. (If transport costs diminished, so that each seller serves a larger exclusive domain, the same would be true, a conclusion that might give us pause.) But, when the number (and density) of sellers increases, will there not be a greater temptation on the part of some to cut prices – not merely to gain business from the next seller down the line, but in order to draw price-conscious customers from more remote areas? Within a large city, a niche develops for discount houses, which live in symbiosis with full-price stores. Within a hamlet, or even medium-size city, no similar opportunity for small-markup stores exists.

Admirers of perfect-competition theory like to point to large-volume, "competitive" sellers who provide a safety valve for the price-conscious consumers and who come into viable existence because of the existence of a sizable number of such consumers. To borrow a term from the unconventional wisdom, such consumers exercise in concert their "counter-vailing power." But, at best, this only establishes the existence of pockets of near-perfect competition.

A story is told about an oriental student who was asked, on his General Examination at Harvard by Professor Leontief, about integrability conditions and violations of transitivity of choice in consumer-preference theory. He was supposed to have replied airily, "Who cares about clazy people?" Well, God cares about price-insensitive consumers and the wastes involved in imperfectly competitive markets that experience the deadweight losses of non-Pareto-optimality. An ideal system is one that serves well the interests of ordinary man and not just those of *homo economicus*.

One of the beauties of perfect competition is that – if conditions suitable to it prevailed universally – under it most of us could relax our pursuit of self-interest, knowing that the existence of a margin of eager beavers sufficed to produce the price uniformity and other optimality conditions that we would all enjoy. A market system of imperfect competition that provides a competitive escape valve only to those ready to pay the price of perpetual vigilance is not an ideal system. To say, "Those who buy at prices well above marginal cost (including, of course, the extra costs of convenience services and differentiation of product) have made their beds. Let them lie in them – they could have chosen otherwise," is to express an attitude: it does not demonstrate that the wastes of imperfect competition under *laissez-faire* are small, or preferable to what would result from some government interference.

All my fine theorems about asymptotic homogeneity of the functions producing a homogeneous output, where the quantities of product of different sellers can be meaningfully added as $q_1 + q_2 + \cdots + q_N$, cannot negate the Chamberlinian insight that wider markets (more ultimate similar consumers) or reduced technical optimal scales (of the q_i^* type discussed above) are likely to permit, and hence induce, further differentiation of products. If electric power permits shorter runs of mousetrap production, consumers with a yen for diverse types of mousetraps will find someone providing a greater variety. Thus larger N may result merely in a finer grid of differentiated products, but without $N \to \infty$ leading to perfect competition.

I personally suspect that increases in N will generally, even *after* they induce the Chamberlinian pulverization of markets, tend to reduce market imperfection on balance. But that does not mean that the limit as $N \to \infty$ is zero market imperfection. Instead the limit may be at an irreducible positive degree of imperfection.

Staying, for metaphorical purposes only, with the spatial analogy, the proper Chamberlinian vision treats enlarged numbers and densities in the following way. As N grows, sellers (say doctors) become more frequent and tighter spaced. Specialists develop – internists, obstetricians, kidney specialists, left-kidney specialists, and so forth. Along a line, the beads or nodes of specialists – or of department stores versus local shops – are more sparse than the beads of general practitioners. On a uniform plane – as Lösch theorized[29] – the fine hexagonal grid of high-markup local stores will be contained in a coarser grid of high-volume stores.

Under free entry it is possible that new complexes of differentiated products can be created at constant costs or better. Investing enough money in advertising and other activities, a group of soap, cigarette, or cosmetic companies can come into existence at no worse than constant returns. After the rents are bid up of factors uniquely gifted to promotion – television networks or station licenses, world champion athletes, golden-voiced announcers – there may appear no extraordinary profits anywhere. Yet this is not to be identified with perfect competition, nor are we justified in regarding the differentiation of product as lacking in intrinsic utility. Most, if not all of the items, are being sold at an excess over marginal cost, such that it would add to the welfare of the universe if an extra item were

---

[29] A. Lösch, *The Economics of Location*, Yale University Press, New Haven, 1954.

somehow sold and consumed at less than market price. Nothing like this would occur in the conventional models of perfect competition, or, for that matter, of monopoly.

As the universe is seen to have more and more solar systems like ours, Nature contrives to perform more and more experiments with varied – or as we might say – differentiated outcomes. That is Chamberlin's imperishable vision.

CONCLUSION

In speaking of theories of monopolistic or imperfect competition as "revolutions," I know in advance that I shall provoke dissent. There are minds that by temperament will define away every proposed revolution. For them it is enough to point out that Keynes in 1936 had some partial anticipator in 1836. Newton is just a guy getting too much credit for the accretion of knowledge that covered centuries. A mountain is just a high hill; a hill; merely a bulging plain. Such people remind me of the grammar-school teacher we all had, who would never give 100 to a paper on the ground that "No one is perfect."

With such semantics, I have no quarrel – provided its rules-of-the-game are clearly understood. However, to those familiar with the history of sciences – how they develop, the role of new and altered modes of thinking in marking their growth, the role even of myth in the autobiography of a science – revolutions are a useful way of describing accelerations in the path of growth. An old theory – or model; or, to use Kuhn's terminology,[30] "paradigm" – is never killed off, as it should be, by a new set of facts. Being prisoners of their own *Gestalts*, scientists (like lovers) abandon an old theory only when they have found a new theory in which to clothe their beliefs. Chamberlin, Sraffa, Robinson, and their contemporaries have led economists into a new land from which their critics will never evict us.

---

[30] T. S. Kuhn, *The Anatomy of Scientific Revolutions*, University of Chicago Press, Chicago, 1962.

Samuelson's Publications in the History
of Economic Thought

ESSAYS AND TECHNICAL STUDIES IN THE HISTORY OF ECONOMIC ANALYSIS

1. "Wages and Interest: A Modern Dissection of Marxian Economic Models." *American Economic Review* 47, no. 6 (1957): 884–912.
2. "Wages and Interest: A Modern Dissection of Marxian Economic Models: Reply." *American Economic Review* 50, no. 4 (1960): 719–721.
3. "A Modern Treatment of the Ricardian Economy: The Pricing of Goods and of Labor and Land Services." *Quarterly Journal of Economics* 73, no. 1 (1959): 1–35.
4. "A Modern Treatment of the Ricardian Economy: Capital and Interest Aspects of the Pricing Problem." *Quarterly Journal of Economics* 73, no. 2 (1959): 217–231.
5. "The Transfer Problem and Transfer Costs: The Terms of Trade when Impediments Are Absent." *Economic Journal* 62, no. 246 (1952): 278–304.
6. "Review of H. Myint, *Theories of Welfare Economics*." *Economica* 16, no. 64 (1949): 371–374.
7. "Modern Economic Realities and Individualism." *The Texas Quarterly* 6 (1963): 128–139.
8. "Economists and the History of Ideas." *American Economic Review* 52, no. 1 (1962): 1–18.
9. "A Brief Survey of Post-Keynesian Developments." In *Keynes' General Theory: Reports of Three Decades*, Robert Lekachman, 331–347. New York: St. Martin's Press, 1964.

447

10. "Economic Theory and Wages." In *The Impact of the Union: Eight Economic Theorists Evaluate the Labor Union Movement*, David McCord Wright, 312–342. New York: Harcourt, Brace, 1951.

11. "Marxian Economics as Economics." *American Economic Review* 57, no. 2 (1967): 616–623.

12. "Understanding the Marxian Notion of Exploitation: A Summary of the So-Called Transformation Problem Between Marxian Values and Competitive Prices." *Journal of Economic Literature* 9, no. 2 (1971): 399–431.

13. "The 'Transformation' from Marxian 'Values' to Competitive 'Prices': A Process of Rejection and Replacement." *Proceedings of the National Academy of Sciences of the United States of America* 67, no. 1 (1970): 423–425.

14. "An Exact Hume-Ricardo-Marshall Model of International Trade." *Journal of International Economics* 1, no. 1 (1971): 1–18.

15. "What Classical and Neoclassical Monetary Theory Really Was." *Canadian Journal of Economics* 1, no. 1 (1968): 1–15.

16. "Irving Fisher and the Theory of Capital." In *Ten Economic Studies in the Tradition of Irving Fisher*, William Fellner. New York: John Wiley, 1967.

17. "The Way of an Economist." In *International Economic Relations: Proceedings of the Third Congress of the International Economic Association*, Paul A. Samuelson, 1–11. London: Macmillian, 1969.

18. "Economic Growth." In *Gendaisekai Hyakka Daijiten*, vol. 1. Tokyo: Kodansha Ltd., 1971.

19. "Marx as Mathematical Economist: Steady-State and Exponential Growth Equilibrium." In *Trade, Stability, and Macroeconomic Essays in Honor of Lloyd A. Metzler*, George Horwich and Paul A. Samuelson, 269–307. New York: Academic Press, 1974.

20. "Optimality of Profit-Including Prices Under Ideal Planning: Marx's Model." *Proceedings of the National Academy of Sciences of the United States of America* 70, no. 7 (1973): 2109–2111.

21. "The Economics of Marx: An Ecumenical Reply." *Journal of Economic Literature* 10, no. 1 (1972): 51–57.

22. Samuelson's "Reply on Marxian Matters," *Journal of Economic Literature* 11, no. 1 (1973): 64–68.

23. "Insight and Detour in the Theory of Exploitation: Reply to Baumol." *Journal of Economic Literature* 12, no. 1 (1974): 62–70.

24. "Rejoinder: Merlin Unclothed, A Final Word." *Journal of Economic Literature* 12, no. 1 (1974): 75–77.

25. "Review of V.K. Dmitriev, *Economic Essays on Values, Competition, and Utility*." *Journal of Economic Literature* 12, no. 2 (1975): 491–495.

26. "The Art and Science of Macromodels Over 50 Years." In *The Brookings Model: Perspective and Recent Developments*, Gary Fromm and Lawrence R. Klein, 3–10. Amsterdam: North-Holland, 1975.

27. "Adam the Immortal." *Pennsylvania Gazette*, University of Pennsylvania, November 1976, 26–27.

28. "A Modern Theorist's Vindication of Adam Smith." *American Economic Review* 67, no. 1 (1977): 42–49.

29. "The Canonical Classical Model of Political Economy." *Journal of Economic Literature* 16, no. 4 (1978): 1415–1434.

30. "Noise and Signal in Debates Among Classical Economists: A Reply." *Journal of Economic Literature* 18, no. 2 (1980): 575–578.

31. "A Corrected Version of Hume's Equilibrating Mechanism for International Trade." In *Flexible Exchange Rates and the Balance of Payments: Essays in Memory of Egon Sohmen*, John S. Chipman and Charles P. Kindleberger, 141–158. Amsterdam: North-Holland, 1980.

32. "Bergsonian Welfare Economics." In *Economic Welfare and the Economics of Soviet Socialism: Essays in Honor of Abram Bergson*, Steven Rosefielde, 223–266. Cambridge: Cambridge University Press, 1981.

33. "A Chapter in the History of Ramsey's Optimal Feasible Taxation and Optimal Public Utility Prices." In *Economic Essays in Honor of Jørgen H. Gelting*, Svend Andersen, Kartsen Larsen, P. Norregaard Rusmussen, and J. Vibe-Pedersen, 157–181. Copenhagen: Danish Economic Association, 1982.

34. "Paul Douglas's Measurement of Production Functions and Marginal Productivities." *Journal of Political Economy* 87, no. 5 (1979): 923–939.

35. "Schumpeter as an Economic Theorist." In *Schumpeterian Economics*, Helmut Frisch, 1–27. London: Praeger, 1982.

36. "1983: Marx, Keynes and Schumpeter." *Eastern Economic Journal* 9, no. 3 (1983): 166–180.

37. "The Keynes Centenary." *The Economist*, 25 June 1983, 19–21.

38. "The House that Keynes Built." *New York Times*, 29 May 1983.

39. "Succumbing to Keynesianism." *Challenge* 27 (1985): 4–11.

40. "Comment (on Axel Leijonhufvud's 'What Would Keynes Have Thought of Rational Expectations?')." In *Keynes and the Modern World*, David Worswick and James Trevithick, 212–221. Cambridge: Cambridge University Press, 1983.
41. "The Normative and Positivistic Inferiority of Marx's *Values* Paradigm." *Southern Economic Journal* 49, no. 1 (1982): 11–18.
42. "Marx Without Matrices: Understanding the Rate of Profit." In *Marxism, Central Planning, and the Soviet Economy: Economic Essays in Honor of Alexander Erlich*, Padma Desai, 3–18. Cambridge, Mass.: The MIT Press, 1983.
43. "Thünen at Two Hundred." *Journal of Economic Literature* 21, no. 4 (1983): 1468–1488.
44. "Quesnay's 'Tableau Economique' as a Theorist Would Formulate It Today." In *Classical and Marxian Political Economy: Essays in Honor of Ronald L. Meek*, Ian Bradley and Michael Howard, 45–78. New York: St. Martin's Press, 1982.
45. "Land and the Rate of Interest." In *Theory for Economic Efficiency: Essays in Honor of Abba P. Lerner*, Harry I. Greenfield, Albert M. Levenson, William Hamovitch, and Eugene Rotwein, 167–185. Cambridge, Mass.: The MIT Press, 1979.
46. "Correcting the Ricardo Error Spotted in Harry Johnson's Maiden Paper." *Quarterly Journal of Economics* 91, no. 4 (1977): 519–553.
47. "Yes to Robert Dorfman's Vindication of Thünen's Natural-Wage Derivation." *Journal of Economic Literature* 24, no. 4 (1986): 1777–1785.
48. "Out of the Closet: A Program for the Whig History of Economic Science." *History of Economics Society Bulletin* 9, no. 1 (1987): 51–60.
49. "Mathematical Vindication of Ricardo on Machinery." *Journal of Political Economy* 96, no. 2 (1988): 274–282.
50. "Wicksell and Neoclassical Economics." In *The New Palgrave: A Dictionary of Economics*, John Eatwell, Murray Milgate, and Peter Newman, 908–910. London: Macmillan, 1987.
51. "How Economics Has Changed." *Journal of Economic Education* 18, no. 2 (1987): 107–110.
52. "Wicksells Werk und Persönlichkeit—Eine kritische Analyse in Moderner Sicht." In *Knut Wicksell: Finanztheoretische Untersuchungen nebst Darstellung und Kritik des Steuerwesens Schwedens, Klassiker der Nationalökonomie*, 25–36. Düsseldorf: Verlag Wirtschaft und Finanzen GmbH, 1988.

53. "Ricardo was Right!" *Scandinavian Journal of Economics* 91, no. 1 (1989): 47–62.

54. "Conversations with my History-of-Economics Critics." In *Economics, Culture, and Education: Essays in Honour of Mark Blaug*, Graham Keith Shaw, 3–13. Aldershot, U.K.: Elgar, 1991.

55. with Don Patinkin and Mark Blaug. "On the Historiography of Economics: A Correspondence." *Journal of the History of Economic Thought* 13, no. 2 (1991): 144–158.

56. "The Fitness Maximized by the Canonical Classical Model: A Theme From Houthakker and R.A. Fisher." In *Aggregation, Consumption, and Trade: Essays in Honor of H.S. Houthakker*, Louis Phlips and Lester D. Taylor, 9–20. Boston: Kluwer Academic, 1992.

57. "Marx on Rent: A Failure to Transform Correctly." *Journal of the History of Economic Thought* 14, no. 2 (1992): 143–167.

58. "Gustav Cassel's Scientific Innovations: Claims and Realities." *History of Political Economy* 18, no. 3 (1993): 515–527.

59. "Two Classics: Böhm-Bawerk's *Positive Theory* and Fisher's *Rate of Interest* through Modern Prisms." *Journal of the History of Economic Thought* 16, no. 2 (1994): 202–228.

60. "The Classical Classical Fallacy." *Journal of Economic Literature* 32, no. 2 (1994): 620–639.

61. "Who Innovated the Keynesian Revolution?" In *Economics, Econometrics and the LINK: Essays in Honor of Lawrence R. Klein*, M. Dutta, 3–19. Amsterdam: North-Holland, 1995.

62. "Isolating Sources of Sterility in Marx's Theoretical Paradigms." In *Essays in Honour of Geoff Harcourt*, vol. 1, Philip Arestis, Gabriel Palma, and Malcolm Sawyer, 187–198. London: Routledge, 1996.

63. "Credo of a Lucky Textbook Author." *Journal of Economic Perspectives* 11, no. 2 (1997): 153–160.

64. "How *Foundations* Came to Be." *Journal of Economic Literature* 36, no. 3 (1998): 1375–1386.

65. "Requiem for the Classic Tarshis Textbook That First Brought Keynes to Introductory Economics." In *Keynesianism and the Keynesian Revolution in America: A Memorial Volume in Honour of Lorie Tarshis*, O. F. Hamouda and B. B. Price, 53–58. Cheltenham, U.K.: Elgar, 1998.

66. "Land." In *The Elgar Companion to Classical Economics*, vol. 2, Heinz D. Kurz and Salvatori Neri, 27–36. Cheltenham, U.K.: Elgar, 1998.

67. "Samuelson, Paul Anthony, as an Interpreter of the Classical Economists." In *The Elgar Companion to Classical Economics*, vol. 2, Heinz D. Kurz and Salvatori Neri, 329–333. Cheltenham, U.K.: Elgar, 1998.
68. "John Bates Clark: America's First Great Theorist." In *John Bates Clark, the Distribution of Wealth, Klassiker der Nationalökonomie*, 55–72. Dusseldorf: Verlag Wirtschaft und Finanzen GmbH, 1999.
69. "A Quintessential (Ahistorical) Tableau Économique: to Sum up Pre- and Post-Smith Classical Paradigms." In *Economics Broadly Considered: Essays in Honor of Warren J. Samuels*, Jeff E. Biddle, John B. Davis, and Steven G, Medema, 47–60. London: Routledge, 2001.
70. "Ricardo, David (1772-1823)." In *International Encyclopedia of Social and Behavioral Sciences*, Neil J. Smelser and Paul B. Baltes, 13330–13334. New York: Elsevier, 2001.
71. "Economic History and Mainstream Economic Analysis." *Rivista di Storia Economica* 17, no. 2 (2001): 271–277.
72. "A Modern Post-Mortem on Böhm's Capital Theory: Its Vital Normative Flaw Shared by Pre-Sraffian Mainstream Capital Theory." *Journal of the History of Economic Thought* 23, no. 3 (2001): 301–317.
73. "Where Ricardo and Mill Rebut and Confirm Arguments of Mainstream Economists Supporting Gobalization." *Journal of Economic Perspectives* 18, no. 3 (2004): 135–146.
74. with Erkko M. Etula. "Two Alternative Hypothetical 'Lost' 1814 Ricardo Manuscripts: New-Century Bearings." *History of Political Economy* 38. No. 1 (2006): 1–14.
75. "Thünen—An Economist Ahead of His Times." *Preface to The Isolated State in Relation to Agriculture and Political Economy*, Part III, Translated by Keith Tribe, Ulrich van Suntum, xii–xiv. Basingstoke, U.K.: Palgrave Macmillan, 2009
76. 'The Harvard Circle." *Journal of Evolutionary Economics*, forthcoming.

COMMENTARIES ON CONTEMPORARIES AND NEAR-CONTEMPORARIES

77. "Lord Keynes and the General Theory," *Econometrica* 14 (July 1946): 187–200.
78. "Harold Hotelling as Mathematical Economist." *American Statistician* 14 (June 1960): 21–25.

79. "D.H. Robertson (1890–1963)." *Quarterly Journal of Economics* 77 (November 1963): 517–536.
80. "A.P. Lerner at Sixty." *Review of Economic Studies* 31 (June 1964): 169–178.
81. "Galbraith." *Newsweek* (July 3, 1967).
82. "Marx's Das Kapital." *Newsweek* (October 16, 1967).
83. "Who's Who in Economics." *Newsweek* (January 19, 1970): 78.
84. "Joseph Schumpeter." *Newsweek* (April 13, 1970): 75.
85. "Lenin."*Newsweek* (December 7 1970): 86.
86. "John Maynard Keynes." *Part III of Geschichte der Politischen Okonomie*, Horst Claus Recktenwald. Stuttgart: Kroner, 1971: 556–565.
87. "Rosa Luxemburg."*Newsweek* (October 25, 1971): 99.
88. "Jacob Viner, 1892–1970." *Journal of Political Economy* 80 (Jan/Feb 1972): 5–11.
89. "Frank Knight – 1885–1972." *Newsweek* (July 31, 1972): 55.
90. "The 1972 Nobel Prize for Economic Science." *Science* 178 (November 3, 1972): 487–489.
91. "Nobel Laureate Leontief." *Newsweek* (November 5, 1973): 94.
92. "Remembrances of Frisch." *European Economic Review* 5 (June 1974): 7–23.
93. "Nobel Choice: Economists in Contract." *New York Times* (October 10, 1974): op-ed page.
94. "Joseph Alois Schumpeter." in *Dictionary of American Biography, Supplement 4, 1946–1950.* New York: Charles Scribner's Sons, 1974.
95. "Alvin Hansen as Creative Economist." *Quarterly Journal of Economics* 90 (February 1976): 24–31.
96. "Nobel Laureates Meade and Ohlin." *New York Times* (October 15, 1977).
97. "Paul Douglas's Measurement of Production Functions and Marginal Productivities." *Journal of Political Economy* 87 (October 1979, Part I): 923–939.
98. "The Year 1983: Keynes, Schumpeter and Marx." *Japan Economic Journal* 11 (January 1983).
99. "The Centennial of Keynes." *Nihon Keizai Shimbun* (June 5, 1983).
100. "Piero Sraffa (1898-1983)." Published as "Un genio con poche opere," *Corriere della Sera* (March 6, 1983).
101. "The 1983 Nobel Prize in Economics."*Science* (December 2, 1983).
102. Article on the MIT Economics Department. *Technique* (Massachusetts Institute of Technology), 1984.

103. "The 1984 Nobel Prize in Economics." *Science* (January 4, 1985).
104. "The 1985 Nobel Prize in Economics." *Science* (March 21, 1986): 1399–1401.
105. "An Economist's Economist." (Obituary for Walter Heller) *New York Times* (June 23, 1987).
106. "Walter Heller Obituary." *The Independent* (June 20, 1987).
107. "Sparks from Arrow's Anvil." In *Arrow and the Foundations of the Theory of Economic Policy*, George R. Feiwel, 154–178. London: Macmillan, 1987.
108. "In the Beginning" (on Keynesian Economics at Harvard). *Challenge* (July–August 1988).
109. "The Passing of the Guard in Economics." *Eastern Economic Journal* 14 (4 1988): 319–29.
110. *Interview by Marjorie Turner for Joan Robinson and the Americans.* Armonk, NY: M.E. Sharpe, 1989.
111. "Trygve Haavelmo 1989 Nobel Laureate in Economics." *Bilanz* (October 1989).
112. *"Remembering Joan."* In *Joan Robinson and Modern Economic Theory*, George R. Feiwel, 121–143. New York: New York University Press, 1989.
113. "Galbraith as Artist and Scientist." In *Unconventional Wisdom: Essays on Economics in Honor of John Kenneth Galbraith*, Samuel Bowles et al., 123–128. Boston: Houghton Mifflin, 1989.
114. "Gottfried Haberler as Economic Sage and Trade Theory Innovator." *Wirtschaftpolitische Blatter* (April 1990).
115. "Tribute to Nicholas Georgescu-Roegen on his 85th Birthday." *Libertas Mathematica* 10 (1990): 1–4.
116. "Sraffa's Other Leg." *Economic Journal* 101 (May 1991): 570–574.
117. "Tribute to R.M Goodwin." In *Celebrating R.M. Goodwin's 75th Birthday*, Massimo Di Matteo. Universita Degli Studi di Siena (May 1990).
118. "Richard Kahn: His Welfare Economics and Lifetime Achievement." *Cambridge Journal of Economics* 18 (1994): 55–72.
119. "Tribute to Wolfgang Stolper on the Fiftieth Anniversary of the Stopler-Samuelson Theorem." In *The Stolper-Samuelson Theorem: A Golden Jubilee*, 343–349. Ann Arbor: University of Michigan Press, 1994.
120. "The To-Be-Expected Angst Created for Economists by Mathematics." *Eastern Economic Journal* 20 (Winter 1994): 267–273.

121. "Gottfried Haberler (1990-1995)." *Economic Journal* 106 (November 1996): 1679–1687.

122. "Some Memories of Norbert Wiener." *Proceedings of Symposia in Pure Mathematics 60: The Legacy of Norbert Wiener: A Centennial Symposium*, D. Jerison, I. M. Singer, and D. W. Stroock, 37–42. Providence, RI: American Mathematical Society, 1997.

123. "Report Card on Sraffa at 100." *European Journal of the History of Economic Thought* 3 (Autumn 1998): 458–467.

124. "My John Hicks." *Indian Journal of Applied Economics*, Part I:7 (October–November 1998). Also published as Chapter 1 in *John Hicks: His Contributions to Economic Theory and Applications*, K. Puttaswamaiah, 1–4. New Brunswick, NJ: Transaction Publishers, 2001.

125. "Sraffa's Hits and Misses." In *Critical Essays on Piero Sraffa's Legacy in Economics*, Heinz D. Kurz, 111–152. Cambridge: Cambridge University Press, 2000.

126. "My Bertil Ohlin." In *Bertil Ohlin: A Centennial Celebration (1899-1999)*, Ronald Findlay, Lars Jonung, and Mats Lundahl, 51–61. Cambridge, MA: MIT Press, 2002.

127. "Edmund Phelps, Insider-Economists' Insider." In *Knowledge, Information, and Expecations in Modern Economics in Honor of Edmund S. Phelps*, P. Aghion, R. Frydman, J. Stiglitz, and M. Woodford, 1–2. Princeton, NJ: Princeton University Press, 2003.

128. "Multiple Priorities in Evolving Scholarly Disciplines." *History of Political Economy* 35 (Summer 2003): 333–334.

129. "Reflections on the Schumpeter I Knew Well." *Journal of Evolutionary Economics* 13 (2003): 463–467.

130. "Abram Bergson, Economist." *Economic Journal* 115 (February 2005): F130–F135.

131. "Franco: A Mind Never at Rest." *Banca Nazionale del Lavoro Quarterly Review* 58 (June–September 2005): 5–9.

132. "Wassily Leontief 1906-1999." *Foreword to Wassily Leontief and Input-Output Analysis*, P. Puttaswamaiah. Vijayanagar. Bangalore: International Journal of Applied Economics and Econometrics, 2006.

133. "Franco Modigliani, 1918-2003." *Foreword to Franco Modigliani, Peerless Twentieth-Century Macroeconomist*, P. Puttaswamaiah. Vijayanagar, Bangalore: International Journal of Applied Economics and Econometrics, 2006.

134. "Reflections on How Biographies of Individual Scholars Can Relate to a Science's Biography" (Co-editor's foreword). In *Inside the Economist's Mind*, W. A. Barnett and P. A. Samuelson, viii–x. Oxford: Blackwell, 2006.

135. "Franco, Dear Friend and Wonderful MIT Colleague." In *Reforming European Pension Systems*, Arun Muralidhar and Serge Allegrezza, 5–7. Amsterdam: Dutch University Press, 2007.

136. "John Hicks: An Economist Ever Greater than His High Reputation." In *Markets, Money and Capital: Hicksian Economics for the Twenty-First Century*. Roberto Scazzieri, Amartya Sen, and Stefano Zamagni, 49–51. Cambridge: Cambridge University Press, 2008.

137. "A Few Remembrances of Friedrich von Hayek (1899–1992)." *Journal of Economic Behavior and Organization* 69 (January 2009): 1–4.

138. "Robert Merton Solow." In *International Encyclopedia of the Social Sciences*, 2nd edn., William Darity. Farmingham Hills, MI: Macmillan Reference, 2009.

139. "The Richard Goodwin Circle at Harvard (1938–1950)." In *Computable, Constructive and Behavioural Economic Dynamics: Essays in Honour of Kumaraswamy (Vela) Velupillai*, 49–55. Abingdon: Routledge, 2010.

Index

accumulation: in fixed-coefficient Marxian model, 248, 252; Ricardo on temporal issues in, 168–9. *See also* growth; saving
Alice in Wonderland (Carroll 1865), 376
alienation, Marx's concept of, 117
Allais, Maurice, 331
Allen, R. G. D., 352
alternative paradigms, and classical political economy, 89
Amoroso, L., 352
Andersen, Hans Christian, 34
antiquarianism, and approaches to history, 5–6, 8, 9, 27. *See also* Whig history
Anti-Samuelson (Linder 1977), 15
Archibald, G. C., 306, 312, 322, 415n5
Aristotle, 322n12, 326, 338, 426n15
arithmetic progression, and Malthus on land augmenting technical change, 109
Arrow, Kenneth, 149
assumptions: in Quesnay's *Tableau Economique*, 61–64; in Ricardo's *Principles*, 184–6; in Smith's *Wealth of Nations*, 118–19, 121–3; of symmetry in monetary theory, 318; technological in Marxian economic models, 229–31
asymptotic homogeneity, theorem of, 441–2, 444
Auspitz, R., 416n6
autarky, and long-run equilibrium in international trade, 54n7
automatic synchronization, fallacy of, 369

Bailey, Samuel, 110
Banking Policy and The Price Level (Marshall 1926), 376
Barna, Tibor, 60, 62, 65–6

Barone, E., 352
Bator, F., 442n28
Baumol, William, 273n10a, 282n16
Beckmann, Martin, 197
Benham, Frederic, 423n12
Bentham, Jeremy, 229, 422n11
Beveridge, Sir William, 406
biological method, Marshall on use of in economics, 419
Blaug, Mark, 6, 32, 110, 114n13, 197
Böhm-Bawerk, Eugen von, 18, 75, 105, 196–7, 237n6, 258, 324–43, 350, 369, 370
Bortkiewicz, Ladislaus von, 15, 34, 109, 236, 237n6, 283, 351–2
Bourgeois pricing regime, 276–7
Bowley, A. L., 352, 360n4
Brems, Hans, 110
Brinkman, Theodor, 212
Bródy, A., 283
Brown, Douglass V., 26
Bullock, C. J., 26
Burchardt, F. A., 145n14
Burmeister, E., 271
Burns, Arthur F., 383
Butterfield, Herbert, 7

Cairnes, J. E., 163
Cambridge Journal of Economics, 30, 31n2
Cambridge University, 379
Can Lloyd George Do It? (Henderson & Keynes 1929), 410
Cannan, Edwin, 28, 110, 352, 365, 406, 409
"Canonical Classical Model of Political Economy, The" (Samuelson 1978), 2, 18, 32–3, 89–113

capital: and accumulation in fixed-coefficient Marxian model, 248; analysis of Böhm-Bawerk's theory of, 324–43; depreciation and Quesnay's use of term "interest" in context of, 79n10; formation of and consumption in canonical classical model, 90; and interest in pricing process of Ricardian model, 168–82; and Marx on equal rates of surplus value and profit, 263–4, 275, 291; and Marx's model of extended reproduction, 295; and Marx's model of simple reproduction, 231–2; and Morishima's critique of Marx, 271; natural wage and Thünen's theory of, 216–17; Thünen's logic on, 220–2. *See also* capital goods; circulating capital; constant capital; fixed capital; variable capital; wage funds
capital formation. *See* saving
capital goods: and Marx on simple reproduction, 262; and Quesnay's *Tableau Economique*, 75–7, 84. *See also* fixed capital
capitalism, and Schumpeter as economic theorist, 373
Carlyle, Thomas, 108, 109
Carrell, Erich, 222n13
Carroll, Lewis, 376
Carver, T. N., 352
Cassel, Gustav, 321–2, 352, 405
Chamberlin, Edward, 352, 360, 412, 413–15, 415n5, 417, 420, 435–7, 443, 444, 445
Chapman, John Jay, 254
Chicago School, 14, 318, 415
Churchill, Winston, 9
circular flow: and competition in Schumpeter's model, 368; in Quesnay's *Tableau Economique*, 72
circulating capital: Böhm's model of, 326; as distinct from fixed capital, 171; and Ricardo on machinery, 189. *See also* wage funds
Clapham, J. H., 412
Clark, John Bates, 64, 94, 105, 140, 141n11, 195–6, 200, 230, 324, 326, 333, 352, 369
Clark, J. M., 352, 383, 413, 424
classical economics: and Great Depression, 400; and land theory of value, 152, 154; political economy and monetary theory in, 305–23; and Samuelson on canonical classical model of political economy, 89–113; technology and theory of consumption in, 136; and time shape of interest, 177
Clemenceau, Georges, 258
Coase, R. H., 430n18
Cohen, Ruth, 330

Cohen Council on Prices, Productivity and Incomes, 379
Collected Scientific Papers (Samuelson 1966–2011), 9, 16, 17
Collery, Arnold, 44
Columbia University, 2, 25
comparative cost, Ricardo's theory of in international trade, 160, 162n26
competition: and Schumpeter as economic theorist, 360–1; use of terms "imperfect" and "monopolistic" in context of, 414. *See also* imperfect competition; perfect competition
competitive imputation, and Schumpeter's zero-interest-rate doctrine, 356–7
constant capital, Marxian concept of, 234, 254, 263
constant cost, and monopolistic competition revolution, 422
constant-elasticity-of-substitution (CES) function, 363
consumer loans, and moral views of interest rate, 326, 426n15
consumption: and capital formation in canonical classical model, 90; in Keynesian economics, 410; and Marx on simple reproduction, 262
contrived scarcity, as distinct from natural scarcity, 425–6
Corn-Law tariff (England), 109
corporations, and Schumpeter's imperfect competition theory, 360, 361
Costabile, L., 12
cost controversy: and debate on nature of competition, 412, 423–4; and Schumpeter as economic theorist, 353. *See also* comparative cost; constant cost; transport costs
cost-of-production relations, and land theory of value, 179–80
countervailing power, and Schumpeter's theory of imperfect competition, 360
Cournot, Augustin A., 196, 360n4, 401, 416, 417, 419
crisis theory, and Marxian economics, 142n13, 149n19

Dandrakis, E., 190
Darwin, Charles, 100n5, 409
Davenport, Herbert J., 352
Debreu, G., 428n17
demand, and labor theory of value in Ricardian model, 136, 151. *See also* supply and demand; tastes

Dempsey, Bernard W., 197, 217n11
determinate macroeconomic system, 384
diagrammatics, of classical growth theory, 105–108
Dickinson, H. D., 239n8
Dietzel, Karl August, 110
differential theory of rent, 140, 149, 153–67
differentiation, and monopolistic competition revolution, 442–5
Dimitriev, V. K., 368
distributive shares, and indeterminacy of wages in Marxian models, 278–81
Divine, Thomas F., 426n15
Dobb, Maurice, 29, 30–1, 237n6
Domar, Evsey, 130, 272
Dorfman, Robert, 1, 110, 271, 299n25, 339
Dornbusch, Rudiger, 45, 46, 49n5, 51, 57
Douglas, Paul, 94, 216–17, 442n28
Duke University, 19

econometric inference revolution, 3, 26
economic analysis: and Marx as mathematical economist, 272–3; mathematics and history of, 10–13; Samuelson's publications on history of, 447–52; Samuelson's view of conceptual unity of, 3–4, 5
Economic Consequences of the Peace (Keynes 1919), 401, 404, 406
Economic Journal, 404, 408n12, 410
economics: impact of Keynes's *General* Theory on, 397–41; and Samuelson's publications on contemporaries and near-contemporaries, 452–6; Samuelson's view of as science, 5–8. *See also* classical economics; econometric inference revolution; economic analysis; history, of economics; Keynesian revolution; Marxian economic models; mathematicization revolution; monopolistic competition revolution; neoclassical economics; political economy; quantum-theory economics
Economics of Imperfect Competition, The (Robinson 1933), 412
Economics of Overhead Costs (Clark 1923), 413
Economists Papers Project (Duke University), 19
Edgeworth, Francis Y., 110, 354, 417
effective demand, Keynesian analysis of, 398, 402
Einstein, Albert, 28
Eliot, T. S., 356
Eltis, W. A., 12, 60, 61, 74n6

"embodied" labor, in Ricardian model, 160
"embodied" land, in Ricardian model, 134, 143, 144, 152, 153
employment, and Robertson as critic of inequality, 393. *See also* unemployment; labor; wages
Engels, Friedrich, 261, 272, 281
equal-organic case, of constant relative prices, 293
equilibrium: long-run in canonical classic model, 90–1, 92–5; long-run in Ricardo's *Principles*, 186–7; Smith's *Wealth of Nations* and restoration of, 126–8
"ergodic hypothesis," 318, 319–20
Essay on Marxian Economics (Robinson 1942), 15
Euler, Leonhard, 102n6
Evans, Griffith, 331
expanded-reproduction model, and steady growth in Marxian economics, 241–4
expectations, in Keynesian economics, 402
exploitation: and Böhm's capital theory, 327; and Marx as mathematical economist, 265–6, 290–1
exponential-growth states, and Marx's discussion of extended reproduction, 268–70
extended reproduction, and Marx as mathematical economist, 260, 261, 267–70, 274–5, 277–8, 295
extensive-margin theory of rent, 140
external economies, and Marshall, 420
external margin, 198

factor intensity, and Thünen's *The Isolated State*, 212–14
factor proportions, and prices in Marxian economic models, 245–50
Farrell, M. J., 442n28
Federal Reserve System, 385
Fellner, William, 190, 239n8
Fermi, E., 26
Fetter, Frank, 327, 352
Firuski, Elizabeth (Boody), 352
Fischer, Stanley, 45, 51, 57
Fisher, Irving, 306, 324, 325, 327, 332, 337, 339, 352, 354, 405, 417–18
fixed capital: as distinct from circulating capital, 171; in Ricardian model, 180, 189. *See also* capital goods
fixed proportions, assumption of in Quesnay's *Tableau Economique*, 62

Foundations of Economic Analysis (Samuelson 1947), 1, 2, 3
Freeman, Ralph E., 382
free trade, and self-correcting gold-flow mechanism in Hume's model, 54–5. *See also* laissez-faire
Frenkel, Jacob, 39, 40n1, 44, 46
Friedman, Milton, 32, 415n5
Frisch, Ragnar, 151, 153n23, 348, 352

Galbraith, John Kenneth, 360
game theory, 428n17
General Theory (Keynes 1936), 309, 378, 397–411
geometric progression, and canonical classical model, 109
George, Henry, 330, 369
Georgescu-Roegen, Nicholas, 134, 149, 352
Gide, C., 59–60
golden age, references to in Smith and Ricardo, 168–9
golden-rule state, and Schumpeter's zero-interest-rate doctrine, 357
Goodwin, Craufurd, 19
Goodwin, Richard, 383
government, and collusive action, 428. *See also* political economy
Gramsci, Antonio, 29
Gray, Alexander, 59
Great Depression, 399–400, 401, 403, 404, 410
growth: diagrammatics of classical theory of, 105–108; investment and Malthusian in Smith's *Wealth of Nations*, 125–6; Smith's model as endogenous process of, 130. *See also* simple reproduction; steady growth

Haberler, Gottfried, 39, 43, 44, 351, 363, 378, 423
Hahn, F. H., 271
Hall, Peter, 197, 212–13, 214, 222n13
Hamilton, Earl, 390–1
Hansen, Alvin, 375
harmonic mean, 339
Harris, Seymour, 348
Harrod, Sir Roy F., 130, 423n12
Harvard University, 3, 25–6, 378
Hawtrey, R. G., 306, 410n14
Hayek, Friedrich von, 105, 272, 324, 325, 326, 331, 341, 361, 362, 369
Heaviside, Oliver, 375
Heckscher, Eli, 28, 57

Henderson, Sir Hubert, 377, 410
Hickman, W. B., 309
Hicks, John R., 190, 191n3, 310, 321, 322, 352, 382, 421
Hishiyama, Izumi, 61, 74n6
historiography: and Samuelson's approach to history of economics, 5–10; and Samuelson's essays on economic science, 17, 25–35
history, of economics: and role of mathematics in economic analysis, 10–13; and role of Samuelson as historian, 2–4; and Samuelson on political ideology, 13–17; Samuelson's approach to, 5–10; Samuelson's contributions to, 1–2, 17–19; Samuelson's publications on, 447–56. *See also* Great Depression; Industrial Revolution; Whig history
history, of science, 5–8, 445
History of Economic Doctrines (Schumpeter 1954), 351
History of Economics Society, 7, 25
Hitler, Adolf, 372, 373
Hollander, Jacob, 2, 12, 25
homogeneous land, and land theory of value in Ricardian model, 141–2, 144–7
Hotelling, Harold, 352
Hume, David, 39–57, 306, 434n20

"iceberg" model, 201, 202, 213
"immiseration," law of, 238
imperfect competition: and monopolistic competition revolution, 432–3, 443–4; and Schumpeter as economic theorist, 360–1
income determination, modern saving-investment theory of, 399. *See also* wages
Indian Currency and Finance Book, The (Keynes 1913), 404
indirect utility function, 203, 207
Industrial Revolution, 258
inflationary gap concept, and Keynesian economics, 402
innovational development, and Schumpeter's zero-interest-rate doctrine, 357–8. *See also* invention; technology
inequality, Robertson as critic of, 393
intemporal pricing, and Böhm's capital theory, 337
interest: and ethical views on usury, 326, 426n15; and liquidity preference in Keynesian economics, 402; and pricing process in Ricardian model, 168–82; and

Quesnay's *Tableau Economique*, 75, 76; and Schumpeter's zero-interest-rate doctrine, 356–62; and wages in Marxian economic models, 229–59

international trade: Hume's equilibrating mechanisms for, 39–57; and Ricardo's theory of comparative cost, 160

invention, and implications of Smith's *Wealth of Nations*, 119–20. *See also* machinery; technology

investment. *See* capital; saving

Invisible Hand (Smith), 121, 127, 155, 240, 246, 325, 332, 403, 422, 434

Iroquois, 393

Isolated State, The (Thünen 1826), 195, 197

Jenkin, Fleeming, 416n6

Jevons, Stanley, 324, 328, 413

Johansen, L., 12, 283

John Hopkins University, 2, 25

Johnson, Harry, 39, 40n1, 44, 46, 60, 72

Johnson, Samuel, 27

Jones, Ronald W., 57

Jorgenson, D. W., 271

Joseph, M. F. W., 438

Joseph Schumpeter: Social Scientist (Harris 1951), 348

Kahn, Richard F., 30, 352, 382, 410

Kaldor, Nicholas, 29, 30, 31n2, 109, 110, 138, 188, 261, 363, 391, 421, 435, 436–7

Kennedy, Charles, 190

Keynes, J. M. (Lord Keynes of Tilton), 19, 255, 309, 325n1, 362, 364, 377, 378, 382, 397–411

keynesian revolution, 3, 26, 397

Klein, Lawrence R., 397n1

Knight, Frank, 105, 144, 215, 324, 326, 352, 359, 362, 363, 369, 398, 420n9

knowledge, and monopolistic competition revolution in economics, 412–14, 425

Koopmans, T. C., 149, 442n28

Kuhn, Thomas, 89, 126, 445

Kuznets, Simon, 91, 120

labor: and Marx's subsistence-wage theory of labor's cost of reproduction, 289–90; and pricing of goods and land services in Ricardian model, 133–67; and Quesnay's *Tableau Economique*, 61, 62–4, 67–9; Smith on specialization and division of, 434. *See also* "embodied"labor; employment; labor theory of value; unemployment; wages

labor theory of value: and differential rent in Ricardian model, 134; and Marxian economic models, 236, 258; Ricardo and failures of, 34, 171–3; and Smith's "rude state," 123–5; and technology in Ricardian model, 136, 150–2

Laffer fallacy, 44

laissez-faire: and Böhm's capital theory, 337; and Ricardo's *Principles*, 188, 190; Smith's defense of, 117

land: and pricing of goods and labor in Ricardian model, 133–67; and Quesnay's *Tableau Economique*, 61, 62–4, 82–4; scarcity of and falling interest in Ricardian model, 176–8; Schumpeter and infinite capitalization of, 365–6. *See also* "embodied" land; homogeneous land; land rent; land theory of value

"Land and the Rate of Interest" (Samuelson 1979), 4

land rent, residual of in canonical classical model, 94

land theory of value, 144–7, 152, 153, 178–81

Lange, Oskar, 310, 321, 322, 352, 425n14

Laughlin, J. L., 43–4

Laughlin fallacy, 43–4, 52

Leacock, Stephen, 187n1

Leibniz, G. W., 412

Leigh, Arthur H., 197, 217, 218, 220, 221n12, 222n13

Lenin, Vladimir I., 281, 330

Leontief, Wassily W., 60, 66n2, 137n5, 144, 147–8, 254n23, 309, 351, 423n12, 443

Lerner, A. P., 352, 375–6, 423n12

level-of-water fallacy, 45

Lieben, R., 416n6

linear programming: and modern interpretation of Ricardian model, 161–7; and technological change under perfect competition, 240

Linear Programming and Economic Analysis (Dorfman, Solow, and Samuelson 1957), 230n1

Lipsey, R. G., 306, 312, 322

liquidity preference, in Keynesian economics, 402

literary appendix, on doctrinal disputes in classical economics, 111–13

"living labor," and theoretical innovations of Marx, 284

location, and Thünen's influence on geography, 216

London School of Economics, 379, 398, 414, 414n3

Lowe, Adolph, 145n14

Lundberg, Erik, 383

luxury goods, and consumption in Marx's model of simple reproduction, 266–7, 286–7

Macaulay, Thomas Babington, 27

machinery, discussion of in Ricardo's *Principles*, 33–34, 108, 183–91. *See also* technology

Machlup, Fritz, 105, 326

Mahalanobix, P. C., 338

Maital, Shlomo, 60, 61, 68, 69

Malanos, George, 60

Malthus, Thomas Robert, 64, 89, 93, 98, 109, 125–6, 128, 137, 141n12, 218, 238

Markov, A., 260

Marschak, Thomas, 197

Marshall, Alfred, 32, 196, 324, 353–4, 376, 377, 393, 405, 407, 416–20

Martineau, Harriet, 318–19

Marx, Karl, 15–16, 18, 34, 60, 89, 93, 101, 106n9, 117, 126, 130, 137, 138, 142n13, 160n25, 175, 186, 190, 218, 229–59, 260–300, 368. *See also* Marxian economic models

Marxian economic models: bourgeois regime of price in, 276–7; and concepts of constant and variable capital, 234, 254, 263; crisis theory in, 142n13, 149n19; expanded reproduction model and concept of steady growth in, 241–4; factor proportions and prices in, 245–50; and labor theory of value, 236, 258; prices and exploitation in, 291–2; prices, wages, and interest in, 229–59; production functions and technological change in, 253; and profit rates, 292; and reserve army of unemployed, 254–7; stationary conditions in, 231–7; steady state in, 288–9; subsistence levels of wages and cost of reproduction in, 289–90; technical coefficients of production in, 285; technological assumptions in, 229–31, 275–8; and theory of simple reproduction, 263–4, 266–7, 286–7; and time-phasing, 287. *See also* Marx, Karl

mathematicization revolution, 3, 26

mathematics: and Böhm's capital theory, 339–43; and canonical classical model, 96–101; and history of economic analysis, 10–13; and Hume model for self-correcting gold-flow mechanism, 55–7; quantum-theory economics and asymptotic homogeneity, 437–42; and Quesnay's *Tableau Economique*, 79–84; and Ricardo on machinery in *Principles*, 183–91; and Smith's *Wealth of Nations*, 121–30; and Thünen's *The Isolated State*, 203–206; and view of Marx as mathematical economist, 260–300. *See also* linear programming

May, K., 12

M'Culloch, John Ramsey, 110

Meade, James, 331

Means to Prosperity (Keynes 1933), 411

Meek, Ronald L., 33, 60–1, 68, 236n5, 282n16

Mercantilism, 117

Merton, Robert K., 196, 347

Metzler, Lloyd, 260, 383

Mill, John Stuart, 39, 89, 90, 91, 93, 105, 178, 190, 308

minimum-effective rate of accumulation, 90

Mirabeau, Marquis De, 59, 60

Mitchell, Wesley, 352, 375

"Modern Treatment of the Ricardian Economy, A" (Samuelson 1959), 128

Modigliani, Franco, 104, 320n9

monetary theory: in classical and neoclassical economics, 305–23; and Schumpeter as economic theorist, 361–2. *See also* Quantity Theory of Money

monopolistic competition revolution, 3, 26, 412–45

monopoly, Marshall and theory of, 416–20

More, H. L., 352

Morgenstern, Oskar, 417

Morishima, M., 12, 261, 270, 271–2, 283, 290n21, 296, 297, 298, 299, 300n25

Mosak, Jacob, 44

multi-good/multi-land economy, and rents in Ricardian model, 159–61

Mussa, Michael, 49n5

Myrdal, Gunnar, 428

Nagatani, Hiroaki, 104n8

Nash, John, 217

natural resources, and Smith on invention, 120

natural scarcity, as distinct from contrived scarcity, 425–6

natural wage, Thünen's doctrine of, 197, 216–17, 224n14

Nazism, and Schumpeter's political views, 372

Negishi, T., 12

neoclassical economics: and Böhm's capital theory, 324–43; and canonical classical model of political economy, 101–105, 109; political economy and monetary theory in, 305–23; and time shape of interest, 177
Net National Product (NNP): and Marx on simple reproduction, 263; Ricardo's definition of, 33, 181; Smith's concept of, 117, 118, 125
Neumann, John von, 126, 417
New Left, 15, 260
Newton, Isaac, 27, 409, 412
Nobel Prize, 4
non-substitutability theorem, 149–50
non-traded goods fallacy, 44
numeraire units, 246
numerical examples, and Marx as mathematical economist, 273–5

O'Brien, D. P., 2, 3, 4
observational instruments, mathematical models as, 12–13
"Of the Balance of Trade" (Hume 1752), 39–40, 41n2
"Of the Jealousy of Trade" (Hume 1752), 41n2
Ohlin, Bertil, 39, 57, 406, 434n20
Okishio, N., 283
oligopoly: and monopolistic competition revolution, 433; and Schumpeter as economic theorist, 360, 361
one-farm-good case, and Thünen's economic model, 199–203
operations analysis, 218
organizational principle, and nature of subjects treated by Samuelson, 18–19
overinvestment, and Robertson on economic cycles, 381

Pais, Abraham, 28
Pareto, Vilfredo, 258, 355, 414
Parris, Scott, 19
participant-observer, and Samuelson on twentieth-century economics, 9–10
Pasinetti, Luigi L., 12, 13, 110, 183
Patinkin, Don, 6n6, 311–12, 321, 322
Pearson, Karl, 354
perfect competition: and monopolistic competition revolution, 414–16, 420–2, 424–32, 435–7, 443–4; theorem about technological change under conditions of, 239–40

perpetual net rental, 94
Petersen, Asmus, 197
Phelps, Edmund, 190, 331, 392n22
Phillips, Almarin, 60, 61, 68, 69
Physiocratic system, 61, 66, 68, 69, 75, 77n9, 95, 128, 134, 152, 263n5
Pigou, A. C., 359, 377, 384, 399n2, 420
political economy: and Böhm's capital theory, 324–43; classical and neoclassical monetary theory and, 305–23; and Samuelson's canonical classical model, 89–113; and Samuelson on role of ideology in history of economics, 13–17. *See also* government; Nazism
positive interest, and Böhm's capital theory, 327
positive rent, and scarcity of land in Ricardian model, 139–41
Prais, Sigmund J., 46
preferences. *See* revealed preference; tastes
price: bourgeois regime of in Marxian economics, 276–7; capital and interest aspects of in Ricardian model, 168–82; equal-organic case of constant relative, 293; and equilibration in international trade, 46–9; of goods, labor, and land services in Ricardian model, 133–67; and exploitation in Marxian models, 291–2; Marx's polemic on Smith's view of, 279–80; in Robertson's economic model, 389–90; wages and interest in Marxian economic models, 232–3, 245–50. *See also* intempulpricing; Quantity Theory of Prices
"Prices of Factors and Goods in General Equilibrium" (Samuelson 1953), 180
Proceedings of the British Academy, 29
production: function of and Quesnay's *Tableau Economique,* 63–4; function of and technological change in Marxian economic models, 253; relations of and monetary theory in classical and neoclassical economics, 312–17; technical coefficients of in Marxian models, 285. *See also* cost-of-production relations; expanded reproduction; simple reproduction; time-phasing
productivity, and assumptions in Smith's *Wealth of Nations,* 121–3
profit: constituents of in real world, 169n1; exploitative rates of in Marxian economic models, 291–2; and Quesnay's *Tableau Economique,* 77–9; and surplus value in Marx's model of simple reproduction, 263–4;

and wages in Marxian economic model, 237–41, 245–50. *See also* transient profits

qualitative theories, of money, 307
quantitative theories, of money, 307–308
Quantity Theory of Money, 54
Quantity Theory of Prices, 42
quantum-theory economics, and asymptotic homogeneity, 437–42
Quesnay, François, 18, 33, 59–84, 261

Ramsey, Frank P., 222–4, 354, 356, 366–72, 407n8
"real-bills" doctrine, 385, 387, 388
Rechtenwald, Horst C., 197
rent. *See* land; positive rent; residual rent; surplus rent
residual rent: and concept of homogeneous land in Ricardian model, 141–2, 143; and long-run equilibrium in classical economics, 93; in Quesnay's "Tableau Economique," 64; and Schumpeter on marginal-productivity relation for land, 372
revealed preference, and Schumpeter as economist theorist, 350
Review of Economic Studies, 352–3
Ricardo, David, 11, 16, 18, 27–32, 33–4, 39, 64, 77n9, 89, 91, 92n1, 93, 99, 101, 102n7, 108, 111–13, 133–67, 168–82, 183–91, 212, 218, 229, 232n2, 263n5, 286, 328
Rist, C., 59–60
Robbins, Lionel (Baron Robbins of Clare Market), 140n9, 369, 381
Robertson, Sir Dennis H., 19, 215, 362, 375–93, 420n9, 423–4
Robinson, Joan, 15, 45, 224n14, 238–9, 261, 280–1, 283, 324–5, 326, 330, 337–8, 339, 352, 360, 383, 393, 411n15, 412, 413, 414, 417, 418, 423, 425n14
robots, and Ricardo on machinery, 184–91
Rodbertus, J. A., 272
Rosenstein-Rodan, Paul, 153n23
Rowthorn, B., 12
"rude state": and doctrinal disputes among classicists, 111; and Smith's labor theory of value, 123–5, 130

Salin, Edgar, 197
Samuelson, Paul: contributions to history of economic thought, 1–2, 17–19; list of publications on history of economic thought, 447–56; role of as historian, 2–4; on role of

political ideology in economic science, 13–17.*See also* specific topics and titles of essays
saving: inequality of investment and lagged Robertsonian, 382–3; and Malthusian growth in Smith's *Wealth of Nations,* 125–26. *See also* zero saving
Say's Law, 98, 114n13, 141, 310, 321, 399
Scarf, H., 428n17
Schabas, Margaret, 7n8
Schneider, Erich, 197, 353n2
Schultz, Henry, 352
Schumpeter, Joseph A., 18, 32, 43, 59, 60, 72, 107, 196, 217–20, 258, 261, 331, 347–73, 421
science, Samuelson's view of economics as, 5–8, 27. *See also* history, of science
self-interest, and Smith's Invisible Hand doctrine, 127
Seligman, Edwin, 25
Senior, Nassau William, 110
Sentimental Fallacy, 220, 223, 225
Seton, F., 290n21, 300n25
Shaw, Bernard, 137n4, 330
Shell, K., 271
Shephard, N., 127
Shove, Gerald, 430
Sidgwick, Henry, 418
Sidrouski, Miguel, 313n4
simple reproduction: and Marx as mathematical economist, 260, 262–7, 273–4, 293–4; and stationary conditions in Marxian economic models, 231–2
Slichter, Sumner, 390
Smith, Adam, 17–18, 34, 59, 89–113, 117–30, 150, 154–5, 168, 169, 172, 263n5, 279–80, 284, 325, 332, 368, 401, 422, 434. *See also* Invisible Hand
sociology, of knowledge, 412–14
Solow, Robert M., 1, 222–4, 271, 299n25, 331, 351, 356, 391
space model, Samuelson's version of Thünen's, 197–9
specialization rings, and Thünen's *The Isolated State,* 198–9, 211–12
specie flows, in Hume's treatment of international trade, 39–57
Spinoza, Baruch, 10
Sraffa, Piero, 12, 13, 16–17, 27–32, 109, 110, 114n13, 283, 286, 325, 326, 329, 330n3, 332, 338, 353, 371, 414, 422–3, 424

Stackelberg, H. F. von, 352, 417

Stalin, Josef, 373

standard commodity, Sraffa's definition of, 34

stationary conditions, in Marxian economic models, 231–7

steady growth, and expanded-reproduction model in Marxian economics, 241–4

steady state, in Marxian economic models, 288–9

Stigler, George, 12, 105, 113–14n13, 425n14, 436n23

Stiglitz, J. E., 271

Stolper, W. F., 66n2, 423

Stokowski, Leopold, 34

Strachey, Lytton, 405

Study of Industrial Fluctuation, A (Robertson 1915), 375, 380

subsistence levels, of wages: labor and cost of reproduction in Marxian economic models, 289–90; and profit rates in Marxian models, 292; and Quesnay's models, 63, 81–2; and Smith on reproduction cost, 122–3. *See also* wages

substitutability theorem, 149–50, 152, 180–1

supply and demand: and Böhm's capital theory, 332, 341; and Morishima's critique of Marx, 270; and Samuelson's reading of Smith, 118; and stationary conditions in Marxian economic model, 233. *See also* demand

surplus rent, 174

surplus value, and profit in Marx's model of simple reproduction, 263–4

Sweezy, P. M., 137n4, 234n4, 236, 238, 349

symmetry assumption, in monetary theory, 318

"Tableau Economique": and Marxian economic model, 233–5; and Samuelson's critique of Quesnay, 59–84

tastes: implications of Smith's theory of, 119; and indirect utility function, 203; and labor theory of value, 291; and monetary theory, 307; and one-farm-good case in Thünen, 200, 201; and price equalization in international trade, 49, 50, 55; and Quesnay's "Tableau Economique," 66, 69, 73, 76, 83; and "substitutability theorem" in Ricardo, 181; and Thünen's space model, 198. *See also* revealed preference

Taussig, Frank W., 105, 110, 237n6, 250, 251, 328, 349, 352

technical coefficients, and Quesnay's models, 63

technology: and assumptions in Marxian economic models, 229–31, 275–8; and labor theory of value in Ricardian model, 136, 150–2; and Schumpeter's zero-interest-rate doctrine, 356; theorem about change of under perfect competition, 239–40; Thünen and one-farm-good case, 201. *See also* innovational development; invention

temporary monopolists, and Schumpeter's zero-interest-rate doctrine, 360

terms-of-trade fallacy, 44

Theory of Monopolistic Competition, The (Chamberlin 1933), 412

Thornton, Henry, 362, 385

three-sector model, and Marx's analysis of simple reproduction, 266

Thünen, Johann Heinrich von, 4, 18, 102n7, 154, 195–225

time: and accumulation in fixed-coefficient Marxian model, 248, 252; capital and interest in Ricardian model, 170–1, 173–4; and Morishima's critique of Marx, 271–2; and Ricardo on accumulation, 168–9; and wage-fund doctrine in Marx, 250–4. *See also* time-phasing

time-phasing: and Böhm's capital theory, 337; in Marxian economic models, 287; of production in Smith's *Wealth of Nations*, 128–30; in Quesnay's *Tableau Economique*, 62, 75, 83. *See also* time

Tinbergen, Jan, 352, 407n11

Tooke, Thomas, 410n14

Torrens, population adjustment assumption, 174–6

Tozer, J. E., 11

Tract on Monetary Reform (Keynes 1924), 405

trade. *See* free trade; international trade; laissez-faire

transfer problem, and Robertson on terms-of-trade, 384

transformation problem, and Marxian economic models, 34, 235–7, 297

transient profits: and canonical classical model, 107; Schumpeter's concept of, 107, 360

transport costs, and Hume on international trade, 41n2, 50, 52–4

Treatise on Money, A (Keynes 1930), 404–405, 408–409, 411

Treatise on Probability, A (Keynes 1921), 407

Triffin, Robert, 424

Truesdell, Clifford, 28

Tucker, Harold W., 126
Tugan-Baronowsky, M. I., 272
Turgot, A. R. J. (baron de l'Aulne), 75, 77, 104

uncertainty: land scarcity and falling interest in
  Ricardian model, 177–8; and monopolistic
  competition revolution, 430–2
unemployment, and concept of reserve army of
  unemployed in Marxian economics,
  254–7. *See also* employment; labor
University of Chicago, 2, 3, 25

value: Marx's alternative regime of, 296–8;
  Smith's labor-command version of
  compared to Ricardo, 111–13; Smith's value-
  added accounting of, 118; and "prices"
  regimes in Marxian economic model, 277;
  and "value-in-use" as qualitative necessary
  condition for market value, 136. *See also*
  labor theory of value; land theory of value;
  surplus value
variable capital, Marxian concept of, 234, 263
Viner, Jacob, 2, 3, 11, 25, 28, 39, 43–4, 110,
  113n12, 141n11, 151n22, 352, 353, 362,
  414, 423

wage funds: in classical economics, 102, 105,
  177; in Marxian economic models, 250–4;
  Ricardo's concept of, 99. *See also* circulating
  capital; wages
wages: in classical long-run theory, 90, 94; and
  distributive shares in Marxian economic
  models, 278–81; and interest in Marxian
  economic models, 229–59; Smith on
  transient rise in, 118. *See also* employment;
  income determination; natural wage;
  subsistence levels; wage funds

Walras, Léon, 59, 94, 140, 172, 254n23, 318,
  350, 354, 401, 413, 416, 420–1
Wealth of Nations, The (Smith 1776), 18, 34,
  117–30, 434
Webb, D. C., 422n11
weighted arithmetic mean, 339
Weizsäcker, Christian von, 190, 298n24, 331
West, Sir Edward, 64, 141n12, 173, 175,
  238
"Where Ricardo and Mill Rebut and
  Confirm Arguments of Mainstream
  Economists Supporting Globalization"
  (Samuelson 2004), 4
Whewell, William, 11
Whig history, 5, 7, 8, 10, 12, 19, 25–35, 350
Wicksell, Knut, 94, 187, 191n3, 196, 237n6, 324,
  326, 352, 360n4, 421, 442n28
Wicksteed, Philip H., 94, 137, 140, 141n11, 200,
  258
Williams, John, 376
Wilson, Edwin Bidwell, 354
Winch, Donald, 3
Winternitz, J., 236
Wittgenstein, Ludwig, 29
Wong, Y. K., 353
Woolf, Virginia, 405
Works and Correspondence of David Ricardo
  (Dobb & Sraffa 2005), 30, 31n2

Young, Allyn, 117, 215, 352, 413, 420n9

Zeno's Paradox, 436n23
zero-interest-rate doctrine, evaluation of
  Schumpeter's, 356–63
zero saving, in Marx's discussion of simple
  reproduction, 264–5
Zeuthen, Frederik, 352

Printed in the United States
By Bookmasters